For Susan and Bob
with love and
affection —
Winston

May 1, 2019

Leonidas Polk

Leonidas Polk

Warrior Bishop of the Confederacy

HUSTON HORN

 University Press of Kansas

© 2019 by the University Press of Kansas
All rights reserved

Published by the University Press of Kansas (Lawrence, Kansas 66045), which was
organized by the Kansas Board of Regents and is operated and funded by Emporia State
University, Fort Hays State University, Kansas State University, Pittsburg State University,
the University of Kansas, and Wichita State University

Library of Congress Cataloging-in-Publication Data

Names: Horn, Huston, author.
Title: Leonidas Polk : warrior bishop of the Confederacy / Huston Horn.
Description: Lawrence, Kansas : University Press of Kansas, [2019] | Includes
bibliographical references and index.
Identifiers: LCCN 2018050290
  ISBN 9780700627509 (cloth : alk. paper)
  ISBN 9780700627516 (ebook)
Subjects: LCSH: Polk, Leonidas, 1806–1864. | Episcopal Church—Bishops—Biography. |
Confederate States of America. Army—Officers—Biography.
Classification: LCC E467.1.P7 H67 2019 | DDC 355.0092 [B]—dc23.
LC record available at https://lccn.loc.gov/2018050290.

British Library Cataloguing-in-Publication Data is available.
Printed in the United States of America

10 9 8 7 6 5 4 3 2 1

The paper used in this publication is recycled and contains 30 percent postconsumer waste.
It is acid free and meets the minimum requirements of the American National Standard
for Permanence of Paper for Printed Library Materials Z39.48-1992.

Contents

A photo gallery follows page 188.

Preface and Acknowledgments

Leonidas Polk, an anomalous man of the cloth who was the first Episcopal Church bishop of Louisiana and was later a Confederate general in the American Civil War, had a precedent in Church of England history. In 1688, Henry Compton, the bishop of London and previously a lieutenant with the Royal Life Guards, escorted Princess Anne as she fled palace intrigues to join her husband, Prince George of Denmark, in Oxford. The historian Thomas Macaulay says of the event, "Compton wholly laid aside his sacerdotal character. Danger and conflict had rekindled in him all the military ardour which he had twenty-eight years before [as] he preceded the Princess's carriage in a buff coat and jackboots, with a sword at his side and pistols in his holsters."[1] What follows is Leonidas Polk's comparable story.

The exceedingly long time (don't embarrass me by asking) I spent writing this biography is matched only by the assistance and encouragement given me by others every step of the way. Initially, Annie Armour, then the archivist at the University of the South, launched me by providing the voluminous letters and papers of Leonidas Polk written before and during the Civil War. Thereafter, Christopher Adde, Frank Osen, and the Reader Services staff at the Huntington Library in San Marino, California, walked beside me. Yes, they rolled their eyes sometimes at my dilatory method, but they never slackened their pace. At length, both Fred Woodward and Joyce Harrison at the University Press of Kansas, learning of my decades-long trudge and emboldened by affirming reviews from four anonymous readers, cautiously mentioned "publication." At the end, Bea Gottlieb, my no-nonsense copy-editor friend from *Sports Illustrated* days, pored over my manuscript with a penetrating eye.

And all the while my family—Polly Lee Carroll, our four sons David Graves, John Goodrich, James Madison, and Joshua Phillips, and our grandson Graham Graves—in many ways large and small, steadfastly kept me focused on my project's ever-receding end point.

To all these people, I extend thanks, heartfelt, with the hope that this book in some measure is worthy of their selfless gifts.

Prologue

It was the twenty-ninth day of June in 1864—the feast day of the martyred Saints Peter and Paul on the Christian liturgical calendar. The people of Confederate Augusta were beset by wartime stringencies and demoralized by the anticipated fall of nearby Atlanta, but the Georgians had risen to the occasion, withholding nothing from the funeral honors they lavished that day upon Leonidas Polk, their own sacred martyr. His upper body, mangled by Indiana gunners who killed him atop Georgia's Pine Mountain with a three-inch, ten-pound ball of iron, was now freshly uniformed and encased in a lead coffin; it rode upon a caisson drawn by four plumed horses, their tack jingling. Along the city's shady avenues the cortege wound, and finally into the fashionable Greek Revival precincts of St. Paul's Episcopal Church. Civilian businesses had shut down, and the military and ecclesiastical tributes to the deceased that were being heaped, one upon the other, were punctuated throughout the day by cannon salutes and tolling bells.[1]

Early arrivals had claimed the pews, while the latecomers who had watched along the streets were obliged to stand outside the church. The parading presence of three brother bishops, a general from the Army of Northern Virginia, a navy commander, a regiment of infantry, a troop of cavalry, a battery of light artillery, and a marching band assured everyone that truly, as a sorrowing journalist had written, "a divine and chieftain has fallen."[2] Nothing less befitted this Rebel commander who was, as well, the senior bishop of the Protestant Episcopal Church in the Confederate States of America. Of course, the hateful Yankees earlier had mocked the fallen hero. "The Gunpowder Prelate," a New York diarist dubbed him; a *Harper's Weekly* cartoonist drew him looking foolish in liturgical vestments upon a prancing warhorse; a Union Army commander lampooned the sainted soldier as The Right Reverend Warrior General Polk. All such attempts at wit were beneath the notice of the anguished people in Augusta.[3]

In a region where Mars and the Christian God were both revered, the military and clerical credentials of this composite celebrity had commanded a social position and a popular deference that few fellow Southern men could match. Leonidas Polk was as fabulous a figure, one admirer felt, as might be drawn from the fertile imagination of Sir Walter Scott; with ancestors indeed from Scott's Borderlands, Polk exemplified "in his life and character the spirit of ancient chivalry as handed down to us in the Morte d'Arthur." Another admirer reckoned no living man plumbed deeper "all the hidden powers and secret springs which move the great moral machinery of the South." Thus, when the West Point graduate, Louisiana clergyman, and master of hundreds of slaves publicly affirmed secession and Civil War, he effectively bestowed Heaven's blessing on the Southern cause. And sure enough, three providential years would pass with no harm coming the bishop general's way on the battlefield. Until the summery day when he was framed in the sights of a Yankee cannoneer.[4]

Beyond its gruesome details, the battleground death had sent a shudder throughout the Confederacy, arousing an anger in one grieving soldier who might have been speaking for many in the note he left near the bloodstained Georgia sod where Polk had died: "You damn Yankee sons of bitches has killed our old Gen. Polk." A kinsman comrade-in-arms observed more poetically that "the manner of his death had something in it suitable to his greatness of soul, and it seems not improper that a shell should open wide the door that let his spirit out." Fanny Polk, his widow, remained simply uncomprehending for years afterward: "Oh, God," she would write in her memoir, "why was he taken and so many worthless left?"[5]

Belligerence animated the funeral preacher, the Georgia bishop Stephen Elliott. Like Polk, he viewed the War between the States as a War between Heaven and Earth, and the trail of blood of "my murdered brother" did not lead merely to the artillerymen who had loaded the powder and lighted the fuse; it led more directly, he railed, to the Christians of the North. It was they who had fanned the "fury of this unjust and cruel war." Elliott vowed to be present when these churchmen cowered "at the judgment-seat of Christ." He would delight in their "fearful retribution."[6]

Elliott's truculence notwithstanding, the proceedings within St. Paul's were not without irony. Leonidas Polk would have been the least downcast of those crowding the chancel and nave. For mankind was born but to die, he had long persuaded himself. The joyous existence awaiting the righteous just beyond the graveyard was ever to be preferred to the existence one endured in this miserable, dying world whose satisfactions were illusory. These were mere fancies, he had said, experienced "bestride a bubble which floats and bursts."[7]

One of the Indiana artillerymen who had shot him dead a few days earlier got it right when he cheerily said: "The old Fifth Battery has got [itself] a big name on this campaign."[8] With the big name now in the coffin before the altar, the choristers and dignitaries rose to honor their slain brother in a hymn so appropriate to the occasion that Polk might have chosen it himself. It had been composed by his fellow cleric, the Reverend William Muhlenberg, and its lyrics began, "I would not live alway—thus fettered by sin, temptations without and corruption within."

Now, after fifty-eight years, the divine and chieftain could *requiescere in pace*.

I

Leonidas—A Name to Daunt the Northern Barbarians (1776–1825)

When he was seventeen years old, Leonidas Polk was appointed provisionally to attend the United States Military Academy at West Point, New York. This occurred largely because his father, William Polk, a wealthy banker in Raleigh, North Carolina, had the right connections in Washington City, especially with Secretary of War John C. Calhoun and President James Monroe. When William Polk was himself seventeen, an officer at the time in the War for Independence, he took through his shoulder a bullet fired by a Tory in Canebreak, South Carolina. With surpassing spunk, Lieutenant Polk, having no blanket and no tent, huddled nightlong with his broken arm through a thirteen-inch December snowstorm, his "bullet holes . . . plugged with tow [cloth] from the shot bags of the Soldiers." The next day, accompanied by a cousin, William repaired by horseback and sled to his headquarters twenty miles distant, where he "was received by his Colonel, in silent sorrow, which was shewn by the big tear trinkling down his manly and furrowed cheek." The seeping from his shoulder, William would later boast, was "the first American blood spilt south of Lexington in Massachusetts."[1]

Home at last, William was confined to his Mecklenburg bed for ten months by the suppurating wound. Finally recovered and nothing daunted, he returned to duty as a major, but while engaged in the Americans' battle against the British at Germantown, Pennsylvania, the amateur officer, now a mere eighteen, was shot yet again, this time "whilst in the act of giving [a] command." The bullet entered his open mouth, "knocking out four Jaw teeth and shattering the Jaw bone." And though he temporarily lost the power of speech, young Polk possessed "an excellent constitution" (as he later evaluated himself) and soldiered on, so little fazed by the rigors of military life that in 1777 he endured the wintry privations of Valley Forge. Provisional Cadet Leonidas Polk sprang from sturdy stock.

On April 10, 1806, Leonidas was born to William and Sarah Hawkins Polk, a descendant, too, of landed colonial gentry and Revolutionary forebears.[2] At a time when his parents fancied the names of historical Greco-Roman celebrities, Lucius Junius Brutus, a founder of Rome, was the namesake of their firstborn; the second little boy's namesake was the warrior-king of Sparta, heroically killed at Thermopylae while defending his homeland against barbarians from the north.[3] If ever a name proved apt, this one did when Leonidas Polk also stood his ground against the Northern barbarians of his day, the marauding Yankees who came marching down into Dixie.

Young Leonidas's academy appointment arrived at the stately Polk home in Raleigh when the future cadet was a civilian collegian off at the University of North Carolina in Chapel Hill. At this fledgling university, scarcely older than the sophomore himself, Leonidas was caught up in club debating, casual learning, and attiring himself, as he noted, in "the tip of fashion."[4] Previously, Leonidas's growing-up was on the order of parental coddling in the midst of Southern luxury afforded by vast land holdings and many slaves. Academic stress and rigid discipline was then in his future. The nearest he had come to that earlier was during his boyhood days at Raleigh Academy under the hated tutelage of the Reverend William McPheeters, the Presbyterian "Pastor of the City" and a tyrant schoolmaster. He drilled scholastic fundamentals into Leonidas and Lucius by employing the "wall book" system imported from England. In a typical lesson, the pupils were required to read from two-foot-by-three-foot sheets of paper the cautionary biblical tale of two she-bears devouring forty-two impertinent children for mocking the Prophet Elisha.[5] In short, Leonidas would later say, McPheeters had ill-served his preparation for college. In the elegant syntax he sometimes affected in his correspondence to his parents, he put it this way: "I have, and with affectionate gratitude shall ever remember it, received at your hands all the advantages our first schools offered for the enlarged culture of my mind." But even though "my opportunities greatly surpassed my diligence," these school experiences, "from a radical deficiency, were not as efficient in attaining their ends as parents generally, and doubtless afterwards many of the pupils, could have wished."[6]

Leonidas's liking for learning was closer to the military sagas of his father and grandfather. The grandfather, Thomas Polk, rich as all the Carolina Polks generally were, was once called a "home-bred lord" and was remembered from Revolutionary War times as "not a little obnoxious" to the Tory Royalists in his North Carolina neighborhood. He was famed in his family mostly for preventing the British in 1777 from melting down for cannon Philadelphia's stock of bells (among them one later christened "Liberty Bell").[7] A youthful Leonidas, soaked in his family's patriot histories, had once enlivened a Fourth of July celebration in Raleigh "in singing the patriotic odes" of the day so melodiously a cappella that he was judged the winner against a competing tenor. Predictably, then, and fortified by martial genes and a letter of recommendation from an admiring North Carolina professor, Leonidas on June 16, 1823, presented himself to Colonel Sylvester Thayer, commandant of the United States Military Academy. To Andrew Jackson, a Polk family friend, it was the best school in the world.

By stage and steamboat, he set out for New York with Washington Thompson, a fellow cadet candidate, and the two young men had time en route to explore the sights of the Northeast. In Washington City, taken in hand by Chapel Hill professor Ethan Allen Andrews, who provided two horses and a guidebook, the tourists made the rounds, from the office of the *National Intelligencer,* whose publisher, Joseph Gales Jr., was formerly from Raleigh, to the Capitol, newly restored after the British set it afire in 1814 and now surmounted by a copper-sheathed dome.[8]

Pressing on to Baltimore, Leonidas and Washington headed for Rembrandt and Rubens Peale's Baltimore Museum and Gallery of Fine Arts. If, alas, no arresting female nudes were on display that week, the boys made do examining the eleven-foot-high skeleton of a mastodon and visiting the Gallery of Heroes from the Revolution and the War of 1812.[9] Washington Thompson headed on for West Point alone, but Leonidas spent the next ten days with his sister Mary, then enrolled in Miss Mallon's Academy for Females in Philadelphia.[10] More museum visits and a few flirtations with Mary's schoolmates followed. Leonidas reached New York City after a journey of some eighteen hours by steamboat and stage. That left him a full Sunday to take in Manhattan. The high point of the layover was attending Price and Simpson's Broadway Circus, a newly opened entertainment in the city.[11]

At six o'clock the following morning, Monday, June 16, Leonidas boarded one of Robert Fulton's steamboats and headed up the Hudson to West Point. Churning against the pastoral river, the paddle wheeler had entered the river's Highlands by midafternoon and deposited Leonidas on the wharf of the military academy. Once Leonidas had made the 190-foot climb to the plain above the Hudson, he was directed to the superintendent's office. He presented his credentials to Colonel Thayer: a transcript of his course work from the University of North Carolina and the glowing recommendation picked up in Washington City from Professor Andrews. Thayer had doubtless known Andrews when both were engaged in coastal defenses in the War of 1812, and his letter, Leonidas thought, "was of much account" in assisting his admission to the academy. Subsequently, as the first order of the following day, Leonidas and the other new arrivals were assigned to ranks and files, squads and platoons. Their makeover from civilian to soldier commenced forthwith.[12]

First, posture. Abner Hetzel, a classmate from Pennsylvania, remembered that morning's basics this way: "To display the Chest, draw in the Corporation [abdomen]; draw the Chin in perpendicular to the Chest; hold the hands down so as to touch the seam of the Pantaloons; & take care don't bend the elbows, keep the Shoulders drawn back & always be sure to keep the feet in an angle of 45 degrees, etc."[13] Once their bodies had been contorted into a shape as presentable as could be expected on Day 1, the anomalously rigid youths were set in motion by their upperclass (and doubtless amused) instructors. Try as the green cadets might, such esoteric commands as "by the right oblique, march" led to the tangles of feet and weapons that have branded raw recruits since the dawn of close-order drill. "Indeed, every new Cadet appeared to have gyves on," Hetzel observed, meaning shackles chained to the legs of felons.[14]

By week's end Leonidas had been academically examined. Two arithmetic problems were so easy that he did not even walk up to the available blackboard to give his answers. Parsing English was another matter. That test somehow determined his placement among the French sections: his knowledge of that subject being but "indifferent," as he put it to his father, he was consigned to the lowest section.[15] All else being in order, his probationary status as a cadet was granted the following Sunday, thereby placing him in the Fourth Class, in which, as a lowly commoner among the student hierarchy, he was designated a Plebe. In his first letter home, he proudly reminded Sarah Polk that his mail hereafter was to be addressed to *Cadet* Leonidas Polk. The "Mr." she had written on her envelope "I have dispensed with since I have been admitted."[16]

Fourth Classman Polk along with most of the corps (third-year cadets got the summer off) marched away from their barracks the following Monday morning, bearing their clothes, muskets, swords, wash pans, tin buckets, stools, and bedding to a nearby expanse of open ground where they erected a city of tents, a simulation of army field conditions. For the next seventy-five days they were immersed in military instructions: infantry and artillery drill, plus the attendant arcana of military lore. Every other day the corps marched in formation to the riverbank where they stripped naked and waded through the shoreline grass to bathe in a cove of the Hudson.[17] Come nighttime, the worn-out young men lay down on the wooden floors of their tents. They had been provided with two blankets only, one to lie on, the other, as Leonidas said, wrapped around them "Indian like, with our knapsacks as pillows. In that style we sleep." Having at his age to worry if he seemed masculine enough (what youthful son of a Colonel Polk would not?), Leonidas boasted to his older brother Lucius that "some of the effeminates complain" about the sleeping arrangements, but "to me it is a pleasure." In short, as he assured his mother, in living the life of a soldier in toto, he was "as well pleased as I or you could wish."[18]

Adding to the plebe's overall satisfaction had been his good fortune in being asked to room with "fine young men" who stood very high in their class. Although this was a time when plebes were not harassed but stood on equal footing with upperclassmen, the invitation still probably testified to Leonidas's winning personality—and perhaps to his father's fame. One roommate was William Bainbridge, the senior cadet officer of the whole corps. Another was Bennett Henderson from North Carolina, who had urged Leonidas to brush up on his French before arriving at the academy. The third, also a second-year cadet like Henderson, was Albert Sidney Johnston from Kentucky and a corps sergeant. The ensuing friendship between Leonidas and Sidney would be a lasting one; nine years later, returning from a European trip, Leonidas brought Sidney an onyx cameo portraying George Washington. In 1862 when the friends were generals and were comrades in arms at Shiloh, Johnston was killed, the South's only full general to die in battle.[19]

The summer encampment of 1823 concluded at sunrise on September 1 when the outdoor community was crisply dismantled. First, drummers commenced a ditty called "Strike Your Tents and March Away." The cadets—in a synchronized, slow-motion ballet set to twenty-second drum-tap intervals—stacked arms, loosened ground pins, lowered tents, rolled canvas, and smartly marched their bundles to the quartermaster's storeroom. The village of cloth standing moments earlier had vanished, the trodden grass of an empty plain left to recover in the morning sun. Leonidas and the others then breakfasted, and afterward, fully uniformed and armed, repaired to their barracks. While a band had played, the event, said Leonidas, had been elegant to behold, the battalion throwing itself into various forms with the utmost ease and precision. He was so exhilarated by the tent drill and the exuberance of the stylish parade to winter quarters that he detailed it all in letters to both Lucius and his mother.[20] Thereon the days, weeks, and months of the next four years of Leonidas's life were as carefully cadenced by Thayer as had been the rat-a-tap striking of the tents. Virtually everything the cadet did in his waking moments had been devised and scheduled by the superintendent, who further had installed a scheme for evaluating and ranking on a daily basis a cadet's academic, military, and social status. Outstanding performance in one area would help offset a deficiency somewhere else, and the cumulative standing at the end of the cadet's four years would determine which branch of the army he would be assigned to, the highest (and rarest) rankings leading to enviable commissions in the Corps of Engineers. Cadets with the next lower scores went to the artillery, and those with the lowest to the infantry.

With one's military future in the balance day in and day out, not every cadet thrived under the grinding regimen. Leonidas usually did. After only ten weeks of class time, and showing himself as much a would-be educator as a soldier, he assured his father that the academy as a center for scientific learning was "inferior to none in . . . the world." And this was not mere boyish enthusiasm, should his father suppose; it was the considered opinion of others, visitors to this place, men of distinction. As for the tight rein Thayer held on the cadets, Leonidas primly believed that it prevented an "evil prevalent in most other colleges. I mean that lazy and idle habit contracted by many students which enables them to be dragged barely at the heels of their classes." And lastly, let his soldier-father rest assured, the military training he was receiving was also very good, and cadets were promoted into office in direct ratio to their application, of which he promised a sufficiency.[21]

Leonidas's sole complaint—it was the frustrated classicist speaking— was the lack of time afforded for literary attainments. He wished there were a debating society such as he had belonged to at the University of North Carolina. For the time being, the only pinch of variety in his military diet was his newspaper subscription. Within a year, though, Thayer gave his blessing to a society for the purpose of literary improvement, meeting every Saturday evening from suppertime till nine o'clock, until further orders. Cadet Polk was a founding member.[22]

At the end of his six-month academic probation (a "fiery ordeal," as he described it to his father with a biblical quotation), Leonidas was holding his own; his math skills put him fourth among his peers. Only French dragged him down. The lower sections in any subject at the academy were holes easier to fall into than to climb out of; he had only a tenuous hold on his status after struggling out of the depths to a position of twenty-seventh in his class of ninety-six.[23] His deportment, suffice it to say, was not yet blemished by any recorded delinquencies, and if he ever took part with other cadets in illicit sorties to Benny Haven's, a nearby place to drink bad wine and smoke cheap cigars after hours, he escaped detection. Washington Thompson, the friend who had traveled with Leonidas to West Point, had had no problem behaving, but he had gotten off to a slow start in math and was so dispirited by his poor beginning that he had fallen increasingly behind. "I have aided him as much as I could, yet all appears to be unavailing," Leonidas wrote; he pledged continued improvement on his own part. No one doubted it: family members agreed in exchanged letters that he was fast becoming "a hard student."[24]

Indeed, the aspiring soldier from Raleigh was thriving. The food seemed to suit him just fine, filling him at breakfast with coffee, bread and butter, smoked beef or ham, and radishes. Dinners, apparently, were not so tasty: mutton and turnips, typically.[25] As for refreshment outside the dining hall, Leonidas chose not to sign a voluntary alcohol abstinence pledge that some straitlaced cadets had gotten up.[26] Leonidas had taken a liking, too, to the surrounding Hudson Valley. As his first winter faded into spring, he rhapsodized over the lushness of the green mountains and bluegrass plains, and he marveled at the river, so covered with sloops and other craft that it seemed one could step across their decks from the west bank to the east. Catching sight of an occasional wheat barge floating southward from the Erie Canal that was soon to link the Midwest to New York City was among his favorite moments. Indeed, he was so pleased with his life that, midway through that spring, he told his mother he was considering not taking a vacation at home until he graduated. With such valuable educational opportunities as the academy afforded, he proposed taking "time by the forelock" and remaining in place.[27]

Along with summertime drill exhibitions, Thayer devised about that time another scheme to fan public enthusiasm for his school: an annual assembly at West Point of a distinguished Board of Visitors. The Visitors— politicians, professors, physicians, and generals—were charged with hearing the cadets examined at term's end and with suggesting how the state and progress of the institution might be improved. To be named to the board was thought an honor, and among those reporting for duty in June 1824 was Raleigh's Albridgeton Burges, MD, a Polk family friend. Burges hand-delivered to Cadet Polk a half-dozen silk stocks, the neck bands then a part of the cadet uniform. Equally appreciated was the savory news Dr. Burges had brought him regarding North Carolina's upcoming gubernatorial election.[28] Another of that year's official visitors cordial to Leonidas was Gen. Edmund Pendleton Gaines, renowned for his bloody War of 1812 exploits against the British in Canada and the Seminoles in Florida (hence, the city of Gainesville). When Gaines was introduced to Cadet Polk from North Carolina, he said, "Ah! Son of General Polk, I presume!" Leonidas hesitated a beat before allowing Colonel Polk's unofficial promotion to stand. "Yes, sir!" he replied.

Having finished his first-year examinations in the presence of the faculty and the 1824 Board of Visitors, Leonidas was joined by his father and sister Mary, the two having just arrived at the academy. All then boarded a steamboat up the Hudson in order to sightsee the Catskill Mountains and, farther north, Albany and the workings of the new Erie Canal. When the touring group broke up, William Polk and his son and daughter steamed down to New York City, and after a few days father and sister departed. That left Cadet Polk on his own in the city until he was contacted by another of his father's friends, the New Yorker James Alexander Hamilton, a lawyer with a growing political interest in Andrew Jackson. In Colonel Polk's Federalist pantheon, James Hamilton was the son of the luminary politician commemorated thirteen years earlier by William and Sarah Polk when they gave up their liking for classical names and chose "Alexander Hamilton" for their next little boy.[29]

Providing a carriage and horse, James Hamilton proposed to Leonidas a round of visits to the city's "curiosities"—a pin factory, a steel mill, and treadmills lately installed at the city penitentiary. Prisoners on the treadmills powered grindstones, an innovation in punishment that proved of particular interest to the budding engineer.[30] With his early-summer leave drawing to a close, Leonidas boarded an Albany-bound steamboat and was soon all-military again, stationed at summer camp. Like father, like son, he arranged to share a tent with a nephew and ward of Gen. Andrew Jackson. A Tennessee upperclassman doubtless sharing similar political tastes, he was Daniel Smith Donelson, a future warrior colleague of Leonidas.[31] Unexpectedly, Leonidas had been made the staff sergeant of the corps. That rank was normally awarded to the cadet standing first in his class (where Cadet Polk stood not), but the precedent had been changed by Maj. William Jenkins Worth when he was commandant of cadets. Worth apparently saw in Leonidas a particular aptness for the job. "I am attached to the Adjutant's Department, and do nothing but write," he informed his father.[32]

Sergeant Polk's writing duties that fall involved him in Colonel Thayer's preparations for the mid-September visit to West Point of the Marquis de Lafayette. Momentous to most Americans, the event was an unwelcome interruption to some at the academy, Leonidas told his father, Lafayette's friend. The visit promised to arouse "a little irritation of feeling . . . of all those in the vicinity of the path of the Marquis."[33] George Washington's famous French ally in the Revolutionary War was now the Guest of the Nation on a thirteen-month-long tour of all the Union's twenty-four states; just before sailing up the Hudson River to the academy, the debonair hero of Brandywine and Yorktown had danced the night away among 6,000 admirers at a gala soiree in New York City. Then he and several hundred convivial friends embarked on the *James Kent*, which, gay with flags, departed up the river at 2:00 A.M. The ladies occupied most of the steamboat's eighty bedrooms, while most gentlemen dozed on the deck. Lafayette shared his stateroom with two American army officers.[34]

Running aground in a dense fog, the *James Kent* was a little late reaching academy waters, but when at noontime Lafayette had been rowed ashore, the cadets with classes suspended were primed, Leonidas said, to "do him all possible military honors," to "stun him with the roar of cannon," and to "drill until he is tired of us." Later the marquis and the corps and all the attendant guests from New York supped in the mess hall, and once Lafayette had departed at day's end for Newburgh a few miles farther north, Leonidas reported that "hosts of tar barrels" spaced along the riverbanks would be set ablaze to light the old warrior's way. As a result of burning so much of a principal export from his home state, Leonidas joked, "North Carolina will thrive!"[35]

Bad colds and sore throats became recurrent nuisances for Leonidas in the winter of 1824–1825, but that was about all the thought he gave them. (They were the precursors, he would later discover, of a serious lung disease.) And he gave no thought at all, judging from the silence of his correspondence, to the new academy chaplain, Charles Petit McIlvaine, who in late spring 1825 had arrived from a church in Georgetown in the District of Columbia. Compulsory Sunday chapel services with their sermonic stress upon perishing souls were numbly endured by Leonidas and other members of the corps; clandestine reading, next to dozing, was the option preferred to heeding eternity's perils. The weekdays' academic trials and successes were what counted most for Cadet Polk, and he took particular notice about that time in discovering his affinity for fluxions. Comprehending fluxionary flow in Newtonian calculus, he explained to his father (who must have been gratified it was not a problem of his), was essential to his wading through an opaque three-volume text on physics that was to be studied during the coming term.[36] The author was Olinthus Gilbert Gregory, an esteemed professor of mathematics and physics at Britain's Royal Military Academy outside London, and the course was so difficult that only the better-qualified cadets at either school could master the material.[37]

Yet another twist of fortune occurred that term that would bear profoundly on Leonidas's future. Jefferson Davis of Kentucky, having survived the probation of his first six months, was admitted to the corps as a full-fledged cadet. Expressing the sectional allegiance he felt then, and that would expand steadily throughout his life, he regretted to his father that only Jeff Davis and two other probationary Southerners had made it through the fiery ordeal of 1824–1825.[38] Thanks to introductions handled by Albert Sidney Johnston—Davis's fellow Kentuckian and Leonidas's steady friend and roommate—Davis had already become a part of the somewhat staid friendship circle Johnston and Polk belonged to. The nuances of a West Point "set," Davis wrote almost sixty years later, were "well understood by those who have been ground in the Academy mill," and he would remember his association with Leonidas as affectionate.[39] Maybe the camaraderie of the Johnston/Polk set was a steadying corrective to the frequent disciplinary troubles that plagued the rebellious Jeff Davis. Even so, Leonidas was being written up himself from time to time: "Using or permitting the use of tobacco in quarters, 3 April 1825; Visiting in study hours, 20 Feb. 1826; Absent from reveille, 2 April 1826"—and more demerits to come.[40] During that summer of 1826, Robert Edward Lee of Virginia arrived at West Point. He never received a single demerit throughout his four years as a cadet, possibly elevating him to a set in which he was the sole member.

Leonidas's second-year final examinations showed he was doing well except, again, in reading French, which, for all his trying, he could not master. As he now stood thirty-seventh in his class of sixty, he regarded the subject with disgust and as a curse upon him. That disappointment, added to the accumulating pressures of regulations and regimen, had by then succeeded in ruffling Leonidas's wonted composure, even eroding the dutiful cadet's conscience. As the son of an affluent banker, his departure from uprightness had to do with money. At his request, his father had that spring sent him $50, welcome funds Leonidas could easily use for necessities and, now and then, a therapeutic excursion to New York City.[41] Leonidas had asked for the money even though he certainly would have known that money sent to cadets from off the post was a violation of Colonel Thayer's determination that cadets make do with their stingy monthly stipend of $28, an amount from which various fees were deducted for clothing, books, and board. Leonidas was typically left with about $6 to pay the tailor, shoemaker, and merchant, as well as his washman. Consequently, he was always deeply in debt, as were, he said, nineteen-twentieths of the corps.[42] Sending the $50 note, not aware it was contraband, Colonel Polk had resorted to the reasonable expedient of the federal mails—a bad idea. Leonidas carelessly opened the letter one April afternoon in the academy post office and was observed by the vigilant postmaster. The "ferret," as Leonidas sneered, reported what he saw to Thayer. For this violation, Thayer sternly admonished Leonidas, who had the good sense to feign contrition while suffering the superintendent's "descanting on the necessity of obeying literally the regulations and such like" and furthermore touching on "merit, conduct, etc."[43] What Leonidas learned soon after, but Thayer never did, was that yet another of Colonel Polk's $50 banknotes had come his way, this time by courier. The father had entrusted the money to his Raleigh namesake, William Polk Boylan, a new cadet appointee who reached West Point that summer.[44] Yet "in consideration of [his] general good conduct," the superintendent's dressing down was the extent of Leonidas's punishment, and he was promoted again that summer, now to sergeant major. Still, not one to forget bygones, Thayer in September wrote "Gen. Polk" to inform him of Leonidas's post-office violation. Thayer deemed it his duty to inform the father thus, "as I am confident the money was not remitted to him with your consent or knowledge." Chagrined to find himself culpable of a military academy crime, Colonel Polk had stoutly assured the superintendent that "such an infraction should not again occur." That promise irked Leonidas all over again. So how, would his father please tell him, was he "to keep himself in flannels"—in underwear?[45]

2

"Opinions . . . Most Awfully Dangerous" (1826)

Being charged with possession of forbidden funds was not the only scrape with the authorities that Sergeant Major Leonidas Polk would have that year. He was downgraded in his drawing class, and his overall "general merit" standing in the corps was likewise diminished. His offense, to which he readily admitted, was placing tracing paper upon an assigned drawing project and marking significant points and lines before undertaking to "sketch off the rest from sight."[1] Cadets engaged in tracing, though it had been long against the rules, and did so with neither subterfuge nor shame; they regarded the shortcut as an insignificant preparation for making the sketch that had been assigned them and would be graded. Gaining advantage over a classmate was thought to be a nonissue. Most of the drawing instructors were themselves indifferent. Colonel Thayer was not, and in the winter of 1825 he decided to put an end to the make-ready tactic. He declared that "the academic board expects every drawing exhibited at the examinations to be produced by the joint labor of the attentive mind, the judicious eye and the skillful hand, and not by a process so mean and mechanical as the one forbidden."[2] Though no mean draftsman, Leonidas was among the half in his class found guilty, and he was given a punitive low grade. His class standing plummeted from ninth place to thirty-second.

Having grown into a young man customarily self-assured and rarely intimidated by any elder's rank or position, Cadet Polk quickly posted a closely written five-page letter to one he hoped would cast a sympathetic judicial eye on what the student perceived as persecution. This was the new secretary of war in Washington,

James Barbour, a public servant whose paternalistic visit to the academy the previous spring had much affected Leonidas. "He viewed us as his children," Leonidas had reported then to his real father, "and had the interests of all and each of us at heart, and should be ever-ready to aid us in our views. He spoke to us very affectionately, and concluded recommending to us to be good boys."[3] Now Leonidas was taking up the secretary on his offer of aid, pleading the injustice and injury to himself and the other draftsmen singled out for punishment in the tracing-paper crackdown. Though angry, he was not insubordinate and had followed military protocol by submitting the letter first to Colonel Thayer. During a subsequent interview with the cadet, the superintendent did not withdraw the demotions but, clearly admiring Leonidas's soldierly pluck, "seemed desirous," Leonidas sensed, "to be thought in a very good humor."[4]

Secretary Barbour decided against intervention and urged Leonidas and the other affected cadets (some of whom, also seeking help from the outside, had written their congressmen) to study hard and regain their lost standing. Leonidas's father, too, had sent him conciliatory words from Raleigh. By April, still aggrieved by the unfairness he had suffered and not the least mollified, Leonidas was nevertheless able to attest gamely that "I am now progressing as cheerfully as though I were first [in my class]."[5] The asserted contentment behind that remark needs to be questioned. Some six decades later, William M. Polk, his biographer son, would say that the drawing-class experience had "brought [Cadet Polk] face to face with an example of official injustice," and he was so embittered that he determined then and there to give up a military career in order to pursue instead a "life of more direct, individual consecration of his powers to the service of his fellow-beings." Accordingly, he "chose the ministry of the Church as the vocation which would put him in closest touch with the object of his desire."[6] Leonidas's son perhaps overemphasizes the drawing episode as the sole cause of a shift in vocation. More positive circumstances in 1826 were inclining Leonidas toward his radical decision.

An epidemic of influenza had shut down the academy that winter, but for a while Leonidas was more preoccupied with his ill temper than with his sore throat; he mentioned the flu outbreak to his father only at the end of the tracing-paper letter. Still, along with 162 other cadets afflicted with a dry cough, he had been excused from duty. "I have myself had it very badly, but am now mainly well."[7] Leonidas was sicker than he thought; he later suffered an "aggravated attack of pneumonia," and an adhesion formed on "one of the lobes of his left lung." Prior to these illnesses, he could "out run, out wrestle and out jump everyone at West Point," his admiring wife would one day claim; from 1826 on, she said, his general health began a slow decline.[8]

When feeling better in the previous term, Leonidas had been absorbing and excelling in comprehending the wisdom of Professor Olinthus Gilbert Gregory. The Englishman's daunting three-volume production of dense text (and lovely drawings) was then in use in the academy's department of natural and experimental philosophy; among other subjects, the books addressed hydrostatics, pneumatics, machinery, optics, and astronomy.[9] If some cadets found the contents murky, to Leonidas they were so readily accessible that he stood fifth in his class at term's end.[10] One other book by Professor Gregory had also gripped Leonidas's thoughts that winter. It had nothing to do with the principles of steam engines, or the conservation of energy, or the laws of falling bodies. Alarmingly, it explicated the Fall of Man and the soul's tortuous path to salvation.

Old Greg (the West Point cadets' parlance for this authoritative gaffer, then barely in his fifties) had himself been a "gentleman cadet" at the Royal Military Academy at Woolwich. He subsequently began teaching there and became widely recognized for his command of mathematics and mechanics. But he was more than that. With singular scholarly breadth, he had served as the general editor of, and furnished three-fourths of the treatises, in *Pantologia*, a twelve-volume encyclopedia known throughout the English-speaking world as "representing a distinct Survey of Human Genius, Learning and Industry."[11] Away from the Royal Academy, Gregory was an active layman in the Baptist Church in Woolwich.

Well-liked by the British cadets, Professor Gregory in his churchman's role had cultivated an agreeable classroom sideline with them, a nonjudgmental exchange of his and their views on faith and reason. As a result of these amiable chats, in 1811 he undertook an effort to reconcile science and religion, to synthesize, as it were, the logic of the first with the romance of the second. His method was to weave into twenty-two tendentious essays both his extensive reading of secular materials and his absolutely literal interpretation of the Bible. About half of the essays were posed as letters to a cadet who had belonged to his popular confabulatory circle, and the collection, which ran to almost 500 pages, was titled *Letters on the Evidences, Doctrines and Duties of the Christian Religion*.[12] Never bothered when combining science's facts, proofs, and logic with his faith, Professor Gregory would fearlessly tackle such intriguing inquiries as whether the corporeal remains of a luckless Christian eaten and digested by a heathen cannibal would be readily available for reassembly on Judgment Day. The scientist-theologian averred they would indeed.[13]

Sometime during 1825, through the efforts of Charles McIlvaine, the new chaplain at West Point, a stack of Gregory's books found an ongoing lodgment in the quartermaster's storeroom; the *Evidences* won few readers, Leonidas Polk notably excepted. As well as being chaplain to the corps, the Reverend Charles Pettit McIlvaine had been hired by West Point early in 1825 to be professor of geography, history, and ethics (taught only to First Classmen). At twenty-six and bringing along Emily Coxe, his wife, he was barely older than the most senior cadets. He was, however, already known for his evangelical leanings in the so-called low-church wing of Episcopalianism. Most West Point cadets would have found it hilarious that the chaplain could testify that before his baptism at fifteen "a profane expression had never crossed my lips."[14]

After graduating from the College of New Jersey (the forerunner of Princeton) and beginning his ministry at an influential parish on the edge of Washington, the United States Senate of the 17th Congress took note of the preacher and elected him chaplain, the youngest minister to fill that post.[15] In whatever pulpit he stood, the evangelist McIlvaine's mission was to alert non-Christians and flabby Christians to heed the imperative of baptism and to thereby steer clear of spiritual ruin. Among the powerful men in the government who heard him proclaim his fearful message one day at the Capitol was Secretary of State (and future president) John Quincy Adams. Secretary Adams drolly summarized the sermon: "[McIlvaine] expatiated with great effort of pathos upon the importance of the soul, and the infinite danger of its loss; but he did not undertake to explain what the soul is. That was above his reach."[16]

Now as the second chaplain hired at West Point, McIlvaine's departure from the political pulsings of Washington to the backwoods of the upper Hudson River had been precipitated by a pulmonary disease that had been worsened by his labors amid the Potomac's dews and damps.[17] And while McIlvaine's health could scarcely have flourished in the Hudson Valley's winter frosts, shortness of breath and chronic headaches became the least of his West Point troubles. It was his psychic health that was soon failing.

He had given up the adoring warmth of his Georgetown congregation in exchange for a "chilling want of any manifestation of sympathy with the Gospel" that he proclaimed to the fidgety cadets where Sunday's services were "looked upon as a weariness." Never did a cadet pay him a visit, and a sneering "infidel" lieutenant provoked him once to walk out of a dinner party. Typically, at any day's end, the dejected teacher would slouch to his quarters where he wondered if Providence had led him into a dead end.[18] In sum, it was vocational failure, more than personal hurt, that weighed so heavily on the chaplain's heart. He was persuaded that "immense danger" accrues to any minister of the Gospel "if one [soul] be lost through our negligence or remissness!"[19]

One April day, in the depths of such gloom, he heard a knock. A cadet named Martin Phillips Parks, every bit as doleful as McIlvaine, was at the chaplain's door, the first such disturbance of his professional solitude since his arrival. Cadet Parks, burdened with grief and guilt, confessed that he had ignored the pleadings of a kind father and not come sooner to see the chaplain lest he be the object of ridicule by his irreligious peers. And now his father was dead.

Heaven sent, here was just the opening Chaplain McIlvaine had been praying for. Once he had ushered Cadet Parks into his underused study and prayerfully buoyed the youth's sorrowing spirits, he dispatched him back to his barracks bearing two self-help publications from the American Tract Society that McIlvaine, drawing from an ample supply, had pressed upon him. The chaplain urged his new friend to read for himself the tract addressed "To One in Affliction." But he should drop off the other, "To An Unbeliever," at any opportune spot in the cadets' lodgings. Young Parks, himself a North Carolinian on comradely terms with Leonidas Polk, obligingly planted the pamphlet in Polk's room in a spot where he was sure to see it.

The contents of the tract hewed to the chaplain's core beliefs: only professing Christians accepting and believing in the Crucified Savior can face with confidence the moral perils and defeats of life and gain the rewards of eternity. And just as McIlvaine had hoped, the bait left by Cadet Parks was picked up and sampled by a wavering skeptic, the cadet whose disbelief was already eroded by his readings in Professor Gregory's *Evidences*. Caught up short in his aimless drift, Cadet Polk was convicted by the tract's alarming message, and on the following Saturday he too walked to the chaplain's home and knocked. McIlvaine's surprise—and delight—must have radiated when on that April afternoon, his day off, he found at his front door yet another cadet unknown to him.[20] Two in seven days! He dared to hope it amounted to the longed-for validation of his campus ministry. Preparation of Sunday's sermon could certainly wait.

"This step was my most trying one," Leonidas would shortly tell his father by letter, but he was soon rewarded by the advice given by "our most excellent minister, Mr. McIlvaine."[21] As with Saul on the road to Damascus, there fell from Leonidas's eyes something like scales. As he would later explain his conversion to his brother Lucius, "The opinions I before entertained were not only erroneous, but the most awfully dangerous; and

. . . my course of life was equally ruinous." He recommended that Lucius hurry and take heed of his own soul's jeopardy.[22]

Leonidas Polk's visit that day made an impression on McIlvaine that would enliven future sermons and letters, and even after the Civil War had alienated the two he remembered the event in fond and vivid detail.[23] Cadet Polk had been close to tears and reduced to fragmented mumbles as he entered the chaplain's study and was led to a chair. McIlvaine, not yet ready to trust in his own good luck, at first suspected that the heaving, speechless youth found himself in deep trouble with the academy authorities—a plausible guess inasmuch as Leonidas had accumulated in the neighborhood of seventy demerits earlier in the term.[24] But academy demerits were not Leonidas's worry; instead, he felt convicted of moral failure before the throne of God. He begged the chaplain for guidance on how to make amends.

As McIlvaine sought to calm him, Leonidas explained what had brought him to this state: how he had begun reading Gregory's book of letters, how he had obtained copies of the two volumes from the post quartermaster, how within their pages he had seen much that caught his engineer's eye, and how he had then picked up and read the tract left in his room by Cadet Parks. Considerably distressed, he knew it was time to visit the chaplain.

Within hours of his Saturday afternoon visit to the chaplain's study, Leonidas was resolved upon his immediate future. On the Sunday morning that followed, in the classroom that served once a week as the chapel, when the Reverend Mr. McIlvaine intoned to the cadets, "Let us pray," Cadet Polk, and only Cadet Polk, slipped from his seat onto his knees. This was the posture directed by the Book of Common Prayer for all intercessions and was one conspicuously ignored by the cadets jammed together every Lord's Day on backless benches. True, as McIlvaine would later grant, "these [benches were] so near to one another that one must be specially determined to kneel in the prayers, or he would think no room could be got for it."[25] But truer still, the majority of the cadets crowded into the borrowed lecture hall on a Sunday were present by coercion rather than conviction. Now here was Cadet Polk defying peers, tradition, and space limitations. "That single kneeling cadet," McIlvaine would still marvel later, was "a thing not supposed to be possible as a cadet that turned to God."[26]

In the first letter to his father recounting his religious turnaround (fully a month after the fact), Leonidas did not allude to any inner turmoil, mentioning only that while growing into manhood he had sometimes pondered questions bearing on eternity. Professor Gregory's logically argued letters to an inquiring British cadet had provided the answers Leonidas could accept. As for miracles, Leonidas told Colonel Polk, Gregory had laid out convincing associations between religion and the sciences, the established facts of the one with those of the other. Claiming to be "guided by reason," Leonidas could no longer withhold his assent. He knew that his father, a confirmed skeptic of Christianity, would not enjoy this letter. He decided to say nothing about the American Tract Society's evangelizing pamphlet that had clinched the argument.

Nor did he inform him, at least in so many words, that two weeks earlier he had been baptized in the academy chapel. In his circumlocution, Leonidas said only that it had taken great moral strength "to bring myself to renounce all of my former habits and associations; to step forth singly from among the whole corps, acknowledging my convictions of the truth of the holy religion which I had before derided, and was now anxious to embrace." The experience would have been unendurable, he said, had he not been assisted by the special favor of Divine Providence, but having that now in abundance, he felt "fully fortified against the opinions of the world."[27] Among those were the negative opinions of his parents. These he most regretted, but he was undeterred.

In the meantime, a leak had sprung in West Point's secular dike. The example of piety set by, of all people, Leonidas Polk—"a larking youth," said McIlvaine, "not over-careful of obedience to the interior discipline of the corps, not unwilling to join in certain not-perfectly-temperate frolics"—was immediately effective. Within days half a dozen other cadets were calling on McIlvaine to profess themselves disciples of Christ, and subsequently students (and even some of the faculty) were coming in such numbers "for instruction, conversation and prayer" that the chaplain's largest room, wholly vacant just days earlier, was filled to overflowing. With Colonel Thayer's approval, nighttime worship meetings were scheduled twice and then three times a week.[28]

Supposing providence might be influencing the goings-on, and respectful of the frequent use of the number forty in the Scriptures, Chaplain McIlvaine would remember that exactly forty days passed from the first time he and Leonidas had met until the cadet presented himself on Sunday, May 28, to receive the sacrament of baptism. (It was actually forty-three days.)[29] At the same service, under the prayer book's heading for "The Ministration of Baptism to Such As Are of Riper Years," another cadet, William B. Magruder, from Jefferson County, Virginia, was also baptized; he was in the shadow, however, of the other, more popular, and livelier fellow. It was Polk upon whom the military congregation focused. The two cadets, in full uniform with belts and sidearms, walked toward Chaplain McIlvaine under the gaze of their transfixed schoolmates. A cadet eyewitness, possibly taking notes, would later provide such details as Polk's and Magruder's uniforms and accouterments in a letter to the *Christian Inquirer*, a Unitarian newspaper published in New York City.[30] They then knelt before a basin of water, an improvised baptismal font. Polk boldly enunciated his responses to McIlvaine's *Prayer Book* questions; Magruder mumbled his. When the sanctified baptismal water had been poured over their heads, the chaplain delivered a direful exhortatory charge to the new Christians: "Pray your Master and Savior to take you out of the world, rather than allow you to bring reproach on the cause you have now professed." With that, "as if he were trembling with new emotion," Leonidas's deep-toned, assenting "Amen!" seemed to come, McIlvaine thought, "from the depth of his heart [and] spoke to every other heart in the congregation."[31]

Cadet Polk's reverberating "Amen!" made waves beyond the chapel and the classroom. McIlvaine shortly learned that there was talk in Washington's War Department of "noisy demonstrations of excitement in the chapel"; that "discipline and order and study were broken up" by religious fervor; that the new chaplain was a loose cannon rolling about the deck of the US Military Academy. McIlvaine warned Leonidas to be on his guard lest he should afford the least excuse for other reports that might ripple through the War Department.[32] McIlvaine's source was James Milnor, rector of St. George's Beekman Street in Manhattan, an Episcopal center of evangelical piety. Milnor was McIlvaine's spiritual adviser, too, and thanks to his political past (he served a term in Congress before being ordained), he was privy to talk making the rounds in the capital. Hoping to dampen the chatter in Washington, Milnor accepted an invitation from McIlvaine to come see for himself the sudden, if scarcely tumultuous, turn the chaplain's ministry had taken. He was thus in the West Point chapel on June 4 when Polk and Magruder, freshly baptized, along with their friend Martin Parks, one professor, one instructor, and "four [other] inhabitants of the Point," received the bread and wine of Holy Communion.[33] The sacramental service being celebrated there, McIlvaine surmised, was another historic first in the academy's history.[34] The cadets involved were elated, and even though the year's final examinations would begin the next morning, instead of cramming they passed the evening in devout conversation with Milnor and McIlvaine. "My mind dwells with inexpressible delight on the transactions of the last Sabbath," Milnor wrote to McIlvaine upon his return to Manhattan. "When I reflect on our evening interview with those dear youths who had given themselves to the Lord, I cannot be sufficiently thankful that I was permitted to witness such a scene."

If subsequently there was joy among the angels of Heaven, there was continued consternation among the politicians of Washington, whom Milnor had not been able to silence. Instead, he urged McIlvaine to prepare "for those difficulties which some are plotting to throw in your way." From various quarters since his return to New York Milnor had heard that in the capital McIlvaine's ministry was imagined to have aroused "a sudden excitement of the animal passions of the young men." Indeed, it was being said, the chaplain's counsel and sermons had "led to actual insanity in one"—Cadet Polk was meant—and to indifferent academic performance in many. Accordingly, while some in Washington were pressing to have McIlvaine discharged, Milnor was working among acquaintances to ward that off; he asked McIlvaine to assist him and to guard, by divine grace, against any useful ammunition falling into the hands of "the enemies of truth." Urge the "dear brethren who have assumed Christ's yoke" to pray for these enemies, he suggested, and to prepare carefully for their examinations lest their preoccupations with religion be blamed for any poor performances.[35]

Then, at the height of the excitement, the Board of Visitors made its annual appearance to oversee the June examinations. The president of the board that year was the Tennessee congressman Sam Houston, a coincidence not helpful to Leonidas. An ardent supporter of fellow Tennessean Andrew Jackson, General Houston was naturally on cordial terms with Colonel Polk, Jackson's power broker in North Carolina. The congressman had, in fact, dropped by the Polks' household the previous spring, spending a night or two. He was a confidant, moreover, of Leonidas's brother Lucius. Consequently, Houston took particular note of Colonel Polk's boy. This cadet, Houston was informed, his eyebrows probably arching, was displaying worrisome signs of religious fanaticism and, among the faculty, was a subject of grave concern. Bearing the news back to Tennessee, Houston related what he had heard to his friend Lucius, who apparently relayed it to the parents. "Silly reports" would be Leonidas's dismissive reaction when asked.[36]

Never mind that the Raleigh Polks were pew-holding Presbyterians. By return mail William Polk expressed his and his wife's upset with their son's embrace of personal holiness (and, in his father's view, effeminate piety). Leonidas had replied with deep regret that his letter on May 11 had been the cause of uneasiness to the family. And though his apology was heartfelt, it was not the alarming letter's content for which he felt remorse; it was its thoughtless presentation. "At the time I wrote [two weeks after the baptism, which he did not mention], my mind was in a state of great distraction which disqualified me for writing with coolness, or dispassionately." This should account for the family's being unduly disturbed, and they might now put their worries aside. Besides, he said, changing the subject, they would doubtless welcome the news that he was coming to Raleigh on summer furlough, a concession granted him by Colonel Thayer. He signed the letter with a tenderness unusual in his letters: "With sentiments of the profoundest respect and filial affection, your son, Leon. Polk."[37] What he had decided not to bring up in this letter was any reference to Sunday's observance of Holy Communion at the academy, nor that prior to the furlough he was to visit New York City with Chaplain McIlvaine. Once their exams were over, the Reverend Mr. Milnor had suggested that McIlvaine bring his handful of converts to the city on Sunday, June 25, and attend services at St. George's. The cadets might then wish to stay over for Tuesday evening's prayer meeting. And among other activities he'd planned, Milnor thought the pious young men—Polk, Parks, Magruder, and the others—would value a visit to the city's wellspring of evangelical literature, the four-story headquarters of the American Tract Society at 87 Nassau Street. How could they not?[38] Leonidas excepted, the cadets returned to the academy bearing large supplies of evangelical tracts.

Leaving behind his notoriety, Leonidas reached Raleigh toward the first of July, particularly delighting his sister Mary. His mother sensed right off that her military son had arrived physically and emotionally drained. The merry stripling who had left town was thus in for some intense scrutiny by other family members and friends. While charmed by the tall sergeant major's natty uniform and chest-out, chin-in bearing, they were puzzled by the religious makeover he was said to have undergone; observing him firsthand, they could wonder if this was in fact the look of fanaticism. For one who had promised to bring his family consolation instead of ongoing worry, Leonidas's behavior continued to be disturbing. His mother, writing about him to Lucius after his return to West Point in August, claimed she had been well satisfied that his enthusiasm arose from his ill health; as his health improved his spirits returned. But still, "he has a fault," she said, sounding as though he were moping in the next room. "He can't bear any allusion to his piety or Christianity in the slightest degree; it even affects him to tears."[39] Sarah Polk took heart a little as the summer progressed. She did not doubt Leonidas was a "sincere Christian," she confided to Lucius, but her maternal hope was that whatever is besetting him "will wear off, and he will settle down a good man, a good member of society."[40]

Fortunately that summer Leonidas had an empathetic Raleigh friend he could turn to, one with intense religious feelings of her own—feelings, moreover, that similarly defied her parents. The friend was Frances Ann

Devereux, nineteen years old.[41] Fanny Devereux was a gently disposed but strong-minded girl who had spent her early childhood in New Bern, North Carolina, some eighty miles from Raleigh. Her Irish father, John Devereux, had married New Bern's Frances Pollock and acquired her sizable inheritance—eight plantations and 7,500 milled Spanish pieces of eight. He had subsequently prospered as a planter, a mercantile trader, and the manager of his wife's fortune. John Devereux's land and slave holdings in the region dimmed even those of William Polk.[42] Although growing up in different towns, the Polk and Devereux children had occasionally met as summertime playmates. For Leonidas and Fanny, play-acting husband and wife games were among their favorites. Often, Fanny wrote in her memoir, "he called me his 'little wife.'"[43] By the time Fanny was about thirteen, the Devereux family had moved to Raleigh, and it was not much later, apparently in 1821, that she had been sent north to Catholic boarding school.

Fanny was the child of a Protestant mother and a Roman Catholic father, both of whom took their religious heritage seriously. Fanny's mother was staunchly Presbyterian, as befitted a granddaughter of the Reverend Jonathan Edwards, one of eighteenth-century America's most esteemed evangelical theologians. Fanny's father had attended a seminary in France before giving up the idea of becoming a Catholic priest. Later the parents agreed on sending their daughter to St. Joseph's Academy for Girls in the tiny village of Emmitsburg, Maryland. Fanny loved St. Joseph's and the Sisters of Charity who were training her and her schoolmates in how to become "good . . . mothers of families." Fanny's mother and father were also pleased with the school, even consenting to Fanny's making auricular confessions to a priest; the girl found the counsel of her confessor a stand in, she said, for that of her parents. But ere long Fanny was affected by the sanctity of the school, so deeply that she wished to become a Roman Catholic herself. Learning that, her parents (at least, her mother) began to wonder if the school was a good fit after all for a great-granddaughter of Jonathan Edwards. With the school term of 1826 drawing to its close, Mother Devereux dispatched her husband and her Episcopalian daughter-in-law Catherine Johnson Devereux to Emmitsburg. They were to fetch the girl and steer her toward enrolling in a secular school in Philadelphia.

With Father Devereux remaining in the background, Catherine and Fanny settled down for heart-to-heart girl talk. The two got along just fine, Fanny dutifully agreeing to the transfer. She resisted, however, any further concessions: she would read only Catholic books and would avoid attending Protestant worship. Two years later, turning eighteen, she became a Roman Catholic. As a result, she knew exactly during that summer of 1826 what Cadet Polk was going through with his own family. The young people's affection for one another began to deepen.[44]

Meanwhile, to get Leonidas's mind off religion, Colonel Polk that summer proposed to his mopey son that he consider becoming a farmer in Middle Tennessee. His inducement was that, after Leonidas's graduation from West Point, his land-rich father would give him, Lucius, and their half-brother, William Julius Polk, adjoining acreage in Maury County. Leonidas, already with a taste for farming and a matter-of-fact concern for his professional future once he had left the military, joined William Julius in agreeing to the plan. With a lighter heart than when he had arrived home, he made ready in mid-August to return to school. As his mother saw him off, she exacted a promise that if his health again declined he would come home straightaway; she left off saying that she suspected his physical illness and religious enthusiasm were cause and effect.

While en route to West Point, Leonidas wrote one letter to his father and one to Lucius. Set side by side they are instructive. To his father it was an amiable four pages: minor travel mishaps, mutual acquaintances he had encountered along the way (one stranger had introduced himself because of Leonidas's striking resemblance to his father), and the assorted financial affairs he had tended to in Baltimore on the family's behalf. Flush with at least $1,500, he paid off a debt here, collected one there, made a bank deposit, and bought grass seed for the Raleigh orchard. Here was a businesslike letter William Polk would be comfortable reading from his truly affectionate son.[45]

The letter to Lucius, by contrast, was devoted to spiritual matters. Leonidas believed Lucius ripe for evangelizing, and that evening aboard the side-wheeler *Constitution*, his writing table trembling with the pounding of the steam engine, his hand nervous with the object of the message, he wrote the first of several proselytizing letters to this newfound prospect. The writing is rushed, haphazard, imploring; he confesses that but a few short months ago he himself had been careening out of control, humoring "awfully dangerous" opinions and indulging in "equally ruinious" conduct, to which he implied Lucius was prone. The unheeding cadet had been avoiding the "but too-sad realities of the truth" that whoever is without Christ is lost. From personal experience, he knew the scorn the world accorded this view; in his own former blindness, he too had been impiously derisive. But all that was before his insights and feelings had been completely revolutionized. Now, he said, "I do not more certainly believe *any* fact [more] than the truth of Revelation." As to Lucius's own plight: "What can I do less then, than *beseech you most tenderly* to examine [Scripture] for yourself . . .

earnestly hoping you will not procrastinate." Leonidas would remember Lucius daily in his devotions, he promised, and especially "it shall be my prayer that you may arrive at, and believe the solemn truths of which I have been speaking." Lucius's reactions—a man of twenty-four much given to a Tennessee planter's diversions of dancing, horse racing, and drinking—can be supposed. At the time he was occupied courting Elizabeth McCullough of Nashville, a great catch, an older friend said, "certainly handsome, intelligent and well concated, [though] her fortune ($30,000) is not worth talking about." Lucius admitted to his sister that he did not answer Leonidas's imploring letter. "I should think he was a little hurt at your silence," Mary primly replied.[46]

3

"Board, Room, Servant, and All Other Like Necessities" (1826–1830)

Just after Leonidas left for the academy, his baby sister Sarah, the Polks' twelfth child, died after six months of chronic illness; of the Polks' thirteen children, Sarah became the fourth to die in infancy or childhood. The older Polk children, sorrowing for their mother, had become relatively inured to the high mortality rate of their brothers and sisters.[1] Sarah Polk then sent word to Lucius that 120 of their slaves would soon be dispatched in two batches from the Polks' North Carolina properties to Middle Tennessee. Their plantation on Bigby Creek, the destination, was situated in the rich farmland of Maury County, "where they can support themselves as they cannot do in N.C.," she said. This was the acreage promised Leonidas—provided he settled on it.[2]

At West Point, Leonidas was disappointed that Charles McIlvaine was absent because of a family crisis (his father and a brother had both died during the summer), but Cadet Polk's popularity with the other authorities had not waned on account of his religious zeal.[3] On the contrary, he was told when he arrived that in addition to an assignment helping orient that term's new cadet candidates he had also been promoted to orderly sergeant. This was Leonidas's third promotion in his first three years, and along with other reasons he was specifically chosen to solve a persistent disciplinary problem. Orderly sergeants were charged with reporting cadets missing from morning roll call. But First Class cadets, exercising heretofore a traditional but unsanctioned indulgence, were frequently still abed at daybreak, snug in the knowledge that conspiratorial orderly sergeants would report them present. It had suddenly occurred to someone at headquarters that Chaplain

McIlvaine's new Christians, bound as they were to enhanced obedience in their own conduct, might even enforce roll-call rules ignored by conniving predecessors. Sergeant Polk, punctilious as expected, did indeed fulfill the superintendent's expectations—to the dismay of slumberous seniors. Then, as with his earlier correspondence with the secretary of war criticizing Colonel Thayer's enforcement of the drafting-class rules, the student undertook to rectify other teaching objectives of the United States Military Academy.

Leonidas had learned—possibly from McIlvaine, whose ox stood to be gored—that Sam Houston's Board of Visitors had recommended that the chaplain's department of geography, history, and ethics "be broken up." Similar humanities courses in those days were fixtures on virtually every American college campus, designed to smooth any intellectual rough edges remaining on seniors about to graduate.[4] But to West Point's Visitors, the humanities subjects being taught did nothing to equip a soldier for warfare. Hedging, the Visitors did not say the studies were "unimportant," but surely they "should be acquired either before the cadets come to this academy or after they leave it."[5]

Since the same Visitors had advised that a proper chapel be built to replace the borrowed classroom in use, their criticism of McIlvaine's courses presumably had nothing to do with the chaplain's disturbing evangelical successes. Leonidas may still have suspected a plot against his mentor. Even if he did not, as a charter member of the cadet's Dialectic Society ("for literary attainments") his educational ideas were absolutely opposite those of the Visitors: the academy was spending too little time on the humanities—on what he described as belles lettres. The approach most beneficial to the academy—and to the country, he added—was not to cancel these courses but rather to add another year to the cadets' tenure. He would far rather spend his "fifth year in a further course in reading than attending [to] the duties of a lieutenant." Many of his classmates, he assured his father, would "make a like choice."[6] Leonidas was fervent on the issue, energized because McIlvaine's liberal arts department had exposed him to Olinthus Gregory's *Evidences of the Christian Religion*. Now he feared the liberal arts courses "were on the verge of expungement."[7]

Aware that since his furlough his religious zeal still rankled his father as it would even two years later when he told his son, "You are spoiling a good soldier to make a poor preacher," Leonidas had learned to maneuver between canny and candid when writing home. One of the few letters he sent during the spring of 1827 shows his more cautious approach. Absent were all mentions of eternity, redemption, and the urgency of Christian commitment; instead the son played to the father's interest in commerce and industry. The Hudson River, he wrote, was aswarm with Erie Canal cargo sailboats; the merchant boatmen, no longer held back by winter's ice, were streaming for New York City markets. Soon to fill the river in the opposite direction, he predicted, would be the summer tourists, booking passage on luxury steamboats rapidly plying the New York–Albany run. Leonidas was so well acquainted with these vessels that he told his father of the improved layout of the boilers, and he reported the main cabin of a newer boat would contain decorative paintings "by the most celebrated of our artists . . . either of a national character or from fancy." With a word or two about life in the Raleigh household, he was done. In a postscript he mentioned he continued to enjoy uninterrupted good health.[8]

Refraining from topics his father would predictably dislike was one tactic Leonidas chose when writing home. But when the bullet had to be bitten, as when he first disclosed his conversion to Christianity, he would approach his intended subject circumspectly by saving the disagreeable news for last. Five days after the steamboat letter, just eleven days before his twenty-first birthday, he wrote about the things that had really been on his mind: his desire to abandon a military career and to devote himself instead to broadening his knowledge of history and other classical disciplines. The engineering education he had gained at the military academy was thin, superficial, and imperfect, he had concluded; even at other colleges, a similar result was to be expected since the reservoir of the world's accumulated knowledge could barely be tapped during only four years of study. He wrote that "apart from his textbooks his familiarity with history and indeed of most other books . . . is exceedingly limited, and I feel great unwillingness to close my eyes to all this light while effort only is wanting for its enjoyment." His desire, then, was "to roam unchecked for a while through the groves of Academe"—or, as he put it with a flourish, "to prosecute farther some of those branches to which my attention has been called, . . . as well as to take up others, hitherto untouched."[9]

Casting the line, he added what he hoped would set the hook. He had been offered a postgraduation job after Colonel Thayer had recommended him: the professorship of the mathematical and physical sciences at a school for boys currently being formed in Amherst, Massachusetts. Required to teach only three hours a day, he would be paid $800 per annum and given "board, room, servant, and all other like necessities." Thus he would have the luxury of ample free time to read the books that would illuminate his mind.[10] Leonidas did not mention a further fact to his father: the new school would promote a religious component that appealed to him. To be known as the Mount Pleasant Classical Institution, it was being shaped to be a feeder school to the five-year-old Amherst College, and among its goals, as its prospectus phrased it, was to inculcate "that moral and religious influence which contributes to fit a man for the high purposes of existence."[11] Inasmuch as Amherst College was itself designed to incubate candidates for the ordained Christian ministry, the teaching situation was one Leonidas could warmly anticipate, and surely his chaplain friend supported him. Leonidas sent home a copy of the fresh-off-the-press prospectus, then awaited results. Notwithstanding William Polk's unquestionable support of schools and schooling, Leonidas was worried that his father would forbid his taking the offered professorship. And he had promised to abide by his decision. Among the factors that he felt might help his chances was Sylvanus Thayer's role. The superintendent's initiating recommendation of Cadet Polk was particularly noteworthy because Mount Pleasant's founders included an influential man among the colonel's Massachusetts kinsmen: Martin Thayer.[12] Martin had bankrolled the buildings and grounds and had joined in the enterprise with two academic associates, Francis Fellowes and Chauncey Colton. Both young men had just received degrees from Amherst College, and Colton—all but assuring Leonidas's esteem—was a fervent evangelical and a future priest.[13] Colonel Thayer also had assured Leonidas that with the United States enjoying a decade or so of relative peace, with only Native American Indians qualifying as enemies, the army was overstocked with graduates from the military academy and would readily grant Second Lieutenant Polk a timely discharge should he request it. That would free him from the five-year obligation that normally attached to a West Point education.

To further win his father's hoped-for assent, Leonidas would now suggest an idea beneficial to the whole Polk family: the Mount Pleasant Classical Institution held such promise for superior education, he said, that his parents would do well to enroll Leonidas's two youngest brothers, Rufus King, thirteen, and George Washington, almost ten. Leonidas was sure that were the two to remain in North Carolina their boyhood education would be just as deficient as his own had been. Leonidas reminded his father that he had often complained "that the schools around you were far from reaching the objects for which [they] were designed." Here was a perfect opportunity for the older brother to assume tutorial control of the boys' schooling; he would happily come fetch them during his vacation break.[14]

Some weeks having passed, William Polk replied. He did not deny his son's application for approval by fiat; instead he raised querulous issues and expressed various misgivings. Leonidas's response in early May refutes his father's objections point by point. While the father hoped to squelch the son's teaching ambitions then and there, Leonidas gracefully acknowledged that he believed the peevish letter had been "prompted by the purest desires." Leonidas, just the same, had an even greater surprise in store.[15]

His father had begun by referring to Leonidas's problematical health. Was it not too fragile for him to undertake such a rigorous regimen of study and teaching? No, Leonidas replied, the feebleness he had exhibited when at home the previous summer had departed. On the contrary, he had "seldom felt better." His father questioned his need for a salary, even one of $800, which was better than an army second lieutenant would receive. If Leonidas's primary object was to continue his formal education, did he not know that his father would gladly provide the necessary funds? Taking a paying job was quite unnecessary for a youthful son of the banker William Polk. To that Leonidas replied that he was not "capable of entertaining the idea that . . . you would think of withholding" funds. He simply believed there was no impropriety in his earning a few dollars, particularly as he would be pursuing an "object out of the way of the ordinary course of education . . . an after-addition to what it is usual [for the parents] to give."

Then William Polk suggested that the characters of the founding scholars deserved closer scrutiny. They may not be men to be trusted. No, dear father, Leonidas informed him; the integrity of the founders was "directly the reverse" of what he suspicioned. Regarding Francis Fellowes, "no one within the range of my acquaintances [is] of a more dignified or correct deportment." Leonidas kept to himself that Fellowes was barely two years older than he was.[16] Finally the father raised the matter of Leonidas's past twelve months at West Point, his pious ardor, and the loose talk about his mental balance discrediting his and his family's station in life. Instead of pursuing the career of a military officer or of a Southern planter, might Leonidas's now settling for a teacher's job nourish slander against all the Raleigh Polks? To a problem completely unforeseen by him, Leonidas expressed amazement at his father's worry. It had never crossed his mind that his becoming a schoolteacher could "throw . . . open a door for ill-founded and injurious inferences" reflecting badly on the Polk name. Had he thought of that, he said, he never would have embarked in the first place on the negotiations with the Mount Pleasant Classical Institution.

After reading through the catalog of his father's fears, Leonidas admitted he had been oblivious to the extent of his parents' anxieties. They must have indeed wondered whether his desire for the professorship had been seized upon while "my mind [was] distorted from its native vigour, and blinded into the adoption of some wild and silly schemes of enthusiasm."

Not so. True, in months past his mind sometimes had found "itself in a complete chaos" and he had "been liable to extraordinary excitability," but all such turmoil was over and done. Serenely, Leonidas assured his father that "for the future you may feel yourself at ease."

If the father was beginning to feel himself at ease, it was but for a fleeting moment. Leonidas continued his letter by declaring he was giving up the professorship idea entirely. But he was now fully persuaded that the Christian ministry was the profession to which he should devote himself.[17] The would-be clergyman could imagine his parents throwing up their hands in dismay. Reassuring them of his mature judgment, he explained that it was only after isolating himself from the influence of outsiders that he had come to his vocational decision. As that process had occurred during the forty days of Lent just ended, Leonidas must have employed the time in prayer and reflection upon his future.[18]

This vocational conviction was bolstered by a new strain of independence. Leonidas had not even suggested that he sought or needed his father's approval to pursue theological studies. His father reacted mildly, wishing only for more detail as to how his son had arrived at this decision on his life's work. He and Sarah Polk also urged their son not to tender his army resignation until he had returned to Raleigh and the three of them could calmly discuss the new situation.[19] Leonidas agreed to that, but curtly, providing them no further illumination: "I can only repeat what I stated in my letter, that it has not been the work of a moment, but of leisure consideration. I will forebear, however, from further mentioning it until I have complied with your [resignation] wishes."[20]

No family member was present when Cadet Polk received his diploma and his commission on Sunday, July 1, his mother's hopes to be there having fallen through. She would have been proud. Leonidas stood eighth in a class of thirty-eight and was therefore entitled to a commission as a brevet second lieutenant in the prestigious artillery. As a graduation present that might soften their increasingly headstrong son, the Polks suggested a tour of the Northeast United States, a refreshing change from his cloistered academy life.[21] The requisite travel funds were hand-delivered to Leonidas in June by Henry Hawkins. Henry was a sixteen-year-old cousin on Leonidas's mother's side from Raleigh and was among that summer's conditional appointees arriving at the academy. Sarah Polk had availed herself of space in Henry's trunk to replenish her son's supply of shirts and pantaloons. As the military authorities thought Leonidas to be a model cadet, he had again been assigned to the newcomers' barracks to help in welcomes and indoctrinations. Knowing Henry's grasp of mathematics to be less than outstanding, Leonidas in his function as a mentor invited Henry to be his roommate. Drilled by the senior cadet, the boy was found admissible, if not with brilliancy, at least with benefit and credit to himself and friends.[22]

As well as money and clothing from home, the handsome young soldier was provided by his father with letters of introduction to two influential New Yorkers: US senator Martin Van Buren (Abraham, his son, was Leonidas's classmate) and Representative Churchill C. Cambreleng. Both men were strong Andrew Jackson partisans, and both had recently talked politics with Colonel Polk in Raleigh.[23] Thus equipped with funds and letters and a furlough document in hand, Brevet Second Lt. Leonidas Polk of the artillery made ready to depart the academy grounds.

His itinerary was a crisscrossing of the Atlantic seaboard, seemingly random, though he may have acquired a tourists' guidebook. If not, his own detailed account of his travels was one in its own way. He went first to New York City, then to Philadelphia, then through New Jersey en route to New Haven. While in New York he shipped to Raleigh a large black trunk containing his accumulations from West Point, along with recent purchases such as a "multiplying writing machine" by which "we are able to obtain two copies of whatever we write at once." He bought two of the instruments, one for his father and one for Lucius in Tennessee.[24] He was off then to Philadelphia, where he toured the recently completed Fairmount Waterworks, whose new hydraulic pumps forced the waters of the Schuylkill River far and wide throughout the city. Leonidas supplied his father with precise data concerning the pipes, pumps, and present and future gallon capacities.[25] That eye-opening experience concluded, he went to Burlington, New Jersey, where he "stopped 2 or 3 hours with a friend." He deemed it best unsaid that Burlington was Chaplain McIlvaine's hometown. From Burlington he proceeded by steamer on Long Island Sound to New Haven and there called on another friend, this one identified. He was Denison Olmsted, Leonidas's chemistry professor at the University of North Carolina and now Yale's professor of mathematics. Though a Connecticut Yankee, Olmsted had taken a liking to Southern ways while in North Carolina (he bought a slave for $350 shortly after moving there) and had become cordially connected to the patrician Polk family. A man of diverse interests and talents, he had just that week (July 21, 1827) patented a "gas light from cotton seed," probably demonstrating his prototype lamp for the inquisitive soldier.[26]

Never one to write legibly, Leonidas's cacography during this excursion was worse than usual. His fingers, he explained, were swollen, and he supposed the condition was due to nervousness brought on by the agitation and excitement of traveling. Out of curiosity he chose Middletown, Connecticut, as his next destination in order to visit Capt. Alden Partridge's American Literary, Scientific, and Military Academy, an upstart institution only a few years old. Captain Partridge had been a cadet at West Point in its earliest days and rose to be its superintendent. But after a controversial term of office he was removed in 1817 by President James Monroe to make way for Sylvanus Thayer. Not leaving quietly, he immediately founded his own version of a military school and predicted it would shortly come to surpass the US academy. In cadet numbers, at least, he soon was as good as his word. By 1826 Partridge had 287 cadets compared to Thayer's 250. That November, to taunt his former employer, he had saucily led forty-one of his strongest boys on a five-day cross-country march through the autumn rain until they reached Poughkeepsie, where they boarded a southbound steamboat to cross the Hudson to West Point. Sgt. Leonidas Polk and other West Pointers had welcomed the marchers on a Sunday evening, whereupon they were fed, shown around, and taken to a chapel service conducted by Chaplain McIlvaine.[27] Now able see Partridge's academy itself, the visitor cast a supercilious gaze over the place. Noting earlier that good books and apparatus were not wanting at Yale, and that its library was remarkably fine, he now sniffed to his father that since the Partridge academy possessed "but little [laboratory] apparatus or library . . . , I am induced to form an unfavorable opinion of the place. I fancy that many who send their sons to it are greatly in the dark."[28]

A succession of travelog letters was dispatched to Raleigh throughout August and September. From Middletown and Captain Partridge's school, Leonidas had headed for Springfield, Massachusetts, where he witnessed (and later described minutely) the manufacture of muskets by water power at the United States armory. He went thence to Worcester and Boston. In Boston Leonidas looked up "friends who had been at the Point with me." He failed to tell his parents their names, but they were probably John Childe of West Boylston, who had just graduated second in his class, and a furloughing cadet from Virginia, Robert Lee.[29] Two years behind Polk and Childe at the academy, Lee was as popular a cadet as could be found in the corps, and the youths would have made an amiable holiday threesome. John Childe's fame as a civil engineer of American railroad systems was ahead of him, but early interest in the subject perhaps led him to suggest that the young men spend a day sightseeing at Quincy.

Here, ten miles south of Boston, a year-old quarry railroad was a drawing card to tourists.[30] The line had recently been built to haul granite blocks for a Revolutionary War monument then rising on Boston's Bunker Hill.[31]

The simple track of steel ribbons spiked to heavy wooden rails ran about thirty-two miles from the Quincy quarry to the Neponset River, where barges then took the stone to Charlestown. Horses, to Leonidas's surprise, were able to "draw an almost incredible weight" down the slightly inclined railroad. Leonidas even included a sketch with his letter home detailing the flanged interface of the carts' wheels and the track over which they rolled. The sight of the innovative transport system seems to have made the impression on the visiting cadets their host had hoped for as Leonidas was moved to patriotic eloquence. Though what Lee remembered as Polk's comment sounds more like a politician's stump speech than an off-hand conversation among twenty-year-old sightseers, Lieutenant Polk addressed Cadet Lee this way: "Lee, we shall probably both live to see the whole country covered by a network of these iron roads and, in my opinion, it will be to them we shall owe the holding together of this immense country under one flag; owe, in fact, the preservation of the Union."[32] Balderdash, that proved to be.

The touring cadets went next to Quincy to view the neighboring homes of two presidents of the United States, John Adams, the second, and his son John Quincy Adams, the sixth and then current president. "I had pictured to myself a fine country seat, occupying an eminence, surrounded by groves, orchards and woodland and all the appurtenances of such a place," Leonidas told his parents. He and his friends were struck, instead, by the thrifty plainness of the presidential birthplaces, clapboard two-story houses standing beside one another on dirt-surfaced Franklin Street. Thomas Boylston Adams, youngest son of John and Abigail Adams, and his wife, Ann Harrod Adams, escorted the visitors through the home of the late president.[33]

On his own again, and again favoring his academic interests, Leonidas traversed Rhode Island, Connecticut, and Massachusetts, visiting three other young schools before arriving in Amherst. There the Mount Pleasant Classical Institution was soon to open without a Professor Polk to run the mathematics department. Leonidas concluded the school was bound to flourish, but he betrayed in his letter no lingering wish to be on the faculty.[34] In Albany, New York, at dinner with the Martin Van Burens, Leonidas talked politics authoritatively with Thomas Ritchie, editor of the Richmond *Enquirer*, another Andrew Jackson advocate.[35] Leonidas then proceeded to Saratoga Springs. Catherine Ann Johnson Devereux (the sister-in-law who tried to persuade Fanny Devereux to abandon Roman Catholicism) was there with her husband, Thomas; the couple were partaking of the resort's salubrious waters and fashionable ambience. Not deigning to tarry by these affects, the young lieutenant was impatient to be off to visit battlefields where soldiers he admired had contended against British, French, and American Indian enemies. "Aside from water and company," he said of the spa, "the place offers few attractions."[36]

Just beyond the gaiety of the spa, Leonidas surveyed the fields of Saratoga. There, after three weeks of battling in 1777, the ragtag Americans had wrested a humiliating surrender from the British and Hessian professionals led by John Burgoyne. It was the turning point of the War for Independence. (And soon he stood upon the nearby Bemas Heights, where the exemplary patriot of Quebec City's near-capture, Brigadier Benedict Arnold, had been wounded yet again assaulting King George III's hirelings. Alas for an unblemished future, he had not been killed.)[37] More galvanizing still was Lieutenant Polk's walk amid the ruins of Fort William Henry in the sylvan recesses of Lake George. His mind was illumined by the portrayal of the French and Indian War in the just published *The Last of the Mohicans: A Narrative of 1757*, in which James Fenimore Cooper had written how Huron Indians with "fatal and appalling whoop" had butchered hundreds of paleface men, women and children, soldiers, and civilians after Britain's besieged fort had surrendered to the French. So awful was the event that Cooper had slyly warned "all single gentlemen, of a certain age," to forebear reading his novel as "it might disturb their sleep." Leonidas's ruminations on the bloody pyre onto which many of the bodies were thrown were offset by the transfixing scenery of azure Lake George.[38]

The traveler was by now moving so fast that he could not match correspondence to mileage, and in attempting to keep his parents and various friends informed of his progress and adventures he was in Pittsburgh in mid-September before he could tell his father of where he had been since leaving Lake George four weeks earlier. The swelling of his fingers, induced he believed by frazzled nerves, had not subsided, and this further slowed his writing. Sailing by steamship up Lake Champlain after stopping at Fort Ticonderoga,[39] he had entered Quebec at St. Jean, thence proceeded by carriage to the isle of Montreal. Observing peasant farmers during his fifteen-mile ride to town, he was told by others in the coach and accepted as fact that these Canadians were "indolent and careless of anything like advancement." In features, language, manners, and dress (roundabouts, moccasins, red sashes around their middles) the "lower Classes" of rural French Canadians were certainly distinct from Americans, but the dress of the townspeople, the patronizing visitor was relieved to see, happily conformed to "ours." Shortly he was headed for Tennessee and home.[40]

The disagreeable summer sun of 1827, which during his stay had baked Quebec and himself, was elsewhere parching the Ohio River Basin in the

United States. When he reached Pittsburgh, as a result, he was told that no travel was available on the dried-up river for those headed south.[41] With no choice but to endure more stagecoach travel, he first rode down to Wheeling, Virginia (now West Virginia), and there swung west into Ohio on the National Road then abuilding, a serendipitous upgrade in his travel plans.

For Leonidas and his coach companions in 1827, the National Road was a comparative improvement over the jolting, rattling roads they were accustomed to, a benefit ascribed to the innovative macadam plan—loose stones scarcely larger than sugar cubes being packed over the roadbed to a depth of twelve inches. This method, the well-informed army engineer already knew, was "much of late praised in England."[42] Such comfort as Leonidas found in the sugar-cube roadway was short-lived; after about fifty miles, his stage outran the macadamized portion and plunged along such rutted coach roads as old Ebenezer Zane's Trace across Ohio. Thereafter it maneuvered west and south through Lexington, Kentucky, and into Tennessee. The route he had taken, Leonidas trusted, would someday become an essential link of the National Road. It was a fond hope. Even then, when its future still looked promising, the National Road was beset by political wrangling among the states and towns through which, with congressional blessing, it might pass. "The roads in this country are wretched in the extreme," he said, the sentiments "of all travelers no matter how much the politicians will disagree."[43]

At last he was safely arrived in Middle Tennessee, welcomed by his brother Lucius, his second cousin Marshall Polk, and various other Polk relations who lived there. Leonidas reverted almost at once to civilian life. He had written out his resignation from the army while making his way south, and now he sent it over to Raleigh for his father to forward to Colonel Thayer at West Point. His tour of the Northeast and Lower Canada had taken him longer than planned, and despite his making haste and even sometimes "declining civilities . . . I should have been glad to have received," he was late reaching Tennessee. Thus, with his furlough about to expire, he had deemed it necessary to waive his promise to talk first with his parents in Raleigh before submitting the resignation. As he blithely informed his father, "I apprehended no difficulty in obtaining your consent to my resigning."[44]

4

"'Minding High Things' Too Much"
(1828–1830)

William Polk was preoccupied in the winter of 1828 with presidential politics, the simmering contest between the patrician incumbent John Quincy Adams, and the people's hero of New Orleans, Gen. Andrew Jackson, Polk's old crony. To free himself for campaigning, the colonel shifted family chores to his and Sarah's oldest sons. Now civilian, Leonidas was to see after Raleigh farming affairs, and Lucius, having come over from Tennessee, was to shepherd young Alexander Hamilton Polk, then seventeen, to New Haven, Connecticut, where the youth was to prepare himself academically for enrollment in the fall term at Yale College.

After Lucius got back to North Carolina, his father took him to Tennessee to help him deal with overdue land rents and lawsuits, contentions seeming always to characterize the Polks' real-estate dealings in the western district. Leonidas, now in charge of the Raleigh household and gardens (including the exotic lemon and orange trees growing in a backyard greenhouse), found the solitary life altogether congenial, he told Lucius, not at all missing the political discussions that filled the Polk home when his father was around.[1]

As a trained army engineer turned civilian planter, Leonidas discharged the orders his father had left him by applying textbook construction skills while supervising slave gangs in rebuilding some creek dikes (which had broken and flooded adjacent fields) and in repairing an earthen dam that held back water used to drive a grain mill. Leonidas also turned his hand to another task devolving upon plantation owners: he restored order with a lash after a number of his father's slaves had made violent threats against one another. The object of the slaves' anger was Frank, himself a slave and the "driver" of a work crew, who had been about to punish one of the younger men under his charge. The other slaves thought the threatened whipping unwarranted and had mobbed around Frank with raised clubs and shouts. They terrified him so, Leonidas reported, that Frank could not sleep that night. "Such [abuse and insults] from Negroes to one another I have never heard," Leonidas admitted, and with his surrogate authority (and nascent ease with violence) he met the challenge by personally flogging all those he thought deserving. In his offhand report of the affray, which is torn in places, he wrote: "I went down the [*torn*] next morning and beginning with Mingo whipped the whole [*torn*] who were [*torn*] engaged in it some way. They have been quiet ever since." The account of the flogging, apparently not a remarkable occurrence in the Polks' plantation affairs, is tucked among news of crops and of family and neighbors.[2]

Lashing the backs of slaves was but one aspect of Leonidas's maturing into a patrician Southron that season. As a baptized Christian coming of age, he made ready to present himself for Confirmation in North Carolina's Episcopal Church. The denomination had spun off from the Church of England and, since the Revolution, had been gradually recovering respectability after its Tory past. In the stern presence of the Right Reverend John Stark Ravenscroft, the first bishop of North Carolina, Leonidas reaffirmed in March the vows he had made two years earlier in the West Point chapel. Bishop Ravenscroft, already well acquainted with Raleigh's Polk family, administered the Laying on of Hands to Leonidas, and likewise to his sister Mary Polk Badger and her new husband, George Badger, at St. John's Church in Fayetteville.[3] Leonidas was by then under the bishop's eye, having made himself useful in church affairs. Shortly after his return from his eastern travels, he was put in charge of the Sunday School program at Christ Church in Raleigh, and he would soon represent the parish at a statewide convention.[4]

Bishop Ravenscroft had a pastoral bond with Sarah Polk as well. One of the town's established benefactresses, she and various of her well-to-do women friends had in 1821 founded the Raleigh Female Benevolent Society. A close-knit society it was, too. Fanny Devereux, Sarah's future daughter-in-law, was treasurer, and Fanny's mother was a member of the board of managers.[5] One day Mrs. Polk invited the bishop to her home, affording Colonel Polk an opportunity to try out one of his theological opinions on a professional. Is it not the case, Polk ventured, that a dying man of clean habits and high morality would as surely get to Heaven as any bona fide Christian? Ravenscroft did not give this heretical notion a moment's thought. "No, sir," he boomed. "He would go straight to hell!"[6]

Leonidas's own religious endeavors that winter and spring dovetailed with the amatory stirrings he had put on hold. Shortly before taking off by sulky for Fayetteville and the convention, he proposed marriage to Frances Ann Devereux. She had turned twenty in March, and these childhood sweethearts had grown up having a number of things in common: their wealth and social positions, their earnest dispositions, and lately their tendencies to brood on religious matters. During their courtship that spring Leonidas helped Fanny sort through the spiritual quandaries still besetting her since she was wrenched by her family from the Catholic girls' school in Maryland. Or as Fanny put it years later in her memoir, he "took such pain to direct my mind aright, which had for a while been entangled in a sea of perplexities and doubt."[7] It was evidently this directing that led Fanny to renounce her ties to Catholicism. In choosing the spiritually uncertain Fanny for his bride, Leonidas may have had to accept a compromise of the spousal ideals he had once enumerated to Lucius: "tenderlings and excellences, frankness, gentleness, industry, good sense and matronly dignity, and above all purity. With such a one poverty would be richness." Poverty, with Fanny at his side, might indeed provide richness, but taking into account the Devereux family's formidable financial resources, why not have richness with wealth thrown in? For her part, what Fanny desired in a husband she had found without reservations; she later described Leonidas exactly as St. Paul had defined the Godhead: he was her "all in all."[8]

Given to privacy about his personal life—it is an aspect noticeable even when he wrote to those closest to him—Leonidas told few family members about the marriage proposal until several months had passed. However, he did confide in Mary and her husband George Badger before he proposed, binding both to secrecy. Mary and George reacted at first to her love-struck kid brother with laughter, probably because of the clandestine air Leonidas had assumed. Hurt, he "put on one of his grave faces," Mary soon told Lucius (violating "woman like" her pledge to secrecy), "and remarked it was no laughing matter, and in less than a week from that time actually carried the matter through." Mary was satisfied with the arrangement. "The Lady in question," she told Lucius, "has left the Catholic Church, and will, I expect, join the Episcopal, so it will exactly suit."[9] (Notwithstanding his usual sharing of confidences with Lucius, Leonidas let six weeks go by before he wrote his brother of his plans to marry "Miss D" and expressing the hope he had made the right matrimonial decision.)[10]

Had Leonidas had his way, the marriage would have taken place later that summer or by early fall at the latest. That was not to be, and he widely missed the mark when he wrote Lucius as late as August 22 that the wedding might take place no later than October or November. In the Devereux household the thinking was otherwise, because that summer Leonidas had been nurturing the idea of attending a theological seminary to train for his ministry in the Episcopal Church. Taking that into account, Fanny "thought it best that our marriage should be delayed." Leonidas, "with great reluctance, acceded to this."[11] One may sympathize with the tensions then ensuing for the husband-to-be. Until their wedding in May 1830, Leonidas and Fanny were able to see one another but for one week in the spring of 1829 and one month that autumn.[12]

At West Point, meanwhile, Chaplain McIlvaine had resigned his captaincy, some of those ranking above him glad to see him go. He had relocated in Brooklyn, New York, becoming the rector of St. Ann's Episcopal Church. With Leonidas's wedding hopes dashed and needing McIlvaine's advice regarding seminary training, he left Raleigh at summer's end for Brooklyn. There he met his brother Hamilton, who had come to the city from New Haven, and with McIlvaine the two attended a convention at Trinity Church in Manhattan. Afterward, the brothers visited West Point before Hamilton was due back at Yale. When he left Raleigh, Leonidas had not firmly determined which of two Episcopal seminaries he would attend that fall, but after four days in the company of McIlvaine, he had decided. Given McIlvaine's leanings, it was no surprise that Leonidas chose the low-church Virginia Theological Seminary rather than the high-church General Seminary in Manhattan. From the Virginia school's beginnings a decade earlier, McIlvaine had been involved in its growth and had many friends among the faculty and trustees. From time to time he also raised money and recruited students to enroll there.

As a precaution, Leonidas made no mention of McIlvaine's influence when he informed his family of his choice; the minister's sway over the planter's son was evidently a sore subject in the Raleigh household. Instead, Leonidas emphasized that he had picked the Virginia school for its forested Fairfax County campus ("high, healthy and retired"), for "the Spirit of the place" (meaning to him its emphasis on missionary outreach), and for the Southern contacts that would serve him in good stead in his later ministry. Which seminary one attended was less important than what one wished to achieve, he explained patiently to Colonel Polk. For one usually respectful of education and learning, Leonidas seemed to hold a patronizing view of some aspects of the academic regimen he was about to enter. Certainly, he conceded, the right courses of study mattered, as did skilled professors to direct the students' inquiries. But the prospect of lectures was worth little to him. "All that professors say can be found already published," he said. "The real labor . . . devolves necessarily on the student." He did grant that, with the proper books placed in his hands, and with opportunities for "rubbing against" other similarly directed students in the seminary setting, he expected to profit from his studies in Alexandria. While in Brooklyn, Leonidas enrolled in a two-week-long cram course in biblical Hebrew. Studies and spiritual satisfaction in order, the farmer-seminarian still had practical matters back in North Carolina to attend to; his corn was cribbed, his cotton soon to be housed, and he had been "gratified" that the slaves he owned were purchased by Lucius—they would soon depart for Tennessee.[13]

Leonidas and McIlvaine had gone to Washington for the late October meeting of the Society for the Education of Pious Young Men for the Ministry of the Protestant Episcopal Church. This society had, not incidentally, given birth to the seminary in Alexandria, and McIlvaine favored the proceedings with a sermon. The visitors then looked in on Congress, and next they had an audience with President John Quincy Adams at the White House, arranged for them either by McIlvaine (whom Adams had once approvingly heard preach in Washington) or by the Reverend James Milnor, the former Pennsylvania congressman and an Adams supporter.[14] At the president's home the consummate Washington politician Henry Clay came gliding through the waiting room and jovially recalled a winter's travel adventure with Leonidas's father six years earlier; deposited on the ocean ice by the ship's captain, the passengers had had to walk to Baltimore on the frozen bay.[15] Then Adams came in. The president appeared to Leonidas "as awkward as Mr. Clay is easy." The dilapidated condition of the president's White House quarters dismayed Leonidas, too. It "looks more like parsimony in the government than anything I have ever seen," he said.[16]

As Leonidas was rarely happier than when touring and sightseeing, once he was settled in Alexandria he did not want for leisure to pursue this non-academic interest: he would idle away study time in his seminary room by observing with a telescope the Capitol comings and goings of President Adams and the members of Congress some six miles distant over the snowy Virginia landscape.[17] Other times he set aside the Bible and theological texts to conduct himself as any well-to-do planter away from home might do—arranging through correspondence agricultural matters and the selling of his slaves to his brother in Tennessee. The bulk of these men and women and children, he said casually, their possessions in wagons, would walk some 500 miles from North Carolina to their new home. As the weather worsened that winter, he did express concern for the people embarked on their "very cold and disagreeable journey."[18]

The gulf between the Christian precepts of self-denial he heard within the seminary walls and the structure of influence and money supporting his own world outside had lately begun to destabilize his moral balance. Knowing his parents were content to be spared his musings, he kept them mostly to himself, and his letters to them were typically filled with light chatter about his daily doings. He did allow himself to sermonize upon the death of Andrew Jackson's wife, Rachel, just as the president-elect was about to be inaugurated. He hoped that the widower, recognizing religion's "necessity," would rule the nation "upon the just and perfect principles of Christianity"—a fond idea, as it turned out.[19] News from his mother included that she had lately given birth to a ninth son, named Charles James Polk, and that his uncle Benjamin Hawkins, "in a fit of derangement," had fatally slashed his throat with a "raisor."[20] No one in the family at this time, least of all the groom-to-be, ever penned a word regarding his recent engagement to Fanny Devereux or how he might be dealing with the heartbreak of their postponed wedding.

The hurt he was feeling more acutely was spiritual, and he poured it out to McIlvaine. After attending a meeting of the school's missionary society, he recognized that, unlike some of his fellow seminarians, his passions were ruled more by rebellion and self-serving than by discipleship. He was pleased to call himself a follower of Christ who had ransomed him from Hell, he said, but his heart and will denied it. "My dear bro.," he wrote, embellishing his letter with excerpts from New Testament epistles:

> I feel that my heart is yet too much set on the things of this world. I don't despise the opinions of men enough, I don't "despise the shame" of many parts of this life a true and faithful follower of Jesus must necessarily lead. I find I am "minding high things" too much, and have not my heart yearning after the low and obscure and the poor enough. I am too unwilling to "count myself of no reputation." This is my fault, my great fault.

His preoccupying endeavors to prepare himself properly "for death and judgment" showed a serious deficit, and he promised to work on mending his ways.[21]

Whatever pastoral advice McIlvaine was able to supply to the troubled seminarian is unknown. As his own diary entries show, McIlvaine was himself sometimes beset by self-condemnations and doubts, some of which he may have admitted to his protégé.[22] All the same, Leonidas's struggle with enjoying—while not wholly wanting to enjoy—the benefits of his high social station was to surface only a few weeks later when he rode over again to Washington to attend with McIlvaine the annual meeting of the American Colonization Society (ACS). The ACS, then about a decade old, was a hopeful, if unrealistic, organization bringing together white people whose interests ranged from those wishing devoutly to abolish slavery (one of whom was Charles McIlvaine) to those wishing just as much to preserve it (one of whom was Col. William Polk, the president of the society's Raleigh chapter).[23] What Northern and Southern members agreed on was the idea of inducing America's freed slaves to resink their roots in their native continent, a policy society members thought good for all concerned. In Liberia there would be free farmland; in America, no black pauperism, no violent conspiracies, and no racial mixing. It was the nation's nineteenth-century expression of ethnic cleansing, as one modern historian has said.[24] Thus Northern abolitionists were members of the ACS; Christian evangelicals were members of the ACS; many of Colonel Polk's slave-owning planter friends were members of the ACS; and the former president James Madison was a member of the ACS.[25]

Attending the society's meeting that winter with his church friends, Leonidas seems to have been infected by the abolitionists in his group. "I believe in the course of not many years one state after another will be willing to abolish slavery," he wrote his father. "From a variety of motives, funds enough will be raised to gradually transport [the freed slaves]" to Liberia. Thus convinced, Leonidas joined the society. Though his optimism was wrong, later when his slaves worked his sugarcane plantation he still participated in ACS affairs, serving as president, at one point, of the New Orleans chapter.[26]

As a soldier comrade from Revolutionary War days, William Polk was personally picked by President-elect Andrew Jackson to parade down the streets of Washington as Old Hickory was ushered in as seventh president of the United States. Ever pragmatic, the colonel hoped while in Washington to put in a good word for Mary's husband, George Badger, who aspired to a cabinet post as US Attorney General.[27] Polk arrived a few days beforehand in early March and, as many other presidential friends were disposed to do, was soon confabbing with Jackson in his suite at the new and fashionable National Hotel on Pennsylvania Avenue. Whereupon First Lt. Edward George Washington Butler of Louisiana entered the room. Lieutenant Butler, formerly a ward of Andrew Jackson, had graduated from West Point in 1820 and knew of Leonidas Polk's having been a cadet as well. In his conversation with Colonel Polk, Butler asked where young Polk was now stationed. "Stationed?" choked Leonidas's father. "Why, by thunder, sir, he's over there in Alexandria at the seminary!"[28]

For all the disappointment the old soldier felt in a favorite son based at a divinity school, Leonidas was nonetheless welcomed to Washington by his father for the inauguration. Just weeks earlier, Leonidas in a letter had primly criticized the new president for his "descending to the removal of petty postmasters in order to replace them with political cronies of unrespectable character." Even though his trust in Jacksonian principles had been shaken, Leonidas cheekily used his White House visit to persuade the president to reinstate to West Point his cousin Henry Hawkins, now eighteen, who had been expelled for deficiency in mathematics.[29] Leonidas then decided spontaneously to accompany his father back to Raleigh for a week's visit. The absence from his fiancée had begun to tell.[30]

Once back at the seminary, bad news awaited. Leonidas's favorite teacher, Reuel Keith, the school's dean and head professor, had left for Florida on short notice because of his wife's illness. The resulting "destitute condition" of the school, as Leonidas saw it, so upset him that he considered withdrawing. He decided to remain only after reflecting that it was a duty he owed the other fourteen students in the school.[31] Keith was a Vermont Yankee, sternly pious and evangelical (like Leonidas), a little sickly (like Leonidas), an avid horseman (like Leonidas), and, to cap it off, a warm friend of Charles McIlvaine. What's more, his intellect, coupled with a wry classroom charm, had appealed to Leonidas and his classmates. Adding to Leonidas's upset was the fact that he had been looking forward during his final term to studying systematic divinity, Keith's specialty.[32] To fill the void, Leonidas increased his studious exertions and complemented book learning with practical experience. He joined fellow seminarians in "harmony and brotherly love" to teach in Sunday schools and ministered to the unchurched of the neighborhood—what one school trustee termed the group's "zealous efforts for the spiritual improvement of the destitute and ignorant in the vicinity of the Seminary." He meant the neighborhood's slave population.[33]

These diversions notwithstanding, Leonidas was increasingly restless with his life, chafing at course work and wanting to find early employment as an ordained clergyman. With grand-sounding phrases usually found only in sermons, he assured McIlvaine that if launched into the ministry "I would only so pass through things temporal as not to lose those that are eternal, but . . . I would mightily set forward the cause of God and the salvation of multitudes of my dying fellow creatures." Might not McIlvaine know of an "appropriate station" for him as a worker in "fields white with the harvest"?[34] His ambition along these spiritual lines was strong, though a taste for things temporal always lurked in the background. Even the day after his letter to McIlvaine, he was thanking his father for a financial favor. Some months earlier, needing cash for books and other school expenses, he asked Colonel Polk to sell off certain plantation land that the father previously gave him. William Polk obligingly bought back a considerable chunk of the acreage for himself.[35] So Leonidas was clearly "minding high things" from time to time, and making little progress in counting himself of no reputation, or not despising the shame of discipleship.

But with his mind made up to apply for ordination as a deacon in the Episcopal Church, he was constrained once more to justify to his father "the cause I have determined to pursue during my life on Earth."[36] His letter opened as though preached to a congregation of one. There was no hope for happiness in Eternity apart from Christian allegiance and "that all therefore who fail of this must be lost." Fully persuaded of that doctrine, and being a caring and dutiful person, he had "determined to use the time and talents allotted me on earth in unfolding and explaining the scheme of redemption and in urging its acceptance" to all and sundry. He understood this might be personally costly. For example, he was now obliged to distance himself from worldly affairs, he said, and he risked, as well, the censure and alienation of friends whom he must now relate to in a "novel . . . and . . . perhaps painful" manner. But so be it; his concern for their spiritual welfare and his own obedience to God would override his reticence to preach to those to whom he felt "ties of natural affection." Cautiously, he pressed on: "That [a rupture] may never occur [among friends] is my sincere desire, but more particularly, my dear Father, that such a change may be effected in our relative condition as entirely to forbid the possibility of its [ever] occurring. These things I have thought it a duty frankly and affectionately to express to you." That William Polk was deeply discomfited reading this indictment can be believed.

Though Leonidas might sometimes temper his evangelical pronouncements when corresponding with his family, the plight of a dying brother in the early spring of 1830 pushed him farther than ever before. Hamilton Polk, the ailing nineteen-year-old to whom Leonidas was devoted, was clearly in desperate straits when he came through Alexandria in January with either severe asthma or tuberculosis, as it came to be known. The family assumed that, whatever his illness, it had been exacerbated by the Atlantic seaboard's winter months, and he had dropped out of Yale and was bound for Tallahassee, capital of the newly acquired Florida Territory. This temperate haven with a growing following among American health-seekers had few residents and fewer amenities (three hotels, two groceries, one grog shop, and a slave auction) but could already boast a social whirl of planters, led elegantly by Prince Napoleon Achille Murat, son of the deposed king of Naples. A famed tubercular visitor in 1827, Ralph Waldo Emerson, noted that "what are called the ladies of the place are in number, 8."[37]

After Hamilton's visit, Leonidas informed their mother that he was convinced his brother "may have, and undoubtedly has the appearance of having, the seeds of our family malady sown within him."[38] Though his training as a minister was in its early stages, he was not reluctant to turn his hand to pastoral counseling. When, for example, his mother seemed to minimize the seriousness of Hamilton's illness, Leonidas became a scold. He was pained by both his own and his family's "earthly attachments," but more so by his parents' reluctance to look death in the eye and prepare for it, as he believed faithful Christians should. "I confess I do not see the wisdom of putting away from our minds the contemplation of things as things are, and must be," he told his mother. He pursued these preachments at some length in his letter before backing off and apologizing for the lecture.[39]

With his spring marriage pending and with Professor Keith away, the once academically fussy student who had wanted to overhaul West Point's curriculum had become a far less resolute divinity scholar. Conceding "that I might spend some months longer in study with advantage," he nevertheless decided to conclude his preparation for the parish ministry little more than eighteen months after entering the Virginia seminary. Comfortable in his opinions, Leonidas held that "in a theological course, a few weeks longer or shorter could not be of material consequence."[40] Richard Channing Moore, his bishop in Virginia, evidently agreed, and Leonidas made plans to present himself for ordination in Richmond (where the bishop resided) and arrive in Raleigh fully certified for ministry and ready for marriage by late April. A May wedding could then take place before Tennessee business would take his father from Raleigh.

Accordingly, having satisfactorily answered the examination questions put to him by Bishop Moore, he was ordained into the diaconate on April 9, 1830. That was Good Friday, and the ceremony took place in Richmond's Monumental Episcopal Church.[41] Two days after his ordination, becomingly vested in surplice and black tippet, the Reverend Mr. Polk was put to another test as he ascended the Monumental pulpit Easter morning. "Though not very well and much excited" (his word for "nervous" in his letter to McIlvaine), he launched his clerical career by reading his Easter sermon to a congregation better known for First Families of Virginia social connections than for piety. Still, the preacher felt "graciously sustained and comforted in the delivery of my message." Left then to fend for himself by Bishop Moore, he preached again on the two following Sundays. Too inexperienced to extemporize, he was "very much fettered by my notes," believing the worshipers deserved a "spiritual, heartfelt appeal from the Gospel" rather than the written essay he had composed. The parish vestry forgave that shortcoming, and within days a job offer from the Monumental Church arrived in the mail. By then he was in Raleigh, and he accepted. "This," Fanny Devereux Polk was to say with bitterness forty years later, "was a great mistake."[42]

5

"At Any Moment Our Brightest Hopes May Be Nipt in the Bud" (1830–1832)

Leonidas Polk and Frances Ann Devereux were wed on Thursday, May 6, 1830. After little more than a further week in Raleigh, the couple left for Richmond where, now employed by the Monumental Church, he was obliged to "enter on the duties of the parish." For Fanny the period of the wedding and honeymoon seems to have been a blur. She remembered mostly that "almost immediately" after the nuptials that they were packed up and traveling north by stage and steamboat.[1]

Whatever fanciful notions of brotherly love the Reverend Mr. Polk had entertained before his immersion in professional parish ministry, he soon downed a dose of reality. He forthwith got in touch with Charles McIlvaine, still in England. Leonidas discerned in the large and fashionable congregation "spirits of every grade and character," few of whom were "decidedly and actively pious." Neither, to his despair, was the "bond of Christian fellowship strong among them," as "the Gospel required." But having visited other Episcopal parishes, he acknowledged that his parishioners' aloofness "was a fault in some degree I have thought general to our Church." Leonidas was privately praying that he might be able to improve the quality of Christian love within his flock. A monthly concert he had set up might also help to bring the people together. One impediment to his goals was the bishop, Richard Moore. Though "kind and affectionate," he is "getting old and is for peace" and "is cautious and admits new plans . . . with difficulty." The bishop was content with "the usual societies" and a lecture now and then.[2]

As for his own ministry, he told McIlvaine, "I trust I am not ignorant of the way to be saved, but how to present it so as to command attention and constrain obedience seems beyond my powers." Leonidas's health no less than his pastoral technique was proving unequal to his goals. Within weeks of his and Fanny's settling into their apartment, he took sick with "bilious fever." Whatever that was, it must have been associated with his old pulmonary problem and was possibly exacerbated by the stressful events of the past months. He became so short of breath that for weeks in June and July he was unable to preach, his primary assignment when the bishop was away. That added new dimension to his feeling "very deeply, at times, distressed and depressed under a sense of the magnitude of my work." He took heart (a little) by reminding himself that Saint Paul had once stiffened the backbone of his young missionary friend Timothy by saying, "Let no man despise thy youth, but be thou an example of believers."[3] Still, he reckoned he could do with a little stiffening from McIlvaine. "Can you find time from your valuable engagements to drop me a few hints?" he pleaded.

Bishop Moore seems to have been oblivious to Leonidas's faltering nerve and health; he dropped the whole running of the parish into his lap in late July and left for a months-long journey. Leonidas coped as best he could, but "he grew more feeble daily," as Fanny remembered it. Then, in the midst of his parochial duties, he was summoned in September to Raleigh, as Hamilton had "insisted upon returning home to die" from his lung disease. Staying close beside Hamilton over several days and nights, Leonidas avoided "anything that looked like teaching" and awaited Hamilton's request for guidance in preparing for death. And then (Fanny recounted) "right joyfully did he preach unto him Christ, and him crucified."[4] Whereupon Hamilton consented to baptism and, shortly before he died two days short of his twentieth birthday, told brother Lucius: "It is my sincere prayer that we may all . . . be reunited in Heaven as on Earth in one family."[5] Leonidas read the Order for the Burial of the Dead over his brother's grave.

Scarcely was he back in Richmond than he learned his infant brother Charles James, scarcely two, had also died. The brothers' deaths afforded Leonidas yet another opportunity to urge his father and his brother to ponder Eternity. Although "our children and our parents are sources of great comfort and happiness to us . . . they are mortal," he reminded his grieving father. Enduring happiness, though sought in the here and now, was to be found "only beyond the grave," and then only by "real Christians" who would be reunited with one another in the Hereafter.[6] His entreaty to Lucius was no less urgent. Expressing his conviction that the deaths of their six siblings had been divine messages to their parents, communicating "a recognition of God . . . as a merciful father [and] the proper object of their highest love," he closed triumphantly: "It is indeed, my bro., a dying world, and every stroke bids us to prepare to meet our God."[7]

Leonidas's diseased lungs during the winter of 1830–1831 caused him renewed pain in his side, fatigue, coughing, and night sweats.[8] He was briefly diverted from dwelling upon his own health when Fanny, late in January, gave birth to their first child.[9] They named the boy Alexander Hamilton after the deceased uncle, and as any new father is wont, Leonidas boasted to Lucius that even during his first fortnight the infant had given "strong indications of both eminence and usefulness." And although little Hamilton's "broad shoulders and . . . prominent chest" suggested to the father that he "might long escape the hands of the physician," Leonidas was gloomily constrained to add that he and Fanny realized that, should God will it, "at any moment our brightest hopes may be nipt in the bud. This I endeavor constantly to realize."[10]

In fact, baby Hamilton thrived, and it was Leonidas's decline that beset the young family. The newborn's liveliness was a part of that problem, exhausting and wearing away at both parents' affection. Leonidas rallied in March as though he had downed a spoonful of a patent tonic. The medicine was news from New York City of a Lenten-season fervor among the city's Presbyterians, but affecting other Protestants.[11] The Reverend David Moore (son of Virginia's bishop, with a parish on Staten Island) thought the religious goings-on might be likened to Europe's Reformation in the sixteenth century, indeed to the biblical day of Pentecost in Asia Minor's first century. To the low-church faithful in the high-church Diocese of New York, the revival was thrilling, and Leonidas was no less energized by what he was hearing. "Oh, how I long again to breathe such an atmosphere," he wrote to McIlvaine. "It is the Elixir of Life, a refreshing shower to the thirsty and parched ground." He begged McIlvaine to write him some details of it all. "It will be news from the seat of war. It will be animating; it will encourage; it will strengthen the feeble knees and lift up the hands which hang down."[12] The revival peaked, and gradually died down, as did Leonidas's vigor. By April, just a year after he had begun at Monumental Church, "he broke down so completely," said Fanny, "that he felt it necessary to resign his post."[13]

The couple almost immediately sold their furniture and returned to Raleigh. Fanny and Hammy—as the parents were now calling him—moved in with the Devereux family. Leonidas felt strong enough, however, to make it back to Virginia, where his diocesan convention was to meet in Norfolk on May 19. At the end of the proceedings, he was elevated from the diaconate to the priesthood by his champion, Bishop Moore.[14] But no sooner had he rejoined his family than his health took another alarming turn. If nothing were done, said Fanny, he felt "he must die," just as Hamilton had.[15]

An uncle (John Hawkins, his mother's brother) advised Leonidas to seek medical help in Philadelphia, unrivaled in those days for the healing arts. Hawkins further recommended that his nephew mosey along getting there; a leisurely trip by horseback in the open air was a popular prescription for pulmonary disorders.[16] Setting out in early June, Leonidas probably expected to be gone a few weeks, but having kissed his wife and child farewell and swung into the saddle, he was off on what would prove to be an absence of eighteen months.

To reach Philadelphia, some 400 miles from Raleigh, Leonidas and his horse took a course that passed through the seminary in Alexandria. Here, to his delight, he found Reuel Keith, now returned to teaching. Leonidas clearly being a favorite of his, the professor dropped everything, and the two rode on together to Philadelphia, where Leonidas called on Dr. John Kearsley Mitchell, a Philadelphia physician famed for the treatment of fevers and a society doctor of the sort Leonidas would seek out.[17] Leonidas was taken aback by Mitchell's prognosis: he would die in a matter of months. Mitchell obligingly had Leonidas seek a second opinion from Mitchell's mentor and former professor, Dr. Nathaniel Chapman, a professor at the Medical School of the University of Pennsylvania.[18] Central to his diagnostic theories was the assumption that every illness was an expression of an irritation in the stomach and that debility and exhaustion depleted the stomach's key assignments to ward off illnesses. Leonidas, afflicted by his coughs and night sweats, was certainly debilitated and exhausted, as Chapman and a colleague quickly observed. The patient was manifestly in need of rest and relaxation, particularly from the accumulated rigors of parenthood, parish administration, and hortatory preaching.

First off, he was to dispense with the vomit-evoking tartar emetic plasters and the weakening dietary regimen that some well-meaning Southern doctor had prescribed. Second, he was to book passage to Europe and spend the coming winter in Italy. The doctors did not mean sometime in the future; they meant now, today.[19] Leonidas and Reuel Keith remounted and headed for a steamship office in New York City.[20] Needing funds for this unforeseen journey, Leonidas turned to accommodating New York bankers familiar with his family and cashed promissory notes from his brother Lucius that, with some fear of the unknown, he had the presence of mind in Raleigh to tuck into his saddlebags.[21] Then, with a day or two at his disposal, he and Keith rode over to Brooklyn to visit McIlvaine, who supplied Leonidas with the letters of introduction "to gentlemen" that he would take to Europe, and so did James Milnor, his New York clergyman friend from West Point days. He also obtained letters from the Reverend Levi Silliman Ives, the rector of St. Luke's Episcopal Church in Manhattan. Weeks earlier, Ives had been chosen bishop-elect of North Carolina, and while he was not an evangelical of McIlvaine's stripe, Leonidas considered introductions over his name worthwhile.[22]

On August 8, Leonidas embarked. His parents, then in Tennessee, knew nothing of his plans. Fanny learned of his pending departure just days before he sailed; a box of clothing she then hurriedly assembled failed to reach him in time.[23] Recalling her husband's startling leave-taking from Hammy and her, Fanny was succinct: "What I felt may be imagined." What Leonidas later felt about the extensive and expensive steps he was about to take to recover was mixed. He admitted he had erred in leaving his family behind. And he disclosed sometimes that he regretted making the trip altogether, since, as Fanny explained, "what an amount of care and anxiety he would have been spared" had he accepted John Mitchell's prognosis and died.[24]

A nineteenth-century New England physician, Dr. William Sweetser, observed that preachers of his day, obliged to strain their voices to reach the back rows of their churches, were especially susceptible to phthisical complaints. Apart from the refreshing open air to be found on ocean voyages, Sweetser held that the real benefit to consumptives sailing to Europe was the patients' vomiting brought on by seasickness. The wracking and heaving and gagging "activates" the lungs, he cheerfully commended in his *A Treatise on Consumption*.[25] On his way to such promised good health, Leonidas spent twenty-one days crossing the pitching Atlantic, and despite Dr. Sweetser's view that it was all to the good, his recurrent bouts of vomiting rendered him miserable by the time he reached Le Havre. It was not until some weeks later in Paris that he could report color returning to his cheeks and that he was "much less nervous."[26]

To bolster his belief that his health was truly on the mend, Leonidas consulted François Joseph Victor Broussais, MD, shortly after arriving in Paris. A colleague of Philadelphia's Nathaniel Chapman, Dr. Broussais was "celebrated," Leonidas told Lucius, "for his skill in the diseases of the lungs."[27] Following the office call, Leonidas felt even better than before: Broussais had pronounced his lungs "perfectly sound." This improvement, Broussais thought, was easily explained by Leonidas's having lain off preaching for several months, giving his lungs the rest they needed. Continue abstaining, Broussais counseled, while taking a leisurely, three-week autumn trip up the Rhine, and follow that by crossing the Alps into Italy.[28] For winter sojourns in the treatment of "invalids with complaints of the breath,"

Leonidas said, Broussais favored Italy over southern France, the more usual choice of doctors in England.[29]

Before leaving Paris, Leonidas had begun keeping a journal, and from it his movements and liturgical notations can be tracked for several months thereafter. On Sunday, October 2, still in Paris, he attended the same church twice, finding the morning preacher "decidedly styled evangelical," thus to his liking. Regarding sermons that did not "affect the practice of the hearer both toward God and man" to be of little use, he pronounced the afternoon's preacher wanting in this regard.[30] The following Sunday found him at the English ambassador's chapel, where he met disappointment with the sermonic efforts of the Anglican bishop Michael Henry Thornhill Luscombe. Moodily he spent the balance of that day alone in his room, thinking "much of my dear wife and little one."[31] He set out by four-horse diligence to Brussels at five o'clock Tuesday morning. Clamped between two mute Frenchmen for several hours, he spent the time in what he felt was profitable reflection. His analysis of the past month: "If pleasure in its most extended sense were the sole object of life, Paris is the place to find it. . . . But if this life is the place to prepare for another, and if the Scriptures are true, one had better live anywhere else."[32]

Continuing on to Amsterdam, Leonidas dropped down to Nijmegen, where he caught a steamboat headed up the Rhine for Cologne—"remarkable" he told Rufus, for its manufacture of "eau de cologne, the watery fragrance initially produced to ward off bubonic plague." He continued to Switzerland, then left the river to travel by diligence to Bern. Near Bern, under the guidance of the director himself, he was able to tour and evaluate Philip Emanuel von Fellenberg's famed progressive Hofwyl School. His appetite for teaching whetted, he accounted that day as one of the most pleasant of his journey, and he picked up ideas he would later put to use in the several educational ventures of his own in the southern United States.[33]

Just before Alpine snows would strand him, Leonidas departed in mid-November by carriage over Simplon Pass, a road more than a mile high that had been built fewer than thirty years earlier by Napoleon Bonaparte. By early December, after brief stays in Milan and Florence, he reached Rome. Like any tourist there, he maintained a satisfactory balance of the little time he had and the abundance of paintings, statuary, and architecture that had to be seen. He kept to himself and the privacy of his journal the solemn thrills he had felt when first absorbing the "Forum Romanorum," whose ruins must have rung centuries before with "the energetic and animated voice of the great Apostle of the Gentiles preaching the Gospel," and next the "astonishing magnificence of the Coliseum," where "on this spot thousands of the followers of Christ were made the prey of wild beasts, by the cruelty of imperial monsters who disgraced human nature."[34] Yet for all the antiquities he was enjoying, his patriot leanings were stirring again, telling his father that his travels had served mainly to teach him "to revere more highly and esteem more devotedly the simple and equitable institutions of our happy country. We are at least a century before this part of the world, and are by their liberals everywhere regarded as a model."[35]

He was alone during the year-end holidays, not even mentioning Christmas in a letter home on December 24. And shortly he shared with his journal a gloomy assessment of the year just closing, chastising himself variously for imperfections.[36] On January 11, feeling fine, he left Rome accompanied by his Italian servant Paul. Sometime since the beginning of his European travels he had employed this man to travel with him and help with the baggage, among other chores. He alludes to Paul in only one of his journal entries. His new destination was Naples, where, apparently breathing easily now, he hoped to arrive in time to see a predicted eruption of Mount Vesuvius. To get there, he and Paul took a carriage on the Appian Way, stopping to admire ruins and churches in Terracina and Fondi. At Fondi, he ran afoul of officious custom agents. He had accumulated so many souvenir prints and books that when his trunks were opened he was suspected of being an unlicensed peddler. He refused to pay a fine of twenty dollars. Four vexing days would pass before the matter was finally resolved in Naples: the fine was "abated two-thirds," and his belongings were returned to him. Still vexed, he wrote: "One is forced to the reflection that a government so unrighteously administered must ere long go to the wall."[37]

During his Neapolitan stay he had caught sight of Sir Walter Scott, another tubercular tourist seeking relief in the city; Leonidas promised himself a devotee's visit to the author's home in Abbotsford, Scotland, before sailing for America. As the weather warmed to the north, he bade farewell to the many physical and aesthetic contentments he had found in Naples and began the travels that would take him home. He would head first up the Mediterranean Coast toward Siena, then veer toward Florence, Bologna, and Venice. By then having experienced Italy more or less comprehensively, he would recross the Alps into France. But barely under way, at the port city of Leghorn, he had an unnerving experience. Disdaining doctor's orders and prevailed upon to preach at a "Bethel meeting among the sailors," he stirred up his slumbering lung disease. "I can't make out my case at all," he wrote later from Nice to McIlvaine. "I look very well and, while silent, feel so. But the least excessive talking . . . brings me quite to the ground again. I sometimes fear that I shall never be able to combat again with the trials of our calling."[38]

By about that time, his brother Lucius back home had arrived at Andrew Jackson's White House in Washington and there, on April 10, was wed to Mary Ann Eastin, a young Tennessean whom the president described to Lucius's father as "my favorite niece."[39] The wedding news would catch up with Leonidas somewhere along his itinerary, and he bought his new sister-in-law a present before sailing for home.[40] Leonidas was the consummate informed tourist as he continued northward through France, skipping little. (He did, by very good luck, miss catching the epidemic cholera that had that year killed 18,000 Parisians; a brief "derangement of the bowels" was his only symptom.) Sightseeing near the Mediterranean port of Marseilles, he spied wagons loaded with bales of American cotton and poked through the bagging hoping to find his father's identifying mark. The cotton, though, had been rebaled along the way, and if any had been grown by Tennessee planters, their trademarks were now missing. Then in the vicinity of Lyon, where the region's centuries-old silk industry was attempting a resurgence, he investigated silkworms feeding on chopped mulberry leaves and visited the adjacent silk factories. His curiosity here was due to knowledge that back home in Raleigh there was much speculative excitement over growing mulberry trees with an eye on the commercial prospects of domestic silk. To Leonidas, the cocoon-to-thread process he saw going on in Lyon had, he thought, a fair prospect of succeeding in Wake County. Furthermore, while on the subject of agriculture, Leonidas suggested to his father that the planting of grapes for winemaking in the mountains of western North Carolina was probably a good idea, too. He had come to this conclusion after observing similar viticulture conditions while his steamboat passed up the Rhine River the previous October. Wrong about silk, he was right about wine: flourishing vineyards nowadays crowd the state's Yadkin Valley.[41]

Leonidas and the cholera reached London almost simultaneously, but its virulence there was relatively benign, and he gave it little thought. Rather, he allowed himself five weeks of leisure in and around London. While he had been enchanted by the pastoral beauty of the English countryside seen on the ride from Dover, he was blasé about the imputed "wonders of this wonderful city." A surfeit of vistas and structures had set in, wearing down the traveler's visual appetite. And the expenses of London (he found himself "constantly pulling shillings from one pocket and pounds from the other") convinced him "I could not, if I would, stay long in such a land." Rather, he was content, as he told his mother, to attend the springtime conventions of the Great Religious Charities that had drawn him to London in the first place.[42]

And he was always ready, of course, to spend time with like-minded churchmen. His particular pleasure, thanks to McIlvaine's letter of introduction, was being invited to the Royal Military Academy home of Olinthus Gregory, author of the textbooks so influential in Leonidas's embrace of fluxions and religion. The two hit it off, and Leonidas "was made an inmate [sic] of his house and stayed for a week."[43] Thanks, too, to McIlvaine's having spread the word two years previously, other doors in Britain swung open to the famed cadet. Leonidas was even persuaded to speak to Bible and tract societies, but was peeved that published accounts of his off-the-cuff remarks were "absolute misrepresentations."[44]

While Leonidas was enjoying himself among his new friends around London, Fanny and baby Hammy, now almost fifteen months old and teething, were in New York City. Anticipating her husband's midsummer return but her own "health being very poor," she would shortly move on to Connecticut to bide her time with Catherine Ann Johnson Devereux, her affectionate sister-in-law. A letter from Leonidas reached her in the city, in most respects resembling those he wrote his parents and brothers—where he'd been, what he'd been doing. He mailed this one from Cambridge, where he made the rounds of all the colleges in the one day he spent there. But it differs from his other family letters by his abruptly and briefly raising the issue of slavery in America. He was in the midst of telling her of his admiration of Britain's pastoral scenery when he expostulated: "And when I think of our vast plantations, with our dirty, careless, thriftless negro population, I could, and do, wish that we were thoroughly quit of them. The more I see of those who are without slaves, the more I am prepared to say that we are seriously wronging ourselves by retaining them." And that was that. He finished by saying, "But I am in no mood for entering into this subject. . . . So, dear wife, good night."[45]

In a lighter mood two days later, the novice priest rode into Oxford, and when his coach paused for passengers at the centuries-old Mitre Inn on High Street, he playfully alighted and turned in. "I thought it might be the only chance I should ever have of being sheltered beneath the Mitre," he told Fanny.[46] He was soon reflective and penitent again. He had now been away from his family a year—departing on horseback from Raleigh on "the journey which I as little thought would have led me to Oxford as it is now likely to lead to China"—and for all the enlarging providential experiences he had sampled in that time, in his unworthiness he had failed to acknowledge the gifts with either a "grateful heart or obedient life." He told Fanny he prayed God would pity and forgive him.

On the following Sunday he visited the New College chapel with his host for the day, John David MacBride, the principal of Magdalen Hall. Among the beauties for which the Gothic chapel was noted was the spectacular west window with paintings on glass of the Adoration of the Shepherds and the Seven Virtues by Joshua Reynolds and Thomas Jervaise. Leonidas admired these works, but being a plain-liturgy clergyman (and more than a little self-righteous) he was critical of the chanted Evensong the two men attended at the close of day. He told Fanny the music was fine but that he suspected insincerity lurked beneath the gloss of choral worship. At least he appreciated the audible responses made by the congregation (in contrast to apathetic mutterings by his own people in Richmond) but worried if it all smacked of Rome and "that Church from whose lapses we profess to have recovered." He attended three services that "holy day" but at nightfall nonetheless felt less than sanctified.[47]

Despite his professed longings for home and his intention to sail for New York in early June, Leonidas simply could not resist the lure of unvisited places to the north. Thus he was soon off to Manchester, the terminus of England's first significant railroad. With his developing fondness for trains, he rode with great pleasure the two-year-old train that carried him to the port city of Liverpool. Assured he had the remaining letters of introduction and his traveling map and roadbook, Leonidas hurried on now to Sheffield to observe the manufacture of cutlery and silver plate, buying in a shop a pair of "first-rate" razors for his father. His greater object, though, was making the acquaintance of an eminent townsman in Sheffield, James Montgomery. A journalist, poet, and missionary enthusiast (and friend of McIlvaine), Montgomery had composed the lyrics for some 400 hymns, "Rock of Ages" among them.[48]

Montgomery and Leonidas got along finely. "I have met with few persons who have more interested me than this excellent man," Leonidas reported to his father. "I spent the greater part of three days with him." Did Montgomery's abolitionist poetry surface during Leonidas's visit? He was known in America for "The West Indies," his epic-length poem censuring the enslavement of Africans and Caribbean Indians. If not that poem, Leonidas would have been sure to approve of Montgomery's world-weary moods as expressed in "The Grave," in which the poet had written: "*I long to lay this painful head, / And aching heart beneath the soil.*"[49]

With his cache of letters of introduction soon exhausted, Leonidas pointed himself north. Coming up from Carlisle (it was now the middle of June), he crossed the Sark River on the Border Bridge and at Gretna Green entered Scotland, the land of Polks and Pollocks—his and Fanny's forebears. The village on the national boundary was then notorious for specializing in weddings for eloping couples from England. Leonidas discovered his innkeeper "filled the two-fold office of parson and host," and in a pithy phrase he told his mother that Gretna Green was "famed for the consummation of the happiness or wretchedness of the truant world."[50]

Then he set about looping around Scotland, first up the eastern coast, then down the western, by stage, gig, and boat, with a succession of requisite tourist stops at such places as Edinburgh, Perth, Inverness, Loch Katrine, Loch Lomond, Glasgow, and probably Dunblane. The last stop, as few travelers would know better than Leonidas, had been the home of Robert Leighton, the Anglican archbishop of Glasgow in the seventeenth century. Close by the walls of Dunblane Cathedral was Leighton's 1,500-volume library of rare books established by him for his clergy. That Leonidas a decade later would bestow Leighton's name on his Louisiana sugar plantation speaks for his high regard for the churchman, a Presbyterian minister before he was an Anglican priest.[51] After Scotland, lest he miss something a self-respecting American tourist oughtn't, he crossed the Irish Sea for quick looks at Belfast and Dublin.

Of all his experiences in the British Isles, his tour overall being a "great delight," the merriest was his calling at Sir Walter Scott's home at Abbotsford. He told his mother about this affecting visit to the Scottish Lowlands in a letter he began while steaming homebound across the Atlantic, thirty-five days out from Liverpool aboard the *Sheffield*.[52] "The castle is seated on the bank of the river surrounded by a high wall with an immense, ponderous gate, with turrets on the posts which look as if they might belong to the Middle Ages," he informed his mother.

> Another enclosure [fences] in a most beautiful piece of woodland composed of small trees of [Scott's] own selection and planting. A winding road leads from the gate on the highway, down through the wood to the house. At this gate I dismissed my boy and gig with orders to meet me in the afternoon at McCross several miles below, and took my route along the road down to the castle. Nothing could exceed the solemn stillness which prevailed within this enclosure. The day was clear and cloudless, the sun warm enough to be pleasant without being oppressive, and not a breath of air was stirring, nor an axe nor a hammer nor the lowing of a single cow was to be heard. I felt odd

and enjoyed the excitement which made me half wish to see at every turn in the road some of the bare-legged Highlanders spring from the bushes; I should have doubtless made a poor defense with [my] umbrella against the claymore of a Roderick Dhu or Rob Roy, but their appearance would have helped out the romance of this feeling and place.[53]

I reached at length the lower gate, and after pulling at the bell until the last hope of getting admittance in that quarter had failed, I turned aside among the bushes to another smaller one which fortunately stood ajar. Here, after thumpting and hallooing, I gained the ear of an old woman. To her I made my obeisance with an humble request to look over the castle grounds. She replied, 'She did na ken if the lassie wha had the keys wa aboot the hoose, but she word see.' The lassie, who proved to be a woman of forty, soon appeared with her clean white apron and spruce laced cap, and announced herself the housekeeper. We mounted by a stone stairway . . .

And here letter and story break off.

Once his ship had docked, Leonidas resumed the letter but added only a few more lines. "Dear Mother, I had written that far before landing, and am sure if I were to attempt a continuation of my little details today, I should fag for want of spirits." Sarah Polk was promised an oral conclusion of the Abbotsford visit when she and her ambling son were reunited in Raleigh. For the rest of us, the conclusion of the charming story appears forever lost. But it was resumed, in a way, during the Civil War when Leonidas was himself likened to the valiant Highlander Roderick Dhu in Scott's The Lady of the Lake.

6

"A Disposition to Be Pulling Down and Fixing Things Better" (1832–1836)

The *Sheffield* arrived in New York on Friday evening, August 17, 1832, after some forty days at sea, slow going for an Atlantic crossing even in those days.[1] By the following Monday afternoon, having cleared customs, Leonidas had traveled by stage sixty miles north to reunite with Fanny and eighteen-month-old Hamilton in Stratford, Connecticut.[2] Leonidas was suntanned and fit-looking— "much more fleshy than I ever saw him," Fanny noticed. And considering how she had been ailing herself and enduring his absence, the improvement in her husband's health was "almost enough to repay me for the long separation."[3] For little Hamilton's part, since his father's departure from Raleigh fourteen months past he had cut all his teeth, and Leonidas found him "full of spirit and one of the best natured little fellows in the world."[4] Fanny saw something Leonidas missed: the boy was "extremely jealous" of his father's attentions to his mother.[5]

From Connecticut, before heading for Raleigh, the Polks visited the McIlvaines in Brooklyn. During Leonidas's absence, McIlvaine had been elected bishop of Ohio, and he proposed that Leonidas consider moving to Ohio as well, to become a parish priest under his Episcopal wing.[6] Leonidas temporized; not only was he unsure that he yet had the stamina for clerical duties, but his father was tempting him with a less spiritual gift of several hundred acres of prime Tennessee farmland should he adopt the life of a country squire. He begged the new bishop to give him time. With Leonidas again on a vocational fence, the Polks moved slowly toward home, first a week in Philadelphia, a day or two in Baltimore (where Leonidas bought two brown horses and had them shipped to Petersburg, Virginia), then on to Alexandria to visit seminary friends. Intending to spend another week in Richmond, the family stayed but one day; a cholera outbreak in the city posed a risk not worth taking. But by leaving Richmond early, they had put themselves ahead of schedule. Thus they were stranded in Petersburg on a weekend while awaiting the arrival of a two-horse carriage dispatched from North Carolina by Colonel Polk and driven by a slave named Henry.[7]

Henry arrived punctually in Petersburg on Monday, and by week's end everyone was in Raleigh. When the excitements and pleasures of homecoming had subsided, Fanny settled down to domesticity in her in-laws' home. She soon learned she was again pregnant, and she busied herself trying to be useful, passing her time with recreational horseback rides and civic good works. As the weeks in Raleigh dragged on for him, Leonidas began to press Fanny to agree to moving to Tennessee, where the gift of a plantation from his father still awaited. There, too, he would be close to Lucius (a desire long deferred), and, while his lungs continued to heal so that he might eventually resume pulpit preaching, he could dabble again in gentlemanly farming. Lucius, setting a good example, had struck agrarian success in Tennessee, "universally esteemed and loved, both by the high and the low," as Colonel Polk had appraised him.[8]

Fanny's parents and Leonidas's mother were initially against the move, hoping, among other motives, to keep their new grandson near. (The dispassionate colonel asserted neutrality.)[9] Grandfather John Devereux, playing his best hand, invited his son-in-law to his plantation at Hill's Ferry and proposed he accept a quantity of productive farmland and its seventy slaves that he and his wife were offering. The plantation he had in mind was situated on the Roanoke River about eighty miles northeast of Raleigh in Bertie County, and he reckoned its overall worth, at the very least, to be $75,000. Land-rich but cash-poor, Devereux was obliged to make the family gift conditional: Leonidas's father would have to assume $22,000 of Devereux's debts.

It never got to that. Leonidas first politely put off a decision and, shortly thereafter, declined outright. Devereux, a perceptive judge of character, was graceful in his disappointment: "I see with pride and pleasure that pecuniary considerations have no influence on Leonidas's decisions," he reported to Colonel Polk. He contented himself further by supposing plantation life in North Carolina might prove "ennuisome" to the setting-out family, whereas "the scene in Tennessee will be novel, and the prospect of happiness highly flattering." To help that prospect along, and so that "these young and inexperienced children" not feel "degraded in their own situations," Fanny's father gave Leonidas $500 expense money for the trip west as well as thirty-four slaves. Hoping "God will bless and prosper my endeavors," Devereux said "that in a little while" Leonidas might come in for thirty or forty more slaves.[10] For good measure, one of Fanny's maternal uncles gave them a carriage and the horses to pull it.

It is not to be supposed that the young Polks embarked on a journey to a make-do farm in some forlorn wilderness where they would be roughing it in classical pioneer style. Rather, Middle Tennessee's bluegrass agricultural region was fast becoming one of the most prized in the United States. It was already sprouting prepossessing mansions, and to a farmer like Leonidas its climate and growing season surpassed North Carolina's. Leonidas's tract was to be carved from his father's enormous holdings of prime Maury County land, which would place him near both the center of the state and his brother Lucius's plantation. In time, two other brothers, Rufus and George, would be given equivalent adjoining portions. Even added together, the sons' tracts were a fraction of their father's Tennessee lands. He had thousands of acres more all over Tennessee and, making a rough guess, once told his wife that he imagined his Tennessee acreage had a value of "something short of half a million of dollars."[11]

In April, with the worst of the Appalachian winter passed, with their furniture shipped ahead, and with a farewell visit paid to the Devereux family in Bertie County, Hammy and his parents and their new supply of slaves departed Raleigh by wagon train.[12] The trip was punishing for Fanny, her pregnancy becoming problematical. "Extremely ill," as she was later to say, she lay flat in their carriage much of the way to Knoxville over difficult roads, and a baby boy was stillborn near that mountain town.[13] The family's arrival on Wednesday, May 15 (about three weeks later than first planned), was a great relief for all—and a major event at Mary and Lucius's Hamilton Place. This was the newly completed mansion on the Mt. Pleasant Road in the Ashwood Settlement that the couple occupied following their White House wedding a year before; their newborn daughter, Sarah Rachel, was there, too.

Moving in, Leonidas and Fanny and Hamilton were given two adjoining chambers upstairs. Their parlors opened onto a breezy central hall that itself opened onto a balcony. Here they would live for eleven months, and it can be easily supposed that in their conversations they imagined themselves in the near future owning a similar home and plantation. In time, indeed, an impressive array of three more Polk sons' palatial homes arose in the Ashwood neighborhood, becoming objects of curiosity and envy to neighbors (even admiration to some Yankee troops who would march past during the Civil War). "Prettiest country I ever saw," a Missouri infantry lieutenant would write in his journal in the summer of 1862.[14]

Settling in, by a Sunday in late May Leonidas and Fanny were sufficiently recovered from their trek west to drive up the Mt. Pleasant Road to nearby Columbia to attend fledgling St. Peter's Episcopal Church.[15] There they learned that Leonidas's father, unannounced, had just arrived in town and was staying with James Walker, a kinsman and a founder of the little church.[16] Colonel Polk was passing by on his way to explore the vast acreage he owned (but had never seen) in far western Tennessee.[17]

Shortly before the elder Polk was to set out on this months-long survey accompanied by Lucius and Leonidas, Fanny approached her father-in-law and assumed a remarkably outspoken stance for a woman of that day. Frankly, said Fanny to her father-in-law, the land he had set aside for Leonidas, being fifteen miles away from Hamilton Place, was too remote from her other, young in-laws. Might not the colonel not find something closer for her husband and herself?[18] William Polk, if maybe taken aback, consented to this and soon deeded to Leonidas about one-quarter of his plantation on the Mt. Pleasant Road, a 5,000-acre expanse he had named Rattle and Snap. Lucius's Hamilton Place already stood on a corner of this tract, and eventually Rufus and George Polk built their homes on the two remaining quarters.[19]

Exploration of the colonel's lands as far west as the Mississippi River would prove wearisome for him and his two sons (by July they were not half done), but their backwoods travels slapping "muskettoes" and dodging cholera outbreaks were not without interesting, even bizarre, aspects. There was their overnight stay with a "steam doctor," one of the region's many amateur practitioners of the era's faddish theory of healing with boiling-water vapors and vegetable medicines containing, for example, cayenne pepper. The well-trained wife of this particular steam doctor cooked the travelers' breakfast; she was thirteen. And then there was their invitation to a community's Fourth of July levee at which their teetotaling hosts saluted the holiday with cold water. Colonel Polk drily, as it were, informed his wife that he "felt sure the cold water steaming will not incapacitate me from tomorrow's work."[20] Soon thereafter Leonidas returned to Ashwood and was satisfied that his cultivated land was producing serviceable crops of cotton and corn. As for the house he hoped would go up the next year, he told his mother that "I am very busy making brick."[21]

In Middle Tennessee, brick was the favorite building material of the rich at that time, and more exactly put, Leonidas was very busy supervising the making of brick, an intensive hand-labor task of digging surface clay from the ground, kneading it with water, forcing it through dies, striking off lumps, molding these to shape, then firing them all in a kiln stacked thousands high and wide. Slaves (with a little help from mules) were the ones who did all that, but Leonidas with proprietary nonchalance took the credit. In October in another letter home he said: "My brick kilns are now at full blast. I shall have burnt all by the middle . . . of next week. I shall then proceed to digging and laying the foundation of my house, which I hope to finish by Christmas." No devil's workshop for idle hands at Ashwood.[22] And with his slaves attending full time to his labors, Leonidas was free to take on executive projects. Once his father was back from the West, he enlisted Leonidas's skill as a surveyor to plot an expedient rerouting of the main Mt. Pleasant Road that passed the Polks' property. Father and son also succeeded in closing entirely one public road that had crossed the tract, thereby consolidating the colonel's, Leonidas's, and Lucius's acreage within one fence. An affected neighbor, "old Mr. McGee" as Leonidas dismissively termed him, protested the closure of the road, but the united Polks prevailed against him and viewed their success with mirth. "Pa will tell you what pleasing excitement McGee and his road gave us all for a week or so," Leonidas wrote to his mother. Accounts of Leonidas's several other enterprises as a beginning planter and Maury County citizen filled the rest of the letter, and it was clear he had found the active life he wanted. As he noted in a jovial mood: "In truth, Ma, I sometimes half suppose that I inherit from you a disposition to be pulling down and fixing things better, to be making new screws or building railroads."[23]

Still, for all the engaging distractions of building a plantation home, the Ashwood farmer's calling to the ministry was never far from his thoughts. So he was ready when the pastor of the Episcopal Church in Columbia, discouraged by his own lack of success, decided to try elsewhere, creating a feasible opening for Leonidas. Daniel Stephens, rector of St. Peter's, had been beaten by a congregation allowing their church edifice to remain unfinanced and unfinished and had largely wandered off to where "other denominations [were] having much more preaching than heretofore."[24] Opportunely, then, Leonidas took steps to transfer his name from the clergy rolls in Virginia to those of Tennessee. Polk's new bishop, James Hervey Otey, wrote in his diary one subsequent evening: "Rev. L. Polk received into Canonical connection with the Diocese. May the merciful Lord make him an instrument of much good."[25]

Polk was thirty years younger than Stephens and was little concerned by competing preachers and stewardship shortfall. He took over the parish on January 1, 1834, helped along by James Walker, the parishioner married to James K. Polk's sister Jane Maria.[26] Probably drawing no salary, Leonidas conducted services on most Sundays, but his infirm lungs still left him "unable to render . . . efficient service" to his charge of seventeen souls. All the same, he was assured of "increasing interest in the . . . church by those" attending, and an increase in their number and their financial support would soon attest to that.[27] To his chagrin, though, the building was still unfinished in April when the annual meeting of the Tennessee Diocese was to convene at St. Peter's. The twenty-six delegates arriving made do with Columbia's Masonic Hall. That some of the things under Leonidas's control fell behind schedule surprised no one, for he kept many irons heating in his fire. In the midwinter, just as he was about to take over St. Peter's, his father died in Raleigh. Of course he sermonized a little in his condolences to his mother, but he noted with some charm that the crusty old soldier had become a little less severe in his declining years ("much more than I had anticipated") and seemed toward the end "to expire like a candle."[28] With that tended to, he put Ashwood's domestic matters into Fanny's hands and ventured off to Mississippi as an "attaché" with his brother Lucius and his half-brother William Julius Polk. In partnership, the three were "exploring" for land to buy.

Leonidas left the brothers after a few days and rode back up into Tennessee's Tipton County, set amid Reelfoot Lake and the snaking Mississippi River. Here he sold off some acreage owned by his father.[29] As one of several treks he would make through West Tennessee before the Civil War, Leonidas would acquire a firsthand familiarity with the land that later complemented the military maps his topographical engineers would give him as he plotted defenses of the Mississippi Valley against Federal gunboats.[30]

Back in Ashwood, he then tried to juggle his, his father's, and Lucius's farming affairs. The bulk of the corn crop had been picked, but seventy-five acres of his father's cotton was yet untouched because of prevailing cold and rain. Sarah Polk had turned to her two oldest sons for advice regarding the estate and the education of her youngest children. Leonidas was unable to leave his parish and plantation to go to her side but did what he could by correspondence, not neglecting to counsel her on religious imperatives of prayer and belief. His father's death was followed in three months (on April 8) by another: the child the young couple were expecting. Fanny, again ailing in her pregnancy, gave birth to a second stillborn child—a "perfectly-formed" baby boy. Though Fanny said "every effort of prudence was made to avert" a recurrence, scarcely a year had passed since the last such mishap.[31] For Fanny and him "the affliction was a heavy one," Leonidas said.

Affording him some comfort, the portion of his farm once leased by his father to a man named Fleming now belonged to Leonidas free and clear. Its "snug and close-built" cabin of logs was improved by Leonidas with an exterior covering of "weather boards," and a spring provided freshwater within a "stone's throw of the door." The house was only four rooms, but the little family gave it a grand name—Mount Breeze—and in late May Leonidas, Fanny, and Hammy left Mary and Lucius in their rambling Hamilton Place and settled in. They lived there for the next three years while their brick manse, more than befitting any other parish priest, rose with glacial slowness above its limestone foundation.

For that project Leonidas had assigned himself the role of architect and contractor. "You see I have the same attachment to carpentry and fixing as characterized my early life," he again reminded his mother. However, as Lucius did and as any of his neighbors would have done, he also engaged Nathan Vaught to help in building the house.[32] And as did Lucius and Mary's house, it testified to its occupants' wealth and position, perhaps to excess. One architectural authority has reckoned that Leonidas's house was even "more pretentious" than Lucius's.[33]

The young and genial planter-priest, now sinking roots into the arable land of Middle Tennessee's Maury County, was not long in entwining himself likewise among the region's people of influence, those whose interests and connections would provide lasting benefits to his future. Francis Brindley Fogg, attorney at law, was one of the best of these. A fast-rising Nashvillian from the North, Fogg had represented William Polk in some of his real-estate litigations, and years later he was an essential benefactor of Bishop Leonidas Polk's University of the South.[34] Fogg's wife, Mary Middleton Rutledge Fogg, was herself a Nashvillian of social note, being the granddaughter of two signers of the Declaration of Independence.[35] On a visit to Maury County in 1834 to attend a church convention, Mary Fogg had taken a liking to Fanny and Leonidas and invited them to visit her in Nashville. In July the Polks spent a week under the Foggs' roof.[36]

Indeed, to anyone attending that convention in Columbia's Masonic Hall, the new rector of St. Peter's would not have gone unnoticed. He clearly had the approving nod of the bishop, James Otey. Bishop Otey was a Virginian with a penchant for teaching and stern morality, as well as a willingness to endure immoderate lengths of evangelical travel. Leonidas had possibly known Otey since his North Carolina college days, when both had attended the university in Chapel Hill, and in the course of the three-day meeting Leonidas was evidently perceived as leadership material himself.[37] He was either appointed or elected to six different committees, including the powerful Standing Committee.[38] In addition to committee memberships, Leonidas was chosen to be a delegate to the national church's General Convention in Philadelphia in 1835, a signal honor.[39] Telling his mother of his recognition, he sent her a copy of the official proceedings. Now that his father had died, Leonidas changed from rarely to often including church news in letters home.[40]

To balance his ecclesiastical interests with secular affairs, Leonidas paid close attention to his plantation's work. And to improve his income, he diverted some of his acreage and workers that summer from cotton to the growing of hemp, or *cannabis sativa*, a plant providing tough stem fibers for twine and rope. Raising hemp for twine, a practice successful in Kentucky, was an agricultural novelty lately catching on with his Tennessee neighbors; their hope was to produce bale rope and burlap bagging to ship their cotton.[41] Restive with only two vocations to occupy his mind, Leonidas would soon take up a third that tapped into his love of trains and railroads. He joined Maury County neighbors who hoped to build a railroad from their county seat, Columbia, to the Tennessee River some seventy miles to the west. What the planter entrepreneurs hoped for was a better and cheaper way to get their cotton to the Port of New Orleans by replacing the often impassable wagon roads to the steamboat wharfs on the Cumberland River in Nashville. With Leonidas writing a promotional pamphlet and pulling strings (especially those attached to his cousin James K. Polk, a Tennessee congressman), the planners' aims, modest at the outset, grew into visions of a transnational network of rails connecting the Mississippi River with the Atlantic Ocean. All that was wanting was government help and, of course, money.[42]

By late October Leonidas and his family, along with Lucius, were on their way to Raleigh to visit Sarah Polk for the first time since her husband had died. Their traveling companion as far as Knoxville was Bishop Otey, his purpose being to visit the sprinkling of Episcopalians inhabiting the eastern mountains and hollows of his spread-out diocese.[43] Leaving the wayfaring bishop, the others hastened on to North Carolina, where Mary Polk Badger was seriously ill. After their arrival, Fanny surmised that Mary Badger's "complaint is decidedly of the liver," complicated by a violent cough, diarrhea, and night sweats. Despite these distressing symptoms, Fanny told Mary Ann Polk back in Tennessee that she was convinced that "nothing is [being] done for her. Dr. Beckwith, it appears to me, is afraid to use any remedies to act upon the liver lest the bowels should become affected and that complaint carry her off speedily."[44]

Mary Badger was a redoubtable patient. She went horseback riding most days and, despite feeling unwell, posed obligingly while she and others in the family had their portraits painted that December. The artist was George Esten Cooke, an itinerant portraitist from Maryland who sought out the patronage of well-to-do citizens in the South. Among these Southerners, Cooke had earned a good reputation and liked to say that not only did his purse prosper thereby but that his "mind [was] elevated by such associations." Lucius, reciprocally, found him "very refined."[45] Cooke had come to prospect in Raleigh while the legislature was in session and struck a rewarding vein when he encountered the Polk, Badger, and Devereux families, all convening themselves that season in Raleigh. Indeed, "we aren't coming home until after Christmas," Lucius wrote Mary Ann, "because Mr. Cooke has not finished" the seven or so paintings the interlocked families had commissioned. Out of their sick sister's hearing, the Tennessee visitors had decided it would do her good for them to remain longer than they had planned. "The fear was that if we left," Lucius explained, "she would sink so rapidly the painter would not have it in his power to complete the picture." Lucius regretted that Mary Ann was not present to sit for Cooke along with the rest.[46] The crowd dispersed from the Polk homestead the day after Christmas. Fanny and Hammy moved to her parents' home. Mary Badger returned to her own home, where George Cooke could apply finishing touches to her portrait. Leonidas and Lucius, Rufus, twenty, George, seventeen, and Susan, twelve, all headed for points north. That left the widowed Sarah Polk with only young Andrew for company; she now felt "much more [lonely] than before they came."[47] On their way north to locate a school with sufficient éclat for Susan, the Polk party stopped in Washington City to see their kinfolks: Congressman James K. Polk and his wife, Sarah Childress.[48] Then parting from the others, Leonidas and Susan continued on to Philadelphia, where they chose for Susan the girls' school operated by "the Misses Smith."

Deep January cold had seized the Northeast, and returning from Philadelphia Leonidas passed an eight-degree night in Columbia, Pennsylvania. Lucius meanwhile reported from Washington that the whole region was "colder than known before in some forty years to the oldest inhabitants," and though carefree "belles and beaux [had] been sleighing" in that city, ice blocks had jammed the Ohio River at Wheeling. Leonidas wisely took a more temperate route south to Raleigh, arriving in mid-February. Reunited with Fanny and his mother, Leonidas found Mary Badger increasingly ill. She languished throughout the rest of the winter, hoping by springtime to visit her brothers in Middle Tennessee to drink the water from the region's limestone wells, the therapeutic tonic in which either she or Dr. Beckwith had now come to put some stock. She died, though, in March, bearing her affliction, as a family friend said, with "Christian meekness and patience."[49] After Mary's funeral, Leonidas and Fanny left for home, insisting that his mother accompany them; Sarah Polk brought along Mary and George Badger's two young children, Sally and Catherine, to spend the summer.[50]

Scarcely back on his plantation, Leonidas had to arrange his affairs to fulfill his elected role as a delegate to the national church convention in Philadelphia in late August. Anxiety over Fanny's health—she was in the last trimester of a third difficult pregnancy—made his leave-taking difficult for the two of them, but he felt obliged to go. As a traveling companion he took along his niece Griselda Gilchrist Polk, daughter of his half-brother William Julius Polk. Grizzie, sixteen, would remain all winter for treatment of an eye disease. She too enrolled at Miss Hawks's school to which her cousin Susan had now transferred.[51]

Though new to the governing conventions of the Episcopal Church, the Reverend Mr. Polk found himself welcomed among old friends. And because he had been making ripples in the parochial backwaters of Tennessee, he was shortly appointed a trustee of the General Theological Seminary in New York City, a prestigious role that would keep him in touch with many among the church's powers.[52] More useful, still, to his future in the church was that convention's main item of business: the neglect of missionary outreach into the western wilderness of the United States. Thus before all the talking and legislating were done the official name of the denomination had been changed to The Domestic and Foreign Missionary Society of the Protestant Episcopal Church in the United States of America. Thus the die of Leonidas Polk's future was cast. Two prime movers of the name-change had been Leonidas's missionary-minded evangelical friends Charles McIlvaine and James Milnor.[53] And to address what was regarded as the crisis of the unchurched thousands settling in Missouri, Indiana, Arkansas, Louisiana, and Florida, a "special committee" was formed, the popular Mr. Polk becoming a member. His committee recommended that missionary bishops be immediately elected and dispatched to the godless West. Among the candidates proposed was a North Carolinian known to Leonidas, the Reverend Francis Lister Hawks of Newbern. His mother and Fanny Polk's mother were friends as well.[54] The convention members desired that Mr. Hawks, once he had been upgraded to Bishop Hawks, would carry the Gospel into certain Southern and Southwestern states and territories, a kind of St. Paul of the Sagebrush across a vastness the size of France. Hawks, however, declined the election a few weeks later because he realized he could not support his young family on the pittance the job would pay. The job remained open.

Meanwhile, Leonidas returned to Fanny's bedside, where his ministrations were beneficial. A living child, this time a daughter, was born to Fanny on November 27. The infant girl was named Frances Devereux, and the parents soon took heart that her care was much easier to manage than Hammy's had been back in Virginia. "She is literally no trouble," her mother mused. Fanny was discovering that young parents usually find life with their second-born less trying than with their first and that having a wet nurse at the baby's beck and call—well, that, too, lightens the load.[55]

Leonidas's congressional cousin, James K. Polk, though by now the influential Speaker of the House, had not proved helpful to his Tennessee relatives' Columbia Railroad scheme. Leonidas and Lucius invested instead in a turnpike company; an ordinary paved road would be built to connect their town to the Tennessee River. Whereupon, Leonidas found yet another outlet for his spirited attention: he undertook to rescue a failing school for girls, the Columbia Female Institute. Apart from his aborted professorship in 1827, it was his first significant venture into the field of education. Fanny summed up his efforts in the winter of 1835–1836: "He devoted himself to raise funds in Maury County for the purpose of building up a school for girls. He succeeded."[56]

At the outset housed in classrooms borrowed from St. Peter's, the reinvented school deserved an inventive building. Leonidas chose a castellated fortress. William S. Drummond, a Washington City architect with a liking for antiquity simulations, was retained.[57] As Leonidas had so fancied Sir Walter Scott's Abbotsford castle, he was pleased with Drummond's preliminary elevations of battlements and towers atop the proposed institute. "Very pretty and rather a splendid plan," he told his mother.[58] When the building opened, the school's catalog boasted that "visitors [were] charmed with its resemblance to the old castles of song and story."

7

"How Happily the Days of Thalaba Went By" (1836–1838)

When not required to be in the nation's capital, Speaker of the House James K. Polk, still some eight years away from the US presidency, lived with his wife, Sarah, in a Federal-style, white two-story clapboard house in downtown Columbia, Tennessee. Cousin Leonidas had been assured by James and Sarah that, whenever his duties kept him late at St. Peter's Church, he was welcome to spend the night at their home. Leonidas had arranged to do just that on an April day in 1836. After presiding at a Wednesday Evensong, he went to the Polks' nearby home and retired in a guest bedroom.[1]

When he awoke the following morning, his left arm and leg were numb, and his head spun with dizziness. "Something very like parallicis [sic]," Leonidas's brother Lucius described it.[2] A member of the household summoned Dr. John Hays, a Columbia physician and a family friend. Following standard procedures of those days, the physician drained a copious quantity of blood from Leonidas and applied a hot dressing of mustard poultice to his feet. Though wobbly, the patient was soon able to return to his Ashwood home eight miles distant. The benefit of Dr. Hays's remedies was fleeting. Leonidas's numbness and dizziness persisted, though he followed the doctor's and Lucius's advice to taper off all exertions and give up preaching altogether. Another nighttime attack, more wracking than the first, left him slurring words and struggling to express himself. To treat this episode, the Polks' regular family doctor, James C. O'Reily, was called in, and Lucius observed the patient being "purged very freely."[3] So while Leonidas cooperated and Lucius looked on disapprovingly, O'Reily prescribed more bleeding, along with hearty doses of nux vomica, a solution containing vomit-inducing strychnine.

Whatever the problem, the medical theory went, ousting a patient's internal fluids would soon dislodge some noxious humor from the buffeted body. An amateur venesectionist himself, Leonidas had a few weeks earlier diagnosed palsy in a slave woman and had prescribed that she be bled. Fanny proudly told Sarah Polk: "[Mr. Polk] had an issue [incision] put in her neck and a blister on the spine which has been kept open, and I am glad to be able to say she is much better."[4] Dr. O'Reily's bleedings and purgings, not surprisingly, did not benefit Leonidas. A day or so later, while dining at home, he became sick and faint at the table and, Lucius reported, "had to ease himself out of the chair on [to] the floor." It was his third spell. A visitor, James Jones, was summoned from another room. Leonidas withdrew a lancet out of his own pocket and directed Jones to grasp it. "Don't be alarmed," he commanded the blenching man. "Open the vein." And straightaway a pint of blood was drained into a basin. After the ordeal, Leonidas "was deadly pale [and] a little sick at the stomach," Lucius said. By now, Lucius had seen enough: he firmly insisted that Leonidas stop taking the "vile medicine" O'Reily had prescribed. Once he did so—not so strange—he soon got better. Lucius took some credit: "I have no doubt if he had discontinued O'Reily as well as the drug, he would not have had the [later] attacks."[5]

Whatever was ailing Leonidas was probably worsened by strain and fatigue, and no small wonder. Easter, for one thing, had fallen on April 3; his preaching responsibilities on that Sunday and the preceding days of Holy Week would doubtlessly have aggravated the condition of his lungs.[6] Further, just prior to the first attack he had learned that financial reverses would shortly befall the senior warden at St. Peter's, the ranking lay member of the parish. He was Adlai O. Harris, a Columbia businessman of Leonidas's age, the husband of James K. Polk's sister Naomi, a helpful connection for his occupational dealings. More directly affecting Leonidas, though, Harris was a friend so valued ("My vestryman, my warden, my right arm in every good work") that Leonidas had cosigned a $15,000 loan made to Harris. That gesture of trust would eventually cost Leonidas the entire amount, but he was magnanimous to the end.[7]

As for fatigue, it was likely that contributing to his ill health was Leonidas's regularly expanding, rarely shrinking, list of pursuits: fulfilling parochial duties expected by his congregation; devoting time to the several committees he served for his diocese and the national church; teaching Sunday School for the slave families on his plantation families; and raising money for the school-castle under construction. That left the plantation. As winter gave way to spring, he was superintending the planting of cotton, corn, and hemp, and with imported experts helping him, he was designing a bagging factory, a rope walk, and a sawmill driven by a steam engine. Lastly, the situation at Ashwood Hall was a worry; Fanny fretted that the house was still not ready for her family after three years.

A jammed schedule notwithstanding, Leonidas had been enjoying himself to the fullest before he fell ill. His particular delight was the hemp factory. From England he had acquired professional rope makers: a Mr. Yates to design the rope walk and install the spinning and weaving machinery, and a Mr. Williams to oversee the cordage manufacture. Both of these men, along with the architect and builder employed to construct the girls' academy, were making themselves at home with Fanny and Leonidas in Mount Breeze, their snug and close-built log cabin.

To operate his factory Leonidas had adopted the idea of using the children of his slave families—the same children he taught "the elements of Christian knowledge" on Sunday afternoons.[8] In a letter to his mother, Leonidas listed all twelve of the boys and girls he had chosen for the work, along with their mothers' names: "Henry (Selma's), Lucy (Ginny's), Minerva (Cleopas'), Cornelius (Olive's), Hunter (Nora's)," the list began. "Some of them [are] most too small," he admitted to her, but all were "handy and brisk." These "small fry" eventually worked in the rope walk and ran the machinery that spun and wove the hemp, having not a care in the world, as their master saw it.[9] Fanny showed an assertive interest in industrialization herself; she was hankering for a 30-horsepower steam engine to drive the hemp machinery and to power a sawmill and grindstones. Up till then, long planks for the future mansion were being laboriously ripped from timbers and balks by two-man sawyer teams using seesaws. The slave sawyers were doing just fine, moving so fast while Leonidas was so much occupied that he found "it was impossible . . . to take an accurate measurement of all the plank they had sawed."[10] Even so, Fanny did the arithmetic and convinced her husband that $1,700 for a used steam engine would soon pay for itself, providing, for example, 2,000 feet of planking per day. Wisely, the amateur engineer listened to his wife; not much later, through a system of belts and shafts, bagging, planks, and cornmeal were piled high.[11]

Following the attacks of illness, Leonidas was advised to remove himself from all clerical, agricultural, and academic affairs for several months. He prevailed upon Bishop Otey to take on the ministry of St. Peter's, and the bishop was obligingly in the pulpit by May 12. Leonidas agreed to read lessons and prayers when he felt up to it, but hortatory preaching was still out of the question and remained so for more than a year.[12] He did venture beyond the plantation now and then, attending, for example, that July's diocesan convention in Pulaski, Tennessee, about thirty miles from his home. His popularity among his peers resulted, of course, in their freedom to pile ever more duties and committee memberships upon him, one of them to see to the publication of a diocesan newspaper, another to help Bishop Otey establish a "Literary and Theological Seminary." A fund-raising drive for $100,000 was getting under way for that, Otey never doubting that planter friends had the money. It was merely a matter of prying it loose.[13]

Leonidas was feeling no better upon his return. Lucius supposed his attending the four-day convention and his abstaining from eating meat (on Dr. O'Reily's orders, most likely) had combined to weaken him further. So the Polk families repaired to Beaver Dam Springs in neighboring Hickman County. The record of how Leonidas passed the autumn of that year of recuperation is sketchy. What is known is that he left Tennessee around October on what was apparently a healthful pleasure and business trip to Kentucky and Ohio, possibly on horseback. In Cincinnati, Leonidas concluded his trip by purchasing bagging machinery for his hemp factory and was back home by Christmas. Having benefitted from his expedition, he was winding up a turbulent year in convalescent ease and domesticity. Being at the time rather flush with new lands and cash from Colonel Polk's estate, he and Fanny awaited shipments from New York of thousands of dollars' worth of furniture, carpets, and tableware for their new home.[14]

"This winter was a happy one," Fanny much later wrote in her memoir. "Indeed, all our life was happy" (a hyperbole she assumed her grown children did not question), "but I enjoyed more of my husband's society than at any period. We lived in a little cabin, our two children were healthy, and in my dear brother Lucius and his admirable wife we had congenial friends. More than all, my husband had leisure to be with me, and the evenings were spent in reading." "How happily the days of Thalaba went by," Fanny rhapsodized, casting Leonidas and herself as the romantic protagonists in the Arabian setting of a Robert Southey poem. "I often said God gave us this time to prepare for storms which must come."[15]

As spring gave way to summer, Ashwood Hall was ready for occupancy; the new household goods had arrived in Nashville by riverboat coming up from New Orleans. Fanny and Hammy had been visiting her parents in Raleigh since early July, leaving Leonidas with baby Frances in Tennessee. Father and daughter and servants moved into Ashwood Hall about July 15. The event seemed to put Leonidas in a chipper mood, reflected in a letter to Sarah Polk. "I have had great pleasure in building it," he said of the house, and his little girl, beginning to talk, brightened the solitude of his dining table with "her little prattle." His health, furthermore, was as good as it had been anytime in the past twelve months, though his strength was far short of what it had been five years previous. "I am quite regular in my habits and . . . moderate in all that I do. I have learned wisdom, *some* wisdom, from living." He could imagine his mother's reading that and thinking it a pity he had not learned wisdom sooner. "I agree with you," he said, that "I have lived very fast and am now, even at the age of 30, beginning to feel it. . . . I am reaping that which I have sowed."

Sarah Polk's children had scheduled an all-family reunion for October in Raleigh—"the fragments of a dispersed family once more under the paternal roof," Leonidas lyrically described it to Bishop Otey back in Tennessee. "Such a meeting has not happened before since the days of our nursery years." Traveling alone to North Carolina by steamboat and stage, he seemed to find his journey a lark. "I traveled 220 miles on one day, from 5 A.M. to 10 P.M. It is like flying."[16] During his absence, the Tennessee plantation had prospered under the care of overseers. Though upon returning he found whooping cough among the hands, the two steam sawmills were clattering and shrieking (and returning to him up to $45 a day), and the hemp spindles and looms were twirling and clicking. He was all set for a good year ahead.[17] The hemp factory's output was sufficient, in fact, for him to launch interstate sales.

Francis Hawks having resolutely rejected the nonlucrative, unappealing invitation to become a missionary bishop to the godless Southwest, church leaders in 1838 at their next triennial convention fixed their gaze upon the Reverend Joseph Hubbard Saunders. Another North Carolinian, Saunders at the time was the much-esteemed pastor of Christ Church in Pensacola, Florida. The Reverend Mr. Saunders was touched by the high regard in which the convention committee held him, but he had only lately begun his Pensacola ministry and had a young, growing family as well. He, too, demurred accepting the far-flung missionary bishopric.[18]

Pastor Saunders would helpfully resolve the Episcopalians' vexing search. In a conversation between convention sessions, Saunders mentioned a name to Levi Silliman Ives, the bishop of North Carolina. Yet another North Carolinian, the man proposed was a determined, self-reliant, and a financially well-off fellow whom Saunders had known and liked when both were twelve-year-olds in Parson McPheeter's Raleigh Academy. If offered the job, he just might take it. It was Leonidas Polk, of course. Ives had known Leonidas for several years and, at that moment, must have thought Saunders's suggestion heaven-sent. And so did his brother prelates once

Ives had passed it along. The bishops shortly voted unanimously that the Reverend Mr. Polk was just the man they wanted. Moreover, as convention business proceeded, Saunders made a little speech to other delegates praising his boyhood friend. The approval by these delegates was unanimous.[19]

Whether for good or for ill, everyone's latest choice for Missionary Bishop of the Southwest was not consulted, not being present at the convention. And when Leonidas Polk in Tennessee learned a few days later what had befallen him, both he and Fanny were dumbstruck, she more than he. At that moment began, she would say years later, "one of the greatest trials of my life."[20] No record explains why Leonidas did not attend the fateful September gathering in Philadelphia. The birth of a daughter, Catherine, in mid-August might well have kept him at Fanny's side, and he had been otherwise pursuing his usual manic schedule.[21]

Feeling still stretched too thin by the many demands he had assumed on behalf of God and Mammon, he resigned as the rector of St. Peter's parish shortly before the 1835 General Convention that would so dramatically change his life. He gave as his reason the continuing difficulty of making the twenty-mile trip between the church and his home.[22] All the more remarkable, then, was that the national church, so desperate to fill the Southwest missionary post, would soon gamble that a part-time country-town priest with a history of illness, an expanding household, and a desire to cut back on church-connected duties was just the man to oversee a ministry comprising half a million square miles with scarcely two inhabitants in each of them. Had Polk himself applied for the job, no reasonable employer would have given his credentials a second glance, but like bearers of bad news two convention delegates brought personal word of the election to the Polk household in Tennessee.[23] Columbia College in New York, having deep Anglican roots as the pre-Revolution King's College, was acting fast, too, and soon notified Polk that he was to receive an honorary doctorate at the upcoming commencement exercises.

Leonidas's reaction to his fate, according to Fanny, was cheerful surrender. She made herself sound game, too, when later she wrote: "There was no struggle in his mind. He never felt anything hard he was called on to do for God. He had done so much for him, and though the acceptance involved loss of property and the abandonment of wife and children for months at a time, he did not hesitate." Facing all that, Fanny had dolefully considered her lot. "Home and all its endearments must be given up, and I left alone to bring up my children." But as the dutiful clergy wife she regarded herself, she cast aside self-pity and steeled her backbone: "Thank God I did not . . .

by any [act or] word influence his decision. I told him he was God's servant and soldier, and I had no right to have even an opinion."[24]

To take part in a kind of dress rehearsal for the pomp awaiting him in his episcopal future, Polk in the fall headed for New York to receive his honorary Doctor of Divinity degree. Now distinguished with an academic degree, Dr. Polk had two months to get ready for his bishop's ordination scheduled for December 9 in Cincinnati. As a man might do when planning a party for himself, Leonidas began by inviting the clergy friends he wished either to participate in or to attend the event. Charles McIlvaine was his logical choice to preach the sermon. Bishop William Meade of Virginia was to preside, and Bishops James Otey and Benjamin B. Smith of Tennessee and Kentucky would present Polk, according to the protocol set by canon law. A friend from Leonidas's earliest days as a novice minister in Virginia would read appointed scripture, and thirteen other clerics would be present.[25] Cincinnati's Christ Church had been chosen for the occasion. Fanny, Susan, and Sarah Polk occupied choice seats in the nave as the service opened.[26] In due course the program moved to "The Form of Ordaining or Consecrating a Bishop," a 300-year-old rite from the Book of Common Prayer. McIlvaine titled his sermon "The Apostolical Commission," and he held forth at considerable length on the godly imperative of the Anglican episcopacy, seasoning his message with a few glancing blows at Roman Catholicism. Such was his warmth for his subject that he dreamed of the day when all Protestants would be Episcopalians.[27]

Eventually, after thirty-five disquisitional pages, the preacher rested his case, directing his listeners to regard Leonidas seated in front of the pulpit. It had been thirteen years, McIlvaine began afresh, since this manly cadet, indifferent to the derision of his fellows, had appeared "in open day" at the West Point chaplain's study door and stammered: "I have come about my soul." "From that moment the young man appeared to take up the Cross," McIlvaine continued. But until the church had lately called him to a courageous enterprise in the Southwest, he had "supposed he had settled himself for the rest of his life, as a preacher and pastor to an humble and obscure congregation of Negroes . . . to whose eternal interests he had chosen cheerfully and happily to devote himself as their spiritual father, with no emolument but their salvation." While McIlvaine may have overstated the lack of ambition the enterprising planter had in mind for his future, it led nicely to the climax of the narrative: "And thus the Chaplain has here met the beloved Cadet again, seeing and adoring the hand of the Lord in that remarkable beginning. . . . I call you Son, in affectionate recollection of the past. I call you Brother now, in affectionate consideration of the present and the future."[28]

It was vintage McIlvaine oratory, and if any in the congregation, blinking back tears or stifling yawns, doubted any detail of Leonidas's conversion experience, their minds were put to rest when McIlvaine paused and three men near the front suddenly stood in their pew. All had been West Point cadets in the 1820s and had likewise "experienced the effects of Mr. McIlvaine's preaching at the academy." They "bowed to testify to [the] accuracy" of the Cadet Polk narrative.[29]

It was an interesting trio. One was Crafts James Wright, then a Cincinnati lawyer and journalist and later editor of the *Cincinnati Gazette*. He had been one year behind Leonidas at the academy, had been one of Jefferson Davis's roommates, and was among the fellows bemused by Cadet Polk's prodigal piety. In later years, with Col. Crafts Wright commanding a US infantry regiment, he was pitted against Confederate Lieutenant General Polk and roughly handled at the Battle of Shiloh in April 1862.[30] In his earlier newspaper account of Polk's consecration, Wright did not name his companions in the Cincinnati pew, but they were probably the Reverend Albert Taylor Bledsoe and the Reverend Martin Parks. Cadet Bledsoe, an "intimate acquaintance," as Polk would later say, had roomed with Leonidas at West Point and had himself been recently ordained by McIlvaine. As for Parks, it was he who had deposited the religious tract that led Cadet Polk to Chaplain McIlvaine's doorstep.[31]

With his vouchsafing friends now reseated, the Reverend Mr. Polk, vested in a floor-length white garment with banded sleeve cuffs, took a position before Bishop William Meade of Virginia and declared himself ready to become a bishop in "Arkansas" and to conform to the doctrine and disciple and worship of his denomination, "so help me God. . . ."[32] Everyone then offered prayers on his behalf, after which he was examined as to his orthodoxy and as to his conviction that he had been "truly called to this Ministration" according to the will of God. "I am so persuaded," Leonidas answered. Then, having been helped by a friend to don a black satin chimere and scarf, he knelt while Meade and the congregation intoned *Veni Creator Spiritus* ("Come, Holy Ghost, our souls inspire . . .").[33]

Leonidas thereby became the thirty-third bishop ordained in the Episcopal Church; moved by the solemnity of it all, he and Bishops McIlvaine, Meade, and Otey pledged themselves to pray for one another every Sabbath from that day forward.[34] Soon thereafter the new prelate would have his portrait painted by George Esten Cooke, the same artist who had done the several portraits of the Polk family in Raleigh. Cooke portrayed the now-illustrious Polk seated in an ecclesiastical chair in a bishop's raiment, looking as youthfully handsome and pleased with the situation as can be imagined. As to intrusive mundane matters, setting out with Fanny by stage for Tennessee, the new bishop left town owing a few bills for incidental expenses. And a year and a half later, when the old debts had become more like irritants than obligations, Leonidas was still stalling McIlvaine by pleading a shortage of funds. He neglected to mention that the shortfall related to his and Lucius's recent decision to buy a plantation.[35]

8

"Not a Common Preacher; He Was Good for Something" (1839–1841)

As the three bishops in Cincinnati intoned the *Veni Creator Spiritus* over the kneeling ordinand, they implored the Holy Ghost to bestow "peace at home upon the Right Reverend Leonidas Polk." The prayer proved less than totally efficacious. On St. Valentine's Day, he and his wife had a front-porch spat just as he was setting out for the six months he would spend on his first missionary sweep through Arkansas, three Deep South states, and the Republic of Texas.

Fanny, still fuming, reported the quarrel to Sarah Polk three weeks later. "I told him I thought he [had] treated me and the children badly," she wrote. "He had no time to tell us his wishes excepting after the stage came to the door." Then, thinking of the many plantation chores and responsibilities he had dropped in her hands—the crops, the slaves, the overseers, the various mills on the place—she jabbed her pen with a harshness unusual for her: "It would be much better if the mills would burn down, in my opinion," forgetting for a moment her earlier avowal that when it came to her husband's new calling she "had no right to have even an opinion." But now "I am sometimes ready to say . . . I cannot bear it!" Fanny, of course, was just now experiencing what many other plantation mistresses would go through in those antebellum days: playing "deputy husband," as the historian Catherine Clinton has aptly termed the trying situation. Fanny's mother-in-law, wisely knowing that Fanny would feel weighed down once Leonidas left home, dispatched to Ashwood Hall a Mrs. Dutton from Raleigh. Fanny soon pronounced her companionship an inexpressible "comfort."[1]

Even if his election to the episcopate was unexpected, perhaps unwelcome, Polk plunged into his new calling. Considering that on the morning of his departure he was still dashing off official letters to be posted once he was gone, the harried husband might have pleaded extenuations for his irritable leave-taking.[2] For weeks he had been rushing preparations for his missionary travels, among them charting an itinerary and writing ahead to those he hoped to visit. (As often as not, the notice provided by his letters would miscarry, and he arrived at some remote southwestern outpost unknown and unexpected.) Before departing, furthermore, he had been confronted by a pile of plantation and commerce temporalities awaiting him when he and Fanny left behind the ordination's involvements and returned to Tennessee just before Christmas. He needed, for example, to give attention to the buying and selling of certain slaves and to protect his investment in the Columbia Central Turnpike, the highway passing by the Polk brothers' plantations, the alternative to their dashed railroad hopes.[3] To this family enterprise was added about the same time the acquisition by Leonidas and Lucius of a plantation of some 500 acres in central Mississippi's Madison County, then a remote area thought to have a future of cotton wealth and prominence.[4] Lastly, Fanny's husband had the hemp mill, the gristmill, and the sawmill to worry about—the mills that Fanny soon wished would go up in smoke. In January an unlikely solution had presented itself to Leonidas, albeit one that seemed to involve as many problems as benefits. A man named Larimore was commissioned by Lucius Polk to go to England to shop for thoroughbred racing stock. While there, Larimore had persuaded an English mechanic named Thomas Brewster to bring his wife and six children to the United States on the chance that he could find employment operating the machinery of Leonidas's three mills. (With no authority to strike such a deal, Larimore was "activated," Fanny surmised, "merely by the desire to make himself of consequence.") When Lucius went to New Orleans to pick up his newly acquired horses, he was introduced to the animals' traveling companions: Brewster and family. As much astonished by Larimore's audacity as by Thomas Brewster's simplicity, Lucius nonetheless accompanied the immigrant family up to Tennessee and presented them as a fait accompli to the bishop. Brewster, by good fortune, had lived next door to the parish church in Worcester, and after letters of reference had been received from the vicar there and from two bankers, the Brewsters were absorbed into the Polk plantation community—and into Fanny's household. She was philosophical. Almost. "The children are really patterns of good behavior and politeness," she conceded, but it "gives me a good deal of trouble" that the large imported family put a strain on her house servants.[5]

With all these material concerns more or less in order, Leonidas by mid-February was finally poised for his immersion into a wilderness where, in Leonidas's words, the people were perishing for want of exposure to the Gospel. His plan was to wend first through the southeastern United States, then head by way of Arkansas toward the Republic of Texas. The church's Foreign Committee had lately conjectured that Texas was not to be missed, and Leonidas, in a sense, agreed. Though having already "within our own borders more than enough [work] to occupy my undivided attention," the new bishop accepted that "the growing importance of this Republic is daily becoming more manifest, and the influence for good or evil . . . is equally certain."[6]

So it was that soon after the set-to with Fanny, the bishop and his attendant, a slave named Henry, climbed aboard a public coach and set forth. A few weeks later the travelers had graduated to a borrowed buggy in Mississippi. Mapless and just at dark on a sodden Saturday they managed to hit Holly Springs. That town, Leonidas reported, seemed "to have sprung into existence as by magic. . . . Three years ago it was a cotton farm; now it numbers its inhabitants by thousands, and spreads its habitations over several miles square."[7] The "magic" that produced Holly Springs's sudden prosperity was Andrew Jackson's banishment of the native Chickasaw Indians in the early 1830s, allowing white men to flood onto the land to build gins and bale presses. During his Holly Springs visit, Leonidas began to hope that the planters and their families being drawn into the vacated region would further "be translated into the kingdom of God's dear Son" by a resident minister he hoped to recruit. Proceeding, then, to Randolph, a Tennessee town on the Mississippi River, he discovered the Reverend Colley Alexander Foster, an Ohio protégé of Bishop McIlvaine.[8] Listening to Polk's Holly Springs blandishments, Foster resigned from his ministry in Randolph that very night and was on the new job in within days.[9]

To assess the spiritual "condition and wants of Arkansas," the bishop and Henry on March 1 took a steamboat from Randolph to Helena across the Mississippi. They docked on Saturday at three in the morning. Helena was a spot where passing Methodist and Cumberland Presbyterian preachers sometimes tarried, so Leonidas, not to be outdone, preached on Sunday. On Monday, March 4, he went on to Montgomery's Point to spend the night. It was not to be a restful evening. Situated at the confluence of the White, Arkansas, and Mississippi Rivers, this scruffy village had begun as a fur-trading post. Except possibly by the lights of the roustabouts and robbers who regularly roosted there, the sole tavern with open sleeping barracks would not have rated one star in a tour book. Having no choice,

Leonidas checked in. At bedtime he pulled off his thick-soled boots, cautiously positioned himself upon a well-used mattress, turned up the collar of his pitch-cloth coat, and, for hygienic buffering, knotted a red silk handkerchief around his head and face. Along about midnight he was awakened by the clumping entrance of a dozen carousing men piling one by one into the remaining eleven beds. Hence, a problem in the making.

"Well, stranger, I am going to turn in with you," No. 12 announced to Leonidas. "You cannot come here, sir," the bishop replied. "There's two to that," said the man; "I am coming." "You cannot come here, sir," Leonidas said again. After a third unfriendly exchange the cursing man began to falter, and his friends, trying to sleep, told him to shut up and find somewhere else to lie; come morning, they would settle the hash of the inhospitable stranger. When the hungover sleepers awoke, however, the stranger was gone, headed up the Arkansas River to Little Rock. His had been a "wonderful escape," Leonidas was assured by Arkansas acquaintances, due, they guessed, to the rugged boots parked beside Polk's bed and the manly weatherproof pitch-coat he was wearing even while asleep. The would-be bunkmate had doubtless decided that "any man who wore such boots and such a coat . . . must be armed to the teeth." Even without weapons and frail in stamina, the bishop did not want for grit.[10]

For five days in Little Rock, Bishop Polk preached a daily sermon in the Presbyterian Church, striding across the town square bedecked in his vestments, a source of amazement to the layabouts. To his own amazement, he found the town contained some 2,500 "highly intelligent people comprising some society as good as is found anywhere."[11] He advised the Board of Missions to send the Arkansan Episcopalians someone with sufficient determination to endure the wear and tear of the locale. A salary of $1,000 a year would be his reward.[12]

Days later the United States mail coach brought Polk and his servant to Washington, Arkansas, athwart the Southwest Trail and, as was sometimes said, one of the "most highly civilized communities in early Arkansas."[13] A promise to visit newly organized church families in Louisiana was pressing the bishop, but he wished to drop down the Red River into Upper Louisiana, and the only available boat would not be under way until hundreds of cotton bales had been loaded. Mr. Dooley's ferry at Fulton was running, however, so Polk was able opportunely to get himself across the river that Sunday afternoon and into the northeast corner of Texas, where he could visit friends from the East recently settled on Pecan Point.

Actually, he was not certifiably in the Republic of Texas. He was close, being somewhere on Lost Prairie, a region then in dispute between the governments of the United States and the republic. It belonged to Miller County, a part of Arkansas, said the United States. No, it belonged to Red River County lying within their borders, said the Texans.[14] More ominously, Polk's missionary's map said he was on the fringe of "Hostile Ground," an area rife with Comanche warriors implacably resentful of white settlers.[15] For the missionary with carte blanche for the whole Southwest, neither hostiles nor whose country he was in much mattered. With a remarkable knack for tracking down acquaintances in the wide-open spaces, the bishop quickly located a few North Carolina expatriates and passed an agreeable night's lodging, catching up on the latest Red River and Texas Republic gossip with Robert Hamilton, a Scot who was now a prosperous titular Texan and among the signers of the Texas Declaration of Independence. On Monday Leonidas boarded the cotton boat headed down the Red River to Shreveport. Travelers from the northwest corner of Louisiana like Bishop Polk were obliged to take the shallow-draft cotton boats that could squeeze past the Great Raft through sidelong creeks and bayous; the river, determined to reach the Mississippi one way or another, had dredged these passages on its own. On this trip the draft of Polk's boat was not quite shallow enough; during the night it hit a snag, and as water filled the hull it settled upon a bayou's bottom. The right reverend passenger, as the story was told by Fanny, called upon his West Point engineer's education and devised a method of raising the stricken craft. The crew followed his advice, and the boat was shortly afloat again and under way.

By then, however, Bishop Polk and Capt. Charles Barnard, a Bible-reading fellow traveler with whom the bishop had struck up a friendship, had hailed another cotton boat happening by; boarding her, they arrived in Shreveport on Friday, March 22. Polk was soon occupied tracking down more far-flung friends from back East; like a bloodhound, he could find them anywhere.[16] Then, with Palm Sunday coming up, he inquired of a town tavern keeper where he might find a place to preach. "Preach?" cried out the man. "We have never had any preaching here, and we don't want any now." The tavener spoke with conviction and, Polk soon learned, was supported by the town rowdies holding similar secular views. Providentially, maybe, the grateful crew of the refloated cotton boat had by now arrived. They reassured the hostile citizenry that their resourceful pastor "was not *a common preacher*." Say what you will about the breed in general, "he was *good for something*." And so it came to pass. Leonidas was allowed to borrow a meeting room in an unfinished building, and Captain Barnard, a fur trader, proved himself an able Palm Sunday acolyte: he rang a summoning handbell in the street and for Communion provided a table draped with musk fur, placing his Bible reverently upon it. All went well.[17]

Bishop and servant reached Natchitoches on Wednesday evening, with Easter just ahead. No Protestant minister was known to live among the town's 2,500 people, and as the congregations Polk managed to assemble contained a number of Creole French Catholics, he concluded that neither was a Catholic priest stationed there full time.[18] Filling the ecumenical gap, he preached and baptized on Maundy Thursday and Good Friday. As his audiences began to grow, Polk's lungs began to falter. So he rested a little on Saturday and Sunday morning, and when the town's Sunday markets slowed down he resumed preaching at noontime to an Easter congregation in the courthouse. He preached again later that afternoon, and he had just mounted the pulpit on Easter night when he was struck with fits of coughing.[19] Exhausted and breathless, he took to his bed and stayed there for two days. By Thursday, April 4, he had rallied and moved on to Alexandria for one day's stay; no preaching, but he had appointments in Mississippi yet to fulfill—Natchez to Vicksburg to Jackson to Raymond, a blur of ministrations mornings, noons, and nights. For variety, at Laurel Hill Plantation outside Natchez he consecrated tiny St. Mary's Chapel, preaching "to a number of slaves of the estate assembled for that purpose." A good (and wealthy) friend of Tennessee's Bishop Otey, William Newton Mercer had the chapel built, at a cost of $20,000, for the families and slaves from surrounding plantations.[20] Upon seeing St. Mary's that spring day, Leonidas very likely got the idea then and there of a plantation chapel of his own in Tennessee.

Polk reentered Louisiana on May 2. Traversing a road that overlaid an Indian trail, he made his way through West Feliciana Parish to The Cottage, the coyly named plantation home in St. Francisville belonging to Thomas Butler. Butler was a planter of considerable magnitude (he owned or had owned eleven other sugar and cotton plantations) and was a judge, a onetime US congressman, a pioneer churchman, and a worthy host.[21] More particularly of interest to the visiting bishop, Butler was a member of the committee that asked Polk to provide episcopal oversight until the Louisiana diocese had its own bishop.

The steam packet *Cuba* departed New Orleans on Friday afternoon, May 10, 1839, bound for Galveston in the Republic of Texas. Aboard were Polk, his slave Henry, and the Reverend David Page, a priest from Natchez.[22] The *Cuba* was an elegant sidewheeler (fare $30), recently reoutfitted for her passengers' safety and comfort. Her luxurious appointments, in fact, added to the letdown many of those disembarking would feel the moment they beheld the cheerless Galveston Island waterfront.[23] Well-accustomed to bleaker places, Polk took no notice and dutifully hurried from the dock to join Galveston's resident Episcopalians at their Sunday afternoon worship. They possibly murmured thanksgivings for their bishop's safe passage aboard the *Cuba*. And none too soon. Thirty days later she wrecked on a sandbar in Galveston Bay and sank.[24]

Bishop Polk spent Monday as any land developer on a business trip might do. Persuaded by townspeople that Galveston was destined for surging growth, he rode out with a real-estate agent to select a lot for a church building. But not to buy it himself. He let it be known that he hoped the town's own developers, as such people elsewhere generally did to "principal religious denominations," would hand the property over to him as a gift.[25] By evening, it was time to move on; he and Page and the Reverend Robert Ranney, the town's pastor, took an overnight boat headed fifty miles up Galveston Bay to the three-year-old City of Houston, the official name by which the locals styled the little village. If inauspicious to look at, Houston was nevertheless the capital of the Republic of Texas, and Polk and his companions wisely sought out the home of a leading citizen, William Fairfax Gray. A lawyer from Fredericksburg, Virginia, he was already known to Polk. He occupied a house on the Courthouse Square and was otherwise at the center of the town's civic, educational, and cultural affairs, the kind of connection much suited to Bishop Polk's missionary objectives.[26] Just weeks before, Gray had collected between $4,000 and $5,000 from various Houstonians to acquire land for the first Episcopal parish in Houston. From this acorn would sprout the subsequent cathedral oak situated on Gray's original site.[27] Polk spent some of Friday, May 17, writing an account of his experiences thus far in Texas, posting it to the Foreign Board of Missions. That evening Millie Gray, his hostess, invited a few of Houston's other civic benefactors to drop in for prayers and refreshments with the bishop.[28] Their chitchat included the laudatory newspaper notice that had run the day before in the *Houston Morning Star* acknowledging the presence in town of Polk and his companions. The news account said in part:

> We understand that it is the purpose of these gentlemen to explore
> the republic with a view of supplying to our citizens ministrations
> of religion from the highly respectable and intelligent body of
> Christians with whom they are connected. We hail the coming of these
> gentlemen whose piety and talents are well known to many of our
> citizens as an augury of the rapid advancement of our country and the
> establishment of its institution upon the best and surest foundations.[29]

All well and good for the journalist to gush, but as Polk had seen in Shreveport, the missionary bishop in Texas sometimes encountered secular skepticism. Was this dignified man possibly a fugitive from United States justice, as not a few newly arrived Texans seemed to be? Well, what then? Fanny remembered that her husband met a former Tennessean in Texas who surmised, "You must be one of the [Maury County] Polks." "I am," said the bishop. "Well, stranger, if it is a fair question, I would give a heap to know what brought you here." Bishop Polk said he was a clergyman and had come to see about preaching to the people. "Oh, my friend, do go back," said the Texan. "We are not worth the trouble."[30]

Encouraged at least by the *Morning Star*'s bracing approval, Polk and Page and Henry left Houston on horseback on Saturday, May 18, and headed south, planning to visit Columbia, Brazoria, Velasco, Quintana, and Matagorda on the Gulf Coast. Over the next seven days the missionary team worked the Texas coastal towns, then turned their horses north across the shadeless prairies stretching toward Austin. That was a summertime mistake. The Southwest sun beat down with such persistence on the land that both Polk and Page were shortly sickened by the heat. (As usual, how Henry bore up is not mentioned by the bishop.)[31] After reviving, but then suffering a recurrence, they gave up this part of their trip. Traveling only in the nighttime cool, they returned to the coast and, on June 10, caught a boat for New Orleans.[32]

Within two weeks Leonidas was safely back in Tennessee. Behind him stretched five months passed, 5,000 miles traveled, forty-four sermons preached, fourteen infants and adults baptized—the hard lot of the missionary experienced almost daily. As he had learned, "it is a grave enterprise to enter the army of the host of the Lord," a weariness for him compounded by his having a wife and children whose welfare was seldom forgotten. "I have often felt strongly," he later admitted, "that a missionary bishop ought not to have a family. He should be literally married to the Church."[33] The joyful homecoming was marred only by Fanny's revelations that she had been almost overwhelmed by the responsibilities that her husband had left her with. The worst of these was the supervision of the many slaves on the plantation, something in which neither she nor Thomas Brewster, the mill mechanic from England, had any experience. "It was unfortunate that [Brewster] had to take his first lessons . . . in my wife's management rather than my own," Leonidas later confided to his mother. "Unfortunate for him, as [slave management] amazed her a good deal," he added, "amazed" meaning "baffled." The Englishman, though, caught on quickly: "The trial is now over . . . and I think he will henceforth be a great comfort to her as a general manager." On other issues his initial hopes for Brewster would shortly fade. By the time he had been able to examine the ledgers, he could see that the plantation's once promising hemp business had not gone well in his absence, Brewster seemingly unequal to running the venture. By fall Polk had sold the steam machinery in which he had taken such entrepreneurial pleasure.

Travel fatigue had vanished within a month's time, however, and the bishop felt so refreshed that he vowed he was ready to sally forth again as soon as he had taken in hand all the family and home affairs awaiting his attention.[34] With his missionary work seldom off his mind, he had written to the Foreign Missionary Society, stressing his conviction that East Texas was ripe for evangelizing. Having noticed the cheapness of Texas land but suspecting inflationary prices were coming soon, he drew upon a biblical text to give the devil his due: "The children of this world are wiser than the children of light," he reminded the society.[35] Translation: prudent Christians with building plans should learn from canny Texan speculators. The time to buy lots for church buildings was right now.[36]

It was shortly after his return to Tennessee that Leonidas began the plantation chapel in Ashwood. It was to command a pastoral rise of land amid a grove of trees where the four farms of the Polk brothers came together. As well as a corner nicked out of their acreage, each brother committed the labor of slaves they owned, and these workers—brick makers, masons, carpenters, plasterers—were set to work in midsummer on what Leonidas described as a building "of chaste and simple Gothic architecture." William Julius Polk, their elder half-brother who lived some miles distant, was persuaded to contribute to the project, giving money for the roof. When finished, the building was free of debt. With the resourcefulness of an accomplished draftsman, the former cadet had consulted architectural books and drawn up the plans himself.[37] A square crenelated bell tower stood at the front, and buttressed sidewalls were pierced by three arched stained-glass windows. The Polk brothers' chapel, still standing, closely resembles elevations and other details found in a generic do-it-yourself church-building book just published by the protean bishop of Vermont, John Henry Hopkins. (Hopkins would later apply another sideline—landscaping—when, as Leonidas's friend, he designed the campus of the aborning University of the South.)[38] Once the chapel was well under way, Leonidas, Fanny, and the children left for Raleigh on September 10. For the bishop it was the first leg of a "flying trip" to Virginia and New York, where he intended to beg shamelessly for missionary manpower and financial support.

Tarrying only to drop off his family with the Polk and Devereux kinfolks in Raleigh, Leonidas worked his way north, preaching and pleading for his lonesome ministry as he went. He reached New York City in early October, and on Saturday, October 12, went to the General Theological Seminary, hoping to inspire a few self-denying volunteers among those close to graduation.[39] Some classes were scheduled for that Saturday night, but as a favor to the visitor they were suspended so that Leonidas was able to make his pitch to the captive students. Shortly thereafter he moved on to New Haven, Connecticut, hoping to recruit among the divinity students at Yale College; his pleadings availed little. Then, with not much to show for his swing through the Northeast, he returned home only to depart on his second mission on January 29, 1840. This time he provided tender farewells on the front porch for Fanny, as well as kisses all around for the three children, Alexander Hamilton (nine), Frances Deverux (four), and Katherine (fifteen months). Fanny was pregnant again.[40]

Wearisome as his tramps through the South and Southwest were for him, few of his duties demanded more of his time than communicating the specifics of his ministry to his employers, the Foreign and Domestic Missionary Societies. Frequent, comprehensive letters were expected from him, all of which were promptly printed in *Spirit of Missions*, the societies' monthly magazine. His quandary—whether to provide his readers with too few or too many details—was brought into arresting focus after he had taken a boat down the Tombigbe River to Mobile on the Alabama Gulf Coast. "I cannot but remark upon the shocking indifference to the value of human life, and the rights of the dead, exhibited everywhere, more or less, on our western streams," he wrote fully after this trip.

> Men are knocked overboard, and flats, and other boats, stove or blown up, by which many lives . . . are lost, producing frequently nothing more than a fleeting show of sympathy, or an idle remark. I have . . . seen the bodies of the dead floating unnoticed among the drifting timber; and I was recently called to notice the humiliating spectacle of a bird of prey feasting on the vitals of a half-consumed corpse. These things . . . betray a depravity dishonorable to us as a people.

He concluded that such behavior called loudly for "active exertion by churchmen, those whose function it is to elevate and purify the moral sensibilities of the nation."

Depraved human nature was but one misfortune he encountered among coastal Alabamans. During the past year the Mobile city treasury had become bankrupt, a yellow-fever epidemic had killed hundreds, and two conflagrations had destroyed several Mobile neighborhoods, altogether a dispiriting loss of life and property along the Gulf. But the bishop could see the silver lining in these acts of God, as he deemed them: "The difficulties . . . seem not to have been lost on the citizens of Mobile," he observed during his visit. "Many have blessed the rod which has smitten them, and [they] have turned unto the Lord with penitence and submission."[41] Later, reaching Natchez in Mississippi, he learned that this town, too, had been devastated in recent months by out-of-control fires and a yellow-fever epidemic killing 235. As before, his piety led him to hope that the "chief Shepherd" of his fellow Episcopalians would "enable them to say, 'it is good for me that I have been afflicted.'"[42]

In such a penitent mood, Polk may have wondered if there was any connection between God's righteous wrath and one of his own trials. Burdened by the defaulted $15,000 loan he had secured for Adlai O. Harris, his Tennessee church friend, he called on Madison Caruthers when he reached New Orleans. Also a Tennessean, Caruthers was now Harris's partner in a Louisiana commission business and had been involved in Harris's earlier financial difficulties. Beyond eliciting friendly promises from Caruthers, who asserted financial straits of his own, Polk got nothing. He reported this to Lucius, a party to the debt, and took a peaceful stance regarding repayment: "I am of the opinion . . . that the proper course is to keep quiet and let them alone. Violence, at least, never yet answered any good purpose."[43] His time in New Orleans was more profitably spent when he paid a comforting call on a cadet friend from West Point days, a man now in a debtor's prison. Such punishment the debt-wracked bishop would never face—by Louisiana law clergymen owing money were exempt from imprisonment.[44]

Since many of the moneyed Protestant planters living in Catholic Louisiana regarded Episcopal Church membership as a social enhancement worth having, a bishop's visit did not go unnoticed. As had happened in Houston the previous spring, Polk was not long in finding himself attended to by influential people. Someone among them extended an enticing invitation, leading Polk to explain (when writing again to the Mission Society) why he had left New Orleans for "the river coast, between the Bayous La Fourche and Plaquemines." As he wrote, "To this point my attention was called by a gentleman whose family belonged to the Church, and who assured me that himself and others—planters—in that vicinity, were very anxious to organize themselves into a congregation, build a church, and settle a clergyman."[45]

The area to which he had gone was the fertile stretch along the Mississippi Delta where both sugarcane and its planters were flourishing. As the guest of the solicitous plantation owners for several days, he began to realize that not only his hosts stood to benefit from this "incipient effort in behalf of the Church"; the effort further "commends itself to the regards of those who feel interested in the welfare of the colored race." But who would undertake this humane task upon such "a large field [of] plantations on both sides [of the Mississippi], owned chiefly by Protestants?" He answered: "An individual disposed to give himself to the work of Christ." Seated in his study in Tennessee while penning these lines to his managers in New York, the bishop was imagining himself as the settled individual best suited to minister sympathetically to the bayous' disparate population of rich and poor, free and bound. Having been at home but four of his eighteen months as a bishop, he had come to see that the scope of the evangelizing task assigned him was, in its magnitude, preposterous. As he confided to McIlvaine, the "ground allotted me by the Church" roughly equaled all of France, and after his two excursions into it he realized that "it [was] quite impossible for me to do anything effectively over so wide an extent of country. [It] would require two years of incessant active labor . . . without one day of rest intervening." Nevertheless, his sense of duty being prodigious, he had no thought of giving up so soon, and after three months gathering strength the bishop went forth yet again.[46]

At the turn of the year, he left Ashwood Hall on the third (and last) of his missionary journeys. He and his servant, now a slave named Armstead replacing Henry, began their journey in a two-horse light carriage—so light that it broke down a few weeks later while negotiating an Arkansas swamp and was left behind. Leonidas and Armstead discovered with pleasure the riding comfort afforded by the carriage horses, one of them "the finest saddle horse I have ever travelled." Equipped with buffalo robes for nights in the open, the companions rode into the wilderness, their principal concern being horse thieves.[47]

Polk's goal was the western reaches of his diocese (the Indian Territory that is now Oklahoma), though he proceeded gradually across Arkansas, stopping to preach to anyone who would listen—especially those "perishing in the wilderness." At length he reached Fayetteville on the far-northwestern corner of the state. On New Year's Day 1841, as had become customary for him, he took time to pen self-chastisements and melancholy reflections on the past twelve months while peering as best he could into a future he was sure would be a trial. The season led him to think he was "standing on the top of a high hill, up which I had been struggling since midsummer." From that vantage, he saw "I have done but too little in accomplishing the ends of my creation in the year that is now gone. I have humbled myself too infrequently before the throne of God. I have watched against the intrusion of a worldly spirit too little." Despite his catalog of moral deficiencies (he counted several more), he had made one amendment to his self-centeredness along the way in Little Rock. Ignoring his indebtedness, he gave $800—a third of his salary for the coming year—to the town's Episcopalians to help them acquire lots on which to build a church.[48]

Fayetteville—the jumping-off point for the Indian Territory—was a rowdy town of street fights and vigilante hangings that no bishop could much care for. He was welcomed by the Reverend William Scull, a recent arrival himself. Scull's ministry stretched over and beyond Fayetteville's horizon to include the US Army's Fort Gibson, a sickly fortification set on the Indian lands some sixty miles farther west; his duties were largely going there to bury the dead, which included both Native Americans and American soldiers.[49] As much to the bishop's liking as the hard-working priest was Fayetteville's Sophia Sawyer, "a pious female" with whom Polk was much taken. She was an independent-minded Yankee who espoused equal education for girls and women, and a few months earlier she had opened her Fayetteville Female Academy, essentially for Cherokee Indian girls.[50] Sawyer had studied at Byfield Seminary in Massachusetts. A classmate's having gone on to found Mount Holyoke College in South Hadley inspired Sawyer to pattern her little school after Holyoke, combining religion and academics. Though she had grown up among New England Congregationalists, Mistress Sawyer pleased the bishop by saying she found the Episcopalians' Book of Common Prayer admirable for enlightening the "heathen mind."[51]

If Polk held any moral pangs regarding Andrew Jackson's forced removal of the Five Civilized Tribes from the southeastern United States to the empty prairies on which he now found himself, he did not express them in any of his known reports or letters. What did concern him was the need to Christianize the Choctaw, Creek, Chickasaw, Seminole, and Cherokee Indians who now lived there. It was an exchange of sorts: deprived of earthly lands and possessions by the United States, the tribes would be offered heavenly dwellings in the hereafter. Or, as his missionary employers were to ask plainly: "Are these immortal beings to be suffered to go to Hell, without an effort on the part of the Church to pluck them from the fire?"[52]

Before he and Armstead could reach Fort Gibson, their first destination, a change in the weather dropped the temperature to 12 degrees below zero, cold not thwarted even by buffalo-robe bedding. The two travelers sought shelter in the vicinity of Tahlequah, the newly established capital of the Cherokee Nation. Polk discovered the layover to be providential. He met with several Cherokee chiefs who were agreeable to his promises to send "the gospel to those parts." One chieftain opened his home for a service, and, with a small congregation gathered, Polk preached. Soon after Fort Gibson, Polk and Armstead reached nearby Park Hill, visiting the printing operations of Samuel Austin Worcester, a radical Congregationalist missionary from Massachusetts who for years (and despite imprisonments) had been siding against state and federal governments on the Cherokees' behalf and had lately been printing tracts, schoolbooks, pamphlets, biblical scripture, and hymns he had personally translated into the Cherokee language. His work, Polk noted in his official report, "was languishing for want of adequate support."[53]

Bishop Polk was probably aware of the bitter—indeed murderous—division within the Cherokee Tribe between members who had approved of the removal from Georgia and those who had opposed it. Polk was treading carefully between the dangerous antagonists. Park Hill was also the home of John Ross. Ross had grown up in northern Georgia, fought beside Andrew Jackson in the Creek War, and vigorously opposed the Cherokees' removal by his former military ally who was now betraying him and his people. Subsequently, in the Indian Territory (now Oklahoma), Ross became the tribe's principal chief.[54] As Ross had been a slave-holding plantation owner in Georgia before the Cherokees' exodus—and near extermination—on the Trail of Tears, he and the bishop may even have found common conversational ground during a convivial evening. Polk reported that Ross was "willing to lend his influence . . . for the education and Christianization of his people and would assist the Episcopalians should they choose to enter that missionary field."[55]

Polk and Armstead arrived at Fort Gibson on about January 21. The place was numbingly bleak in the dead of winter. Since more than enough missionaries of various denominations were already milling among the tribal peoples, Polk's heart was most pained observing the unchurched Caucasian Americans. Dolefully he wrote: "In no other part of my field of labor have I seen a people [so] perishing for lack of knowledge. They have no one to say to them 'this is the way, walk ye in it.' They [lack] guides [to] go forth into the wilderness to seek for the sheep of Christ 'dispersed abroad,' in the midst of this naughty world."[56] Moving on, he paid a second visit to northeastern parts of the Republic of Texas in February, this time contacting his Hawkins kinfolks.[57] He then descended the Red River again, and in Shreveport he preached as before. To his dismay, the townspeople related "the remarkable fact that not a solitary sermon had been preached in the village since my visit two years before."[58]

If former friends and relations along his wearisome track helped bolster the missionary's resolve, there were times the whole enterprise was hard to endure. Near the end of this third trip, he wrote to his mother, "I have had, as you may suppose, some rather rough fare. A few nights ago I had to pass the night in a cotton-house on the top of a pile of cotton, with dogs and Negroes lying around, and a hamper-basket to hang my clothes upon." With blankets and buffalo robe "I manage, on the whole, to make myself comfortable."[59] At last he reached New Orleans, where the homes and beds of friends—and the pulpits of parish churches—awaited. He bought for his mother a paper bedspread ("a specimen of the growing national extravagance") and sent Armstead back to Tennessee alone. Lucius was in the city for company. So were those importuning him to resign his rambles and become the settled diocesan of Louisiana. More exhausted than won over, he wrote his sister Susan that he was "fatigued in mind and body." And he vowed to Fanny that "this is the last time I shall be so long away." What he longed for was to be in his library with his "chickens" on his knees, playing "riding gemmen" and "running way wid stage."[60]

9

"As It Is My Duty to Live Here, I Will Try My Best to Like It" (1841–1849)

While some Louisiana Episcopalians were maneuvering to have Polk declared their diocesan bishop by the national church, others, influential landowners along Bayou La Fourche who knew of Polk's reputation as a Tennessee cotton and hemp planter, were hoping for a bishop who might be disposed to become a neighborhood planter as well.[1] Polk's wealthy friend Judge Thomas Butler had been especially eloquent on the subject. He urged Leonidas and Lucius before leaving the state to visit the La Fourche region (where one of Butler's many plantations lay) and to size up its agreeable prospects for residency and profit. Butler recommended especially Thibodauxville,[2] a pretty place a couple of years old just forty miles west of downtown New Orleans, where citified culture and cane cultivation thrived in equal measure.[3] Butler's blandishments notwithstanding, when Leonidas and Lucius boarded the steamboat *Augusta* in New Orleans on March 26, they were of a mind to return directly to Middle Tennessee and home. What happened over the next day or so, as the vibrating sidewheeler churned and corkscrewed up the Mississippi, can be imagined by those who have initially resisted, then succumbed, to an impulse purchase. "The boat shakes so terribly that I can scarcely recognize my own hand writing," Lucius wrote his wife, Mary, the second day out, but he was able to make plain that his and Leonidas's scheduled arrival in Ashwood in four or five days would be delayed many weeks. Mutually stoking one another's imaginings of owning sugar dynasties, the brothers, though already 300-odd miles along their way, changed their homeward plans in midstream. They disembarked the *Augusta* when it called at Vicksburg, then took another boat back down the Mississippi to Donaldsonville on the river's Louisiana side, retracing practically the whole of the route they had just traveled. At Donaldsonville, where a large bayou forked off the main river to flow south and west toward the Gulf of Mexico (hence "La Fourche"), they boarded a bayou boat. "We are only going to look, not to buy," Lucius stressed to his wife (by making the point twice). He added, "We would be dissatisfied with ourselves if we did not."[4] Lucius was already disenchanted with growing cotton in Middle Tennessee, just as Leonidas was giving up on hemp farming. He was even less keen to plant cotton in Mississippi's semilawless-frontier Madison County, where he and Leonidas had recently bought their 500-acre plantation. In the county seat an officer of the law was murdered recently in full view of Lucius and other townspeople, an event giving him pause. Mary Polk nailed the situation: "The state of society must be dreadful."[5]

Leonidas did not suppose the brothers' midstream turnaround was of much import; he did not even mention it in a letter from La Fourche to their sister Susan. He merely noted he had thought it not amiss "to look a little . . . after my private affairs."[6] To that end, he and Lucius were by that time enjoying the Deep South hospitality at the "fine estate" of James Porter in Thibodeauxville. Porter had formerly lived in Tennessee, had known some of the Polks there, and like Lucius had raised and raced thoroughbreds. From Porter's home about a mile outside the village the brothers ventured up and down the waterway, plantation shopping. Canny Judge Butler had guessed right: the bishop was smitten by the place. Describing it to Susan, Leonidas wrote: "From . . . Donaldsonville down to Thibodeauxville 40 or 50 miles, [the bayou] is a continuous village of small French farmers with occasionally an American planter among them. The bayou is about as wide as an ordinary street in one of our cities, and is navigable by large steamboats which . . . seem to pass just by the door. . . . Shrubbery grows finely, and the orange is in perfection."[7]

And what's more, with the Western world's sweet tooth growing insatiably since the seventeenth century, the opportunist bishop-investor would have cast an approving eye on the seemingly endless fields of sugarcane that bordered the stream, everything green and flourishing in the heat and humidity while packet boats laden with hogsheads of raw sugar and barrels of molasses plied the bayou's length. And should he have paused a moment to picture himself situated here as a planter, he knew that it would place him solidly in the social station of the Southern squirearchy. It was these people living so well on the frontier whose money would allow him to fulfill his prayers of nurturing his Protestant faith in this domain of Cajun

Catholicism, these Anglo people who surely had the wherewithal to buy land, construct churches, and pay the clergymen's salaries. Lastly, the contemplation of producing an exotic commodity like sugar—the wondrous result of chemistry and physics, of crushers and boilers and evaporators—fascinated the engineer-bishop. Thomas Butler would have succeeded as a real-estate broker; he had expertly matched locale and prospect. What's more, while James Porter was making Lucius and Leonidas feel welcome in his home, he was simultaneously on the lookout for a plantation buyer. His wife having recently died, Porter was ready to sell everything he had: land, house, outbuildings (including a pigeonaire), a cane mill, sugar boilers, and his workforce of thirty-two slaves.[8] The price for 1,500 acres fronting on the bayou and the slaves was $107,000, and to Leonidas it was irresistible, especially as he had access to $50,000 that Fanny had recently inherited from her maternal uncle, George Pollock.[9] Porter and Leonidas, during their talks that April, reached a tentative agreement hinging on the near certainty that Polk would become the bishop of Louisiana.[10] With all that now understood, the Polk brothers resumed their aborted homeward journey. Once arrived, Lucius, shorter on funds than Leonidas, had decided he would stay put in Tennessee a while longer.

Reasonably sure as time passed that he was destined to live in Louisiana, Leonidas spent the spring and summer tidying up both his and his mother's business affairs in Tennessee. Significantly, by midsummer he and his brother Andrew Jackson Polk had begun discussing Andrew's purchase of Ashwood Hall. In September the bishop took his family (including a wet nurse for baby Sarah) to North Carolina. They would travel by "private conveyance" (a carriage, a buggy, and a wagon), and before they set out he joked in a letter to his mother that the caravan would contain "women and children and much cattle. See account of the journey of the Israelites from Egypt into Canaan."[11]

In Raleigh, three daughters and the servants were left at the home of Fanny's parents, and then Leonidas, Fanny, Sarah, and Hamilton, now almost eleven, proceeded in early October to New York City for the church convention where Leonidas would officially become bishop of Louisiana. In early business, convention delegates gathering in St. John's Chapel on Varick Street were informed that, after three years of scholarly research, the church historiographer was able to affirm that Jesus Christ was indeed, as belief had it, "most probably" born on December 25 in the year 1.[12] Convention delegates then moved on to religious events transpiring that October day and, in due course, unanimously elected Leonidas Polk as bishop of Louisiana. Whereupon, the erstwhile missionary bishop rose and happily resigned his cure of the Diocese of the Southwest, handing over the care of that sprawling wilderness to James Otey.[13]

An eye affliction bothering the bishop had by December healed enough for him to risk travel, so the Polks returned to Raleigh. Fanny settled in with her parents; she and the three daughters remained until the birth of yet another daughter, Susan, in April. Leonidas meanwhile made preparations to transport to Tennessee the slave gang he and Fanny had acquired, the men, women, and children bequeathed from Fanny's uncle George Pollock.[14] As 1842 began, the North Carolina slaves set out in wagons bound for Tennessee. Subsequently, most were moved to the Polks' Louisiana plantation on Bayou La Fourche, arriving grimly aware, no doubt, that their futures growing cane and making sugar augured an even harder life then they had previously known. Their master, meanwhile, in cheerful anticipation of presiding at his first convention of Louisianan Episcopalians, took a different route for New Orleans. His plan was to reach the city by combining tried-and-true stagecoach travel with that of a modern railroad. Any hope he had for a dignified, on-time arrival was frustrated in Georgia somewhere southwest of Atlanta. The public stage broke down, and he was compelled to plod on to the nearest station of the new Montgomery & West Point Railroad on a mule.[15]

The appointed beginning of Leonidas's full-time Louisiana ministry got off in slow motion, too. On the convention's opening day, January 19, 1842, so few delegates (including the tardy bishop) showed up at brand-new St. Paul's Church on the corner of Camp and Bartholomew that the proceedings were adjourned for lack of a quorum. The next morning at 11:00, when it was closer to full strength (one bishop, five clergy, seven lay delegates), Polk, running late, called the convention to order. Judge Thomas Butler, instrumental in arranging Polk's presence, was there to lend support.[16] Standing tall behind the lectern, dishabille and travel-weariness surely evident, the bishop gave his new flock a forceful call to action. The paramount job for him and his colleagues was "to establish in the minds and hearts of our hearers a sense of their ruin; and point them to their remedy"; that is, to nurse Louisiana's dehydrated unsaved on a hearty diet of "'the sincere milk of the Word.'" That appeal, plus Polk's hope to enlarge the clergy ranks of the understaffed diocese, constituted the long and the short of the convention. "We may scarcely hope to find [enough such men] willing to come among us from aboard," the realist bishop conceded, "abroad" meaning Northern men not likely to accept the low-paying jobs on the Louisiana frontier, the uncomfortable climate, the high incidence of disease, and the slave economy. How, then, to find right-minded clergy? "Rais[e] them up from among ourselves!" the bishop declared.[17] He had no sooner wound up the convention on a Thursday, and then preached twice the following Sunday, than he was felled again by inflammation of the lungs. (Probably a relapse of the pleurisy he had suffered in Alabama in March 1840.) His preaching now definitely proscribed, the latest affliction, he said, "disqualified him for all official duties for the next six weeks."[18] While recuperating, Polk was at least able to see to the settlement of the several hundred slaves from North Carolina and Tennessee who had lately arrived at La Fourche. Otherwise, he was teaching himself the rudiments of growing sugar, a pursuit he found recreational. By this time, Polk had decided on the name he would give his plantation: Leighton Place, to honor Archbishop Robert Leighton, whose home and library he evidently visited in Dunblane, Scotland, in 1832.[19]

By mid-March the bishop was feeling well enough—just—to resume limited preaching. He did so on Palm Sunday to his own slave population, "a devout congregation." A week later—Easter Day—he was in New Orleans preaching twice, and by mid-May, having seen to the planting of his first crop of cane, as well as the organization of the Church of the Ascension in Donaldsonville, he took passage on a northbound steamboat, not to return until December. An equitable exchange, on balance: the underfed Episcopalians were getting from their bishop just slightly more in ministry than they were paying him, which was nothing at all.[20]

During the seven months of his absence in 1842, Polk had to pack up household belongings in Tennessee, gather up family and left-behind slaves, and move everyone and everything to Thibodeauxville. Since Fanny and the children (including their new daughter, Susan, whom he had not seen) were all in North Carolina while the household things were in Tennessee and the left-behind slaves were in both places, his responsibilities had complications. He went first to Ashwood, and on two Sundays he preached to "the colored people" at the just-finished St. John's Chapel. On a Thursday evening he went up to Columbia, where he officiated at St. Peter's Church at the wedding of Virginia Otey, the bishop's daughter, and Benjamin Minor. Then, with George and Rufus Polk, he departed for Raleigh, and the Tennessee Polks returned to Maury County at the end of July. Since Leonidas was soon to leave for Louisiana, the Polk brothers determined to donate their little St. John's Chapel to the Diocese of Tennessee. The gift was commemorated worshipfully for four and a half hours on September 4. The racially mixed congregation of more than 500 then watched as George Washington Polk and Rufus King Polk were baptized. Leonidas noted, happily, that the two were now "doubly his brothers: brothers by blood and brothers in Christ."[21]

But Rufus, though appearing to be in good health, was dead of "pulmonary consumption" within six months. By then he was the father of an infant daughter. His body returned to St. John's churchyard in a coffin. Leonidas's grief was lessened somewhat when Lucius gave up his long indifference to baptism, an attitude probably picked up at the knee of his essentially irreligious father. Bishop Otey officiated, and now certain that eternal life was the legacy of at least four of his brothers (Hamilton had been baptized before dying in 1830), Leonidas felt a weight lifted from his heart. He told Lucius: "I have desired of earthly blessings for myself nothing more than to see this result brought about." Leonidas even dared to suppose that Lucius's financial troubles might soon lift a little, too. "Doubtless . . . you will find that God will bless you," he assured him, "bless you in mind, body and estate. For truly Godliness is profitable for all things, [in] the life that now is, as well as that which is to come."[22]

Leonidas's and Fanny's preparations for the upheaval to Louisiana were made with contingencies. To make a definitive move with no looking back was intimidating; it might be best to be able to come and go. So they would hold onto Ashwood Hall for now, delaying Andrew's purchase. The US Congress, on the other hand, had just passed a tariff bill highly beneficial to American sugar producers, and that made Leonidas sanguine about the future. He would detach twenty-five slaves from his Ashwood force and take them, too, to Leighton Place. That would bring the number of Leighton's field hands to 150. "Not a hand too many for the capital I have in land there," he had been advised. Then there were his children to think about. A Mrs. Porter, "a very elegant and accomplished lady" (not known to be related to the Louisiana Porters), was coaxed from the faculty of the Columbia Female Institute to go with the family as governess. She agreed to a salary of $350 a year, which has the sound of a bargain for the Polks. All the more so, when one considers she may not have known that Fanny was once again expecting. Daughter number five, Elizabeth Devereux, would be born back in Tennessee the following June.[23]

With departure arrangements all in order by November 17, 1842, Leonidas and Fanny and Mrs. Porter and the children got under way from Ashwood by carriage. At Memphis they boarded the steamboat *Edwin Hickman*. By December 4, the second Sunday in Advent, the bishop's lungs felt fine and he was ready to get back to work. As the vessel steamed down the Mississippi toward New Orleans, he conducted Morning Prayer and preached in one of the sidewheeler's saloons, raising his voice above the machinery's throbbings amidships. On Christmas Day, with the family more or less settled in at Leighton Place, he preached for the townspeople in Thibodeauxville's courthouse. He was in his element.[24]

When Lucius and Leonidas had previously showed up as house guests (and as prospective buyers) at James Porter's home in early 1841 they were much taken by the outdoor surroundings, appealingly luxuriant with springtime's sprouting cane plants. Porter's was one of the bigger plantations in La Fourche Parish, stretched along the bayou's western bank for three-quarters of a mile. His house of one and a half stories (standing today) was a clapboard building with dormers, ten wooden pillars, and an open gallery across the front. It was situated back a little from the levee, with rose hedges and mossy oaks growing on the sloping lawn. Far from being pretentious, it suited a young bishop just starting out. The Polk brothers could see, though, that the house betrayed neglect by Widower Porter. Upkeep had scarcely improved since the bishop had taken ownership and settled in with a number of slaves to begin sugaring. Nor had Leonidas properly prepared Fanny for what to expect when she saw her new home. It was not a gladsome moment.

Not long after moving in, she proclaimed her unhappiness to her confidante in Tennessee, Mary Polk, Lucius's wife. To accommodate her family of four daughters, the governess, their nephew William Polk, and the assorted servants, the dilapidated house was unacceptably crowded, and "everything is in confusion and out of repair. It will need both time and labour and money to make the place even comfortable, the two latter things we cannot now command, and therefore cannot expect to be very comfortable for a long time to come." Plus, the rainy winter weather was "more disagreeable" than the chill she had endured in New York, and even the flat, watery scenery disappointed her. The rosebushes in the front yard were a minor consolation. Don't let "your good man buy a La Fourche plantation," she warned Mary. "It certainly has but little to recommend it . . . although I have no doubt as a place for making money it is very desirable." In short, she told Mary, "as it is my duty to live here, I will try my best to like it."[25]

For Fanny, the house did improve with the passage of time, and with it, so did her mood. The effervescent Leonidas was happy from the outset, dilapidation notwithstanding. Though feeling a little unwell at times, he was soon caught up in his first sugar production, from the planting of seed cane, to the rolling of the canes, to the boiling of the juice. His field hands and sugarhouse workers produced 480 hogsheads of sugar and 700 barrels of molasses, and while it was a shorter crop than he had hoped for, he felt he had surpassed his neighbors.

Mostly detached from the Louisianans in his first year on the job, the new bishop had exercised executive restraint. By the beginning of 1843, however, returning with fresh ideas, he was not reluctant to act and speak with force to his people. He would shortly overturn a parish election in Baton Rouge, for example, because women communicants financially supporting St. James Church there had been denied the vote.[26] But on this January day, again running late to his convention, uppermost in his thoughts was the spiritual neglect of the state's slave population by his church and by the owner-planters. As was the case when Polk was a Tennessee farmer, his slaves at Leighton were excused from work on Sundays—an unpopular notion among his planter neighbors.[27] No work, maybe, but the slaves were still obliged to attend Sunday School sessions overseen by Polk's full-time chaplain to the slaves, the Reverend William Spencer Wall. As Fanny described the Sunday School, the pupils were "taught orally the principal events of the Bible, the great truths of our religion, . . . and many hymns." She added that "gladly would they have been taught to read but for Louisiana law prohibiting it." For that she blamed "the conduct of the abolitionists." Not mentioned by Fanny, but logically taught on Sundays, was the *Prayer Book*'s Catechism. Catechumens at Leighton would be taught the *Question*: "What is thy duty towards thy Neighbour?" And the *Answers*: "To submit myself to all my governors, teachers, spiritual pastors and masters" and "to order myself lowly and reverently to my betters." Useful precepts to pacify the restive slave.[28]

The more zealous ministry to the blacks that the bishop envisioned for his second year was expressed in language almost lyrical: "It is one of the chiefest charms of the Gospel of Christ," he began, "that it seeks to equalize the human condition; and to compensate, by the richness of its spiritual provisions, for the disparities existing in the worldly circumstances of our race. It is eminently, therefore, the property of the poor." The charge he was laying before his clergy, in short, was for them to expand an uplifting ministry to the masses locked in poverty and captivity. And lest the white owners be alarmed, the ministers must make clear that "we are not political crusaders, but simple and guileless teachers of the Gospel [to] those to whom we go."[29]

When the convention closed, winter planting of Polk's next sugar crop was under way, even while his duties throughout the state (and auxiliary assignments in Mississippi and Alabama) took precedence. It was evidently on this roundabout trip that he went to Woodville, the Mississippi home of Jane Cook Davis, the mother of his West Point chum Jefferson Davis. Here he confirmed Jane Davis at St. Paul's Church, to the comfort of her son, then a planter living at Davis Bend, near Vicksburg.[30] The sugar prospects at Leighton Place, meanwhile, continued to be encouraging, and Leonidas, in residence for a spell, typically took much of the credit. "My crop," he exulted to his own mother, "is by dint of the most extraordinary exertion on my part, a decidedly good one. The stand of cane is remarkably fine and the whole is in excellent condition and growing well." He calculated that in the coming winter he might make as many as 800 thousand-pound hogsheads of sugar and hoped to realize five cents a pound, or $50 each. To this cheering prospect he added that his health was never better.[31]

Fanny in the early spring of 1843 had left Bayou La Fourche and went up to Ashwood Hall with the children and Mrs. Porter. In the seventh month of her pregnancy, she was glad to be out of the gathering sweaty heat. Leonidas caught up with his family once he had seen to the plowing of his 600 acres of ripening cane before the fall harvest. He reached Tennessee just a few days after Fanny gave birth to Elizabeth Devereux Polk on June 29. That summer's other high point arrived in August when Lucius and George came to him wishing to seal their recent baptismal vows by confirmation and to receive Holy Communion for the first time. Writing Bishop Otey afterward, Leonidas confessed that professional composure had almost failed him. "I am sure you would have been deeply affected," he wrote, "as well as highly gratified, had you been with me yesterday. . . . And how, my dear bishop, can I describe the feelings which were excited by this service? Overwhelming, as you may imagine, to the last degree."[32]

Less ennobling and far more onerous were other events that summer, among them dealing with bankers and debt. Paying off the note he had cosigned for his now-bankrupt friend Adlai Harris, he told his mother, had proved to be "a dreadfully severe year upon me, taxing all my ingenuity and energies to the utmost capacity."[33] He had managed—manfully, as he would have seen it—because he had drawn again on the all but inexhaustible strength he found in his religion, the remedy he was always pleased to recommend to others. He braced his beloved Lucius years later to bear up under his own debts, typically advising: "No man ever knows whether he has pluck in him until you put him in real difficulty. . . . It takes a *man*, when assailed by misfortune, to turn round square upon his adversary and face and conquer him. As the Apostle says, we should as Christians 'learn to know how to be abased as well as how to abound.'"[34]

By selling off some of his West Tennessee acreage, negotiating with the bankers, and borrowing $25,000 against that year's growing crop, Polk thereby lightened his financial woes. "The good providence of God has blessed my exertions and I have . . . been enabled to meet the crises in every particular," he told Sarah Polk. Things hadn't looked so good in five years, he said, "and if I should be able to work anything like fair crops. . . ." That "if" would prove to be a big question as the goodness and mercy from above was soon failing here below. His nephew William Polk, the transplanted Tennessean who had lately been managing the cane at Leighton, notified him that the Louisiana sugar country was baking under rainless August skies, and the once-promising cane was rustling in the drying wind. Along the Polk property, William had a ditch cut through the La Fourche Levee to let in bayou water, but nevertheless, he warned Leonidas, June's promise of 800 hogsheads had better be revised downward. Offsetting this estimate was the hope that scarcity throughout the region might drive up the price. Leonidas conceded the uncertainty of all such calculations: "The amount of the crop and the prices at which it may be sold," he now wrote his mother, "is all a matter of the merest speculation in the world, as you very well know from your own exercises as a planter."

But having provisionally dug himself out from his debts, he had learned something about money management and was anticipating a more worry-free financial future, come what may. "I have not an account at the store of Fancy Free, nor do I hereafter mean to have one," he reassured his mother in a picturesque turn of phrase. "I mean hereafter to pay as I go, and when I cease to have the means to pay with, why then I shall cease to go."[35] In that expectant mood, he herded his family back to Louisiana in November, anticipating the winter grinding of cane under William's supervision.

The moneyed communicants of Thibodeaux's St. John's Parish—the congregation Polk had lately organized—were tiring of services in the courthouse and desired a church building befitting their lofty station. Accordingly, they subscribed the construction funds and began building on land donated by George Seth Guion, one of the town's richest (and most magnanimous) Episcopalian planters.[36] The bishop (the rector of the parish, too) dedicated the cornerstone on New Year's Day 1844. Polk's personal imprint on the building was to be evident from that stone up: the four Doric columns supporting a pediment above the twelve-foot-deep front portico, the routing of stovepipe flues within the nave, the positioning of the pulpit and holy table, and the guttering to carry off resolute Gulf Coast rain from the slate roof all conformed to proposals submitted in writing to the building committee by their engineer-bishop.[37] His Greek Revival design was "remarkably neat," as he termed it, merrily. Glumly unecumenical, the Reverend Charles Menard, the new Roman Catholic pastor in town, held a three-pronged opinion of the brick structure, its Protestant builders, and their style of worship: "This year the Episcopalians finished their 'temple,'" he recorded, "where about a dozen rich Americans who came from the North go for their preaching. The less-rich Americans, who don't drive such handsome teams, have built a wooden temple for the use of all the [other] denominations."[38]

During the bearable Gulf Coast winters, life was pleasant for the Polks. Leonidas's particular pleasure in an enlarging circle of friends was evident when he told Lucius that "we are getting up a very good state of social intercourse with our neighbors," and he rattled off a host of names. These attentions evidently flattered the bishop, but Fanny, still in a pout regarding her situation, thought them illusory. "We have a good many callers for the night when Mr. Polk is at home, but *friends* very few."[39] The pleasures of socializing along the bayou were offset by the death of Sarah Polk in Raleigh in December 1843. Her son used the occasion, as he usually did when some family member died, to reiterate to the living the imperatives of penitence and commitment to Jesus. Susan came in for the special attention of a letter on this subject. That bad news was followed with the report that Leighton Plantation, stricken by drought, had produced far less than the hoped-for 800 hogsheads of sugar. They might eke out only 500. (At about $50 each, the crop did return the $25,000 borrowed against it.)[40] Then, with the sugar and molasses finally on their way to market, the settled planter became the roving missionary again, leaving in February for Galveston, Matagorda, and Houston in his auxiliary role as acting bishop of the Republic of Texas. His out-of-the-ordinary duty in Matagorda on behalf of the Episcopalians was to consecrate their church building recently shipped from New York prefabricated and unassembled.[41]

Polk was at home most of March and half of April minding his cane fields, but he then left for a six-week trek through western Louisiana. At about this time—July 1844—Fanny's father died, and she inherited 100 of his slaves. John Devereux's will specified the slaves were not to be under her husband's control, but all the same the couple's mutual holdings now amounted to some 400 men, women, and children.[42] This abundance of slaves now living under the thumb of a man of the cloth would occasion criticisms of Polk as an eccentric bishop, if not something worse.

The gossip extended overseas. Of particular interest among the antislavery English was the fanciful Louisiana sugar plantation they had read about, farmed by would-be-missionary slaves. Another was the baseless rumor that on Bishop Polk's frequent forays to out-of-the-way plantations he would discreetly sell off decrepit slaves to pay for his travel. Samuel Wilberforce, an abolitionist Church of England cleric at work in the 1840s on a history of American Episcopalians, was once discussing the proposed plantation with a visitor and said it "had come to his knowledge from good authority" that Bishop Polk "had taken his old slaves on a visitation, and sold them so profitably that he paid all the expenses of his visitation." The visitor, the Reverend Richard King of Dorset, was familiar enough with Polk to protest that the second story must surely be slander. He promised to write his American friend William Whittingham, the bishop of Maryland and an acquaintance of Polk's, to back him up. Wilberforce's subsequent history excoriated the American church for its silence and indifference to slavery: "The bishops of the north sit in open convention with their slave-holding brethren," he wrote with distaste. The alleged plantation school he described as an "evil" enterprise, and while Polk escaped being named, a review of the book in the United States would inferentially connect him. The Episcopal Church is not only "a mighty buttress" of slavery, the reviewer wrote, but "certain of its Bishops its reckless and unblushing champions."[43] Wilberforce did not allude to Polk's selling his old slaves, evidently supposing the story was false.[44]

In April the Sixth Annual Convention of the Diocese of Louisiana opened in Natchitoches. The agenda item of particular interest to the bishop was a plan finally to pay him a stipend for his ministry. Of more interest to the delegates, however, was their bishop's account of the latest eruption of gossipy controversy fomenting the nation's Episcopalians: those of the low-church party offended by church ceremonial (candles, bells, and such—too "Romish!") and those of the high-church party defending their rituals on Church of England precedent. Ignited on Christmas Eve by seminarians in New York who rang the chapel bell at midnight to celebrate the Nativity, their high-church hijinks led to their immediate expulsion.[45] A kind of inquisition of the General Seminary faculty was then launched. Often the target of high-church smears, Low-Church Trustee Charles McIlvaine led the way in rooting out suspected heretics. Even the saintly Clement Moore, teaching at the seminary before composing *The Night Before Christmas*, was roughed up a bit in the scuffle.[46] To his convention, Polk tidily glossed over the details of the agitation, merely urging his flock to put away their fears. Usually traveling the middle of the road during these liturgical storms, Polk assured his convention he and they would continue to adhere to Reformation principles in Louisiana, and he urged his people "to exhibit a spirit of kindness toward those with whom we differ."[47]

Called away for an ecclesiastical trial in New York at year's end, Polk did not return until early January 1845. During his absence, the sugarcane rolling season had commenced, a time when many planters were accustomed to taking their meals and sleeping in the sugarhouse where the boiling pots were bubbling.[48] Awaiting him, too, in his office was a seven-months' pile of accumulated diocesan work. To the good, he now resolved the question of where he was to settle his family. They had decided to sell Ashwood Hall to Andrew. While Tennessee was a welcome retreat from Louisiana's humid summers and diseases, the costly back-and-forth river journeys were wearing them out.

With summer getaways to Tennessee no longer an affordable option, the family sweltered through succeeding seasons on the bayou. In 1847 Leonidas established an in-house academy for sixteen-year-old Hamilton and eleven-year-old Fanny, drilling them both each day from 9:00 A.M. until 2:00 P.M. "in mathematics and the classics (Hamilton alone in the latter). Their advancement . . . I would fain believe, [is] quite as decisive as it has hitherto been under instructors less interested in their improvement," he told their Aunt Susan. Hamilton had been withdrawn from the Flushing Institute, and his father "determined that [he] shall not go to college for a year yet, as I think he can spend that time more advantageously under my roof." The four daughters were "under the tuition" of a private woman teacher two days each week. As little dancers they were learning the "art of motion," and their father thought them "fit subjects for the appliances of the art." Furthermore, everyone was accomplished at singing. "Should you hear us," he told Susan, "sometimes accompanying the piano to 'The Old North State,' you would think we were hearty lovers of all her simplicity, her honesty and her pines. As we assuredly claim to be."[49]

Good health and spirits had returned by 1848. The bishop was particularly cheerful about the increasing success of his diocese. It had grown during his eight years from three parishes to twenty-three, a gain he reckoned in a boastful letter to McIlvaine at "very nearly six hundred per cent." "You will, I know, pardon my bringing to you notice of my affairs thus unblushingly," he said, "but I cannot but speak to you of what so interests my own heart." He went on to expand on his hope to establish a parochial school in every parish in the state. "From the [plan] we expect good results in counteracting the system of Rome." Polk was more pragmatic than prejudiced, not evincing the intense animus toward Roman Catholicism that marked many of his fellow evangelicals. In the same letter, indeed, he expressed what sounded like a cordial, if competitive, relationship with Antoine Blanc, the other bishop in New Orleans: "I was at work yesterday, Sunday, all day side by side with my brother Blanc, the Romanist bishop of their diocese," he wrote. "They are moving everything to extend their power and to maintain their ancient influence. . . . The actions of our church have stimulated them greatly. It is the only form of Protestantism they seem to be concerned about, and as by the blessing of the Lord, we have not been without success. They may be said, perhaps, not to be without grounds of uneasiness."[50]

Solon Robinson was a travel writer and essayist in the 1840s for the *Ameri-*

can Agriculturist, a long-running magazine published in New York. Solon, as he signed his articles, had a knack for producing chatty reports, focusing on innovative farming methods for his gentlemen readers and tasty regional recipes for the ladies. On the junket he undertook in the winter of 1848–1849, he set out from St. Louis to explore cotton and sugar plantations in the Deep South. His writer's instincts and curiosity pulled him toward the sugar-making bishop of La Fourche Parish, and he showed up at Leighton Place in February 1849.[51] All the Polks were at home, and Robinson eventually sent his publisher a sunny account of the prospering situation he found on Bayou La Fourche. Upon his arrival, he was given a census of the slave population—370 men, women, and children. Of these seventy were children under ten, and not a few others were "entirely superannuated," leaving "an effective force of field hands [of] not more than one third of [the total] number." Robinson marveled at this aggregation of black people: a "host to feed and clothe, and all to be looked after and provided for by the care of one man!" It was "quite enough to frighten a New England farmer." The bishop, Robinson declared, was quite the agricultural innovator, too. His workers, for example, used a plowshare especially fashioned for Leighton's soil. Robinson reported that Polk had designed the implement. The previous year Polk had experimented by having leaves stripped from maturing cane stalks on certain acres (some of the seventy children were given this job), and the stripping had resulted in a larger yield of juice compared to other acres. Polk had also tried grinding the bagasse—the cane leavings—a second time, obtaining enough additional juice to justify the effort. Robinson was also impressed by Leonidas's tinkering skills: "Bishop P. has made an improvement upon his mill that I like." It had to do with how the cane was fed between the steam-driven rollers.

Plantation expenses averaged $8,000 per year, and almost everything was made on the place, from shoes to tools to summer and winter clothing. But the bishop's plan to raise pigs to feed the hands was ill-advised, Robinson had decided. "The labor bestowed upon cane, instead of corn, will buy more pork than the corn will fatten," he firmly informed his readers. Robinson questioned the economy, too, of producing homespun cloth and clothing at Leighton, but Leonidas justified that by saying it was work assigned to the elderly, the invalids, and the convalescents and to mothers just before and after childbirth—to those, in short, unable to work in the fields or the house. Robinson did commend the bishop's strict policy of keeping the Sabbath day work-free, even during the critical rolling season, and concluded his report by "bearing testimony to the high character, both as a gentleman, an improving agriculturist, and a kind master to those whom

Providence has placed him in charge of, which is universally accorded to Bishop Polk." But his "most excellent wife" struck Robinson in the main. With a gallant flourish he wrote that "she is certainly such a one as a great many planters' ladies might well imitate."[52] The magazine ran Robinson's piece in November 1849. By that time a local epidemic, later becoming nationwide, had swept through the springtime cane fields of Leighton Place and claimed the lives of scores of the Polks' slaves. Robinson had to amend his report to say the deaths had in consequence "seriously injured [that year's] growing crop."

Asiatic cholera was a spectacular disease: it turned its victims' vomit black, their stools white, and their skin blue—chromatic symptoms that as often as not carried off the afflicted straightaway. Physicians did not yet suspect contaminated water as the cause, but many pious Americans in the 1830s and 1840s averred it was God's judgment upon the nation's immigrants, people thought to lead irreligious, intemperate lives in their crowded slums. Sure enough, during the first eleven days of December 1848 three ships—one from France, two from Germany—dropped anchor in New Orleans. During the crossing some forty of the steerage passengers had died, and cholera was the suspected cause. The passengers who survived, and millions of Vibrio cholerae organisms clinging to them, came ashore. The stowaway bacteria began to spread rampantly across the state and through the intestines of numerous Louisiana citizens.[53] Weeks later Bishop Polk drafted the address he would give at that spring's diocesan convention, focusing on the epidemic and the divine displeasure it bespoke. As the God of old had righteously leveled Europe with the bubonic plague in the fourteenth century (he wrote), so now the Lord was on the attack in the New World, and "demands of us to 'hear the rod and who hath appointed it.'" Indeed, "the scourge of the nations is upon us, and we may well expect to be called upon to bear our part in the calamities with which our people generally will be most probably visited. Our sins, national, social, and personal, have ascended up before God, and justly provoked the wrath and indignation which is so significantly expressed by the pestilence now prevalent among us." The bishop did not enumerate the sins God had in mind, but hoping to mitigate the impact of the visitation he "set forth a form of prayer which I have caused to be distributed over the diocese for general use."[54]

He was probably too ill himself to arrange for his doomsday prayer to be published by a New Orleans newspaper, for on Sunday evening, April 15, after an arduous day the bishop was himself felled by the pathogenic Vibrio. While he shivered and vomited in the darkened bedroom of a friend's

New Orleans home, the convention opened on schedule without him, his address read by another. Polk's New Orleans caregiver was James Robb, the prominent banker with whom the Polks had begun a long and intimate friendship. During this crisis, having called in the best physicians available, Robb took time off from work and personally stood guard in an anteroom outside the sickroom. His concern was that Polk's clergy and friends gathered from out of town for the convention, "not realizing the danger in [his patient's] seeing 'just this one,'" would talk their way past Robb's servants. Responding to Robb's care, the bishop was soon shakily on his feet and back in Thibodaux.

Penitential prayers to the contrary notwithstanding, the cholera was far from done with the bishop. It had soon worked its way up the Mississippi River and into the bayous of the region and, in early May 1849, pounced lethally upon Leighton Place. Dr. William A. Booth, a medical researcher, visited La Fourche Parish shortly after the epidemic first struck and reported on the cases at Polk's plantation.[55] Already attending the sick at Leighton was Dr. Thomas Williams, a physician friend and St. John's member. (If normally a man to be trusted, the physician was declared inebriated during at least some of his doctoring of the epidemic's victims.)[56] Drs. Williams and Booth made the rounds of La Fourche, and Booth gave accounts of some of the deaths. The first, on May 3, was a slave child of two years. She "died in an hour, without prescription." The second case, on May 5, concerned "Todge, a Negro man, worked till 12 o'clock, without complaint, was found in collapse by [the overseer] at half-past 1 o'clock." "May 5, 3rd case, Matthew, a Negro man, was attacked at 9 o'clock, P.M., found . . . in collapse at 10 o'clock, P.M. . . . May 24, Haywood, a boy five or six years old. At quarter of 6 A.M., got up, vomited a very large worm, and had one large, watery passage. At twenty minutes after 6 A.M. he was pulseless and cold." Concerned for squeamish readers, Booth explained that "these cases are not selected on account of their violence. They are as mild as any that occurred."[57]

The rational scientist seemingly dismissed the divine scourge theory, yet it must have crossed his mind to wonder whether the estimable Leonidas Polk might in fact have grievously offended his God. "[The fever] was malignant from the beginning to the end at Bishop Polk's; while on neighboring plantations all was well."[58] Polk's overseer, a Mr. Boatner, wondered if the atmosphere had been to blame. "There were several showers, and one heavy rain with a good deal of wind," he told Booth, "but, as a general thing, the weather was very fine." Of the 356 slaves on the place, by Boatner's count, 273 contracted the disease and sixty-nine died, at least one old

man in the bishop's arms. Of the resident white people (the Polks, the Boat-
ners, Chaplain Spencer Wall, and others), ten were sickened. That number
included Leonidas again, and two of his daughters. Boatner's wife would
die.[59]

As far as Dr. Booth was concerned, the bishop's second attack should
have killed him. After 220 people had suffered primary attacks at Leighton
Place in the first two weeks, the doctor counted

> not less than 50 or 60 re-attacks. I do not mean by re-attacks, relapses.
> I apply the term to those who had been treated for cholera, whose
> bowels had been regulated, and who were dismissed as cured, and
> remained so from one to two weeks. The re-attacked generally died
> speedily. This was the main peculiarity of the cholera at the Bishop's. It
> seemed as though the poison never would exhaust itself. It attacked and
> re-attacked the victim. It raged doubly as long as it did at [a plantation
> eight miles distant], and three times as long as the same form did on
> any other plantation. Adding re-attacks to the number of primary
> cases, the sum total of cases would not be much less than the whole
> population of the place, which was about 375.

Even another physician's best intentions had fanned the infectious flames
at Leighton. As devised by Erasmus Fenner, MD, an experimental "preventive" dose of "quinine, compound tincture of capsicum, laudanum, and
brandy" was fed, apparently by Dr. Williams, to some of the Polks' slaves
still supposed to be healthy. To the bishop's dismay, a "number" of them
immediately became sick, and a few died. "The Bishop firmly believes,"
Booth wrote, "that [the mixture] developed the disease in some who would
otherwise have escaped an attack; and in others it determined to [collect
in] the stomach, thereby provoking . . . that most unmanageable symptom, vomiting." Greatly mortified at this unhappy outcome was the editor
of Booth's report who publicly took the blame, publishing an astonishing
footnote to Booth's account in the *Southern Medical Reports*.[60] Considering
the shocking failure of Fenner's experimental nostrum, it is a wonder that
Bishop Polk was said to have joined later with a pharmacist friend named
Rabe to develop and advertise their own putative remedy for the disease.
There is no evidence that this concoction succeeded, either.[61]

The household in Louisiana being almost too preoccupied to notice,
word came of the death of Fanny's ailing and aged mother, Frances Devereux, in North Carolina. Mrs. Devereux bequeathed a number of slaves
valued at $20,000 to her daughter, but because they were in family groups

Fanny and her husband, cash-poor though they were, decided against selling any of them and thus separating individuals "from their kindred . . . for no fault of their own." As for Frances Devereux, she was "far better off than in this miserable world," Leonidas assured his sister.[62]

Miserable, at least, was the nation as the epidemic raged on into the summer, spreading or traveling by riverboats up the Mississippi and its tributaries and by covered wagons across the continent as the Gold Rush 49ers headed west. Facing the increasing certainty of his mortality, Bishop Polk wrote out his last will and testament after taking Hamilton to Trinity College in Hartford. His soul he offered to God, his body to the graveyard beside little St. John's Church in Tennessee, his library to the Louisiana diocese, and his estate, still of some substance at that point, to his children and Fanny, "the best friend I have ever had." But with the promise of that summer's corn and cane crops far from realized (combined, they were to have fed his people and to have paid off much of his debt); with his workforce decimated twice over; with $5,000 owed his physicians; and with other plantation expenses exceeding $50,000—the financial resources of Leonidas Polk had sprung a hemorrhage he could never stanch. A codicil was added to his will on September 1, 1858, when he was destitute. It reads: "Since writing the above, the misfortunes which came upon me have deprived me of my property. . . . To my children, I leave a Father's blessing."[63]

10

"From This Time Forward We Were Beggars" (1850–1857)

Gulf Coast weather, rarely benign, was behaving especially badly the week of May 8, 1850. That Wednesday the annual convention of the Diocese of Louisiana opened in Bishop Polk's St. John's Church in Thibodaux, but before dawn, over on the Mississippi River in St. James Parish, wind gusts from the west blew with sufficient force to dismantle the roof and walls of one plantation's sugarhouse, leaving only its chimney standing.[1] Still, by afternoon, all was sunny and pleasant throughout the region. Then, before first light on Thursday, high winds rose again, this time a little closer to Thibodaux, and struck downtown New Orleans. "Violent Tornado" read a front-page headline in that morning's *Daily Delta*. The accompanying story by an early-rising reporter gave a thrilling account: "Between 4 and 5 o'clock this morning," he wrote, "one of the most violent gales of wind which was ever witnessed in New Orleans, sprung up. The angered elements seemed to mock at all impediments; and with the rain, which descended in a deluge, the fearful vividness of the lightning's flash, and the hoarse rumblings of 'heaven's artillery,' a scene was presented, which was, indeed, terrifically sublime. The damage done by this tornado is immense."[2]

Once more the storm subsided as quickly as it had come, and when by Saturday afternoon the churchmen in Thibodaux had wound up their final day's business with "devotional exercises," the town was shining "with all the brilliancy of a Southern spring," the Reverend Charles Goodrich recalled. He, along with the other clergy and laypeople, then got into their buggies and repaired to Leighton Place, where the bishop's wife and a repast awaited them.

The dining-room table gleamed with the crystal and china the Polks reserved for such occasions.[3]

Seated at the table, Goodrich was surprised to observe through the open windows "a dark and heavy cloud just risen above the horizon." Scarcely had he mentioned the cloud's worrisome appearance to the lady at his side "than the air became chilled, and soon the rattling of hail on the roof of the house with a violent gust of wind told me that the storm was on us." A servant hurried into the dining room with a hailstone on a plate; it was an inch in diameter and was passed around the table to the guests' astonishment. By now the wind itself was bringing hailstones into the room, "driving [them] through the open windows like balls from a battery," Goodrich remembered. Attempts to shutter the windows failed, and the guests scrambled from the room while the wind sent their dinner and tableware scudding to the floor. At an adjoining plantation a neighbor planter and his wife who had been invited to the Polks' dinner party, but "for fear of life" had decided not to venture out, were dodging the window-glass fragments and hailstones flying though their own house. The "frightful shower of [hail] lasted perhaps fifteen minutes, although it seemed an age," the husband said.[4]

The Polks' guests were by now cowering in the central hallway, afraid the shuddering house might fall in around them. No wonder: the wind outside had lifted the roof off the sugarhouse "like a balloon, and lodged [it] 60 yards from the walls." Trees crashed down, leaves were stripped from bushes, "fowls great and small, exposed in the garden or fields, were killed, the stables were wrecked and some slaves' cabins were overturned." The hail by now lay so thick and white upon the grass that Goodrich was put in mind of "a winter day in Canada."[5]

Once the wind (family members differed in terming the storm a "tornado," "cyclone," or "hurricane") had begun to slacken, Bishop Polk, wrapped in an overcoat, hurried outside, slipping and sliding on the ice.[6] He wanted to learn the fate of the men and women who had been at work in his cane fields when the storm moved in. None had been seriously injured, he was told, and, satisfied by that, he next sent a messenger to inquire how his next-door neighbors had fared. By the time Polk returned to the main house, and to his guests, so had tranquility. Grass had emerged from the melting hailstones, and the sun shone serenely as though nothing was amiss. Only the damage remained to be reckoned: it came to a staggering $100,000. Fanny Polk was all but prostrated by this latest onslaught and, shortly thereafter, removed to Pascagoula in Mississippi to bathe in the lapping waters of the Gulf of Mexico, gradually regaining her composure.[7]

The bishop, too, had been despairing during the height of the storm, but as the cleanup and rebuilding commenced he recovered the philosophic pluck that was his second nature—"his usual cheerful submission," to use Fanny's phrase. Then the Gulf Coast weather assailed him again. While he was in Cincinnati that autumn of 1850 at another General Convention, the heat of summer gave way to a premature, cane-killing frost. To that was added Hamilton's being taken sick at Trinity College; he had to be brought home by his father for a winter's convalescence. Those troubles were compounded when the bishop obtained a $60,000 mortgage on Leighton Place to pay off remaining Tennessee debts; the broker to whom he entrusted the loan payments, Fanny reported, "appropriated the money to his own use." Leonidas refused to prosecute the man (for what was a prison offense in Louisiana). In Fanny's telling, her trusting husband supposed the broker had not "intended to defraud [and] hoped to be able to repay the amount." As Fanny recalled Leonidas's remarkable resilience, "to all this, the bishop only said, 'I have done all I could. I must leave the future in God's hands.'" Fanny put less blame on God than on the Diocese of Louisiana, pointedly noting that it did nothing to help its bishop recover from his financial difficulties. She sized up their dwindling affluence this way: "From this time forward I felt we were beggars."[8]

Though Leonidas Polk may have shared as early as 1850 his wife's perception that they had become destitute (or were rapidly sliding into that state), poverty for him was more an inconvenience than a cause for despair—a setback, not a defeat. He had enjoyed the greater successes of his sugar making over those of his neighbors (as he liked to boast to Lucius on the few occasions that he could), but he liked to think as well that his plantation and his planter's life were primarily a platform for promoting his religious and educational ambitions.[9] Having chafed under his own boyhood schooling, Polk now truly longed to launch throughout Louisiana a system of parochial schools crowned by a university. England's Oxford adapted to American ways was the vision that kept rising in his mind. That picture had successively flickered, brightened, and faded ever since Polk's days in Tennessee when he and James Otey had worked closely establishing schools. Now in Louisiana, the rising stridency of abolitionists in the North (apostate Christians, as Polk regarded them) gave urgency to Polk's desire to properly educate the Southern young. Repeatedly he would include in his annual convention addresses an appeal for parishes to establish schools run by the clergy, emphasizing that "the education of our children should be in our hands," thereby insulating these "precious objects from the evil influences of indiscriminate association in the ordinary schools of the country." How reassuring, then, for him to visit parishes where just such exemplary schools were up and running. He ticked off four, including the Reverend David Kerr's St. John's School for Boys in Thibodaux (where the Polks' second son, William Mecklenburg, usually called Meck, was doubtless enrolled). Nevertheless, clergy teachers cast in the Southern mold were in short supply, and those adverse Southern circumstances—climate and slavery—thwarted effective recruitment in the North. The solution, as Polk kept saying, was to train already acclimatized and properly brought up Southerners. In his mind was a *Southern university*.[10]

Way back in the spring of 1845, just after that year's convention, Polk heard opportunity knock. A college in the village of Jackson came on the market. It was known as the College of Louisiana, and it owned some fine-looking buildings. Seizing the day, Methodists bought the property shortly thereafter—and got an even better bargain. Renamed Centenary College, it is thriving still in Shreveport.[11] Distressed by the loss, the bishop nevertheless bucked up and, six years later, challenged the convention in 1851 to consider establishing a seminal academy for boys from scratch; by "safe and judicious management" it might become "a seminary on a larger scale." Polk formed another committee, which soon set to work for their "beloved Diocesan."[12] After many months and many resolutions and speeches (one even tracing education in England through fifteen centuries), the committee called for establishing *someday* a high school for boys later to be expanded into a college for young men, as well as a seminary for aspiring clergymen.[13]

Setting Southern education to one side for the moment, Leonidas and Fanny spent a therapeutic three months away from Louisiana, part of the time in Newport, Rhode Island, with their fashionably wealthy banker friend James Robb. The pleasures of the Polks' recreational summer were tempered when they returned to Leighton to face what the bishop described as "the most distressingly dry fall I have ever experienced in this country." With drought came empty cisterns and depleted wells—and the necessity for workers to drink from less reliable sources, some of them cholera-infected. A number of Polk's slaves were again laid low by sickness, and it was only because he could make arrangements to borrow workers from other planters that he could get his ripe sugarcane through the rollers. For the time being, he was feeling optimistic about his financial future. But not about his hopes for schooling Southern youths.[14] The need was for more action and less rhetorical grandstanding by convention delegates. In "fashionable" out-of-state schools, Louisiana's "children, baptized at our fonts, are cruelly offered in sacrifice to the god of this world, that they may shine in the gay ranks of folly and dissipation," one speechifier declaimed. Worse, just beyond these school walls lay a sinister snare: "The Roman

Catholics!"[15] Thoroughly exasperated when the purchase of yet another bargain-priced Louisiana college fell through, Polk dispensed with committees and took charge of building a university himself. Often as not, he had wryly come to realize, a convention resolution was merely a "convenient vehicle [to pass it along] to the 'earnest consideration' of some future convention."[16]

Forthwith, as Fanny remembered, he began collecting "information related to the educational systems of England, France and Prussia," even ordering Prussian textbooks. In addition, he began to "consult with some of his friends as [to] their opinion of the feasibility of founding a University of the South."[17] Typically letting go of nothing else, his research was simply piled atop the backlog of responsibilities he already had. He assessed his situation to Lucius: "No man in America, I don't care who the other man is, has been more crowded for time for the last few years than I have been, and I will venture to add no man has had more to do, or more places to go to, or a greater variety of people and things to deal with." A complaint? Why, not at all. Having God's "kind and ever-present arm . . . always about me and under me," he bore his burdens "triumphantly and cheerfully onward."[18] A wealthy planter fondly recalled the bishop's work in organizing Christ Church up the bayou road in Napoleonville early 1853. Upon arriving, he "turned his attention to the early supply of our spiritual wants"; calling "a meeting of the fathers, mothers and young people of both sexes," he explained his object in the "genial manner which no one possessed in a more eminent degree." The new parish soon raised up a costly ($10,000) Gothic Revival church building, testifying for all to see, boasted a worshipful communicant, to "the wealth, intelligence and public spirit of the neighboring planters."[19] It was that inspiriting "genial manner" that evidently endeared Polk throughout the state. On a spring day during Holy Week 1853, a woman named Clarissa Town was making butter, starching collars, finishing Maundy Thursday's dinner, and otherwise busying about her kitchen in West Baton Rouge when "in walked the Bishop." A meal was quickly got up for him. Grandma Town next day was present at Christ Church when the bishop delivered "the best sermon I ever heard him preach." Then, fortified by the jelly pies and peach tarts that she baked on Saturday, the bishop on Easter morning "preached a better sermon than on Good Friday!"[20]

At least for the time being, Polk had reason to be pleased with himself as well. His health "was never better, nor my conscience more at ease." A vigorous stand of sugarcane waved in the humid heat across 900 of his acres as well, and during the past year twenty-six children had been born to his slaves—to him another sign of providential favor. On a Sunday evening in July he would baptize twenty-two of that infant crop of workers. Polk's good fortune faded when summer sickness returned, foretelling Louisiana's share of a worldwide yellow-fever epidemic. Unusually dense swarms of mosquitoes (the unsuspected carriers of the disease) were clouding the sweltering air of New Orleans; the city's worst epidemic ever carried away 8,000 citizens, about 10 percent of the resident population. As he had during the cholera epidemic, Polk thought of himself in league with "holy men of old" who regarded plagues as "divine displeasure," as God's wielding "rods of correction."[21] The bishop composed a prayer he hoped would succor his wicked city. Lift, oh God, "the ravage of the pestilence wherewith, for our iniquities, thou art now visiting us," he urged all citizens to pray. The plea was published on August 24 in the New Orleans *Daily Picayune*.

In his own way, an editorialist for the *New-York Tribune* agreed with the bishop: the South *was* being punished—but for the sin of slavery. At home, Polk was mocked by Theodore Clapp, New Orleans's iconoclastic Unitarian minister. "We have been gravely reminded, that the epidemic ravaging the city is the display of God's anger," he wrote in his response, also in the *Picayune*. "Is the Bible God a being the human heart can neither love nor respect?" the minister queried. "Can that which befalls all earthly beings, irrespective of character, fills all time, and spreads before the eye of Heaven such an uninterrupted scene of mutability and decay, be the ordination of infinite vengeance? Nothing can enter the human mind so horrible as this supposition. There is as much of God's love in New Orleans today as ever before, or ever will be hereafter." Polk was not swayed by Pastor Clapp's liberal theology. Two years later, in the midst of yet another epidemic, he declared afresh that such scourges seem "to be one of God's great agencies to keep himself visibly before the world's naughty heart."[22]

In early September 1853 Polk left Louisiana for the Northeast to attend that year's triennial national convention. He had barely arrived in New York when he learned that the yellow-fever epidemic had moved on from New Orleans and invaded Thibodaux and Leighton Place. Polk reached his home on Bayou La Fourche on October 20. Before the fever ran its course at Leighton, two of the Polks' children and several of their slaves were sickened. Three of his clergy, after ministering to victims of the fever, took sick themselves and died. One was Alexander Dobb; another was Archibald Lamon, Clarissa Town's son-in-law. Despite these reverses, Polk thanked God that he had been spared more suffering "during the terrific visitation of this neighborhood." Although no one understood why, the visitation ended with the first frost. It had killed the mosquitoes.[23]

For Polk, the respite was fleeting, and he was soon beset with more travail. Yet like Job tested by Yahweh, he was gamely submissive and did not admit a loss of faith. First off, as Louisiana's 1854 spring awoke, so did mosquitoes from cisterns, bayous, and swamps. Some 2,500 New Orleanians would subsequently perish in the 1854 epidemic, and when the yellow fever again reached Thibodaux, nearly 150 of its population, black and white, would die. Then, though Polk had been promised an annual salary of $4,000, the miserly diocese paid him less than half that amount (and had paid him barely a third of that amount the year before).[24] Not that full payment of what was due him would have mattered much. Sagging under their accumulated losses from drought, wind, cold snaps, financial mistakes, and malignant diseases, Fanny and Leonidas acknowledged that their debts had become insurmountable.[25] Their recourse was to sell Leighton, now amounting to almost 2,000 acres, and 189 of the Polks' slaves. The buyer, for $307,000, was John Williams, a New Orleans businessman from Tennessee turned planter and a hefty supporter of Thibodaux's St. John's Church. Within a few years of buying Leighton, he was outproducing all his sugaring neighbors along the bayou.[26]

The Polk parents and children and domestic staff remained in the Thibodaux house for the time being while Williams took over the farming and made a $10,000 profit his first season. Reporting that success to James Robb, Leonidas did not betray the least resentment. He merely repeated a dictum of his theology: "We must take things as they come, so long as we are in the way of duty."[27] A few days later in the way of duty, he paid a pastoral call on a dying friend. He then went directly "from the sick chamber . . . to my own home, where I was taken ill of the prevailing fever, and was sick nigh unto death."[28]

After selling Leighton Place and paying his debts, Polk had retained only about $34,000.[29] All the same, he had held onto 160 slaves and installed them along with Hamilton, his son newly married, at a small cotton plantation he had bought in late 1854 in Bolivar County, Mississippi.[30] The money for this transaction apparently came from Fanny's inheritance. What's more, the bishop had landed a second job: affluent parishioners at Trinity Church in New Orleans, without a rector since the yellow-fever death of Alexander Dobb, asked Polk to add to his bishopric duties by succeeding Dobb. The church building was imposing, brand-new, and half paid for, and since the Trinity people promised him a reliable income (another hope soon to be dashed), Polk accepted the call. Rising unsteadily from his sickbed, he moved the family to New Orleans. As a management priority, his new parishioners asked that he do something right away about the congregation's choir, said to sound pathetic.[31]

For his family's move into New Orleans, Bishop Polk had rented a spacious home on Fourth and Magazine Streets. This put them in the city's architecturally stylish Garden District. The house was close to Trinity Church and had been occupied some years earlier by the Mexican War hero Gen. Persifor Smith, whose subsequent military career had taken him from Louisiana.[32] The Polk parents and children were pleased that they would soon have James and Louisa Robb and their four children as neighbors. The Robbs were building in the same neighborhood a mansion suited to a banker of Robb's prominence. With its grounds, it would occupy a full city block, and its $65,000 tax assessment would set a record in New Orleans. Louisa Robb would not live out that year, but Fanny long after would fondly remember her Garden District neighbors, James especially: "I loved him more than any friend we had."[33]

Once established in his new role as parish rector (and likely having retuned the off-key choir), Polk hired an assistant, Chauncey Colton, a reliable minister who had filled an emergency with Charles McIlvaine after young Mr. Polk had turned it down. With his help, the bishop said he was better able to take on the "multitude of cares inseparable from episcopal residence in a great city from which before [in Thibodaux] I was comparatively exempt."[34] Considering that in the past the overextended bishop had failed to run a plantation successfully, a son would later observe, "he ought always to have lived [in the city]."[35]

Among the bishop's multitude of cares was the establishment of new parishes in the diocese. As he was particularly keen to evangelize free blacks, he was gratified during his first month in the city to help consolidate a parish of some twenty families of free black men and women. He thought them a "highly intelligent . . . class of persons" and supposed that the modes of worship of the Episcopal tradition would "prove, under God, abidingly instructive and profitable to them."[36] The faithful congregation named their church after St. Thomas and got off to a good start under enthusiastic shepherding by the Reverend Charles H. Williamson, a white Church of England priest from Canada who felt certain that the new parish was a "good work not to be repented of."[37]

It was a good work built on sand, however. One member of the new parish was Thomas Jennings (or Jinnings), a professional man (a physician or possibly a dentist) who gave money and time to the congregation as a vestryman. Pastor Williamson was so impressed with Jennings that he had taken the "liberty of subjoining a few remarks [by my] colored brother" into the legislative proceedings of the 1855 diocesan convention. What Jennings had said was that "the establishment of this church has . . . filled a void that has been too long in existence, and promises to be the harbinger of good, to a large and interesting portion of the colored people of this city; and we, therefore, express our gratitude to God for this special mark of His favor."[38] As the racial tensions of the years leading to the Civil War increased in New Orleans, St. Thomas's congregation soon fell apart; it was last mentioned in the diocesan journal in 1858.

Late in 1860, as white New Orleans was calling for secession, Thomas Jennings was arrested for expressing "sentiments of a nature calculated to produce discontent among the free colored population, and to excite insubordination among the slaves." In May 1861, he was arrested again when he and his wife arrived at a charity fair sponsored by a white Episcopal parish with which his Sunday School was affiliated. Jennings was charged (according to a casually edited newspaper report) with "intrading himself among the white congregation . . . and conducting hisself in a manner unbecoming to the free colored population of this city, and in a manner to create insubordination among the servile population of this State." He was released when white parishioners testified that he and his wife had been welcome guests and had behaved civilly.[39] Bishop Polk was in Richmond at the time to take up his commission as a Confederate general. It can be safely supposed that he too would have interceded on Jennings's behalf had he known of his plight.

Along with supporting the free blacks' congregation in 1855, Polk had involved himself anew in the American Colonization Society. Unmentioned in his correspondence since the 1830s when both he and Charles McIlvaine had championed the society's early efforts to relocate American free blacks to Liberia, Polk now found himself president of the society's Louisiana chapter. While the chapter's less-than-benign objective was to rid Louisiana of its numerous free blacks, Polk's reengagement suggests that he found himself still unsettled over race and slavery. Possibly, as one historian has suggested, the bishop's resumed interest in the ACS, whose popularity was waning in the South, was a sign of his continuing "racial empathy." Despite benefiting from slavery for years, Polk now was reportedly telling confidantes that slavery "in its origin was a crime" and the slave trade was an "atrocity."[40]

Polk's critical judgments did not exempt him from a racial ambivalence that remained unresolved for the rest of his days. During the period in which he was attempting to revitalize Louisiana's Colonization Society, he expressed bitter frustration about race to Georgia's Stephen Elliott, the brother bishop in whom Polk confided most openly. "Talk of slavery," he fumed in a letter. "Those mad-caps of the North don't understand the thing at all. We hold the Negroes and they hold us." Blaming the victims for his own peevishness, he plunged on: "They are at the head of the ladder. They furnish the yokes and we the necks. My own is getting sore."[41] What had provoked his ill mood that day he did not say, but it did not fit well with his usual assertions that introducing the unchurched African to Christianity was a welcome obligation. Indeed, priests in Polk's diocese regarded unfree blacks as an evangelical blessing. At the 1855 convention a committee extolled the thirty-one "country congregations of persons of color," meaning the 3,600 plantation slaves to whom the Episcopal Church ministered.[42]

By midsummer 1856 Polk was devoting what little discretionary time was left to him on the university's planning, which probably infringed on demands of church and family. The letters he would shortly be writing to such friends as James Robb and Kenneth Rayner fairly pulse with his enthusiasm. Think of an intellectual factory that, "on the higher ranges of human learning, . . . shall embrace and teach those things deemed important by the race," he would typically write. The imagined library alone, "covering the whole field of the literature and science of the past . . . shall be filled with Southern men and women, as those of the Bodleian and Louvre are, elaborating treatises in Science and Letters, and contributing to the cultivation of a home intellect." The idea of jointly enrolling women and men in American colleges was almost unheard of at the time, but Polk endorsed the innovation and expansively supposed his coeducational university would come to rival, as he variously visualized it, an Oxford, a Cambridge, a Göttingen, a Bonn, a Harvard, a Yale, a University of Virginia. It was high time to prove it.[43]

In late June, on the verge of departing on another of his routine absences from home, Polk planned to send off a circular letter printed as a pamphlet to nine fellow bishops of the Southern dioceses; it ran for sixteen pages, setting forth his rationale for the Southern university that was obsessing him. Brimming with ideas slowly gestated but now hastily delivered, the letter is less than polished. Words and sentences sometimes tumble over themselves in syntactical enthusiasm, and the organization is loose and repetitive. But it was passionate, and at its heart, though he circled around the issue, was Polk's growing conviction that the disunion of the United States, as well as of the Episcopal Church, was inevitable.

His main points were these:

- Bishops of the Episcopal Church vow at their consecrations to serve the spiritual welfare of everyone in their jurisdictions, churchmen and nonchurchmen alike. And next only to preaching the Gospel the Episcopalian way ("the religion of Christ," as he unblushingly termed it), a bishop's sacred duty is to provide both "academical and theological education to the lay and clerical public."

- In the realm of education, Southern bishops have been derelict. Young men searching for decent schools are allowed to wander off to the North unsupervised and unchurched.
- A single Southern bishop might lack the funds to build a college, but in union with the others he could help raise up a university as great as any anywhere. Here laypeople and aspiring "native" clergy would be educated "amidst the peculiarities of our social condition," Southern values thus preserved.

Having indicted the past failings of his brethren, Polk showed them how easily they could redeem themselves: build a university in the Allegheny highlands of southeastern Tennessee. "Trade, with her lynx-eyed vigilance for commercial advantage," had already created a crisscross of railroads knitting the mountainous region providentially to all the Southern states. His mind chock-full of pertinent data, Polk even cited the track mileage of every Southern railroad.

Lastly, he noted that within the national church's episcopacy he and his Southern fellows lacked political significance and suffered from personal loneliness. Living where we do, he said, we are "virtually deprived of" and "substantially debarred" from the cozy get-togethers. Yankee bishops in the compact Northeast enjoyed meeting regularly for "interchange of opinion, . . . exchange of sympathy, and the refreshing influence of Christian intercourse." With national disunion in mind, he wrote that, once he and his brethren had their own university, they could meet annually at commencement time, "burnishing our zeal in the cause of Christ."[44]

Assuming that Northern bishops would eventually read the pamphlet, Polk judiciously kept its contents nonincinderary. He saved his inflammatory candor for a private letter to Stephen Elliott. "Northern fanaticism" and a "state of feeling," he wrote, "is every day getting stronger among Northern clergymen and teachers—Churchmen though they may be—on the subject of coming South to labor." Suspicious Southern parents, meanwhile, withheld their college-age sons from Harvard and Yale but were "twitted with the deficiencies" of existing Southern schools. Nevertheless, "parents are, in their own language, 'done with northern colleges.' They would rather their children should go half educated than send them thither."

Disquiet affecting the states and the nation's colleges were just two issues.

Polk foresaw a falling-out as well among Northern and Southern Episcopalians over slavery. Avowing the "extremest reluctance" to discuss the matter, he discussed it anyway: "[We are] cut off in feeling and sympathy and fact from the dioceses of the North with a wall as high as the heavens between us," he told Elliott. "We revolt at the humiliation to which the impotence of our position and resources subject us." Doubting that America's "states can continue united," he believed that such an outstanding university as he envisioned on the southern "side of Mason's and Dixon's line" will be "indispensable for our protection, our security, [and our] prosperity."

Polk was equally confident that funds to build the school would be easy to raise. As he assured Elliott, "there ought to be enough of a love of learning and religion in the Church itself to found and endow the institution we would establish, amply." In any case, the bishop had a fallback: "We have happily another influence at our disposal which I do not doubt will supply the lack of service of the others. The negro question will do the work," he underlined. "It is an agency of tremendous power, and in our circumstances, needs to be delicately managed. But it is in hand, and in great force to be used by somebody. It will be used. It insists upon being used. It insists upon being allowed to throw its strength into a development of its power to take care of the education of Southern youth." He then cautioned: "If we—Churchmen—do not let it have its own way and operate through us, it will cast us aside and avail of the agency of others."[45]

Less than won over by Polk's funding optimism, Elliott replied by reminding Polk of his own failure to establish his Montpelier Institute in Georgia (a girls' school that, while it lasted, had depended in part on slave labor for its support).[46] In his jovial, if sweepingly derogatory, reply Polk assured his friend that his loss was a valuable learning experience, and he reiterated confidence that Episcopal churchmen in the South constituted the best of all organizations, whether governmental or ecclesiastical, for creating a university. They alone, he said, had the administrative mastery and the requisite social position. The Presbyterians he dismissed as only marginally able to establish such a university. As for the Baptists and Methodists, well, "they have not the bearing, or the social standing or prestige." Similarly, Roman Catholics lacked sufficient influence in the Protestant stronghold of the South.[47]

By now his enthusiasm for the school was having repercussions at home. Fanny Polk "from this time [on] felt as if I had lost my husband and my children their father. Upon one occasion I remember saying, 'I hate the University,' greatly to his amusement. I said I was willing to give him up to a Parish [or] to the Diocese, but this seemed outside, and I felt as if I was cheated of my rights."⁴⁸ Four in the family, however, were facing health problems: two daughters, who had been debilitated by yellow fever; Fanny, whose vision had been affected by her own bout with the disease; and the bishop himself, whose steady worry and work was beginning to wear him down. So the family took their doctor's advice and in August repaired by railroad to Virginia's Allegheny Mountains, where a cluster of sulfur-spring resorts catered to the elegantly ill.⁴⁹

Refreshed "to great advantage" by the vacation, Fanny and Leonidas then made ready to attend yet another General Convention, this one in Philadelphia in early October.⁵⁰ Game companion that she was, Fanny tried to maintain interest in the university goings-on. Before their arrival in Philadelphia her husband expressed "amazement when I suggested that he would find his plan opposed by his Northern brethren. 'Impossible,' he replied. 'I am sure Bishop Potter [Alonzo Potter, who had visited the Polks that spring and with whom they were to stay in Philadelphia] will endorse it, and do all he can to forward it.'" Polk did agree that neither Potter nor any of the other bishops of the North would go so far as to "enable the South to feel entirely independent."⁵¹

Fanny would remember years later that her pessimism had proved true. During the Philadelphia convention "his plan met not only no encouragement, but decided disapproval," she wrote in her memoir. "He could not believe till then that the educated men of the North, while abusing the South for its want of what they were pleased to call education, should, from interested motives (for even then he was slow to believe that it was hatred of the South which influenced them), object to our youth being provided with means [of] education at home." Her gorge rising while writing these words in the 1870s, Fanny broke off abruptly: "Of this I will say no more."⁵²

Fanny's chilly recollection does not square with how the sunny husband later described the Philadelphia gathering to his Louisiana colleagues, and in the following days and weeks he often seemed at odds with himself. The choler evident in his January letter to Elliott had either evaporated or he was dissembling when he reported he had attended "one of the most important Conventions ever held since the organization of our church." That "Mason's and Dixon's line" he had mentioned to Elliott? It seemed no longer an issue, and Polk thanked God "that this large body, representing every part of our widely extended country, [came] together warm from the bosoms of their respective local communities, rife as they were at that moment with the most intense political excitement, and holding its sessions in the theatre of chiefest contention, should have been able to pursue the even tenor of its way, shutting out all agitation of a political character." The united effort by Northern and Southern churchmen so collegially at peace in Philadelphia nourished a "vast increase of reciprocal respect throughout the Diocesan Confederacy" (as he termed it) and furthered the "glory of God and the salvation of man."[53]

If Polk in Philadelphia heard any opposition at all to his Southern university (which is more than plausible), he may have sloughed it off it while contenting himself with the wholehearted support he elicited from his Southern brethren. These nine neighboring bishops, before departing Philadelphia, had signed their names to the proposal, had taken on committee assignments, and in their subsequent "Address to the Southern States" (a revision of Polk's original letter) they broadcast their good pleasure to the laymen and laywomen and clergy of their home dioceses.[54] In his hearty letter to Elliott just after Christmas, Polk had a message for Habersham Elliott, one of the Elliott children: "Say to Haby, my young friend, I expect him to be very diligent and successful in his studies as we shall be wanting him for a professor or president of the university . . . when he gets old enough, especially as we have concluded to be done with the Yankee boys altogether."[55] But what he might say one day did not always match what he would say on another. Writing that summer to his congressman brother-in-law Kenneth Rayner—a "Union-loving man," as he described him—Polk seemed a most amiable Unionist himself. The university "will do more to compose and reconcile the national feeling through the Church than anything, or all things, that Episcopalians have attempted heretofore," he wrote with several underlines.[56] A few months later he even conceded to Rayner that, while the university might seem to be "catering for our immediate wants, it breathes a spirit of broad nationality."[57]

Fanny, beset by an eye disease, remained in Philadelphia while Polk returned to New Orleans.[58] The best place to put the university, and the money needed to put it there, were the first issues he undertook, and in short order he was well on the way to solving both. The site both he and the Tennessee bishop James Otey favored was the Cumberland Plateau of southeastern Tennessee above Chattanooga, a village handily served by Southern railroads. On the airy plateau, furthermore, the lethal summer plagues besetting the South were said to be absent.

The financial wherewithal was confidently expected to flow from the wealthy parents who were eager to support a bastion of Southern independence of whatever construction. A little more conciliatory toward the North than Polk was wont to be, Otey assured a friend that "the establishment of such a seminary as we hope to found will go far towards perpetuating the Union (I think), and if the worst comes to the worst it will, at all events, materially aid the South to resist and repel a fanatical domination which seeks to rule over us."[59]

To guard against Polk's infectious enthusiasm, his fellow Southern bishops decreed that nothing concrete would be done until they had in hand an endowment of at least a half a million dollars. Bishop Polk's early successes suggested this might not take long. Among pledges he had obtained by early 1857 was one for $25,000, and he believed, "if things go well," a certain other gentleman might "give three, perhaps four times that sum."[60] Promises and dollars continued to accumulate through the winter and spring, so a daylong celebration on the Fourth of July was convened by the bishops atop Tennessee's Lookout Mountain. Of course, that day was chosen intentionally as a way of declaring the dawning independence of Southern youths from the perfidy of Yankee and/or abolitionist teachers. Polk phrased it more artfully: "to emancipate our posterity from the disabilities of their position."[61]

Naturally, among those happy to subscribe funds for a Southern university were men who gave thought to how they themselves might benefit financially. Foremost among these was John Armfield. This gentleman of the Old South was flourishing as a slave trader in Alexandria, Virginia, in the early 1830s when by chance he met a persuasive evangelical seminarian from the local theological school. The lad was Leonidas Polk, who promptly induced the slave trader to join the Episcopal Church. How Armfield's brutish business was affected, if at all, by his newfound religion is not recorded, but the pair's acquaintance grew into friendship. At some point, moreover, Armfield became friendly with Polk's Tennessee colleague, James Otey.[62] To an Englishman who had once seen Armfield during his early years escorting a coffle of 200 chained-together male slaves south from Virginia, Armfield was "a compound of everything vulgar and revolting."[63] Otey and Polk viewed the man far more charitably. One reason was that Armfield, seeking a higher social station in his affluent middle years, gave up the selling and shipping of slave families throughout the Southern states and reinvented himself as an affable Tennessee real-estate investor and philanthropist (and slave *owner*, merely). During the 1850s, consequently, he was busy cultivating prominent, vacation-minded Southerners, some of whom were planters who had previously purchased his other wares.[64]

In his new role, Armfield had lately acquired on Tennessee's Cumberland Plateau a dilapidated resort hotel set amid medicinal springs and gorgeous scenery. As luck would have it, the resort was close by the general neighborhood where, it was rumored, Polk and Otey might desire to build their university. Armfield's place was called Beersheba Springs (pronounced

"BUR-sheba" by the locals), and as he restored the hotel and cottages and refreshed the springs he came to see the advantages, as any visionary innkeeper would, of having the fledgling university built on the neighboring tract of upland then owned by the Sewanee Coal Mining Company.[65]

How, then, to proceed? In January 1857, eleven months before a site for the school would be officially fixed, Armfield wrote to his Tennessee bishop friend, inviting Otey to visit his mountain resort and look around. Armfield desired that the bishop while there would select a site for a vacation cottage of his own. Pleased with the invitation (but admitting in his reply he could not afford a second home anywhere), Otey promised to come in late spring and suggested that Armfield propose a similar inspection by Bishop Polk.[66] Armfield was in New Orleans at the time, and soon Bishop Polk was sent an invitation and offered a building site at Beersheba Springs. But what good is a building site to yet another man of the cloth strapped for cash? In due course, cottages were built for both bishops, gifts from other donors with their own agendas.

Armfield may have held an edge over others competing for the university site, but nothing was yet decided. Towns applying for consideration were Huntsville in Alabama, Atlanta in Georgia, and four other communities in Tennessee: Chattanooga, Knoxville, Cleveland, and McMinnville. A decision would be reached by the nine bishops in November, and Otey, being a man of high ideals, believed that in the meantime "all selfish narrow-minded considerations connected with sectional preferences" would dissolve "if we concentrate on this noble and worthy object." Lest others think him unfair, Polk took pains to visit each contending community and appointed a neutral "Commission of Engineers" to evaluate each area with an eighteen-point checklist. Unbeknown to the hopefuls, Polk was already sold on Samuel Tracy's Sewanee Coal Mining Company lands, which draped over the plateau like a blanket and were connected to the valley below by a spur rail line. Whetting Polk's appetite was Tracy's promise of one million board feet of lumber and 20,000 tons of coal. While exploring the region for the first time with Armfield and some other interested parties on a midsummer's day in 1857, Polk reined in his horse within a grove of forest trees and, sounding like Brigham Young at the Great Salt Lake, declared: "Gentlemen, here is the spot, and here shall be the university!" Other trustees might need convincing, but John Armfield, calculating, was entirely pleased. He promised Polk an annual gift of $1,000 for twenty-five years.[67]

Settled in his own mind of the future, Polk now busied himself pursuing academic excellence by turning to the president of the United States.

As "our object [is to] collect the experiences of the past . . . and to digest a system applicable . . . to our social and political position," he proposed to James B. Buchanan that the US State Department should be enlisted in the cause. That is, could not US embassy officials in Europe collect academic documents for the future school's benefit? Not expecting a refusal, Polk provided the president a list of his requirements:

A. Our minister at the Court of France to procure the constitutions, by-laws and regulations of French Imperial colleges and academies into which the University of France is subdivided.
B. Our minister at Berlin to procure the constitutions, regulations, etc., etc. of the Prussian universities and gymnasiums.
C. Our minister at Vienna the same as to Austrian universities in general, particularly those of Vienna, Prague, Padua and Pavia. [Never mind England, Polk concluded; the American bishops had their own sources there through their Anglican brethren.]

The Democrat Buchanan, beholden to Southern states for his recent election, obliged the bishop forthwith. Minister John Young Mason in Paris, for example, was thus informed by Acting Secretary of State John Appleton: "I have it in charge from the President to request you, as I do now, to use your best endeavors towards complying with Bishop Polk's wishes on this subject."[68]

Polk then turned to the matter of fostering publicity for the university. He would personally carry the word to the upcoming meeting of the highly influential Southern Commercial Convention (SCC). A movement then about fifteen years old, the SCC brought together from across the rural South professional men seeking to enhance their economic interests. Polk's brothers Lucius and Andrew and his banker friend James Robb were among those who attended from time to time. Initially the delegates discussed such practical objectives as developing trade relations with Europe and South America, as well as extending the South's railroad system to the Pacific. Even Bishop Otey had addressed the 1853 convention in Memphis, championing spiritual enrichment by missionary expansion into South America's heathen Amazon Basin.[69]

With disunion sentiment growing throughout the region, malcontents with political axes to grind had lately begun to dominate the conventions. The issue of states' rights, the preservation of slaveholding ways, and the purging of Yankee schoolbooks began to eclipse the earlier search for independence and prosperity.[70] It was into such a simmering pot that Polk ventured that August. Leaving Fanny and some of the children in the coolness of Beersheba Springs, he and some 700 other delegates convened in Knoxville, Tennessee. While getting his bearings he was nonplussed by the goings-on.

Though hardly a neophyte in the give and take of conventions, he afterward told his friend Elliott that "as this was my first appearance on that stage, I reserved to myself the privilege of seeing what was to be seen, chiefly, and confining myself to the office of a looker-on. The Conv. was not the most dignified body I have seen. Something of its complexion may be assumed from its consuming a good part of two days in determining whether or not to admit Black Republican reporters," the Southern pejorative applied loosely to Yankees suspected of abolitionist tendencies. Once the alien journalists were granted seats on the convention floor, another debate erupted on reopening the slave trade (outlawed since 1808). Overall the climate in Knoxville, Polk said, "was sufficiently fire-eating to satisfy the most ardent spirit of that class." Polk also found it "remarkable" that the delegates from Virginia "far outstripped [those from] South Carolina in passionate denunciation of the North" and in professing their "interest in, and devotion to Cuffy." Polk's exceptional use of a derogatory term for black people was surely mocking the Virginians who used the word.

The bishop being a likable man and valued by many of the delegates for his pedigree, the "looker-on" in due course found himself co-opted and named to (and made the chairman of) the convention's School Book Committee. Dedicated to providing Southern children with homegrown textbooks devoid of the North's "fanatic teachings," the committee included William McGuffey, a professor famed in early America for his "Eclectic Readers for Children." Another member was a rich Louisiana planter named John Perkins Jr. While Perkins's taste in schoolbook contents is unknown, he was a Yale- and Harvard-educated judge and politician who advocated reopening the slave trade and was recognized at SCC conventions as a fire-eater. Polk's use of "ardent spirit" aptly fit John Perkins. When U. S. Grant's Yankees approached his vast plantation in Tensas Parish in 1863, Perkins defiantly set fire to his own mansion and 2,000 bales of cotton.[71]

Since Polk had mainly gone to the convention to generate goodwill (and funding) for his university plan, the floor fights and vilifications that marked some of the sessions (and rewarded the Black Republican reporters) made him uneasy. He debated, he told Elliott, "whether we would gain or lose by throwing [the University] into the vector and seeking [the convention's] blessing. I wondered whether it would not be better, looking at the outgoing aroma of the convention generally, to let well enough alone and give it the go-by." As matters turned out, Delegate Polk's hesitation paid off. He was subsequently appointed to the relatively sedate Committee on Business, and that gave him an idea. If he confined his promotional remarks to the businessmen's deliberations, he reckoned the university would not be associated with the radicals fulminating elsewhere on "reopening the slave-trade and extreme views generally." His strategy worked. "We have their endorsement heartily given," he assured Elliott, "and have escaped being mixed up in any particular way with the other doings."[72] Polk's pleasure in this last accomplishment was tempered by a journalist who criticized the convention's endorsement of the Southern university. A churchman from Baltimore with a respectable editorial reputation, the writer was Hugh Davey Evans, and shortly after the convention he wrote in his paper *The Monitor* "that we neither wish nor expect [the university's] success." The school was liable to failure, he said, because it was being concocted full-blown instead of being planted in the germ and developed. Evans *hoped* it would fail, he said, because its sectional nature was divisive and at odds with his church's role as reconciler.[73] Alluding to Evans in a subsequent letter to Elliott, Polk scribbled a four-word postscript taken from the Bible's Isaiah: "Let the potsherds strive. . . ." Elliott would have known the balance of the fragment: " . . . with the potsherds of the earth." Isaiah's biblical text was a warning to impious humans who took issue with their Creator, likening them to pottery scraps questioning the potter. Evans was but a potsherd in Polk's estimation and had presumed to question the creator-bishop's ability to build his Southern university from scratch.[74]

I I

A University Takes Root in Terra Incognita (1857–1860)

Fanny's complaint that she lost a husband, and her children a father, to the evolving Southern university was true. To improvise a center of learning from the ground up required of him, as he said, "in the mean season, constant supervision and energetic action that all have endeavored to see supplied." And though Polk was able to put aside many of his diocesan and parochial duties, a succession of demands requiring his personal involvement kept him far from home throughout the autumn of 1857. At least young Meck, having been packed off to a boys' school in Alabama, was able to see his father from time to time as Polk traversed that state attending meetings.[1]

The most decisive of these meetings convened in Montgomery in November, at which the trustees argued at great length about where to build the school and what to name it before bowing to the made-up minds of Polk and John Armfield. The board had by then made Armfield a trustee—the welcome extended to someone pledging $25,000; the cottages he and others had built gratis for Polk and Otey were appreciated but were deemed insufficient inducements.[2] Even more to the board's liking was the promise by Samuel F. Tracy, president of the Sewanee Coal Mining Company, to give the university 5,000 acres for a campus, and to that gift would be added an almost equal amount pledged by eleven other landowners in surrounding Franklin County. And moreover, as the trustees had to concede, the coal company's spur line snaking up from the Nashville & Chattanooga Railroad's main line at the base of the plateau was indeed a modern touch that would connect the outside world to the woodland university—or, as New York's *Journal of Commerce* put it in a picturesque phrase, an iron-rail link to "terra incognita."[3]

Some trustees remained dubious, and to sway them Polk was compelled to argue that the coal company's land provided amenities found together nowhere else: a bucolic range where drinking water, heating fuel, construction limestone and timber, cool summers, mild winters, and disease-free air all coalesced in bountiful supply. "Shall we urge parents to send their children to a school in the Southern lowlands where they would be always liable to intermittents?" Polk asked Stephen Elliott rhetorically. (Posing the same question to F. A. P. Barnard in Mississippi, he winked that Southern children "can have chills and . . . bilious fevers and stay at home.")[4]

Still not sold, some trustees worried that with no settled town nearby the students would have no place to live. Polk assured them that housing students properly would present no obstacle. The plateau, suited to a resort, would work like a "magnet of great power to attract not only students but family settlers." These families would build homes on university land, and once licensed by the school they might provide rooms and board for up to twelve students. Presumably because Polk the cadet had merrily exploited the permissiveness of dormitory life, Polk the bishop was opposed to unsupervised residences for his students.[5]

Adding to these wholesome arrangements the planners devised an innovation having to do with calendar and climate. The Southern gentry in large numbers customarily fled the Deep South in summer, seeking relief from heat and disease in the mineral springs and recreational cities of the world: White Sulphur Springs, Newport, Saratoga, Paris, and lately Tennessee's Beersheba Springs. But what was one to do with one's adolescents at home on school vacation? Stephen Elliott understood the snag and the solution. As most vacationing parents were reluctant to introduce their sons "at that immature period of life" to the dissipated society of watering places, the university was to schedule classes straight through the summer months, able to do so because atop "its lofty table land" the summer's "cool nights and mornings will restore the energies which have flagged under [daytime] application." Explaining further, Elliott rhapsodized to the trustees:

> The proper vacation of a [Southern] University is the winter, that
> season when our planters and merchants and professional men are
> surrounded by their Families upon their homesteads; when the
> cheerful Christmas fire is burning on the hearth, and mothers and
> sisters and servants can receive the returning student to his home, and

revive within him that holy domestic feeling which may have decayed amid the scholastic isolation of a College.

Equally advantageous, a winter vacation would provide the youth an opportunity "to engage in the sports which make him a true Southern man, hunting, shooting, riding." And finally, having thought of just about everything germane, Elliott would remind parents that the work of field hands being pretty much on hold in winter, the vacationing collegian "can mingle freely with the slaves who are in the future to be placed under his management and control."[6]

By such arguments the Montgomery delegates were gradually won over—or worn down. Wearying of the question after seventeen ballots, the Sewanee opponents joined their fellows in a unanimous vote. The unanimity was less than sincere. Alabama churchmen, following the rejection of Huntsville, attempted to reopen the issue six months later. Polk was irritated by their "merely selfish and local feeling," sniffing that "I suppose I have counted too largely on the capability of human nature, even when purged by Apostolic baptism." Only when a full year had passed could Polk report that "all opposition has died out."[7]

The trustees had next to agree on an official name. The University of the South was chosen over the Church University and the University of Sewanee, pleasing Polk because it deftly defined the character and location of the institution "without affording, in the least, just ground of offense, to the most sensitive." That left only the vexing problem of funding. A nationwide financial panic that summer had put the squeeze on the pocketbooks of Southern planters, so Polk and Elliott and the endowment committee "resolved not to enter upon their work, until another crop shall have been realized." Once the 1858 harvest was gathered they would "prosecute" their money-raising mission "with activity and energy." And so they did, for in due course when the South and the planters were flush again the trustees accumulated the half-million-dollar endowment they deemed necessary before they would commence building.

With well-honed skills at selling and self-delusion, Polk and Elliott produced a solicitation brochure in 1860 that reminded wealthy readers that "the world is trying hard to persuade us that a slaveholding people cannot be a people of high moral and intellectual culture." Just the opposite was true, they declared. With slave labor providing the leisure, slaveholding families were enabled to devote themselves to the "elegance of literature, and to such culture as shall make" Southern civilization "the envy of all lands." A donation to the glittering university for "the wise, good and the cultivated" was just the way to put the lie to Yankee slander.[8] Similarly, as Polk had told his convention in 1858, let thanks be to God "for having thrust down into our cotton zone, a plateau so accessible, and so admirably adapted, in every particular, as a refuge for our children."[9] One clergyman swooning would equate the aura of "Sewanee mountain [to] the same spirit that first hovered and went forth from the top of Calvary."[10]

While the bishop himself extolled the providential benefactions raining down on the Sewanee plateau, the delegate from St. John's parish in Thibodaux—Col. Braxton Bragg—did not hearken to his words. Bragg owned a sugar plantation just across Bayou La Fourche from Leighton Place, and although he and Polk were on amicable terms (and not the sneering antagonists they would soon become in the Confederate Army), Bragg at the time was involved with an embryonic college competing with Sewanee for Louisiana's well-to-do sons and their parents' money. This was the State Seminary of Learning & Military Academy that was then taking shape in Alexandria, Louisiana.[11]

In the waning years of peace, Polk's salutary refuge for Southern boys on the Sewanee plateau had grown to some 9,500 acres of more or less untracked wilderness. The donated acreage was now at the disposal of the university's trustees—subject, naturally, to the deed entanglements, surveying disputes, and self-serving altercations that real-estate dealings generally entail. To place the land and its inherent problems directly under his oversight, Polk hired the civil engineer Charles R. Barney to survey the acreage, plot roads, and generally wrestle the unmapped wilds into comprehensible shape. To assist Barney, Polk retained a consultant, Josiah Gorgas, a West Point graduate and later chief of ordnance for the Confederate Army.[12] Over the coming months, Polk fed "My Dear Col. Barney" a steady stream of advice and orders. In one typical letter he told Barney to have trees and brush cleared along the Sewanee Railroad right-of-way and "especially cut away the timber where the cars stop at the tank," alluding to the spot where the steam engine paused to resupply its boiler water. Polk's marketing instincts were sharp; here he was making sure that visitors aboard the train were given ample opportunity to drink in the scenery, so that they might decide then and there to build on school property or at least send their sons as students.[13] Driving Barney as hard as he drove himself, Polk seldom thought to praise his on-site engineer for satisfactory work, let alone the slaves providing most of the muscle. One exception occurred after Barney's progress was threatened by an interfering claim upon certain of the university lands. Polk's approval of Barney's handling of the matter resulted in Barney's response in language rarely seen in an engineer's report: "I was considerably revived by the all-conquering spirit with which you animate me to meet the thick array of hindrances that prevent your glorious enterprise from having a firm footing and a local habitation on this chosen spot," he assured the bishop. "It requires more philosophy and Christian forbearance than I can command to witness quietly and unmoved the low plotting and counter-plotting, the mean trickery, littleness . . . and short-sighted selfishness of this faithless community."[14]

Polk ordered 5,000 copies of a handsome 1,000-feet-to-the-inch topographical "plat" of the Sewanee domain that Charles Barney had drawn. To demonstrate "that the men who have charge of this [university] are not dealing with it as with a petty affair in which they have no confidence, and to which they have given little thought and labor," a hundred of these maps, the size of small tablecloths, were hand-colored for added impact and were to be scattered across the South to potential donors "like the leaves of the trees." Later, smaller versions of the map highlighted placenames—"Otey's Prospect," "Polk's Lookout," "Point Elliott," and the like.[15]

Finally, a grand picnic was scheduled to cap the campaign in August 1958 when the property would be shown up close to potential benefactors and rural neighbors. As Polk envisioned the fete, railway cars would transport an editorial corps and hundreds of guests up from the valley to the raw mountain campus, while buggy roads would be provided for others. Tents were to stretch over "the tables of good things," and a wonderfully "broad flat rock" would be canopied with tree boughs for such of the younger guests "as may wish to amuse themselves by dancing."[16] Instrumentalists for the dancing had to be imported from Nashville because John Armfield, not so obliging in this instance, forbade the loan of the band of musicians then engaged at his Beersheba Springs hotel. They could not be spared, he said, because the lucrative summer social whirl was at its peak.[17]

Whether raising money, planning picnics, or attending committee meetings, Polk was by now so caught up in university affairs and stretched so thin between Tennessee and Louisiana, where the bulk of endowment money was to be found, that he had scarcely time for anything else, even to having a care for himself.[18] He must have believed it imperative, then, that he slow down long enough on the first day of September to acknowledge calmly the ruins of his former prosperity by penning at the bottom of his 1849 last will and testament a two-line codicil. His library was to go to the Diocese of Louisiana, his body to St. John's graveyard in Tennessee, his blessing to his children. (Some modest budgetary optimism would come his way a year later when the trustees awarded him $5,000 to defray the expenses and to cover the sacrifices he had borne already establishing the school. The catch: the money, and a like amount for Bishop Elliott, was to come from funds the two men were obliged to raise themselves.)[19]

In short, for practical and economic reasons, the deflated bishop and his wife decided to give up the rented house in New Orleans on Magazine Street. They hoped eventually to resettle in Beersheba Springs, where the promised house was under construction, or on the university grounds— University Place, as the post office had just been named. As Kate Polk, the oldest child, had married William Dudley Gale of Nashville the past December and was now touring Europe with him and her sister Frances, the youngest Polk girls and Fanny were in the meantime to live for a "twelve-month" at 1234 Chestnut Street, Philadelphia. Still troubled by her eye disease, Fanny was to resume her treatments under Dr. Isaac Hays.[20] To complete the family uprooting, young Meck Polk, just turned fifteen, had been withdrawn from the school in Alabama and was sent in September to Col. Francis H. Smith's Virginia Military Institute (VMI) in Lexington, a change the boy found agreeable. The VMI faculty was predominantly Episcopalian (with the notable exception of Major Thomas Jonathan Jackson, a bristling Presbyterian), and the school was additionally pleasing to Meck's father because "in very many respects [it was] quite equal to West Point." Otey was sending his son William Newton Mercer Otey to VMI, and Meck's cousin Rufus Polk, the son of Rebecca and George W. Polk, would shortly enroll there too.[21]

On their way to the Northeast, the bishop, his wife, and their young daughters stopped first in Raleigh as was their custom. Leonidas called on his longtime friend from college, David Swain, now president of the University of North Carolina, and apprised him of the Tennessee university coming into being. The family went on to Richmond for the sixteen-day convention. Although sectional tensions continued apace throughout the United States, Polk would later remark on the "strikingly harmonious" mingling of Northerners and Southerners in Richmond, reminiscent of Philadelphia three years earlier. An artistic engraver was equally impressed by the camaraderie. He would produce a group portrait portraying all thirty-five bishops present—as well as six who were not—congenially assembled.[22]

Having Fanny again settled in Philadelphia with the girls, Polk continued through Vermont, New York, Massachusetts, and Rhode Island, alert for ideas useful to his university. To open the right doors wherever he stopped, he had acquired in Washington letters of introduction from Alexander Dallas Bache, a fellow cadet at West Point. Bache was a great-grandson of Benjamin Franklin and was now an eminent American scientist and author of a definitive work on European education. While Polk was dining in Bache's home, his host had invited in Joseph Henry, the founder and director of Washington's Smithsonian Institution. Henry later took Polk on a tour of his museum, and Polk soaked up all he could. "I examined his work thoroughly," he reported to Elliott. "Many of the best of [Henry's] plans may be appropriated with great advantage by us." With his introductory letters in hand, Polk then palavered his way with such other renowned educators of the day as James Walker, Louis Agassiz, Benjamin Peirce, and Cornelius Conway Felton, all at Harvard, and Alexis Caswell at Brown.[23]

On his way home, Polk managed to visit his son briefly at VMI. (To Meck's annoyance, his father's pass through was so hasty that he failed to pay the cadet's laundry bill.) The school was still abuzz with talk of John Brown's aborted attack upon the United States arsenal at Harper's Ferry, Virginia, an event not mentioned in Polk's known correspondence. Brown was to be hanged on December 2 in Charles Town, and Virginia's governor, fearing rescue attempts by armed abolitionists, called upon Colonel Smith's boy soldiers.

Winding up his travels at Stephen Elliott's home in Savannah, Polk and the trustees, aiming to codify a constitution for the university, spent three weeks shuffling and sifting an accumulation of printed materials and handwritten notes (with a translator at hand to make abstracts of the texts in German and French): notes Polk had made of personal interviews; materials supplied at President Buchanan's request from America's embassies in Europe; and advisories by Church of England friends. At hand, as Polk was to phrase it, was knowledge of "the working machinery of the most eminent institutions of learning in our country and in Europe," allowing the eight trustees to assemble a document tailor-made for Sewanee. Polk's praise was lavish: "I think posterity will say we have drawn up one of the most complete systems of University education that has ever been produced."[24] With the school now established on paper, the trustees at the same gathering—and at subsequent confabulations—began to think aloud about what eminent man they should hire to run it. One "unhatched" idea bandied about, as the bishop of Mississippi reported, was to enlist Col. Robert E. Lee to become vice chancellor and president of the university. Lee was still much in the news for having commanded the marines who had retaken the Harper's Ferry arsenal from John Brown.[25]

The Christmas season had arrived by then, and with no family nearby, Polk, accompanied by Elliott, went up from Georgia to the Tennessee mountaintop and set up light housekeeping in cabins that had been hastily built on the campus under Barney's direction. Expecting more discomfort from the cold, Polk said they were "agreeably disappointed" by the mildness of the winter weather. Well organized as always, Polk rented a milch cow at the going rate of 10 cents a day. Already occupying a campus cabin was John Hopkins, the bishop of Vermont now serving as Sewanee's visiting landscape gardener. After conversations with Hopkins in New Orleans back during the winter of 1856, Polk had been authorized by the university trustees to hire someone to design the campus and in late 1859 had gone to Hopkins's Burlington home to press his suit.[26] The offer was $1,500 for Hopkins to spend six months in Tennessee devising a campus layout. Hopkins agreed to this plan partly because of his friendship with Polk, but mainly because he urgently needed the money to complete the building of a chapel at his own school, the Vermont Episcopal Institute for Boys in Burlington.[27] During these days Polk thought of himself as something of a landscape expert, too. When in New York City in the fall of 1859 to welcome daughters Kate and Frances home from Europe, he had taken a critical look at the city's Central Park now being constructed. He dismissed the 778 rural acres that were being reclaimed from bogs, rocky thickets, and pigsties by architect Frederick Law Olmsted as "no very great affair after all."[28]

Once on the job in early 1860, with Tennessee's hardwood trees seasonally bare of leaves, Bishop Hopkins could easily discern the landscaping task Polk had set him. He liked what he saw. "If Lake Champlain could be thrown in," he wrote his wife in Burlington, "it would be absolute perfection."[29] He had lavish praise for Polk as well. As Polk more fully unfolded the design of the university for him, Hopkins later said, "I was amazed and delighted at [his] combination of original genius, large enterprise and Christian hope with the utmost degree of practical wisdom, cautious investigation, exquisite tact and indefatigable energy. [It] far surpassed all that I could have conceived within the bounds of human efficiency." He concluded: "I was almost carried away by my admiration."[30]

Upon a gentle saddle horse provided by Barney, Hopkins began to visualize his own designs. The campus proper of some 1,000 plateau acres was to be circled, as Polk would later describe it elegantly, by a five-mile, 100-foot-wide "grand Corso [with] a grand Avenue right through the center of the grounds equidistant from the Corso."[31] The bisecting road was to become University Avenue, and cross streets were to be named for the ten Southern dioceses participating in the university's creation. Natural landmarks—the springs and scenic overlooks abounding on the land—would honor the founding bishops and such benefactors as would make significant donations. Hopkins undertook to render about two dozen watercolor sketches of the scenery that he found so appealing, but before long he realized he had taken on more work than he could finish. Skinflint Vermont churchmen were defaulting on $3,000 in pledges toward reviving the financially ailing Episcopal Institute for Boys, so Hopkins had to return home after only three months at Sewanee. That cut his proposed engagement in half. The $900.51 he received went directly from his pocket into the school's building fund in Burlington.[32]

As Polk's fund-raising had fared better than Hopkins's, he could soon confide to Lucius that the trustees at a February 1860 meeting in New Orleans "were all delighted with my work as to plan of organization, etc. . . . I think I shall succeed fully in [the] matter."[33] That good feeling may have lasted up until the receipt of the late March letter from Colonel Smith at VMI. Though handling his studies satisfactorily, Meck had accumulated seventy-three demerits in two months' time, the fruit, in the view of Colonel Smith, of "great carelessness and maybe criminality." The boy, moreover, "is disposed to be extravagant." Smith ventured to suppose that "perhaps some excess of [parental] indulgence has fostered this." Polk surely was not accustomed to hearing either himself or Fanny upbraided on Meck's account.[34]

In July the superintendent informed Polk that Meck's steadily accumulating demerits had resulted in his dismissal from the institute. "I need not say to you how much pain [the news] gives me," Polk replied and, without protest, enclosed a check for $200 so that his "mindless" boy be provided with "a citizen's outfit" and sent packing to his father in Beersheba Springs. During the exchange of letters, however, Meck somehow avoided expulsion. In Smith's hopeful perception, Meck had awakened to the mortification he was causing. More accurately, Meck had awakened to the fact that he had been incorrectly charged with twice as many demerits as he deserved. He then had asked for, and obtained, reinstatement. As he did often, he promised to do better—but it was a promise hard for him to keep for long. Meck's ongoing delinquencies intruded, of course, upon his father's more worthwhile organizational tasks. Even as he was directing Colonel Smith on August 3 to expel the miscreant forthwith, he was at pains to post to an architect acquaintance his own pencil sketch of the floor plan he envisioned for the proposed Central Building on the Sewanee campus.[35]

Fanny and the girls in Philadelphia were now about to head for their new mountain home in Tennessee, the bishop having to prepare for their arrival. After adjourning the convention, he had the family's New Orleans household goods put aboard the steamboat *Scotland*. Little was left behind; the inventory listed 158 boxes and several "Negroes." All were sent meandering up the Mississippi River to Louisville, and from there baggage cars of the

Louisville & Nashville and the Nashville & Chattanooga Railways carried the cargo to the mule-drawn wagons that would finish the transfer to Beersheba Springs.[36] Reunited at the Tennessee resort, the family started putting down roots, at one point literally. The bishop asked Susan in Raleigh for her husband's "receipt for a compost such bed as they make in N.C. I want it . . . for our garden on this mountain."[37] Thwarting that bucolic plan, Polk decided the cottage at Beersheba, though provided free, was proving to be too far from the university site. Polk had a house built for his family right on the campus. Everyone was settled there by Christmas 1860.

All the while, enough planning had been accomplished and enough capitalization secured that the trustees felt it was high time to lay a cornerstone. Such an event, of course, would be accompanied by as much public notice and festivity as could be managed. First, a small iron safe was acquired for the campus storage of maps and documents, and a sundial was ordered for meteorological readings.[38] Then assignments were made: some people were to haul a huge stone and others to assemble a huge crowd at the top of the mountain. An undressed block of marble, six tons of it, was brought by wagon from the plains below, a task requiring the efforts of eighteen yoke of oxen borrowed from neighboring farmers and, as the young surveyor bossing the operation put it, numerous of "my father's trusty darkies." Bishop Elliott's young son Haby—the child Polk had invited to become president of the school when he grew up—rode atop the stone on the final leg. The stone was then polished and hollowed out to receive the ceremonial documents planned for it. Since there was as yet no architect's finished plan for a building, the marble box was maneuvered onto a makeshift foundation of native sandstone.[39] Needed now, the bishop reckoned, was an appreciative audience.

The business attendant to the ceremonial laying of the cornerstone fell to Polk. His correspondence throughout the summer of 1860 included cordial bids to the dignitaries he hoped would attend the event. Among these was one West Point roommate, the Reverend Albert Taylor Bledsoe, now teaching mathematics at the University of Virginia. Bledsoe, a longtime "intimate friend," was appropriately evangelical and was being courted by Polk for a faculty position. Two other hoped-for guests were F. A. P. Barnard in Mississippi and Benjamin Smith, the bishop of Kentucky. Smith, as the prelate of a border state, had not been asked to join the ten Southern bishops founding the Sewanee university, but Polk thought solidarity with the border-state bishops was useful. James Robb, the banker, was urged to come and make a speech about commerce.[40]

In other dedication arrangements, Polk indulged his usual watchfulness of Colonel Barney's engineering work. Early that fall he gave him step-by-step directions for laying out a main access road from the campus heights down to the valley town of Cowan below: "I think that you should begin at the gate beyond Hawkins' spring," Polk wrote, "and run right across his field towards a large poplar tree. . . . I think I would pass the poplar to the right, then go across Hawkins' woods lot until you strike Trowell's field . . . through [the] cornfield . . . to the right of the graveyard . . . up the ravine by the peach orchard." Barney was permitted to plot the rest of the way to Cowan "in any way you think best."[41] Other particulars to which the bishop applied himself included obtaining free railroad tickets from Nashville for servants hired for the occasion; ordering the food; constructing shelters and privies; and even the hiring of a family band of part-time musicians from Nashville whose everyday occupation was painting signs.

With most things close to being ready, even to supplying sleeping quarters with cots for those staying over, the crowd, said to number about 2,000 and drawn "from New York to New Orleans, from Chicago to Charleston" in Polk's euphonious summation, began to arrive by rail, in carriages, or, for those from the neighboring hollows and highlands, on horseback and on foot.[42] Williamson Hartley Horn's Silver Band entertained on the railroad cars from Nashville, and on the night of October 9, the eve of the celebration, the Reverend Charles Quintard, a postwar chancellor of the university, rehearsed the band musicians and an ad hoc choir in the hymns and canticles that would be used in congregational singing the next day. The official program for October 10 listed the procession that would lead the way to the cornerstone's site: at the head would march the Silver Band, followed by secular dignitaries in uniforms and mufti (including a group of architects competing among themselves for a design prize), followed by clergy in vestments. A witness lamented that the absence of Colonel Lee, who had declined a proffered academic office, was the lone blemish on an otherwise perfect parade. Almost as good, though, was the presence of the heroic Gen. Winfield Scott; he had brought along the Episcopal prayer book that, reportedly, he carried in the War with Mexico. It went into the cornerstone.[43]

Before the ceremonial day was turned over to the requisite orations, dining, and the evening's merrymaking, Bishop Polk, in the name of the Holy Trinity, tapped the cornerstone three times with a mason's hammer and dedicated the university to "the cultivation of true Religion, learning and virtue, that thereby God may be glorified, and the happiness of man be advanced." Into the marble stone Bishop Elliott then deposited a Bible, General Scott's Book of Common Prayer, a copy of the United States

Constitution, and the charter of the school. (A quantity of coins also was rumored to have been sealed in the stone. Though probably seeking, but finding none, wartime marauders later broke the cornerstone to pieces.)[44] The proceedings then concluded with a curiously prophetic twist supplied by John Smith Preston, a heated secessionist and flowery speechifier. Peering at Polk sitting peaceably, he intoned: "When it pleases God . . . to stay your radiant and strong right arm from His battlefields on earth . . . our grateful country will read on your gravestone, 'The Founder of the University of the South.'"[45] With the setting of that commemorative building block, Bishops Polk and Elliott established *themselves* as the foundation stones of the Southern Episcopal Church—its decisive leaders as their nation and their denomination began to come apart.

12

"My Dear General, Consider Me at Your Service" (1860–1861)

Although the Southern bishops' university had been conceived and gestated during rumblings of disunion and war, the university's future looked sanguine as 1860 wound down. Holding 9,525 acres on top of their mountain, the trustees had a goodly amount of money to work with ($363,000 given, $112,000 reliably promised), and would-be residents of University Place were already applying for leaseholds while their cabin construction was under way. Charles Anderson, a provisional campus architect picking up where Bishop Hopkins left off, had been retained after winning the design competition for the Central Building; his prize was $400, though he failed to be chosen as the building's architect.[1] Within a fortnight, however, Abraham Lincoln was elected president of the United States, a bad omen for the school's secessionist-minded administrators. There is no direct record of the rancor that Leonidas Polk probably loosed to his friends, though his wife just days before the election portrayed herself as holding a moderate perspective. "I cannot believe that we are such egregious fools as to allow of disserverance [sic] of the Union," she wrote in one of her otherwise affectionate letters to her close friend James Robb, then living amid Yankees in Chicago. "But you people at the Northwest must not drive us to measures which all may regret."[2] Driven just so, her husband remained in such a bad temper three weeks after Lincoln's election that his more placid bishop friend James Otey took him to task: "To what quarter shall we look when such men as you and Elliott deliberately favor secession? What can we expect . . . when . . . the Ministers of the Gospel of peace are found on the side of those who openly avow their determination to destroy the work which our fathers established?" How Polk replied to this scolding, the first of two that Otey would deliver that winter, is not known.[3]

With Bishop Polk's absentee oversight of his Louisiana diocese entering its fifth month, he left the Sewanee mountain and resumed pastoral duties in New Orleans in early December.[4] Vexations on a national scale aside, he found on his New Orleans desk a letter of sixteen pages upbraiding his episcopal leadership. The writer was the Reverend John Rowland, the Welsh-born, Cambridge-educated rector of St. Stephen's Church in Pointe Coupee Parish. His grievances included the bishop's lackadaisical conduct of liturgical services, his mispronunciations of certain biblical names, and his toleration of diocesan meetings that reached levels of "nigh levity." Rowland was so spiritually undone that he subsequently returned to New Jersey whence he had come.[5] Polk doubtless shrugged off the pique of a parish priest and focused instead on an opinionated letter of his own: his advice to James Buchanan, the hapless lame-duck president of the United States. The thrust of Polk's counsel to Buchanan, written the day after Christmas, was that he and others in Washington would be well advised to let the South break away in peace. Polk spoke, he assured the president, with authority, because he was thoroughly attuned to the determined mind of the Deep South. Furthermore, he let the president understand, "there will [not] be the remotest prospect for the reunion of the two sections as long as slave labor shall prove advantageously applicable to the agricultural wants of the Southern Confederacy." With the letter on its way to Washington, the bishop set his mind next to drafting a prayer to be used by his clergy in the threatening days ahead. Strangely conciliatory after the gauntlet flung at Buchanan, he entreated God "to save us from all ignorance, error, pride and prejudice" and "to compose and heal the divisions which disturb us."[6]

As over the ages countless girls and boys and women and men have observed New Year's Day by beginning a diary, so did Leonidas Polk in 1861 (and like most other diarists, he soon gave it up). "A New Year!" he exclaimed that evening across page one. "May the Almighty Father of us all have mercy on me, and take me into his holy keeping during all its days and hours and moments, for the sake of Him who has loved me and given himself for me." The bishop had earlier paid a cordial holiday social call on Col. Braxton Bragg, now resident in New Orleans (and later Polk's antagonistic superior officer in the Confederate Army). Two days after visiting Bragg, Polk left New Orleans to rejoin his family in Sewanee, where Fanny and the children had holidayed with the Stephen Elliotts and Colonel Barney. Worship, eggnog, and charades filled Christmas day and evening, and the youngsters frolicked in a snowfall four inches deep that descended on the Cumberland Plateau as the old year ended. After but a fortnight's family reunion, which included a winter picnic at a "Natural Bridge" with the Thomas Adamses, university benefactors from New Orleans, Polk prepared to return to Louisiana. Before leaving, and after leading Sunday's prescribed prayers for his friends, he "had the thought," he wrote, "that it was the last time I should pray for the President of the U.S. forced upon us. It was a deeply solemn thought."[7]

War signs by then were breaking out across Louisiana. Governor Thomas O. Moore had commenced sending his state's militiamen, Colonel Bragg among them, to seize various US military properties in Louisiana—arsenals, forts, barracks, and the like—and to expel from the state officers and enlisted men loyal to the United States Army.[8] In a political move Polk and his secessionist friends heartily welcomed, Louisiana was about to follow the examples of South Carolina and other Deep South states and secede formally from the United States. That occurred on January 26.

Four days later Polk began drafting a militant pastoral letter to his clergy and laypeople, and when he was done he had it published. Just as Louisiana had cut herself free from the Union, so too, he declared, would Louisiana's Episcopalians go their own way rejoicing. ("Separated, not divided," he quibbled.) Though love of Northern clerical brethren continued, "the Church must follow nationality," Polk preached. By virtue of his dictum, Louisiana's parishes were no longer in communion with the Protestant Episcopal Church of the United States of America. They now constituted the independent Diocese of Louisiana. In the 400 or so years of Anglican Church history, this separation of a diocese from a national body, Polk proudly declared, was the first.[9] Polk was betraying an astonishing change of heart. According to one listener, Polk had once preached a sermon to his convention in which he had said that the unity of the Church was a sacred, inviolable component. "It was on that occasion," the delegate remembered, "that he compared the Church on the earth to Christ's body, and used the remarkable expression, 'That he who would do aught to divide it, was crucifying the Body of Christ anew, was driving again the nails in our Savior's hands, was again thrusting the spear into His side.'" So much for absolutes.[10]

For the time being, Polk was pretty much on his own; other Episcopal bishops in the South adopted a wait-and-see strategy as the Union unraveled. Whether Polk's singular declaration of independence was based on inspired insight into canonical law or was simply unadorned hubris on his part was much debated, then and for a long time afterward.[11] Testing the waters, perhaps, while returning by train to Sewanee, Polk spent five hours between trains in the Memphis home of James Otey. Polk's March 14 diary entry recounts the afternoon this way: "Talked of the taking of my position. Saw no reason for changing my ground." Neither, apparently, did Otey see any reason for changing his. In his second letter of anguish, rebuke, and appeal written after Polk's departure, Otey raised theological and constitutional issues across ten impassioned pages. He could find nothing redeeming in what Polk had done and suggested it portended devastating shame upon the Church comparable to the Philistines' capture of Israel's sacred ark in the eleventh century.[12] Unmoved by Otey's fuming, Polk five days later joined Stephen Elliott at University Place in addressing a cheerful circular letter to all the Southern bishops, including Otey, summoning them to a meeting in Montgomery, Alabama. At that time, the city was the temporary capital of the Confederacy, and the meeting's agenda was to be "the course to be pursued by the dioceses of the seceding states"—the formation, as it turned out, of the Episcopal Church in the Confederate States of America.[13]

Eventually Polk got back to Otey privately. "On reading your [March 18] letter," he began, "I saw at once that you had mistaken my position and purposes."[14] No matter, as the mistake was soon rectified. With secessionist heat rapidly rising across the South, Otey's moral compass had begun to swing wildly. By May 1861, on the verge of affirming secession and positioning himself shoulder to shoulder with Polk and Elliott, Otey posted a letter to Abraham Lincoln's secretary of state, William Henry Seward, pleading that Seward "urge [the President] to desist from all hostile measures and efforts to compel an unwilling obedience to his Government." Soon despairing that his letter had had any effect in Washington, Otey was not long in blessing his son Mercer's enlistment in the Confederate Army. The three mitered apostles of Southern brotherhood now locked arms against all those who had chosen Abraham Lincoln to be America's president.[15]

In the fiercely Unionist mountains of East Tennessee, meanwhile, where the bishops' university was taking shape, the troublous winter of 1861 careered toward an even bleaker springtime when members of the Polk family fell victim to an attack. In the midnight stillness of Friday, April 12, some hours after Confederate cannoneers had opened fire on federal soldiers in Fort Sumter in Charleston Harbor to ignite the Civil War, figures glided from woodland shadows and approached the residential cabins clustered on the Sewanee campus. While Fanny, her daughters Sally, Lilly, and Lucia, and their male servants slept in their log structure, firebrands were tossed through an open window onto a guest-room bed.

"I cannot describe to you the feeling that came over me when I realised [*sic*] from the horrible roaring and lights that the house was on fire," Fanny reported to her husband a few days later. "I passed through the parlour which was full of red light from above, went into Sally's room, saw flames, a perfect sea, in the front room and overhead. Tried to get through to call the boys [the servants] who were in the most danger, found the door locked . . . , retraced my steps (remembering to close the doors after me)."

Maintaining admirable presence of mind, Fanny made sure all children and slaves had been roused, then ordered one of the men to carry out a basket of silverware and "told the girls to save what they could." Lucia, thirteen, "came crying. Told her to be quiet and get her clothes out of the drawers." Fanny plunged back into the burning rooms to pull from the walls oil portraits of her parents. She had returned "for Mr. Robb's [portrait] when the flames burst through the door and drove me back." At last remembering her own clothes,

> I went into my room to try to save them. . . . I did not realize I was in danger. . . . While trying to get to my wardrobe, Alti [Altimore, a slave] came in and said "Mistress, you must leave the house. This roof may fall in a moment." I objected, when the roof over the hall fell in and flames rushed to the end of my room. I did not see them and Alti just carried me out.

As he bore her to safety through the library, Fanny said to her books, "Farewell, old friends." Then, with flames consuming scores of letters between Leonidas and her from the beginning of their marriage, Fanny saw that the vacant house of the Elliott family nearby was also burning to the ground. Fanny's neck "burned red," all her jewelry lost, a gift of fine lace no more ("which I am woman enough to deplore"). Fanny apologized for sending "a very egotistical letter, dear husband." She could not withhold one last thought: the Diocese of Louisiana "ought, for very shame, do something for you, but I do not expect it . . . after the way they acted in '50 after the tornado." Fanny wrote she supposed the fires were "the work of some Abolitionists."[16]

And the arsonists' motive? The Sewanee University historian Merritt Blakeslee believes the "crime was directed not solely against the persons of Bishops Polk and Elliott but more generally against everything that the University-as-Idea represented." He quotes a New Orleans newspaper account probably based on information obtained from Bishop Polk: "The University movement being recognized as a special exponent of Southern views and purposes, fixed the attention of the [perpetrators who] resolved to purge themselves of its presence." Weighing contradictory speculations and hear-say, Blakeslee cautiously concluded that one or more white residents of the Sewanee region were the arsonists. Bishop Polk's own theory was that one of the family's slaves was involved.[17]

Since early in April the bishop had been making parish visitations in the northwest interior of Louisiana, so he knew nothing of the fire until a full two weeks had passed. Fanny was coping with the disaster while Polk was feeling invigorated because the nascent Civil War was steadily gathering momentum, and on his return to New Orleans he wrote a buoyant letter to his wife. Refreshed by an overnight's sleep in a steamboat stateroom, he was "glad to see that we are at last to have the border states" as Confederate allies, and because one of them was Tennessee, he supposed Fanny and the girls in their Sewanee retreat were in a "safe and secure place, and need have no apprehension." Then, after opening his accumulated letters, he learned of the Sewanee arson and, stunned, became "sick at heart." "Was there ever in all the world such a hellish proceeding?" he now raged to Fanny by re-turn mail. "The spirit of hell itself was never more exhibited . . . prompted by the spirit of Black Republican hate." Then abruptly he calmed down. At least no one was hurt in the fire, and his "beloved, thoughtful wife" had had the practical good sense to buy insurance "just before the fire." He was moved to "most heartily thank God" for putting the idea in her mind.[18]

That the bishop was as collected as he was is noteworthy. While out on his visitations he had recently had to deal with the unanswered correspon-dence he had brought with him. The worst of these letters—some many weeks old and evidently not yet read—concerned more of Meck Polk's miscreant deportment at VMI. Facing up to the bad news, the beset father decided to withdraw his son then and there lest, as he wrote Colonel Smith, he "continue a career which may end in fastening on these habits fatal to his future life." But days after posting that directive to the superintendent, the news that P. G. T. Beauregard's bombardment of the Charleston fort had precipitated the war reached the harried father in Shreveport. Immediately he wrote Smith again, saying he had changed his mind about Meck. Cancel his withdrawal, inasmuch as "all the young men of our Southern Country must be sooner or later involved [in the war], and in such a case I would pre-fer my Son to be connected with a corps such as yours."[19] Filled now with paternal pride and martial ardor, Polk was delighted by the bellicosity and adrenaline rushes he observed all around him in Shreveport, as scores of eager volunteers from Louisiana's backcountry were boarding steamboats for New Orleans, where trains would take them to Virginia. Pitching in to do his pastoral bit, he "addressed and blessed" Shreveport's Caddo Rifles shortly before they embarked, and then a little later, after blessing a troop of 100 larking enlisted men—"the very best men of the highest social position in the state," he noted with patrician satisfaction—he boarded his own steamboat in Alexandria. Immediately he began to express his anger again. The coming war would turn "the truth of God against [the] presumptuous and arrogant infidelity inaugurated by Abraham Lincoln," Polk wrote excitedly to James Robb from the steamer *Hodge*. "We hurl defiance at our enemies," he underlined. As Polk would shortly learn, his former benefactor, whose portrait Fanny had been at pains to save from the arsonist's fire, had a different view. Another New Orleans friend reported that in Chicago "[our] neighbour Robb is on his high stilts, all for Lincoln, furious and zealous for the North. Is it not strange, with all his good qualities . . . he is governed by his surroundings?"[20]

Still trying to get his family's life in order, by early May Polk had lost all track of his cadet son and had heard nothing about him from VMI. The most recent letter from Meck was dated April 18, and it contained Meck's breathless account of a recent altercation in Lexington between the corps of cadets and a mob of the town's Unionists. Meck omitted one detail: when VMI's commandant, Maj. William Gilham, intervened in the near riot, rambunctious "Billy Polk, with a musket in his hands and spoiling for a fight," witnesses would later report, "came near shooting the Major." Though spared that unnerving intelligence, the bishop could relax only after learning that Meck and the whole VMI cadet corps were now quartered in Richmond, where the schoolboy soldiers had become emergency drill instructors of recruits even greener than themselves. A novice Virginia cavalryman would recall years later the May afternoon when he was "standing there on the railroad track" and Cadet William Polk put him through the "rudiments of the finger & cap salute until I could give it with tolerable grace." The instructor's name stuck in the soldier's mind because he "had once heard [Bishop Polk] celebrate a religious service, and greatly admired him."[21]

Louisiana's Episcopalians assembled routinely in convention that spring, this time in St. Francisville. The distracted bishop pushed himself throughout the midnight's hours preceding the convention's opening to write the obligatory Bishop's Address. ("Oh! That I could get those reports ready at an earlier day," he would lament that evening in his diary. "I must do that hereafter. The Lord help me in this!")[22] At last prepared, he followed the set agenda matter-of-factly, making no mention of the arson attack on his family and expressing his confidence that his university stood poised "to be put into operation, so soon as the state of the country shall be sufficiently settled."[23] That sunny outlook faded rapidly as the Union dissolved, so the bishop began a transformation himself, the West Pointer again emerging. As his ruminations led him, he considered how, were he personally in command of Confederate forces in the Mississippi Valley, the region and the port city of New Orleans might effectively be defended against invasion from the North. He had an idea or two, and he so informed the Confederacy's provisional president, Jefferson Davis. He was sure his academy friend of old would welcome his thoughts on these and divers military issues.

Writing from Vicksburg, as critical a river city as there would be during the coming war, he began his letter: "My dear Gen'l, I write to tender you my sincere sympathy, and so far as I may be able to, my cordial support in the trying position in which our countrymen have placed you." Polk assured the president he had the necessary "qualities to take you through the emergency," but he was constrained to express his concern for the "military condition of the Mississippi Valley." Polk trusted Davis "would allow an old friend the liberty of making a suggestion in regard to what passes under his own eye." First of all, Davis should know Louisiana Confederates were planning to place Col. Paul O. Hebert in charge of defending New Orleans and the Lower Mississippi. Manifestly flawed thinking, said Polk. Granted, Hebert was a well-meaning military man (a West Pointer who graduated first in his 1840 class), but, Polk said, putting it nicely, while his "heart and will are found in abundance . . . what is wanting in the valley is a head."[24]

The bishop had further advice for the president. His and Davis's longtime friend from West Point, Albert Sidney Johnston, ought to be made the Confederacy's general in chief as "a better man could not be found for that post." Here, Davis probably agreed with Polk. As cadets, the three young men had bonded, and later Davis and Johnston had served side by side during the War with Mexico.[25]

The bishop's boldest idea, in whatever capacity the president might think fit, was to offer himself to the war effort. "I beg you will consider me at your service in any way, compatible with my office, you may think me competent to support our cause—a cause which I hold to be the cause of God and his truth against the most ruthless and fanatical infidelity." Without mentioning his family's Sewanee escape, he felt it pertinent to inform Davis vaguely that "Black Republicanism has thought it worthwhile to burn me out in the mountains of Tennessee, an event which I accept as a part of an inevitable history at such hands."

President Davis did not share Polk's edginess about the Mississippi Valley's security, thinking it perfectly safe for the time being. Long a resident of humid Mississippi and probably sweltering just then in Montgomery,

Alabama, Davis wrote confidently that "people of the northwestern States have so great a dread of our climate that they could not be prevailed on to march against us." He demurred, too, at replacing Paul Hebert, who was to prove as ineffective as Polk promised. Davis nevertheless assured Polk "it would gratify me very much to see you." The Confederate government would be moving from Montgomery to Richmond shortly, and from the sound of it Davis just might have a proposition in mind for his estimable friend. Meanwhile, he bade the bishop "accept my thanks for pious wishes."[26]

All but certain that the cause of the Confederacy was the cause of God, the bishop of Louisiana would shortly become irrevocably convinced he was right. A few weeks after he first presented his compliments and offered his advice and services to Jefferson Davis in Montgomery, Polk traveled to Virginia to minister to green Louisiana troops dispatched to turn back the Yankee invaders. As he had in Shreveport, he found the young soldiers praiseworthy, "a fine, gallant lot of fellows, . . . the flower of our youth."[27] A side trip down the Virginia peninsula had a greater impact at the now quiet battlefield around Big Bethel Church where outnumbered Confederates had defeated 4,400 Federal troops. After strolling amid the broken trees and flattened farmers' fences where the war's first field fight had taken place, he wrote Fanny that he had "examined [the battleground] in detail. The hand of God surely seemed revealed."[28]

By the end of that summer of 1861 the affray at Big Bethel seemed trifling, but that the warrior God might find it useful to have Leonidas Polk in a military uniform had already occurred to the bishop; as an idea it was not yet fully formed, but it had been gestating for several days. Just before he went to Big Bethel, Polk had paid a campground call on a New Orleans friend, a society lawyer freshly turned colonel in command of Louisiana's 7th Infantry, the Pelican Regiment. Col. Harry Thompson Hays was encamped near Norfolk farther down the peninsula and received the bishop in his command tent, stylishly attired "in dressing gown and slippers for the purpose."[29] At this relatively benign juncture, the young war might still be fashioned to fit one's accustomed lifestyle. Colonel Hays possibly offered his guest cigars and a glass of port, and it is evident that the civilian visitor admired the military swagger his host projected. Polk may have mentioned that his younger son was off to the war himself. Meck had written that he was drilling recruits in Tennessee and serving as a "sort of aide de camp to Brig. Gen. Felix Zollicoffer," a family acquaintance.[30] Polk could have reflected as well on the exploits of his own father in the American Revolution.

Civilians North and South were just then daily exchanging mufti for uniforms, and if merely a second lieutenant in the artillery forty years earlier, and for only a few weeks at that, Polk was lately showing by his assured temperament that he was as qualified as just about anyone for the transition. Now the self-appointed consultant on military affairs to Jefferson Davis, he had used his trip to Virginia to pause in Nashville and counsel the secession-minded citizens there. The Tennessee capital was rapidly gearing up for war (the state's ordinance of secession would be approved by voters within a fortnight), and on arriving Polk drafted another of his advisory letters, this one to Leroy Pope Walker, the Confederacy's new secretary of war. Whether or not Walker needed coaching by Polk, the bishop began his letter as a primer on matters to date: "Mr. Lincoln," Polk wrote, "has stifled Maryland and paralyzed Missouri. His next victim in order is Kentucky. What is to be done?" Here the fragmentary copy of the letter breaks off, but presumably Polk then suggested how best to defend "this portion of our borders, the Mississippi Valley." Polk was not to be put off by Davis's conviction that the valley's defenses were just fine, and he was looking for Confederate allies to make his case.[31]

His next move—well-meaning and possibly once more officious—was to offer his consultant skills to Isham Harris, the secessionist governor of Tennessee. Harris had weeks before defied Lincoln's call for troops to help subdue the seceded states and was working hard to persuade reluctant Tennesseans to vote themselves out of the Union altogether. Harris was also devising strategies and military preparations to defend against invasion once the secession he favored was a fact.[32] He had already organized the Provisional Army of Tennessee, considered the best state militia in the South. Destined soon to be enrolled officially in the Confederate Army, the militia's men were woefully short on arms and were having a hard time getting help from the Richmond government. Four cannons, two of them unserviceable, constituted the artillery store.[33] Rightly guessing the bishop's usefulness, Harris gave Polk a wish list of cannons, which Polk would carry to the Confederate capital.

The refugees from Sewanee—Fanny Polk and her daughters and servants—were now staying with family in Maury County. Polk visited there, then resumed his journey east. Along the way to Chattanooga he left his train at Cowan and went up to the Sewanee plateau and the deserted campus. He tended to business matters, saw that important papers were locked in the safe, and poked through the ashes of his and Stephen Elliott's pine-log mountain homes. Thoughts "of the past . . . bemoaned me," he said, and if his secessionist convictions ever wavered, the scene surely would have reaffirmed them. Once in Richmond, he postponed for the moment his pastoral objective—the spiritual needs of the homesick Louisianans camped near Norfolk and Yorktown—and went right to work lobbying lawmakers and war-department bureaucrats for munitions.

Success was his within days. On June 19 he telegraphed the news to Governor Harris, who by then had persuaded the people of Tennessee to ratify secession. Polk had obtained eighteen six-pounder artillery pieces, compliments of the state of Virginia. They were on their way to Nashville and Memphis, and more were in the offing. Altogether he obtained enough ordnance for seven batteries of four guns each, the makings of almost a full artillery corps. Warming to work unfamiliar to most bishops, Polk had explicit advice for Harris on staffing the batteries (a first, second, and third lieutenant for each); on the proper construction of gun carriages ("white ash [or] any other tough wood that is light" and axles and wheels of Pittsburgh iron); on the outfitting of Tennessee's cavalry regiments ("I think it would be well for you to have imported from New Orleans as large a number of Spanish saddle trees as you are likely to want"); and on the retooling of old muzzle-loading muskets by rifling the smoothbore barrels. "No better arm, with the Minié ball, can be found," Polk declared, his expertise sounding undiminished by his seminary training.

Polk's high regard for the fearsome and recently developed Minié ball was well informed, too. The diameter of the bullet was slightly smaller than the bore of a rifled barrel and could be quickly rammed home. Because of its conical shape and hollow base, the malleable lead bullet expanded when fired, gripped the spiral grooves in the barrel, and went spinning toward a distant target with an accuracy that could not be matched by smoothbore shoulder guns. When it struck a soldier's body the damage inflicted was usually considerable. Proving Polk's point, the Minié and the rifled musket were to become the great killers of the Civil War.[34] Finally, the militant bishop could even recommend that Tennessee's cavalry troops follow those in Virginia who carried domestic revolvers and double-barrel shotguns. "I have ascertained from the highest authority," he warned, "that we must rely on ourselves and cease to look abroad for arms."[35]

While he was negotiating his ordnance deals for the Tennesseans, the clerically garbed bishop of Louisiana became an unlikely celebrity in the hallways of Richmond's capitol, sought after by soldiers and civilians alike. He discovered that there "is a great wish on the part of my friends that I should take part in this movement," particularly in military service defending the lands and waters of the Mississippi Valley, the backyard of his diocese. The wayfaring missionary had traversed the area for years. He described these solicitors as "persons of consideration." On their heels came a delegation of planters and businessmen from Mississippi and Louisiana. To these men name recognition may have been the bishop's best qualification, but doubtless urged on by Jefferson Davis (who had in mind by now a reduced role for Col. Paul Hebert) they were so insistent that their encomiums, as Polk confided both to Elliott and to Fanny, made him "feel rather sheepish" and "embarrassed me not a little." To his wife, he dared "not write what is said . . . of my capacity to serve the country in this emergency," but he was candid enough to admit that he himself held a "low estimate of my ability, and should fear to attempt what I could not well execute."[36]

Polk plausibly minimized such misgivings when welcomed as an honored guest into the councils of Richmond's most important leaders. He dined twice with the president and cabinet members and had "several chats" with Gen. Robert E. Lee, the commander of Virginia's state forces at that early date and military adviser to President Davis. As Polk had known Lee at West Point, he judged him to be "highly accomplished." But he did not share the more pronounced enthusiasm for Lee that was being expressed by so many in Richmond. He remarked to Fanny that "my friend [Albert Sidney] Johnston is his superior," and he claimed his opinion was shared by many a Confederate with military insight. Indeed, to some observers, both Polk and Johnston seemed cut from the same cloth of heraldic weave. While Polk, as an adoring kinswoman had said, exhibited "the spirit of ancient chivalry as handed down to us in the Morte d'Arthur," Sidney Johnston was to the Confederacy "as royal Arthur [was] to England's brave romance."[37]

During his two long conversations with Davis, Polk expounded generally on Confederate strategies "with great freedom and fullness," and his views, he told Fanny, were certain to be "productive of good results." Among them, he had recommended again that Johnston be given oversight of the critical Mississippi Valley defense. But, protested the president, Johnston "was not in the country," being just weeks before on the California coast with the US Army. With Johnston beyond reach (although making his way to Richmond even then), it was during these talks that Davis persuaded Polk (according to Polk) to assume a merely temporary military role as a brigadier general in the Provisional Confederate Army. Polk says the offer was made at least twice.[38]

Inasmuch as Polk told Fanny he was convinced by then that the US government—the same government, he ruefully reflected, that had given him an education—was bent on destroying "Christian civilization," the wonder is that he hesitated in immediately saying yes. Yet along with doubting his own ability, Polk admitted to Fanny that he was a little uneasy about the propriety of his mixing up warfare with his religious calling. But to this disquiet he had fortuitously discovered one helpful antidote in the person of Charles McIlvaine, his onetime beloved mentor. To Fanny he wrote: "I understand [the bishop of Ohio] said at Cleveland the other day he felt ready to shoulder his musket in defense of his cause. I see no reason why I might not shoulder mine in defense of a much holier cause."[39] His mind then about made up, Polk three days later disclosed to Stephen Elliott a little more of how, peaceable ordination vows notwithstanding, he had made ready to march off to war.

As he said in his letter on 22 June, he had

> just returned from a visit to old Father Meade [William Meade, bishop of Virginia]. We talked over everything connected with Church and State. He is right, wonderfully right, all the way 'round. I was delighted with him. He is a regular old Roman. He is down on . . . McIlvaine and all, and is quite ready to be Southern all through. He is keen for a down-right good fight, and wants the Yankees to feel the weight of our arm. He is for no half-way measures, and so was very refreshing.

> And what did Meade make of Polk's determination to accept the Confederate commission? "He says as a general rule he could [not] sanction it, but that all rules have exceptions, and taking all things into consideration . . . he could not condemn my course if I should accept the appointment." Apparently braced by Meade's quasiapproval (the decision, Polk said, he reserved for himself), "I have therefore told Davis that while I should be glad to be excused from the responsibility, still if he can find no one . . . better, I will not shrink from it, notwithstanding an unfeigned diffidence of my capacity to do it as it should be done. I hope . . . I shall have grace to do my duty."[40]

Jefferson Davis years later would slightly recast Polk's account of the visit with Meade. The president recalled Polk's telling him that "I wanted a view of the matter from [Meade's] standpoint," wondering if Meade thought the Episcopal Church was "likely to be injured by his connection with the army." Furthermore, Polk's characterization of Meade's bellicosity is strangely at odds with a sermon Meade preached just five days before Polk's visit. In the Day of Fasting observance, Bishop Meade rebuked churchmen North and South for shamefully fomenting the disunion. "It is sad to think how the mistakes of the most pious, in every age, have contributed to the wars which have desolated the earth," he had lectured.[41] Puzzling, too, is

Meade's letter to Polk a few weeks after their tête-à-tête. Meade is vague on just where he really stood. Polk's claims that Meade was "keen for a down-right good fight" and egged on Polk's combative intentions seem to overstate the matter. Rather, Meade wrote that reports in the Northern papers of his and Polk's meeting gave the impression that, to Polk's intentions "to engage in the war, I was not much opposed. This is . . . about the right conclusion," he says blandly.[42]

However the conversation with Meade had transpired, Polk was flattered by the Mississippi Valley delegation. Back in Richmond, he struck a more militant pose than his diffident-sounding letter to Elliott suggested. He announced to the president that, as "resistance to tyrants is duty to God," he believed he had a providential commission as well and was reporting for duty.[43] Davis's recollection of this conversation is no less picturesque. He remembered Polk speaking in Ciceronian Latin, saying he could accept the commission because of his *"amor pro aris et focis"*—his love for one's altars and hearths. Nothing in their interview impressed the president more than the "confidence manifested by this great and holy man that he had a sure correspondence with his God, and was treading in the path approved by Him." Davis, religiously attuned himself, had become equally sure that Polk's commission was approved from on high, and before awarding a battlefield command to a civilian with nothing more than classroom experience, Davis even decided to up Polk's rank from brigadier to major general. Tender feelings may have figured in the mix as well. As Davis would later declare, Polk was not only "my esteemed friend; but I will add . . . I loved him."[44]

13

"I Am Afraid of the Polkism of Your Nature" (1861)

During the days before his commission was signed by the War Department, the bishop was roaming about the Richmond capitol precincts, head to head with munitions-minded capitalists and government officials.[1] One of these officials was Albert Taylor Bledsoe, courted months earlier by Polk to teach at the University of the South; since then he had resigned from the faculty at the University of Virginia to become assistant to Secretary of War Leroy Walker. Sharing Bledsoe's new office was an observant clerk named John Beauchamp Jones. John Jones missed little (maybe nothing) that passed before his eyes, and he made a diary entry for every day of the Civil War. For June 21, 1861, he wrote: "A large, well-proportioned gentleman with florid complexion and intellectual face, who has been whispering with Col. Bledsoe several times during the last week, attracted my attention today. . . . Colonel B. informed me it was Bishop Polk." Possibly lifting an eyebrow, Jones penned an underlined entry: "He had just been appointed a major-general."[2] Yea, verily, a Northern church paper sneered a few days later: a "mitred major general."[3]

In fact, in one of his first press interviews, the new general sounded more like the old bishop. He was motivated to accept the commission, he told a Richmond reporter, by an even loftier ideal than the protection of Southern altars and hearths. That was the safeguarding of slavery. "We fight," he said, "for a race that has been by Divine Providence entrusted to our most sacred keeping." Among other newspapers saluting the appointee was Richmond's *Southern Illustrated News*. While conceding Polk was in his fifties when other such elderly men were fading away, a reporter decided the general's "elastic step and erect carriage would indicate he was still in the vigor of manhood." For its illustration the paper provided a woodcut apparently based on an oil portrait of Polk by James Reeves Stuart of South Carolina. Like children with paper dolls, engravers had variously removed the civilian jacket portrayed in Stuart's portrait and replaced it once with a bishop's surplice and stole, and as now with a military jacket collar showing stars, brass buttons, and epaulets.[4]

Right after the appointment, a dinner for General Polk and other friends was hosted by Jefferson and Varina Davis in the Executive Mansion. Davis proposed a toast, alluding to his and Leonidas's cadet days together, life coming full circle, et cetera, et cetera. Wine glasses were being lifted to "the new general," when a puzzled guest whispered to her neighbor, "What is it all about?" "The bishop, you know," she was told. "And as it dawned upon me [who the man was], I showed such a revulsion of feeling that Mrs. Davis sent me a scrap of paper with the words, 'Don't look so disapprobative.'" Margaret Sumner McLean, the daughter and the wife of military men, managed to recover her composure that afternoon and, over time, had a complete change of heart as the bishop-general "forever established his claims to my highest respect and admiration."[5]

Polk and Davis might believe that the pairing of bishop and general was a match made in heaven, but disbelievers other than Mrs. McLean expressed their doubts (as, of course, "old fogies of the red-tape school could be expected to do," suggested the *Memphis Appeal*).[6] The Confederate brigadier general Edward Porter Alexander—no old fogey—would shortly become a critic with credentials. After considering Polk's generalship at the Battle of Shiloh in Tennessee and the Battle of Chickamauga in Georgia, Alexander had his say: "Now the Lord had made [Leonidas Polk] a splendid bishop & a great & good man. So all our pious people, with one consent & with secret conviction that the Lord would surely favor a bishop, turned in and made him a lieutenant general, which the Lord had not."[7] More recently a biographer of Jefferson Davis has said the appointment was "easily Davis's worst and least explicable command decision of the year . . . , a foolish choice." That appraisal was just the kind of thing Stephen Elliott had promised Polk he could expect: "If you succeed, you will need no defenders; if you fail, such is the world, you will have a pack of curs at your heels."[8]

While remaining persuaded that he had acted justifiably in patriotic and religious duty, Polk soon realized that "many of my most judicious friends thought that in this I did an extreme thing," a concession he shortly made to his friend Sidney Johnston. These negative reactions soon caught up with him. Elliott informed him that among his Southern clergy there was "a general feeling . . . against what he had done."[9] A New Orleans priest, both a staunch secessionist and an affectionate friend (he had named a son Leonidas Polk Leacock), was expressing more than a general feeling when he wrote Polk to say "the whole cannonade of the North could not awaken me more. . . . I stood the fire because I had confidence in my leader [but] you have shaken me to the very core of my being." The writer, William T. Leacock, went on: "Now, I never was afraid of you before, but I am now because I know your propensities. . . . I am afraid of the Polkism of your nature." Leacock had known Polk for some thirty years, and Polkism was his delicate term for his bishop's tearaway tendencies.[10] As for dismayed clergy in the North, Bishop McIlvaine sounded far from being someone ready to "shoulder his musket," as Polk had heard him to be. McIlvaine instead told a friend, the Reverend Charles Wesley Andrews, "I deeply lament Bishop Polk's course. It has wounded the Gospel greatly." Andrews was a far more zealous secessionist than Ohio's Yankee bishop seemed to appreciate and certainly did not share McIlvaine's criticism. As youthful ministers, Andrews and Polk had been protégés of Virginia's two bishops. They now shared fury touching on the "North's making war upon the South," and hostility toward foreign-born soldiers in the Union's armies was pointedly evident in Andrews's sermons and in the official pronouncements Polk would soon be addressing to his nativist troops. So it was not so much the Gospel that had been wounded as Andrews's pride of authorship when he learned that a popular sermon he had preached to Virginia's Confederate soldiers was sometimes credited to the hand of General Polk.[11]

The Northern secular press, to no surprise, made sport of Polk's commission. *Harper's Weekly* was quick to publish a caricature of the "Right Reverend Major-General" in clerical vestments upon a rearing horse, waving a crozier while a scabbarded sword dangled from his waist. Elsewhere, a newsman posted to Virginia by the *Herald* of London told his readers that the "singular appointment of Bishop Polk . . . has been the subject of much comment and even of some merriment for several days past." It was a "strange circumstance," he thought, "savoring too much of the chivalric spirit of the Middle Ages, when the cowl of the priest was combined with the armor of the warrior." A colonel, a military professional in the Confederacy, joked to the journalist that with Polk now a general he himself might "apply for a chaplaincy in the Southern army."[12]

Obliged to shrug off criticism from whatever quarter and get on with his job, Major General Polk's first duty was to prevent any incursions by Federal ships and soldiers into the Confederacy's western borderlands and waterways south of Cairo, Illinois. He held authority over the brigadiers and other major generals already on duty in the Mississippi Valley.[13] Under the weight of his responsibility, Polk could take heart because the burden, as he understood it, was for the time being only. President Davis had promised that, as soon as it could be arranged, the command would go to Albert Sidney Johnston or some other experienced professional soldier not then available. Some months later, Polk had this understanding in mind as he sought to soothe John Fulton, his New Orleans protégé; like Leacock, he was another of the bishop's astonished friends. "I took the office only to fill a gap," Polk told him. And despite "unceasing toil and anxiety" while he "waited in vain for [a] man to take my post and let me return to my cherished work," he had tirelessly "labored as though I regarded my employment as permanent." Polk had come to think of himself, as he wished Fulton and others to do, as a minister tending to a parish while the congregation sought a permanent pastor. "I have always regarded myself as a *locum tenens*," Polk told Fulton, using clergy shoptalk for a temporary curacy.[14]

Short-term or long, Polk had his hands full from the moment he took over the Confederacy's newly devised Department No. 2, an expanse eventually to include portions of West Tennessee and northern Alabama, the Mississippi counties along the Mississippi River, all of Arkansas and Missouri, and the river parishes of northern Louisiana. Together it amounted to about a third of the Confederacy.[15] Polk was long accustomed to being dwarfed by the immensity of the territory and work assigned him; here he was back in a familiar area and among the people he had come to know during his crisscrossing travels as a missionary bishop. As a going-away present, Lucius presented his brother with a blanket of two homegrown sheepskins sewn together. All set to command, the novice general was now, at least in the view of Thomas Connelly, a knowledgeable historian, "the most dangerous man in the Army of Tennessee." (For balance, when John Frémont took command that July of Federal forces in Missouri, a Union general remarked that "Frémont's arrival in St. Louis was a national disaster.")[16]

Among his first official acts, Polk set about assembling a staff. An early aide he chose was Lt. William Orton Williams. Williams's father, George, was an 1824 West Point graduate killed in the War with Mexico, and young Orton was a US Cavalry officer before the Civil War. He was a near cousin of Mary Custis, Robert E. Lee's wife, and had recently been romantically involved with the Lees' daughter Agnes. Though Williams was later described by one acquaintance as being "ultra-military, spectacular and erratic," General Lee assured Mary Lee he fully approved Polk's choice: "I should have liked to have had him with me. . . . He could not have gotten [himself] a better man."[17] Polk's opting for this one aide soon proved problematical; within a few months of his appointment as aide-de-camp, Orton Williams showed himself not only ultra-military but also ultra-unbalanced. By then stationed in Columbus, Kentucky, which Polk's troops had lately occupied, Williams encountered a fledgling sentry whom Williams killed on the spot for the recruit's failure to salute him properly. Williams's written report explained: "For his ignorance, I pitied him; for his insolence, I forgave him; for his insubordination, I slew him." Unpunished but now a bit of a pariah, Williams subsequently transferred out of Polk's command, but not before gifting his boss a box of candy on September 9.[18]

The essential task next facing Polk was the composition of his official greeting to all the Tennessee and Mississippi soldiers now under his authority. The document he wrote was published as General Orders No. 1, issued from the Memphis Headquarters of Department No. 2. It was meant for his soldiers' ears, but a far wider audience, Polk knew, would be reached through the South's newspapers. Drafting his order, Polk began in the third person, tiptoeing into his subject: "In taking [charge of] the department assigned him, the general in command cannot forebear remarking that the war which has forced us into arms is not of our seeking. We have protested against it in the fair of mankind. We have been the parties assailed . . . for the assertion of our birthright." A few more sentences in, and he paused. His phrasing must have struck him as mealymouthed. As a military document, it had about as much bite as a bishop's year-end pastoral letter to a flock of Episcopalians.

Setting aside what he had written, Polk the soldier squared his shoulders, sat up straight, and commenced afresh: "The general in command is constrained to declare . . . that the war in which we are engaged . . . is indefensible and of unparalleled atrocity. We have protested, and do protest, that all we desire is to be let alone, to repose in quietness under our own vine and under our own fig tree [like biblical Jonah of old]." This was, indeed, a "merciless war" that, on the "shallow pretense of the restoration of the Union," had "no motive except lust or hate." He was striding now. It was a "war against heaven, as well as a war against earth," Polk continued vigorously. His own cause, "which has for its object nothing less than the security of civil liberty and the preservation of the purity of religious truth," was "the cause of Heaven." Polk's heaven, like Polk's South, was also comfortable with slavery.[19]

The righteous ill will expressed by the bishop-general was broadcast far and wide, all of it more grist for the mill of Yankee scorn. To a Unitarian editor in Boston, it was "to us of the quiet North very much like raving."[20] But for many Southerners his words were a benediction. A friend since boyhood wrote Polk to say his General Orders No. 1 reminded him of nothing so much as the sermon Peter the Hermit preached in 1096 to help ignite the First Crusade (not mentioning the inconvenient fact that Peter and his followers were crushed by the Muslims). A Memphis newspaper rejoiced that General Polk combined the likes of such biblical warrior-heroes as "Jephthah, Gideon, and David . . . marshaling his legions to fight the battle of the . . . Lord of Hosts!"[21]

His motivational speech now delivered, General Polk commenced his first military moves against the South's tormentors, among them some civilian Southerners he saw as treasonous. Living more than 300 miles from the Mississippi River Valley, these people in the mountains of East Tennessee, with few slaves among them, were mostly antisecession and anti-Confederacy. The only disunion many contemplated was how they might break away from the rest of Confederate Tennessee. More serious than these people's politics was the threat to an essential railroad providing Polk's army with a link to Richmond that ran through their homelands. The "Lincolnites," as they were being called, had begun to set fire to the wooden bridges owned by the Tennessee & Georgia and the East Tennessee & Virginia Railroads, and Polk had observed firsthand the discontent of the East Tennesseans. When returning in June from his commissioning in Richmond, his train passed through Knoxville and Chattanooga, and he later reported to Davis that he had "examined the case thoroughly." Enmity to the Confederacy was so pronounced that some citizens were letting it be known that an occupation of the region by Federal troops would be welcome. The New-York Times had lately been recommending the same thing.

Polk urged Davis to act first by ordering a Confederate occupation of the region with a force of soldiers under Brig. Gen. Felix Zollicoffer. A Tennessee newspaper owner before the war who had then held Unionist sentiments, Zollicoffer had been a delegate to the failed Peace Convention in Washington the previous February but became an avowed secessionist after Fort Sumter. Polk, feeling he fully understood the mountaineers' mind from his months of living among them while founding his university, surmised that their Unionist feelings could be effectively placated by putting Zollicoffer's iron fist in a velvet glove. To assist his "fraternal words and unfeigned kindness," Polk enlisted four civilian peace emissaries to try to coax the easterners into the Southern fold, and by late July Zollicoffer (with 6,000 troops behind him) had arrived in mountainous Bristol, exuding charm and waving an olive branch.[22] Though Polk may have hoped his right flank and his rail link with Richmond had been made secure by Zollicoffer's presence, Unionists soon proved him wrong, setting fire to five of the region's railroad bridges.

In his Memphis headquarters, Polk had other concerns to deal with. One was the harvesting of bat guano. With gunpowder already in "great want in the South" at that time, Polk dispatched two chemists to assay the deposits in the prolific guano caves of Arkansas, from which saltpeter, essential to gunpowder, could be extracted. Getting a favorable report, he recommended to Jefferson Davis "that these caves be taken possession of immediately, and worked on Government account." He estimated the powder could be produced at ten cents a pound by the government; private companies were charging twenty-five cents.[23] In the meantime he had supervised the setting up of an armory in Memphis to manufacture rifles. Being a bishop more used to giving orders than asking anyone's permission, he had proceeded on his own on this project, not bothering to consult state authorities in Nashville—except to bill Tennessee's Military and Financial Board for the armory's start-up expenses. That did not sit well in the capital city, moving board members to advise Polk to "suggest to your subalterns to be a little more respectful in their communications."[24]

When necessary, General Polk would work through channels. He did so with David Currin, a member of the Confederate Congress from Memphis. Obliging a Polk request, Currin in Richmond would shortly push through a $160,000 funding bill for the construction of two ironclad gunboats, the CSS *Arkansas* and the CSS *Tennessee*. Polk deemed the vessels essential to defend his base of operations from enemy gunboats on the Mississippi River. It became another ill-fated enterprise in which the inexperienced general did not succeed. That occurred after John T. Shirley, a Memphis shipbuilder, got the contract and set to work, hoping to be done by Christmas. He was immediately hindered by shortages of labor and materials. Polk provided only "six or eight men, when I wanted 100," Shirley testified later during a Navy Department investigation. "He persistently refused to detail any more."[25] Consequently, the boats were still on the ways in Tennessee in April 1862 when New Orleans fell to the Federals. Fearful that Yankee gunboats would now ascend the Mississippi to Memphis, Confederate authorities ordered the unfinished CSS *Arkansas* to be launched, towed, and hidden in Mississippi's swampy Yazoo River.[26]

Once East Tennessee's Tories were being watched over by Zollicoffer, Arkansas guano was being harvested by slave labor, and the Memphis gunboats were abuilding by Shirley, Polk could address himself to recruiting a large labor force to construct fortifications along the banks of the Mississippi River and to install underwater explosives in its channels. His idea, if not appealing to the self-interest of every citizen under his sway, was to have planters in the region volunteer their slaves. One planter defined the notion as "a most villainous call, one [Polk] has no right to make, & is the beginning of a despotism worse than any European monarchy."[27] Probably unfazed by such outbursts, Polk proceeded with lethal efficiency to get in touch with Commander Matthew Fontaine Maury, a friend and a budding torpedoes expert.[28] Now resigned from the United States Navy, Maury was tinkering in Richmond with experimental underwater barrels and boxes of gunpowder designed to obliterate ships and their crews; he had conducted miniature tests of the device in a washtub in his bedroom. Lt. Isaac N. Brown, a navy colleague, described Maury's Richmond experiments among "the many fine things preparing here for the enemy." Now Polk was in hopes that Maury could be attached to his western command. The secretary of war did not agree to this proposal, but by December 1861 Maury was able to send Polk thirty-one of his latest-model submarine batteries to be planted in the Mississippi flowing past Columbus, Kentucky; if time allowed, Maury promised to come in person to "see that everything is right in their planting."[29]

While strengthening the fortifications along his stretch of the river, Polk had also been maturing plans to invade Missouri and Kentucky. These two border states were neither Yankee nor Rebel in the summer of 1861, but if the Confederates could claim them Polk would gain important advantages for controlling traffic on the Mississippi. Kentucky, pending legislature elections on August 5, was claiming neutrality. Belligerents from neither side were welcome, at least officially. Left to its neutral self, Kentucky buffered Tennessee from invasion along its northern border—a buffer, someone reckoned, worth 50,000 Confederate riflemen strung out in a defensive line.[30] Biding his time, Polk learned on August 6 from an agitated civilian (a West Point graduate, as it happened) in Blandville, Kentucky, that the Union brigadier general Benjamin M. Prentiss had been heard predicting "to two of our citizens" that, once results from the elections were counted, the state's "neutrality would go up." Prentiss then reportedly said he "expected orders to occupy Kentucky" and would send "reconnoitering parties into Kentucky to watch the enemy in Tennessee." He further warned that, once his troops were in the state, people should "change to Union men or keep their mouths shut." Sure enough, the vote went solidly to the Unionist candidates—just the pretext Polk needed to make his own contemplated move into the state.[3]

Across the Mississippi River, the state of Missouri presented Polk with different headaches. Two contentious state governments were asserting their primacy, Missouri thereby being both half-in and half-out of the Union and the Confederacy. Skirmishes erupted between rival soldiers mobilizing in the state almost daily. Further, for Yankees intent on invading Confederate Arkansas to the south, the little village of New Madrid on Missouri's southeastern boot heel straddled a good road like an open door. Brig. Gen. William J. Hardee, one of the Confederacy's most eminent military minds and a Jefferson Davis favorite, sent word via an influential railroad president that Polk would do well to occupy New Madrid promptly. Hardee had allowed, too, that he would "like it very much" to serve under Polk's command, something that "would give great satisfaction" to his friends.[32] Polk was doubtless pleased to hear himself so admired by the renowned professional soldier.

Determined now to drive out the Union forces who had come into Missouri from the outside, Polk took stock of his resources. They did not augur success. One problem was the insufficient number of equipped soldiers he had been given in July. While there were probably enough to defend his assigned Mississippi Valley territory, and maybe enough to launch offensives into either Missouri or Kentucky, there were too few to manage all three simultaneously.[33] Polk's other marginal resource was his second in command, Brig. Gen. Gideon J. Pillow. The weeks ahead were to be a learning experience for Polk; his cheeky assistant, a retired officer from the War with Mexico, would serve as tutor.

Shortly after Polk took command of the Mississippi Valley defenses, Tennessee turned over to the Confederate government its Provisional Army and all its war matériel. That gave Polk more than $2 million worth of supplies, as well as some 22,000 troops. These soldiers had been recruited, organized, and commanded up to then by Pillow. The brigadier had been the Polks' former neighbor in Maury County, Tennessee, where he was a prosperous planter and had practiced law in Columbia with Polk's cousin, James K. Polk, the former US president.[34] Alas for Polk, who knew the man well, Pillow was like a comic officer in an opera, vain and ostentatious, puffed up with "officious zeal," and a "reckless egotist," as Polk would later say of him. Earlier that spring, a Polk kinsman had said that "I am dreadfully afraid that Genl. Pillow will have command of our [Tennessee] troops." Pillow did possess great patriotic energy, but his service in the War with Mexico had elicited scoffing reviews and the derision of fellow officers. A political cartoonist had depicted him as a "self-inflating Pillow."[35]

When secession had been looming, Governor Isham Harris of Tennessee had given Pillow, a major general in the militia, command of the state's mobilization. All spring and early summer of 1861 Pillow accordingly committed himself to building up his sizable army of volunteers to defend the western region of the state and its edge along the Mississippi River. He also nursed a posturing and politically unwise plan to invade neutral Kentucky.[36] Pillow was understandably indignant that, after handing his troops to Polk, the Confederate government reduced his rank from major general to brigadier. Nor were his feelings soothed by finding himself under the authority of a church minister recast as a genuine major general. Pillow was no parish priest submissive to episcopal authority but rather a battlefield veteran who, behind Polk's back, was calling him, not respectfully, "The Bishop." And being far less concerned than Polk over the disruptive Unionists in East Tennessee, he was irked when some of the manpower he had assembled for western operations was siphoned off to go there. All this combined to generate an animus between Pillow and Polk that compared well to their shared dislike of Yankees. Even so, Polk, with misguided goodwill, suggested to the War Department that Pillow's usefulness would be enhanced by his being restored to his previous rank. Jefferson Davis demurred, rightly supposing Pillow would misuse his rank to Polk's disadvantage.[37]

To the extent that they would ever be of one mind on anything, Polk and Pillow made common cause toward the end of July. With some reservations, Polk agreed with Pillow's "cherished plan" to invade southern Missouri after Confederates had established a riverbank foothold at New Madrid. The Federal troops in the state were undermanned and were led from St. Louis by John C. Frémont. Though famed as a wilderness explorer, Frémont was a maladroit administrator appointed to the command as a political favor. (Even less experienced than Polk in the role of a major general, he would be fired by President Lincoln a hundred days after he started.) Polk and Pillow, assisted as it were by Frémont's mistakes, were correct in guessing their invasion would scatter the Yankees and tilt the unruly citizenry firmly into the Southern camp.

Missouri's secessionist governor, Claiborne Jackson, visited Polk and Pillow in Memphis on July 22. He promised them that a formidable force of Missouri militia stood ready to welcome a force of Tennessee Confederates invading their state.[38] As the invasion was envisioned, the Tennesseans would be joined by Arkansas Confederates under William Hardee and Ben McCulloch, as well as the Missouri militia under M. Jeff Thompson and Missouri Confederates under Sterling Price. In a rampage north, the combined Rebel horde hoped to extinguish the political influence of Unionist sympathizers, disperse pockets of Yankee soldiers, and enlist would-be Rebels into their ranks. Success would be crowned by seizing St. Louis.[39] Once that was accomplished ("a blow paralyzing" the Yankees, Pillow assured Polk, "more than if Washington was captured"), the jubilant Confederates would sail down the Mississippi and force their way through the rear of Cairo, Illinois. This strategic town, bounded by the confluence of the twisting Mississippi and Ohio Rivers, would be teeming with unsuspecting Union soldiers intent on penetrating the Confederacy southward by water and land and unconcerned about their vulnerable rear. Cairo's capture, the Confederates reckoned, would surely put an end to any Federals' designs on Nashville to the east and Memphis to the south.[40]

Hastily, then, on Saturday, July 27, Polk ordered Pillow and 6,000 of his Tennesseans onto eight steamships and sent them across the Mississippi. Pillow found the flotilla "a beautiful sight," and the next day, to cheering crowds, his men occupied New Madrid. Because, like Polk, he was scornful of the immigrant Germans manning Missouri's US regiments, Pillow called his campaign a "Dutch hunt," and the jaunty dateline of his first telegram back to Polk read "Headquarters Army of Liberation."[41]

As for the ongoing success of the Missouri invasion, it would depend upon good intelligence, good communications, good cooperation, and good luck. In each and every one of these desirables, Polk and Pillow came up short. No sooner had Pillow set foot in Missouri than Polk learned that Governor Jackson had "greatly exaggerated" by as much as 50 percent the number of troops awaiting Pillow.[42] Added to that, the several commanders in Arkansas and Missouri of the Confederate and state militia units were not under Polk's control, and each was soon exercising his independence. Lacking that command authority, Polk became cautious lest Pillow push forward too fast, but he was equally concerned that a delay would imperil the campaign. While Polk was cheered that Confederate forces in Virginia had stunned a Federal army at the Battle of First Manassas (the Yankees took flight like "a covey of partridges," Jefferson Davis was heard to tell a crowd of well-wishers in Richmond), he feared that the beaten enemy might now prefer to pick its next fights in the Mississippi Valley. If so, they would "probably commence active operations in Missouri," he advised the War Department.[43]

Gideon Pillow was indifferent to Polk's edginess. He resented being stuck in New Madrid and wanted to advance rapidly toward Cape Girardeau and St. Louis, boasting, "I am in possession of the river."[44] In reply, Polk courteously reminded his brigadier that "my position here [in Memphis] makes it easier for me to know of the movements of the enemy than for you. We must, in some degree, shape our operations by his." Polk had learned, for example, that rising water in the Ohio River had allowed the Yankees to float three new gunboats over the falls near New Albany, Indiana. Farther downstream heavy armaments had then been added to the vessels, and they were now nearing Cairo. Understanding Frémont to be "a man of energy and enterprise," Polk concluded he would soon descend "the river in boats so as to attack our forts, that is, Island No. 10, Fort Pillow, and Fort Randolph." Though Pillow had scoffed at the likelihood of any of this happening, Polk ignored him and directed that "Lieutenant [Jonathan Hanby] Carter . . . place [a] chain across the river at the first moment he can be spared." It is not clear where Polk desired the chain installed as a means of entangling Yankee vessels descending the river, but within a month or so the chain, or one like it, had been draped on barges across the Mississippi from Columbus in Kentucky to the opposite bank in Missouri. Each link weighed 19 pounds, and a 16- by 14-foot anchor held the chain to the Kentucky soil. Polk proudly displayed the contrivance to Sidney Johnston when he paid a visit to Polk's headquarters.

Carter, a North Carolinian like Polk, was among the first graduates of the Naval Academy at Annapolis. At the outbreak of the war he resigned from the United States Navy, becoming an officer in the Confederate Navy. Polk took a liking to the man, and after the chain was in place he sent Carter to New Orleans to convert a civilian sidewheeler into a Confederate gunboat, another of Polk's marine experiments. Polk had bought this boat for eight thousand Confederate dollars, and when it was being reinvented by Carter from a "mere shell," the *Ed Howard* was rechristened the CSS *Polk*. A gunboat bristling with "six or seven guns," it steamed that December into Polk's military domain ready for battle, with Carter at the helm. All to the good—but too late. Carter was in time only to assist Polk in an unplanned troop evacuation from New Madrid.[45]

Though most of Polk's projects prospered and the bickering between him and Pillow was doubtless an entertainment to some, it was not so to a regimental physician in Polk's army named Lundsford Yandell Jr. As a Kentuckian who regarded the Union soldiers filtering into his state as "fiends incarnate," Yandell despaired to realize that "Genl. Polk keeps his own council and we do not know one day what we may do the next."[46] Sometimes Polk might not know either, as his intelligence tended to be catch-as-catch-can. Thomas Yeatman, a distant kinsman, wrote him from Louisville claiming "peculiar facilities for obtaining information on the Yankees' intentions in Missouri."[47] Whether his tips were helpful is not known, but on August 7, having learned from some source that the Ohio River was rising and that a sizable force of Frémont's Yankees was steaming down the Mississippi, Polk ordered Pillow to evacuate New Madrid at once and fall back to the three forts below. No flotilla arrived because most of Frémont's army was engaged in a losing battle against Ben McCulloch in southwestern Missouri, but Pillow's flight down the river had unwelcome consequences for Polk. William Hardee, left hanging without Pillow's support for an assault on Ironton, Missouri, complained to Jefferson Davis, and the president was soon scolding Polk. "Why was [New Madrid] occupied, and why was it abandoned?" he asked, framing a double indictment. "The occupation was probably an error, but abandonment, if the result of apprehension, was a more fatal mistake." Polk chose to brush off Davis's rebuke, and Polk's son, for his part, surgically excised the critical sentences from the Davis text when he wrote his father's biography.[48]

Polk was somewhat buoyed, at least, by Ben McCulloch's success at Wilson's Creek, Missouri, on August 10, an early Confederate victory comparable to First Manassas. With the Yankees now thrown for a loss in Missouri, Polk had Pillow swing his troop boats around and return to New Madrid. His new orders were to try again to unite with Hardee in northeastern Arkansas. The peevish Pillow countered that the plank road that led to Hardee was out of repair ("rotten" and "full of holes") and soon announced he would instead strike off for St. Louis on a road of his own choosing.[49] Before Pillow could get under way, Polk crossed the river himself, something he might well have done earlier. His resolve to take his deputy in hand wilted as Pillow and his staff officers persuaded him that the enemy's strength along their route to St. Louis and Cairo was negligible. Polk later admitted that it was only "with reluctance that he acceded to their views and sanctioned their plan."[50] Yet scarcely was Polk on his way back to his Memphis headquarters on the steamboat *Mohawk* when he was told that yet another Federal force, this time said to be 10,000 strong, was bearing down the Mississippi, with Pillow's army and Island No. 10 as its probable targets. Once again Polk commanded Pillow to return his army to Tennessee. Or, more precisely, he again politely asked Pillow to follow his orders. Given the faulty intelligence he had received earlier, Polk was perhaps losing his nerve to issue decrees. In a dispatch somewhere between an order and a plea, he huffed "I am clearly of the opinion that your duty is to cross the river into Tennessee with your whole command at once." Toward the end of the message, he entreated again: "My opinion therefore is, I repeat, that you cross the river forthwith."[51] At that point, Pillow evidently concluded from Polk's tone that in the contest between brigadier and bishop, the brigadier was now ascendant. His mind was made up to stay put in Missouri and to proceed to St. Louis. "For God's sake, don't hold me back!" Pillow blurted to his wavering commander.[52]

As though conspiring with Pillow against Polk, the rumored Yankees once more did not appear. Now sounding apologetic, Polk told Pillow that "in regard to compliance with [last night's] order, you are left to conform your action to the exigencies of the case."[53] Pillow must have decided he now had carte blanche. For a day or so later when Polk sent the Fourth Tennessee Infantry up the river to occupy Island No. 10 and the boat stopped at New Madrid en route, Pillow pulled rank on the officers on board. He ordered Col. R. P. Neely and his regiment to disembark and attach themselves to his own St. Louis invasion force. Maj. R. A. Stewart's battalion of artillery was also ordered off the boat. Dumbfounded, Colonel Neely sent Polk a plaintive note: What was he to do?[54] The answer, from Polk's headquarters to Pillow, directed that Neely and Stewart "will immediately repair to Island No. 10 . . . and remain there."[55] They did not. Pillow replied with insolence that were the impressed troops recalled it would "greatly imperil the forces already 40 miles from me. . . . If I am to be allowed no discretion, I certainly cannot but regard it unfortunate that I yielded to your wishes, and accepted a command my feelings so strongly prompted me to decline."[56] At that, Polk's slow-burning fuse set off his powder.

14

"I Beg Leave to Tender My Resignation" (1861)

Not having experienced such defiance while a bishop, Leonidas Polk maintained his dignity by communicating with his brigadier through his adjutant, Lewis DeRussy. As DeRussy rebuked Pillow, "[You] usurped an authority not properly your own, by which you have thwarted and embarrassed [the commander's] arrangements and operations for the defense." General Polk, he continued, "feels it his duty to submit the whole matter to the War Department."[1] Polk never followed up on this threat, having two days later been soothed by a pseudodiplomatic response from Pillow. Pillow in fact was meanwhile informing the War Department himself that the bishop's "varying views and countermanding orders, repeatedly made, [have been] crippling my operations."[2]

While Pillow and Polk tentatively began to cooperate with each other in their mission to rid Missouri of Yankees, Gen. John Frémont was considering how he might make the whole issue moot: he would split the Confederacy asunder and settle the war forthwith. As Frémont envisioned the near future, his Army of the Mississippi, an understrength and ill-equipped collection of soldiers in Cairo, Illinois, would sail down the Mississippi River, capture New Orleans, proceed eastward from there and encircle Dixie counterclockwise, marching triumphantly through the Carolinas and thence into Richmond. It was "the pipe dream of an amateur," as the Frémont biographer Andrew Rolle puts it.[3] All the same, Polk did not doubt that his and Pillow's hold on a fraction of western Missouri was increasingly tenuous. He had received "reliable information" from Col. Lloyd Tilghman of a pending attack on Pillow's stretched-out front and both flanks.[4] Toward the end of

August 1861 he and Pillow reached one of their rare accords and scaled back their campaign to a mere holding operation at New Madrid. Their truce notwithstanding, Samuel Tate, an exasperated Memphis business- man, had seen enough and was driven to write Congressman David Currin in Richmond that "our army matters here [in Tennessee] are in a terrible condition. . . . Polk and Pillow are at loggerheads, Polk giving a command and Pillow countermanding it by the same messenger." He pleaded that Currin "go to President Davis and Secretary Walker and insist upon their sending a practical military leader here." The only nice thing he had to say was that "Polk is a sensible gentleman, and will do well if he had proper co-operation."[5]

The sensible gentleman, however, at that exasperating period was look- ing beyond cooperation. Retirement was his apparent goal. Fed up with Pillow and brooding that he had taken "the office only to fill a gap," Polk wrote to Jefferson Davis on August 29 to say that if the defenses of the Mississippi Valley were "to be directed wisely, harmoniously and success- fully, they should be . . . placed under one head." He named again Albert Sidney Johnston, who "would give universal satisfaction" and who stood, in Polk's opinion, above Robert E. Lee. As Polk would have known, Johnston held command in San Francisco of the Pacific Department of the US Army, but he had resigned on April 10, posting his letter to Washington that day by Pony Express. Settling his pregnant wife, Eliza, and their children in a village just north of Los Angeles (the future city of Pasadena), he and thirty Southern sympathizers began a transcontinental trek by horseback across the California and Arizona deserts, avoiding along the way the Federal troopers who wanted to arrest him as well as Apache who might kill him. On the day Polk was commending him to Davis, Johnston was entraining to Richmond, where service in the Confederate Army awaited.[6]

In Davis's reply to Polk on September 2 the president made no mention of Johnston. Instead he wrote, "I regret to learn that you find an unwill- ingness to volunteer for the [duration of the] war." What prompted this remark? Published versions of Polk's August 29 letter contain no reference to resignation. Possibly Polk's "unwillingness" was passed on to Davis by an emissary, or perhaps Polk had said so himself in a dispatch now lost that he sent Davis two days later.[7] In any case, having expressed his regret, Davis hurried on in the letter to notify Polk that his overall authority was now expanded to include Arkansas and Missouri. By that stroke he was making the reluctant Polk "the single head . . . for the defense of Arkansas and the relief of Missouri."[8]

Apparently sure he could keep the restless amateur at his post, Davis, the more experienced soldier, did take the occasion to tutor him with a couple of command tips: (1) "Employ anyone who disturbs the harmony [he surely meant Pillow, about whom Polk must have complained] near to your headquarters, and under your more immediate supervision"; and (2) "Keep me better advised of your forces and purposes." It was then that Davis tacked on his displeasure with New Madrid's earlier "abandonment."[9]

Pillow's impertinence, Davis's second-guessing of his decisions, and the faulty intelligence with which he was routinely supplied were the irritants that came with Polk's job. He also had to deal almost as frequently with civilian distractions. Faintly remembered women, for example, on different occasions asked him to deliver personal letters to loved ones whose military whereabouts they supposed were within his purview. "You knew me as 'Miss Brockenbrough,'" a member of his 1832 parish in Richmond typically reminded him, enclosing a letter for her son-in-law, a Captain McIntosh.[10] After that, a Mrs. Stafford in Alabama hoped the bishop, after delivering her letter to her soldier son surrounded by the temptations of the camp, would "speak a kindly word" to the boy and "stimulate him to a pious and upright life."[11] Mrs. MacGregor of Louisville, for the sake of "auld lang syne," desired "Brigadier [sic] Genl. Polk" to recommend to the War Department her nephew, a recent graduate of medical school, as he needed a paying job as military surgeon.[12] S. B. Hawkins of Cowan, Tennessee, probably associated with the now-abandoned Sewanee university, wanted Polk to write him an introduction to Jefferson Davis—no reason given. Old Father Meade would be much obliged if Polk wrote him a letter "once a week about your movements and prospects." A few lines from the harried general would suffice, Meade assured him.[13]

Polk then heard from a clergyman who wrote seeking Polk's help in obtaining a parish ministry; his patriotic job as a Confederate army chaplain was paying too little.[14] A further touch of Polk's graciousness was to benefit another priest, an outspoken Unionist. He was James Edward Purdy, residing in the town of Washington in southwestern Arkansas. His parish, Grace Episcopal Church, was a nest of prayerful Confederates. When Purdy refused "peremptory orders" by his flock to lead prayers for President Jefferson Davis (a violation, he rightly deemed, of the Book of Common Prayer), he was expelled from his pastorate, arrested as a spy, and jailed in Memphis. It was his good fortune that the prisoner's father was Lucius M. Purdy, also a priest and one who had served under Bishop Polk in Louisiana in the 1840s, when the son would have been about eleven years old. After learning of the younger Purdy's predicament, Polk had him freed from jail and given a pass through military lines.[15]

After most of Pillow's "Army of Liberation" had returned, thwarted, to Tennessee at the end of August 1861, the bumptious brigadier was far from beaten. He was given free time, in fact, to pursue another of his cherished schemes: to bring neutral Kentucky into the Confederacy by an invasion. Since almost the beginning of the war, Pillow had dreamed of occupying Columbus, a railroad hamlet in northwestern Kentucky situated on a high bluff beside the Mississippi River. Properly furnished with artillery pieces, it would be a formidable deterrent to enemy boats attempting to ply the river southward. The fact that Kentucky had declared its neutrality meant little to Pillow, and after numerous secessionist citizens in Columbus invited him in June to occupy their town, Pillow promptly marched up from Tennessee to oblige. He thought better of the visit and reversed course when confronted in Columbus by a small military force led by Simon Bolivar Buckner, the inspector general of the Kentucky State Guard.

Pillow could be deterred—but not denied. With Polk now ranking over him, Pillow needed the approval of his commander to fulfill his Columbus ambitions.[16] The neutrality that Kentucky declared for itself at the outset of the war had no more constitutional standing in the United States than did secession, but North and South at first went along with the idea, desiring to win Kentuckians to their side by persuasion, not force. Pillow was dubious about the effectiveness of that strategy: he believed that the Confederates' physical possession of the border state was essential to "the ultimate safety of Tennessee from devastating invasion." Abraham Lincoln was no less possessive: he reportedly said that he hoped to have God on his side, but "I *have* to have Kentucky."[17]

While selling his Kentucky invasion schemes to Polk, Pillow had become charmingly convincing. He won Polk's assent after some of Frémont's troops—not yet on their way to Richmond—were seen prowling the banks of the Mississippi near Belmont, Missouri, a village opposite Columbus. Whereupon Pillow showed his taste for the theatrical and Polk his confidence in acting on his own authority as a bishop. Together, hand-in-hand, they proceeded with an incursion into Kentucky that was poison to the political instincts of both Jefferson Davis and the Tennessee governor Isham Harris. It was "a political blunder of the first order," the Pillow biographer Nathaniel Hughes has written, "that the subsequent onus of 'violation of neutrality' and 'invasion' stuck to Polk like tar." But the canny Polk would soon show that he was able to slough off even tar.[18]

The war for Polk was fast becoming a battle of wits as well as bullets. Months before the Confederates' incursion, Kentucky's claim of impartiality was cloaking a fiction. The pro-Union state government, recently elected, ignored the fact that loggers in state-owned forests were supplying timber for Federal gunboats. A Yankee vessel in August had even seized a steamer "employed in the rebel trade while it was tied up at Paducah on the northwest edge of the state." Elsewhere, Unionist recruits by the hundreds (maybe thousands, Polk thought) were drilling at Camp Dick Robinson in central Kentucky. To some ultra-Southerners, such accommodations to the enemy's interests in their border commonwealth were inflammatory. General Polk's Tennessee nephew, James Hilliard Polk, was one such. As a twenty-year-old Confederate cavalry officer posted to Kentucky in the winter of 1861–1862, he declaimed: "Oh, my hatred to Kentucky is bitter, and I wish this whole state were in one perfect mass of ruins. I want our men to burn every house in which a Union man nestles, and leave the owner to perish in a fiery death." Even for Kentuckians wearing Confederate gray, he had no liking: "[They] are treacherous scoundrels, and will betray us," he wrote to his sixteen-year-old sister, Sallie.[19] If without the homicidal vehemence of Jimmy Polk, General Polk was determined to counter the Federal brigadier general Prentiss should he make good his promise to send "reconnoitering parties into Kentucky to watch the enemy in Tennessee." Nor were Pillow and Polk wrong to suspect that the Yankees seen poking around Belmont across the Mississippi were poised to pounce on Kentucky soil at any minute. To keep an eye on the Federal troops, Polk established a regimental outpost called Camp Johnston on the river's Missouri bank. Frémont had by then notified his brigadier, Ulysses S. Grant, to be prepared to send troops into Columbus once Frémont gave the word.[20]

Frémont miscalculated his timing. On the night of September 3, even while Jefferson Davis was still sorting through the snarl Polk and Pillow had wrought in Missouri, and knew nothing of their current plans and plots, Pillow landed his Tennesseans at the riverbank town of Hickman, Kentucky. Next day, joined by other troops Polk had previously sent up from Union City in northwestern Tennessee, Pillow proceeded a little farther north to his Columbus destination, where the tracks of the Mobile & Ohio Railroad terminated, linking the place to much of the South. The town consisted of little more than a few brick buildings near the base of fortress-like river bluffs rearing above. Its citizens for the most part were secessionists so brazen that a Federal naval commander scouting the Mississippi had informed Frémont on September 2 that they were flying "the secession flag from the top of a lofty pole in the center of the village in defiance of our gunboats. What shall I do with Columbus?" The taunting flag was hoisted to welcome General Pillow's anticipated arrival.[21]

Polk was serene in his Union City headquarters, while reactions to Pillow's occupation of Columbus ranged from apoplexy in Richmond and Nashville to "astonishment" and consternation in Frankfort, the Kentucky capital. For some time previous, President Davis had been quite sick and out of touch with his refractory western commander, and his plea that Polk "keep me better advised of your forces and purposes" was a day late in reaching him. Still, had it arrived in a timely fashion, it is unlikely Polk would have complied differently. Thinking himself bound to take action, he told Fanny later that he had seen a "path of duty" stretching before him. "I could do nothing else than tread firmly in it"—a specific application, evidently, of his military mission's being divinely guided, as when he told Davis he "was treading in the path approved by [God]."[22]

When word of Polk's "forces and purposes" reached Nashville, Governor Isham Harris, who previously wanted to convince Kentuckians either to stay out of the war or, preferably, ally themselves with the Confederacy, now "hoped" Polk would order Pillow out of the state "instantly, unless [his] presence there is an absolute necessity." More insistently, Harris told Jefferson Davis of his dismay, saying the movement was "unfortunate" and "calculated to injure our cause in the State." General Polk blandly (but with seeming duplicity) replied to Harris that he himself had authorized the invasion "under the plenary powers delegated to me by the President" and that he did not concur with Harris's overwrought views.[23]

More precisely, it was with Polk's views that Davis did not concur. Writing directly on the telegram just received from Governor Harris, Davis at first directed his secretary of war to "telegraph promptly to Genl Polk to withdraw troops from Ky—& explain movement. Answer Gov. Harris, inform him of action and that movement was unauthorized."[24] These unequivocal directives were taken care of that same day.[25] Polk, still down in Union City, thought it not amiss to let the president in on his campaign in Kentucky. He so informed Davis by a lengthy justification, which he telegraphed on September 4.[26] The president was apparently calmed a little by Polk's reasoning and wavered in his earlier determination to respect Kentucky's neutrality. Again he wrote his reply to Polk directly on the incoming message: "Your Telegram Rec'd. The necessity must justify the action."[27] And that means? Was Davis saying that Polk's reasons for invading Kentucky *had better justify* the action he had taken? Or was he conceding that necessity *may have justified* the invasion? Polk decided the second construction suited his purposes just fine. In his thinking, at least, he had rearranged Davis's six cautionary words, modifying tense and deleting "must." Davis was now understood to be saying, "The necessity justifies the action." (This recasting of the telegram is what appears in *The War of the Rebellion: A Compilation of the Official*

Records of the Union and Confederate Armies. Unmentioned is that this is a doctored copy of the president's message, forwarded by Polk's staff to the Confederate War Department on September 11. Polk had "clarified" the original to his satisfaction.) Polk replied to the President with "great relief [as] the military necessity is fully verified and justified by [enemy] movements . . . on Paducah [Kentucky]."[28] To bolster himself further, Polk wired the Kentucky governor, Beriah Magoffin, on September 8, tweaking tenses and baldly dissembling by assuring him "the President of the Confederate States [has said] 'the necessity justified the action.'"[29]

As Polk now made ready to join Pillow in Columbus, Grant in southern Illinois was in the process of launching a countermeasure. Charles de Arnaud, a Yankee spy, had just reached Grant after being caught snooping, and shot at, by sentries at Polk's Union City headquarters. Though "desperately wounded and neglecting all medical attention while [riding] night and day to reach Cairo," de Arnaud alerted Grant between pants that Pillow's Confederates had occupied Columbus and were marching toward Paducah.[30] Grant immediately loaded a quantity of Illinois soldiers onto steamboats and headed forty-five miles upstream to Paducah at the confluence of the Ohio and Tennessee Rivers. Grant's reaction would seem to scupper Polk's assertion to President Davis that Yankee movements on Paducah were already under way when Pillow reached Columbus.[31]

To both sides, little Paducah loomed large. Not only was it at the confluence of two major rivers; it was also only fifteen miles west of Smithland, Kentucky, where the Ohio River met the Cumberland River. The town thus resembled a tollgate athwart the water highways that led into the heart of the western Confederacy. As Grant's boats pounded up the Ohio, the few Confederates resident in the town departed on an early-morning train (keeping the train in the bargain), and the Federal soldiers soon scrambled into Paducah without firing a shot. Grant later learned that 3,800 Confederates had meanwhile been marching over from Columbus, but they turned around on hearing that Paducah was overrun with Yankees.[32] The taking of Paducah had been played out like a gentlemanly game of chess: Knight's C3, say, to Bishop's D5.

Polk's cadet son, by then a lieutenant in his father's forces, would write later that Polk was greatly upset by the loss of Paducah, irritated at himself, perhaps—or more likely at Pillow, who had been on the scene. Certainly at Grant, who capped his success by having his engineers string together coal barges to create, in less than three weeks, a floating bridge crossing the Ohio from Paducah to the opposite shore in Illinois. At almost a mile, it was the longest such bridge then in world history.[33] One can easily imagine

Polk's upset turning to fury had he known that Grant was aware of the number of infantry regiments, siege guns, field artillery batteries, and battalions of cavalry that the Confederates had assembled in Columbus and that he got his "information from an official of Maj. Genl. Polk, brigading this command." Who his informant was Grant did not say, but among other intelligence tidbits he provided was a copy of Polk's "General Orders, No. 19," in which his Columbus field brigades were nicely detailed.[34] Spared this chagrin Polk, arriving in Columbus on Saturday, September 6, would shortly receive Capt. Orton Williams's welcoming box of candy.[35]

Whoever composed President Davis's September 5 telegram proved both nimble and prescient. Davis was shortly calling criticism of his friend Polk "stupid censure," and by September 13, even as the Unionist state government of Kentucky continued to demand the "ordering off of Confederate troops," Davis was adjusting his earlier demands and agreeably meeting his raw commander halfway. "Your occupation of Columbus being necessary as a defensive measure," he wired him, "will of course be limited by the existence of such necessity."[36] It may be supposed that mordant comments concerning Polk and Kentucky were soon to be heard along War Department hallways in Richmond. That suggests why, when Secretary of War Leroy Walker resigned his post in mid-September, someone in the administration suggested that the loose cannon out west might be just the man to replace him: it would hawser him to a cabinet desk. Though at least one newspaper reported the proposed appointment, nothing came of it. Polk's known correspondence makes no mention of such an appointment.[37]

A more speculative version regarding Polk's future has it that he was considered for still another cabinet seat: secretary of state. It is related by William G. Stevenson, a youthful New Yorker working in Arkansas in the spring of 1861. On threat of being hanged as a Unionist by a vigilance committee, he was coerced into "volunteering" for Knox Walker's 2nd Regiment, Tennessee Infantry, under General Polk's command. Escaping later to his Northern home, Stevenson would shortly compose an entertaining account of his infantry and cavalry duty, which he published as *Thirteen Months in the Rebel Army*. Stevenson had served as a sergeant under Polk and included in his book a description of his commanding officer. "Major-general Leonidas Polk is a tall, well-built man," Stevenson wrote in the summer of 1862, "about fifty-five years of age; hair slightly grey; wears side whiskers, which are as white as snow, aquiline nose, and firm mouth. His voice is a good one for command." Stevenson felt bound to tell his readers that he had sometimes heard "the militant bishop and general criticized." He wrote that Polk's "having a West Point education,

. . . it was expected he would make a skillful general; but the people were much disappointed by his display of generalship in the Western Department, and many clamored for his removal. It was at one time thought he would be called to the Confederate cabinet as Secretary of State; but this was never done." Furthermore, as one who evidently avoided coarse talk himself and the company of those who used it, Stevenson went on to say that "many of [Polk's] old friends and admirers were pained to hear the report circulated that the good bishop indulged in profanity when he got too deep in his potations; and as these are in part confirmed, his reputation suffered greatly."[38]

Alleging that "many clamored" for Polk's removal in the fall of 1861 is perhaps an exaggeration on William Stevenson's part, yet despite Davis's brushing off Polk's stated unwillingness to continue through the duration of the war, the bishop had not given up his idea of resigning. And when he heard from Davis on September 13 that "General A.S. Johnson is en route to join you," Polk's spirits soared. As he shortly informed Fanny, "Genl Johnston has (to my very great relief) taken command . . . in the Miss. Valley."[39] To Davis's relief, too. Sidney Johnston accepted a full general's commission and took responsibility for a newly defined Department Number Two, now an immense area embracing seven states stretching from the mountains of Appalachia to the plains of the Indian territories, an expanse many times larger than Polk's original command. Even before urging Davis in August to give Johnston a command, Polk had privately urged him to leave California and come to the aid of the Confederacy and—as irony would have it—had ably assisted Johnston's high-level assignment by his own faulty management precipitating the political hubbub in Kentucky.[40] As the Kentucky dissension worsened, with Federal troops flooding into the upper half of the state and the state government rejecting secession, Davis could see that his expansion of Polk's authority to include Missouri and Arkansas was not the solution. Militarily, the bishop appeared to critics to be in over his head, putting the vulnerable heart of the Confederacy increasingly at risk. Polk's own instinct was right: Sidney Johnston, a native Kentuckian like Davis, was indeed situated to "give universal satisfaction" as overall commander of the western Confederacy.

While hoping and waiting for his replacement, Polk had not been idle. He worked dutifully, "as though I regarded my employment as permanent." Throughout September and October he transformed Columbus into what enthusiasts were terming the "Gibraltar of the West"; it bristled with guns on the Mississippi's bluffs and was ringed by earthworks on its rearward land approaches to the east. Defending himself at the same time, he attempted to mollify Kentucky's legislature, providing, he thought, "abundant justification" for having invaded the state. The day after Polk's writing that, the government in Richmond "admitted [Kentucky] into the Confederacy"—or, more exactly, admitted secessionist Kentuckians.[41] The state senate was having none of it. Weeks before, the Kentucky legislature had dropped all pretense of neutrality and aligned itself officially with the United States.[42]

To General Polk's immense displeasure, Grant's hold on Paducah and Smithland, along with his monumental floating bridge to Illinois, had rendered Confederate Columbus of limited military value. Unless defenses were quickly constructed on the Tennessee and Cumberland Rivers, the Yankees could easily penetrate the South's western midsection. And there were still those Yankees running loose in Missouri and eyeing Columbus from across the Mississippi. A further irritant included the Federal gunboats on the Mississippi that came steaming by from time to time to "throw shells" at General Polk's men constructing gun emplacements. Not in the least irritated, however, was the artillery captain Marshall T. Polk, the general's young cousin from Tennessee. Like a boy at play in war games, he found one such visit by the Yankee navy exhilarating: "Two Lincoln gunboats [were] blazing away with shot and shell and our big dogs [were] belching forth a surly defiance whilst our light rifled cannon rattled away like bells. . . . I never felt so [stirred] in all my life. The smell of the powder seemed to act like magic, and with the energetic commands of Gen. Polk, excited me so that I was actually wild and just shouted."[43]

Davis's advice to Polk to keep Pillow close was paying off. Though Polk had scarcely any time to write to his family waiting for word in Memphis, in the cheerful letter he at last got off after his first week in Columbus he had some mildly encouraging news regarding the brigadier. "I find I get on better with our neighbor when I am near to him, than when I am remote," he told Fanny. "Things are getting along in a way which is satisfactory enough, at least as much so as, in the nature of the man himself, is possible." Polk's slave attendant Atkinson, Fanny would also be happy to hear, was proving a great comfort to his master, and their son Hamilton would soon be brought up from Memphis as a first lieutenant to join his father in the artillery. He signed off sending "bushels of love."[44]

That same day, General Johnston, attended by his staff, arrived in Columbus. Polk first led his friend on a welcoming walk around the fortress he was building. He assured his new commander that he had a choke hold on navigation down the Mississippi River, one enhanced (until the current would carry it off) by Lt. Jonathan Carter's mile-long chain strung across it.

The two later confided personal matters. Polk is known to have unburdened himself by bringing up the criticisms that newspaper editors and politicians were leveling about his generalship in Missouri and Kentucky. What he may have known or suspected of army talk behind his back is not recorded, but that, too, was nonetheless going on. An infantry major and his circle were suddenly "delighted at being under [Johnston]," as Edward George Washington Butler Jr., informed his mother, a Louisiana sugar-plantation mistress well known from prewar days to the Polk family. "I see Generals Polk and Pillow from time to time," Butler continued candidly. "They are very polite and kind to me always. The army has no confidence in neither of them."[45]

That evening Johnston listened to and consoled his former roommate. "Never mind, old friend" he said. "I understand and appreciate what you have done, and will see that you are supported." Good as his word, Johnston, before leaving, enlarged Polk's command, giving him subordinate command of the western portions of Kentucky and Tennessee, the region now designated the First Division of Department Number Two. Johnston remained in Columbus for three weeks. During his stay a Yankee gunboat came down from Cairo to lob a few harmless shells at the Rebels' fort. Johnston expressed no concern. Further, one observer noticed, discipline and orderliness of the camp improved considerably during his stay—the result, no doubt, of his prodding Polk's more lackadaisical subordinates. Johnston then left for Bowling Green in central Kentucky, where he had established his headquarters.[46]

Johnston's first job was to protect Nashville, the principal industrial center of the South, as well as the rest of the Southern states below that city. It had become a daunting assignment with the buffer of Kentucky now nullified. He had neither adequate troops nor weapons to equip them; all he could do was to stretch an exposed, thinly manned, 500-mile defensive line in zig-zags across the breadth of Kentucky, dipping here and there into Tennessee. His center at Bowling Green was held by 4,000 troops under Simon Buckner, now turned Confederate brigadier. Polk in Columbus anchored the left wing with 11,000 troops; Brig. Gen. Felix Zollioffer anchored the right wing at Cumberland Gap with 4,000 men. Most worrisome to Johnston were the two incomplete fortifications he had inherited on the Cumberland and Tennessee Rivers, waterways that offered the North easy avenues into the Confederacy's vitals. Begun in the spring of 1861 when Kentucky's impartial stance was still under observation by the South, Fort Donelson and Fort Henry were hastily situated in Tennessee some ten miles south of the Kentucky state line. Confederate engineers would shortly regard the chosen sites as far from ideal. The forts stood where the Cumberland and Tennessee Rivers flowed parallel to one another, and like bookends eleven miles apart on the neck of land between the two rivers, they had their rears to each other. Their fronts—one facing east, one west—overlooked their respective rivers. Not initially under Polk's administration (he was preoccupied with invading Missouri and fortifying defensive sites along the Mississippi), the forts' early construction by slave labor had proceeded sluggishly. Johnston now gave Polk the responsibility of seeing to their speedy completion. That task accomplished, Polk then had to tell Johnston that the forts were garrisoned by too few infantrymen and too few experienced artillerists. What's more, heavy ordnance was in short supply and difficult to obtain from the Confederate government.[47]

By now Grant had occupied northern Kentucky, and enemy encroachments into Tennessee from both Paducah and Smithland were not only possible but likely. Federal troops had established a foothold in eastern Kentucky too, a good stage by which to enter the Unionist stronghold of East Tennessee. Should the Federal forces on either wing break through Johnston's defensive line, he would then have the enemy behind him. As at Columbus, gunboats were already taking potshots at Fort Henry before scooting off, but while Polk's gunners might have fired back, the chagrined commander forbade them to do so for fear of revealing the inadequate range of his best thirty-two-pounder guns.[48] Not noticeably downhearted by the shortages and inadequacies in his command, Polk was telling Fanny at that time of his grandiose intentions to carry the war beyond Kentucky and into the Yankee homelands, his resignation shelved.[49]

Polk's visionary thrusts northward would have to wait, though, while soldiers assisted by slaves supplied by planters slowly and ineptly built up the Mississippi River forts also under his command. For example, Asa Gray, Polk's topographical engineer, was ordered to design earthworks and install gun batteries on Island No. 10, a mile-long strip of sand that lurked like a half-submerged crocodile in the middle of the Mississippi. After asking nearby planters to provide 500 slaves for two weeks of construction work, Gray at one point had only sixty, and among them the slaves had only twenty shovels.[50] Gray diplomatically stated the case to his inattentive general: "The multiplicity of matters surrounding you at Columbus has caused [the imperative to fortify Island No. 10] to become of much less consideration than it really deserves."[51] Construction of the river forts in Tennessee was similarly behind schedule, but Lt. Col. William Mackall, Johnston's plainspoken chief of staff, did not beat around the bush the way Asa Gray was apt to do. "General Johnston directs you to hasten the armament of the works at Fort Donelson," he wrote Polk, "and reminds you that Island No. 10 should be occupied by at least a regiment."[52]

Now separated from wife and daughters, Polk urged his homeless family to rent a house in Nashville, a city he was fond of and half of which, by Johnston's realignment, now fell under Polk's military jurisdiction. In the wartime city, "hired" houses (as Polk termed rentals) were in short supply, but a search was ably handled by Russell Houston, a Tennessee attorney related to the Polks by marriage (the brother-in-law of President James K. Polk). When a suitable dwelling became available, Houston won out over four or five other applicants. The Polks' household goods left behind in New Orleans, as well as a young slave named Betsy, were immediately brought up by train, the little girl arriving with an "Adams Express" label pinned to her cape. The general was pleased with the overall arrangement, but he urged Fanny to run a strict household economy. Her three soldier menfolks—himself, Hamilton, and Meck—had combined annual salaries of $7,560, he told her, and this was sufficient, he hoped, for the family's needs. Sending her $1,000, he said, "We must put everything on a war footing and cut down on expenses. . . . This being done, you will live happily and feel that you are doing your duty in that state of life in which it has pleased God to place you," his consolation a nostrum from his prayer book. Even in nearby Nashville, Fanny's separation from her husband was an ongoing torment to him. "I should like exceedingly to see you," he wrote. "I hardly ever wanted to see you so bad, but all in good time." He would have had in mind the very thing to bring about the reunion: his hoped-for resignation.[53]

In the next few weeks, with Fanny settled safely and armed conflict in his district having subsided for the moment, General Polk displayed the kind of boldness that had prompted his invasion of Kentucky. He advised the secretary of the navy that he had been shopping for steamboats to be "speedily converted into armed gunboats," vessels that would be "indispensable to our defenses." Finding three that suited, he submitted to the secretary a bill for $44,000 to close the deal. Among his purchases (for about $12,000) was the sleek 280-foot *C. E. Hillman*, renamed CSS *Eastport*.[54] He needed weapons for his regiments, too. He told Davis that "in view of the very slow progress made in obtaining them from our own manufacturers," he had decided to supply his wants in Havana, Cuba. He was willing to assume full responsibility, provided the president approved, and had already "made an arrangement with gentlemen . . . for buying arms and bringing them into the country" by blockade runners. He had efficiently arranged, as well, to borrow the money to carry out the enterprise, to be refunded at the pleasure of the government. He sent his aide-de-camp, Lt. William

B. Richmond, to the capital bearing the proposal. He could answer any questions Davis might have.[55] The president must have found Polk's self-starting endeavors heartening.

Not everyone did. Doubtless taking pleasure in his various new schemes, Polk had added to them an idea to detach certain regiments of his to bolster Gen. Jeff Thompson's renegade partisans, who were stirring up trouble in Missouri. This triggered another criticism of his performance written by Johnston's adjutant, William Mackall; its bluntness was not what the bishop of Louisiana was accustomed to. "I am instructed by [General Johnston] to advise you that your force is not now, nor in his calculation likely to be, more than sufficient to do the work assigned you," Mackall telegraphed. "Furthermore, to swell [Thompson's] ranks by detachments from your command . . . would destroy its character and not increase its usefulness." A West Pointer, Mackall was an experienced soldier from the War with Mexico and had been Johnston's adjutant in California; his imperious tone would have grated on Polk. On the same day, Polk sent his own counsel to Johnston. He begged leave to advise the general that the building and management of Forts Henry and Donelson would be better served by someone other than himself, that is to say, someone of "large experience and military efficiency." Polk nominated Lloyd Tilghman.[56] A civilian railroad engineer recently made a brigadier general (he had graduated from West Point twenty-five years before), Tilghman would rue the day that he had caught the eye of his endorser.

There soon followed yet another affront to General Polk's self-estimation. Though Johnston had just said that he thought Polk's Columbus garrison was barely "sufficient to do the work assigned you," he ordered Polk four days later to detach 5,000 soldiers (about a third of his strength) and send them with Pillow to Clarksville, Tennessee. Here they were to apply a patch to one of the weaker points in the Confederate's strung-out defensive line. No mention was made of the previous countermand with respect to Jeff Thompson. Grudgingly Polk began to comply, but he did not shrink from informing his superior directly that he and his staff thought depleting the garrison was a mistake on several grounds, most especially "the large [enemy] force now being concentrated in our front." Protection of his flank, were the garrison reduced, he deemed "impossible." Polk's complaint was carried to Sidney Johnston by Pillow and was "duly considered by the general," Mackall coolly assured him. Mackall closed by saying that Columbus was to follow the original order as received.[57] Polk was within rights to grit his teeth.

By the next day these chain-of-command aggravations were on his mind as he sat composing one more important letter. It was addressed to the president, and again Polk would have it delivered by courier, this time by his son Hamilton. The note reiterated his desire to resign from the army. While it remains unclear how Davis back in September had learned of Polk's "unwillingness to stay the course of the war," this new message was in black and white: both a draft of Polk's letter and a published official version survive. In his draft, from which the finished letter varies but little, Polk begins by reminding the president of his hesitancy the previous June to accept the commission in the first place. But because of Davis's "difficulty in finding a commander [to whom] to entrust the department," and because of his own "conviction 'that resistance to tyrants is duty to God,'" Polk had agreed to turn "aside from employments far more congenial to my feelings and tastes." Now, having devoted himself with "untiring constancy" for four months, the unhappy man hoped he might be allowed to resume his former pursuits: "I beg leave, therefore, to tender to you my resignation of my office of major general of the Provisional Army of the Confederate States." Circumstances for his resignation were propitious, too, he said. The department was in the trusted hands of "our mutual friend, General Johnston," and the fortifications at Columbus, "this very important point," were nearly complete.[58]

The centerpiece, high on a bluff at Columbus, was the fort's outsized rifled cannon. With a barrel ten feet long and a breech "almost the size of a flour barrel," as an admirer noted, it could hurl a 128-pound conical projectile three miles. Someone had named the monster the "Lady Polk."[59] Satisfied that he had framed his argument persuasively, Polk intended to dispatch it the following day, November 7. But just a few miles north, up the river in Cairo, Ulysses S. Grant had been drafting a document of his own, marshaling 3,000 of his troops for a surprise attack on the regiment Polk had assigned to surveillance duty around Belmont, Missouri, across the river from his Columbus headquarters.[60] Now about to be confronted by this emergency, Polk's efforts to cast off his uniform and return to "former pursuits" attired in cassock, surplice, and preaching scarf would again clearly have to wait.

Bishop Polk, recently consecrated, was painted in 1841, probably in New Orleans, by George Esten Cooke, an itinerant artist favored by the Polk family. (Courtesy of University Archives and Special Collections, The University of the South)

Clean-shaven before the war, Polk as a Confederate general was described as "bearded like the pard" (or panther) by a military admirer familiar with Shakespeare's As You Like It. *(Courtesy of University Archives and Special Collections, The University of the South)*

A Genealogical Tree of the Polk Family, *artist unknown, shows Leonidas Polk's branch on the middle-right side of the tree. The drawing is dated circa 1849. A photostatic reproduction was made by the Huntington Library in San Marino, California, from a copy owned by a Mrs. F. P. Walkup.*

July 27, 1861.] HARPER'S WEEKLY. 467

It would be a solemn vindication of the power of the Government. It would be an earnest to the world that it meant to maintain itself; and to loyal citizens that it meant to restore its authority and protect their rights.

We all owe it to ourselves and to the rebels to show that we mean the supremacy of the Government and the punishment of all who lead the fight against it in the same way that, when the laws are broken by a riot, the Government proceeds against the ringleaders.

If this were a war with a foreign nation, when soldiers were taken prisoners they would be shipped home again and the officers retained upon parole, and exchanged as opportunity offered. But we can not ship our prisoners out of the country; and we certainly do not want to be perpetually fighting the same men. Therefore, to deal with their leaders as they shall be found to merit will dishearten and weaken the men.

RETALIATION.

If the Government punishes traitors—if it hangs pirates, for instance, will not the rebels retaliate?

Very possibly: and what then? Which is best, that every man who takes up a musket or ships upon a privateer to shoot and rob honest American citizens shall know that he does so at his extremest peril, or that it is a game in which if he be caught he will be let go again?

A Government that fears retaliation is not sure of itself. When Washington was personally entreated by André, not to spare his life, but to mitigate his sentence, the Commander-in-Chief was deeply pained by the sad necessity of refusal; but his duty to a people was stronger than his pity for a single man, and he exacted the utmost penalty.

Did he do wrong? Did he not endanger the lives of American prisoners in the enemy's hands? Did he not court retaliation? At this day we all sigh over the tragedy of André—but do we blame Washington? Do we not know that to have done otherwise than he did would have been a betrayal of the cause confided to him? Do we not know, as he did, that sharp severity is often the tenderest mercy?

LIEUTENANT-GENERAL.

A friend at the West writes to know why General Scott, who was a Major-General forty years ago, is supposed to be advanced in rank by the title Lieutenant-General?

A wiser friend in the East replies that the rank of Major-General is one of the regular grades of army promotion; but the Lieutenant-Generalcy is a rank of honor especially created by Act of Congress for General Scott.

HUMORS OF THE DAY.

IRISH FERTILITY IN EXCUSE MAKING.

An Englishman, traveling in Ireland, remarked to the driver of a coach upon the tremendous length of the Irish miles.

"Confound your Irish miles! Why, there's no end to them!"

"Sure, Sir," said the coachman, "the roads are bad about here, and so we give good measure."

A Pretty Home Truth.—Man may be the Head of the Family; but, far better than that, Woman is the Heart of it.

A shoemaker was taken up for bigamy and brought before the sitting magistrate. "Which wife," asked a bystander, "will he be obliged to take?" Brown, always ready at a joke, replied, "He is a cobbler, and of course must stick to his *last*."

When Louis XIII. passed through the little town of Languedoc, the mayor and the consuls were very much embarrassed about his reception. They consulted a butcher of the place, who was reckoned a very Solomon. The fellow, proud of being sought after, offered his services to introduce them to the king, and performed his duty by saying, "Sire, as I am a butcher by trade, I bring you a few of my beasts." The mayor and the consuls then made a low bow, and the ceremony ended to the general satisfaction of all.

A WONDERFUL MAN.

A Turin letter, describing the new Italian Minister, declares *inter alia*—

"M. Ricasoli never feels fatigue. Four hours' sleep, a piece of bread and butter, and a glass of water, are sufficient to supply his daily wants. He has no court, but he displays a greater haughtiness than Louis the Fourteenth. Rarely is he seen to laugh. He is generous, but is feared. His peasants tremble at his approach, yet he has made them rich and comfortable. Never was a character more strongly marked."

This is quite exact as far as it goes, but it is incomplete. We are glad to be able to finish the description from an equally accurate source:

"For his appearance—M. Ricasoli is seven feet high, but has the delicate feet and hands of a child of four years old. His hair is snow-white, his eyebrows, whiskers, mustache, and beard of the jettiest black.

"For his temperament—it is bilio-sanguineo-lymphatico-nervous. He will weep over the pages of Manzoni, but did not shed a tear when his mother died.

"For his habits—he hates pomp and form, but never goes out without four running footmen, and insists upon being served upon the knee.

"With an annual income equivalent to £10,000 19*s.* 4*d.* in English money, his personal expenditure amounts to 1¼ pauls (5½*d.* English) daily. He is at once silent and loquacious, amiable and sulky, impetuous and cold-blooded, tall and short, young and old—in one word, he is exactly the man whom clever correspondents delight to paint, but whom nobody ever met with."

It will be interesting to lovers to know exactly the difference between a kiss and a treading on the toe—as to the time each demonstration takes, that is to say, in making the lady aware of it. Science has lately decided that the nervous sensation travels one hundred and ninety-five feet in a second, and that a touch on the cheek, therefore, is communicated to the brain one-thirtieth of a second sooner than the pressure on the toe.

A man in Kentucky killed a cow a few days since, in whose stomach was found a large brass pin, a hair pin, and a quantity of hooks and eyes. It is inferred that the old cow swallowed the milk-maid.

"Is this your house and home?" asked a traveler of a farmer as he saw him boarding up a pig-sty. "No," replied the farmer. "I'm only *boarding* here."

"How much can you pay us?—what can you offer in the pound?" demanded the creditors of a bankrupt farmer. "Alas! gentlemen, all I really have is a donkey in the pound," replied the ruined agriculturist.

"I'll let you know when I come again," as the rheumatism said to the leg.

"Well, Patrick," asked the doctor, "how do you feel to-day?" "Och, doctor, dear, I enjoy very poor health intirely. This rumatics is very distressin' indade; when I go to sleep I lay awake all night, and my toes is swilled as large as a goose hen's eggs, so whin I stand up I fall down immediately."

A man down East has invented yellow spectacles for making lard look like butter. They are a great saving of expense if worn while eating.

An emigrant to Port Natal, writing home to one of his friends, says, "We are getting on finely here, and have already laid the foundation of a larger jail."

An empty bottle must certainly be a very dangerous thing, if we may judge from the fact that many a man has been found dead with one at his side.

"Very good, but rather too pointed," as the fish said when it swallowed the bait.

Why is a fool in high station like a man in a balloon?—Because every body appears little to him, and he appears little to every body.

The following is a true copy of a letter received by a village schoolmaster: "Sur, as you are a man of noledge, I intend to inter my son in your skull."

Water isn't a fashionable beverage for drinking your friend's health, but it is a capital one for drinking your own.

The man who "challenged contradiction" got into an awful fight, and was severely beaten.

A man, whose son ran away for "parts unknown," advertised him in the papers, describing him as "red-haired, blue-eyed, and having a turned-up nose." One evening, while the anxious father was, as usual, inquiring of every one he saw concerning his runaway son, a wag, who was standing by exclaimed,

"I'm positive your son will turn up soon, my man."

"Have you seen him, my friend?" asked the father, grasping the other by the hand.

"You say his nose turned up, don't you?"

"Yes, yes; but have you seen him?"

"No, I haven't; but if his nose turned up, he'll turn up too; for every one must follow his nose, you know."

The father groaned at this poking fun at misery.

Fancy Sketch of Right Reverend Major-General Bishop Polk heading his "Division."

DOMESTIC INTELLIGENCE.

CONGRESS.

On Tuesday 9th, in the Senate, a bill passed to refund and remit duties on fire-arms imported for the use of a State. The bill to increase the army was reported from the Military Committee with an amendment to increase the new regiments to the same number as the old ones. The death of Senator Douglas was announced, and after eulogies upon the character of the deceased by Senators Trumbull, M'Dougal, Collamer, Nesmith, Browning, and Anthony, the customary resolutions were adopted and the Senate adjourned.——In the House, a bill appropriating $6,000,000 for the payment of militia and volunteers was passed. The Chairman of the Committee of Ways and Means reported a bill for a national loan. The Committee on Commerce reported a bill closing the ports of entry of seceded States, to collect duties on shipboard, and to seize and confiscate all vessels belonging to rebels. It was ordered to be printed and recommitted. Mr. Lovejoy again brought forward his resolution declaring it to be no part of the duty of the army to capture or return fugitive slaves, and it was adopted by a vote of 92 to 55.

On Wednesday, 10th, in the Senate, much time was occupied in debating a resolution approving of the acts of the Administration with reference to the suppression of the rebellion. An amendment, declaring that nothing shall authorize the permanent increase of the army or navy, was agreed to, and the further discussion of the subject was postponed. A bill authorizing the President to employ volunteers to aid in suppressing the insurrection and protecting property was taken up, and, after some discussion, was passed by a vote of 34 to 4.——In the House, the bill refunding and remitting duties on arms imported by States since the 1st of May, or until January next, was passed by a vote of 135 to 10. The House then, after an hour's debate, passed the bill authorizing a loan of $250,000,000, by a vote of 149 to 5. The bill authorizes the Secretary of the Treasury to borrow on the credit of the United States, within twelve months from the passage of the act, a sum not exceeding two hundred and fifty millions of dollars, for which he is authorized to issue certificates of coupon, or registered 7 per cent. stock, or Treasury notes. The House also passed a bill which provides that whenever it shall, in the judgment of the President, by reason of unlawful combinations of persons in opposition to the laws of the United States, become impracticable to execute the revenue laws and collect the duties on imports by the ordinary means, in the ordinary way, at any port of entry in any collection district, he is authorized to cause such duties to be collected at any port of delivery in said district until such obstruction shall cease; and in such case the surveyors at the ports of delivery shall be clothed with all powers and subject to all the obligations of collectors at ports of entry.

On Thursday, 11th, in the Senate, various bills, all having reference to a vigorous prosecution of the war, were presented and referred to the appropriate committees. The Loan Bill was referred to the Committee on Finance. Bills for the employment of volunteers in the navy, to regulate the marine force, to increase the navy in time of war, increasing the number of paymasters in the navy, and in relation to the Naval Academy, were introduced, and all referred to the Naval Committee. The House bill for the payment of the volunteers was amended by making the appropriation five and three-quarters, instead of six millions, and the bill was passed. The resolution offered on Wednesday for the expulsion of the rebellious Senators of the seceded States was called up, and, after some discussion, adopted by a vote of 32 yeas to 10 nays. Senator Saulsbury, of Delaware, gave notice of his intention to introduce a resolution for an amendment of the Constitution, with a view to the adjustment of the present difficulties. The Senate took up the resolution approving of the acts of the President, which elicited lengthened remarks from Senators Polk of Missouri, and Powell of Kentucky, in opposition, which were briefly replied to by other Senators, when further action on the resolution was postponed till Friday. The bill for the better organization of the military establishments, with its several amendments, was ordered to be printed. The Senate then held a short executive session, and adjourned.——In the House, bills were reported making additional appropriations for the legislative, executive, judicial, and civil departments of the Government; to promote the efficiency of the army, and for the employment of volunteers, which were referred to the Committee of the Whole and ordered to be printed. In Committee of the Whole, on the Army Bill, for the appropriation of six hundred millions of money and five hundred thousand men to uphold the Government, a warm debate arose, in which several members participated, after which the bill was reported to the House and passed. The Naval Appropriation Bill was also passed, and the House concurred in the Senate's amendments to the bill for the payment of the militia and volunteers.

On Friday, 12th, in the Senate, the Force bill, after considerable discussion, was passed, by 36 yeas to 6 nays. The previous vote on the bill authorizing the employment of volunteers was reconsidered, some amendments made, and the bill again passed—yeas 35, nays 5. A bill was introduced relative to the Sanitary Commission, and referred to the Military Committee. Notice was given of a bill to be introduced authorizing the Federal Government to take possession of personal property in the rebellious States where the owners have been found in rebellion. Senator Saulsbury, of Delaware, offered his previously noticed resolution for an amendment to the Constitution, with a view to putting a stop to the present war. It is in substance the Crittenden Compromise of the last Congress. On the presentation of the credentials of Mr. Frederic P. Stanton, appointed by the Governor of Kansas to fill a supposed vacancy from that State, understood to be caused by the appointment of Senator James Lane to a command in the regular army, Senator Lane demurred to being ousted from his Senatorial functions before his military nomination had been confirmed, and the matter was referred to the Judiciary Committee. Various bills received consideration, all having in view the strengthening of the administrative arm of Government.——In the House, the bill came up authorizing the President to accept the services of five hundred thousand volunteers for the prosecution of the war, and appropriating five hundred millions of dollars to pay for the same, when a spirited discussion took place, participated in by various members. The bill finally passed the House. It has yet to pass the Senate. Mr. Vallandigham, of Ohio, offered a preamble and resolution, declaring vacant the seats of such members as have accepted commands in the militia of their several States, which occasioned a lively passage of words between various representatives, when the matter was tabled by 92 to 51. A resolution was adopted requesting the Attorney-General to lay before the House a copy of his opinion in relation to the suspension of the writ of *habeas corpus*.

On Saturday, 13th, in the Senate, a bill was introduced providing for an Assistant Secretary of the Navy. Senator Johnson, of Tennessee, presented the credentials of Messrs. W. B. Wiley and J. S. Carlile, Senators elect from Virginia, in place of Senators Mason and Hunter respectively. Senator Bayard, of Delaware, moved to refer the credentials to the Judiciary Committee before administering the oath, which was disagreed to by yeas 5, nays 35. The new Senators from Virginia were then sworn in amidst suppressed applause from the spectators. The $250,000,000 Loan Bill was taken up, and several unimportant amendments, proposed by the Finance Committee, were adopted. Senator Saulsbury moved to make the sum $150,000,000, as that amount would be sufficient till the next session of Congress. The motion was rejected—yeas 4, nays 36—and the bill was then temporarily laid aside. The bill to increase the present military establishment was discussed, and reported to the Senate. The Senate, after an executive session, then adjourned.——In the House, Mr. Blair offered a preamble setting forth that John B. Clark, a member of the House from Missouri, held a commission in the rebel State Guard of Missouri, accompanied by a resolution declaring that said Clark has forfeited his rights as a representative, and that he be forthwith expelled. After some debate the resolution was adopted by a vote of 94 to 45. The bill to promote the efficiency of the army, by retiring disabled and infirm officers, was passed. The bill to make good the loss of private property incurred by soldiers in going from Fort Moultrie to Fort Sumter was passed. The amount involved is $1120. A message was received from the President, stating that he had signed the bill providing for the payment of troops called into service up to 30th of June last.

On Monday, 14th, in the Senate, John W. Forney was elected Secretary; he received 26 of 36 votes cast. The Army Appropriation bill and the bill providing for an increase of the military establishment were passed. The resolution approving of the acts of the President with reference to the suppression of the rebellion was, on motion of Senator Breckinridge, made the special order for 15th, when he said he would make a speech on the position of public affairs. The $250,000,000 Loan Bill was taken up, and several of the Finance Committee's amendments were adopted. A bill providing for the confiscation of the property of rebels was introduced. After an executive session the Senate adjourned.——In the House a large amount of business was transacted. A resolution requesting the Secretary of the Navy to supply a sufficient force to suppress rebel privateering was adopted. Ben Wood, of New York, offered a resolution providing for a National Convention, to devise measures for the restoration of peace to the country. It was laid on the table by a vote of 92 to 51. Bills to increase the efficiency of the army were reported and referred. A select committee was ordered on the subject of a general bankrupt law, to report to the next session of Congress. Mr. Vallandigham offered resolutions condemning the President's action in reference to the war, but they were promptly laid on the table. A bill to define and punish conspiracy was passed by a vote of 123 to 7. A resolution was adopted directing the withholding of money due on account of the steamer *Cataline* until the Select Committee on Contracts report thereon. A resolution directing the Committee on Elections to inquire whether Hon. Henry May, a member from Maryland, has been holding criminal intercourse with the rebels, and to report what course should be taken in the premises, was adopted. The Senate's amendments to the Volunteer bill were concurred in, and the House adjourned.

THE BATTLE OF RICH MOUNTAIN.

A brilliant battle, resulting in a complete success, signalized the opening of the campaign of General M'Clellan in Western Virginia. It occurred on Thursday afternoon at Rich Mountain, where a force of 2000 rebels were strongly intrenched under Colonel Pegram. The official dispatch of General M'Clellan to the War Department, dated from Rich Mountain, states that he dispatched Brigadier-General Rosencrans, a young and able West Point officer of engineers, with four regiments of Ohio and Indiana troops, as an advance-body, through the mountains from Roaring Run, a distance of eight miles, over which route they had to cut their way through the woods. After a march of nearly twelve hours, General Rosencrans came on the rear of the rebels, and, after a desperate fight of an hour and a half, completely routed them, driving them in the utmost disorder into the woods, and capturing all their guns, wagons, and camp equipage, or, as General M'Clellan says, "all they had." They also took several prisoners, many officers among them. Sixty of the rebels were killed, and a large number wounded. Of the Union troops twenty were killed and forty wounded. General M'Clellan had his guns mounted to command the rebel's position, but he found that the gallantry of Rosencrans spared him the trouble of going into action.

SURRENDER OF PEGRAM.

A dispatch was received at Washington from General M'Clellan a few hours after the receipt of the news of the above battle, containing intelligence of the proposal of Colonel Pegram to surrender his whole force, who are represented as being quite penitent, and resolved never to serve again against the Federal Government. The following is General M'Clellan's dispatch:

"Head-quarters, Beverly, Va., *July 13, 1861.*

"*Colonel E. D. Townsend, Washington, D. C.:*

"I have received from Colonel Pegram propositions for his surrender, with his officers and the remnant of his command, say 600 men. They are said to be extremely penitent, and determined never again to take up arms against the General Government. I shall have near 900 or 1000 prisoners to take care of when Colonel Pegram comes in. The latest accounts make the loss of the rebels in killed some 150.

G. B. M'Clellan,

"Major-General Department of Ohio.

ROUT OF GARNETT'S CORPS D'ARMEE.

The rebel forces, under General Robert S. Garnett, a native of Virginia, and formerly a Major in the United States Army, while retreating from Laurel Hill to St. George, were overtaken on Sunday by General Morris, with the Fourteenth Ohio and the Seventh and Ninth Indiana regiments. When within eight miles of St. George, at a place called Carrick's Ford, the rebels made a stand, a brisk fight ensued, and they were completely routed and scattered by the troops of General Morris. While General Garnett was attempting to rally his men he was struck through the spine with a rifle ball, and fell dead on the road. Two hundred of the rebels are said to have been killed in the recent actions in this quarter, a large number wounded, and more prisoners secured than their captors can take care of. The flight of the rebels is represented as a most disastrous rout.

THE PRIVATEER "JEFF DAVIS."

This city was startled last week by the news that a Southern privateer has been making sad havoc among our merchant ships in the vicinity of Cape Hatteras. The audacious vessel sails under the name of the *Jeff Davis*, and is heavily armed, and commanded by an ex-officer of the United States Navy. She succeeded in capturing five vessels—one ship, two brigs, and two schooners—and sending them with prize crews toward some Southern port. Captain Howard, of the United States Navy, despatched three revenue cutters from this port in search of the privateer, and two other cutters started from Boston on the same errand. The gun-boat *Iroquois* also left in pursuit.

THE PRIVATEER "SUMTER."

Information reached us last week of the seizure of eight more vessels, bound for American ports, by the privateer *Sumter*, off the southern coast of Cuba, seven of which were run into the port of Cienfuegos, and one burned off the Isle of Pines. The *Sumter* was formerly the *Marquis de la Habana*, one of Miramon's Mexican steamers, which was seized by the United States squadron at the time of his bombardment of Vera Cruz. We published a portrait of her a few weeks since.

A NEW GOVERNOR TO BE CHOSEN IN MISSOURI.

The political and financial condition of Missouri is so desperate that a call for a Convention has been issued, to meet in Jefferson City on the 22d of this month, for the purpose of nominating a Governor and Lieutenant-Governor and other State officers, in place of Governor Jackson, who is a fugitive, and the others who are not willing to act under the laws and Constitution of the United States. It is thought that a full Provisional Government of loyal men will be appointed by this Convention, to act in the present crisis.

PERSONAL.

Major-General Polk, *alias* Bishop Leonidas Polk, of Louisiana, who has superseded General Pillow, is to have command of all the rebel land and water defenses of the Mississippi River from the mouth of the Red River as far up as the Union forces will permit him to come. What is to be done with Pillow does not yet appear.

FOREIGN NEWS.

FRANCE.

RECOGNITION OF THE KING OF ITALY.

Napoleon's note of recognition to Victor Emanuel as King of Italy had been published. He does not in it approve of the past policy of the Cabinet of Turin, will not recognize acts of aggression which threaten the peace of Europe, and will retain his troops in Rome "so long as the interests which took them to Rome are not guaranteed."

JUDGMENT IN THE PATTERSON CASE.

The Imperial Court of Paris delivered judgment on the 1st of July in the Patterson-Bonaparte case. The Court, assenting to the argument of the Procureur-General, declared that the suit instituted by Madame Patterson and her son Jerome Napoleon Bonaparte was not maintainable, and condemned them to pay the costs.

The national newspaper Harper's Weekly, *as did some other Northern journals, seized upon Bishop Polk's promotion to a Confederate general as ready-made for ridicule. (Huntington Library, San Marino, California, July 27, 1861)*

Death of Gen. Polk, Pine Mountain, Kennesaw. *Pencil drawing on paper by Alfred R. Waud, 1864. (Morgan Collection of Civil War drawings, Library of Congress)*

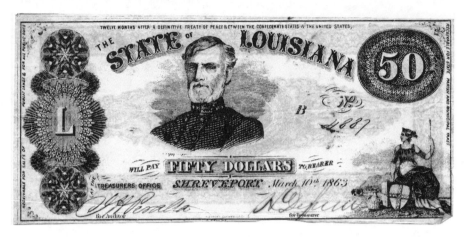

The state of Louisiana, largely under Federal occupation by 1863, tentatively issued its own currency in Shreveport. This $50 banknote, picturing Polk as a Confederate general, contains the wishful promise that "Twelve Months after a Definitive Peace Between the Confederate States and the United States," Louisiana will pay the bearer fifty dollars. Polk's image is reversed on the note; he parted his hair on the right side.

15

The Battle of Belmont—Strutting and Bonhomie (1861)

In his cabin aboard the steamer *Belle Memphis*, Gen. Ulysses S. Grant at about two o'clock in the morning on Thursday, November 7, was awakened by an aide. Having the week before been ordered by John Frémont to menace but not to attack the Confederates occupying Columbus, Grant and his bedded-down troops on transports and gunboats were rocking restfully at anchor on General Polk's Kentucky side of the dark Mississippi River. Now alert, Grant was told that during the previous day "a reliable Union man" had observed numerous Confederates, well-nigh under Grant's nose, crossing the river from Columbus to Belmont. There Polk's surveillance regiment was already quartered.[1]

What the Union man had seen, or thought he had seen, is not easy to say. Few of the Confederates in Columbus could have been spared to cross the river that day. Polk was already under orders from Sidney Johnston to send 5,000 reinforcements east to Clarksville, Tennessee, and these soldiers were on the point of departure. It has been argued by some of Grant's biographers that the 2:00 A.M. dispatch from Frémont was in fact fabricated by Grant afterward, for in his initial report of the Battle of Belmont—the engagement with Polk he would fight later that day—no such message is referred to. Mention of the dispatch is first introduced thirty months later in Grant's revised report. Since Grant had provoked the Battle of Belmont seemingly against Frémont's previous order that he demonstrate only and, further, since Grant previously had not fared all that well against the Rebels, a report of an enemy's threatening movements could prove useful in justifying his independent decision. That is essentially how Grant would later explain matters. Having Frémont's message in hand, the brigadier had determined that come the dawn he had better attack. So he did, making his battlefield debut as a Civil War combat commander.[2]

For pleasing symmetry, it was at almost exactly the same middle-of-the-night hour that General Polk, sleeping peacefully in his Columbus headquarters after penning his resignation to President Davis, was himself roused by an aide-de-camp, Maj. Henry Winslow. The aide came into Polk's bedroom accompanied by a courier from Gen. Jeff Thompson in Bloomfield, Missouri. Thompson had sighted Yankee columns in his neighborhood and thought them a little too close for comfort.[3] Bloomfield is about forty miles west of Columbus, so the information was important, but to Polk it evidently was not overly worrisome; he doubtless composed a reply and rolled over. Yet hardly had he resumed his slumber when Winslow woke him again with more arresting news. On the brightening river, just around the bend and beyond the reach of the Confederates' artillery, Federal gunboats and transports were landing troops on the Missouri bank near Polk's outpost (Camp Johnston). This amounted to an eyes-wide wake-up call to Polk, and it got him smartly out of bed and into the saddle. Gen. Leonidas Polk now had a battlefield debut of his own to make.[4]

By chance that morning, a little before the Yankees had been spotted piling off their boats (they numbered about 3,000), Gideon Pillow's division of 5,000 Tennesseans finally set off for Clarksville to plump up General Johnston's attenuated defensive line from Columbus to Cumberland Gap. The previous day, Pillow's soldiers had supplied themselves for what was regarded as a rather hazard-free march. When the sun came up, they were a few miles along the way. Polk, by then having weighed the gravity of the situation developing across the river, hastened a messenger to the marching column and fetched it back on the double. As the Tennesseans came trotting into camp, they were directed down to the river landing. Steamboats, boilers pressured, awaited them, and four of the regiments were hurried to the opposite shore. Most of these men were facing a hostile enemy for the first time in their lives, and their fate was in the hands of the quirky Pillow.

Polk deemed the 3,000 men now embarked to Belmont sufficient to the task at hand. By a reasonable calculation, he believed the goings-on at Belmont were merely to distract him; the real attack, he reckoned, would come later against the entrenched backside of his Columbus stronghold. His scouts and others had dutifully reported conspicuous Yankee maneuvers, suspected to be misleading, in the vicinity of Paducah.[5] Polk already had galloped out to inspect his rear earthworks, and he was pleased that all was in defensive readiness, the trenches occupied. Meanwhile, the bristling artillery high up on the Columbus bluffs was dueling with two provocative gunboats in the river below. Once the boats had retired upstream after half an hour of futile shooting, Polk positioned himself Janus-like on high ground where he could keep one eye on the backside of Columbus and one on Belmont across the river. As no land attack upon the Columbus fortifications is known to have been planned by Grant, tying down thousands of Polk's troops facing east was precisely what Grant was relying on while he himself was busy in Missouri.[6]

Neither worth defending nor acquiring, Belmont was "a name rather than a place," one historian has said of it, a river landing with a couple of shacks adjacent to cornfields and a wood yard selling fuel to passing steamboats. It was, however, connected by wagon roads into Missouri's interior, so its potential lay in eventually being linked by ferry to the railroad terminus in Columbus. On November 7 its only significance was Camp Johnston, the tent city occupied by Col. James Tappan's 13th Arkansas Infantry, a battalion of Mississippi cavalry, and 150 artillerymen in Daniel Beltzhoover's six-gun Watson Battery from New Orleans. A miserable place even for a tent city (the occupying troops suffered from dysentery and other sickness), the camp merely served as Polk's eyes and ears on the Mississippi's western bank.[7]

By about 9:00 A.M. Pillow and his four regiments had clambered up on the Missouri bank of the river, their number pretty much neutralizing any initial advantage Grant had over Colonel Tappan's forces alone. While Pillow's men were disembarking, Grant was moving 2,500 men from their boats south and slightly east on farm roads leading toward Camp Johnston. Initially Grant's objective at Belmont was to erase the reconnaissance post Polk had established eight weeks earlier. Camp Johnston faced west, its rear against the riverbank and its front and sides protected by an abatis of felled trees poking defensively outward. There were no trenches. Before Pillow's arrival that morning, James Tappan had set his infantry and field artillery pieces in defensive positions out beyond the abatis, aligned just inside the edge of a sheltering wood. Pillow, with seniority and for reasons never satisfactorily explained, modified this arrangement, pulling Tappan's men back some forty yards so that their line was now exposed, running across an open field.[8] Pillow then arrayed his own four regiments in a 400-yard line attached left and right to Tappan. With their backs to Camp Johnston and the river, and hearing the Yankees coming on and firing through the screen of timber, Pillow, Tappan, Beltzhoover, and their collection of amateur soldiers awaited events excitedly. Or as Grant would cheerily describe it, when his skirmishers first began trading shots with Pillow's pickets somewhere deep in the woods, "the Ball may be said to have fairly opened."[9]

Still persuaded that the day's greater danger lay not in Belmont in front of Pillow but in Columbus behind himself, Polk listened and watched. For those on the Belmont scene, of course, there was immediate danger aplenty. Illinois and Iowa soldiers came thrashing forward from tree to tree, wrestling field artillery pieces through the snagging underbrush. When the Federals reached the edge of the woods they saw, probably to their surprise, that they were in gunshot range of the exposed line of Confederate targets that Pillow had arrayed for them. Pillow's exposed men were gradually driven back in a series of hard assaults (an unusual situation in the Civil War's later battles, in which defenders dug in and were not usually put to flight). One Confederate soldier told his colonel afterward that at the time he felt like he was fighting a lopsided duel, his opponent firing from behind a tree, he standing in an open field. The colonel later told Polk, "No worse arrangement of our forces could have been made."[10] When Pillow's men ran low on ammunition (filling their cartridge boxes earlier, they had anticipated the march to Clarksville, not the battle at Belmont), Pillow resorted to a bayonet charge. This, too, failed to stop Grant's momentum.

With zeal and morale flickering, the Confederates fell back through defiles in their abatis into the relative safety of Camp Johnston. Given this respite, Pillow hoped he could regroup them. At about the same time, however, a cavalry troop and the 27th Illinois Infantry Regiment under Col. Napoleon Buford (a cadet chum of Polk's from West Point days) discovered a roundabout, unguarded road that took them behind the Confederates and up to the southern edge of Camp Johnston. Arriving, they shoved aside the few defenders they met. With other Federal regiments ringed around the western and northern sides of the camp and Buford's men about to weave through the fallen trees, the Confederates were almost surrounded. Confederate cannoneers on the Columbus heights thereupon opened fire, overshooting their beleaguered brothers in the camp across the river and targeting the Yankee-infested woods behind. The tactic was ineffectual, shattering trees but sparing the soldiers beneath who began to pour into Camp Johnston and drive the Rebels out in disorder. Among other loot, the six prized brass guns of Beltzhoover's Watson Battery now fell into the enemy's hands.[11] Exuberantly, the captors hoisted "the Stars and Stripes, the flag of our Fathers," and to hear Sgt. Henry Smith of the 7th Iowa tell it, the farm-boy soldiers "swarmed around the flagpole, cannon and tents like bees around an overturned hive."[12] As the Confederates fled, the Yankees shot at their backs. One member of Buford's regiment "felt as cool as though I was shooting chickens."[13] Those surviving sought shelter by sliding down the high riverbanks behind the camp.

From the opposite shore Polk now realized the dismaying turn the battle was taking and Pillow's obvious need for help. He dispatched Col. Knox Walker and his 2nd Tennessee Infantry, immigrant soldiers for the most part whom Pillow had previously disparaged for not being sufficiently "American."[14] The men in Walker's regiment were a rowdy bunch of Memphis Irishmen, as little awed by the prospect of Yankee shot and shell as by their own officers' attempts at discipline. The 2nd Tennessee splashed to shore from their steamboat even before it tied up, and their enthusiastic arrival momentarily disrupted the Yankees' pursuit of Pillow's cowering men. Unfortunately for the fresh troops, the enemy in Camp Johnston had swung around four guns of the captured Watson Battery, and their fire badly mauled the Irishmen. Like those they had been sent to rescue, they sought cover. The commander was forced to conclude around 11:00 A.M. that even further reinforcements had become necessary under the riverbank.

The fortunes of Polk's men continued to deteriorate. So "with great reluctance" (for he was still "apprehending every moment an attack in my rear on Columbus"), Polk began to borrow yet more troops from his backside defenses and inject them across the water. First it was the 1,000 members of the 11th Louisiana and the 15th Tennessee; shortly afterward he ordered his resourceful brigadier general Benjamin Franklin Cheatham to try to organize and rally the dispirited soldiers clinging to the riverbank. Cheatham and his horse leaped from their steamboat, hitting the Missouri mud on the run, the general shouting a promise to lead the men "to hell or victory." Soon thereafter, Polk himself followed on another steamer, escorting Cheatham's 1st Brigade.[15]

By the time Polk's second and third waves of reinforcements were about to come sprinting up the Missouri banks, most of the Yankees had given up chasing the Rebels and returned to Camp Johnston. They might have done better to be making plans to go home, Belmont being untenable as long as Polk's Columbus guns were trained on the place. Instead they joined their fellows in a late morning's celebration of their achievements: bands played, officers made speeches, and ruffians ransacked the acres of abandoned tents belonging to Tappan's Arkansas regiments. Seeing at length that his officers could not quell the uproar and learning that steamboats chockablock with fresh Confederates were coming his way, Grant ordered the tents and stores to be put to the torch. As the flames became visible in Columbus, gunners on the heights, assuming correctly no Confederates were present, aimed plunging shot onto Camp Johnston's parade ground. The "Lady Polk" cannon set the pace, its shells resembling a "lamp post," one flinching Yankee observed.[16] The merrymaking marauders promptly took notice and commenced lining up and clearing out. The barrage, in Polk's view, was instrumental in "turning the fortunes of the day." His chief of artillery, Maj. Alexander P. Stewart, thought the battle itself "was really won by the 'big gun.'"[17]

The barrage from the Columbus guns and the dispatch of Polk's reserves had begun around noon. By about two o'clock the regrouped Confederates had halted the Federals wheeling around them, then reversed the counterclockwise flow. What were the Yankees to do? Said Grant later, by then sounding imperturbable: "I announced that we had cut our way in and could cut our way out just as well." That took some doing. Reenergized by reinforcements and Frank Cheatham's heartening leadership, the Confederates moved inland through cornfields and timber and launched a series of costly attacks upon the vulnerable right flank and rear of Federals racing for their transports. Though many of these were "deliberately loading and firing as they retired," as Col. Jacob Lauman of the high-casualty 7th Iowa reported to Grant, a Confederate officer exulted that "now it was our turn for mayhem."[18] The retreating Federals, exposed as they passed on the road, were easy prey for snipers hidden by the roadside trees. Polk, by now appalled by the number of dead and wounded lying in the roads and fields, tried to curb the killing. A captain from Memphis heard him say it was "too cruel to shoot fellows who were running for their lives."[19]

Similar compassion spared the life of General Grant and arguably changed the outcome of the war. Two unidentified Federal officers that afternoon, one wearing his overcoat and the other carrying his, were seen running from a field hospital, heading for the shelter of a cornfield. When Confederate soldiers saw them and cocked their muskets, General Cheatham nearby ordered them not to fire. Afterward, Cheatham learned that the two defenseless "stragglers" were Grant and his quartermaster, Capt. Reuben Hatch.[20] Amid the quantities of abandoned equipment and clothing that littered the road to the boats, a mess kit bearing the initials "U. S. G." was retrieved by a Confederate. He assumed it was Ulysses S. Grant's.[21]

The breakout fight continued down to the water's edge, pursuers and pursued exchanging fire at close range as the Federal soldiers reached the safety of the transports and scurried aboard. A reserve soldier not in the fight was told by returning friends that it was a rout all right, but no panic. "Nine out of ten of the men came on the boats laughing and joking," he was told. "They had been fighting six or seven hours, and cannon and musketry couldn't scare them any more." The boat captains, by contrast, not so inured to shot and shell, were frantic to shove off.[22]

Once under way, the gunboats and two fieldpieces dragged on board the transports continued the fight with the Confederates lining the shore. Only when all the shooters were beyond each other's weapons did the firing cease. As the sun set, almost 200 men and boys lay dead, and more than 800 on both sides combined had been wounded. But for Polk's intervention, it could have been worse for Grant.[23] Perhaps remembering only the morning's success, Grant later claimed himself the day's victor. For the afternoon's pell-mell pursuit of the Federals, Polk took the credit. Objective historians have reckoned Belmont a tie. In any event, except for those who had to die there, it was of no particular importance to North or South.

Margaret Sumner McLean, who six months earlier had expressed to First Lady Varina Davis "a revulsion of feeling" that an Episcopal bishop had taken up warfare, chanced to arrive at General Polk's Columbus wharf as the Belmont battle was winding down. Her husband, Maj. Eugene McLean, a quartermaster officer, had just been posted to Polk's command, and before the couple's passenger steamboat could tie up, it, like the *Prince*, had been ordered across the Mississippi River to help carry home the casualties. The genteel Mrs. McLean was aghast again, this time to behold the thirty or so blanket-wrapped Confederate bodies brought onboard and laid side by side, their faces uncovered on the deck. "I had always heard that persons dying of gunshot wounds preserved a happy expression," she would later write, "but on those ghastly faces was fixed anger, revenge, suffering, and one man with a demoniac stare in his eyes, had his right hand raised and clenched, as if to defy death itself. Of all who lay there, I saw but one who seemed to have died in peace: a young boy of about 17." Then she brightened:

> When General Polk and his staff returned, flushed with victory and proud of the day's deeds . . . the old General, with his head thrown back and his eyes sparkling with the fire of youth, seemed more like a paladin than a bishop of the Church, and it would be difficult for anyone in his presence to condemn his exchange of the miter for the sword, so thoroughly is he persuaded that he is right.

Later in the evening Margaret McLean discretely watched Polk as he ministered to Maj. Edward Butler Jr., a Louisiana family friend brought to Polk's headquarters gravely wounded. Butler had been shot through the liver while leading his regiment in a charge and was initially attended where he fell by a Federal surgeon.[24] Mrs. McLean now saw Polk praying over the man and decided that "the bishop-general was the right man in the right place . . . , as true to the [miter] as to the [sword]. To my mind, he elevated both." She then heard Butler, who six weeks previous had expressed the army's lack of confidence in both Pillow and Polk, declare before dying that Polk was "one of the noblest men God ever made."[25]

Whatever others might now think of him, for Polk the stimulating acclaim he had reaped from friends and well-wishers the previous June was waning, the swagger he had displayed right after he was commissioned had worn off. He was still at heart more a bishop than a general, and—his relative success at Belmont notwithstanding—he was telling himself perhaps his true calling did not lie on the battlefield. And so, as he had intended before being interrupted by Grant, he now dispatched his son Hamilton to Richmond with the penned resignation. Furthermore, enclosing a copy of his letter to the president, he wrote to Johnston also, affirming his intention to resume his episcopal vocation. He was more candid with Johnston than with Davis. He rehearsed how he had succumbed to Davis's blandishments, how it was "not a matter of my own seeking" but "the prompting of our friend, the President," how acceptance was "done with great reluctance," how only on condition of Johnston's arrival had "I accepted to fill the gap," and how, surely, Johnston "can find among the general officers under your command one who can fill my place far more satisfactorily than I do." Unequivocally and guilelessly, he wished his tenure over.[26]

Maybe it was the relief of simply having survived that was affecting the generals, but the next few days found Polk and Grant both bragging of defeating the other. "We drove the Rebels completely from Belmont," Grant blustered to Brig. Gen. Charles Smith in Paducah. "The victory was complete." Polk thought he'd won "a brilliant victory," he assured his daughter Kate. He wired Johnston that the enemy "have a flag [of truce] here to-day to bury their dead, and admit they were badly whipped." He even passed along to Davis the unfounded story that "General Grant [was] reported killed." The whole text of Polk's telegram to Davis ("A complete rout," it read in part) was sent to Confederate commissioners in London as diplomatic ammunition that might help sway Great Britain toward recognizing the Southern government. "It was gratifying to receive this official contradiction of the Northern account of the battle," an English diplomat wrote Secretary of State Robert M. T. Hunter several weeks after the battle. For Polk, it all went to prove (as he proclaimed anew a cherished battle cry from the American Revolution): "We can and we will be free!"[27] Once Grant's own posturing had subsided, a military note to Polk simply mentioned the recent "skirmish." Polk the general forgot clergy decorum (or so an Ohio war correspondent reported) and cut loose: "Skirmish!? Hell and damnation! I'd like to know what he calls a battle!" In reply to Grant he tamely alluded to "the affair of the 7th."[28] Apart from the vanities of the generals, the valor of the fighting men engaged has never been in dispute. General Johnston's son would later say equitably of the day: "Federal and Confederate alike may look back and feel that there was nothing to be ashamed of in the fighting at Belmont."[29]

Though Polk was doubtless disappointed that the saber and the modish French-style kepi he had ordered from New Orleans did not reach him until just after he had left the field, he still had battlefield mementoes.[30] A solid cannonball was retrieved inside his frame-house headquarters in Columbus, and from the Belmont side of the river his soldiers had brought him the locked trunk, camp stool, and portable field bed of Gen. John McClernand. McClernand had fancied passing Thursday evening refreshing himself with his brigade in captured Camp Johnston. Polk shipped the prizes to his family in Nashville, telling his daughter he just might use the bed himself someday.[31]

Strutting was not the only behavior the combatants indulged afterward. The courtly manners of those early, palmy days of the Civil War dictated that the battle's social aftermath could be as sanguine as the event itself had been sanguinary, neither side taking their losses too hard, nor their enmity too seriously. Now that the dead and suffering had either been buried or hauled out of the woods and cornfields, the ranking officers from North and South several times came together under flags of truce to discuss an exchange of prisoners—at that stage an informal negotiation between commanders not yet officially sanctioned by any treaty between the belligerents.[32] Indeed, the officers' post-Belmont gatherings were often marked less by weighty negotiations than by dining and drinking, their brass buttons loosened, midstream on the Mississippi. A tipsy Cheatham, after one long evening with Grant, thought it best to delay his report to Polk until the morning after.[33] Polk partied on the river, too, once taking along his admiring lady friend, Margaret McLean. A typical truce meeting, as a newspaper reporter summed up the diversions, was proving to be "altogether . . . a most delightful time."[34] "To George Washington, the Father of his Country," said a Yankee colonel during one such get-together, raising a luncheon toast aboard the Confederate Navy's CSS *Charm*. "And the first Rebel!" General Polk riposted merrily. Laughter all around.[35] Off in Nashville, setting Missouri's bonhomie warfare to a catchy 4/4 beat, composer Joseph Benson dashed off "The Belmont Quickstep," known, too, as "The Lady Polka."[36]

The civility went so far that Polk exchanged General Grant's captured hostler, Francis M. Smith, for Colonel Tappan's captured "colored servant, George."[37] "How strange," Polk mused to Fanny, "that such men should have yesterday been engaged in pouring into each other's lines the most murderous fires, and today so agreeable and amicable, and tomorrow ready to return to the same work of wholesale and sweeping destruction." Polk had met face-to-face with Grant a time or two regarding other prisoner exchanges. "He looked rather sad," Polk told Fanny, "like a man who was not at ease and whose thoughts were not the most agreeable. I talked pleasantly and succeeded in getting a smile out of him." Thinking back, Polk continued smugly: "I confess I was not much impressed by him. I think him rather second-rate, though I dare say a good man enough." Polk had unknowingly come close to causing the murder of his adversary. With the battle winding down, Polk remarked to the men milling around him, "There is a Yankee," gesturing toward an overcoated Federal soldier on horseback walking alone across a cornfield. "You may try your marksmanship on him if you wish." No one felt inclined to shoot a man in the back—and General Grant at that moment was spared certain assassination.[38]

Such pleasantries between enemies were interrupted on the Monday following the Thursday battle. Polk was observing a demonstration of the prowess of the outsized "Lady Polk," the general's favorite ordnance. As a consequence of accumulated mistakes, the cannon and some 700 pounds of gunpowder blew sky-high that afternoon. The Dahlgren gun had been hastily manufactured in Richmond that summer, then positioned atop the Columbus heights. It had not been fired prior to the Belmont fight; consequently, in the heat of the morning battle, while Maj. Alexander Stewart's gunners watched rampaging Yankee soldiers swarming into the Confederate's abandoned tent city across the river, they discovered that the ammunition supplied with the "Lady Polk" did not quite fit the gun's 8.5-inch rifled muzzle. Attached to the base of the iron shells was a copper saucer with tabs. Called a sabot, the tabs spun the fired projectile as it traveled up the gun's rifling. The tabs supplied were slightly too wide for the grooves, but by filing the excess metal from the tabs, the gunners were able to fit them into the barrel and fire the gun. The heat of the burning gunpowder soon solved the fit problem. The barrel expanded so that the oversized ammunition matched perfectly. By now the cannonade from various Columbus guns was raining destruction on Camp Johnston, and the celebrating Federal soldiers began to clear out fast. At that point, Major Stewart saw his own Confederates entering the camp and might themselves soon be imperiled by the barrage. He ordered a cease-fire. "Lady Polk," on the point of firing again, was left loaded. As it cooled, the barrel shrunk back to its original size; the sabot down in the barrel became clamped, as in a vise.

Accounts of subsequent tragic events regarding "Lady Polk" are inconsistent, eyewitnesses providing different details and sometimes portraying Polk in an unflattering light. The account in William Polk's biography was supplied by General Polk's lieutenant of engineers, E. W. Rucker. As Rucker tells it, four days after the battle General Polk, accompanied by Lt. [Samuel?] Snowden, stopped at the huge gun to compliment the battery's commander, Capt. William Keiter, who then asked permission to fire the loaded gun. General Polk assented. With sixteen other officers and men looking on, Polk mounted the parapet with Capt. William D. Pickett on his left and Lieutenant Rucker on his right. "Captain Keiter . . . came up and saluted General Polk," Rucker said.

> I remember distinctly General Polk's [saying], "If you are ready, go ahead." Captain Keiter stepped to the rear and gave the command "Fire." The gunner pulling the lanyard, the gun immediately exploded and was broken all to pieces. There were several hundred pounds of powder or more which exploded. General Polk and I were hurled about twenty five or thirty feet back, and fell together. . . . As I picked myself up I felt someone by my side. I touched him and inquired, "Who is this?" and the answer came, "General Polk." It was as dark as midnight. . . . The General, Pickett and I were the only ones left to tell the tale. Captain Keiter, about nine of his company, and Lieutenant Snowden were killed.[39]

A version portraying Polk with impatience and bad judgment was subsequently published in the *Confederate Veteran* magazine in March 1904, the author giving only his initials, "A. G. G." This was probably Asa Gray, a captain on Polk's staff known to be fond of his commander. The passage of time notwithstanding, "A. G. G." claimed "a distinct recollection" of the event. As he told it, after the battle General Polk came to the parapet where the "Lady Polk" had been installed, desiring to see an example of the eight-ton gun's range and accuracy. Brig. Gen. John Porter McCown, an experienced artilleryman, was summoned to the scene. He explained to Polk that the unfired projectile was doubtless frozen in place; if fired, the gun was likely to burst. "General Polk could not well conceal his annoyance," "A. G. G." writes. "When McCown had finished, he remarked: 'I think we shall have to make the attempt.' To this, McCown said: 'You will excuse me if I do not remain to witness it.'" Whereupon the gun was fired, it and an adjacent powder magazine exploding. To this narrative, Capt. William D. Pickett, also writing in the magazine sometime later, strongly disputed Polk's having overruled General McCown.[40]

By his own spare account in a letter to Fanny the next day, Polk says, "My clothes were torn to pieces, and I was literally covered with dust and fragments of the wreck." But "I was only injured by the stunning effect of the concussion." To comfort his wife, he added that "I write you . . . with my own hand that you may see I am safe." Fanny nevertheless came up from Nashville for a spell to nurse him.[41] Whoever was to blame for the deaths, the debacle climaxed mistakes made at the Richmond foundry where the gun had been cast. Confronted with a shortage of high-grade pig iron, the regarded Tredegar Iron Works in Virginia had resorted to buying supplies from the secondary Graham & Son blast furnace in southwestern Virginia. As a Tredegar owner informed the Grahams three days after the blowup, "Several of the guns manufactured [by us] with your metal have recently burst, the one at Columbus Kentucky with results that are distressing."[42]

Polk's injury seems to have been more than he let on to Fanny. One recent historian, usually professionally correct but playing the event for laughs, wrote: "The explosion blew away the bishop's breeches and unhinged his mind for a month."[43] In fact, Polk shortly afterward issued or wrote numerous perfectly coherent letters to army personnel and to his daughters and his wife. But at least one of these letters, as his son points out, was "written from his bed," and in another the handwriting is not his own (though the complimentary close and signature are). And while he quickly resumed his amiable prisoner negotiations with Grant and Buford, he admitted to Sidney Johnston two weeks later that "my head and nervous system generally has been in such a state . . . I have been unable to do more than a little at a time of anything."[44]

When at last he could say he hoped to "assume command again" in a couple of days, Johnston must have sighed with relief. Pillow all this time had been in control of Polk's whole department. Pillow naturally took histrionic advantage of his temporary duty and brought a pot of dubious alarms to such a boil that only two days after the explosion he was able to spread fear across three states. He had heard, he reported on November 13, that the Yankees would shortly "invest [Columbus] with 30,000 men." He next reported, "we are soon, very soon, to have an immense force on our front, and anticipate being entirely surrounded." Pillow then warned the governors of Tennessee, Mississippi, and Alabama that "immense numbers of the enemy are gathering on my front." But rest easy, governors: "We will fight . . . to the last extremity." Pillow's excitement amplified Polk's concussive jitters. He, too, assured Richmond the enemy will "attack me in a few days with an overwhelming force. I beg . . . re-enforcements."[45] Not one of the perils foretold by either general ever presented itself at Columbus. Playing the harum-scarum, Pillow provoked another outburst from Sam Tate, the influential railroad president in Memphis. If Polk is too ill to command, replace him with someone better than Gideon Pillow, Tate insisted to Johnston. "No one here [in Memphis] has the slightest confidence in Pillow's judgment or ability, and if the important command of defending this river is to be left to him, we feel perfectly in the enemy's power. . . . The battle of Belmont has not in the least changed opinion about Pillow."[46]

As the upset to Polk's body and nervous system subsided, so to some extent did his desire to seek his immediate replacement. Perhaps his head was turned by friends' congratulations flooding in after Belmont, or he found the flatteries and cajolings arriving from Richmond heartening. Soothingly and sermonically, President Davis reminded him:

> You are master of the subjects involved in the defense of the Mississippi and its contiguous territory. You have just won a victory which gives you fresh claim to the affection and confidence of your troops. How should I hope to replace you without injury to the cause which you beautifully and reverently described to me when you resolved to enter the military service as equally that of our altars and our firesides? Whilst our trust is in God as our shield, He requires of us that all means shall be employed to justify us in expecting His favor.[47]

Secretary of the Treasury Christopher G. Memminger, maybe egged on by Davis, entreated Polk with a little theological arm-twisting of his own. In a letter written the same day as Davis's, he intoned that "the President is, in his high office, the minister of God for the State; and when, in the discharge of his office, he calls upon you as best qualified to defend the altar of God and the homes of your people, it seems to me to become an indication of Providence." Appreciative of such high-flown sentiments, Polk's resolution to quit died down a little, smoldering.[48] Then, too, Fanny's coming for a conjugal nursing visit had left him with "a sweet memory" and "a sense of greater settledness." After her departure for her rented house in the Tennessee capital, Polk wrote to confess to her his remorse for past failings as a husband and father and thanked her and their children for their loving and long-suffering support. Before putting it away for safekeeping, Fanny wrote on his stationery: "A precious letter."[49]

On November 28 Polk notified Johnston that "I have waived my resignation since Davis seems opposed to it."[50] "Waived" did not mean he'd capitulated, admitted defeat, come crawling—nor much of anything. Just two days later, November 30, he unaccountably renewed his request, mentioning to the president his similar request on November 6 and Davis's subsequent refusal to accept it on November 12. Davis's reaction (presumably another denial) is unknown. Stymied, Polk put off informing Davis of his lukewarm willingness to stay on, finally writing, "I have determined to retain my office so long as I may be of service to our cause." That resolve lasted fewer than sixty days.[51]

16

"I Have Saved the Army from Divers Disasters" (1862)

With or without Gideon Pillow's flawed performance, Sam Tate and his business-minded friends in Memphis were justified in their anxieties: it was just a matter of time before their city, the river flowing past it, and indeed the whole state of Tennessee would be controlled by the Union Army. In the time left, General Polk had resumed full command of the First Division, Western Department. He had decided yet again (fluid though his mind-set could be) to remain in uniform and so bent himself to the further work of strengthening his fort on the cliffs of Columbus.[1] His so-called Gibraltar of the West had lately been given classical status by one of Polk's general officers, who was now calling it the "Thermopylae of the South." The officer conveniently overlooked that, in 490 B.C.E., Sparta's King Leonidas was slain while defending Thermopylae.[2]

Still convalescing from his "Lady Polk" infirmities, Polk was pestered by Pillow, who now designed to capitalize on the commander's diminished fitness. Pillow proposed yet again his long-held ambition to attack Grant in his lair in Cairo. Fending off Pillow and coping with administrative chores coming at him from all directions, Polk confided to Fanny—albeit sounding happy—that "I am as busy a man as there is on the face of the earth."[3] Somehow he found time to order forty-five silk, Christianized battle flags of his own design from Memphis. Priced at $15 each, the flags bore a St. George's cross, red against a blue field sprinkled with eleven white stars, one for each Confederate state that Polk deemed deserving. Kentucky and Missouri, dithering on the North-South border, he regarded as unworthy of stars.[4]

The Christmas plans General Polk then had in mind were disarranged a little on December 23 when his smooth-shod horse slipped and fell on frozen ground. The general's left leg was severely bruised when pinched beneath his saddle. Displaying festive pluck, Polk was hobbling around by Christmas Day, sporting a yellow silk sash an admirer in New Orleans had fashioned in her sewing room and sent as a Christmas gift.[5] Caught up in the mood of the day, he wrote Fanny that he had been reminded of heavenly hosts singing "glory to God in the highest, peace on earth, and good will towards men." He was so buoyed by the Nativity spirit that he even forgave his abolitionist enemies, "wretched fanatics" that they were. "I can and do feel the full force . . . of the [angels'] song towards them," he mused, "notwithstanding the unrealistic purposes in their hearts. I feel no unkindness towards them . . . and would bless them and pray for them all if they would let me."[6] Merrymaking aside, the partying general remained attentive to the enemy's intentions, little understood as they were. Christmas furloughs had been strictly proscribed, and one twenty-five-year-old kept in camp, Regimental Surgeon Lunsford Yandell Jr., noted that both Polk and Pillow anticipated an attack. In plain language he contrasted the two generals in a letter to his father: "Polk is said to be very nervous about it. Pillow is too egotistical and arrogant to doubt any undertaking in which Pillow le Grand has a hand. He has the courage and confidence of a fool."[7]

Like Sam Tate in Memphis, Polk was nervous for good reason. He had been wisely told by a gunnery expert that, "unless you have the opposite bank fortified," even the 150 guns mounted on the river bluffs of Columbus could not stop Federal gunboats from squeezing downstream on the far western side of the Mississippi. Lt. Col. Edward Fontaine, chief of ordnance for the state of Mississippi, further suggested that the bishop obstruct the Mississippi's channel at Columbus by driving piles into the mud and lashing trees against them. Polk's engineers were already erecting pile obstructions in the river at Fort Pillow above Memphis, and the officer in charge there, Capt. Montgomery Lynch, was "confident of success," though admitting to Polk the plan had been "condemned by many." Lynch was "anxiously waiting to witness the effect of high water upon them."[8] Meanwhile, Polk was "paving" the river bottom with torpedoes, as he jokingly told Fanny, and his "tremendous heavy chain" remained in place from bank to bank. Mr. Lincoln's gunboats, he assured her, would be well taken care of.[9]

In late December Polk became fascinated with a scheme dubbed the "River Defense Fleet." Passenger boats, tugs, and other civilian steam vessels plying the Mississippi would be fitted with iron rams and, like wasps, would flit amid an enemy flotilla to sting and sink its slower warships. After hearing the seemingly suicidal proposal explained by its two creators, J. H. Townsend and James. E. Montgomery, Polk said the men "impressed me very strongly," and he hastened them on to Richmond. President Davis was swayed; in short order $1 million was forthcoming from the War Department, and fourteen vessels fitted with iron prows were soon afloat and causing such mischief as they could.[10]

Pillow all the while had continued plotting offensive designs on Cairo while unwilling to submit gracefully to Polk's caution and authority. As Polk observed, Pillow conducted himself toward his commander "generally as towards a rival, to be undermined and supplanted, rather than towards a brother officer . . . to whom a manly patriotism required he should give a generous support."[11] On Christmas Eve the two had engaged in one of their routine quarrels (this time over forage for horses and mules), and, on the day after Polk's Christmas staff party (which Pillow presumably attended), Pillow got in touch with Sidney Johnston in Bowling Green. In a note that seems not to have been cleared by Polk, Pillow advised Johnston that on his own he was ready to send 3,000 soldiers from Polk's Columbus garrison to shore up Johnston's undermanned forces in central Kentucky. No account of how Polk reacted when he learned of this unilateral offer has been found, and he seemingly took it in stride; on December 30 Polk himself authorized the sending of about 5,000 men to Johnston.[12] But something determinative soon surfaced in Pillow's teeming mind. Before year's end, he submitted his resignation to Polk. His complaint (according to Polk) was that, while he clearly deserved promotion from brigadier to major general, his many military gifts had also gone unappreciated by President Davis. Accordingly, he would suffer no further humiliation by him and the other oblivious bureaucrats in Richmond.[13]

With that, Pillow hurried home to Tennessee to vent his spleen. When his anger was evidently not appeased when aimed at Jefferson Davis, he simply turned it against Polk and posted a four-page harangue on the subject of Polk's leadership to Secretary of War Judah P. Benjamin. Polk was an inept military commander, Pillow said, by turns a martinet and a heedless procrastinator (he had let horses and mules die for want of forage!). When defied by subordinates (the humane ones who would feed the starving livestock), Polk's rage "exceeded anything I had ever seen in a sane man." That was hardly the worst of it. During the Battle of Belmont, while wringing his hands for hours on the opposite shore, the heartless Polk had forsaken Pillow and his overwhelmed regiments, leaving them to their bloody fate. Pillow ignored that Polk had officially praised Pillow's "courageously supporting and encouraging his troops by cheering words and personal example."[14] In due course Pillow's vilifying letter crossed the president's desk, where it got a chilly reception. Davis dryly informed Polk that Pillow "has sought to invest you with his [own] attributes, and give to you a character not your own."[15]

Probably because Polk did not suspect that Pillow from his Tennessee home would soon be so busily defaming him to the secretary of war, Polk initially had reacted to Pillow's leave-taking with little more than a shrug. "Pillow has resigned, as you have seen [in the papers]," he wrote Fanny. "Because Davis has not given him the place of a major general. Whether he will succeed in his wishes by resigning remains to be seen."[16] A few weeks later, though, reflecting on his own command successes, Polk had harsher things to say about his departed brigadier. "I have thus far fulfilled my mission . . . which was to hold the Miss. River against all comers," he reminded Fanny. "I have also saved the army from divers disasters which the headlong folly of [erasure] would have inaugurated." This letter, in the Polk Papers at Sewanee, is not in Polk's handwriting. It doubtless is a copy by a staff member who delicately erased Pillow's name.[17]

However prone to folly, Pillow did possess something that Polk still wanted for himself: separation from the army. So on January 30, 1862, Polk wrote to Davis yet again, his third resignation appeal, this time "insisting" on release from the military yoke.[18] Departing from his usual practice of letting Fanny be one of the last to know of his plans, he explained to her early on that he was optimistic that his army days were numbered. "You see [P. G. T.] Beauregard has been ordered here. That suits me very well as it will furnish the ground of my insisting on Davis's allowing me to retire. But this is a secret. I presume he cannot now decline."[19] A telegram having been sent ahead, Polk had his resignation request carried to Richmond by Capt. Hamilton Polk, the tactic he had used before to play upon the president's sympathies. While Ham was on his way, Polk next wrote his friend John Fulton a revealing letter that said his military "life [was] one of unceasing toil and anxiety. . . . How I stand up under it is a matter of surprise to many, not less than myself." He dared hope it was about to wind down.[20] Polk misread the president again. Just as Polk used his son to personalize his plea, so Davis again enlisted Richmond colleagues to lean on Polk's wavering resolve. Soon Polk received two letters from the wartime capital with the president's hand evident in both. John Perkins Jr., Louisiana's Confederate congressman, mixed many a compliment and gracious phrase with a scolding to play on Polk's patriotism and guilt: "I sincerely trust that . . . having once assumed a prominent position in defense of our country, you may not [now wish to] weaken our cause by even a seeming reluctance to continue in its service. . . . I have feared you might not realize fully the effect that a surrender of your command would now have upon the success of our arms."[21] The second letter was from Albert Bledsoe, Polk's West Point roommate and a spiritual companion during the religious enthusiasms fostered by Chaplain McIlvaine. Bledsoe was now the assistant secretary of war. He employed wounded friendship and piety: "I am deeply grieved . . . that you have some thoughts of retiring from the service. I hope, and beg, and pray that you will not do so." Preaching now, he continued, "You know, and you feel, that you have engaged in as great and as sacred a cause as ever enlisted the service of man. . . . Turn not back, I implore you."[22]

Joining his allies, Davis made his pitch as well:

When you gave yourself to the military service, the moral effect was most beneficial. Now you have gained an amount of special information of great importance to the defence of the Mississippi Valley, and at the moment when clouds are gathering over the field of your labors, we can least afford to lose you. . . . You have been overworked, and I can appreciate the condition of one whose cares follow both his waking and sleeping hours.

Davis supposed Polk might be soothed by Beauregard, his fellow Louisi-anan.

Release from duty hadn't worked for Polk when Sidney Johnston had come on the scene, and now it didn't work when Beauregard—the hero victor at First Manassas in Virginia—was posted to the western theater to augment the beleaguered generals in Tennessee and Kentucky. His expertise "as an able engineer . . . full of resources," as Davis put it, was also regarded as a benefit to the best defense of Columbus. "He will, it is hoped," Davis told Polk, "divide your troubles and multiply your means to resist them."[23] On the verge of complying, Beauregard was stricken with a throat infection in Virginia ("nervous affection of the throat," he termed it) that was so severe that in early March he was still achingly ill on his way to Polk's Columbus headquarters. He got off the special train in Jackson in West Tennessee. Major General Beauregard then summoned Major General Polk to come to his sickroom.[24]

Jefferson Davis's midwinter high hopes aside, troubles of late had been multiplying faster than remedies in the western Confederacy. First, at the Battle of Mill Springs in eastern Kentucky in late January, Federal forces under George Thomas defeated Maj. Gen. George C. Crittenden (allegedly thoroughly intoxicated at the time).[25] In that battle, Federal soldiers killed Brig. Gen. Felix Zollicoffer and sent the whole Rebel right wing fleeing back into Tennessee. (Zollicoffer's death did reignite the Southern patriotism of Gideon Pillow, a fellow Tennessean. He promptly swallowed his pique toward Davis and Polk and reenlisted, reporting to Sidney Johnston at Bowling Green; as before, he fell under Polk's command.)[26] Close behind Johnston's right wing being lost in eastern Kentucky, Fort Henry and Fort Donelson in West Tennessee were next to fall. Ulysses S. Grant, conceding that his bishop adversary atop the Columbus citadel had pretty much succeeded in closing off the Mississippi River to Union gunboats, had begun focusing instead on targeting the two unfinished forts, one on the Tennessee River, the other on the Cumberland. Although Polk, as the overarching commander of the region, was initially charged (albeit indirectly) with the forts' construction, he had failed to see to their completion. About all that could be credited, he had directed that several barges loaded with stone be sunk in the low-water Cumberland River to prevent the "Lincoln gunboats" from steaming out of Kentucky and upstream into Tennessee. But one other specific task assigned to him by General Johnston—to finish construction of a place called Fort Heiman, a complementary fort on high ground directly opposite Fort Henry on the Tennessee River—seems to have slipped Polk's mind altogether. With anger toward his friend courteously constrained, Johnston was nevertheless "very much excited" when in late January he burst out in the presence of Col. William D. Pickett: "It is most extraordinary—I ordered General Polk four months ago to at once construct those works; and now, with the enemy on us, nothing of importance has been done. It is most extraordinary, most extraordinary."[27]

Maj. Gen. Henry W. Halleck, a renowned military professional who had succeeded John Frémont as Grant's commanding officer, gave Grant on January 30 the go-ahead to move on the river forts. Grant's staff, cooped up in Cairo, raised such an exuberant ruckus at the news—kicking over furniture, flinging their hats about—that Grant shushed them, saying they might be overheard by the enemy down at Columbus.[28] A few days later, Flag Officer Andrew Foote sent gunboats on the Tennessee against Fort Henry and its more or less up-and-running satellite, Fort Heiman. Grant meantime was landing 17,000 infantry and cavalry on the rain-drenched banks of the Tennessee River, while the river, doing its part, had risen and was flowing into Fort Henry's walls, ineptly situated on the river's floodplain. Within the fort, water in some spots stood waist deep. Lloyd Tilghman, a brigadier general chosen by Polk the previous October for the doleful task of commanding the sodden fort, soon concluded the place was doomed. With seven Federal ironclads approaching the front, ramparts at eye level, Tilghman dispatched most of his troops out the backdoor and off eastward to Fort Donelson. With Tilghman himself then assisting a shorthanded gun crew, a sacrifice garrison of artillerymen held the ironclads at bay as long as they could, and by midafternoon he and some eighty men and their officers surrendered to Flag Officer Foote. The telegraphed news of the opening of the Tennessee River into the heartland of the Confederacy was soon on its way to President Lincoln.

Then, with fifes and drums playing, Grant proceeded east toward Fort Donelson on the Cumberland: Polk's Columbus force on the Mississippi was now about to be severed from Sidney Johnston's Kentucky defense line. The Confederates in Donelson were able to stymy Grant for five days. But within the fort, now besieged, the various generals had fallen to bickering among themselves (newly returned Pillow, naturally, prominent in the disputations), and while they fussed Grant retook lost ground and closed off most of the defenders' escape routes toward Nashville. Pillow, John B. Floyd (a brigadier as inept as Pillow was pompous and who was later censured and dismissed), and Nathan Bedford Forrest did manage to extricate some of their troops before Simon Buckner was put in charge by Floyd on the morning of February 16. General Buckner thereupon unconditionally surrendered the fort and a remaining force of some 15,000. During the surrender formalities later that day, Grant questioned Buckner, a friend from West Point days. Grant: "Where is Pillow?" Buckner: "He thought you were too anxious to capture him personally." Grant: "If I had captured him, I would have turned him loose. I would rather have him in command of you fellows than as a prisoner."[29]

The fall of the Tennessee forts—decisive in the "inexorable progression that led to Appomattox," the historian Bruce Catton has written—also bequeathed to General Polk a legacy of civilian discontent.[30] With eleven companies of Mississippi soldiers captured at either Henry or Donelson, many home-front Mississippians became increasingly demoralized by the war, and during the winter of 1863–1864, when Polk had assumed command in Mississippi, Unionism and anti-Confederate passions there had turned widespread and murderous.[31] More immediately, Polk was engaged in a battle of words in his Mississippi Valley bailiwick with two high-ranking Yankees, Flag Officer Andrew Foote and Brig. Gen. George Cullum. On Sunday, February 23, Foote and Cullum dispatched "an armed reconnaissance" of five gunboats, two mortar boats, and four troop transports of 1,000 soldiers down the Mississippi River from Cairo "to see the condition of things" at Polk's Columbus fortification. With his deck guns loaded with shot and shell and coiled hawsers and folded canvas hammocks wrapped around his boilers and machinery for extra protection, Foote sailed beneath Polk's ramparts top-heavy with artillery and pronounced it "a pretty sight." As the convoy drew nearer to Columbus, an unarmed Confederate steamer appeared under a flag of truce. Foote and Cullum "hoped it was to surrender." Not at all; it was just making a courtesy call. Polk's chief of staff, Capt. Edward D. Blake, presented a letter to his enemies requesting that certain ladies aboard his boat be allowed to pass through the Yankee lines to visit their imprisoned husbands, Mrs. General Buckner foremost among them. Not amused, Foote and Cullum declared in subsequent letters to Polk and others that Blake's mission had been a "mean artifice," a "frivolous pretext," and an "abuse . . . of the sacred character of a flag of truce" disguising Polk's devious design to glimpse the enemy flotilla up close and estimate its strength. Foote's hauteur was partially a pose: "We shall write a withering letter to the right-revered general tomorrow. . . . We will give the bishop a hit," he had told his wife. Polk's reply to the letters to him was composed in seemingly genuine, but possibly feigned, high dudgeon: "I would be unwilling to believe such a suspicion could be entertained by any mind except one conscious of its [own] capacity to venture upon such an abuse. I have the honor to be, gentlemen, your obedient servant, L. Polk." As for the visits by the prisoners' wives and families, they were disallowed for the time being. Foote, for his part, had gotten an eyeful and deemed his reconnaissance highly successful.[32]

While battlefield reversals were in store for thousands of his comrades, Polk was obliged to consider the welfare of his family cowering in the doomed Tennessee capital. Nashville was a key Confederate rail center, and a bulging storehouse had been left largely unfortified while the city enjoyed the economic boom of wartime. Now, with Fort Donelson no longer protecting the city, Sidney Johnston had William Hardee hurry his Kentucky forces down from Bowling Green, then pass through the panicking capital. Headed there as well were Federal troops in overwhelming numbers under Brig. Gen. Don Carlos Buell, while gunboats on the Cumberland and Grant's forces on the land were closing in on Nashville from the west. The city was now engulfed in pandemonium. Hamilton Polk had stopped in Nashville after carrying his father's latest letter of resignation to Richmond and was able to help his mother, his ailing wife, Emily, and his sisters pack up and flee. In a flair of independent spirit her husband could admire, Fanny did not follow his suggestion that she and the girls go to his brothers' homes in nearby Maury County. Rather, late on Sunday, February 16, on one of the last trains to pull out of the city—by then in an uproar though the looming and leisurely Yankees were still a full week away—

Fanny, Hamilton, and the others were hustled out of town by the solicitous "commander of the post," a Captain Lindsay. They headed for the safety of New Orleans, temporary haven though that would be, where they were sheltered in the households of three friends. Fanny later noted that she lost "12 pounds flesh" over the succeeding weeks.[33]

General Polk was by now reporting to Beauregard in Jackson, not the least bit disappointed at being upstaged; if Beauregard's arrival had not effected the discharge Polk wanted, it had lifted from him the weighty command of the Mississippi Valley district. And despite the fates of Henry and Donelson, he remained proud of his fortifying accomplishments at Columbus (he had made the Yankees "stand at a respectful distance," he boasted) and wanted to hold on there with whatever it took, with whatever he had. "I went there to stay, and I feel it my duty to do what I went for," he declared to his family in mid-February.[34] More unnerving to Polk's resolve was Beauregard's passing on to him the doomsday conclusions of his staff engineers after they had picked apart the fortification's strengths. On several grounds, they informed Beauregard, Columbus was far from being the formidable stronghold Polk claimed it to be. With its troops "imperfectly organized" and with lines overextended and "defectively" located, it possessed "alarming weakness" and was particularly vulnerable to an attack on its landward rear. Whereupon Beauregard forthwith declared that Columbus "not meet the fate of Fort Donelson with the loss of the entire army—a hazard contrary to the art of war" and ordered Polk's pride and joy torn down.[35] Beauregard said later (when Polk was long dead) that Polk "concurred in the opinion that [Columbus] could not long withstand a determined attack," but this perception is at odds with what Polk boasted to Jefferson Davis just eleven days after the Jackson meeting, a view later shared by the Yankees. Columbus, by then empty of Confederates, had been "well-nigh impregnable," Polk told Davis, "a solid barrier shutting out the enemy from the Mississippi Valley by the river." Polk had acted the professional soldier in carrying out the "trying" withdrawal, but, aware of the coolness existing between Davis and Beauregard, he surely wanted the president to read between the lines and vindicate him—and the forsaken fort.[36]

Polk's shutdown of the Columbus works was accomplished clandestinely and swiftly. Though Foote and Cullum had claimed the success of their shipboard reconnaissance, they seem to have missed the dismantling of the fort until it was all over. "In five days we moved the accumulations of six months," Polk said, including 140 guns. What could not be moved, or was not worth the effort, was destroyed. "This is my last day and hour," the general wrote in a mournful note to Fanny on Sunday, March 2. "All are gone except myself and staff." A day or so later his spirits had improved. "I felt as if I was leaving home," he admitted to a daughter, but harking to advice learned from St. Paul, the bishop in him expressed serenity: "We may have some reverses, but what of that? We must acquit ourselves like men if we expect the blessing of God. And you women must hold up our hands and strengthen our hearts by cheering us on and praying for us."[37]

The Federal soldiers moving in right behind the departing Rebels on Monday were more impressed than Beauregard's engineers by what they found. "The works are of very great strength, consisting of formidable tiers of batteries," Flag Officer Foote wrote the secretary of the navy. Gloating a little, General Cullum, himself an engineer of coastal fortifications, told his commanding officer that "the Gibraltar of the West is ours!" He regarded the strength of the works as "immense" but said the Confederates had nonetheless abandoned the place in panicky haste, leaving behind "desolation . . . everywhere." When this letter later appeared in Northern and overseas newspapers, Polk harrumphed: "The [panic] reports are inflated, do injustice to the truth, and are intended to act upon and influence the world's mind," he assured his own War Department. Polk's version was that "we removed [enough] to supply my whole command for eight months." Why, only two unwieldy thirty-two-pounder cannons were sacrificed in a "remote outwork [and] were spiked and rendered useless."[38]

Polk would set up his next headquarters in Humboldt, Tennessee, some seventy-five miles south of Columbus and fifty-five miles east of the Mississippi. When packing to leave his borrowed home in Columbus, Polk or a member of his staff would doubtless have prepared for safekeeping the silk banner and staff sent him just days earlier. It was a gift from his friend Sarah Dorsey, a Mississippi author then living at Oakwood, her plantation in Lake St. Joseph, Louisiana. Dorsey had stitched on the banner the monogram of Christ, the Chi-Rho the Emperor Constantine put on his battle standard. Thereby proclaiming that the South's rebellion was nothing less than a Christian contest against the infidel North, Dorsey let herself go in an accompanying note: Here, she told Polk, was a replica of the "first Christian banner ever unfurled on earth and under which [Constantine] was never defeated." Because she recognized "the holiness of our cause, I have not feared to use the sacred Christian symbols, especially as I designed to put them in the hands of a Christian Apostle. . . . We are fighting the Battle of the Cross against Modern Barbarians [and] we beseech you to remember that women and children are behind you for whom your noble heart must make a living shield."[39]

Probably not much resembling Constantine's triumphant march into

Rome in 312 c.e., Polk's evacuation from Columbus was still not a headlong flight down the Mississippi. He was soon relocating part of his army in Humboldt, while the remainder filled the ranks at his other fortified emplacements along the river: New Madrid, Island No. 10, and Fort Pillow nearer Memphis. The best that could be hoped for was that collectively the three fortifications would delay the Federal army's hopes of taking over the Mississippi Valley.[40] That promise obtained only briefly before superior enemy forces compelled the Confederates to pack up yet again their garrisons and guns and retrench farther south. They had about a week to make ready.

Polk from Humboldt and Beauregard from his more distant sickbed in Jackson kept up a steady tattoo of telegraphic good advice to their officers bracing to face the inevitable enemy encroachments. The first fortifications to fall were the two small forts at New Madrid. Peering along at the river's huge hairpin turn below the town, Rebel gunners had earlier enjoyed spotting Yankee boats, both coming and going, as excellent targets. But the forts themselves were equally vulnerable from their landward rears. Because most of the heavier ordnance brought down from Columbus had been repositioned at Island No. 10 another ten miles downstream, the Federal major general John Pope elected to sample first the easy pickings at New Madrid, now under the command of Brig. Gen. John P. McCown. Transplanted from the Columbus frying pan, McCown was soon in the New Madrid fire he had fallen into. With the enemy coming overland in overwhelming numbers (wrestling along a siege gun that required twenty-six horses to drag it into place), McCown implored Beauregard and Polk for reinforcements. He began asking for 40,000, then 30,000, then dejectedly was settling for 20,000.[41] With few soldiers to send, Polk sent instead a number of slave laborers with shovels and a supply of rat-tail files. Should McCown's command be overrun, he could spike his guns with the files.[42] In Humboldt, Polk displayed a bravado strangely at odds with McCown's gloom in New Madrid. On the day he sent the rat-tail files, Polk on March 9 wrote a cheery letter to a daughter in New Orleans saying that "the river is as safe now as it ever was, and my opinion is it will be many a long day before you hear of a gunboat of the enemy down at New Orleans."[43] Polk's optimism was betrayed in nothing flat. McCown evacuated the island four days later.[44] When Meck Polk, having been on hand at New Madrid, next wrote to his New Orleans family he was candid: "It was more like a rout than an evacuation."[45]

Next to go was Island No. 10, a mile-long crocodile of mud and sand crouched in the river. As recently as March 9, Polk had proclaimed that the works on Island No. 10 were "as formidable . . . as we had at Columbus." Perhaps, but to no avail. Polk probably had not reckoned on the combined efforts of the Union Army, the Federal Navy, and its nascent air force, more properly known as the Balloon Corps. Aloft in the *Eagle*, a silk balloon inflated with hydrogen, the aeronaut John Steiner and Col. Napoleon Buford—Polk's bad penny friend again—floated 1,200 feet above the fray directing artillerists on the ground to drop their thirteen-inch mortar shells precisely on the Rebel's gun emplacements. The island was thus surrendered on April 8 with a cost of 109 cannons and mortars, 5,000 small arms, and 4,500 prisoners, one being General Polk's own nephew, Lt. Rufus J. Polk.[46] By then, Leonidas Polk and his army had been ordered to Pittsburgh Landing on the Tennessee River where the Battle of Shiloh was about to commence. The Federal Navy, meanwhile, had captured New Orleans on April 25. That was about three weeks after Polk had penned his jaunty letter promising "many a long day" would pass before New Orleans fell.

17

Shiloh (1862)

Less than a month before the April 1862 Battle of Shiloh, Jefferson Davis, in an "unofficial" letter to Albert Sidney Johnston, confided that "we have suffered great anxiety because of the recent events in Kentucky and Tennessee, and I have been not a little disturbed by the repetition of reflections upon yourself." What the president was talking about were "wholesale assertions" made against Johnston connecting him to the calamitous bad endings at Mill Springs and Columbus in Kentucky and at Forts Henry and Donelson in Tennessee. The result was Johnston's having to abandon Bowling Green and Nashville. (As to pending bad endings, Davis had yet to suppose that New Madrid and Island No. 10 were soon to be in the Yankees' hands.) Taking a positive stance, the president wound up by saying he hoped soon to visit the deteriorating western scene. But it was not to assume Johnston's role as commander. His intention, rather, was "to effect something in bringing men to your standard." Johnston, with plenty to do just trying to organize the amorphous collection of troops then coming together in northeastern Mississippi (a motley group serving variously under Generals William Hardee, Braxton Bragg, and Leonidas Polk), welcomed the president's intervening role with "unfeigned pleasure."[1]

General Johnston's largely untested amateur soldiers, about 30,000 of them, had been withdrawing from Kentucky and Middle Tennessee by railroad and on foot, and their columns were now flowing as through a funnel southward and westward. To unite with Polk's forces coming down from Columbus since early March, Johnston had brought his Bowling Green columns through Nashville, then sent them across the Tennessee River at Florence, Alabama. At length, they all came together during the middle weeks of March just below the Tennessee–Mississippi state line. This was in and around Corinth, Mississippi, where two other rail lines vital to the Confederacy crossed one another—"the vertebrae of the Confederacy," as the secretary of war in Richmond would have it.[2] Already arrived in Corinth from the Gulf Coast were 10,000 troops serving under General Bragg, Polk's former sugar-plantation neighbor and a St. John's Church vestryman from Thibodaux. Bragg was not happy with his reassignment, faulting others (but not yet the bishop) for the Confederacy's current troubles. Thinking of "the great strait" to which the South was reduced by the abandonments of Forts Henry and Donelson and of Nashville, Bragg wrote glumly to a friend that he had been obliged to sacrifice Pensacola to the enemy, stealing away in secrecy so as to connect with the outflanked Rebels backing out of Kentucky and Tennessee.[3] To bolster the assembly in Corinth, Gen. Earl Van Dorn was on his way from across the Mississippi with 20,000 of his infantrymen from Arkansas and Missouri.

Their hopes finally high, Johnston, Bragg, and Beauregard would shortly agree to name the largely green collection of Rebels under their joint command the "Army of the Mississippi."[4] They then devised the organization—one less than wieldy, it has been said—of the many elements they commanded, dividing the army into four corps: semi-independent "bodies" of infantry, artillery, and cavalry constituting divisions, brigades, regiments, and battalions. The commanders of these new corps were to be Polk, Bragg, Hardee, and John C. Breckinridge, vice president of the United States until his term ended in the spring of 1861. In his new undertaking, Breckinridge was given a brigadier general's rank. He replaced Maj. Gen. George Crittenden, whom Bragg had had arrested for intoxication, Crittenden's alleged handicap before, during, and after the Confederates' sobering defeat at Mill Springs.[5]

Polk's corps was composed of two divisions, each with two brigades. Completing his force of about 9,500 was a cavalry troop and an unattached infantry regiment.[6] Polk was pleased to point out in a later report that the vast majority of his troops were from Tennessee, the state in which he had begun his adult life as a priest and planter.[7] The First Division, the one then at Corinth, was commanded by Brig. Gen. Charles Clark, a Mississippi politician-turned-general. Clark's brigade commanders were Col. Robert Russell and Brig. Gen. Alexander Stewart, both West Pointers from Tennessee.[8] The Second Division was under Frank Cheatham, the experienced Tennessee soldier who had helped pull Pillow and Polk out of the fire at Belmont. Cheatham's brigades were commanded by Brig. Gen. Bushrod

Johnson, a West Pointer (but from Ohio), and Col. William H. Stephens, a Jackson, Tennessee, lawyer.[9]

The Yankees were as keen to possess the Corinth railroad junction as were the Rebels to hold onto it. So while the hoards of Southerners settled in (thirteen trains of twenty cars each filled to the brim with troops arrived on March 19), General Grant was hoping to assemble at least 30,000 Union soldiers from bases in Ohio, Kentucky, and central Tennessee; these were already conflating, too, into the southwestern Tennessee region. To attack the invading columns piecemeal before they could merge into a mass was an essential defensive objective for the Confederates. But the enemy, as they approached Corinth, paused at a steamboat landing on the Tennessee River. It was twenty-some-odd miles from the railroad junction by several dirt roads, all of them thoroughly churned by the Confederates passing through under rainy skies; its name was Pittsburg Landing. A few miles west of the landing, among the half-dozen buildings making up the insignificant community thereabouts, was the Shiloh Meetinghouse, a Methodist church built of logs. Its name, borrowed from the Bible, was associated with peacefulness. General William T. Sherman, late of seminary superintending in Louisiana, set up his headquarters near the church, and once Grant had surveyed the surroundings he made the sunny calculation that since the "great mass of the [Rebel] rank and file are heartily tired . . . there is but little doubt but that Corinth will fall much more easily than Donelson did when we do move." Grant got it wrong that time. What lay ahead was a singular onslaught, some thirty-five hours long and costlier in American casualties than the nation's combined losses in the War for Independence, the War of 1812, and the War with Mexico. Lloyd Lewis in his 1932 biography of Sherman has described the pending calamity as well as anyone else: "Two great mobs of innocents ripe for slaughter . . . two herds of apprentice killers, pathetically eager to learn their trade."[10]

The peacefulness surrounding the Shiloh church prevailed for a few weeks. Being a score of miles southwest of Grant's headquarters, Polk described himself to Fanny as "comfortably situated" in Corinth, his headquarters since leaving Humboldt on March 21.[11] Moreover, their sons—Hamilton and Meck—had joined him in Corinth. Notwithstanding that Meck (also called Willy) was among the Confederates lately driven pell-mell out of New Madrid by Gen. John Pope, the father beamed that "Willy is looking very well, and has had a good experience at New Madrid. He behaved very well and grows more strait and tall every day." Meanwhile, Polk had asked another member of his family—William Dudley Gale, the husband of daughter Kate—to join his Corinth household as his military secretary. For both, it was an exceptionally good match. Becoming Polk's confidant, Gale wrote wartime letters to Kate Gale that frequently lauded the general, and after Polk's death Gale remembered with scant restraint his father-in-law as possessing "chivalry as bright as that of Bayard, courage as true as that of Belisarius, and Apostolic faith and zeal like that of one of the Twelve."[12]

By virtue of his earlier days tracking over Tennessee and Mississippi with his father, and then as a planter and missionary bishop, Polk had knowledge of the local geography that certainly could have been of value to the generals with whom he was stationed. Yet his name is rarely mentioned in official correspondence passing among Johnston, Beauregard, and Bragg as those military professionals conferred on how best to deal with the invading enemy armies massing behind them at Pittsburgh Landing. As for the West Pointer Bragg, his indifference to Polk as a military colleague began to spill over into churlish disdain. Recently promoted from brigadier to major general by the Confederacy (he had been an officer in Indian wars and the War with Mexico), Bragg was still outranked by the bishop-general because Major General Polk had held his grade a few months longer. Johnston, doubtless aware of Bragg's irritation in being subordinate to the recently civilian bishop, made Bragg his chief of staff, giving Bragg the authority to issue orders to Polk in Johnston's name.[13] Bragg nevertheless disparaged Polk in letters to his wife, Elise. He was unimpressed with Polk's command of the Mississippi River forts, boasting that his own soldiers were better led, and whining "but Polk ranks me." Being a strict disciplinarian, he assured Elise that, compared to his own soldiers, the troops that Johnston and Polk had brought to Corinth were no better than a "mob, poorly disciplined and given to plundering civilians." Indeed, he said, "the good Bishop sets the example, by taking whatever he wishes."[14] Elise knew just the kind of responses sure to please her fretful husband. "Beauregard is an egoist—Polk a wild enthusiast & both rank you," she wrote him. In whatever sense Elise applied the word "enthusiast" to Polk (extravagantly religious? delusional? prophetic?), it was not complimentary. She was even thinking, she told her husband, of calling on Jefferson Davis in person and telling him "the plain unvarnished truth" regarding the personality disorders of Bragg's fellow generals.[15] Bragg, in one of his more saturnine moods, had scornful words for Beauregard as well. After Beauregard had recently made a famously theatrical call for all Southern planters to donate their plantation bells for casting into cannons, Bragg thought the appeal pretentious and told Elise that the Confederates already had more cannons than trained cannoneers to fire them and that there was casting metal aplenty to be had in New Orleans.

(In a semipatriotic response, just the same, one of Bishop Polk's Louisiana congregations—the people of Mt. Olivet Church in Pineville—kept their bell but donated their iron fence to the cause.)[16]

While the Braggs indulged their gossip, General Polk went about his business, his usual sangfroid self. With Gale at his side, he dictated for Johnston's full understanding his version of the slow rise and sudden falls of Forts Henry and Donelson (that is to say, the finger of blame should not be pointed at him). And he apprised his friend the president on the state of affairs in Corinth. "The enemy are preparing to make a powerful demonstration near Eastport, on the Tennessee River," he wrote, alluding to the Federals swarming like locusts toward Pittsburg Landing. Confident that his own army, small as it was compared to the others, was equal to any other at Corinth, he concluded: "My army, with General Bragg's and General Johnston's, we hope to concentrate in time to meet him."[17]

The hoped-for encounter was decided on two weeks later. Polk's receiving visitors and enjoying housekeeping leisure ended abruptly when Johnston ordered on Tuesday, April 1, that all his armies "be placed in readiness for a field movement and to meet the enemy within twenty-four hours."[18] Around 10 P.M. the next day, Frank Cheatham, commander of Polk's division then at Bethel, about twenty miles north of Corinth and three miles west of Pittsburgh Landing, raised an alarm. He reported to Polk that he was "being menaced" by the Union general Lew Wallace's division, an enemy concentration camped a few miles north of Pittsburgh Landing at Crump's Landing. The Federal cavalry troopers spotted by Cheatham's pickets were only on reconnaissance, so the "menace" was negligible, but it got things moving in the Rebels' lair. Polk promptly relayed the news to Beauregard, who took it to mean that at least some of the Yankees flooding into Tennessee were pressing westward, possibly intending to seize the Mobile & Ohio Railroad at Bethel, or maybe to march on to Memphis.[19] Through his adjutant, Col. Thomas Jordan, Beauregard accordingly recommended to Johnston that "now is the moment to advance and strike the enemy [still] at Pittsburg Landing." Strike, he meant, while Wallace was still detached from the others and before Grant and Sherman could be reinforced by Don Carlos Buell, the latter coming on strong down Middle Tennessee highways with a force of 25,000.[20]

Armed with Cheatham's alert and Beauregard's interpretation of it, Johnston crossed the dark street to Braxton Bragg's sleeping quarters, rousing this officer in his "dishabille."[21] By 1:40 A.M. on Wednesday, April 2, Bragg, Polk, and Hardee had all been told by Colonel Jordan (speaking for Johnston, "the commander of the forces") "to be ready to advance upon the enemy [Thursday] morning by 6 A.M." Each soldier was to carry cooked food sufficient for five days in the field along with 100 rounds of ammunition. The same order was telegraphed to John C. Breckinridge at his headquarters nearby in Burnsville, Mississippi.[22] General Beauregard and Colonel Jordan then wrote out detailed orders for the line of march (or so Jordan asserted later).[23] As Johnston and Beauregard envisioned the movement, their Army of the Mississippi would proceed smartly out of Corinth at the appointed time (subsequently set ahead to 3:00 A.M. for Polk). The three corps (with Breckinridge's reserve corps bringing up the rear) would march along the two roughly parallel roads meandering toward Pittsburg Landing on the Tennessee; by Thursday evening everyone would have reached Michie's Crossroads, a staging area where the two avenues intersected.[24] Thereafter, during the night, officers would pull together their various regiments, and on Friday morning, in a battle formation four corps deep, the Southern army would pounce on the unsuspecting, breakfasting enemy: six divisions milling around a camp without entrenchments and hemmed in by the Tennessee River, swamps, and several creeks.[25]

A fond hope, as it turned out. The Confederates' logistics were based on the belief that their 40,000 officers and men (not to mention their wagons and mules) could extricate themselves on short notice from the congestion of little Corinth and flow in good order and undetected up the Ridge Road and the Monterey Road to Pittsburgh Landing. But the two roads proved a snarl, their usefulness compromised by their merging some six miles farther along, and then branching off again closer to the landing. The roads proved inadequate to the severe uses placed on them by the Confederates. Human shortcomings were manifold, too.

The scheduled dawn departure got going in fact a little after noon when General Hardee and his corps of 4,500 men began to move. (The exodus from Corinth was meant to take place in relative secrecy: spies and the merely curious presuming to observe the huge parade of men and munitions would do so at their peril. All caught looking, General Bragg had decreed, both white and black, were to be "seized and sent to the rear . . . until the object of the present movement is accomplished.")[26] With Hardee off late, the other corps' assignments to follow at prescribed intervals ran later still. The resulting chain reaction magnified confusion and holdups, and to this day which generals (or which circumstances) were responsible have not been clearly sorted out. Early on, Polk blamed Hardee; Hardee blamed Bragg; and Beauregard blamed Polk, maybe the least blameworthy of all. Taking the Ridge Road later that evening, Hardee had aimed for the destination prescribed for him at Michie's Crossroads, about eight miles from

Pittsburg Landing. He arrived not on Thursday night but sometime on Friday morning. Polk's corps of 9,000 had been poised since early Thursday morning to follow Hardee's at a half-hour's distance; Polk's tail end did not clear Corinth until that evening. Bragg's corps, larger and more unwieldy than the other two (he had almost 15,000 men), had left by the shorter Monterey Road but was behind schedule as well. Bragg's initial progress was immediately slowed, he said, by "bad roads [and] insufficient transportation badly managed."[27] Consequently, Hardee was finding himself too far ahead of the others, while John Breckinridge, bringing up the rear from below Corinth, was impeded by the mud churned up by those ahead. Heavy rain had commenced by Friday night. For those in the vanguard, where the two main roads to Pittsburg Landing branched and converged and criss-crossed, schedule problems were further compounded by darkness and the torrent. At one time or another just about everyone stumbled into everyone else's way, and those who didn't were lost. When Bragg admitted on Saturday afternoon that the whereabouts of one of his divisions was unknown to him, Johnston exploded: "This is perfectly puerile! This is not war!" Johnston then rode off to find the missing column himself.[28]

On Saturday afternoon, April 5, Johnston's whole army at last reached the outskirts of Pittsburgh Landing, though now some twenty-four hours behind schedule; Hardee was still maneuvering as late as 3:00 P.M.[29] The army then squared itself roughly (and noisily) into shape, in line for battle. But daylight was waning fast and a successful Saturday attack was now out of the question, with nothing much left but to eat supper and try to fashion a good night's rest. Alas for Polk's men, those options weren't all available; his troops had "practically exhausted their five days' rations in three." For them, night brought empty stomachs amid falling rain and hail.[30]

Enough of Saturday's daylight had remained for the higher-ranked generals to convene and indulge in their first round of blame-fixing before deciding what to do next. Beauregard was particularly irritable and disheartened, sure that the element of surprise had been squandered by the army's lateness and the commotion it had made. (Wondering if their guns would work in the damp weather, many soldiers tested them by firing them off while a cavalry troop with two pieces of artillery pushed forward without authority and collided with the enemy; no particular notice was taken by the Yankees.)[31] In the impromptu five o'clock roadside meeting, Beauregard began by berating Polk, assigning to him the blame for causing the traffic snarls and for ruining his punctilious timing.[32] Brushing aside Polk's defense, Beauregard said further that he wanted to call off the whole expedition and return to Corinth; the enemy, he calculated, was by now "intrenched [*sic*] to the eyes and ready for our attack." Bragg, listening in, and put out of sorts himself by the blundering and unsoldierly delays, doubtless took satisfaction seeing the bishop-general being dressed down. Though out of character for this usually pugnacious soldier, Bragg apparently endorsed Beauregard's inclination to go home.[33]

At this point General Johnston rode up. After hearing Beauregard and Bragg argue for withdrawal, he asked for Polk's opinion. Doubtless peeved by Beauregard's singling him out for criticism, Polk asserted withdrawal would "operate injuriously upon his troops" who "were eager for battle." He declared, "We ought to attack." Presently, Johnston brought the discussion to a close: "Gentlemen, we shall attack at daylight tomorrow." Then, in an aside to his brother-in-law, Gen. William Preston, he said, "I would fight them if they were a million." That was not mere bombast; Johnston had reckoned that the more enemy soldiers boxed in by the river and creeks surrounding the field at Pittsburg Landing, the more they would get in one another's way and subject themselves to entrapment. Thinking then of his long-ago roommate standing nearby, he added to Preston: "Polk is a good soldier and a true friend." If Beauregard and Bragg overheard the encomium, they would have been in a mood to disagree, if not audibly snort.[34]

After dark the generals reconvened to make final plans, this time around a campfire. William Stevenson, an aide-de-camp for John Breckinridge, observed the scene: Beauregard presided, walking about, gesticulating and waving his arms; Johnston stood off to the side; Breckinridge took his ease stretched upon a blanket on the ground; Polk, hatless, "sat on a camp stool at the outside of the circle, and held his head between his hands, seeming buried in thought." Stevenson was impressed. "What a grand study for a Rembrandt was this," he later mused. In the frontispiece of Stevenson's wartime book is an engraving portraying the generals' campfire conference as described by the author. The artist signed himself "N. Orr."[35]

Amazingly—and contrary to Beauregard's perfectly reasonable assumptions and fears—the encamped Yankees that Saturday evening were neither dug in nor very much concerned about the Rebels looming just out of sight.[36] Rather, General Grant had decided the welfare of his undertrained recruits would be better served in drilling than in throwing up earthworks that might provide an illusion of safety. Grant, in fact, had not been around Pittsburg Landing since Friday. He had returned to his headquarters house at Savannah, a river hamlet a few miles downstream where, nursing a badly bruised ankle after his horse had fallen on him, he was getting about the house either by hopping or on crutches. William T. Sherman, meanwhile, having been cavalier regarding the rumors of enemy activity reported to him, did not bother with patrols on the camp's perimeter.[37]

Equally nonchalant was the Union brigadier general Benjamin Mayberry Prentiss, commander of the Sixth Division. But one of his colonels, acting as a brigadier general, was showing more enterprise than anyone else. He was Harvard-educated Everett Peabody, and having paid attention to reports from his own men (they had seen a handful of Rebels peering from a thicket before slipping away), he concluded that any enemies prowling in the neighborhood were up to no good. Rebuffed by Prentiss as an alarmist, Peabody sent out a scouting party in the predawn dark of Sunday morning. Sure enough, at first light his patrols ran smack into skirmishers advancing from Hardee's corps.[38] The Confederates drove the startled Federals backward, and in mounting numbers the Yankees were soon dispersed on the outskirts of their campgrounds. The vigilant Colonel Peabody, with five gunshot wounds, would die shortly, and before 9:00 A.M. his camp had been overrun.[39]

The whole of the Federal encampment seemed ripe for destruction. With the soldiers' tent cities unprotected by earthworks, and bunched willy-nilly among rough and wooded plains and plateaus, the Yankees had the Tennessee River behind them and, on their flanks, three creeks swollen with rain. The Owl and the Snake curled around the army's northern right flank like a cradling arm; Lick Creek flowed along its southern flank. Moreover, the division under Gen. Lew Wallace that was camped at Crump's Landing on the far side of the Owl and the Snake was not readily at hand for Grant's use; Wallace could join Grant's other regiments only by boarding river transports to Pittsburg Landing or by filing over a bridge across the Owl. Given these circumstances, the Confederates supposed they had the Yankees in the trap General Johnston had envisioned. To spring it they hoped to curve the enemy's left wing away from Pittsburgh Landing. The maneuver would isolate the Federals from supplies and back them against the unfordable creeks. Johnston predicted, "There, they'll have to surrender."

Having slogged for two days up the rainy roads from Corinth, the weary and hungry Confederates were scarcely in top fighting form as Sunday dawned dry and bright. But therapeutically the day ahead beamed with "the sun of Austerlitz," as General Johnston's son was to characterize it, likening the weather to Napoleon's fabled victory under cloudless skies in Moravia six decades earlier. The springlike weather proved a tonic to the soldiers, their morale already bolstered by the address their commanding general had ordered read aloud to them once they had set out from

Corinth. "I have put you in motion to offer battle to the invaders of your country," Johnston braced his troops through their commanders. "With . . . valor becoming men fighting, as you are, for all worth living or dying for, you can but march to a decisive victory over agrarian mercenaries, sent to subjugate and despoil you of your liberties, property and honor." (Taking his place amid this horde of despoilers was the 22nd Ohio's Col. Crafts James Wright, who at Polk's consecration as a bishop had vouched for his friend's holiness.)

By "agrarian mercenaries," Johnston was expressing his conviction that the invaders intended to hand over conquered plantations to the slaves, a subtlety possibly over the heads of some of the rank-and-file soldiers. But certainly they all would have responded to what he said next: "You are expected to show yourselves . . . worthy of the women of the South, whose noble devotion in this war has never been exceeded in any time."[40] Brimming with that worthiness himself that sunny morning, General Johnston settled into his saddle with a prophecy on his lips. "Tonight," he said to his staff, "we will water our horses in the Tennessee River." Some cavalrymen under Polk's command, not Johnston's, were among the few Confederates able to fulfill those words.

At the beginning of the battle, 40,000 Confederate troops were arrayed in deep ranks three miles wide, and like an ocean sweeping a beach they fell upon Grant's awaking army in successive waves. With the Confederates facing an enemy estimated at 35,000 men (Lew Wallace's division of 7,500, still camped north of Pittsburg Landing, failed to reach the scene that day), the battle would bring together the largest aggregate of soldiers ever seen on the continent. Intended to burst serially upon the Yankees through thickets, woods, cleared fields, ravines, creeks, and gullies, the several Rebel corps were arranged atypically. A more orthodox formation—the several corps side-by-side with some semblance of control for their officers—was what Johnston had originally had in mind, but Beauregard, for reasons never fully explained by him, devised the unusual placement, and that, for the most part, was what was followed.[41] Thus, the Confederate III Corps under William Hardee, the prewar Federal officer who had written the US Army's most current manual on infantry tactics, led the way;[42] Braxton's Bragg's II Corps followed 1,000 yards behind; and Polk's I Corps, coupled with John Breckinridge's Reserve Corps, brought up the rear. In no time, the men in the successive corps began to intermingle, orderly command soon giving way to confusion. In William Polk's metaphorical phrasing, the Confederates' "behavior was much like that of a team of balking horses: as one command went forward, the other was standing still."[43]

As for Polk, he and his staff (including Capt. Hamilton Polk, his aide-de-camp and son) had ridden toward the front with an escorting bodyguard detached from Lt. Col. Richard Brewer's Mississippi and Alabama Battalion.[44] They entered the battlefield from the southwestern corner. For his own reasons, Polk at the outset had arranged his soldiers in columns abreast, consistent with Johnston's original side-by-side plan but at variance with Beauregard's design. Polk's troops advanced along the road that passed Shiloh Church and that led to Pittsburg Landing. His I Corps's assignment was to support the right wing of Bragg's corps, now running on ahead.

As the Rebels approached the front, at least according to a diarist in Bragg's 3rd Brigade, they could "hardly be restrained from rushing up to the fray." They were "all laughing and huzzaing, shouting 'Hurra, boys, the fun has commenced now in earnest.'" Early on (the diarist made timely entries throughout the battle) he noted that "General Polk's Battle Flag has been shown to the boys," a tactic helping troops reckon that they were where they were supposed to be.[45] (Sometimes flags were put to less commendable uses; the Federal general John McClernand charged in his official Shiloh report that during the battle Confederates attacking his left were seen "bearing an American flag . . . as a means of deception.")[46]

Having initially sent a brigade to support Bragg's right wing, Polk was subsequently directed by Johnston to tend to Bragg's left. Sidney Johnston had ridden up to Polk unattended by his own staff or escort, and Polk obliged his friend by quickly dispatching Alexander Stewart's 2nd Brigade, the nearest unit at hand.[47] Recklessly, Johnston then led Stewart's men to the front himself, the soldiers on the run through camps recently abandoned by retreating Yankees. It was 7:00 A.M., and shortly thereafter Polk was ordered by Beauregard to send another brigade to support Bragg's opposite wing, the left. Polk dispatched Frank Cheatham and his brigade on this mission. Now having but two brigades remaining (Robert Russell's and Bushrod Johnson's), Polk awaited further orders. (It was close to this time that one of Polk's artillery captains, Marshall T. Polk, a cousin of whom he was fond, was wounded and taken prisoner when his battery was overrun. This was not an anomaly: among the Confederates and Federals contending at Shiloh, sixteen were descendants of the patriarch Robert Polk; Lucius Eugene Polk, General Polk's nephew, was shot in the face.)[48] Subsequent orders sent to Polk directed him to send his remaining reserves to support Bragg's center, then under heavy fire from forces commanded by Generals William T. Sherman and John A. McClernand. (It was Brigadier General McClernand's camp bed that Polk had claimed as a trophy after the Battle of Belmont.) With Polk's and Bragg's once-separate corps by now thoroughly intermingled, the two generals resorted to an ad hoc arrangement, one to oversee the left, the other the right. Such management was to create a problem; as the day progressed, the Confederates were succeeding in driving the Federals backward—but with an ironic outcome.

Johnston's basic battle plan had been to fold back the Federal left upon itself. Thus, both Sherman and Grant would be driven away from supplies and reinforcements at Pittsburg Landing, and the soldiers would be crowded into a pocket formed by Owl Creek and Snake Creek. "They can present no greater front between those two creeks than we can, and the more men they crowd in there, the worse we can make it for them," he had reasoned. But because the Confederates attacking the Federal right were moving faster than their fellows attacking the Federal left, the Yankees were being bent back toward Pittsburgh Landing, the opposite of Johnston's hope to pin them against the creeks where no escape was possible.[49] The to and fro of the day's running fights was concisely stated by a Union officer's recollections of his unnerving Sunday: "Surprised at seven, and our front line broken; reinforced and confident at ten; stubborn at twelve; desperate at two; our lines crumbling away at three; broken at four; routed and pulverized at five; at six, rallying for a last desperate stand."[50]

No fewer than 229 accounts of the two-day Shiloh battle were later published in *The War of the Rebellion*, ranging from the banter of the Union colonel John Logan of the 32nd Illinois Infantry (his "boys gave [the Confederates] such a dose of blue pills that they sickened at the stomach and changed their course") to the factual terseness of General Polk ("the resistance at this point was as stubborn as at any other on the field").[51] Otherwise, Polk supplied few details of his own whereabouts during the two days of fighting. In general, he seems to have been perilously close to the front, where, apparently, he relished the danger. Alexander Walker, editor of the ultra-secessionist New Orleans *Delta*, covered the battle for his paper with the flair of a publicist. "[Leonidas] Polk, . . . as ardent and enthusiastic as a young soldier in his first skirmish, pushed forward his brave Tennesseans, with his splendid batteries," he wrote. "A nobly appearing chief, he dashed along the lines, inspiring his men by his brave and self-possessed bearing."[52] Beauregard remained in the rear all day, apropos of his role as commander, but his report also puts Polk close to the front-line shooting when he writes that all four corps commanders "repeatedly led their commands personally to the onset upon their powerful adversary."[53] Polk's son Meck, an artillery officer in the battle, says about the same. His father "held a position well up against his line, arranging and placing commands as the hotly contested points in his front demanded. . . . On four occasions placing himself at the head of his troops, he led them in desperate charges against their gallant foes."[54] It was on one of these forays that the man at General Polk's side, his orderly, was killed. Similarly, Polk presumably exposed himself to lethal gunfire when Lt. Col. Andrew Blythe, leading the Mississippi regiment he had recruited himself, was shot. "The gallant Blythe . . . fell under my eye, pierced through the heart, while charging a battery," Polk wrote in his report.[55]

Polk was clearly far more in the midst of the fighting than he had been at Belmont when he felt obliged to remain on the Kentucky side of the Mississippi, lest Columbus be attacked from the rear. This "disposition to personally supervise important matters [was] so characteristic of the man," William Polk would later write. Moreover, his son thought, the general was so convinced that day that the fate of the whole Confederacy "hung almost in the balance" that he exposed himself to dangers that "might better have been left to subordinates." After division commander Brig. Gen. Charles Clark was disabled by a shot in the shoulder and his troops began to falter, Polk's "frequent exposure of himself to the hottest of the enemy's fire tended greatly to reassure" Clark's men and boys; like most everyone at Shiloh, they had scant or no battlefield experience.[56]

For all his derring-do, Polk (and even his horse) came through the battle remarkably unscathed. Of the four corps commanders, all of them mounted, he alone was so lucky. Two horses were shot from under Bragg, Hardee was "slightly wounded, his coat rent by two balls, and his horse disabled," and Breckinridge was "twice struck by spent balls."[57] The troops of Polk's I Corps fared far worse than their leader. "My corps suffered a good deal, about 2,000 killed and wounded," Polk would report to a daughter, sounding oddly proud of the toll of fallen. He boasted: "That showed where we were."[58] For his own deliverance "from the thickest of the storm," Polk gave credit to God. "It was he who 'covered my head in the day of battle,'" he told his wife, quoting Psalm 140.[59]

Polk and his soldiers, as was true of other units, were not constantly entangled in fighting during the two long days. Awaiting further orders around lunch time on Sunday, men of Capt. Thomas Stanford's Mississippi Artillery Battery caught their breath in a deserted Yankee campground still redolent of abandoned breakfasts. One soldier reported they "all got a good dinner already cooked, which the well-supplied enemy had not time to eat in the morning." Probably short on rations himself, he noticed a difference. "They fare far better than we do. We found an abundance of cheese, potatoes, dried fruit, honey and almost every substantial that is intended for an army."[60]

Across the broad field of fighting, in one notable exception, the back-tracking Yankees showed a fierce obstinacy. After fleeing their camp, soldiers of the remnant Sixth Division under Brigadier General Benjamin Prentiss came by chance at midmorning to an eroded wagon track.[61] Curving convexly across the battlefield along a ridge, it was a ready-made, elevated line of breastworks. Learning of it, Grant would order it held "at all hazards." It has since been observed by military historians that a modern army would divide immediately and bypass such an obstacle, subduing it from the rear. Instead, the Confederates attacked the line head-on repeatedly and disastrously. (Prentiss was subsequently gracious in his praise of the attackers: "Their bravery . . . is testified to by the devotion with which they stood forward against fearful odds to contend for the cause they were engaged in.")[62]

Joined in support by the less-battered divisions under Brigadier Generals Stephen A. Hurlburt and W. H. L. Wallace, 11,000 men with thirty-eight field guns crouched for a good half-mile behind the road's hunched shoulders. A shield of roadside thickets and underbrush gave the Federals further protection. Thus arrayed, they methodically wounded and killed hundreds of infantrymen in Polk's corps who were ordered (by Bragg, primarily) to run through a hail of shells and a buzz of bullets toward the almost invincible position. The surviving Confederates, stymied for hours, called the center of this awful place the "Hornet's Nest" (also known as the Sunken Road), and its stubborn defense, some of it "to the very muzzles of our guns; some of it in hand-to-hand combat," so delayed the Confederate advance throughout most of Sunday afternoon that Prentiss's soldiers would be credited for saving the rest of Grant's army from almost sure destruction.[63]

An even greater setback for the Confederacy (that day and forever after) occurred elsewhere on the field in midafternoon: Sidney Johnston was mortally wounded. Trying to help dislodge the Yankees by setting an inspiring example, he was himself often close to the front, at one time heartily promising another officer that "a few more charges and the day [is] ours."[64] An hour or so later in a peach-orchard fight to the right of the Sunken Road, he was still putting himself in danger, exhorting faltering Tennessee soldiers to charge with their bayonets. "I will lead you!" he had cried. Although unhurt in that episode, shortly thereafter a spent bullet or shell fragment severed an artery in Johnston's booted leg. Initially unaware of the severity of the wound, he tried to make light of it, telling Isham Harris: "Governor, they came very near putting me *hors de combat* in that charge." By then frantic aides had begun a futile search for the hidden wound. Within the half-hour, the general bled to death. Getting the news, Beauregard ordered it be suppressed, fearing its effect upon morale; he then assumed full command of the Army of the Mississippi.[65]

Late in the day in the Hornet's Nest a Union regiment, separated from its own brigade and apparently forgotten, was finally encircled by the relentless Confederates, among them men of Polk's corps.[66] At that point, explained James Geddes, the colonel of the Eighth Iowa Infantry, his regiment was being shot at from three directions while tree limbs severed by shells from Federal gunboats on the river rained down on the men's heads. With all that, for Geddes it "became absolutely necessary, to prevent annihilation, to leave a position which my regiment had held for nearly ten consecutive hours of severe fighting." Having already lost 200 killed or wounded, Geddes led the remnant of his command some 300 yards back from the Sunken Road, whereupon they met, blocking the way, "a division of the rebels under General Polk thrown completely across my line of retreat." It was now about six o'clock in the evening, and being captured on the spot with most of his survivors, Geddes later claimed "the honor for my regiment of being the last to leave the advanced line of our army on the battlefield of Shiloh on Sunday, April 6."[67]

Polk's men, who had become a juggernaut at the center, encountered another Iowa regiment harder to encircle than Geddes's. Capt. Samuel Edgington of Company A, Twelfth Iowa, had just assumed command after Col. Joseph Woods had been disabled by two wounds. At this point, with his regiment's ammunition exhausted, "a rebel officer rode up to me carrying a white flag and demanded a surrender of my command." Captain Edgington was a stickler for protocol: "I asked [the man] his rank and he told me he was a lieutenant on the staff of General Polk. I promptly ordered him away, saying to him I would confer with no officer below my rank." Firing was resumed, Edgington's account continues, "[and] after a short interval another rebel officer rode up to me . . . demanding a surrender of my command, gruffly saying he could not hold the fire of his men. He informed me he held the rank of captain. I replied to him that I had no thought of surrender . . . and not to send any more demands . . . as I would shoot down any officer attempting again to approach me with a white flag." Edgington had fondly supposed that men from Grant's "army down by the river . . . would rally and come to our rescue." Alas "they came not," and by sunset the Twelfth Iowa had ceased to exist as a fighting unit, all 700 members having been either killed, wounded, or captured by General Polk's forces. Sam Edgington, at least, had his dignity intact. A fellow captive watched as Edgington surrendered his sword to Polk, "who returned the salute with it, and then handed it back to him."[68]

The troops of Polk's I Corps weren't yet finished. Scarcely had several Iowa infantry regiments surrendered than Polk's First Mississippi Cavalry dashed ahead to capture a Michigan battery completely limbered and just about to fly to the rear: four guns, all the horses, officers, and some fifty cannoneers. This was Battery B of the 1st Michigan Light Artillery in its first Civil War battle—and last until the prisoners were exchanged six months later. (In the *Chicago Tribune's* thrilling, if fabulous, account, the capture of Battery B "was under the immediate direction of General Beauregard . . . who received a bullet wound in the arm.") The guns of Battery B were ordered delivered to General Polk for his personal approval. By a mistake surely irksome to Polk, they were sent to Bragg.[69]

Meanwhile Polk had taken Benjamin Prentiss in hand with about 2,200 other prisoners. Prentisss' sword was handed to Pvt. T. M. Simms, who had been with Polk in Columbus, and the private escorted the captive general (a descendant of a Mayflower family) to Col. R. M. Russell of the Twelfth Tennessee; Russell turned over Prentiss and his sword to Polk.[70] Prentiss was more easily captured than cowed, "the public enemy" being the derisive name he gave to Confederates. And as he listened to the hoorays of his captors, he tartly said: "Yell, Boys, you have a right to shout for you have captured the bravest brigade in the U.S. Army."[71] The correspondent Whitelaw Reid, covering the battle for the *Cincinnati Gazette*, would write that even earlier in the day Prentiss's beleaguered men had "held their position with an obstinacy that adds new laurels to the character of the American soldiers."[72] With Prentiss having that sort of reputation, it's understandable why Polk was a little nettled that early reports of the battle said the renowned Yankee had been captured by troops under Bragg. The error was "of small consequence," Polk told his daughter Fanny, but the fact that he brought it up at all was another instance of the sore feelings between him and Bragg.[73]

After the fall of the Hornet's Nest, the remainder of Grant's army was crowding or cowering along the Tennessee River's western banks; it was not done fighting, however. Compressed into a compact ball near their supply depot, these all-but-beaten (yet uncaptured) Yankees were now underneath the shelter of a semicircle of the fifty guns that Grant had ordered into place on a ridge. Gunboats, moreover, were nudging up to the mouth of Lick Creek and lobbing seven-inch shells onto the attackers; the bombardment was maintained all night.[74] Confronted by this array, the pursuing, but exhausted, Confederates slowed to a walk.[75] Possibly—certainly, in the critical opinions of Polk, Hardee, and Bragg—with a little more daylight they could have decisively won the day with a last-gasp effort, but on Beauregard's orders the fight was called off at dusk. "The victory," in his words, "[was] sufficiently complete, and would be consummated the following morning."[76] That night General Prentiss saucily said otherwise to the Confederate officers with whom he was quartered: "You gentlemen have had your way today, but . . . we'll turn the tables on you in the morning."[77]

Tossed about during the course of Sunday's fighting, separated units of Polk's corps spent Sunday night on various parts of the battlefield. Some had dropped to the ground where they were when Beauregard called a halt; some, in Cheatham's Second Division, had enough strength (and hunger) to return for the rations and ammunition left in the bivouac they had occupied Saturday night. The camp was roughly a mile and a half back from their farthest advance.[78] General Polk joined Cheatham's troops for the night, "to insure their being on the ground at an early hour in the morning."[79] Steady rain and random cannon fire from the gunboats fell across the battlefield during the night. The rain, at least, was a balm of a kind, the surgeons said, since it bathed the wounds and wet the throats of the casualties suffering everywhere in the open.[80] A particular blessing for Grant was the longed-for arrival of reinforcements. Gen. Lew Wallace's Third Division of 7,500, who had spent most of Sunday on back roads vainly seeking ways to cross Owl and Snake Creeks, had by dawn Monday finally found their way to the battlefield, and Don Carlos Buell's fresh Army of the Ohio, 25,000 strong, had arrived from Middle Tennessee during the night. Thus supplied, the Federals were now in shape to reverse the course of the battle just as General Prentiss had foretold. As word spread of the arriving reinforcements, Prentiss chuckled that morning to Thomas Jordan: "Ah! didn't I tell you so! There is Buell!"[81] Indeed, with Buell's troops leading the way, Monday unfolded as an ironic replay of Sunday, the roles of drivers and driven transposed. Still, though the Confederates had been greatly depleted by Sunday's losses, and were now largely on the defensive, their resistance from dawn Monday until midafternoon was formidable. Some of the firmest opposition was provided by Polk's corps.

Polk would say later that he had distinctly informed Beauregard that he was spending the night at Cheatham's bivouac, but Beauregard evidently lost track of his corps commander's whereabouts and began to suppose "that the commander of his First Corps had been captured." Not until about 9:30 Monday morning, with fighting already at full tilt, did he learn that Polk was with Cheatham somewhere near Shiloh Church. With that, he fired off a summons, "and rather an imperative one," in the words of Alfred Roman, Beauregard's aide-de-camp. Polk was "to hurry back to the front and plug the gap caused by his absence between General Breckinridge's left and General Bragg's right." And hurry back he did, reads Roman's fulgent text as approved by Beauregard:

> Dashing forward with drawn sword, at the head of Cheatham's fine division, [General Polk] soon formed his line of battle . . . where his presence was so much needed and, with unsurpassed vigor, moved on against a force at least double his own, making one of the most brilliant charges of infantry made on either day of the battle. He drove back the opposing column in confusion, and thus compensated for the tardiness of his appearance on the field.[82]

Polk's own report, dated September 1862, modestly omits mention of his dashing swordplay in the four-hour fight, though he may have had it in mind a few days after the fighting when he assured his wife that Shiloh had been a "magnificent affair." Having been battle-tested initially at the smaller-scale conflict at Belmont, he now "felt somewhat more accustomed" to witnessing carnage on such a large scale: 23,746 casualties.[83]

Possibly on the defensive, however, he did point out in his official Shiloh report that, long before Beauregard's irritable summons reached him Monday morning, he and Cheatham had got "in motion" toward the renewed battle at dawn, their march delayed only "to arrest for some time a stampede [of fellow Confederates] which came from the front." In most generals' official reports, self-serving elements are routinely included, but in this case Bragg thought Polk went too far. He termed this account of the two days' fighting Polk's "Romance of Shiloh."[84]

The fortunes of the battle shifted throughout Monday even as they had on Sunday, but inexorably the Federals' greater numbers prevailed. By early afternoon, Beauregard's adjutant general, Col. Thomas Jordan, aptly described his army to his chief as "a lump of sugar thoroughly soaked with water, but yet preserving its original shape, though ready to dissolve."[85] Lest the lump crumble while he did nothing but watch, Beauregard prudently put an end to the fighting around 3:00 P.M. The Army of the Mississippi, having sustained 10,500 casualties, limped back to Corinth, the train of wagons and men eight miles long. Grant's army chose not to pursue. William T. Sherman would later reportedly say: "We had quite enough of their society for two whole days, and were only too glad to be rid of them on any terms." The two days, in short, had put many to death but decided little. Except that the western Confederates, as one historian would put it, were now well on their way down a "Via Dolorosa" stretching from Shiloh to Durham Station in North Carolina.[86]

Among the walking wounded on the rainy retreat to Corinth that night was an idealistic twenty-year-old named Conrad Wise Chapman. Born in Washington, DC, but living since a young boy with his family in Rome, he was already an accomplished landscape artist when he determined to leave Italy in the early summer of 1861 to enlist in the Confederate Army. While fighting on Shiloh's second day in the ranks of the Company D, 3rd Kentucky Mounted Infantry, a bullet had buried itself under Private Chapman's scalp. Gravely wounded, he now dragged himself along until, exhausted, he reached a roadside house, the floor of which, he said, was already "covered with wounded men." The timing of the artist's desire the summer before to become a mere private soldier had coincided with that of Bishop Leonidas Polk's decision to become a general; now the general had reached the makeshift hospital a little before the private. "One woman was nursing a young fellow on the only bed in the place," Chapman noticed. The soldier "seemed a great friend of Genl Poke's [sic], who wished to cheer him up, and in fact all of us, by recounting the looks of the battlefield after the fight. Our troops were still in possession [Polk was saying], and there were at least three blue coats stretched out for one gray." Chapman only then "learned of the death of our noble Commander." Still assuming that his side had won the two-day battle, he lamented that victory had come at the cost of "a frightful sacrifice."[87] In the nighttime, as Private Chapman finally slept, a wagon rolled down the muddy road outside toward the Mississippi state line. It bore the most singular corpse among the day's thousands: the hastily embalmed body of Leonidas Polk's West Point friend Sidney Johnston.[88]

18

"I Am as Happy as I Generally Am" (1862)

Confederate patriots lacking Leonidas Polk's flourishing esprit de guerre found the winter and spring of 1862 fully disheartening. The commander of Polk's corps, though, was not of a defeatist mind. Let others dwell upon the war's trials in the western Confederacy: the evacuations of Bowling Green, Nashville, and Columbus and the successive defeats at Mill Springs, Fort Henry, Fort Donelson, and New Madrid. And the two terrible days at Shiloh? Deemed by most impartial reckonings as no better than a tie, Polk was his usual sunny self: "We have dealt them a terrible blow and taught them a lesson!" he chirped to daughter Frances.[1]

Once New Orleans became theirs on May 1, 1862, the Federals not long after occupied Memphis. By then General Polk seems to have become almost inured to Confederate setbacks, rarely if ever losing heart. Yet bearing up in Corinth, where he found himself for the next two months, took some doing. The town on the Tennessee–Mississippi border had become a huge, miserable hospital for some 49,500 ailing military men, either Shiloh's wounded or those otherwise diseased and dying. Initially, almost half the town's population were patients, most of them suffering and bearing tales from the front lines. "I was shocked at what the men have told me about some dead Federals that they saw on the battlefield," Kate Cumming, a doughty war nurse, wrote in her diary. "They say that on the bands of their hats was written, 'Hell or Corinth;' meaning, that they were determined to reach one of the places. Heaven help the poor wretches who could degrade themselves thus."[2]

Polk, of course, was never one for gloom. "I have at no time ever doubted our ultimate success," he assured his sister Susan.[3] He did not seem to despair even when receiving a melancholy letter from his wife in New Orleans written four days after Easter as she related the isolating woes in her family's New Orleans home. As she reported, the city was practically in the hands of the "Lincolnites," calamitous news to her, and she had "sent the silver to a place of security" (it was Liverpool, England). Worst of all for Fanny, her daughter Frances "seems entirely prostrated by anticipated evils." As for herself, she "was not much of a hand to express [her] feelings" but longed to see her husband once more. The truth was, the lamenting wife continued, she had endured the accumulating pain of their separation "for nearly five years"—ever since her husband first set out to build the University of the South. After that, she said, "your time has been so taken up that all our former companionship, except at rare intervals, ceased, and I felt as if I had to face everything alone. Now there is nothing to look forward to on earth." Her morbid consolation, she concluded, was her hope that she, her husband, and the children would all be reunited once they had all died and gone to a heavenly rest.[4]

Even while the general was absorbing these dispiriting ruminations, more bad news came up from New Orleans. For one thing, the city's cotton stores, held by brokers and valued at some $2 million, had been set afire by patriot citizens (the bales were sloshed with whiskey) to keep them from falling into the hands of the approaching enemy. Sugar, rice, and molasses were dumped, much of the business district was looted, and as New Orleans author George Washington Cable would write of these days from his boyhood, "the glare of . . . sinuous miles of flame set men and women weeping and wailing thirty miles away on the farther shore of Lake Pontchartrain."[5] Polk, still owner of a cotton plantation in Bolivar County, Mississippi, was among the heaviest losers, the fire effectively destroying what remained of his and Fanny's fortune.[6] Compunding the bad news, Polk would soon be obliged to authorize the burning of his cotton already baled in Bolivar County, lest it fall into Yankee hands.[7]

In another defeating incident, as David Farragut's and David Porter's ships edged up the Mississippi River closer to New Orleans, the defenders had launched the CSS *Louisiana*, a highly menacing ironclad being built specifically to keep the Yankees away from the South's key port city. It was, alas, minus its intended engines and propellers. A few months before, at Polk's "very earnest solicitation," the Confederate Navy had agreed to build the gunboat, and more lately Polk was personally championing the vessel with proprietary zeal to President Davis. "On this boat I have been relying very strongly," he wrote on April 15, and to train a crew to fight on this novel vessel he recommended that the president name as captain a former

US Navy officer now on Polk's staff. The friend of several years was First Lt. William B. Richmond, "a man of coolness, nerve and judgment, . . . whose whole heart is in our cause."[8]

While Polk awaited a reply,[9] the Yankees' naval threat was mounting, so the unfinished *Louisiana*, four weeks shy of completion, was slid off her ways. As she had at least sixteen guns mounted, she was tugged downstream to assist two riverbank forts attempting to hold back a fleet of seventeen Union gunboats. The desperate defense did not succeed, the *Louisiana* firing only twelve shots, and on April 28, hours before New Orleans was formally surrendered to David Farragut, the ship was furtively set afire by her crew, there being 10,000 pounds of gunpowder in her hold. Then, while other Confederate officers discussed surrender terms in David Porter's cabin "as coolly as if at tea-table among their friends," the *Louisiana* exploded nearby in spectacular, vengeful fashion. The Yankees' anger at being deprived a prize was only a little less explosive.[10]

As several other naval enterprises had caught Polk's fancy in the first months of the war, the military use of steamships seemed to be a fascination that was fed as much by his longtime love of steam power—whether harnessed to trains, sawmills, cordage spinners, or paddle wheelers—as by his determination to protect the Mississippi River. Like the CSS *Louisiana*, however, most of his steamboat schemes had come to naught. The one more remaining up his sleeve would be scuttled before he could launch it some months later by a bureaucratic Braxton Bragg.[11] Yet even as the debris of the demolished *Louisiana* was floating down to the Gulf of Mexico, the general was his old self again, displaying his remarkable brio. In a letter meant to lift the sagging spirits of young Frances, he assured her heartily that "except that I am separated from my family and grieved with the disturbed state of the country, I am as happy as I generally am, and you know that is not miserable."[12]

Five days after Shiloh, President Davis had elevated Maj. Gen. Braxton Bragg two ranks; he now became, like Beauregard, a full general. Most pleased of all by this event was Elise Bragg. "You are relieved from obeying the commands of our vain glorious Bishop!" she wrote to her husband, though it is unlikely that Polk, even with the slight edge of seniority he briefly held over Bragg, had ever commanded the experienced soldier to do anything. But now that Polk was expected to obey the commands of Bragg, formerly a mere parishioner under the bishop's authority, the reversal of roles became recurrently disagreeable to both men.[13] For the time being, there was concord between the two, both cooperating with William Hardee and Earl Van Dorn in the execution of a masterful departure from Corinth.

Confronted in late May by 125,000 Federals troops under Henry W. Halleck, who had been cautiously approaching the Rebel front ever since Shiloh, Beauregard and his generals had unanimously concluded that their armies, outnumbered now two-to-one, were facing certain entrapment.[14] To avoid that, the generals determined to cozen the Yankees, doing so when the entire command stole away from their camp town in the middle of the night of May 29, essentially undetected. To preserve secrecy of the clandestine operation, Beauregard had earlier forbidden all publications and letters to mention troop arrangements and ordered all journalists to stay twenty-five miles away from Corinth. And to stoke his soldiers' martial fire, Polk was pleased that the Reverend Benjamin Palmer, a visiting Presbyterian preacher friend from New Orleans, had come to read aloud to the men of one brigade the "Woman's Order" just issued by Gen. Benjamin Butler, the military governor of the occupied city. Infuriating Southern manhood, the order was meant to curb the escalating harassment of Federal troops by the city's inhospitable Confederate women. Butler's General Orders No. 28 declared that "when any female shall, by word, gesture, or movement, insult or show contempt for any officer or soldier of the United States, she shall . . . be treated as a woman of the town plying her avocation." The reaction by one corporal in the ranks hearing the words of the artful order—"Oh! monster of iniquity!"—was just what the preacher would have wanted. "Not a word was spoken," the soldier, John Gordon Law, told his diary, "but the firm, resolute look, the compressed lip, the flashing eye of every soldier, said plainer than words could say that the insolent invaders of our sacred soil should never cross our entrenchments without walking over the dead bodies of sixty thousand determined and indignant men." Given that "Beast Butler" was among the enemies most despised by Polk, he helpfully supplied his men with words matching their fierce looks. Polk had promised the soldiers, Law related, that "we would go into battle with this motto: 'Our mothers, our sisters, our daughters, our wives, our country and our God.'"[15]

Beauregard's troops, energized by either a preacher's rhetoric or the hoped-for pleasure of deceiving their hated enemies, carried off the ruse almost flawlessly. (Like a schoolmaster to children, Beauregard had required his generals to repeat after him the detailed instructions he had just given them.) At about eleven o'clock on the night of May 29, columns of soldiers began their muffled departure along roads leading south out of the town, some 14,000 in Polk's I Corps alone. Campfires with no one around them were left burning along the Rebels' front lines. Two locomotives towing empty strings of cars rattled repeatedly into and out of town, their arrivals greeted by cheering troops as though fresh reinforcements were pouring in. Loaded trains departed in silence, bearing the sick and wounded, food, stores, guns, and ammunition. A single band played "Taps" at various places, sure it would be heard by the Yankees' pickets. Gen. John Pope was thoroughly hoodwinked: At one o'clock in the morning he telegraphed Washington: "The enemy is reinforcing heavily, by trains, in my front. . . . The cheering is immense every time they unload. . . . I have no doubt that I shall be attacked in heavy force at daylight." Pope's only daylight attack might have been by apoplexy. Five hours later, when skirmishers from the 36th Indiana Volunteers were ordered forward to the Rebel works, they "found them entirely abandoned by the enemy."[16] Pursuit, desultory at best, was soon given up.

Having evaporated in Corinth, Beauregard and his corps commanders reanimated themselves some fifty miles south, in Tupelo, Mississippi. Though tactically justifiable, the Confederates' withdrawal deeper into Mississippi left a defensive hole in the region; that situation led successively to the fall of the Mississippi River's Fort Pillow and ultimately the city of Memphis. Vicksburg was now the Confederacy's only remaining Mississippi River stronghold, and these Western Department losses so exacerbated the ill feeling the president already held toward Beauregard that, while Beauregard was on sick leave, Davis assigned his new four-star general Bragg "permanently as commander of Department No. 2."[17] Exercising rearrangement of the armies he had inherited, Bragg put Gen. William Hardee in command of his main force and assigned Polk "second in command of the forces." Unbeknownst to Polk, however, four days before Davis modified the command structure Bragg had written to Adj. Gen. Samuel Cooper in Richmond that of all the major generals under him, Hardee alone was "a suitable commander"; he was thoroughly dismissive of Polk, lumping him with some other generals he regarded as "incumbrances . . . better out of the way." Polk's promotion to "second in command," accordingly, was certainly a "dubious title," as noted by the Army of Tennessee historian Thomas Connelly.[18]

Even if divining that he numbered among Bragg's encumbrances, Polk propounded satisfaction with his lot. He assured his family, then coping with their own privations in occupied New Orleans, that his army's getting out of noisome Corinth, and relocating in Tupelo, was a move much to the good. The new tent city where wells and fresh latrines had been dug, kitchens set up, and ovens constructed comprised "a delightful [woodland] camp." More bucolic still, there were no enemy guns being fired at them. Polk wished Fanny and the girls could "look in on me and see how comfortable I am."[19]

A visitor to Polk's camp about that time was the polished Camille Armaud Jules Marie, Prince de Polignac, a French national and a lieutenant colonel on Beauregard's staff. He was fond of war, wine, women, and epicurean dining. His journal entry for June 14, 1862 reads: "Rode to Gen. Polk's hd.-qrs. where I was engaged to dinner. Dinner good. I say 'good,' and yet if I had been served such a dinner in Paris at any restaurant I should have raised a bustle, abused the 'garcon,' cursed the owner . . . flung my towel right into the plate, gone off in a hurry without paying, lost my temper and probably my umbrella. . . . All is comparative in this world."[20]

Polk's nephew, Capt. James Hilliard Polk of the 6th Tennessee Cavalry, looked in on the general too now and then and reported on his uncle's campground contentment to his own family. "If you could see him in his shirt sleeves—white sand floor and cloth roof to his house—enjoying a *cob* pipe every day—you would be amused. He has a good many of these rustic mereshaums to supply friends. Says, whenever 'simmons gits ripe, he intends to have some beer.' I spend some very pleasant hours with him whenever I get off camp."[21]

That same lightheartedness was evident when Polk wrote his sister, Susan Rayner, in Raleigh, telling her that he was getting on just fine. Evidently he had finally tamped down his wish to be relieved of military duty. He, indeed, had at last adjusted to the radical change from bishop to general. "Things now go very naturally," he said, adding with a little pride a homely expression: "As our Western people say, we manage 'to curry up our corner of the cabin.'"[22]

There were limits, all the same, to perfect adjustment. The everyday coarseness of army life surrounding his little patch did not sit well with the gentlemanly homebody. He shared this discomfort with his Tennessee bishop friend James Otey. After a decade's residence in Memphis, Otey was in failing health and was convalescing with church friends in Mississippi.[23] Gladdened that Polk was planning to visit him at the home of Margaret Johnstone, the widowed mistress of Annandale, a plantation with its own chapel in Madison County, Otey replied in mid-July to a letter from Polk the previous week.[24] To the army camp bishop's complaint of withering in a moral desert, Otey sympathized, paraphrasing the condition as Polk's "thirsting for Christian intercourse and communion."[25] The coming visit, Otey hoped, should revive his needy friend, but in the meantime he confided that, for his part, during "musings of the midnight hour" he would often experience Polk's "image risen before me, and the communings we have had together have come up to remembrance." Since Otey was persuaded that divine displeasure was the source of sorrows on earth, he would wonder during these wakeful séances what had the Lord seen in his brother bishop's conduct that He had found "it necessary to correct by laying upon you so heavy a burden."

The afflicting burdens, as Otey saw it, were Polk's "separation from your family, even for a whole year and more," and his being cast "among men of turbulent and lawless passions, men often of no principle, their lives deformed by crimes and their hands stained with blood." It was a society, in short, rife with hard men who supposed battlefield heroism an acceptable substitute for Christian piety. Quoting a Hebrew Psalmist surrounded by ungodly barbarians, Otey lamented: "You have been constrained to cry out 'Woe is me that I dwell in Mesech!'" Polk's campground woes, of course, were worsened by greater villains yet: Yankees whom Otey saw as the "authors of all the misery and suffering and anguish which have filled up our cup for the last year."[26]

If Otey's doleful letter failed to slake Polk's thirst for Christian communion, his Mississippi visit with the aging bishop may have provided the looked-for refreshment. Upon his return to camp life, Polk caught up on overdue correspondence, sounding in fine fettle while composing for history an acerbic and sometimes droll eight-page defense of his generalship at the Battle of Belmont. Sent to Richmond, this was his official reply to the charge by Gideon Pillow that Polk had left his troops without ammunition or reinforcements in the face of the enemy. To which assertion Polk responded: "How General Pillow could have risked himself in making such a statement . . . when he knew that witnesses abounded who could disprove [it] . . . is difficult to account for, except upon the principle that the power to believe one's own inventions, like all other powers, grows upon what it feeds, and is strengthened by exercise."[27]

General Pillow had written his letter of resignation two months after Belmont, telling the secretary of war that he was all the more hurt by Polk's abandonment because he had "enjoyed an intimate friendship with General Polk for twenty-five years." To this claim by his former Tennessee neighbor, Polk rejoined archly:

If any intercourse which was the fruit of what he regarded as an 'intimate friendship' during that period has been profitable or gratifying to him, I am glad of it. I am compelled to say, however, that while I must confess an acquaintance for that length of time, so far from its inducing me to admit him to relations which might be dignified by friendship, I have every year found increasing reasons for caution in exposing myself to an unguarded intercourse, and my army experience has not diminished my sense of the importance of such vigilance.

With Pillow now put in his place, Polk could go back to enjoying his campground comforts—until an attempt by a party or parties unknown was made a few days later to evict him from his cozy "corner of the cabin."

As recounted by the general and his son William, sometime during July the War Department in Richmond ordered Polk to drop everything having to do with commanding 14,000 troops in Tupelo and report to Jackson, Mississippi. His new assignment was to serve on August 12 as president of a court of inquiry, a legal proceeding involving an officer or soldier. Polk's previous judicial experience was limited to serving on ecclesiastical courts weighing the peccadillos of erring brother bishops; that trifling background probably led him to discredit any suggestion that his legal expertise had recommended him for the assignment. Rather, he believed that someone wished him shunted from his corps command. A few days later, Richmond authorities rescinded the assignment, and thereafter Polk never doubted that the someone behind the original order had been Braxton Bragg. Or as Polk's son phrased it in a recollection after the war, his father had concluded the order was an "emanation from Bragg" who "designed engineering [Polk] on the shelf and so out of the army."[28] No official records of the court of inquiry summons could be found, but General Polk's conclusion is plausible.[29]

It is further most likely that it was Polk whom Bragg was defaming a few weeks later at a private dinner. Surrounded by his staff, he referred to one of the generals under his command as an "old woman, utterly worthless." A visiting military friend at the table (a former brother-in-law, as it happened, of Jefferson Davis) was astonished by Bragg's openly declared disdain for someone the friend considered "widely respected and admired." Lt. Gen. Richard Taylor afterward chided Bragg for his language, suggesting his words were sure to get back to the insulted general. (Taylor related the incident in a book he published years later but inserted a short blank line instead of Bragg's name.) "I speak the truth," Bragg harrumphed. And almost certainly the words did get back to Polk. To a daughter he later gibed his pitying and "lofty contempt" for Bragg, a man he said he had "dry-nursed . . . for the whole period of [my] connexion with him." While their mutual dislike continued to fester, the two managed to display a surface civility toward one another, but it must have been Polk's "lofty contempt" that lay at the root of his subsequent, even recurrent defiance (when not actual insubordination) of Bragg's authority.[30]

While the enmity between Bragg and Polk was taking its own course, Don Buell's Army of the Ohio abandoned Corinth. Having no one to shoot and nothing but time on their hands, the Yankee soldiers had been ordered in mid-June to move toward Chattanooga in southeastern Tennessee, primarily, orders read, to dislodge "Kirby Smith and his rebel force from East Tennessee."[31] Wresting Chattanooga from Confederate hands had been on the Federal government's wish list for some time, President Lincoln himself weighing in to offer advice to his generals.[32] As it happened, a brigadier in an expedition possibly not yet noticed by Lincoln had been marching down from Nashville that same week and had shelled the city from across the Tennessee River for most of two days. The men of Brig. Gen. James Negley's brigade of infantry and cavalry had reached their destination by tramping across the fallow campus of Bishop Polk's University of the South.[33]

As for Buell's proposed assault on the town, while proceeding en route across northern Alabama, he was to repair the vital, war-wrecked Memphis & Charleston Railway as he went. It was well into July 1862, consequently, before he had reached Stevenson, Alabama, just west of Chattanooga. He was too late to push aside Kirby Smith's now reinforced army. Buell, accordingly, paused beside the Tennessee River to await further, unpredictable Confederate developments. Unnerving to any Yankees in the region, for example, were the swirling and destructive cavalry raids being carried out that summer by Cols. John Hunt Morgan and Nathan Bedford Forrest—a plague of marauding throughout Middle Tennessee and bluegrass Kentucky such that Federal politicians in the Tennessee capital became jittery to the point of seeing things. Reports circulating in Nashville had it that Generals Polk, Cheatham, and Hardee and their infantry commands had entered Chattanooga on the Fourth of July. In fact, all these Rebels had celebrated Independence Day 200 miles away in Tupelo, Mississippi.[34]

A feisty young diarist in Harrodsburg, Kentucky, meanwhile, fed up with the insolent Yankees occupying her state, pleaded to her diary: "Tell the Southern soldiers, for Heaven's sake to come and deliver the women and children of Kentucky."[35] Surrounded by civilian Unionists, fence-straddlers, and bushwhackers, Lizzie Hardin belonged to Kentucky's Secesh minority, but her Rebel sentiments were shared ardently by Braxton Bragg in Tupelo and Edmund Kirby Smith in Knoxville. Even as she pined for deliverance, these two like-minded generals were making militant plans to lift the women and children of Kentucky (and those of Tennessee) from beneath the Yankee heel. Kirby Smith had weighed the imminent danger of Buell's approaching army against his outnumbered Army of East Tennessee and wrote to Bragg on July 20 to say "your cooperation is much needed." He wrote more urgently four days later asking Bragg to "take command in person" and wage "a brilliant summer campaign."[36] Bragg had lately sent John McCown's division to bolster Kirby Smith and, further, had already determined to leave Mississippi for Chattanooga. Then and there, Bragg locking arms with Kirby Smith, the two of them would drive all the Yankees flying out of the South's heartland and never stop until they reached the Ohio River. Accordingly, on July 21 Bragg ordered his Army of the Mississippi—34,000 strong and efficiently drilled and reorganized by William Hardee—to begin leaving Tupelo for Chattanooga "with the least delay practicable."[37] Cavalry, wagons, and artillery struck out directly cross-country along dirt roads; the infantry went roundabout by railroad through Mobile, Montgomery, and Atlanta. Left behind to keep tabs on Ulysses S. Grant were sizable forces commanded by Sterling Price and Earl Van Dorn.[38] Bragg and his staff hurried ahead, and presently he and Kirby Smith confirmed their plans. Step one: they would wrest Tennessee from the invaders by looping into the state in Buell's rear, then severing the supply lines essential to Buell in Tennessee and to Grant in northern Mississippi. Step two: they would invade occupied Kentucky and reclaim it as well from the Yankee invaders, just as Lizzie Hardin had proposed.

The Confederate generals' agreement—loosely sketched in correspondence in June before being mutually solidified at their face-to-face Chattanooga meeting on July 31—began to unravel a week or so later. Bragg's wagons, creaking overland, had yet to arrive, and Kirby Smith was champing to be off. (As historian Thomas Connelly assesses Kirby Smith, he "was a good leader, but not a follower; he could command, but not cooperate.")[39] The time was never more better, Kirby Smith believed, for thrusting his Army of East Tennessee into Kentucky. He would first duck around the Union brigadier general George Washington Morgan's iron grip on Cumberland Gap, the historic roadway at 1,600 feet tying together Tennessee, Kentucky, and Virginia. (Daniel Boone had traversed it in 1775.) Avoiding Morgan, a friend from prewar days, Kirby Smith would then weasel his way into eastern Kentucky through the less accessible Big Creek Gap and Roger's Gap and there await the arrival of the Federals, drawn out of Middle Tennessee as if by magnetism. Since that was approximately Bragg's personal aspiration as well, Kirby Smith in a letter to Jefferson Davis hinted disingenuously that he had Bragg's support for his unilateral movement.[40] Bragg in fact was opposed but was reluctant to pull his rank of full general in Kirby Smith's military department. Resigned to his fate instead, Bragg urged Kirby Smith to be careful and hoped "we may all unite in Ohio."[41] Kirby Smith and two divisions left Knoxville on August 14 at 4:00 A.M.

After two weeks of back-and-forth struggle through bushwhacker country and roadless mountainous terrain (Kirby Smith compared his army's trek to Cortez's burn-the-ships-and-don't-look-back conquest of Mexico's Aztecs), his Army of East Tennessee entered Kentucky's fertile bluegrass region. Haplessly raw Federal troops sent to head off these determined Rebels near Richmond, Kentucky, were disastrously swept aside on August 30 (5,300 of the 6,500 Yankees involved were either killed, wounded, captured, or missing). Then, having chased the survivors and officials of the state government out of Frankfort, the capital, and sent them packing to Louisville, Kirby Smith set up headquarters in Lexington. He had snatched back most of central Kentucky from the enemy, and while awaiting Bragg's arrival from the south, he intended to enlist secession-minded Kentuckians into his fold.[42]

Bragg made ready to move into Tennessee, reorganizing his army yet again by dividing it into two wings. Hardee commanded the left, Polk the right. To what extent the "utterly worthless old woman" Polk was consulted on this and other decisions by Bragg is not known, but Polk would later express his contrary opinions on the merits and execution of Bragg's Tennessee and Kentucky invasion. Probably aided by hindsight (and, like most generals, having a knack for self-embellishment), Polk later boasted to his brother-in-law Kenneth Rayner that from the outset he had expected Bragg's and Kirby Smith's combined operation to fail (which by then Polk had seen happen). Had *he* been in command, he said, he would not have moved the army to Chattanooga, as Bragg had, but would instead have ordered a "more rapid and energetic campaign" by marching the Confederates straight up the middle of Tennessee from their Tupelo base, "falling on first one corps of the enemy, and then on another, thus destroying them in detail."[43] This was exactly an option Bragg had considered and discarded. Polk's second-guessing raises the issue of whether he was always as guileless as a bishop might be expected to be. Just before setting out from Chattanooga, he had evinced collegial enthusiasm with Bragg. To Susan, he had written that "we have a fine army, and are on the eve of attacking a Federal force under Genl Buell. We . . . hope to take Tennessee and Kentucky from under the heel of the tyrants."[44]

Bragg's army of 30,000 began crossing the Tennessee River, headed west, toward the end of August. For Polk, the march began in a region fully familiar to him from his exploratory roams when founding the University of the South, and it had the added pleasure, as he told Susan, of a family outing: among his 15,500 soldiers were his two sons ("Hamilton and William, two fine fellows") and four of his Polk nephews: Lucius Eugene Polk ("now a colonel of a regiment, and a gallant man") along with George's sons, James and Rufus, and Lucius's son William.

Before crossing the mountains and dropping down into the plains of Middle Tennessee, Hardee's left wing and Polk's right wing both had first to thread up the Sequatchie Valley in the Cumberland Plateau. Like much of eastern Kentucky, East Tennessee was a region of Unionists. Or as General Orders No. 1 spelled it out to the men, the region in which they found themselves was a "country . . . infested with a cowardly and insidious foe, seeking opportunity to assassinate single persons and small parties." As one safeguard, when nature called a man on the march, he was instructed to first get permission from his captain to leave the ranks, to entrust his musket to a comrade, then to make haste to finish.[45]

Don Buell, meanwhile, had repositioned his Army of the Ohio, arraying it across Middle Tennessee and bracing for Bragg's assault. Buell was assuming that Bragg would head for Nashville. The Confederate commander had indeed contemplated that destination, but he had since changed his mind, persuaded by Kirby Smith that "a junction with my command" in Kentucky promised "certainty of success."[46] The Confederate columns, therefore, once through the valleys and passes of the southern Appalachian Mountains, angled northwest away from Nashville on a line that would take them to Glasgow, Kentucky. But their whereabouts so mystified the Yankees that President Lincoln himself was compelled to ask Buell: "What degree of certainty have you that Bragg with his command is not now in the Valley of the Shenandoah, Virginia?" Buell, guessing, assured the president that Bragg was "certainly this side of the Cumberland Mountains with his whole force." That night, a spy let Buell know he luckily had it right.[47]

By now rumors were moving faster than Bragg's forced marches. "The enemy have advanced on Cincinnati and threaten an attack!" an officer in Louisville reported, and the city was said to "be in consternation."[48] Buell was in motion too, racing sideways and north so as not to wind up behind Bragg and hoping as well to find a way to hit Kirby Smith in Lexington. Thus began a series of crab-walk steps between the two armies, avoiding immediate contact, but on a roundabout collision course toward Perryville, Kentucky.[49] In a mood jovial for him, Bragg had laudatory things to communicate, even to Polk: "We are pleased to hear of your progress, and trust we shall soon be together again," he telegraphed. "The enemy are moving on a line parallel to us from Nashville to Bowling Green. They are striving hard to be ahead, but you have the advantage, and I trust will avail of it. Yours very truly, Braxton Bragg."[50]

Of the thirteen white stars on the Confederates' official flag, one of the dimmest stood for Kentucky. Aiming to add luster to it, Bragg had decided that his current invasion must be as much a public relations campaign as a military expedition (just as Robert E. Lee hoped his Army of Northern Virginia's invasion of Maryland that same month would tip another border state into the Confederate fold). The time was ripe, Bragg was sure. "A Louisville paper . . . represents Cincinnati . . . in consternation," he told Polk happily and urged him as he progressed into the state to use his hortatory pulpit talents to "arouse the people to join us."[51] For his own idea of arousing Kentuckians, Bragg after reaching Glasgow issued a recruitment broadside seasoned with sexual innuendo that Kentucky's yeomanry would not fail to grasp. "We come . . . to punish with a rod of iron . . . to avenge the cowardly insults to your women," he proclaimed. "If you prefer Federal rule, show it by your frowns. . . . If you choose rather to come within the folds of our brotherhood, then cheer us with the smiles of your women. . . . Women of Kentucky, your persecutions and heroic bearing have reached our ear. Banish henceforth forever from your minds the fear of loathsome prisons or insulting visitations." And let the ladies "scoff with shame" any Kentucky man "who would prove recreant in his duty to you."[52]

The prospects for the Confederacy's protecting the honor of Kentucky's belles and winning over the hearts and minds of the state's waffling menfolk seemed bright. Kirby Smith's army, for one thing, had managed to get in the rear of George Morgan in Cumberland Gap. With supply lines cut off, Morgan was soon short of food; consequently, one of the best friends East Tennessee Unionists had was obliged in mid-September to skedaddle with his brigade across southern Kentucky. Kirby Smith, by now occupying Lexington, had become justly renowned after routing the Yankees at Richmond (Kentucky). With Bragg's Army of the Mississippi now flooding into the state like a runaway river, captured Yankee mail revealed the writers, by Bragg's reading anyhow, as "greatly demoralized, disheartened and deceived; utterly in the dark as to our movements."[53] Bragg's sunny humor was soon overcast when the legions of fired-up Kentucky recruits he had hoped for did not materialize. Contrarily, too, some of his own soldiers, relaxing from their avenging mission, were now giving thought to recreational pursuits. A brigadier in Polk's wing, tied down by duties, complained to a friend that though his campground was "distant only a few miles from the 'Great Mammoth Cave,' however anxious we may have been to visit it, we had no time just then to do so."[54]

After both armies paused for a few days at arm's length—the Rebels in Glasgow, the Yankees in Bowling Green—the two resumed moving north on parallel courses in the direction of Louisville, shadowing one another almost amicably, as though in a dance promenade. What General Polk thought of these maneuvers at the time is not recorded, but he would say later (again to Kenneth Rayner, continuing his second-guessing of Bragg's Kentucky leadership) that Bragg should have ordered a "cross march, falling on [Buell's] flank and crushing him before he could get to the relief of Louisville."[55]

Still sidestepping slowly north, the armies eventually clashed at Munfordville, a town whose salient feature was its handsome stone-pier trestle where the Louisville & Nashville Railroad's trains crossed the valley of the Green River (or occasionally did, whenever the bridge, repeatedly blown up and rebuilt, was intact). In mid-September, without authority and with more audacity than wisdom, Brig. Gen. James Chalmers, Polk's subordinate in the lead of his columns, led his brigade against the Yankees' dug-in garrison at the crossing. The Confederates were repulsed with heavy losses. In immediate response, to teach the insolent enemy a lesson and to bolster the morale of his own men, Bragg drew his entire army off its intended route to join Kirby Smith and surrounded Munfordville's recently victorious garrison of 4,000 Union officers and men. Now intimidated by the number of their foes, some Roman Catholic soldiers sought out the Indiana chaplain Peter P. Cooney to hear what might be the last confessions of their lives. Father Cooney and the soldiers constructed a makeshift confessional in an open field, their blankets draped over propped-up muskets. "I sat eight hours without getting off my seat," the confessor priest told his brother in a letter.[56]

Next day, without a shot being fired, Col. John R. Wilder wisely accepted Bragg's demand for unconditional surrender.[57] The Federal prisoners were then paroled and escorted under flags of truce to Buell, a tactic designed to embarrass the Federal commander as much as to oblige him to shelter and feed them. The Confederates then settled into the captured earthworks and bathed themselves in the Green River, the first opportunity for such a luxury since crossing the Tennessee back in August.[58] At that point, "the entire army was in the best of spirits," said Gen. Joseph Wheeler, leader of Hardee's cavalry. "I met and talked with Generals Hardee, Polk, Cheatham, and Buckner; all were enthusiastic over our success . . . in getting Buell where he would be compelled to fight us to such a disadvantage."[59] Bragg was equally eager. Should the Federals now wish to come along and give him battle, Bragg boasted to a Unionist Munfordville citizen, his army would regard the encounter as no "more than a breakfast spell [and] could eat Buell's up alive."[60]

Buell, however, parked in Cave City ten miles south of Munfordville while awaiting reinforcements from Nashville, did not present his army for Bragg's breakfast, nor for any other meal. And as for the Rebels' other appetites for friendship and food, the population was hostile and the "country barren and destitute of corn for the men and fodder for the animals." Thus, on September 20, Bragg was obliged to retire from the picked-over neighborhood around Munfordville, marching fifty-nine arduous miles northeast to Bardstown, where plentiful provisions awaited. The rendezvous with Kirby Smith's army, then in Lexington, was closer at hand.[61]

The Kentucky maneuvers, up to then, were anticlimactic for Federals and Confederates alike. For failing to engage Bragg around Munfordville, Buell was subjected to criticism throughout the North, rumors in the ranks even asserting that he and Bragg were brothers-in-law. Bragg was criticized, too, accused of skulking away from a fight, and preposterous as the brothers-in-law rumor was, it was an explanation that fit each general's lack of bellicosity toward the other. St. John Richardson Liddell, a brigadier in Kentucky under Bragg, and never his apologist, said simply: "I have frequently heard it said that Bragg *ought* to have fought Buell at Munfordville. But the truth is he could not wait [there] without starving."[62]

Was Bragg in fact too diffident in not carrying the fight to Buell? And was his siege of Munfordville simply bravado or a judicious use of the Confederates' time and resources? Either of these elements, it has been argued, would have been better spent in joining Kirby Smith earlier and in capturing still-defenseless Louisville. (The time spent in Munfordville included a day off observing, on September 18, a "day of thanksgiving and prayer," proclaimed throughout the Confederacy by Jefferson Davis; in part, it was a tribute to Kirby Smith's victory at Richmond, Kentucky.)[63] The wisdom of the whole enterprise has long been debated by historians, beginning with General Polk's son William. The most judicious weighings of the facts, and the least censorious judgments of Bragg, are those recently made by the historians Grady McWhiney and James Lee McDonough. McWhiney, for example, says that up to the time Bragg left Munfordville he "had made no irreparable strategic or tactical mistakes." The Southern historian McDonough, demurring, thought "Bragg's failure to fight at Munfordville was one of the great crises of the whole war—probably the greatest moral crisis."[64]

With the roads to the west now open, Buell hurried his army north, some of his columns passing unchallenged through Munfordville. And once in Louisville he thoroughly strengthened the city's defenses against what had been feared as an almost certain attack by Bragg and Kirby Smith. (One military observer reported that some citizens, on the verge of fleeing the city, were "not over-assured that Bragg might not follow them all the way to the Great Lakes.")[65] Bragg, however, had public relations plans that took precedence over immediate aggression and pursuit. While his soldiers rested around Bardstown, he resumed his efforts at enlisting young Kentuckians into Confederate ranks and at persuading their families and other civilians to declare Confederate allegiance. As his campaign to win friends was not going well (he had brought 15,000 muskets into Kentucky and still had few volunteers to shoot them), he hit upon an ingenious recruiting idea: once he and Kirby Smith had reinstated the exiled secessionist government in Frankfort, Bragg could then claim the legal authority to *draft* Kentucky men into his army.[66] Perhaps this was a fabulous notion, but as the general informed the War Department in Richmond: "Unless a change occurs soon, we must abandon the garden spot of Kentucky to its cupidity. The love of ease and fear of pecuniary loss are the fruitful sources of this evil."[67]

Bragg and his staff set off on the political mission on September 29. About the only encouragement along the way came the next day from Polk, left behind. Information reaching Bardstown, though filtered and tainted by Rebel hands, was that Abraham Lincoln's Emancipation Proclamation, issued in a preliminary form a few days earlier, was causing "great demoralization of Buell's army." To distract his disgruntled troops, Buell was supposed likely to come out of Louisville to pick a fight. Not intimidated by that prospect, Polk did begin to hope adverse reaction to the proclamation might actually be the undoing of the Union war effort. "This does not look very promising for their cause," he wrote to Bragg.[68] (His dispatch does not reveal Polk's personal feelings regarding the freeing of the slaves—feelings that, as we have seen, may well have been conflicted.) Still, it was a downcast Bragg who called on Kirby Smith to gather his army at Frankfort and join in the inaugural ceremony. He conceded to Polk his discouragement: "Recruiting [is] at a discount; even the women are giving reasons why individuals cannot go."[69] Northern sentiments were at play against him too; at about the same time, the Kentucky Home Guards, instead of joining the Confederacy as had been hoped, enlisted almost to a man in Buell's army.[70]

While away politicking, Bragg at the outset had kept a light check on Polk's reins—too light, he would learn, as Polk elected a day or so later to exercise defiance.[71] Among the principal towns then occupied by Bragg and Kirby Smith, each manned by forces of various sizes, were Bardstown,

Harrodsburg, and Danville to the south and Lexington and Frankfort to the north; together they described a rough triangle in north-central Kentucky with Louisville, now Buell's new base, about thirty miles west and north of the triangle. At Danville east of Bardstown on Tuesday, September 30, Bragg directed Polk politely ("I consider it best . . .") to move the army out of Bardstown and to relocate northward in the direction of Louisville. This would place the men, their rations growing short again, closer to grain mills and leave them, Bragg said, "the better to invest Louisville."[72]

Yet once Bragg's directive had reached him, possibly not until Thursday, October 2, Polk did not follow its terms: instead of relocating the whole army, he sent but one brigade. Bragg's low-key phrasing probably gave Polk the latitude he enjoyed when being ordered about by his disesteemed commander; in any case, Polk decided the logic of the order had been upended by events changing faster than the transmittal of messages between the generals.[73] On Wednesday, he had learned that heavily manned southbound columns of Federals had left Louisville on roads clearly leading toward Bardstown. He concluded, therefore, not to put his own army in motion on a northward slant that would expose it broadside to Buell's approaching forces. Polk's caution was sound enough; the greater fact was that since Wednesday others of Buell's columns had been moving east. On a front sixty miles wide, Buell was indeed approaching both Polk in Bardstown and Kirby Smith in Frankfort. Informed of the enemy's nearing Bardstown by his cavalry chief, Gen. Joseph Wheeler, Polk notified Bragg on Thursday: "I shall keep the enemy well under observation, and my actions will be governed by the circumstances which shall be developed. If an opportunity presents itself, I will strike." Barring that, he would fall back defensively eastward toward Harrodsburg or Danville, an emergency tactic previously approved by Bragg. He closed by advising the absentee commander: "It seems to me we are too much scattered."[74]

While this update was wending its way to Bragg (it took almost another two days to cover the sixty miles),[75] Bragg had become convinced that Buell's main thrust was not aimed at Polk in Bardstown but instead at Kirby Smith in Frankfort. And scarcely supposing on that Thursday morning that Polk had largely, on his own, elected to stay put in Bardstown (a point not made clear in their exchanges), Bragg now dictated that Polk hasten north: "It may be a reconnaissance, but should it be a real attack we have them. . . . Hold yourself in readiness to strike them on the flank." His morning message was followed by another at 1:00 P.M.: "The enemy is certainly advancing on Frankfort," Bragg said. "Put your whole available force in motion . . . and strike him in flank and rear." Receiving this order the next day, and supported by Wheeler's information and by the concurrence of his wing and division commanders, the prudent William Hardee among them, Polk once more chose not to obey Bragg. He had no adequate force "available for such an assignment," he protested.[76] Far from striking the enemy flank and rear as Bragg desired, Polk and his officers agreed that their shrewdest move was for all their forces to fall back toward Harrodsburg, thirty miles east, and unite there with Kirby Smith. This they did, and Polk's message, deserving urgency, was sent to Bragg on Friday afternoon by "a relay of couriers . . . at intervals of 10 miles."[77]

The irony in all this was that the Yankee column under Gen. Joshua Sill that seemed to endanger Smith in Frankfort was not Buell's main thrust but rather a diversionary force; it numbered about one-third that of the Confederates. Buell, for his part in this confusion, believed that Bragg's whole army was in the Bardstown vicinity, not spread out eastward. And so, as the Army of Tennessee historian Stanley Horn put it: "Seldom in the annals of warfare have the commanders of two contending armies been so completely befuddled as to the locations and plans of the other. . . . The result was that [Bragg] left Polk with 16,000 men to fight 58,000, while he took [Kirby Smith's] 36,000 to meet Sill's 12,000."[78] At least Polk and Wheeler had got it about right, and Buell was more right than wrong.

Bragg did not protest the withdrawal agreed to by the several generals on the scene. Critics, though, have been hard on both Bragg and Polk for the series of previously ignored, delayed, and misunderstood messages, as well as the flawed information that passed for military intelligence that first week in October. The perspective of one contemporary sideline witness, Maj. Edward Turner Sykes, was about as accusatory as it was forgiving of the two generals: "On arriving at [Frankfort]," he would write after the war, Bragg

> determined on making a *coup de main* on Louisville with [Kirby] Smith's troops, sufficiently supported, whilst Polk [in Bardstown] was ordered to make a flank movement, so successful in Stonewall Jackson's campaigns, and turn the enemy's right. Had this been done, the result and issue of the contest might and most probably would have been different. But there are marplots to be found in every household, cabinet or council. General Polk saw fit (and it may have been best; it is not for me to say) to disregard the order until he could communicate with General Bragg by courier and suggest the propriety and, as he deemed, necessity of remaining with and protecting our very large and important supply train. The delay in communicating, at the distance

they were apart, was valuable time never to be regained; the enemy had changed position, and hence Bragg realized a sad disappointment, by General Polk's conduct, in the full fruition of his hopes.[79]

Concealing that sad disappointment, Bragg was civil to Polk after accepting word of the withdrawal toward Harrodsburg. In his reply Saturday morning, October 4, he asked only that Polk "keep the men in heart by assuring them it is not a retreat but a concentration for a fight."[80] That fight, at Perryville days later, would forever dash the ambitious general's hopes of winning Kentucky for the Confederacy.

19

Perryville—"The Most Exciting Few Moments of My Life" (1862)

While General Polk's wagons, herds of cattle, and men began to evacuate Bardstown on Saturday morning, October 4, Braxton Bragg up in Frankfort proceeded with plans for a ceremony to reinstall Kentucky's exiled Confederate government. The honoree was Richard Hawes, a onetime US congressman who had been lately elected by fellow Kentucky secessionists and whose new station was approved in Confederate Richmond, Virginia.[1] The affair began at noon and did not go very well for long. Yankees not far off were no more inclined to cooperate with Bragg than was General Polk. Distant cannon fire was heard to the west of Frankfort at the height of the goings-on (it was Joshua Sill's noisy Yankees on the march from Louisville), and the remainder of the day's scheduled activities, including an evening ball, were canceled.

A Union journalist, amused by the disruption (and equally amused by his own banter), passed the news to his readers. "There was something inexpressibly ludicrous in the rebel proceedings at Frankfort inaugurating a 'Provisional Governor' of Kentucky," he began.

> To read [General Bragg's] grandiloquent "programme" of the ceremonies one is reminded of descriptions of some pompous Oriental pageant, attendant on the coronation of some high and mighty potentate claiming kindred with a whole celestial firmament of stars and planetary orbs. The "installation" took place; "Governor" Richard Hawes donned the ermine robes of office; a whole constellation of the starred rebels bowed in recognition of the new authority; and, in less than

six hours afterward, Governor Hawes, . . . followed by his be-spangled and rag-tag military servitors, took to their heels and ran off toward Lexington. . . . They are still on the run.[2]

As the Northern press guffawed at the cancellation of Bragg's inaugural ball in Frankfort, among those jeering elsewhere was one of Bragg's own brigadiers, who termed the abbreviated ceremony an absurd formality.[3] But for balance, at least, instances of disrespect to the officer class were not confined to Confederates that weekend; some Kentucky Yankees were also given a dose. Bardstown, like many another middle Kentucky small town in the late summer of 1862, was subjected to a series of occupations by first one army and then the other. As though by prearrangement, the bulk of Polk's Confederates had scarcely pulled out when a squadron of Federal cavalry, in a show of bravura, came clattering down Bardstown's deserted main street.[4] Uh-oh. Col. John Wharton's CSA cavalry, a troop composed of Terry's Texas Rangers and the Tennessee 4th, was still in town. The Confederates immediately captured a portion of the incoming Yankees, including a major, a captain, and a lieutenant. They sent their commissioned trophies to General Polk. St. John Richardson Liddell, one of Polk's brigade generals, picks up the story a little later:

> I stopped at a house to receive some orders from Gen. Polk [and] he placed in my charge [the] three Federal cavalry officers. . . . For some cause of retaliation, he directed me to dismount them and turn their horses over to the quartermaster. The saddles (McClellan "trees") were to be specially reserved for him and his staff. . . . I could not help observing General Polk to be in the highest spirits. . . . I proceeded at once to execute the orders, to the disgust of the three mounted prisoners. Two of them I found to be Kentucky Union men. Like all traitors, they used very abusive language against the South. They were captured in their own town (Bardstown) when they attempted to enter at the head of their squadron for *effect* with their friends, particularly female friends.[5]

The chagrin of one of the officers must have been especially acute. Polk reported to Bragg that he had reason to believe the man had already been captured once before and was now in violation of a parole. That offense probably triggered the retaliation Liddell had detected in Polk.[6]

By this time, Sunday, October 5, Buell's Army of the Ohio was pressing across middle Kentucky on a sixty-mile-wide front. Harassed by intervening Confederate cavalry, the three Yankee columns moving south had been unable to overtake Polk, his men staying just beyond their reach.[7] But catching them for a showdown battle was not General Buell's only objective. His other purpose on that parched October weekend was to find drinking water for his men and animals "for the want of which our men suffered exceedingly."[8] The infrequent rains and dried-up landscape had made the search problematical for both moving armies. Sips from the standing water in creek beds, even from hog wallows, were what many were reduced to. Thirsting and enterprising infantrymen of the 64th Ohio, for their part, found an abandoned still house and were filling their empty canteens with Kentucky bourbon when a totally unsympathetic general came along and ordered it all poured on the ground. Almost as disheartening, the heat and supporting dust were well-nigh overpowering, a member of the 64th Ohio reported: "Night and still no water, except here and there a stagnant pool, from which the exhausted soldiers swept off the thick scum."[9] With no sign of rain, an ample autumn sun beat down equally on Yankee and Rebel marchers, and for shade a wilting Confederate surgeon marching at the rear of his regiment had lifted a parasol over his head. "Well, sir," said Gen. William Hardee to the doctor, "just imagine the whole army with umbrellas!" The doctor put it away. A more authentic casualty of that debilitating autumn season was Capt. Hamilton Polk, the general's son, who had been felled one day in September by sunstroke. He eventually returned to duty (and was among the last Confederates in North Carolina to surrender after Appomattox) but was said to have died eight years later of the aftereffects of the sunstroke.[10]

General Polk himself seemed to be in relative comfort when on Tuesday, October 7, he wrote a brief and uncomplaining letter to his wife, who was still in New Orleans with their younger daughters. Polk's army had passed through Perryville and reached Harrodsburg, a town with an adequate water supply. "We have come here to concentrate our army with E. Kirby Smith," Polk said. "It has been done and now we shall give the enemy battle wherever he presents himself. The Lord be with us and bless our arms! . . . In him is all my trust."[11] His news and easygoing tone were curious, given the facts. No actual concentration with Kirby Smith had yet been effected; Kirby Smith and his Army of Kentucky were still somewhere near Frankfort, at least thirty miles north of Polk. There, expecting to be hit by Buell's main thrust, Kirby Smith was pleading to Bragg for reinforcements on October 7.[12] General Liddell, moreover, says "no one, not in on the secret, knew precisely where Kirby Smith's command was. Common opinion was . . . that it was within striking distance [of Perryville]."[13] And though

Kirby Smith and Bragg both still thought Buell's march toward Perryville was a feint and that the danger lay elsewhere, Polk presumably thought otherwise. He says in his official Perryville report that on October 7 (the same day he wrote to Fanny) that he was well aware of the danger posed by the looming Yankees approaching Perryville from the west. "We had reason to believe that much the larger portion of [Buell's] force . . . followed our retiring army in the march to Perryville," he wrote. What Polk thought of Bragg's contrary view may be suggested by Polk's reminding Hardee months later that on October 7 "I already knew . . . that four-fifths of Buell's army was before me."[14]

If Polk truly knew, but withheld from his wife, the fact that his little army of 16,000 was about to be confronted by some 55,000 members of the Army of the Ohio, he was gallant for sparing her worry. But was he himself concerned? At 11 P.M. on October 6 he had sent Bragg an update on Buell's movements west of Perryville: "I have directed General Hardee to ascertain if possible the strength of the enemy which may be covered by his advance. I cannot think it large."[15] (He would explain later that he thought the *advance* force was not large. A few historians accept Polk here at his word; others score the statement as disingenuous.) In any case, if Polk was merely guilty of loose syntax, an occasional flaw that appears in Polk's letters and dispatches, the night of October 6–7 was most inopportune for ambiguity: Bragg seized on Polk's saying "I cannot think it large" to affirm his own theory that Buell's greater force must be headed to Frankfort and Lexington. As a result, tricked by Buell's effective ruse and ill-served by Polk's and Hardee's vagueness (betraying, perhaps, their own uncertainties), Bragg weakened his army by dividing it.[16]

As the critical need for water was still afflicting both armies, and with pursuing Yankees closing on his heels, Polk had directed General Hardee on Tuesday, October 7, to turn and face the enemy outside Perryville. Skirmishing farther west was already occurring when defensive positions closer to the town were chosen with care.[17] Perryville itself was little more than a crossroads ten miles west of Harrodsburg, but Polk decided to make a stand there primarily because the riverside hamlet sat athwart the Chaplin Fork of the Salt River. Three less-significant streams just west of the town— Doctor's Creek, Wilson's Creek, and Bull Run—made Perryville the best source of water for miles around. By guarding this water, the Confederates would slake their own thirst and render the Federals all the more miserable. When Bragg was informed at his headquarters in Harrodsburg on October 7 that Gen. Charles C. Gilbert's III Army Corps was on the Perryville horizon, he reacted as though Gilbert was a mere annoyance. He notified

Polk that afternoon at 5:40 P.M.: "You had better move with Cheatham's division to [Hardee's] support and give the enemy battle immediately; rout him, and then move to our support at Versailles [a village just southwest of Lexington]."[18] On his own, Polk determined to pay very little attention to the casually phrased order.

It may be that Bragg, for all the demeaning remarks he freely uttered behind Polk's back, found dealing forthrightly with his former bishop intimidating. Though Bragg had been active as a layman in the church in Louisiana, and his marriage in 1849 was solemnized by one of Polk's priests (because a friend of both the bride and groom, the Tennessee bishop James Otey, was unable to be there), he sat rather loose to religion. For example, he had never seen fit to be baptized.[19] Still, Polk had been Bragg's bishop in Thibodaux; even if he now resented doing so, Bragg might suppose he still owed Polk some deference. Assuming that possibility, Bragg had chosen reflexively to cajole Polk rather than to dictate to him. Bragg's restraint, if any, was often wasted. His circumlocution late that September—"I consider it best" that Polk vacate Bardstown and maneuver toward Louisville—had availed him little. Polk barely budged. Similarly, Polk now chose to pay no mind to the mildly worded dispatch to "move to our support at Versailles." When he later found himself in trouble with Bragg for disregarding the order, Polk scoffed to his friend Hardee: "What order?" Bragg's loose phrasing had given Polk the elbow room he needed to declare the dispatch was not peremptory but merely advisory. Polk's subordinate commanders, as well, had joined him in that reading.[20]

Polk's high opinion of his own military judgments, especially when they might improve on Bragg's (as was the case this time), inured him to how close he came to insubordination, a grave offense. (He may even have fancied how he would enjoy boasting of them later to Kenneth Rayner, his admiring in-law in Raleigh.) For Bragg, though, the recurrent clashes with Polk gnawed at him, and his distemper showed eight months later in a letter to Jefferson Davis recounting the Kentucky campaign of 1862. Mindful that he was criticizing the president's very close friend, Bragg wrote: "With all his ability, energy and zeal, General Polk, by education and habit, is unfitted for executing the orders of others. He will convince himself his own views are better, and will follow them without reflecting on the consequences." The Bragg biographer Grady McWhiney has drily observed that Polk probably had been a bishop too long to be a successful subordinate. But in this instance, William Hardee would disagree forcefully. Had Polk followed Bragg's instructions at Bardstown, said Hardee, the army would have been destroyed.[21]

If doing little more, Polk did send the reinforcements to Hardee outside Perryville that Bragg stipulated in his 5:40 P.M. message. Polk then rode down from Harrodsburg to Perryville himself. Before leaving, he informed Bragg that the reinforcements were insufficient by his reckoning and that he wanted James Withers's division placed at his disposal. To this Bragg objected, Polk said later, on the ground that Kirby Smith had informed him that the enemy was in force in his front, and no more troops could be spared for Perryville.[22] Off to the west, though, as the sun went down, advance units of Charles Gilbert's III Corps, a juggernaut, had ascended the low hills west of the town and spied the trickles of creek water at their base. They also espied Hardee's infantry and artillery units arrayed on the opposite hilltops. Brig. Gen. St. John Liddell, who had placed his Arkansas regiments in a relatively weak forward position on high ground east of Doctor's Creek, had concentrated what strength he had where he expected to be hit hardest: near the few available pools in the creek bed. The Yankees, accordingly, made ready for a battle and a drink.[23]

Hardee and Polk by now were increasingly troubled that Bragg seemed insensitive to Perryville's pending danger. Every bit the professional soldier Bragg was, Hardee wrote him a note around 7:30 P.M., which was carried to Bragg by an officer. Putting the case as delicately as he could ("Permit me, from the friendly relations so long existing between us, to write you plainly"), he believed that the commanding general was making a big mistake by failing to gather all his forces in one place to make the blow effective. Between it and Versailles, Perryville seemed the better choice: "I could not sleep quietly to-night without giving expression to these views," Hardee finished, signing himself "Your sincere friend." Bragg's response was to come Wednesday morning to Perryville himself—but not to alter the allotted concentrations of Polk's and Kirby Smith's troops.[24]

Months later, after both Polk and Hardee had been criticized by Bragg for their disobedience at Perryville, Polk recollected his thinking on that October Tuesday night to his cocommander (and coconspirator, as Bragg saw it). "I was, I conceived," Polk told Hardee in a self-justifying letter three pages long,

> left at liberty to exercise such discretion as sound sense and the facts
> before me demanded. . . . I [was] under the deep and painful conviction
> that the force at my disposal was totally inadequate to perform the duty
> assigned it; and while I must attempt that duty I should do it in such
> a way as to prevent the wreck and destruction of the little army with
> whose conduct and safety I was charged.

To have taken Bragg literally when he received the 5:40 P.M. dispatch Tuesday night meant to Polk that he was to assault Gilbert's III Army Corps immediately—and in the gathering dark. And that, Polk said, would have "not been judicious." He resolved to await daylight and looked for somewhere to sleep.[25]

Since leaving Tennessee in July, Polk was frequently in the company of his surgeon-chaplain friend, the Reverend Charles Quintard. That October night, sharing blankets in a Perryville barnyard, Polk and Quintard dozed while west of town, by the light of a harvest moon, Yankee skirmishers and Rebel pickets exchanged musket fire. Infantry commanded by Col. Daniel McCook drove the Confederates off a lightly defended rise known as Peter's Hill and away from Doctor's Creek. The water they had been guarding belonged now to the enemy, who helped themselves at last to refreshing swallows. What lay ahead was forty-eight hours of frequent face-to-face fighting—awful encounters, in the experience of one Tennessee soldier, where bayonets and butts of guns were used with death-dealing effect.[26]

The Yankees at Doctor's Creek fought off a counterattack by Liddell's Arkansans around Wednesday sunrise. Thinking in the Federal high command soon concluded that the Confederates, now falling back in some places, might be in disarray. If not all that confused, they were clearly not of one mind on how to proceed.[27] From Perryville at 6:00 A.M. Polk notified Bragg in Harrodsburg that the enemy seemed disposed to press that morning. "Understanding it to be your wish to give them battle, we shall do so vigorously." Within moments, Polk's mind amended "vigorously" to mean "cautiously." He just might be obliged to fall back, he advised Bragg, should his hunch prove true that plenty of reserves were behind the Yankee advance.[28] To Bragg, all this must have sounded straightforward enough. Yet no sooner was this dispatch on its way than Polk and his senior officers had a breakfast confabulation in which Polk expressed his even truer position: an attack was imprudent. As he had at Bardstown, Polk again argued that they collectively disregard the instructions in Bragg's 5:40 P.M. dispatch. He carried the meeting; all his subordinates agreed that rather than falling on the enemy vigorously they had better wait and see. As Polk would later term their caution, it was resolved, in view of the great disparity of forces, to adopt the "defensive-offensive." Hence, to be guided by developments.[29]

Bragg had learned during the night that the enemy had slowed its advance on Kirby Smith, so at 9:45 A.M. on October 8 he rode into Perryville, straining to hear the vigorous attack Polk had promised. The surrounding quiet and sporadic shooting off in the distance were not what he had in mind. Instead of mounting an engagement, according to his singular account, recollected by Thomas Claibourne fifty years later, Generals Polk, Hardee, Buckner, and Cheatham were about to remove themselves from the town just as Bragg arrived.[30]

Colonel Claibourne, a staff officer under Simon Buckner, remembers the moment this way: Having "played his troops into columns for withdrawal," Polk and the three other generals were

> ready to march [northeast] to Harrodsburg. I had just ridden up as
> Bragg addressed General Polk. I state substantially: "What are you
> doing, General Polk?" "I am retiring as the enemy are too many."
> General Bragg quickly and on no further inquiry into conditions,
> replied. "Bring on the action with small arms." General Polk and
> the others present seemed for a moment astonished; but recovering
> quickly, he waved his arm and ordered that his troops . . . should be
> deployed on the lines they had just left.

Claibourne at this point, having gone two nights without sleep, was permitted by Buckner to "snatch a little"; he later resumed his duties as Buckner's aide. Kenneth Noe, author of a meticulous study of Perryville, terms this recollection by Claibourne "suspect" and not substantiated in any other record. Possibly the colonel was too drowsy that morning to get all the facts straight.[31]

If in fact Polk had intended to retire to Harrodsburg, and was prevented from doing so by Bragg's arrival, Polk had not been idle beforehand. He had arrayed four infantry divisions in and about Perryville across a front a little more than two miles wide. For their part, the Federals were either in place on the low hills west of town or were still approaching on roads from the southwest and northwest; the sporadic exchanges of nighttime gunfire had picked up since first light. In two specific orders, Polk at midmorning had sent word to Brigadier General St. John Liddell, precariously advanced in the middle of this front, to fall back to a safer position; and had dispatched Gen. Joe Wheeler's cavalry to clear the Lebanon Road (which came into Perryville from the southwest) of an approaching enemy column.[32] It was the 20,000 men of II Corps of the Army of the Ohio under Gen. Thomas Leonidas Crittenden. The spirited attack by 1,200 of Wheeler's cavalrymen so unnerved the Federals tramping up the road (and so misled them, leaving them to think that the mounted soldiers were the advance of a huge Confederate force) that II Corps was effectively nullified from the rest of the day's fighting.[33]

After Polk met Bragg and his staff trotting into town—whatever contretemps may have next ensued—Bragg presumably let Polk lay out his defensive-offensive argument. Bragg then undertook his own examination of the troop deployments Polk and Hardee had arranged. Bragg's first report of Perryville, written four days after the battle, says merely that he suggested some changes and modifications that General Polk promptly adopted. In a second, more detailed report written the following May, irritation surfaces: "Orders were given for some changes deemed necessary . . . and Major-General Polk was ordered to bring on the engagement."[34] Then, "impatient at the delay after this order, I dispatched a staff officer to repeat it to [Polk], and soon thereafter I followed in person and put the troops in motion." Stewing still over Polk's alleged lack of aggression that October morning, Bragg inserted in this May 1863 report that even the enemy's commanding general, Don Carlos Buell, had been surprised that no morning attack had been initiated by the Confederates while Charles Gilbert's III Army Corps "was isolated." Bragg: "Polk and the general officers at the meeting about daylight who resolved on . . . delay must have acted without correct information and in ignorance that my orders were urgent and imperative for the attack."[35]

Now that he was on the scene, Bragg had to make a significant decision: an adjustment to meet the thickening and lengthening mass of Yankees taking place to the northwest of town. To strengthen the Confederates' right wing (and so to prevent the enemy's circling around it and putting themselves between Polk and Kirby Smith's army up toward Frankfort), Bragg switched Gen. B. F. Cheatham's First Division from the extreme left flank to the extreme right. The maneuver covered about a mile and took an hour or so, but, once situated, Cheatham and John A. Wharton's Texas cavalry were a reliable anchor on the Confederates' right. Bragg then left Polk more or less in charge, insisting only that an assault begin promptly. But promptness, as usual, was a relative concept in the two general's thinking: "It was now near 1 o'clock," says Polk, "and . . . by [General Bragg's] direction, orders were given for a general movement throughout our whole line." Bragg's peeved version reads: "The action having at length commenced after noon."

At whatever time it commenced, no sooner had Polk directed Cheatham to advance straight ahead against Gilbert than a warning arrived from Colonel Wharton's cavalry: reinforcements belonging to Alexander McCook's I Corps were still streaming down a road northwest of town, attaching themselves to Gilbert's left flank. After consulting with Bragg, Polk took a calculated (if not cautious) risk, stopping Cheatham's men in their tracks and biding his time at his headquarters until McCook reached Gilbert and settled in. Polk explained his thinking: "Concluding that our chances of success were greater against the line in my front, even when re-enforced, than it would be by attacking it as it stood and exposing my flank to the approaching force, I awaited until the re-enforcements got into position. The attack was then ordered."[36] Bragg himself would now express satisfaction: "The engagement became general . . . and continued furiously from that time until dark, our troops never faltering and never failing in their efforts," he wrote in his first report.[37] His second report is equally warm: "Our troops [fought] with a gallantry and persistent determination . . . which the enemy could not resist . . . though he was largely more than two to our one."[38] Indeed, however much displeased he may have been with Polk on Wednesday morning, he had mellowed sufficiently by the following Sunday, October 12, that he could praise him and Hardee and several other commanders for brilliant achievements on this memorable field.[39]

With Hardee managing the Rebels' left, Polk was occupied during the afternoon principally on the right. (Buell, the Federal commander, was scarcely busy at all; five miles to the rear, out of earshot, and not informed of the goings-on in Perryville, he was holding in reserve three times the Confederates' manpower and was planning to start the fight the next day.)[40] John Wharton's cavalry (the Tennessee 4th, the Kentucky 1st, and the Texas 8th) worked themselves around the Yankees' far-left flank. "Wharton charged the enemy's extreme left with great fury," Polk would report, gaining "a skirt of woods and an eminence of great importance to our success on our right."[41] Then Cheatham's three infantry brigades under Daniel Donelson, Alexander Stewart, and George Maney were thrust to the front. On this Polk struck a pleasing note: "They mounted the steep and difficult cliffs of Chaplin River in gallant style and moved upon the enemy's position with a most determined courage." Undaunted "by a storm of shot, shell and musketry from several batteries strongly posted and supported by heavy masses of infantry, . . . our troops pressed forward with resistless energy." Considering the disparity of their numbers and the "havoc which was being made" in their ranks, Polk supposed his men's advance would "compare favorably with the most brilliant achievements of historic valor."

Years later, Cheatham was still thrilled by the spectacle. From the sidelines of Gen. George Maney's brigade, he watched as Maney urged his command against Federal troops who resisted but slowly gave ground: "As his men fired they would take one step forward to load, which assured me they were making progress under [a] terrible storm of artillery and musketry. It was the most exciting few moments of my life."[42] Other officers— Confederate and Union alike—also found Perryville stirring. Watching from a hilltop, St. John Liddell thought the "contending forces in the valley had the appearance of actors in a great amphitheater. . . . The advance, the repulse, the charge, the retreat, the fire from the numerous batteries, the incessant rattling of musketry . . . rendered the spectacle interesting in the extreme."[43] A Yankee officer elsewhere on the battlefield was equally delighted by the aesthetics of the carnage" "Riding toward our left, . . ." he related, "we came upon an open knob, where we found General McCook and all his staff watching some beautiful artillery practice." By "beautiful artillery practice" he meant that the safely positioned gunners were coolly "firing up a wide ravine upon [Confederate] cavalry moving up a road to our front."[44]

Wednesday afternoon wore on with the Federal lines nearly everywhere being pressured backward and away from the water they needed. And confusion was as thick as the smoke. Col. A. S. Marks, for example, in command of the 17th Tennessee Infantry, had run out of ammunition after a "heavy and incessant" hillside face-off with the enemy. Once the Yankees had withdrawn a ways, Marks detached a company of his men to go for more bullets and powder, "but before [their] return I was ordered by a staff officer, unknown to me, to move forward." With nothing to shoot, Marks had his men fix bayonets and trot up the hill. "When I had arrived near the crest of the hill the same officer ordered me to have my bayonets taken off." Protesting that this command left his men no useful weapons, Marks was then ordered to turn around and descend the hill. At that point, "Major General Buckner came up . . . and ordered me to hold the hill at all hazards." With no ammunition and buffeted by those ranking him, the obliging Colonel Marks and his men hunkered down on the shell-pocked hill "until night closed the conflict."[45]

Disarray reigned elsewhere late in the day and came near to ending the military career of Louisiana's bishop. (It did, unfortunately, end the lives of a large number of Hoosiers fighting for the Union.)[46] At the time, twilight was mingling with moonlight, and gun smoke was obscuring vision across the battleground, making it "difficult in the melee to distinguish friend from foe," as General Hardee would put it. Lt. Col. Daniel Govan's 2nd Arkansas Regiment, a part of St. John Liddell's infantry brigade, was firing somewhat aimlessly while advancing toward another line of infantry twenty-five paces ahead. Liddell says in his memoir that then "a distressing cry came from the dark line before us, 'You are firing upon friends; for God's sake stop.' In an instant everything was still." Puzzled, Liddell was "about to give the order to [go] forward with bayonets fixed when General Leonidas Polk rode up." During the next quarter-hour or so, the bishop-general's life brushed so close to a conclusion that word of his breathtaking experience was soon humming along the Southern grapevine.

After Liddell reported to Polk the distressing cry he had heard—leading Liddell to think other Confederates were being fired upon by Colonel Govan's men—Polk exclaimed: "What a pity, I hope not." With all his aides out on other missions, Polk then said to Liddell, "Let me go and see." Colonel Govan was opposed to Polk's taking the risk, insisting that the "friends" out there in the dark were indeed Yankees. Undeterred and "quite in doubt," Polk demanded of Liddell: "'Open your ranks!' It was done. The brave old man spurred his horse with a jump through the opening."[47]

Mercer Otey, later told the story by Polk himself, continues the narrative:

[Polk] started off on his faithful old roan, Jerry, to investigate for himself. Fortunately, his grey uniform was concealed by a linen duster, and favored by the gathering gloom, he rode to the officer standing a little to the right of the line, and inquired: "What troops are these?" Promptly, the officer replied: "The [Union] Twenty-second Indiana. Lieutenant-Colonel Tanner, commanding!" General Polk was staggered only for a second, when he at once replied: "Colonel, cease firing, don't you see you are firing into your own troops over there?" Colonel Tanner blurted, "I am damned sure they are the enemy." "Enemy!" said Polk. "Why, I have just left them myself. Cease firing, sir!" "But who are you who gives this order?" inquires the Colonel. Bending over his horse's neck, [Polk] seized the Colonel roughly by the shoulder and remarked in his imperative manner: "Cease firing this instant, sir, or I will have you arrested and court-martialed for disobedience of orders in the enemy's front." This so staggered the Colonel that he instantly gave the order: "Cease firing!" General Polk then with remarkable presence of mind rode slowly down the line of the regiment till he gradually zig-zagged his way back to his own lines.

Otey later asked Polk how he had felt for the few moments his retiring figure was exposed to the line of Indiana infantry. "'Well, my son,' Polk said, 'I felt like a thousand centipedes were traveling up and down my backbone.'"

Having rejoined his fellows, shaken but unscathed, Polk "cheerfully" called out to Govan: "Colonel . . . they are the enemy. Give it to them." Liddell remembered Polk's saying to him, "General, every mother's son of them is a Yankee." Liddell: "The news was circulated loudly, 'Yankees!' The trumpet sounded to 'fire.' A tremendous flash of musketry for . . . nearly one quarter of a mile in length followed." "I assure, you sir," Polk reportedly told the British journalist Arthur Fremantle months later, "that the slaughter of that Indiana regiment was the greatest I had ever seen in the war." William M. Polk, reprinting most of Fremantle's version, thought it best to omit the heartless remark attributed to his father.[48]

As the carnage of the 22nd Indiana subsided, Polk called it off; shooting in the dark merely wasted ammunition. By then, casualties to the unsuspecting 22nd Indiana had amounted to some 50 percent: of 300 engaged, the regiment's toll was fifty-two killed and 137 wounded and captured. Among others wounded and captured was Michael Gooding, commander of the 13th Brigade. His bad luck was not over. While a prisoner that evening, he was almost murdered by a sword-wielding Confederate officer convinced that Gooding, as a ruse, had shouted: "You are firing upon friends; for God's sake stop." The overwrought Confederate was possibly Col. C. M. McCouley of the 7th Arkansas who called Gooding "a fiend in human shape."[49]

For the sake of his impartial account, Fremantle used dashed lines to obscure the identity of the Union officer who had missed a chance to take Polk prisoner and was in turn tricked by the Confederate general; Samuel Watkins repeated the dashed lines in his account. With the passage of some twenty-five years, Mercer Otey did not scruple to reveal a name. In his *Confederate Veteran* article, he said the ill-used Yankee was Thomas B. Tanner, acting commander of the 22nd Regiment, Indiana Volunteers.[50] In a footnote in his published diary, Fremantle considerately added: "If these lines should ever meet the eyes of General Polk, I hope he will forgive me if I have made an error in recording his adventure." Polk did take exception to a rumor reaching him after his close call. Liddell had told others he had heard Polk say, "Give them Hell, General!" The alleged expletive, Liddell says, was disputed weeks later by a blustering Polk, and Liddell assured him he could not recall ever hearing the bishop-general's using the *H*-word. "I was amused," Liddell recorded, "at the absurdity of the thing, as well as the good General's theatrical manner." (Liddell was not present at Belmont and so had missed Polk's reported "hell and damnation" outburst upon hearing that Ulysses S. Grant had called their daylong battle a "skirmish.")[51]

If the bishop's alleged gloating over the Hoosiers' fate was un-Christian on his part, Polk's better instincts were later shown in a letter expressing his regret that the Southern army's lack of chaplains contributed to his soldiers giving vent to vengeful feelings toward the Yankees.[52] More telling still, while burial details moved over Perryville's desolate battlefield where neither side could claim a decisive victory, Polk and the Reverend Charles Quintard obtained the key to St. Philip's Episcopal Church in nearby Harrodsburg, and the two went there alone. Quintard as a physician had spent the day of the battle, and straight through until half-past five the next morning, "incessantly occupied with the wounded" until "I dropped, I could do no more. I went out by myself and leaning against a fence, I wept like a child." Now as priest he donned the local rector's vestments and, standing before the altar, read the Litany and other prayers. Polk, as worn out as Quintard and possibly lamenting his pitiless deception of the Indiana regiment, knelt at the chancel rail and wept himself. His prayers were magnanimous, as he petitioned God for "peace to the land and blessings on friend and foe alike."[53] Bragg by then had ordered the Confederates out of Kentucky.

Surviving Perryville uninjured, Polk was soon pitched about by ecclesiastic troubles. Far from Perryville, in Federal-held New Orleans, the Union general Benjamin Butler—the "Beast Butler" most despised by Polk—had lately imposed vindictive martial law on six of Polk's favorite clergymen: secessionist-minded parish priests whom Butler colorfully regarded as "contumacious" hirelings of "the Rt. Rev. Warrior Gen. Polk."[54] In obedience to their bishop off at war, the men had refused to lead their congregations during Sunday worship in prayers for President Abraham Lincoln. Seditiously (said Butler) they instead encouraged the faithful to pray silently for Jefferson Davis. Butler sentenced the three reputed ringleaders to brief terms in a military prison in New York and further expelled all six from the city for the duration of the war.

Elsewhere, Episcopalians up North in convention in New York were no longer the harmonious brethren with whom Polk had mingled three years previous. Instead, they had taken to defaming the absent bishop of Louisiana in legislative deliberation and ridicule. Mounting one attack (if locking the barn door too late), the Reverend Dr. Daniel Goodwin proposed a resolution that church law forbid any bishop from leaving the ministry to take up arms. Opponents—not necessarily siding with their absent brother—objected to the political tilt of the resolution and defeated it.[55]

Legislative debate was then set aside when a minister from the rich and powerful Trinity Church on Wall Street rose to speak. He was Francis Vinton, who had been a first-year cadet at West Point during Leonidas Polk's term.[56] He now held a letter whose author he declared was Bishop Polk and that was purported to be a personal attack on Garret Davis, a US senator from Kentucky.[57] Vinton read the letter aloud, and when a delegate desired to know if it was authentic, Vinton replied that he had long been familiar with Polk's handwriting and had seen the original. Vinton's assurances notwithstanding, the preposterous letter could not possibly have come from either the mind or the hand of Leonidas Polk. The wording is coarse, clumsy, and misspelled, and the handwriting of the original (preserved in the Chicago Historical Society's collections) can be read with no trouble whatsoever. That's another way of saying it bears no resemblance to the daunting scrawl of Polk's penmanship, a style he himself once accurately compared to hieroglyphs. The forgery was the work, perhaps, of a soldier in Polk's army or of some Kentucky secessionist. But if too lampoonish to have been believed by any but the most gullible delegates, the letter had a future. After the convention adjourned, it was passed along to William Lloyd Garrison's weekly abolitionist newspaper in Boston. Its text (punctuation and spelling errors now corrected) was then set in type, cited as a delectable specimen of Southern piety, and centered on *The Liberator*'s front page.[58]

Once the delegates were done laughing at Polk, they moved to the more contentious matter of addressing the American public concerning the Civil War. Again, Leonidas Polk did not fare well once Bishop Charles McIlvaine of Ohio had expressed the several bishops' mind through their pastoral letter. As for the personal score he had to settle with his former protégé, he got to that in his third paragraph. "We do not attempt to estimate the moral character of [Southern churchmen supporting rebellion] . . . except as to one matter," he wrote.

> When the ordained ministers of the Gospel of Christ . . . do so depart from their sacred calling as to take the sword and engage in the fierce and bloody conflicts of war; when in so doing they are fighting against authorities which, as "the powers that be," the Scriptures declare "are ordained of God"; when especially one comes out from the exalted spiritual duties of an Overseer of the flock of Christ, to exercise high command in such awful work—we cannot, as ourselves Overseers of the same flock, . . . refrain from placing on such examples our strong condemnation. We remember the words of our blessed Lord . . . for the special admonition of His ministers: "They that take the sword shall perish with the sword."[59]

Five thousand copies of McIlvaine's letter were then published, and one copy he sent to the White House. A reply came from Lincoln's secretary of state, William Seward: "The bishops' claim of an intimate connexion between fervent patriotism and true Christianity seems to the President equally seasonable and unanswerable."[60]

20

"I Believe I Have Been of Some Use to the Republic" (1862–1863)

Don Carlos Buell had begun the encounter at Perryville in October with some 36,000 troops dispersed throughout the area. Braxton Bragg had concentrated only 16,000. Now, with little more than a draw to show for it, Buell hung back cautiously as the Confederates on October 9 began to extricate themselves from the possibility of subsequent annihilation—and from Kentucky altogether. Perhaps, as a Bragg biographer says, the battle was a "limited tactical success" for the Confederates. It was a victory for the Yankees, anyhow, to the extent they had cleared the state of their enemy's forces. For the 7,500 Federal and Confederate officers and soldiers killed, wounded, or captured, however, it was merely tragic. The report to Abraham Lincoln from a Union general in Louisville that Bragg and Frank Cheatham might be among the slain was doubtless cheering news in Washington but erroneous withal.[1]

The fact that Bragg otherwise had been shaken by the battle's outcome was evident, as attested to by Leonidas Polk and William Hardee. Late on the night of October 8, Bragg conferred with these two at his headquarters in Harrodsburg. Sitting beside a fireplace, Polk and Hardee exchanged "glances of astonished concern" as Bragg "paced the floor rubbing one hand over the other." To his subordinate generals, he seemed robbed "of power of clear thinking"; and even self-control appeared about to desert him, according to William M. Polk.[2]

Failing after ten weeks of personal entreaty to bring any significant number of Kentuckians into the secessionist fold, Bragg had no further use for the state. His losses in battle were not even offset by the 2,000 Kentucky recruits he had corralled, half of whom had already deserted. Ignoring Gen. Edmund Kirby Smith's impassioned opposition, he turned his army toward Tennessee and home on October 11; Kirby Smith's soldiers reluctantly fell in at the rear.[3] General Polk, though later singled out by Bragg as the man most responsible for the military reversals in the Kentucky campaign, was put in charge of the snarl of departing columns and trains that soon clogged the Appalachian country roads leading south.[4] With a keen sense of what was most appropriate to the new situation, Chaplain Charles Quintard, who had bolstered a drooping commander with prayer at St. Philip's Church after the battle, now adopted another useful tactic to strengthen the dispirited infantrymen he rode beside. "Every morning, I filled my canteen with whiskey and strapped it to the pommel of my saddle to help the wearied and broken down keep up the march."[5]

Along the homeward route, provisions and water were scarcer than Quintard's whiskey. Yankee cavalrymen, meanwhile, kept pressure on the retreating columns. But ahead lay Cumberland Gap, now evacuated by Gen. George Morgan's starved-out Yankees. Once through that pass, the departing Kentucky invaders would be safe. Among the more resolute plodders along the track was General Polk's dairy cow, a fixture at his headquarters. "Fat and sleek," she would soon be supplying Polk's mess with "plenty of fresh milk" in Shelbyville, Tennessee.[6]

Many in the ranks headed south were bitter that their armies' foray into a border state had come to such a sorry end. Particularly unreconciled to the withdrawal was a disgusted Kirby Smith. Threatened from behind by the pursuing enemy, and daunted ahead by dwindling supplies and wretched mountain roads, he wrote pleadingly to Polk on October 17: "Cannot we unite and end this disastrous retreat by a glorious victory?" An aide riding in Polk's mounted escort would recall that Polk was similarly unhappy. Sometimes, Col. Philip Spence wrote in a memoir, Polk

> would stop to make little encouraging talks when the boys . . .
> resting on the roadside, would cheer him as he passed. On one of
> these occasions . . . a fine-looking, sun-burned veteran, who had seen
> much service and hard fighting, was sitting on the fence and called
> out, "General, don't you think it would be a heap better if our faces
> were turned toward that firing we hear in the rear?" alluding to the
> skirmishing with our rear guard. This created a laugh amongst these
> old soldiers, always willing to go forward but never willing to retreat.
> General Polk made no reply. He doubtless hated the retreat from
> Kentucky more than any soldier in that grand army.[7]

While Polk was on the road from Kentucky, the Confederate War Department and Congress promoted him to lieutenant general (doing the same for his friends Kirby Smith and Hardee).[8] Polk's spirits were lifted even more when he reached Knoxville on October 23 and was met by a cousin, Thom Polk, with cheering news of his family in Louisiana. *"Laud Deo! Laud Deo!!* Forever be His holy name blessed and praised," the general exulted the next day when writing Fanny. It was God, he was certain, who had led her, their five daughters (Frances, Sallie, Susan, Lillie, and Lucia), and their four slave servants out of New Orleans. Among the servants was Winny, her surname unknown, who was the wife of Altimore, General Polk's army companion and body servant.[9] The refugees had boarded a flatboat and, under a flag of truce, had sailed away from the occupied city through Bayou St. John and across Lake Pontchartrain. They then had passed through Federal lines and reached Jackson, Mississippi, by train. There, at Poverty Hall, a plantation nearby, they joined Fanny Polk's eldest daughter, Kate Polk Gale. Her husband, William Dudley Gale, was one of General Polk's volunteer aides.[10]

Though any port would have suited the storm-tossed Polks and their servants, the Gale family was having its own troubles. Federal soldiers occupying their region had sawed through the Mississippi River's levies, creating a seventy-mile-wide stream; the flood had inundated the Gales' plantation, Holly Bend, on the Yazoo River. The family had removed to Poverty Hall, an unoccupied log house owned by a Gale relative. But they counted their blessings because Fanny and the girls were at last "out of the clutches of the Beast," as William Gale put it. That, of course, was a reference to Gen. Benjamin Butler, the despised military governor of New Orleans. Since his arrival, it had become an abiding amusement of the occupied citizens to portray Butler as either contemptibly cruel or stupidly ridiculous. For many, his likeness was to be found painted on the interior bottoms of their chamber pots.[11]

With Fanny safely out of Louisiana, her husband thought it best that Hamilton continue to recuperate with his mother and sisters. He was now married and the father of two sons, a four-year-old and a barely-one-year-old, and, leaving Tennessee, presumably took his family to Mississippi.[12] As for the General himself, for all he had been through in Kentucky, he "was never in better health, as everybody says. I believe, too, I have been of some use to the Republic. At least, they all say so."[13] Many, perhaps, but hardly all. One to say otherwise, for example, was Dr. David W. Yandell, a prominent Louisville surgeon and the medical director of William Hardee's corps. With that status, he was privy to certain military confidences and "enjoyed opportunities for seeing orders [and] hearing opinions . . .

such as are not vouchsafed to every doctor." Thus informed, he concluded after Perryville that, at best, Polk was a military misfit. In a letter to William Preston Johnston (Jefferson Davis's aide and the son of Polk's late friend Sydney Johnston), the surgeon spelled out his thoughts. Polk "threatened wonders [and] was positively ferocious, but he can't be relied on, bishop and lieutenant general as he is. . . . I saw enough of the old greybeard at Shiloh and Perryville to cause me to place no great confidence in him." And furthermore, Polk "will prevaricate. When I was a boy I called it by another name." On second thought, Yandell modified this last aspersion a little. Polk was merely guilty of saying "he was going to do this, and going to do that, but the old man forgets." In sum, Yandell recommended that the president remove Polk from all battlefields, assigning him instead to a desk job, preferably heading a court of inquiry. Yandell's assessment of Polk was almost flattering compared to his opinion of Braxton Bragg ("either stark mad or utterly incompetent"), but in the letter he urgently beseeched Johnston to do *something*: "Will, if Bragg isn't removed or Polk transferred to house duties we will all go to the Devil out here."[14]

In the first days after Perryville, and the dispiriting departure from Kentucky, Bragg had not yet seen fit to find a scapegoat. Rather, he put the best face he could on matters. He even extolled Polk and other generals for their "brilliant achievements on this memorable field. Nobler troops were never more gallantly led," he told Richmond in his first official report. "The country owes them a debt of gratitude."[15] The Confederate country, however, was more critical than grateful for Bragg's army conduct. Not only was Kentucky now lost for good. The Army of West Tennessee under Earl Van Dorn, whom Bragg had left behind at Vicksburg earlier in the summer, had just been defeated at Corinth, Mississippi, by Gen. William S. Rosecrans. For the time being, therefore, Federal troops could stay put unmolested in northern Mississippi and West Tennessee. Plus they now had the run of Kentucky.[16] The unkindest cut would come from the commander's usually loyal wife, Elise. She now added her voice to the rising clamor of second-guessers. "You have, it is true, made a very rapid march but without defeating your wary foe," she scolded. "I had hoped [General Buell] could have been overtaken & driven out [of Kentucky]. . . . So much was expected of your army."[17]

From Knoxville, where his "much shattered" army was resting before moving to Murfreesboro in Middle Tennessee, Bragg was immediately called to Richmond by Jefferson Davis.[18] Surely smarting by now, Bragg over the next several days used part of his presidential conference to indict Polk for the overall failure of the Kentucky campaign. Polk, meanwhile, was left to reorganize the army, establishing Polk's and Hardee's two wings into two corps. Polk's other task was to prepare for the move west. Once Bragg had returned from his interview with Davis, Polk was summoned to give his side. He went to Virginia on November 7 and, as if on vacation, took along Fanny and two daughters, Susan, twenty-one, and Lucia, fourteen, all of whom had come up from the Gales' Mississippi plantation.[19]

Polk's conversations with the president included complimentary remarks about General Bragg—he was a fine organizer and disciplinarian, and so on and so forth. But, in short, the man was "wanting in the higher elements of generalship." Subsequently, Polk reportedly shared his discontents with friends in the Richmond Congress.[20] Davis had responded carefully to Polk, saying, "I can make good use of him here in Richmond," a remark Polk would not let Davis forget.[21] Caught between his pets, and having to sympathize equitably with their charges and counter-charges, Davis must have thrown up his hands.[22] In the end, he tried to resolve the quandary by installing Gen. Joseph Eggleston Johnston in the role of a super-commander of the Department of the West, placing him above both Polk and Bragg. It was a stopgap measure, Davis soon restoring and enlarging Bragg's authority. With that edge, Bragg tried months later to have Polk court-martialed for disregarding his orders at Bardstown and Perryville. At this ploy he did not succeed, but he was not done defaming the bishop.[23]

Before returning south to the Army of Tennessee (the command's new name as of November 1862, when the Army of the Mississippi and the Army of Kentucky were combined), Polk and Fanny and the girls detoured through Raleigh for a family visit. They stayed in the mansion of Leonidas's boyhood, occupied now by his sister, Susan Rayner, and her husband, Kenneth, the former US congressman. Wherever the visiting Polks might go, they were a delight to the home folks. Fanny widened their eyes with Beast Butler stories, including the details she supplied to a lurid tale already making the rounds throughout the South. The received account concerned a no-nonsense New Orleans matron and a Yankee soldier. After "one of Butler's beasts" kissed her in the street, she had pulled a pistol and shot the man dead. "That's almost right," Aunt Fanny Polk informed her niece, Catherine Ann Edmondston, who wrote it all down. More precisely, Fanny recounted, the accosted woman had plunged a knife into the scoundrel's throat. Passing by just then was a noble Yankee officer—a species so rare as to be hardly imaginable. He had helped the cutthroat damsel flee the scene, escaping the certain vengeance of General Butler.[24]

Uncle Leonidas, meanwhile, engaged in his man-to-man talk with Kenneth Rayner, explaining how he would have succeeded in the Kentucky invasion where Bragg had botched it.[25] After Rayner passed along the gist of this "confidential chat" to a prominent member of the North Carolina judiciary, it is plausible to reckon that word of Polk's averred military acumen was then noised quietly around his hometown. In any case, a prominent Yankee in faraway Middle Tennessee was spreading a variation of Polk's opinions about Kentucky and Bragg's leadership. Two Confederate deserters had given the Federal commander in Gallatin an earful, which he passed along to his superiors in Nashville. The Rebels were "all disgusted with the Kentucky campaign," Maj. Gen. George H. Thomas was told, and were "very much frightened after the battle at Perryville." What's more, "General Polk in a speech told his division [sic] that he had always been opposed to going into Kentucky." *And* "all the men enlisted in Kentucky have deserted!" General Thomas thought the ex-Rebels' story "very plausible," passing it along to his chief of staff "for what it is worth."[26]

As the Polks prepared to return to Tennessee, young Lucia was enrolled at St. Mary's School for Girls in Raleigh. The school was known for molding future Christian women with a thoroughgoing academic education. Once the remainder of the family was homeward bound, they passed through Asheville in western North Carolina, whereupon it was decided that Fanny and the rest of the girls should soon return to make their home a "resort for many charming, cultivated people, and so far little touched by the war."

By mid-December 1862 Fanny and Susan had found a large house in Asheville, one occupied at the time by a smaller family willing to let the Polks have it for a year. They could scarcely have asked for better accommodations: eight furnished rooms plus two unfurnished in the garret, as well as an outside garden, an orchard, and a cow. Soon the other girls came on from Mississippi, and close behind came Hamilton with his wife and two little boys.[27] Fanny, while in New Orleans, had sometimes despaired of ever again finding happiness in her mortal life, but now she expressed herself surprisingly restored to good humor. On that note, Leonidas told his wife that "the finger of God seems to have pointed to [the house] and led you all there." Having first discerned divine intervention in the Confederates' victory at Big Bethel, Virginia, early in the war, the bishop could now recognize a sympathetic Providence at work on a family level.

With the new home obtained, Polk assumed the role of an absent but dutiful husband and father, promising to stock the Asheville household cupboards with "flour, hams, lard and possibly candles (if I can get them)." Not much later, he arranged for twenty male slaves "and their families" to be moved from the Mississippi plantation he still owned. Mules, too, were sent. About his only family worry now had to do with Hamilton: "Quiet is absolutely indispensable to his recovery," he told his daughter Frances. Polk had equipped his son with a magneto-powered medical instrument providing "General Electrization." Some physicians of the day recommended the device for a wide variety of maladies, including impotence and writer's cramp. Relief from "congestion of the brain and paralysis" was the promise for Hamilton. "He ought to use the electric machine quite constantly so as to get well," his father prescribed.[28]

During their general's absence in Virginia and North Carolina, Polk's army had traveled from Knoxville by rail and on foot to redeploy in a sizable semicircle outside Murfreesboro, a mainline railroad town in Middle Tennessee. Thirty miles southeast of Nashville, it was situated beside Stones River, and Bragg valued it as a military base and rail depot. The place had lately been wrestled away from a Yankee garrison by Nathan Bedford Forrest and his usually irresistible cavalry brigade. Forrest had taken 1,200 prisoners in the raid. Happy with that turn of events, Bragg assured the War Department that Middle Tennessee's welcoming citizenry, "having felt the yoke of Abolition despotism, could now be depended upon for warm support and enlistments."[29] Polk caught up with his officers and men outside the town about November 27; in the meantime, his young friend Mercer Otey had joined Polk's staff as a Signal Corps lieutenant.

In early December, Jefferson Davis arrived at Murfreesboro, paying, as Polk termed it, a "royal visit"; it was the president's first trip to the western theater since the war had begun. During his weekend there, Davis reviewed Polk's corps; the spectacle was greatly enjoyed, especially by a young sergeant raised on an Alabama cotton plantation (who with his four brothers had become Confederate soldiers). "The Brigades were drawn up in line of battle, one behind the other," James Hall rhapsodized to his father.

> The President, General Bragg, General Polk, Cheatham, Withers and other Generals with their escorts were drawn up in beautiful array on the brow of a hill in front of us. When all was ready the President with [James] Withers by his side (because Withers' Division was being reviewed), followed by a host of generals, rode slowly down the front of each Brigade. Each Battalion presented arms as he rode by them. I knew Marse Jeff as soon as I saw him. The President then took his original position on the brow of the hill. We then marched by him in column company, the officers saluting him as they passed. The whole division then saluted by presenting arms and giving three hearty cheers. This was the Grande Finale of the review.[30]

Polk was mighty pleased with the performance himself. They were "the best-appearing troops [Davis] had seen," which judgment was "very gratifying to me, as you may suppose," Polk told his wife.[31] Then at dinnertime on Saturday, Bragg's assembled generals kept their customary spitefulness in check and passed an amicable evening with the commander in chief, their collective opinion apparently minimizing the threat of any worrisome winter offensive from Nashville by William Rosecrans's XIV Corps (shortly to be renamed the Army of the Cumberland). Was that wishful thinking or merely the officers' needing to appear well-informed? According to one report, the president promised Polk's troops they would themselves be in Nashville by Christmas.[32] In fact, from the president on down, the Confederates were merely guessing at Rosecrans's next move. But refreshed by his generals' hearty assurances and bonhomie, Davis left in good humor Sunday morning, December 14, for Chattanooga and Mobile. Then, counting on Rosecrans to hibernate in Nashville, Davis would shortly siphon off 7,500 of Bragg's infantrymen and dispatch them to Mississippi, much to Bragg's pique: the President had denied him the strength he knew he would need against Rosecrans.[33] But that was a problem for later. Though considerably outnumbered by the Yankees marshaled in Nashville, the carefree officers and men in Murfreesboro continued their holiday partying.[34] Most of those in the higher ranks were accordingly on hand later that Sunday when the celebrated guerrilla cavalryman John Hunt Morgan, thirty-seven, married pretty Mattie Ready, twenty-two, of Murfreesboro. Morgan had been promoted the day before by Davis to brigadier general.[35] Never one to put off duty, he scarcely had time before the ceremony to dust himself off after completing a dazzling raid in which his troopers captured the entire Yankee garrison at Hartsville, Tennessee.

Now, with the Right Reverend Lt. Gen. Leonidas Polk presiding (in full military uniform, he was bending, if not breaking, his wartime vow to forgo clerical roles in public), the social event of the season proceeded. A friend of Mattie took note of the wedding's musical aspect: "It is certainly the match of the Times," he mused. "'The Belle of Tennessee' and the dashing leader whose name rings throughout the civilized world." During the ceremony, Morgan's brother-in-law and right-hand assistant, Col. Basil Duke, seems to have paid as much attention to the bishop-militant officiating as to the matrimonial couple. "Clad in his uniform of Lieut. Genl., I thought him one of the noblest looking men I had ever seen," Duke recalled, "and I was impressed with his grand and benignant manner. He was one of the finest specimens of the ante-bellum gentleman I ever saw." A merry dinner and ball followed the ceremony. Whether one can trust an engraved, postwedding illustration showing the guests dancing a Virginia Reel upon a United States flag the size of a parlor carpet cannot be said for sure. It is nevertheless certain that other fun took place in the drawing room. By popular demand, the surgeon David Yandell did his renowned impersonations of Polk and Bragg.[36]

About this time, Polk dispatched William Richmond, a favorite aide-de-camp, to Asheville to help the Polk family settle in. He was a man of surplus energy and capacity ("One after my own heart," is how Polk described him).[37] Richmond reported back bearing welcome letters from two of the Polk girls. Having the family safely moved in kept Polk in good spirits. He confessed relishing, as well, the prospect of a future major battle against William Rosecrans, "feeling perfectly confident of our ability to thrash [him] whenever he will come out and give us battle." Daughter Frances, however, was downcast because of the war and the attendant hardships of her recent flight from New Orleans. In a bracing letter, her father urged her to remember always to trust in the loving providence of God, "a well-spring of life, a talisman of defense." Moreover, he assured her, the days of "these pesky Yankees" were numbered. "We shall as surely conquer them, as the sun rises in the East and sets in the West. Their successes, such as they are, are purely temporary." He predicted "peace we certainly shall have before the winter is over," adding, "I am only afraid it will occur before we have killed that miscreant Butler and this vulgar braggart Andy Johnson," the Federal military governor of Tennessee.[38] Whether Polk's malicious remark was facetious or sincere is unclear, but Jefferson Davis had genuinely lethal designs of his own on Benjamin Butler. On Christmas Eve he issued a proclamation decreeing that, should Butler ever fall into Confederate hands, he was to be hanged on the spot. Such was the war's deranging effect on former political cronies: the Confederate president's ire was directed at a man who in 1860 had proposed Davis run against Lincoln for president of the United States.[39]

Polk spent Christmas Eve and Christmas Day attending to the routines of his command. On December 24 he got word from his cavalry officer, Brig. Gen. John A. Wharton, asking where army deserters should be sent for trial. "Someone," said the soldier at odds with the season of goodwill towards men, "must be shot from this command, and that speedily."[40] On Christmas evening, a Thursday, Polk wrote his wife that he had "had rather a plain time today." No clergyman had appeared at Murfreesboro's Episcopal Church for Christmas worship, so the bishop's one pleasure was the company of a colonel and a lieutenant, both from Asheville, whom he had invited to share the holiday table in his quarters.[41]

Before the fighting broke out along Stones River on December 31, General Rosecrans was all business. On the Feast of St. Stephens, December 26, under rainy skies, he ordered some 44,000 soldiers out of their entrenchments around Nashville and marched them south toward Murfreesboro. Because neither the Confederates' actual positions nor their intentions were clear to the Federals (would they stay dug in at Murfreesboro or, as some of the Federal brass figured, back off speedily southeastward to Shelbyville?), Rosecrans sent his Army of the Cumberland down a network of hard-surfaced and country dirt roads that led one way or another to the vicinity of the town. Yet hardly had the Federal troops ventured outside Nashville than they encountered roving Confederate cavalry units sent by Bragg to spot and hamper their progress.[42] Having just enough numbers and fire-power to be dangerous, the mounted Rebels, supported by three infantry brigades, would repeatedly force the Federals to stop and deploy into skirmish lines. Then Joe Wheeler and John Wharton's men would gallop off, a couple of miles this way, a couple of miles that way, and set up another harassment. After three days of coping with these deadly cavalrymen, along with the occasional quagmire road (one Federal brigade, bogged down in mud, had to return to Nashville and start over on a different route), the dogged Yankees finally reached their destination, scarcely thirty miles from the start. Bragg in the meantime had begun to compress his own infantry and artillery into a tighter, more formidable perimeter around Murfreesboro. In all, his troops numbered about 38,000.[43]

Isolated and occasional skirmishing and artillery exchanges would punctuate the next forty-eight hours, the probing and testing that anticipated the battle that erupted on New Year's Eve 1862. The cannonading and shooting had resulted, as Polk reported, in many losses on both sides, "an appropriate introduction to the great battle of the ensuing day." It was during this period of preliminary tension that General Polk was reported to have granted his soldiers license to "dispose of any prisoners [they] had trouble taking care of" in the coming battle. The accusation surfaced months later in a Unionist newspaper, the *New-Orleans Era*, under the headline "How the Rebels Treat Their Prisoners." The item was then reprinted in the Cincinnati *Daily Commercial* on May 19, 1863, where it startled a vigilant reader: the Ohio bishop Charles McIlvaine. According to the news story, which McIlvaine clipped and then mailed to Polk, a Confederate captain "who lately served in the rebel army under General Bragg" said that, on

December 30 in Murfreesboro, "General Polk rode along the lines of his corps, addressing the regiments in person. In his speech to the regiment to which I belonged he said: 'If you find any trouble in taking care of prisoners, and wish to dispose of them in any other way, I will not scold you.'" The captain's recollection goes on: "This, too, from the lips of a Christian bishop! A minister of the gospel of peace! While some were disposed to cheer the remark, others exclaimed, with astonishment, 'Who would have thought that of General Polk!' This I heard, and I shall never forget the chill of horror that passed through my veins when it was uttered." With Benjamin Butler in mind, the captain then concluded: "If Jeff. Davis can pass a sentence of death on a Northern General, and order his execution if captured, ought not President Lincoln to pass a like sentence on the pious Bishop of Louisiana?"

McIlvaine addressed Polk with surface cordiality. "Sir, Deeply as I deplore your present situation," his letter began,

> I am not desirous making it worse without other than anonymous evidence, to such allegations against you as are contained in the enclosed extract. Other statements injurious to your habits and character I have steadily denied and refused to believe. I should be glad to deny this [one] on other grounds than my belief of the impossibility of its truth. As [the story] will have a wide currency, I will with great pleasure give a wide circulation to your denial, should you favor me with it.

There is no evidence that Polk replied.[44]

The battle at Murfreesboro, usually termed the Battle of Stones River, commenced in earnest at dawn on New Year's Eve, a Wednesday. Eyeing one another on Monday and Tuesday, December 29 and 30, both armies had found their places and settled in along a three-mile front. The enemies were arrayed this way on Tuesday night: West of the river and facing east in a line running more-or-less south to north, the Federal right wing was under Maj. Gen. Alexander McCook; the center was under Maj. Gen. George H. Thomas; the left wing was under Maj. Gen. Thomas L. Crittenden. Facing Crittenden from across Stones River was the Confederate right under Maj. Gen. John C. Breckinridge's division; facing Thomas in the center (and, like him, west of the river) was Polk's partly entrenched corps; Polk himself was quartered in the home of "the Widow Zane."[45] Adjacent to Polk on the Confederate left and opposed by McCook was Hardee's corps. (A brigade commander under Hardee was Brig. Gen. Lucius Eugene Polk, Leonidas

Polk's nephew.) As for Confederate cavalry, John Wharton's brigade was under General Polk; Joe Wheeler's brigade was under General Hardee. The notion that Wheeler's cavalry was fit to be useful in the hours ahead is a wonder. From Monday evening through the following day and night his brigade had displayed its rugged versatility. Instead of attempting to slow the Yankees' forward progress, 4,000 troopers set out on a counterclockwise whirlwind circuit behind Rosecrans's whole army. That was where his supply lines stretched back to Nashville, and along the way of continual riding and fighting, the men under young Wheeler (he was twenty-six) captured and paroled about 1,000 stragglers, destroyed or crippled four wagon trains, cut 1,000 mules free from harness, rounded up fresh horses for themselves, and for thirty-six hours raised hell aplenty along Rosecrans's backside; their losses, apparently, were slight.[46] Rosecrans penned not a word of this humiliation in his Murfreesboro report.[47]

The "geography of the [Stones River] battlefield contained a matrix of elements" (to borrow the historian David J. Eicher's elegant phrasing): woods and cedar thickets, cultivated fields, rocky outcroppings, half a dozen crisscrossing turnpikes and lanes, a railroad, and Stones River itself, wadable provided the rain held up.[48] Rosecrans made no determined attack on Tuesday, as Bragg had expected him to do; indeed, an incongruous harmony prevailed over the region that cold night. Both bands of the bivouacked armies, after exchanging taunting renditions of "Dixie" and "Yankee Doodle," subsided in mutually mournful versions of "Home, Sweet Home." In a memoir recounting that moment beside Stones River—"Reader, I tell you this was a soul-stirring piece"—a Confederate soldier on the front would portray the night with a borrowed poem:

> Whose sad, slow stream, its noiseless flood
> Poured o'er the glancing pebbles
> All silent now, the Federals stood,
> All silent stood the Rebels.
> No heart or soul had heard unmoved
> That plaintive note's appealing,
> So sweetly, "Home, Sweet Home" but stirred
> The hidden fount of feeling.[49]

First thing Wednesday morning, December 31, acting on a suggestion offered by General Polk at a staff meeting, Bragg had determined to carry the battle to the Yankees; he would strike Alexander McCook on Rosecrans's right flank. By coincidence, Rosecrans had directed the divisions of Horatio

Van Cleve and Thomas J. Wood on the Federal left to cross Stones River at dawn and attack Bragg's right flank, a position manned in relative isolation by John Breckinridge's single division. The Federals hoped with their superior numbers to drive Breckinridge into Murfreesboro and captivity. Had Bragg and Rosecrans's two attacks gotten off simultaneously, they would have given the battle a furious clockwise swirl just northwest of Murfreesboro.

But William Hardee on the Confederate left was up and moving first, falling on the Yankees by daybreak as Van Cleve was attempting to wade his division across the river. Thus the Rebels, advancing through morning fog, got the jump on Rosecrans, who at about that very time was in a small tent beside his headquarters marquee receiving the Communion Host from Chaplain Peter P. Cooney of the 35th Indiana Infantry. And with that, the Peace of the Lord was finished for that day. William Bickham, a Cincinnati war correspondent in Rosecrans's camp, described the swelling din of the Confederates' onslaught that soon reached the commanding general's ears:

It was nearly seven o'clock. Suddenly all hearts were thrilled by a sound sweeping from the right like a strong wind soughing through a forest. Now a deep reverberation like thunder rolling in a distant cloud. Directly, a prolonged, fierce, crepitating noise, like a cane-brake on fire. Ears that once hear that appalling sound never forget it. Days after the rattle and rumble of a wagon will startle and thrill you.[50]

By catching the men on the Federal right just stretching awake or cooking their breakfast on New Year's Eve morning, the Confederates' hope was to bend the enemy lines back on themselves, driving them across the east-to-west turnpike to Nashville that was their essential supply line (and escape route).[51] At Bragg's direction, the movement was to be so well-coordinated that his left and center divisions under Hardee and Polk would be ranked in rows several hundred yards apart and would pivot clockwise like wheel spokes two miles long. The spokes were meant to sweep relentlessly around to the northwest. "Keep up the touch of elbows to the right, in order that the line may be unbroken," Bragg instructed his soldiers. Should all go well, the Yankees would be compressed and captured—or annihilated.[52]

Bragg's hoped-for parade-ground precision on a landscape rippled by plowed fields and punctuated by cedar thickets proved as unrealistic as his later report was embellished. "The enemy was taken completely by surprise," he wrote to higher-ups in Richmond. "A hot and inviting breakfast of coffee and other luxuries, to which our gallant and hardy men had long been strangers, was found upon the fire unserved, and was left as we pushed on to the enjoyment of a more inviting feast, that of captured artillery, fleeing battalions, and hosts of craven prisoners begging for the lives they had forfeited by their acts of brutality and atrocity." Bragg's exhilarated recollections seven weeks after that first morning are remarkable when set beside the words of William Bickham, the Cincinnati journalist. To communicate the awfulness of Murfreesboro to his own readers, he would shortly write: "A week of horrors, a week of carnage, a week of tremendous conflict—and battle still raging. My God, when will it end!"[53]

As of Wednesday morning, the Confederate left presented 10,000 men against Major General McCook's 16,000 on the Federal right. Yet the surprise of their attack gave the Rebels an advantage, said by some, as nearly equivalent to twice their actual numbers. "No troops in the world could have withstood [it]," one Illinois colonel said, and the attack put some of Hardee's opponents in mind of his daybreak rout of Federal troops at Shiloh the previous April.[54] The Union's Brig. Gen. Edward Kirk was mortally wounded almost at the beginning, and not much later Brig. Gen. August Willich, mistaking Rebels for Yankees in the confusion, found himself a captive. John Wharton's cavalry at the same time was curling around the right flank of the Federals; coming at the Yankees from behind, his 2,000 troopers took some 1,500 prisoners. As the Confederate wheel thus rolled clockwise, Polk's front-line divisions at the pivot began to move somewhat uncertainly toward Gen. Philip Sheridan's division on McCook's left—that is, near the left-center of Rosecrans's front. The element of Yankee astonishment was gone by then, and Sheridan's infantry and artillery were all set at the edge of a woods when Polk's people arrived. Sheridan had bent his line to an acute angle to counter the Rebel advance, and to his favor otherwise was the open ground in his front and the bulletproof limestone outcroppings his men were crouched behind. Delays and a rearrangement of units on Polk's right stalled the Confederates' momentum, not counting one private's laconic observation that on that midwinter holiday "John Barleycorn was general-in-chief."[55]

To the Yankees' good fortune, as Polk would later point out, Confederate elbows had not long stayed in touch with one another. Not only were his men moving targets of the Yankee muskets ahead and the cannons on the flanks; the running soldiers were simultaneously having to negotiate ground broken by "a ridge of rocks, with chasms intervening, and covered with a dense growth of rough cedars."[56] Furthermore, the exacting attack times set by Bragg could not be scrupulously followed by his subcommanders. So for all of Hardee's early success against McCook, by midmorning the idealized sweep of Confederates like a scythe through hapless Union ranks had begun to falter and come apart. Now uncoordinated, the Confederates were repeatedly thrown back with high losses once they encountered Philip Sheridan's division, "intrenched behind stones and covered by thick woods," as Polk described the scene.[57]

As had happened at Perryville, disorganization in the Rebel ranks added to confusion as to who was shooting at whom. While members of the Confederate 4th Tennessee Infantry debated whose artillery was raining "murderous fire" upon them (thinking maybe the battery puffing off in the distance was manned by fellow Confederates), Polk related how Sgt. Thomas B. Oakley, a Rebel color-bearer, with "cool courage . . . did march out with the flag of his country some 8 or 10 paces in advance of his regiment. Holding the flag conspicuously aloft, he exposed himself to the far-off cannoneers, who presently turned their attention and their shots at the flag-bearer." That settled the question that the gunners "were no mistaken friends of ours." The following summer, an anonymous private picked up Polk's account: General Polk was inspecting the 4th Tennessee and sought out Sergeant Oakley, and as "he ungloved his hand, said, 'I must shake hands with you.' Then raising his hat, the general continued: 'I am proud to uncover in the presence of so great a man.'" With that "a great shout rent the air."[58]

Having some of his key officers killed or disabled, Sheridan was at length driven backward, Polk reported, "with the rest of the fleeing battalions of McCook's corps." But it had cost the Rebels dearly. In one charge, Polk said, "the horses of every officer of the field and staff of [Col. A. J.] Vaughan's brigade, except one, and the horses of all the officers of the field and staff of every regiment, except two, were killed." Vaughan's 4th Brigade lost also one-third of its force, 105 men killed outright.[59] Sheridan lost almost a third of his 6,500, including 72 officers wounded or killed (among them three brigade commanders).[60]

Like a farmyard gate swung wide, two-thirds of Rosecrans's front had been folded to a right angle of its original position. The Yankees still controlled the vital Nashville Turnpike—the hoped-for prize that might have won for the Rebels a clear-cut victory. (Had the Confederates succeeded in securing the pike so essential to the Yankees' survival, they would have captured Federal ammunition trains and been in a position to attack General Thomas's corps front and back.) Soon the sharp bend in Rosecrans's front was crammed with infantry and artillery, a lethal apex aimed at the approaching Confederates like the point of a spear. Moreover, the salient was dominated by a compact thicket rising a few feet higher than the surrounding fenced-in corn and cotton fields. Studded with boulders and draped with the low-hanging branches of cedar trees, the wood was called the Round Forest by the locals. Now that Generals Rosecrans and Thomas had estimated its defensive possibilities, the area was bristling with some fifty guns situated on a ridge high enough to fire over the heads of their own infantrymen, who were themselves shielded by the thicket's rocks and trees.[61] Little daunted, Bragg commanded his troops to do what they were becoming known for: heedless attacks against virtually impregnable positions. After only a few of the subsequent vain attempts to drive the Yankees out of the Round Forest, the Confederates gave a new name to the place: Hell's Half-Acre.

Shortly before midday, Bragg ordered Brigadier Generals James R. Chalmers and Daniel S. Donelson and their Mississippi and Tennessee brigades to charge in successive waves across some 400 yards of open ground. (It was General Donelson who as a cadet had been General Polk's tent mate at West Point in the summer of 1824.) Reenacting their success in the lethal Sunken Road at Shiloh, the Yankees held steady against the oncoming Rebels. The grove they shared with birds and rabbits then quickly became for the soldiers an arena of wounds and death inflicted by flying bullets, clubbing musket butts, thrusting bayonets, and ramrods. Among the first to rush the salient, some of Chalmers's men in the 44th Mississippi, with no working muskets to shoot, inflicted what injuries they could with sticks.[62]

Close behind, leaping or sidestepping the slain, wounded, and stragglers of Chalmers's brigade, Donelson's men dashed through an open cotton patch. In the din, some were seen to pluck cotton from the bolls underfoot to stuff into their ears. In the tumult and breakdown of coordination, Col. John Houston Savage's 16th Tennessee found itself with no support on its left. Unable to advance and unwilling to retire, as Polk would report, the 16th Tennessee held on for three hours and sustained 207 casualties among its 402 men.[63]

If the assault on the Round Forest seemed all but hopeless to the men being thrown against it (what few penetrations of the woods were achieved were never more than momentary before counterattacks repulsed them), never mind. Bragg was determined to force the issue right there, irrespective of other, more favorable prospects elsewhere on the field. Thus, with mounting losses and exhaustion now weakening Polk's divisions, Bragg at midafternoon sent him reinforcements from John Breckinridge on the eastern side of the river. (Because Rosecrans had called off his intended attack on Breckinridge, these fresh reserves had been unengaged up until then.) Unfortunately, the four brigades sent to Polk were not marshaled effectively after fording Stones River. Polk blamed the brigades themselves, saying they came to him tardily "in detachments of two brigades each, the first arriving nearly two hours after Donelson's attack, the other about an hour after the first."[64] Then, just as Chalmers and Donelson had been fed piecemeal to the Round Forest defenders, so were these brigades. Having to cross several hundred yards of open ground raked by artillery and rifle fire, they ran against the salient's concealed defenders as though driven down a chute in an abattoir. According to a sympathetic Indiana infantry chaplain watching his enemies' distress: "We could see their men falling like leaves, but the broken ranks were filled and they held their ground with a heroism worthy of a better cause." He observed, too, less heroic acts by "several of their men. When the firing was hottest they fell upon the ground, and when the rebel force fell back these men skipped across to our lines and surrendered."[65] Polk himself later provided what he hoped was an extenuating alibi: "The opportune moment for putting in these detachments had passed." Contrarily, a Federal colonel on the scene thought Polk's "error . . . was so palpable as to render an excuse for failure necessary."[66]

Whether Polk's fragmentary use of the Breckinridge reserves was due to ineptitude or to necessity is a Stones River issue debated still.[67] In any case, the fortunes of both the attacking Confederates and the defending Federals, as measured by Ohio's Col. William Hazen, "oscillated from front to rear the entire day."[68] But Hazen's 2nd Brigade, absorbing the repeated impacts of the Rebels, held. The defensive strength of his brigade had been "doubled," he estimated, by the "little crest [it] occupied." And though sorely tested by the day's incessant pummeling, his command rested that night "where it had fought, not a stone's throw from where it was posted in the morning."[69]

In sum, nothing conclusive was gained by either side on December 31 (the casualties, too, were equivalent), and the fate of Murfreesboro and Stones River hung balanced that joyless holiday night. The Confederates had won on their left but lost on their right; the Federals had won on their left but lost on their right. (Polk's son William, an artilleryman, believed that the Confederates would have succeeded on the right too had their guns been able to keep pace with the infantry, but "entangled in the cedar thickets [many batteries] accomplished but little.")[70] As it was, early on New Year's Day morning 1863 the Federals withdrew from the smoking ruin of the Round Forest to better consolidate themselves, while Polk's forces took possession of scarred rocks, bloody rills, and splintered cedar trees. Such was the cost of missed chances and, perhaps, obstinacy by Braxton Bragg.[71]

As the night of New Year's Eve had found both armies close to wreckage, luckier than some among the wounded were those who had fallen within reach of a troop of compassionate Confederates who laid them in rows, friends beside foes, and minded through the night campfires lighted between the rows "to prevent the poor fellows from freezing." And yet, though some 14,000 dead and dying men strewed the battlefield—the temperature dropping around them, rain falling on them, the ground freezing beneath them—Braxton Bragg's perspective was that of a holiday reveler in his cups. He telegraphed Richmond that "God has granted us a Happy New Year. Rosecrans was badly mauled." Bragg supposed the enemy would surely retreat (which, some think, is what Bragg would be doing were he in Rosecrans's predicament),[72] and, thus comforted, he drifted into sleep with no expressed plan for either the conclusion or the continuation of the conflict around him.

On the holiday that often led him into solemn introspections, it sufficed for Polk at Murfreesboro to ruminate that the previous day's battle had "developed in all parts of the field which came under my observation the highest qualities of the soldier among our troops." Possibly before retiring himself he was preoccupied with tending to a wounded family friend and future son-in-law, William Huger, engaged even then to Elizabeth Polk, known as Lilly. Huger was a Louisiana infantry officer whose leg was amputated after the battle. Polk subsequently sent him south by boxcar in the care of Charles Quintard, who exercised during the trip his dual role as a regimental surgeon and chaplain. "I held the stump of his thigh in my hands most of the journey," Quintard related. "When we reached Chattanooga, I was more exhausted than my patient."[73]

By the time January 1 had dawned in Murfreesboro, Rosecrans's soldiers had backed out of the Round Forest point (thereby reducing the dangerous exposure on their bent front line). Polk's brigades then moved into the vacuum, making them "masters of the field," as Polk rather dramatically described the transaction. Bragg's optimism to the contrary, Rosecrans was not retreating; he was regrouping. And wisely, while the Confederates paid little heed, he sent at dawn the Third Division from Crittenden's Corps to claim an unoccupied rise of ground on the eastern side of Stones River. Up to then, the Confederates had thought this to be their side of the stream, but Crittenden's division, now in place, glared down on John Breckinridge's brigades situated about a mile to the southeast; in addition, it could fire into the flanks of Polk's other forces west of the river.[74] The Third Division had become a serious threat to Bragg's whole stalled right wing.

After a day of relative inactivity by both sides, Bragg on Friday morning, January 2, decided to drive the intrusive division off its perch and back across the river. He ordered Breckinridge to do the job. Breckinridge thought it was a little late for that; he had already examined the lay of the land and the elevated, entrenched enemy facing him. He argued against Bragg's order. Even if his brigades succeeded in dislodging the Third Division's infantry, ranks of Yankee artillerymen on the western side of the river would then have the Confederates' exposed flanks in their sights. He was not alone in his dissent. Roger Hanson, a fulminating brigadier under Breckinridge, was so certain of the murderous futility of Bragg's order that he had to be restrained from going to Bragg's headquarters after vowing he was aiming to kill the general forthwith.[75] Not dissuaded by his subaltern's dissent (not only was Bragg anxious for a telling victory; it has been suggested that such was his enmity for Breckinridge that he may have thought him worth sacrificing), Bragg ordered Breckinridge to begin the eastern-bank assault at 4 P.M. He likewise directed Polk, situated on his western-bank position, to distract the enemy by opening his own artillery at the same time. "Shell out of the woods . . . any sharpshooters who might annoy [Breckinridge] while approaching the river," as Polk phrased the order. Polk did so with three batteries but came a-cropper. The Yankees reacted so vigilantly to Polk's "distraction" that they drove his brigades clean out of the Round Forest and reoccupied it.[76]

Though his infantry would regain it one more time (with a bayonet charge the next morning), Polk's loss of the Round Forest on Friday afternoon was not the only thing that went wrong with Bragg's eastern-bank attack. Able to watch the Rebels' preparations in full view, the Yankees had seen the attack materializing—and they were dug in and braced. True, the Breckinridge brigades numbered more than 5,000 men (including men of the famed Orphan Brigade of Kentucky and another of Tennesseans led by Brigadier Gideon Pillow).[77] And they were initially successful against the Third Division, though their losses were significant.[78] In the struggle that followed, reduced sometimes to hand-to-hand combat and point-blank shooting, they drove their enemies off their hill and back across Stones River.[79] The Federals, scattering "like blackbirds, even collided head-on with a too-little, too-late force sent to their rescue." But now that their routed comrades were no longer in their line of fire, Yankee gunners behind forty-five cannons arrayed practically side by side on the elevated opposite bank, opened predictably on the left flank of the prematurely jubilant Confederates.[80] Hopelessly exposed, the Confederates were beginning to back away from their vulnerable exposure when a counterattack manned by fresh Yankee infantry charged back across the river and sent them fleeing even faster.

Brigadier General Roger Hanson was himself mortally wounded in the artillery barrage when a shell fragment severed an artery in his left leg. Polk offered him an encouraging word or two as he was carried to the rear, and Hanson gamely declared it was "glorious to die for one's country." As night fell, Breckinridge's people (excepting his 1,700 killed and wounded) were back where they had started the attack at 4:00 P.M. Breckinridge was seen by Lt. Col. Joseph Nuckols "raging like a wounded lion," furious at Bragg. With Hanson dying, and his Orphan Brigade cut to pieces, he bewailed: "My poor Orphans! My poor Orphans."[81] In the words of the historian Kenneth P. Williams, "Bragg had himself been a proud U.S. artilleryman; [he] should have known better than go up against that concentration of enemy guns."[82]

The week of horrors and carnage bewailed by the Cincinnati journalist had at last come to an end, though Braxton Bragg was still bellicose when he went to bed.[83] He was in the same temper in the middle of the night while reading a message from two of his subordinates, Maj. Gens. Jones Withers and Frank Cheatham, who had sent it up the chain of command through Polk. They were urging that the Confederates prudently consider getting out of Murfreesboro while they still could. Polk, having seen "the effect of the operations of to-day," added to the paper an endorsement and sent it to Bragg by Lieut. William Richmond. Bragg cast drowsy and dismissive eyes on the message and told Richmond to "say to the general [Polk] we shall maintain our position at every hazard." Getting that distressing reply, Polk at 3:00 A.M. wrote Hardee to inform him of what was going on, adding that he considered Bragg's decision "unwise . . . in a high degree." Less the autocratic bishop he sometimes had been and now more the obliging lieutenant, Polk told Hardee: "I shall, of course, obey his orders and endeavor to do my duty."[84]

But the next morning a little before noon, with Stones River rising from the rain (threatening to cut Bragg's army in two), Bragg, after receiving an erroneous estimate of Rosecrans's strength and another, correct report that Federal reinforcements were pouring in from Nashville, called Polk and Hardee to his headquarters. The commanders now concurred that a withdrawal was in order; it would commence under the cover of the coming night.[85] Almost a third of Bragg's army had been lost at Murfreesboro, and some 2,000 of his wounded and sick and their medical attendants were to be left behind. As press reports from the battle area were delayed, Southerners in Richmond, Charleston, and Memphis were still celebrating Bragg's proclaimed victory as the Army of Tennessee began to slouch off toward the southeast of the state.[86]

Shortly, it would be Rosecrans, not Bragg, who could more justifiably claim success. He had so skillfully managed to blunt William Hardee's early advantage that William Polk himself praised the Federal commander's generalship: "He did it so well that ultimately he held the field, and if he had never done anything else, his conduct at Murfreesboro should secure him a high place as a commanding general."[87] Abraham Lincoln was thankful just for the stalemate and would later say that the whole fate of the Union had teetered precariously as the mayhem of Stones River had swept first one way and then the other. Mindful of the 13,000 Federal casualties at Fredericksburg, Virginia, that same December, the president said "a defeat instead, the nation could scarcely have lived over."[88]

21

General Rabbitt Escapes a Guerrilla Snare (1863)

Just as they had done following Perryville and the failed Kentucky campaign, the subordinate generals in the Army of Tennessee resumed fixing fault within days after withdrawing from the ruins of Murfreesboro. Now quartered in the relative safety of Shelbyville, Tennessee, not far from Chattanooga, Braxton Bragg's dedicated vocal critics—William Hardee, John Breckinridge, Patrick Cleburne, and B. Franklin Cheatham (and, somewhat more on the perimeter, Leonidas Polk)—warmly engaged in what had become their favorite pastime. Bragg, meanwhile, holed up in new headquarters in nearby Tullahoma, was thinking himself unappreciated by his officers. Ineptly, he soon managed to exacerbate the generals' ill feeling even more.

Further bothering Bragg were what he regarded as unjust disparagements by Confederate congressmen, the South's public, and its press. All were denouncing Murfreesboro's awful casualties (among the greatest of the Civil War) and were angered that the town and its earthworks and rifle pits had been handed over to General Rosecrans's Yankees. Had not Bragg told the South on New Year's Day that God had given them a victory? And though his subsequent withdrawal from the town had its military logic, even affirmed by Jefferson Davis, it was a reversal hard for most civilians to accept.[1]

One Louisiana man with good reason to feel dismay, but attempting to understand Bragg's thinking, was John Middleton Huger, a Louisiana planter well known to Polk: it was his son Willie who had lost a leg at Stones River and was to marry Lilly Polk the next year. The elder Huger, a soldier in 1835 against the Seminole people in Florida, had served briefly under Bragg in Pensacola at the outbreak of the Civil War.[2] Now, some weeks after Stones River, and little suspecting General Polk's low opinion of Bragg, Huger wrote him asking to be assured that the conduct of his former chief "did not deserve the injurious" clamor making the rounds. Esteeming Polk as a bishop no less than as a general, he trustingly said: "It is a necessity of your nature to seek the truth and . . . to do justice must be imperative to an especial degree." Huger admitted that, immediately after the Murfreesboro retreat, while "heartsick from disappointment," he too had maligned Bragg. But now he felt remorse. He entreated Polk "to lend me assistance" in rolling back "this wave of popular error, and brush[ing] off the aspersions which now dim the bright shield of your brother warrior." Huger's letter crested with a flourish: "How true it is that the praise accorded to a man . . . is uttered in a 'still small voice,' whilst blame comes trumpet-tongued and leaps like live thunder from peak to peak, filling all space to the very echo."[3] Polk's reply to Huger's pleading must have tested his diplomatic skills (it has not been found), but, as a hero to many Louisianans like John Huger, Polk was soon to be honored by the state's issuing a $50 banknote bearing an engraving of his head and shoulders in uniform. (Polk was in good company; George Washington graced another Confederate fifty.)[4]

Continued criticisms of Bragg's generalship kept surfacing. Some were patently unfair, the Chattanooga *Rebel* often in the lead. A daily paper widely read by Confederate soldiers (and sometimes employed to mislead Yankee readers), its editor, Henry Watterson, was among Polk's friends and had briefly been a member of his military staff. Watterson was a youthful gadfly—sometimes a soldier, other times a journalist (and the first postwar editor of the prestigious *Louisville Courier-Journal*). He inveighed regularly against Bragg, as when he reported (incorrectly) in mid-January that "the retrograde movement from Murfreesboro was made despite the disapproval of Bragg's general officers." The truth was exactly the opposite.[5]

Justly angered by this distortion amid a "deluge of abuse," Bragg sent a circular letter to the generals expecting them to "cheerfully attest . . . in writing" that their "verbal decision to withdraw from Murfreesboro on January 3 had been arrived at collegially." Emotionally vulnerable at that point, Bragg had also asked his most fractious lieutenants—Polk, Hardee, Breckinridge, Cheatham, and Cleburne—to tell him if he had "lost the good opinion of my generals, upon whom I have relied as upon a foundation of rock." Bragg urged them to "be candid."[6] As one Army of Tennessee historian drily observed, "Seldom has a correspondent received more wholehearted co-operation from those he addressed."[7]

Those who hastened to reply did craft their letters with care, not failing to mention their "high personal respect" for their commander, and so forth and so on. But to be candid they soon were affirming that Bragg had indeed lost his generals' good opinion.[8] Why on earth, a perplexed Jefferson Davis would say later, "Genl Bragg should have selected that tribunal and invited its judgment upon him, is to me unexplained."[9]

When Bragg's circular was posted on January 11, Polk was on furlough in Asheville with his family. An affecting diversion for him those days was time spent with five-year-old Frank Devereux Polk, Hamilton's son, who called his grandfather "General Rabbitt" after a bedtime story invention of Polk's named Jenny Rabbit.[10] Sinister goings-on were meanwhile brewing for the grandfather. Unionist sympathizers in East Tennessee had somehow learned of Polk's Carolina whereabouts away from his troops, and some guerrillas had put out the word they would capture him when he attempted to pass through their mountains on the return trip to Shelbyville. Bragg's letter reached him on January 17. Then, evading the guerrillas' snare (apparently warned of the danger by William Gale), Polk was back in Shelbyville by the end of January.[11]

For the comfort of himself, his son Meck, and some other staff members, Polk had appropriated (presumably paying the owners) several rooms of the spacious town house of the Gosling family. (The tornado that passed through Shelbyville on the night of March 7, lifting roofs from houses and churches, spared the Goslings' sturdy home.)[12] William Gosling was an Englishman, and before the Confederate government cut off his supply of dyes (as it was just about to do), he was manufacturing gaily colored cotton goods in his water-driven mill on Shelbyville's Duck River. Understanding that he and his wife held Unionist sympathies, the Confederates courteously spread throughout their house, sleeping between sheets every night and finding them to be "very nice quiet people." As the weather warmed, Mrs. Gosling even supplied Polk's mess with lettuce and asparagus from her garden, while the headquarter's cow did her particular part.

When exigencies of the service required the corps commander to move outside to a tent (as when he later removed to Chattanooga that summer), General Polk took along many of the comforts of home. He described to his family "an excellent table on a new plan which incorporated folding legs and was supplied with split-bottom chairs," and at mealtimes a cloth and napkins were laid out. "Our table furniture is all silver, alabastrine tureens [and] dishes, . . . plates, goblets, sugar dish and cream jug, syrup jug and all. We have the nicest tea and little tea kettle you have [ever] seen." Polk's portable bedstead, though, as he mused one late August evening, was a mixed blessing. It is "just wide enough for me alone," he told Fanny in as near an intimate allusion as to be found in all his surviving correspondence. "As I look upon it, it seems to have a very lonely bachelor look about it." Or, as he said to a daughter after his wife had just returned to Asheville from a conjugal visit in Shelbyville: "Tell your mother that I miss her amazingly, and that thinking of her yesterday [a Sunday] I came as near having the blues as I have ever done since I have been in the army. It is terrible to be cut off from you all. . . . Indeed, indeed."[13]

By the time Polk had returned to Shelbyville, the hostile clique of Hardee, Breckinridge, and Cleburne had pretty much unloaded their requested candor on Bragg, assuring him they spoke for others. Cheatham alone had withheld putting in writing his opinion of Bragg's competency. Polk showed similar restraint. Possibly he thought Bragg pathetic, the "lofty contempt" he might express for the man at other times being tempered now by pity. As he would later say to a daughter and his wife, it was his fated role to be Bragg's "dry nurse."[14] Polk began his response to Bragg's request on January 30 with a fussy summary: "There seemed to be two points of inquiry embraced in your note." The first he listed as Bragg's requesting of his fellow commanders that they refute the slander against him by writing out their support of the army's withdrawal from Murfreesboro. (Most had already discharged this specific item.) The second was "whether you had lost the confidence of your general officers as a military commander." This second inquiry, Polk continued, "though not so clearly and separately stated [as the first], nevertheless is, to my mind plainly indicated." As he knew Cheatham and some unnamed subordinates to be more uncertain as to Bragg's intent, Polk was asking for clarification.

Bragg could scarcely have felt anything but chagrin reading the frank answers supplied by Hardee and the others to his "confidence" question. He now shifted his ground. Replying argumentatively the same day to Polk by letter, Bragg said "to my mind that circular contained but one point of inquiry . . . and that was to ask . . . what had transpired between us in regard to the retreat from Murfreesboro." A half-truth at best, but Polk let it go, and in his reply he said only that—as Bragg well knew—Polk had supported the retreat. The "opinions and counsel expressed at the time" he "would give again under the same circumstances."[15] (For his diplomatic pains, Polk was now in trouble with Hardee and the others who had spoken plainly to Bragg. Polk's slippery correspondence with Bragg, they grumbled, had cast them in the role of "mere 'discontents.'")[16]

But within days, writing now to Jefferson Davis, Polk was as pointedly critical as ever. Bragg's circular asking for "candid replies" was "ill-judged," and the subsequent correspondence among Bragg and the other generals was "unfortunate." Worse was Bragg's future leadership of the Army of Tennessee, which Polk could not bear. The very fate of his beloved Confederacy was at stake. Polk sent the president seven documents touching on the circular and its aftermath and assured Davis that his critical opinions were shared by his division commanders; they, in turn, agreed with the unfavorable assessments by "officers of the other corps." In some ways Polk tried to be gracious. Bragg's "capacity for organization and discipline, which has not been equaled among us, could be used by you at headquarters with infinite advantage to the whole army," he said. And let the president recall, Polk went on, that only months ago he himself had said that "I can make good use of him here in Richmond." Summing up, Polk allowed that were the man even "Napoleon or the great Frederick he could serve our cause at some other points better than here." Secure in his unofficial relationship with the commander in chief, he signed off: "Faithfully, your friend."[17]

To take Bragg's place, Polk had recommended to Davis the urgent appointment of Joseph Eggleston Johnston, already the supreme commander of the combined Armies of Tennessee and Mississippi. Polk confided to Johnston his recommendation in a private meeting. Since Johnston's cadet days at West Point (where he overlapped with Polk), he had been an outstanding, aggressive soldier fighting Indians and Mexicans, and he was now unhappy, telling a close friend in the Confederate Congress that even in his enlarged role he had been "laid on the shelf in an administrative post." Rather than put up with such a desk job, he said, "I should much prefer the command of fifty men."[18]

But it turned out that Johnston's sense of propriety would not allow him to entertain succeeding to the command of the 80,000 men already belonging to Braxton Bragg, an idea already being broached by the president. Davis was properly worried about the "condition of things in the Army of Tennessee" and, in late January, sent Johnston to Bragg's headquarters in Tullahoma "to decide what the best interests of the service require." And as the "General Commanding," Johnston was reminded by Davis, he had the authority on his own to decide what to do. Johnston found the condition of interpersonal relationships in Bragg's army about as messy as rumored, but after two weeks of nosing around he reported himself quite pleased overall with Bragg's administration. Bending backward as far as he could, Johnston even asserted that "the operations of [Bragg's] army in Middle Tennessee have been conducted admirably . . . evincing skill in the commander and courage in the troops." Internecine bickering notwithstanding, he thought "that the interest of the service requires that General Bragg should not be removed."[19] Should Davis disagree (the Southern papers were full of gossipy speculation that Bragg's days were numbered), Johnson declared that "no one in this army, or engaged in this investigation, ought to be [Bragg's] successor." That number would include Generals Polk and Hardee, but more particularly he meant it to include himself.[20] That left Davis with little to choose from, a situation "very embarrassing to me," Davis admitted to Johnston.[21]

Johnston's recusal, despite his desire for an active job like Bragg's, was for him a matter of honor. Having played the investigator, he wanted no part in anointing his own balding forehead (Johnston styled what hair he had in a frontal comb-over arrangement) as Bragg's successor. Here was an ethical squeamishness, says the Johnston biographer Craig Symonds, that would not have been felt by Ulysses S. Grant or William T. Sherman in the least.[22] Here, too, was an overly "delicate idealism" that annoyed Jefferson Davis, who wanted Bragg replaced. Polk in February had told Davis that "I am sure [Johnston] will be content to assume the command." Polk now complained in a March letter marked "PRIVATE" that he thought Johnston's contrary feelings were "morbid" and "misplaced."[23]

Then, presumably at Davis's behest, Bragg in early March was summoned from Tullahoma to Richmond by Secretary of War James Seddon—certain to be reassigned, the rumormongers believed. An accomplished gossip, Gale passed along to Polk that he had learned from some of his well-connected Richmond contacts that Bragg's just-released Murfreesboro report had created "quite a commotion" in army and political circles and stirred up "a storm in Congress," and because he had censured Breckinridge, Cheatham, and McCown, Breckinridge was ready to resign. "The Tennesseans can stand [Bragg's] pitching into McCown, but not into [their own] Cheatham," Gale reported.[24] Breckinridge cooled off, and Bragg did not go to Richmond; Joseph Johnston held up the order because Bragg's wife, Elise, was still recovering from typhoid fever in nearby Winchester, Tennessee. (Never too removed from his pastoral instincts, the bishop in Polk had written to Bragg about that time to say that "I am glad to know . . . that Mrs. Bragg is out of danger, and hope she will, as the genial Spring opens, speedily regain her usual health.")[25] Furthermore, while Mrs. Bragg was on the mend, Johnston himself was ailing, the effects of slow-healing bullet and shrapnel wounds suffered at the Battle of Seven Pines in Virginia. So you can see, Your Excellency, Johnston impressed upon the president, General Bragg cannot be spared.[26]

Davis in the meantime had resorted to another tactic to deal with the maladjusted Army of Tennessee; he sent his aide and troubleshooter, Col.

William Preston Johnston, to the western theater to sniff out "the condition of the army." The son of Albert Sidney Johnston, and a Polk family friend (but also close to Bragg), Colonel Johnston and Polk "had long talks" over a weekend at the Gosling house. A beaming Polk also entertained him with a review of his corps, 20,000 strong. "I never saw them march so well," Polk said later. "I felt proud [for] in their hearts is embodied as large and as intense an amount of rebellion as was ever concentrated in the same number of men. It is a pleasure to command such men. [Colonel] Johnston was highly pleased."[27]

Invigorated by his exchange of confidences with the president's emissary (whose subsequent report to Davis on Bragg's contentious relations with his generals was probably delivered orally),[28] Polk reached for pen and paper and wrote yet another of his insistent advisories to Davis. He again urged Bragg's removal from Tennessee: "Col. Johnston informed me he thinks Genl J. desires to keep Genl B. in his present position," Polk wrote. "I think the case would be more properly stated by saying that [General Johnston] does not wish to be, or seem to be, the cause of [Bragg's] removal." But were Bragg transferred to Richmond and given the promotion and prestige of inspector general of "all the armies of the Confederacy," much would be gained. Especially considering how to Bragg army desertions and evasions of military duty are particularly irksome. With Bragg in Richmond, Polk enthused that "the whole family of idlers, drones and shirks of high and low degree, far and near, would feel his searching hand and be made to take their places and do their duty." Polk's certainty that summer was that winning the war and "achiev[ing] our independence was essentially a matter of mobilizing the many men capable of serving, but not yet wearing Confederate uniforms." Should Davis not fully appreciate what else Polk was getting at, he concluded: "The way is clear for assigning Genl J to the command of the army, [giving] universal satisfaction to officers and men."[29]

One historian has noted that Davis "had a deeply rooted aversion to advice," and though possibly tempted by Polk's logic, here was advice aplenty—which may explain why he did not acquiesce.[30] Further, if the president should be too insistent, Johnston might resign. Davis at length dropped the matter, leaving Bragg in Tennessee. Joe Johnston's foot-dragging had done the trick, and Davis's decision produced few future benefits to the Confederacy.

Bragg was not the only general in Tennessee whom Polk was hoping to clear out of his way that spring. The other project being hatched—even more problematical than War Department politics—was the proposed kidnapping of Gen. William Rosecrans. The Federal commander was to be snatched from the handsome Edwin Keeble house back in Murfreesboro, the red-brick headquarters-residence that Rosecrans had acquired for his own use after its secessionist owner (indeed, a Confederate congressman) had fled the town.[31] By whom the abduction scheme was conceived is not known for certain, but it seems to have been primarily the work of an Alabama cavalry lieutenant colonel named James C. Malone Jr. This officer came in from the field to meet with General Polk on March 14 and to get his opinion regarding "the lawfulness and expediency of the plot." Having sketched the kidnap proposal to Polk, which Malone seems to have developed while galloping about Murfreesboro, the trooper was to await Polk's considered judgment of the plot, and three days later he had it. Polk thought the idea had much to recommend it and urged that, along with Rosecrans, the abductors grab all the papers in his adjutant general's office.[32] Polk wrote Malone there was little he was not willing to do to thwart the Federals' "campaign of extermination against the South." Polk had lined out in his draft version the words in which he accused the Yankees of a "campaign of desolation and wholesale murder," but Malone was still sternly admonished not to reciprocate the Yankees' "extermination" tactic by harming Rosecrans, let alone by assassinating him. (Polk had first drafted "Should his life unfortunately be taken," thought better of having considered that possibility, and lined it out.) "We owe it to ourselves to be true to our own good word," Polk wrote. "From the work of assassination we would recoil with just abhorrence."[33] (Polk's concern for Rosecrans's welfare arguably belies the extraordinary rumor at Murfreesboro that he had countenanced no-quarter executions of enemy soldiers taken prisoner.)

To deliver his incendiary letter to Malone, Polk sent his swashbuckling aide-de-camp, First Lieutenant Richmond. More than a mere courier, Richmond had already signified his desire to help lay hands on Rosecrans. As he was a former sailor, Richmond on Polk's recommendation had been poised to assume the captaincy of the CSS *Louisiana* when that prized ironclad was deliberately blown to pieces on April 21, 1862, just before New Orleans fell to the enemy. Now Richmond evidently hankered for any derring-do that came his way while possibly angling for additional notice and approval by his mentor. For at that very point in his bachelor life, Richmond had set his cap on one of the sisters of Henry Clay (Harry) Yeatman, the husband of General Polk's niece Mary Brown Polk; like William Gale, Richmond was another of his volunteer aides-de-camp. Between Richmond and his suit, however, stood William Gale. He regarded Richmond as a fine fellow in many respects, but (as he gossiped to his wife, Kate) he found "many things connected with his family that would render a match between him and any well-bred girl of good family a thing not to be thought of. I feel much sympathy for him." What Gale knew about the Richmond family, and what Harry Yeatman thought of Richmond's courting his sister, is not known, but Army Nurse Kate Cumming, an esteemed Southern heroine, knew Richmond well enough to declare him a man who "in every respect adorned the Christian character."[34] The kidnap plot was now thickening. After assuring Polk that Rosecrans would not be hurt (rather than harm the man, Lieutenant Colonel Malone vowed, he would abort the escapade), the colonel and the lieutenant stole off toward the Keeble mansion in Murfreesboro. Alas for this narrative account (but fine for Rosecrans), the adventure then petered out and came to naught. Alas too for William Richmond; he also failed to kidnap the heart of Miss Yeatman.[35]

Unlike Richmond, who nursed an ardent dislike of Yankee prisoners (cowardly abolitionists and "unadulterated negro-worshippers" and the like), Polk was at least protective of the hapless prisoners in his care. Through he too termed the Federal soldiers "Abolition prisoners," he was angered that, through either carelessness or intentional neglect, the prisoners were not fed for a prolonged time after their arrival and confinement on the courthouse square in Shelbyville. Pending an investigation of that oversight, Polk had ordered the arrest of a lieutenant colonel, Theodore Francis Sevier, an inspector general on Polk's staff whom he considered responsible. Although Sevier had evidently given proper orders respecting the feeding of the prisoners, the food was not delivered (heavy rain hindered the cooking fires, among other delays), and Polk's surmise was that Sevier "did not look after the matter as closely as he would have done had the men been a detachment of our own army." Writing Maj. Thomas Jack, his assistant adjutant general, Polk denounced the maltreatment as inexcusable: "As the feeding of a large body of men devolved directly upon [Sevier], he should have pursued the matter until it was accomplished, whether by night or day." And if the "indifference to their wants [was] because they belonged to the ranks of the enemy, then it was a grave error." What further concerned Polk was the effect "this seeming neglect [would have] on the people around, and on our reputation for humanity. If others are cruel and inhuman, it is bad example and should not be followed." Polk ordered the colonel's arrest lifted ("he has been a diligent officer heretofore") but rebuked him personally the next day. That ended a disciplinary episode for an officer not known himself to follow orders scrupulously.[36]

Military matters that winter and spring had not prevented Leonidas Polk from tending to his family with his usual husbandly and fatherly care. Worried about undue pressure on his younger son, he had reduced the artillery responsibilities of eighteen-year-old Meck and sent him on a restorative furlough to Asheville bearing assorted gifts. For the general's wife, daughters, daughter-in-law, and granddaughters, there were dress patterns and variously configured homespun cottons, produced in Gosling's mill at fifty cents a yard. These were some of the last colored goods Gosling produced before running out of dyes, and General Polk imagined the fabric would "make up" very prettily. A hogshead of Tennessee bacon would soon be en route too. As for his own situation he was well pleased, and the army was in better condition than of late. His optimism regarding the fortunes of the Confederacy remained unshaken. "The general prospects of peace are increasing, though we must have some battles yet before it is effected," he said. Even so, he thought the war would end before the summer did and "perhaps not [continue] beyond the spring."[37]

Polk remained buoyant for several weeks after that February letter. While writing soon thereafter, he had a tidbit to tell he was sure would interest the family: he had just been handed a photograph of William Rosecrans. (The unnamed sender had possibly been connected with the proposed abduction of the general.) Polk's quick study of the picture, he said, confirmed what he had supposed all along: Rosecrans's looks revealed him to be "pert," "smart," "cute," "wiley," and "contriving." Polk's satisfied conclusion: "It is a great thing to know your man." His mocking tone would then turn churlish. Eight weeks later he would grouse to a daughter: "[Rosecrans] is rather an indifferent specimen of humanity and we have scant respect for him." Similarly, since confronting U. S. Grant at Belmont, and discussing prisoner exchanges with him after the battle, Polk's disdain for that general had ripened. He could now prophesy that Grant would fail in his drawn-out efforts to take Vicksburg, where Joe Johnston would soon "fall on him and crush him out root and branch."[38]

For successes of his own, Polk was happy to tell the home folks that, by pushing himself to work well into the morning hours, he had finished writing his official reports of recent battles. Though almost a year had passed since Shiloh, his version of that battle had been admirably drafted, he thought: "Everybody hereabouts [is] very much pleased with it." The self-historian did concede that friends of General Beauregard might not be very well content with his less-than-flattering limning of their hero's battlefield exploits. "I shall leave him to take care of himself." Moreover, for his reports on Perryville ("clear and precise") and Murfreesboro ("carefully composed"), he took a bow. The reports' pending publication, he did not doubt, would be received by welcome reviews. "If they accomplish nothing else, they will . . . furnish so much towards the history of the war that is entirely reliable, and that, in a land of puffs and disparagements, is not without its virtue."[39]

Because without fail some readers in every time and place will not share an author's high regard for what he or she has written, Polk would shortly hear of several factual or typographical mistakes he had made; in one regrettable instance, some readers felt he had not portrayed certain Alabama and Mississippi soldiers at Murfreesboro as accurately as he should have. Feelings, he was informed, had been hurt. Polk's apology was calculated to put everything aright in the regimental ranks. As it must have done. "I would rather weave garlands of well-earned fame around these soldiers' brows," he wrote their commander, "than to be the occasion, even by inadvertence, of the loss of a single leaf from the chaplets with which they deserve to be crowned."[40]

Except for routine cavalry-skirmishing near their respective front lines, and for the steady visits by spies and informers to both sides, the Federals and Confederates kept their distance from one another throughout the Shelbyville spring. April 10 was Polk's birthday, and his grandson Frank in Asheville would soon send a week-old Easter egg to "Gen. Rabbitt" as a present. Polk's birthday reflections the next day betrayed a bishop, a soldier, and a husband deep in melancholy. "Just to think, I am fifty-seven," he wrote Fanny. "I have spent many of these years as I would not again, but in many of them I have tried to do my duty." Five days later, Bragg and his staff visited Polk's command and were "highly pleased." Horses, mules, and men were all prospering now with plenty to eat, and "as far as the fields before us are any indication, there never was such a wheat harvest." In a singularly rare addition, he signed off the first of these letters home lightly mentioning his body servant: "Altie is quite well, and sends his respects to his mistress."[41]

With his reassignment deferred but with partisan congressmen in Richmond still second-guessing his Kentucky campaign, Bragg determined to put his idle springtime to good use by settling an old score, namely by deflecting Kentucky criticism of himself and placing it squarely on Polk. It may be recalled that Bragg, when first reporting on Perryville, had lauded Polk's and Hardee's "brilliant achievements on this memorable field." It was an assessment, Bragg said later, that even Polk thought too effusive.[42] But that was then, this was now, and Bragg was setting out again on a fishing trip. In mid-April he posted another of his circular letters to subordinate generals. Quoting extracts from Polk's published Kentucky documents, Bragg cited Polk's two councils with his commanders that resulted in his deciding to contravene Bragg's orders: Polk's resolving "to pursue a different course at Bardstown on October 3," and "to be guided by events at Perryville on October 7." Bragg now asked the letter's recipients, artlessly it would seem, to confess "to what extent you sustained the general in his acknowledged disobedience."[43]

As was prudent, Patton Anderson equivocated or did not remember; he supported Polk, however. William Hardee refused to "enter into details"; Simon Buckner was constrained from answering to sustain his "self-respect"; and Benjamin Cheatham said his "sense of duty compelled him to decline" to reply. Several of Polk's fellow generals who did comply provided him with copies of their answers. Hardee floated the suggestion to Polk that "if you choose to rip up the Kentucky campaign, you can tear Bragg into tatters." Not ready to take so drastic a step—but convinced he had a dangerous adversary in Bragg no less than Rosecrans—Polk replied to Hardee that "when I said to you I felt it to be quite as necessary to watch Tullahoma as Murfreesboro, you will see I was not mistaken in my estimate of . . . the character of others."[44] Polk was "permanently antagonized," as one historian put it, while Bragg proceeded to assure Jefferson Davis that at Bardstown and Perryville Polk had shown he was "unfitted for executing the orders of others." He added that he found it no longer possible for "cordial official confidence to exist between him and his corps commanders." Even so, his scheme to bring down Polk this time died aborning. He would, therefore, continue to bide his time.[45]

Remarkable in this peevish environment, Bragg and his chief lieutenants continued to observe surface amenities—dining at one another's headquarters, sharing parade-ground camaraderie, attending worship services together, exchanging civil correspondence. They were unusually congenial on the June day that General Bragg was baptized; gathered around the font were several of his most diligent antagonists, all on their best behavior. As Charles Quintard was looking to win for Christ soldiers of whatever rank, he had skillfully engineered the event unbidden. The chaplain admitted being intimidated by a general known to be "so . . . sharp in his sarcasm that many men were afraid to go near him," but he steeled himself to confront Bragg and to plead that baptism was indispensable for salvation of the commander's soul. Bragg was so stirred by the presentation Quintard made that tears appeared in the general's eyes and, grasping the chaplain's hands, said, "I have been waiting twenty years to have someone say this to me."[46] Bishop Polk, it may thus be supposed, had been remiss in failing to broach the matter when Colonel Bragg was attending St. John's Church in Thibodaux, Louisiana, in 1858, and though unredeemed, the colonel was reckoned worthy to represent the parish at Polk's diocesan conventions.

All was soon ready for General Bragg's formal admission to the Church. Georgia's Stephen Elliott, Polk's longtime friend from Sewanee days, had just come to Shelbyville as Polk's guest, and on his first Sunday he had preached on a parade ground to "nearly 3,000 soldiers who listened to him with the most profound attention," one member of the congregation allowed. Now he was scheduled to administer the baptismal sacrament at Shelbyville's Episcopal Church of the Redeemer.[47] Just as the ceremony was about to begin at 4:30 P.M. on Tuesday afternoon, June 2, in strode (in riding boots) Lt. Col. Arthur James Lyon Fremantle of the Queen's Coldstream Guards. The Englishman was just back from an all-day jaunt in which he had inspected the Confederates' front lines beyond the town. Lodged for several days in a tent set up next door to the Goslings' home, Fremantle had taken a liking to Chaplain Quintard's leading morning and evening services, complete with hymn singing in which "General Polk joins [in] with much zeal."

Fremantle was glad he was in time for the auspicious baptism. It was "an interesting ceremony," he said, "peculiar to America . . . performed in an impressive manner by Bishop Elliott." The bishop took the general's hand in his own (the latter kneeling in front of the font) and said: "'Braxton, if thou hast not already been baptized, I baptize thee,' &c. Immediately afterwards he confirmed General Bragg, who then shook hands with General Polk, the officers of their respective Staffs, and myself."[48] Bragg was deeply affected, later assuring Quintard: "I shall never cease to be grateful. My mind has never been so much at ease; and I feel renewed strength for the task before me."[49] Among Colonel Fremantle's most satisfying recollections of his Shelbyville visit was the discovery that such Southern gentlemen as had attended Bragg's baptism radiated in their upper-class diction their "descent from Englishmen." The colonel discerned in the Confederate officers the highborn qualities found in his aristocratic friends back home. Polk he likened to a feudal lord—"a grand seigneur," in his words—and the general's cavalry bodyguard comprised "young men of good position in New Orleans, most [of whom] spoke in the French language, and nearly all [of whom] had slaves in the field with them." Lest the Briton suppose himself déclassé amid this distinguished company, William Gale had thoughtfully loaned him his own slave Aaron, as well as a horse.[50]

Though General Polk had proclaimed Gen. William Rosecrans to be "pert," "wiley," and "an indifferent specimen of humanity" when this Yankee commander at the head of 70,000 infantry and cavalry troops moved out of Nashville on June 24, a scoffing Polk and his fellow Confederates were in deep trouble. Rosecrans's initial thrust was straight ahead toward the 44,000 Rebels strung across the southeastern corner of Middle Tennessee, the positions they had taken since withdrawing from Murfreesboro. Polk's corps, strongly entrenched, held the left at Shelbyville; Hardee's corps, less formidably, held the right at Wartrace. Cavalry units were stationed to the west and east of the infantry. The center, Bragg's headquarters, was farther south at Tullahoma and sat astride the railroad to Chattanooga, the Confederates' main supply line. Between the advancing Yankees and the situated Rebels was a range of high foothills cut by defiles through which three roads ran between Murfreesboro and Tullahoma.

Would the wiley Rosecrans attack the enemy head-on down these roads? Yes and no. Yes, that appeared to be his plan. No, it was merely a feint. While making a strong show toward Polk in Shelbyville, the bulk the Army of the Cumberland swept around Hardee east of Wartrace and fixed its sights behind him on Tullahoma. To Tullahoma, accordingly, both Polk and Hardee judiciously hurried. Or, more accurately, they slogged thence through the mire of rain-soaked roads. Once arrived, many of the infantrymen, thoroughly drenched and unfed for at least a day, were set to strengthening half-finished fortifications along muddy ditches. As W. S. Worsham would remember, "The boys began to get wrathy and hot, but the rain, which kept falling in continuous showers, kept us cool." At least the misery was egalitarian, with generals and privates alike in the ditches. "During one of the heaviest rains that fell," Worsham saw "General Cheatham on a stump, sitting as complacently as if in the sun, with one shoe off and one of his big toes sticking out through a hole in his sock."[51]

During the generals' Tullahoma meeting to decide their next move, General Polk, fully acquainted with these Tennessee regions, was among those urging a further withdrawal; Hardee demurred for a while. Lt. Mercer Otey remembered the Tullahoma discussions graphically: "Gen. Bragg was pacing up and down the piazza of his headquarters nervously twitching his beard," Otey wrote. "His indecision was finally determined by the advice given by Gen. Polk to the effect that expediency required our retiring to Chattanooga, as to remain where we were would place us in the position of a rat in a barrel with the bunghole closed." The bunghole, Otey explained, was "the Cowan railway tunnel in our rear, through which our subsistence must necessarily be transported. . . . No prudent general like Rosecrans would attack when he could flank us."[52] At length, Bragg acceded to withdrawal, nimbly extricating his army from looming envelopment by putting it in motion up and over the Cumberland Mountains and across the Tennessee River to the temporary safety awaiting in Chattanooga. Sympathetic as a chaplain should be, Quintard found General Bragg at tiny Cowan, south of Tullahoma, on Thursday, July 2, in conference with Polk. "My dear General," Quintard said to Bragg, "I am afraid you are thoroughly outdone." As though confessing to his priest, as indeed he was, Bragg admitted: "I am utterly broken down." Having given up Tennessee (and its burgeoning fields just coming to ripeness) to the Yankees, he whispered to Quintard: "This is a great disaster."

Quintard was in an irrepressible mood and would not hear of it. "General, don't be disheartened, our turn will come next." The chaplain's pastoral confidence had been fortified upon arising that day, July 2, when he had dutifully read three psalms appointed for Morning Prayer. Now leaving Bragg to his disconsolation, he approached Lt. Col. Harvey Walter, resting crumpled by a roadside fence and presenting to Quintard "the very picture of despair." "My dear Colonel, what is the matter with you?" asked Quintard jovially. "How can you ask such a question?" the colonel replied. "My dear Colonel," said Quintard, "I am afraid you've not read the Psalms for the day." When Walter asserted that indeed he had not, the chaplain proceeded to quote the first verse of Psalm Eleven: "In the Lord put I my trust; how say ye then to my soul, that she should flee as a bird unto the hill?"[53]

It may be that Colonel Walter was thereupon thoroughly emboldened by Quintard's ministrations. Polk's other infantrymen, however, were already fleeing as birds unto the hills. Their hasty march taking them over the mountains would lead them straight onto the forlorn grounds of University Place, the shuttered home of Polk's Sewanee school. Polk had been preceded up the mountain days earlier by Col. John Wilder, whose Yankee garrison had been humiliated the previous September by Polk at Munfordville, Kentucky. Now able to humiliate reciprocally, Wilder and his Indiana "Lightning Brigade" had galloped roughshod across the overgrown campus, setting fires to boarded-up homes and destroying the coal-mine railroad to Tracy City as they went. Their frolic added zest to his troopers' satisfactions at being able to run amok in the enemy's rear.[54]

During the afternoon of July 3, Polk, accompanied by Lieutenant Otey, arrived at this sylvan but ravaged place, its once bright promise brought to a standstill two years back. Unseen by the Confederates passing through that afternoon, but remarkably found a few days later by a Union chaplain exploring the abandoned grounds and buildings, were "reams of old letters and papers left over from the university's founding days." Amid the "rubbish lying about" were sermon manuscripts and letters addressed to Mercer Otey's father, James, the cofounder with Bishop Polk of the school.

"Desolation reigned," the affected chaplain said of the scene, "and silence that might be felt, but not described." The only living things he saw were "two cats [and] a hen with little chickens."[55]

In Polk's later correspondence no mention can be found of his layover atop the Tennessee plateau he could properly call his own, not a word of the despair that must have filled him. Lieutenant Otey, though, remembered well how he and his general beheld the vestiges of the once-landscaped campus, the marble cornerstone in the midst of weeds, the ashes of Polk's own house set afire in 1861 by arsonists while his wife and daughters were sleeping. Otey wrote about that July day decades later, when the postwar university was well on its way to being reborn. "Weary and dispirited," Mercer Otey related, "we climbed the mountains."

> When General Polk reached the plateau he called his body servant Altimore to fetch his cane chair from the headquarters wagon, and had it placed at a point that had been cleared of surrounding trees (called "Inspiration Point," I think), commanding a full view of the great valley stretched at our feet. He then sent for [Quartermaster George R.] Fairbanks . . . to inquire if he could supply us with any buttermilk. Here we rested for an hour or more . . . and together talked of the hopes and plans that he and my father had entertained for the building of the great university that now adorns the spot. No wonder the good general lingered and pondered on the scene before him.[56]

Along with most of his soldiers, Polk moved on toward Chattanooga later that day. (Not a few, however—mostly recent Middle Tennessee conscripts not much for soldiering in the first place and, by now, pretty much done for—trudged back down the way they had come, handing themselves in as deserters to any Yankees they met.) Rosecrans's people ascending the plateau were meanwhile so close behind the Confederates that after midnight Polk's rearguard cavalry was unsure whether the Yankee cannon fire they heard was "intended for shelling the woods or [for celebrating the] Fourth of July."[57] Then all through Independence Day on the mountain's western flank and summit, cavalry and mounted infantry units on both sides contended with one another.[58] Confederates descending the eastern flank toward Chattanooga, meanwhile, hoping to slow the Federals' pursuit by felling trees across the roads, called for axes. Polk's quartermaster could supply less than a dozen, rendering the soldiers' barriers less than insurmountable.[59]

With the Rebels departed, Col. Luther Bradley's 3rd Brigade took their place on the university campus for a few days thereafter in July and August. Upon the summit of "the grand Southern University that was to have been," a Yankee commissary officer found it to be "one of the best camping-grounds I know of." It was "delightful and cool" with "the clearest and finest water I ever drank"; he wanted "to spend the whole summer there." The Indiana captain could have been taking the words right out of the mouth of Bishop Polk. Back in the 1850s he had extolled the same summertime amenities when promoting the school to parents sweltering in the Deep South.[60]

Polk by this mid-July was in Chattanooga and thus spared from knowing about the fate of the university cornerstone that he had solemnly blessed twenty-six months before. Some of Bradley's soldiers, seeking gold coins rumored to have been sealed in the cornerstone, used mauls or gunpowder to break open the marble box. The coins, if any, were pocketed and the stone chips saved as souvenirs. Colonel Bradley was said to have "taken steps to ferret out the perpetrators of this sacrilege, and will bring them to punishment." Whether he was successful is not known, but a marble fragment, carved to resemble a tiny Bible, was returned to the university's chapel in the 1890s, courtesy of a youthful marauder once in Rosecrans's army.[61]

22

"I Am Somewhat Afraid of Davis" (1863)

To his family, General Leonidas Polk was soon putting a hearty face on Bragg's "great disaster," the army's hasty retreat from Middle Tennessee the previous autumn, now a summertime basket brimming with ripening foods left to the Yankees. Polk told some in his family that it was a judicious move and all for the best.[1] Not just prudent, but "well and wisely done," he burbled to daughter Kate Gale: "Our position has been strengthened, . . . and we have only lost control of a portion of territory which may be regained as it was before." Though Fanny and two other daughters had come over from Asheville and were at Polk's side in Chattanooga ("enjoying their visit to the camp"), Polk, as summer 1863 waned, was not feeling his earlier rosiness. For one thing, the civilian news from Mississippi and Louisiana was that thousands of cotton bales were being burned lest they fall into the hands of the enemy—a financial loss for Polk that amounted to "the finishing blow to what remained of his fortune."[2] Added to this news was the downward course of both the Confederacy and Jefferson Davis's presidency; the general was so alarmed that sweet submission was not an option. "Nothing is clearer than that we are approaching a crisis in the history of our affairs," he wrote that month to Kenneth Rayner, the brother-in-law in Raleigh to whom he regularly confided military opinions and political anxieties. Marking his letter "PERSONAL AND CONFIDENTIAL," he wrote: "That we have lost ground in the last few weeks is patent to all," meaning in Middle Tennessee, Gettysburg, and Vicksburg. Before U. S. Grant's July 4th victory, Vicksburg had been the Confederacy's control point on the Mississippi River, an irreplaceable funnel for supplies to its armies west of the river. In addition, almost 30,000 Confederates had been captured there by Grant, Polk's old adversary from Belmont whom Polk had mocked, predicting he would be crushed in Mississippi "root and branch" by Joseph Johnston. As for Robert E. Lee's disastrous foray into Pennsylvania, that, he told Rayner, was "very ill-advised."

Polk was at least sanguine about his own Army of Tennessee. "While we may have occasional desertions, we have no fear. . . . [The army] may be relied on. But it is not strong enough." Dismaying to Polk was the *public's* lack of resolve. Throughout the Confederacy he perceived a tendency by the people "to let down their support of the war effort." There was despondency in Mississippi, clandestine "reconstruction talk" in Alabama, and in Polk's hometown the Raleigh *Standard* was editorially advocating "yielding and returning to the old Union." Polk exclaimed to Rayner, incredulous and underlining the sentence, "all of this . . . calls for immediate attention on the part of those who do not mean to allow our efforts to rid ourselves of Yankee rule to fail." The solution he had in mind was an alliance with the French emperor Louis Napoleon.[3] His frustration with the South's war effort had not moderated the next day when he not only mailed to Bishop Stephen Elliott a copy of his Rayner letter but also, in a separate letter, wrote a diatribe against Jefferson Davis.[4] Fully revealing Polk's disquiet at the time (and his insubordinate streak) are the criticisms in this letter that Polk levels against the commander in chief. "It is the law of God's providence to aid those who aid themselves," Polk writes, taking a theological stance Elliott was sure to share. "This is as true in efforts to succeed in things temporal as things spiritual." The trouble was that the temporal aid being provided by the bureaucrats in Richmond was insufficient to win the war. Polk was at the end of his patience with the lot of them, beginning with the president, whom just days before he had extolled personally in a flattering, almost fawning, letter.

Probably underlying Polk's anger were real or imagined slights by the harried Confederate president. Lately, Davis had not responded when Polk in July sent him his proposed overhaul of the Confederacy's western armies. All generals (privates, too) sometimes think they may know better than anyone ranking them. Polk always did. He was so sure of his reasoning that he said the recent so-called successes of William Rosecrans in Middle Tennessee and of U. S. Grant at Vicksburg would shortly be shown to be fleeting, never amounting to much. Meanwhile, Polk had reorganization ideas of his own to send to the Confederate president some three weeks after the Army of Tennessee had relocated to Chattanooga. "My mind . . . finds not much relief in prosecuting our campaign in the west on the present plan," he began. He advised these things: first, Gen. Joseph Johnston's Army of Mississippi and Eastern Louisiana would be brought to Chattanooga and combined with Bragg's Army of Tennessee and with Simon Buckner's Army of East Tennessee, then situated in Knoxville. Polk supposed this fattened legion might "foot up 70,000 to 80,000 men"; sweeping back into Tennessee under Johnston's leadership, it would easily overwhelm Rosecrans, reclaim the whole occupied state for the Confederacy, then snatch back from Federal control the Mississippi River from Columbus, Kentucky, to Memphis. And with that accomplished, perhaps the thousands of Confederates paroled after the fall of Vicksburg (set free on their pledge not to resume fighting until exchanged) could then be re-enrolled and rearmed and folded into the whole of this western juggernaut.[5] Even without the Vicksburg veterans, Polk was sure the gloating days of Grant would be over and "the prestige of his Vicksburg conquest [erased]."[6]

Polk sent virtually the same letter to his friend William Hardee (who, to get away from Bragg, had just had himself placed under the command of Joseph Johnston in Mississippi), adding opinions he had tactfully withheld from Davis. The western army, Polk said, "is the *important* army of the Confederacy, and has a higher mission [than Lee's Army of Northern Virginia]." His peroration was heartfelt: "In short, [my plan would] place us where we have ever desired, and been attempting to be, since this war began."[7] What he heard back from Hardee was not encouraging. General Johnston, despite his vaunted reputation, was not the skilled manager Hardee had hoped for. He was deficient, Hardee told Polk, "in all those particulars in which you feared he was," and he had a "very inefficient staff to match." Plus, the strength of his Mississipians had been exaggerated, Hardee said.[8] Polk did not let this news discourage him. Hearing nothing back from Davis, he soon pressed him again to consider his ideas. He granted that Hardee's disillusionment in Johnston's manpower "puts a different face upon the matter," but "we all feel here we are in the midst of a crisis." He now had an amended plan for Davis that would still help effect "our deliverance." In addition to reorganizing the western army, greater energy should be expended by the Richmond government in conscripting every civilian man under forty-five; it might be best, indeed, "to do away with all exemptions from conscripted service." And the drive to re-enlist and re-equip that idle hoard of paroled prisoners from Vicksburg needed pushing. "The military necessities of our condition require that our efforts should be directed to gather such a force for these purposes. To my mind, such a movement is more full of promise than any other now open to us." It was beginning to sound like a lecture.

Then, with an intriguing twist that showed how he could rise above personal pique, Polk strongly recommended that Gideon Pillow, that nemesis of old, be given the job of running a national conscription department. (Pillow was then at Bragg's behest successfully enlisting volunteers, drafting other civilians, and chasing down disabled soldiers and stragglers and deserters in Alabama and Tennessee.) "Of my opinions of Pillow as a man and a soldier you are fully informed," Polk reminded Davis. "They have not changed in the slightest degree, nor are they likely to change. . . . Yet he has a certain description of talent in high development, and that talent qualifies him preeminently for filling the [conscription] department . . . beyond any man I know in or out of the army. . . . I think his services to the cause would be invaluable." Polk recommended, too, that Pillow be promoted from brigadier to major general, and he warmly wound up the letter by saying: "I write . . . as you have several times asked me [to do], freely, and remain very truly your friend."[9]

In this same letter Polk had assured Davis that "I think, my friend, you may have all the grace and strength and wisdom required to guide us safely through the difficulties which surround you." This effusion was presumably sincere (more or less) when he wrote it, yet in the next six days Polk's high opinion of Davis plummeted again. In his rant to Stephen Elliott on August 15, Polk no longer proclaimed Davis as having "grace and strength and wisdom." (He still had not answered Polk's second letter, though he had scarcely had time to do so.)[10] "The truth is, I am somewhat afraid of Davis. I do not find myself willing to trust his judgment." Further: "I am afraid also of his forecast. He certainly has shown himself deficient in both qualities, and I do not feel like risking everything on the legacy or procedures of any man who has so many temptations to pull the trial of his individual strengths to the extreme points." Polk's psychological profile of the president had other disturbing aspects. "Davis is proud, self-reliant and, I fear, stubborn. . . . He is not quick to perceive coming events, and he is very apt to invest others—even the whole people—with [the belief] that things are possible which history has shown are not possible, nor even probable." Little wonder an exasperated Polk did "not think such a mind should be allowed the . . . untrammeled and final action of leading the Confederacy."

By Polk's lights, Davis was not alone in being out of his depth in Richmond. Others "at the helm" (unnamed by Polk to Elliott) distressed him. "I think what [these] people have been doing for two years, they will go on to do to the end of the chapter, and this makes me afraid." It did not make him a quitter, though. "We have had, abundantly, the means to defy the Yankees and their posterities forever, had they been judiciously used." True, it was getting late, but not too late. Worthier secessionists such as he and Elliott, Polk reminded his friend, "are deeply interested in the issue" and, by being denied "a hand in shaping measures," are adversely affected. All well and good that Davis proclaimed fasts, humiliation, and prayer, but it would be better "were [he] to lean a little less on his own understanding and to believe that there were some minds in the land from which he might obtain counsel worth having." Polk did not need to spell it out that one such preeminent mind was his own.[11]

As far as is known, Jefferson Davis never got around to replying to, or heeding, any of Polk's insistent advice, and the Army of Tennessee idled away the summer. No reorganization of the western armies. No appointment of Gideon Pillow (a man with few supporters in Richmond) to the conscription post Polk recommended.[12] As for Emperor Napoleon III, he too disappointed the political instincts of the general in never deigning to recognize the Confederacy's political existence. Polk's discouragements were lightened, at least, by the company he had that summer: Fanny, two of their daughters, and the ailing son Hamilton all came visiting from Asheville. He and a "very pretty daughter" were spotted on July 19 in Chattanooga's St. Paul's Episcopal Church by Kate Cumming, an admiring army nurse singing in the choir. Charles Quintard, she noted also, preached the "very fine sermon." As with the Eleventh Psalm, the preacher understood his Old Testament text to be applicable to the Confederacy: "We are journeying into the land which the Lord hath said I will give it you."[13]

While awaiting word from the president that never came, Polk and several other discontented high-ranking officers sent to the War Department a letter urging Adjutant and Inspector General Samuel Cooper to "earnestly implore" Jefferson Davis to "take prompt measures to recruit our wasted armies by fresh levies from home." The officers reckoned at least a quarter-million soldiers might thus be found and put into the ranks. The letter, signed even by Braxton Bragg, argued among other things that the Confederacy's liberal exemption system, which excused from military service certain civilian men "thought necessary for [society's] comfort and convenience," was defeating the South as assuredly as was the enemy. Granting such workers might well be essential in peacetime, they were needed elsewhere, the letter said, during "the mighty upheaval of a great revolution." To the "lasting reproach upon their manhood, hearty vigorous young men, rather than take the field, eagerly seek fancy duty which could be performed by women or disabled soldiers." There was a second concern incensing the letter's manly signatories: "The friends of timid and effeminate young men are constantly besieging the War Department, through Congressional and other agents, to get soldiers . . . transferred to safe places."[14] General Cooper's reply, more sympathetic than remedial, arrived within a fortnight. The officers' complaints had been passed along to Jefferson Davis, but to no effect.[15] In the meantime, some of these same discontented officers organized themselves into the Comrades of the Southern Cross (CSC), a secret Christian brotherhood. The CSC was the idea of the remarkably capable Patrick Cleburne, a sometime poet and hymnist from Ireland who in Confederate service had soared from private to major general in just two years. He was joined in establishing the society (intended, it was said, for intelligent and righteous soldiers and officers) by Chaplain Quintard, Polk's emissary to the founding meeting. The Comrades pledged themselves to helping indigent Southern victims of the war while fostering reenlistments in the army. Quintard had a hand in composing the group's constitution, but his initial optimism at length gave way. Candidly, Quintard conceded that after the "bottom dropped out, . . . the Order of the Southern Cross—like the Southern Confederacy—went to pieces."[16]

While Rosecrans consolidated his Middle Tennessee gains on the far side of the East Tennessee mountains, the Confederates summering in Chattanooga were relatively secure and relaxed.[17] Pettiness also managed from time to time to intrude on their collegiality. Once in a discussion among Bragg and his generals as to what Rosecrans could be expected to do next, St. John Liddell was called upon. Liddell speculated that the Yankee commander might well act rashly: he "must have lost all caution after having flanked us so easily out of Middle Tennessee." Liddell would later say he intended no criticism of Bragg's recent generalship in Tennessee, but Polk's ears picked up the pinch to their commanding officer. "General Polk, with a perceptible smile at my thoughtless hit at Bragg's policy, bowed assent," Liddell noticed.[18]

Lest they now be surprised by the enemy meandering in their rear, Polk had put his Signal Corps friend Mercer Otey in charge of four mountaintop observation posts. (One was on Lookout Mountain, where six years before Bishops Otey and Polk and their supporters had gathered on the Fourth of July to consolidate their visionary plans for a "liberating University of the South free of Abolitionist cant.") Facing northwest where the Yankees were massed, Mercer Otey's lookout stations spanned some thirty air miles, the signalmen being in contact with one another by telescopes and flags, and, at night, by coal-oil torches. On August 21, Mercer's men dutifully flagged word that Yankees were to be seen unlimbering artillery across the Tennessee River on the heights of Springer's Ridge. As it happened, it was once again those bedeviling Hoosiers under Col. John T. Wilder, his "Lightning Brigade of mounted infantry."

General Bragg was convalescing at the time "from a general break-down" at a spa hospital in Cherokee Springs, Georgia ("in very bad health," according to the nurse Kate Cumming), and his headquarters staff back in Chattanooga dismissed Otey's artillery sightings as fanciful.[19] That Friday, being a Day of Humiliation, Fasting, and Prayer for the nation's Confeder-ates, found many attending church services when the Indiana shells began falling explosively onto Chattanooga's hushed streets, proving Lieutenant Otey correct. The pastor of Henry Watterson's church was not to be de-terred from the worship service already under way, but the anxious journal-ist reckoned the minister intoned "the longest prayer I ever heard."[20]

Within days of the Yankees' shelling Chattanooga, Gen. Simon Buckner had been forced to give up Knoxville. With Bragg unable to reinforce his little Army of East Tennessee, Buckner avoided sure defeat at the hands of Maj. Gen. Ambrose Burnside by moving south into Georgia. He arrived about the time fellow commanders had concluded that their campgrounds beneath Yankee artillery were no place to find themselves and that the whole Tennessee army ought to seek shelter in northern Georgia. Or, as Mercer Otey would summarize: "There was nothing left for us but to ske-daddle, and skedaddle we did," leaving Tennessee soon in Federal hands.[21]

Skedaddling, yes, and all in dignified good time. General Polk seems to have been more blasé than some, describing Colonel Wilder's barrage as a feint, not a crisis. "A few shots exchanged in the evening of the day you got off amounted to nothing," he reassured Fanny. Why, as custodian of the troops quartered around Chattanooga, he had slumbered unperturbed that night in the new nightshirt Fanny had left him.[22] Two nights later, from his tent a mile outside Chattanooga, he again wrote again offhandedly of another light shelling by the Yankees: "One [citizen] had his arm broken . . . and 3 privates were killed, and one officer wounded in the trenches."[23] He went on to spell out for Fanny his predictions of what Rosecrans and the Federals were likely to do next. They would, he believed, seek a place to cross the snaking Tennessee River somewhere upstream from Chatta-nooga, where the land northeast of the town was relatively level and acces-sible. Rosecrans "has not crossed at Bridgeport [where Confederates had destroyed a railroad bridge and were keeping watch], and I think will not, nor any place below [i.e., downstream] Chattanooga. He will wish to cross at a place where, when he gets over, he will find no mountain obstructing him."[24]

So much for Polk's boast of knowing his man. The wiley Rosecrans—

mountainous terrain notwithstanding—did in fact cross the Tennessee River at various places downstream from Chattanooga in late August and early September: at ferries and shallows and at Bridgeport, twenty-eight miles west, where the Yankees replaced the partially collapsed railroad trestle with a bridge of planked-over pontoons. (To obscure their enterprise, other workers had slyly thrown short lengths of boards into the river *upstream* from Chattanooga; to the Rebels, the boards floating past suggested that enemy pontoon bridges were being assembled north of the town, not south.) Once over the river by these various routes, the Federal army was soon on Bragg's flank and rear, but sightings of the movements were at first regarded at Confederate headquarters (as with Mercer Otey's semaphore alarms) as "incredible."[25] To disbelieve was reasonable. The corrugated countryside of northern Georgia, largely uninhabited at the time, was not made for casual marching or for sustaining thousands of soldiers living off the land. Forage and water were hard to find, with some lucky Yankees discovering drinking water in an abandoned coal mine.[26]

The region into which Rosecrans had insinuated his army, prowling now unseen in the Confederates' rear and threatening their supply lines from the south, comprised four gnarled mountain ridges. Roughly parallel like three fingers and thumb of a right hand palm, they point southwestward away from Chattanooga and the Tennessee River. The daunting landscape did shield the Yankees from the Rebels' eyes, an advantage Bragg had glumly conceded even before Rosecrans crossed the river. "A mountain is like the wall of a house full of rat-holes," he complained to corps commander Daniel Harvey Hill. "The rat lies hidden at his hole, ready to pop out when no one is watching. Who can tell what lies behind that wall?"[27] The Federals, for their part, were not all that pleased with their situation either. The historian Peter Cozzens summed it up: "It was hard to say which would prove the greater obstacle to [their] taking Chattanooga—the Army of Tennessee or the terrain."[28]

With the Yankees across the river soon shelling the valley town again, by the first week of September the whole of the Confederate garrison had begun slipping southward out of Chattanooga for Georgia. (On Monday night, September 7, Mercer Otey's torch wig-waggers, their coal oil depleted, "got out of lights and quite a trouble was the result," Lt. William Richmond reported.)[29] General Polk and his staff left with Bragg the morning of September 8. Henry Watterson, the editor of the Chattanooga *Rebel* who was Polk's friend and Bragg's affliction, had intended to travel with the group until learning Bragg was included, and so he bowed out. The last of the Confederates departed on the morning of September 9, whereupon

Maj. Gen. Thomas Leonidas Crittenden's Federal troops took possession of the town before the sun went down.[30]

With both armies soon to be dispersed throughout Georgia's northeast woods and mountain recesses (near the outset, Rosecrans's three corps were spread across forty miles), Lieutenant Richmond summed up the situation in his journal: "We are in utter darkness so far as the enemy's whereabouts in force . . . and his movements are concerned."[31] The enemy was little better off, supposing that the Army of Tennessee might be in full flight for the safety of Atlanta or Rome. This rumor flourished, helped by Bragg's reputation for retreating and supported by bogus Rebel "deserters" infiltrating Yankee encampments.[32] The Federals' unknown whereabouts did not appear to bother General Polk. The day after giving up Tennessee but camped "not far from Chattanooga," he wrote Fanny to remark on the good spirits in which he found himself, his soldiers, and even his normally sour commanding general. Polk's optimism was credible.[33]

Among other things, three generals highly regarded on other battlefields had lately joined the Army of Tennessee. One was Lt. Gen. Daniel Harvey Hill, who had been reassigned from Lee's Army of Northern Virginia. Another was Maj. Gen. Thomas Hindman, recently commanding Confederates in Arkansas; he had been given a division in Polk's corps. Hindman lost no time wearing out his welcome to some already in Georgia. Shortly after his arrival, on the testimony of one of his own officers, he had proved "himself to be a regular low-life rowdy by what he done. . . . Our division was on the march until about two o'clock in the night," the officer recounted. "When we halted, General Hindman found Polk's staff camped on the spot where he had picked, and he went up and roused them, calling them a set of 'unprincipled curs.' To say the least, he was challenged to a duel which he did not accept."[34] Lastly, Lt. Gen. James Longstreet had also been detached from Lee's army and was hastening to Georgia by the South's rickety railroads. Satisfied by these developments, Polk's only complaint was personal: "My old enemy"—the sciatic nerve on his right side—was acting up. That said, he cheerfully reminded his wife that "we look for our gallant women for support to the last. I cannot but feel that all will be well yet."[35]

Polk's upbeat letter, written on a Thursday, was scarcely on its way to Asheville when his prediction on the course of the war took a turn for the worse. The Confederates had discovered that 4,000 or 5,000 Yankee troops belonging to Maj. Gen. George Thomas's XIV Corps had wandered into a mountainous bowl called McLemore's Cove; furthermore, they were separated from the main body of Thomas's corps. Bragg reckoned luck was with him: Yankee rats were in an escape-proof trap. Taking personal command, Bragg chose Hill and Hindman to do the trapping. Hindman was especially esteemed by Bragg for his leadership in the fighting at Shiloh in 1862. Too bad for high hopes, for neither Hindman nor Hill was able to perform as Bragg had ordered and hoped. The upshot was that Thomas's soldiers escaped from the cove virtually unharmed, hieing off to the safety of Lookout Mountain.[36] In William Gale's telling, probably reflecting how Polk characterized the matter in his hearing, "both armies lay on their arms all day, Thomas afraid to move and Hindman afraid to attack, until night when the Yankees slipt off and left us in the lurch."[37] Or, to use William Richmond's even more unsympathetic analysis of the event, "the bird had flown and the farce was complete."[38] The moderately silver lining for Bragg, as Capt. William Polk observed after the war, was that the "blow [that] had been aimed at Thomas . . . sent him up the mountain and still further away from his companion corps."[39]

Bragg at the time was "in high resentment at his headquarters at the failure of his anticipated coup," Gale reported to his wife. Having reserved his usual right to hold himself blameless should things go wrong in the cove, he would subsequently scapegoat Hill and Hindman roundly.[40] The two newcomers, consequently, were not long in becoming members of the anti-Bragg clique. General Polk, in contrast, had been camped at Dr. Peter Anderson's farm ten or so miles from the miscarried trap and emerged blameless. His grumbling that week centered again on his "rheumatism," but he would be next in line for a blast of Bragg's anger.

While General Thomas and the men of his XIV Corps were repairing rapidly to the top of Lookout Mountain, Maj. Gen. Thomas Crittenden and 16,000 men of his XXI Corps were approaching the Confederates from Chattanooga.[41] Supposing the Army of Tennessee 35,000 strong was on the run to the south, General Crittenden's columns were themselves meandering southward, not wishing to encounter the tail end of the retreating Rebels without first reconnecting with the missing XIV Corps. The Yankees were wrong on two counts: The Confederates were not on the run; and Thomas's corps was not, as was thought, awaiting Crittenden on the western bank of Chickamauga Creek somewhere near Lee and Gordon's Mills. The dangerous separations of General Rosecrans's army continued.[42]

Maj. Gen. Alexander McCook's XX Corps, meanwhile, was camped below LaFayette near Alpine, his position somewhat obscured from prying Southern eyes by the surrounding mountains. Though he too posed a potential threat to Bragg, Crittenden's approaching columns were isolated and "out in the plain," as Capt. William Polk put it, presenting a tempting target for the Confederates. Hoping to redeem the escape of General

Thomas from the cove, Bragg now designed to fall upon Crittenden and cut off any attempt by him to return to Chattanooga. While pondering how best to go about this, Bragg had added Polk's corps to his concentration of troops in LaFayette. On the next day, Saturday, September 12, however, he sent it back the way it had come. Polk's assignment was to meet Crittenden head-on.

Unbeknownst to the plotting Confederate commanders, the vanguard of Crittenden's columns had reached Lee and Gordon's Mills on Friday afternoon, discovering that Thomas and his XIV Corps were not there. Rather, as night fell, Confederate "campfires could be distinctly seen on the other side of the creek." Writing in his diary, 2nd Lt. James Chapin of Indiana noted that "their light told that the foe was present in considerable force."[43]

Whatever Rebel fragments were close to Lee and Gordon's Mills were greatly augmented throughout Saturday as General Polk's corps took position at Rock Spring Church, a crossroads about five miles south of the mills. Because Bragg that weekend had vacillated as to which Federal force he thought posed the greatest threat to LaFayette, Polk's corps had been obliged to retrace the route they had taken on Friday, trudging yet again through nine miles of gagging dust. The ten-minute shower Saturday evening did little more than muddy the air.[44] Sometime during that retrograde march, Polk was observed by a New Orleans artillery officer, a churchgoer acquainted both with the clergyman-general and the works of Shakespeare. "The change in his appearance from a clean-shaved white-robed bishop to a soldier 'bearded like the pard,' and wearing a black slouch hat and a faded gray uniform, is very striking," he noted in his diary.[45]

Once arrived at Rock Spring Church, Polk began arranging his troops across the three roads down which Crittenden's corps was said to be advancing.[46] The enemy, Polk was told by his cavalry, was marching toward Pea Vine Church, two miles due north of Rock Spring Church and well east of Chickamauga Creek.[47] As battlefield deployments could be thankless chores for commanders who were often second-guessed by their subordinates, sometimes openly, Polk's directions to one of his generals—the bushy-bearded, ferocious-looking Maj. Gen. William H. T. Walker—even turned confrontational. Walker, according to Brig. Gen. St. John Liddell, was "well-known to be a crackbrained fire-eater, always captious or caviling about something." On this occasion, proving Liddell correct, he was raising "pertinacious quibbles about the battle dispositions made by 'Old Polk,'" Walker's behind-the-back dismissal of a man about ten years his senior. (Walker had taught tactics at West Point, and as Bragg's classmate at West Point, he may well have shared some of Bragg's disesteem for the bishop's generalship.) Polk was "good-naturedly perplexed," says Liddell, and endured Walker's rants and oaths, "trying to explain and alter [his troop alignments] to suit Walker." At length, having "pretty much exhausted rhetoric and expletives," Walker went "grumblingly away," leaving General Polk "completely badgered."[48]

Supposing that the approaching Federals held a numerical advantage (for so he had been erroneously informed by his cavalry reconnaissance), Polk late in the evening alerted Bragg rather picturesquely that "the enemy is moving with steady step upon my position—it is a strong one—and will no doubt attack early in the morning." Wishing he were stronger himself, Polk requested that General Buckner's corps be immediately sent to Rock Spring "to make failure impossible."[49] The courier William Richmond, urged by Polk to make haste, delivered the request to Bragg "eight and a half miles off, in 35 minutes." Bragg was still unsure of McCook's hostile intentions (if any) below LaFayette but reluctantly released Buckner's corps to Polk, exhorting Polk in a midnight dispatch not to wait for Crittenden to reach Rock Spring but instead to initiate the fight. "Finish the job entrusted to you," he scolded. "Action, prompt and decided, is all that can save us."[50]

Now in the late hours of that Saturday night, while his entrenched soldiers slept on their arms, their seminary-trained general, in the parlor of Susan Park's home, composed an order that would serve admirably as an inspiriting homily for the dawning Lord's Day. His troops upon arising should realize that "in the battle now before us," profound issues hung upon the result.

> If we are successful the star of the Confederacy rises in the ascendant. The sprits of our friends everywhere will be cheered and our homes made happy. The thorough defeat of the enemy now would blast the prospects of our cruel invaders. The lieutenant-general knows that the troops he has now the honor to command . . . will not fail to remember that this is the enemy by whom their property has been destroyed, their hearthstones desolated, their women insulted and outraged, their altars profaned, and they will sternly avenge their wrongs.[51]

Polk's sermonic flourishes were for naught, his nighttime rhetoric cooling rapidly in the silence and dew of daybreak. The steady step of General Crittenden's columns hours earlier had swung wide to the northwest, halting at Lee and Gordon's Mills on the far side of Chickamauga Creek. The corps was thus five miles short of Polk's entrenchments, and when at first light Confederate cavalry rode out from the Rock Spring crossroads east of the creek, there was no one there.[52] Lt. Gen. Daniel Hill summarized the nonevent: General Crittenden "with delightful unconsciousness" had not known "that he was in the presence of superior strength, and had he kept coming south, he would have collided fatefully with Polk's bristling lines."[53] And so, no Southern star was to rise in the ascendant, no cruel invaders were to be sternly avenged.

General Bragg and his staff galloped upon this empty stage at midmorning. "Expressing great disappointment, [Bragg] had not a word of censure to offer General Polk," according to Captain Polk, who was present.[54] Disappointment notwithstanding, Bragg curiously chose not to order Polk with his 26,000 rested troops to advance upon the enemy now camped on the far side of Chickamauga Creek; instead, at day's end, he returned to LaFayette. Polk's corps followed Monday. Later, as Captain Polk would write, "reports began to circulate through the army that [Bragg had indeed] blamed General Polk for the failed attack." Bragg's official report intimates the same, making no mention of Crittenden's unforeseen veering off to the western bank.[55]

Some historians side with Bragg.[56] But while Captain Polk's bias is understandable, he points out plausibly that even as General Polk, on Bragg's orders, was marching to LaFayette on September 11 and then back to Rock Spring Church on September 12, Crittenden had twenty-four hours to cross Chickamauga Creek undetected. (Bragg's disingenuous official version has it that Polk was dispatched to Rock Spring *immediately* [emphasis added] after the September 10 debacle in McLemore's Cove"; Polk was, in fact, recalled to LaFayette on September 11 and sent back to Rock Spring the next day.) Moreover, Captain Polk questions Bragg's unwillingness to launch an attack Sunday morning that could have crushed Crittenden's XXI Corps.[57] In short, William Polk says evenly, both Confederate leaders had been outwitted, as no such force had been in Polk's front the night before, as had been reported to him, and as he reported to General Bragg.[58] No particular admirer of Bragg, St. John Liddell may have at least sympathized with the commanding general's being twice disappointed that week, first by Hindman and then by Polk. Since Bragg's generals typically viewed their leader with disdain, Liddell suspected that in carrying out Bragg's orders "zealous cooperation on their part was wanting." Liddell had even imagined after the Battle of Murfreesboro that "if [Bragg] had caused one or two of us to be shot, I firmly believe the balance would have done better."[59]

Bragg in Georgia had none of his officers shot to improve the remainders' performance, but to soothe his spirit a little he did arrest a war correspondent whose criticisms of his generalship (like those by Henry

Watterson) had become a constant irritant. The journalist was John Henry Linebaugh, formerly an Episcopal priest. Again like Watterson, he was a confiding friend of General Polk, having served under Bishop Polk in Louisiana in the 1850s. Lately, he had been a frequent visitor at Polk's wartime headquarters in Shelbyville, Tennessee, and probably in Georgia too.[60] Bragg's charges of treason lodged that September against Linebaugh (his detailed dispatches to the *Memphis Daily Appeal* regarding the Army of Tennessee's recent movements had been deemed too precise and his estimates of Bragg's generalship too derogatory) were subsequently dropped.[61]

Given his mercurial nature, Bragg liked having it both ways with the wartime journalists around his camps. On at least two occasions earlier that summer, with the connivance of the Chattanooga *Rebel*'s editor Henry Watterson and publisher Franc M. Paul, Bragg's provost-marshal, Col. Alexander McKinstry, had planted false stories in the newspaper widely read by soldiers on both sides. The misinformation purported that Maj. Gen. John C. Breckinridge's division had been "sent back to Middle Tennessee to reinforce Bragg against Rosecrans." (Breckinridge was on loan to Joseph E. Johnston in Mississippi at the time Vicksburg fell. He did in fact return to Bragg's command in Georgia on September 2, just in time for Chickamauga.)[62] Subsequently, after Henry Watterson had become editorially impertinent, Bragg banned the sale of the *Rebel* to his soldiers. Further, Bragg demanded that Paul fire his star reporter. Since army readers were the *Rebel*'s mainstay, Paul acceded to Bragg's high-handedness.[63]

Denied an encounter with Thomas Crittenden's XXI Corps at Rock Spring Church, General Polk and the Army of Tennessee spent the next few days clustered around Bragg's headquarters in LaFayette waiting for Bragg to plot his next move. General Rosecrans usefully spent the time pulling his three scattered corps closer to one another along the western bank of Chickamauga Creek. Bragg's spirits had nonetheless been bolstered, knowing that Lt. Gen. James Longstreet and his I Corps veterans were soon to arrive in Georgia. Famed for their successes in the Army of Northern Virginia, the reinforcements had departed on a train journey that made use of sixteen different railroads and every kind of rolling stock available as they zigzagged around Yankee-held territories. Longstreet's arrival was expected on September 18, and, preparatory to taking on Rosecrans across Chickamauga Creek, Bragg on September 17 sent Polk's corps yet again back to Rock Spring Church. (Since the previous weekend, the nine-mile dust track between the two points had now been traversed by Polk's soldiers five times.) General Polk took lodgings once more with the accommodating Susan Park.

As Rosecrans expected an attack any day, he gave priority to protecting two open roads to Chattanooga—his escape routes should they be needed. The roads figured prominently in Bragg's preparations as well; he planned to cross the creek at Lee and Gordon's Mills and hit Rosecrans on his Chattanooga side—that is, on his left flank—and thereby cut off his escape access to the city. Assuming that plan worked, he would then drive the Federals southward toward McLemore's Cove, the trap yet to be sprung and set for a second attempt. Polk had discussed with Bragg a similar strategy. While a strong demonstration was made at Lee and Gordon's Mills, he proposed that "under cover of this feint, . . . the remainder of the army should march rapidly by the right flank, and at Reed's Bridge move to occupy Rossville on the west bank almost 10 miles north of Lee and Gordon's Mill." Bragg reportedly agreed with Polk in principle; it too was a tactic involving a sequential wheeling movement of the kind that Bragg liked, but he stuck to his preference to concentrate on the crossing at the mill rather than focus on Rossville farther north.[64] Bragg had lately reorganized the Army of Tennessee into five corps under Generals Polk, Walker, Buckner, Hill, and Longstreet but decided to move without waiting for Longstreet. The Confederates would cross Chickamauga Creek at several points well south of Rossville: at Alexander's Bridge, Lambert's Ford, and Reeds Bridge, for example. Bragg's assumption was that Rosecrans's left rested near the mill and would be vulnerable to turning. At the time, it was true enough.

The crossings would begin at six o'clock on Friday morning, September 18. Columns were assigned specifically to either the major-road bridges or secondary-road fords spanning the creek; they were to head for the western bank of the Chickamauga more or less simultaneously with "the utmost promptness, vigor, and persistence."[65] Once over, the columns farthest to the north (Brig. Gen. Bushrod Johnson crossing at Reed's Bridge; Maj. Gen. William H. T. Walker at Alexander's Bridge) were to wrap around the Yankees' left flank like a noose. Assisted by comrades meanwhile attacking the Federals' center and far right, the encirclement would then tighten southward, tidily corralling the hapless Yankees into the cove.

General Polk left Susan Park's at 6:30 A.M., setting up new headquarters closer to Lee and Gordon's Mills in the home of Dr. Peter Anderson. Not far into the day, the Confederates' idealized plan began to unravel, not surprisingly, from stiff Yankee resistance on both sides of the creek. Generals Johnson and Walker (the latter's troops stymied at Alexander's Bridge by John Wilder's brigade firing seven-shot repeating rifles) did not get over the creek until late afternoon. By then, Maj. Gen. John Bell Hood, with the first of Longstreet's Virginia divisions, had come running onto the field.

Ranking Bushrod Johnson, Hood assumed command, and the combined troops, latecomers included, were among the first Confederates in force to reach the Chickamauga's western bank. The balance of Bragg's men crossed throughout the night.

The dust raised by the Confederates' movements throughout Friday had been clearly visible to signal stations on Lookout Mountain. Thereby roughly informed of the Rebels' whereabouts, Rosecrans that night parried their various creek crossings that now overlapped his left flank; he shifted Maj. Gen. George Thomas's corps two miles through the woods to the north, extending and heavily strengthening his left flank near Reed's Bridge. (It was the second shift to the left the Federals had made.)[66] The result was that by morning of September 19, both armies were ranged west of the Chickamauga along parallel lines some five miles in length and about a mile apart. The LaFayette/Chattanooga road tilting to the northwest ran between the opposing soldiers through a mix of woods, thickets and cleared fields, the ground littered by leaves and grass dried by that autumn's drought. It was deadly fuel soon set ablaze by the pending battle and the soldiers cooking fires.[67]

As Rosecrans had hoped, General Thomas's extension to the left had gone largely unnoticed in the dark by the Confederates; whereas at sundown Friday only rabbits and blue jays were in their front, at sunrise Saturday they beheld in the distance the men of John M. Brannan's and Absalon Baird's divisions. The Federals' left wing was now far stronger than Bragg had anticipated; as for Thomas, at the head of one of the largest infantry brigades in the Union Army, he supposed it easily equal to whatever came its way.[68] Brannan and Baird were dispatched to bear down on Nathan Bedford Forrest's dismounted infantry at Reed's Bridge, driving these particular Rebels back into the creek they had recently crossed. The Battle of Chickamauga was now fully in play, and General Thomas, thoroughly pleased, heartily informed Maj. Gen. John M. Palmer: "We can, I think, use them up."[69] Forrest sent to Polk for support and dug in.

Bragg was too far removed from the early fighting near Reed's Bridge to know what was happening; indeed, he was not yet aware that the enemy, shifting leftward, had significantly strengthened itself on his right. Rather, he was about to begin an attack on his own front near Lee and Gordon's Mill. He asked Polk for a status report. The status was not what he had expected, and Bragg was now obliged to send reinforcements from Polk to the beleaguered Confederates near Rossville. Among those arriving was Polk's aide, Lieutenant Richmond. "Alive to the urgency of the situation," as Captain Polk put it, Richmond showed ad hoc generalship by providing advice to Lt. Gen. Alexander Stewart (one of Hood's generals just in from Virginia and unfamiliar with the lay of the Georgia land). Stewart then struck Maj. Gen. Joseph Reynolds's Yankee division so hard that he "swept it out of the way."[70]

In a letter to his wife two days later by William Gale, another of Polk's aides-de-camp, the altering fortunes of Polk's wing during the day were told with refreshing candor. "The attack was begun on our right, our object being to cut them off from Chattanooga," he wrote. "They guessed this and hurled against our right large masses. [Maj. Gen. William] Walker fought them for three hours and was whipped, then [Maj. Gen. B. F.] Cheatham went in and got whipped, the enemy advancing all the time and our men giving way. Walker went in again and was whipped again, then Cheatham tried once more and barely succeeded in holding his own. By this time it was 4 P.M., and both sides seemed willing to stop. Not so your father, who commanded in person." (Polk had left Lee and Gordon's in early afternoon, crossing the creek at Hunt's Ford, and arrived dramatically on the battlefield with Thomas Hindman's reserve division. Major General Hindman himself, ailing, did not catch up with his division until three o'clock that afternoon.)[71]

Brig. Gen. Pat Cleburne, still east of Chickamauga Creek, made ready to respond to an order from Polk to report to him immediately on the western bank. Instead of crossing at Thedford's Ford some miles distant from his bivouac, Cleburne expedited his arrival by sending his men, holding their trousers aloft and naked below their waists, through the hip-deep waters.[72] Subsequently, Gale's account continues: "General Hill was hurried up from the rear, and Liddell and Cleburne went at them. During the lull, the Devils had got logs and stones and made breastworks, but our men went at them with a yell and [had] driven [them] back about a mile when it became so dark . . . they were ordered to halt."[73]

Capt. John Frank Wheless, another member of Polk's staff, would recall in a postwar letter Polk's cheerfulness in the face of determined Federal resistance at Chickamauga. At about 5:30 P.M. with a certain brio, Polk had said to Wheless: "Find Bragg and say 'I feel certain, from the prisoners captured, we have been fighting Rosecrans's entire army.' That 'I am now placing Cleburne in position on the right, will advance in a few minutes upon the enemy, and expect to drive them before us.' Present my compliments to General Bragg, and assure him *et al* that 'I feel confident of success tomorrow.'" Bragg was braced upon hearing Polk's report, confirming to Wheless that, as Polk's prisoners had said, Rosecrans was unquestionably arrayed in full force against the Confederate front. Bragg's meeting that night to discuss the next day's plan would require Polk's presence, and as Wheless departed he was assured that a staff officer would show Polk the way.[74]

Turning back to Polk's headquarters, Wheless could hear the "sharp rattle of musketry" as Clebourne's attack got under way. With the sun commencing to sink, General Polk had kept pace with his troops on horseback, and when "it became so dark our men could not distinguish friend from foe," said Gale, "the two armies bivouaced in sight of each other."[75] Captain Polk summarized the day more waggishly: "General Thomas, finally realizing that General Polk was about to turn the tables and 'use *him* up,'" retreated until he reached the position from which he had started out in the morning.[76]

Captain Wheless would subsequently overhear various of Polk's general officers involved in the late-afternoon fighting characterize it "as the severest they had ever witnessed, not excepting the charge of Cheatham's division of Polk's corps at Perryville."[77] To the extent their commander appreciated the valor of his officers and men, it was one of the few things that Leonidas Polk could feel good about for some time to come. Within days, he was arrested for what Bragg alleged was his dereliction of duty.

23

Bragg's Designs for a Satisfying
Sabbath Disintegrate (1863)

Alongside Frank Cheatham's division, Patrick Cleburne was driving his troops with urgency as the Chickamauga sun went down. "He rode like a fury from brigade to brigade. . . . I never saw Cleburne before or after so demonstrative as on that evening," marveled a fellow officer.[1] And once their shooting into the dark had become clearly futile, Cleburne's men fell asleep on their arms. But for all the carnage left in the smoldering thickets and fields that night, the Confederate lieutenant general Daniel Harvey Hill would choose a dismissive metaphor at Braxton Bragg's expense: the day's fighting had been but "the sparring of the amateur boxer," Hill would say, "and not the crushing blows of the trained pugilist."[2] Bragg expressed his own satisfaction, saying Saturday "night found us masters of the ground, strewn with corpses and dying men though that ground was." Then, before retiring, Bragg confidently reshaped his army into two wings (a "hazardous experiment," Hill would later sniff), still intending, as he had from the outset, to envelop William Rosecrans's left flank and force the Yankees into the waiting trap of McLemore's Cove.[3] Lt. Gen. James Longstreet, catching up with some of his Virginia troops that had arrived on the scene earlier, was expected momentarily and was assigned the left wing. Bragg assigned the right wing to Polk. Now Polk's command comprised six ample units: four divisions under Cheatham, Cleburne, St. John Liddell, and John C. Breckinridge, and two corps under Hill and William H. T. Walker. (Thomas Hindman's division, ordinarily attached to Polk's Corps, had been assigned to Longstreet.) Artillery was under Melancton Smith, Rice Graves, and T. R. Hotchkiss; the Orleans Light Horse Troop served as Polk's escort and courier service.

Late that evening, at his headquarters at Thedford's Ford on the south edge of the battlefield, Bragg explained his rearrangements with his two senior generals. He met first with Polk, who left for his own camp before 11 P.M., then with Longstreet, who came in just after that. Longstreet was lucky to be there at all. After detraining in early afternoon at Catoosa Station near Ringgold, and with no welcoming members from Bragg's staff, nor even any guides, he and two aides had set off uncertainly toward the sounds of battle some miles distant. Feeling their way through the moonlit darkness, they rode smack into a Federal picket line. "A sharp right-about gallop, unhurt by the pickets' hasty and surprised fire, soon put us in safety," Staff Officer Maxley Sorrel, having caught his breath, reported later. Thereafter, "another road was taken for Bragg," about whom by this time, said Sorrel, "some sharp words were passing among the three riders."[4]

The after-midnight hours shrouding Bragg's candlelit tent had become all but opaque as cold fog rising off Chickamauga Creek mingled with warm smoke from thousands of campfires. It had "the bewildering aspect of some enchanted forest," an elegiac Confederate colonel was moved to say.[5] And partly as a result of that atmospheric condition, certain events occurring during the next six or seven hours remain today every bit as murky. What is clear is that what unfolded the next day dramatically changed Leonidas Polk's army future. For the obscuring fog—combined with innocent misstatements, selective memories, and self-serving concoctions by participants in the night's passage—confuse everything leading to the upshot nine days later, when Bragg had Polk arrested and relieved of his command. What follows is an attempt to reconstruct events as they may credibly have unfolded after Bragg's late-night conferences with Polk and Longstreet.[6]

At the end of the conference, Bragg directed Polk orally (no written order was made) to resume the battle early Sunday morning. Bragg specifically mentioned his well-known intention of turning the enemy's left flank southward into McLemore's Cove. Polk had demurred during the conference, saying that Rosecrans's forces, unlike their situation eighteen hours earlier, were now massed in greater numbers on the Rebel right. Polk argued that, with stout effort, the enemy might be driven backward but might not be so easily turned. To this worry Bragg had dissented, then declared that the right wing turning attack was to be launched as he desired "at day-dawn." Hill's Corps was to lead the way, and Polk was to advise Hill of his assignment.

Polk, perhaps feeling diffident (a novel experience for him), was uneasy with this last order. Bragg's new two-wing structure placed Lieutenant

General Hill, a professional soldier, under the far less experienced Lieutenant General Polk. To Polk's mind, a perfectly workable arrangement had been followed all that previous day when he and Hill had fought side by side on an equal basis, both generals serving as corps commanders. Now, far from supposing himself as qualified as Hill in military competence, Polk regarded Bragg's new scheme "an injustice and needless affront to Hill."[7]

An affront, though, might well have been Bragg's intention in placing Hill under Polk. The relegation would serve as a subtle reprimand for Hill's earlier miscarry at McLemore's Cove and, for added measure, a slap for what Bragg regarded as Hill's "querulous and insubordinate spirit," the abrasive manner Hill evidently took little pains to conceal when dealing with Bragg. (Bragg, brooding, would remember and bring up Hill's surliness a full eight years after the war.) Further, Bragg did not personally inform Hill of his reduced status, and to Hill's lasting pique he would learn of the implied downgrade thirdhand. Probably the truculence Hill would display even toward Polk all day Sunday was the result.

Now bearing into the foggy dark the oral instructions with which he disagreed, Polk left Bragg's tent and rode about a mile toward his own headquarters, located inconspicuously within a cedar thicket near Alexander's Bridge. The woodsy setting, as some men that night came to believe, was more like a hideout than a headquarters.[8] Along the way, with Maj. Gen. John Breckinridge riding at his side, Polk happened to meet General Hill's chief of staff, Lt. Col. Archer Anderson. When asked about Hill's whereabouts, Anderson said he was at Thedford's Ford—to Polk's surprise, having just left that vicinity. Polk, now obliged to act for better or worse, directed Anderson to tell Hill that he was now under Polk's authority and that Polk desired to see him presently at his own headquarters to discuss particulars.[9]

At this point, General Bragg's designs for a satisfying Sabbath, so dependent on others, began to disintegrate. In Polk's version of his roadway encounter with Archer Anderson (as he related it later to Bragg's adjutant, George Brent), Polk implies—but does not say specifically—that he made Anderson to understand that Hill should attack at daybreak. But in a note to Hill some days later, Polk says unequivocally that he *did* mention "daybreak" to Anderson.[10] Even so, Anderson and two staff officers with him at the chance meeting with Polk later certified in writing that Polk, in their hearing, made no reference to a dawn attack. Just as puzzling, John Breckinridge, astride his horse close by Polk, said no dawn attack was mentioned, and Hill would later tell Polk that Anderson said nothing whatsoever to him regarding *any* attack, let alone when it should be made.[11] According to Hill, he was told by Anderson only that he was now under Polk's command and of Polk's wanting to see him during the night.[12] It may be, then, that Polk misremembered how much he revealed to Anderson of Bragg's confidential order. The Hill biographer Hal Bridges makes the plausible suggestion that Polk, as a matter of discretion, held back details of the attack and its timing, fully expecting to see Hill himself later in the night. Some two decades later, Archer Anderson tried charitably to wrap up the whole snarl by saying, "It was easier to order an attack for daybreak than to bring it about. . . . Many annoying miscarriages that night combined to prevent it."[13]

After Archer Anderson and his two companions went looking for Hill to pass along however much, or little, Polk had told them, Polk rode on to his bivouac on the eastern bank of Chickamauga Creek. Members of Polk's escort had been posted at key roadway positions in the vicinity to tend to signal fires and to direct those looking for Polk.[14] Reaching his camp about midnight, Polk immediately dictated Bragg's oral orders to his chief of staff, Lt. Col. Thomas Jack, addressing the written versions to Polk's three field commanders: Hill, Cheatham, and Walker. Their troops were to be "amply supplied with ammunition before daylight," the orders read, and the attacks themselves were to take place "to-morrow morning at daylight."[15]

A little after midnight, a courier named J. A. Perkins, who belonged to Polk's escort troop and had been posted at a signal fire at Alexander's Bridge, led Maj. Gen. William Walker into Polk's camp. Walker's orders—that he was to hold his division in reserve during the daylight attack—were then handed to him.[16] Perkins was sent back to the bridge by Polk to watch for Hill; he remained there until 2:00 A.M. dutifully minding the fire.[17] Meanwhile, once the dictated orders for Hill and Cheatham were ready, Colonel Jack asked Charles Gallway, a private in Polk's Orleans Guards escort, for "two intelligent couriers to be entrusted with their delivery."[18] General Cheatham "was immediately found," Gallway says (at about 1:00 A.M., Cheatham would later confirm), "but the courier bearing the dispatch to General Hill rode until one o'clock, and not finding him reported back to headquarters."[19] Gallway's assertion that the courier *returned* at "one o'clock" must be either a faulty recollection or careless handwriting, because the courier in question, John H. Fisher, said in a sworn statement that he vainly searched for Hill for about *four* hours and upon his return to headquarters "did not report to Col. Jack, as I understood from his clerk . . . I was not to disturb him."[20]

While Courier Fisher had been searching in the dark for Hill, two officers on Hill's staff (presumably neither Archer Anderson nor his earlier companions) were drawn by firelight to a fork in the road near Alexander's Bridge; there they were directed by Trooper L. Charvet, the soldier posted at this fire, to Polk's cedar thicket. General Polk and William Richmond (the last night Polk's aide would be alive) were talking beside a campfire. Hill's officers told Polk they had themselves been looking for their leader futilely for almost four hours. (The consensus of historians is that Hill at the time was resting somewhere near Thedford's Ford.) Polk sent Hill's staff officers back out into the smoky fog to continue their search in order to inform Hill of the urgency of the ordered daylight attack.[21]

By now Polk must have begun to worry in earnest about locating Hill in time. Between first light and sunrise he summoned a sleeping captain on his staff, John Frank Wheless, to serve as yet another courier.[22] Beyond bothering now with the chain of command, Polk addressed the attack orders directly to Hill's subordinates, Patrick Cleburne and John Breckinridge, and sent Wheless off.[23] (It's easy to suppose that Breckinridge, having spent several predawn hours at Polk's campfire, would have already been aware of the timetable and in need of no additional order, but accounts of that night are replete with just such inexplicable details.) Polk's orders to Cleburne and Breckinridge now read: "Having sought in vain for Lieutenant-General Hill, [Lieutenant General Polk] gives you directly the following orders: Move upon and attack the enemy as soon as you are in position."[24] If this easygoing periphrasis lacks the insistence of Bragg's "daylight attack," Polk was at least anxious enough that he handed duplicate backup orders to another trusted captain, J. Minick Williams, and hurried him off behind Wheless.[25]

Wheless found Hill—and by chance. As dawn was breaking, Hill was conversing around a breakfast fire with Cleburne and Breckinridge, Wheless's two intended quarries. To Captain Wheless's borderline impertinence that the lieutenant general sitting before him could not be found during the night, Hill curtly rejoined that it was *Polk* who could not be found when Hill had gone looking for him at Alexander's Bridge. The posted courier Polk had promised to have at the bridge, Hill said, was not there to show him the way when he arrived around 3 A.M. Wheless, trying tact now, rejoined that he "knew General Polk had couriers placed at the bridge; that they remained there until late, but the hour I did not know."[26]

Captain Wheless clearly asserts, moreover, that either Breckinridge or Cleburne, having read the order addressed to him, then handed the paper to Hill. Odd as this may seem, Hill would later claim that it was not until eight o'clock that morning that he learned (and from Bragg's mouth) "that an attack had been ordered at daylight." As for Polk's written order that

John Fisher had spent four hours trying to deliver to him, Hill would later say he "saw [this] order for the first time nineteen years" after the fact.[27] Besides, as written, the order could not be complied with. Either Breckinridge or Cleburne, according to Wheless, "remarked that the men could not go into the fight until they had their rations"—that is, their breakfast. To this, says Wheless, Hill consented, whereupon Hill busied himself making adjustments in his lines while his soldiers ate.[28]

The consequence of all these misaligned communications was that Hill's division was making its whereabouts known to the enemy not by cannonading and musketry at dawn but by the clatter of breakfast utensils. Back at Polk's headquarters, as he and his staff and escort troopers were about to ride to the front, Yves LeMonniere, a jaunty Cajun private in the Louisiana troop, spotted John Fisher, the unsuccessful courier. Fisher was now warming himself by a fire, the bridle of his worn-out horse draped over his right shoulder. "I cried to him," said LeMonniere, "'the General wants you,' and added devilishly: 'You are going to catch hell.'" Fisher jumped into his saddle and hurried to Polk's side to explain his nighttime misadventures. Catching up with the two, LeMonniere heard a snatch of Fisher's alibi "'. . . and, having no answer, I stopped at the fire to warm my hands, and did not think I was doing wrong.'" At that, said LeMonniere, "General Polk spurred his horse, and we followed at a rapid gait. We knew then by his face and movements that something was wrong. 'Ah, le quart d'heure de Rabelais!'" LeMonniere added as a Creole jest at Fisher's expense.[29]

Riding off to get things moving as Bragg had directed, Polk and his retinue went looking for Hill. They learned along the way from the returning courier, Frank Wheless, that Hill's soldiers would not be ready for battle for at least an hour. Finding Hill himself at a little after 7:00 A.M., Polk said (according to Private LeMonniere): "'General, why have you not attacked?' General Hill answered: 'General, my men are drawing rations, etc.' 'Sir,' said General Polk, 'this is not the time for eating; this is the time for fighting. Attack immediately; attack immediately.' And without waiting for an answer from General Hill, General Polk whirled his horse around and, galloping along his line, to every major general said: 'General, attack immediately.'" LeMonniere could hardly believe that the refined cleric he had known in New Orleans could wax so wroth. "The mask had fallen," he realized. "That Bishop Polk, a man *par excellence* of suavity and manners, should have so spoken to his first in command . . . denoted a terrible strain on the man's mind." Normally Polk "was without exception 'un chevalier de la noble ecole,' brought up in a Parisian parlor."[30]

If more colorfully recollected by Private LeMonniere, Polk's outsized anger at the dallying Hill was noted too by another Polk partisan, Charles Gallway of the Orleans Guards. "Why General Polk did not at once arrest [Hill], I cannot see," the soldier wrote to friend Willie Huger. Had he done that, he "would have entirely exonerated himself from the charges Bragg would shortly level."[31] Of course, there is Hill's side to take into account, baffling though it is. For the record, he would later write, "General Polk made no objection to the breakfast delay."[32]

Because of Hill's tardiness, Polk at the very least was put out with his colleague, but Bragg proved livid with Polk. After having had to accept that his daybreak attack was a lost cause, his customary scorn of Polk was kindled afresh by an apparently duplicitous member of his staff. Indeed, if the missed chances at McLemore's Cove had seemed farcical to Lieutenant Richmond, now farce in fact ensued. In the early morning, Maj. Pollock B. Lee had been sent by Bragg to find Polk and to learn just why the battle had not been joined. Upon his return, Lee concocted a fabrication sure to please Bragg. He reported (according to Bragg) that he had found Polk sometime after sunup dawdling on the front porch of a farmhouse three miles behind the front lines. Far from being up and at General Thomas, he was relaxing in a rocking chair, reading a newspaper. Hearing this fatuous tale, and maybe only half-believing it, Bragg found it useful. He was to repeat it several times: shortly thereafter to General Hill, and subsequently twice to his wife, Elise, who as always delighted in hearing any slander against her former neighbor. To further substantiate the smear, Bragg next placed *himself* on the porch, telling Hill: "I found Polk after sunrise sitting down reading a newspaper at Alexander's Bridge, two miles from the line of battle, where he ought to have been fighting."[33] Similarly, Bragg told Jefferson Davis: "I sent to Genl Polk and found him after seven o'ck two miles in rear of his line in the house where he slept." Bragg would continue to embellish the story for years after, telling an army friend in 1873 that, while rocking and reading, Polk had informed Major Lee that he was waiting for his breakfast. But for Polk's lackadaisical behavior, Bragg assured Edward Sykes, "our independence might have been gained that very morning." A tasty bit of gossip, the story was naturally bandied about among the troops with enriching details, one soldier regaling a civilian cousin with the news that, on the morning of September 20, "instead of finding [Polk] in Thomas' rear, [Bragg] found him and [his] staff in bed!"[34]

Had not common sense sufficed, all these fanciful tales were subsequently put to rest by Capt. William Polk, who would later record that, when Pollock Lee did in fact find General Polk, Polk was in his headquarters "camp in the woods at Alexander's Bridge"; the sun was not yet up (sunrise was 5:47 A.M.); there was no farmhouse nearby; General Polk had already breakfasted; and he and his staff were already mounting their horses. Captain Polk would further say (quite logically) that, had General Bragg *believed* the rocking chair story, he should have had Polk arrested "without a moment's hesitation," as "any other commander . . . would have." Arrest was "the only punishment adequate to the offense charged," he noted.[35]

Two weeks later, Pollock Lee reportedly denied to a member of Polk's staff that he was the source of the rocking chair canard.[36] Suspiciously, though, for almost a year previous there had been bad blood between Major Lee and two young kinsmen of General Polk. They had together forced Lee to back out of a duel challenge. It may have been motive enough for Lee to try to defame Polk out of spite.[37]

The fogs, foibles, and mistakes during the night of September 19–20 having finally dissipated, Sunday's daylong battle along Chickamauga Creek commenced some three hours later than Bragg had desired. Early or late, the Army of Tennessee fought well and, eventually, victoriously. Opposite Polk's right wing, at least, General Thomas's Federals upon a ridge behind chest-high breastworks of logs and rails ("the ringing of axes had been heard all night," said Hill) had for hours presented an almost impenetrable front, a regular "crochet of eight interlocking divisions."[38] General Hill's opening attack in this area was initially repulsed with heavy losses, and it would be hereabouts that later in the day steadfast George Thomas earned his soubriquet "The Rock of Chickamauga." But when about noontime Rosecrans rushed more defenders to stiffen Thomas's resistance to Hill's corps, he inadvertently opened a costly half-mile gap opposite the Rebels' left wing. James Longstreet and John Hood and their transplanted Virginians (among others) opportunely rushed into this opening with devastating effect: the Union right wing began then to break apart. Subsequently, Longstreet wheeled to his own right, a direction not in accord with Bragg's left-wheeling entrapment plan but one that further overwhelmed the enemy. As word of the rout reached the devout Federal commander, General Rosecrans was seen to make the sign of the cross upon his chest, alarming an observer from the Washington War Department. "Hello," Charles Dana said to himself after witnessing Rosecrans's devotional act. "If the general is crossing himself, we are in a desperate situation."[39]

Elsewhere on the Confederate right, in the midst of delivering progress reports throughout the afternoon "at the top of my horse's speed," Maj. William W. Carnes witnessed a worrisome incident of battlefield strife between colleagues rather than enemies: Generals Polk and Hill. It was at about 2:00 P.M. during a lull in the fighting when Carnes, with a message from Brig. Gen. Patrick Cleburne, rode up to Polk's field headquarters. There he found Polk and Hill sitting on a tree trunk. Carnes had dismounted and was standing at a respectful distance to await Polk's notice when the generals' conference suddenly turned contentious. Polk rose abruptly from the trunk, and Carnes heard him say "with considerable warmth of manner: 'Well, Sir, I am sorry that you do not agree with me, but my decision is made, and that is the way it shall be done.'" Carnes would later include this snatch of conversation in a newspaper account of Chickamauga which he wrote for the Atlanta *Constitution*, but he provided his postwar readers with selective details only. As he acknowledged to William M. Polk in 1884: "I did not put into print an additional remark made by General Polk after he left General Hill, which was heard by me, and showed [that] what he had met in General Hill [was] certainly not cooperation. General Polk said, as if [in] half-soliloquy, though spoken aloud, 'That is certainly the most pig-headedly obstinate man I ever met in a general's uniform.'" Carnes had reckoned "that General Polk's effort to arrange a programme with General Hill had met with no success, and that he had determined to proceed from that time on his own judgment." William Gale was doubtless reflecting his father-in-law's feelings too when he himself accused Hill of "stubborn disobedience" that afternoon "in declining to move forward upon the pretext that his flank was not protected." Gale reported that General Polk "said more than once, 'Oh! this man, Hill! He is enough to drive me mad!'" As for himself, Gale's recollections of General Hill at Chickamauga aroused long after everything from sputtering rage to imagined mayhem. He would declare in 1884 that Hill "should have been decapitated for his unaccountable abandonment of his command that [Saturday] night [and] for his stubborn disobedience of [Polk's] orders Sunday in declining to move forward."[40]

The quarrel that exercised Gale had commenced over how best to continue the assault against George Thomas. Subsequently, at 3:30 P.M., Cleburne was ordered by Polk "to advance my heavy batteries and open on the enemy," a second attempt after both he and John Breckinridge had been repulsed by Yankees secure behind the sturdy log works they had spent all night constructing. Hill had characterized the Confederates' initial effort as a "desperate 'forlorn-hope.'"[41] Now, in Polk's plan, Hill with three divisions was to attack the Federal left flank. Presumably because Hill disagreed on some points of this tactic, he (in the words of Polk's son, a witness) "was very much opposed to executing [Polk's orders] and showed a singular unwillingness to act." Hill had to be urged on twice more, according to Captain Polk.[42] Curiously, in his rather mellow 1884 recollections of Chickamauga, Hill gives no particulars of any differences between him and a lowering Polk; instead he graciously summarizes the vicious fighting of Sunday afternoon by saying: "It probably never happened before for a great battle to be fought to its bloody conclusion with the commanders of each side [Rosecrans and Bragg] away from the field of conflict. But the Federals were in the hands of the indomitable Thomas, and the Confederates were under their two heroic wing commanders Longstreet and Polk." Hill was being more than complimentary toward Polk. For it had come to pass after their dispute and Polk's tongue-lashing of Hill, as overheard by Carnes, that Polk had placed Hill himself more or less in charge of the whole right wing.[43] A benefit inherited by Hill was the noteworthy initiative displayed that afternoon by Polk's nephew, Brig. Gen. Lucius Eugene Polk.[44]

In sum, the irresistible Rebel forces left and right gradually overcame the unmovable Yankee objects, contradicting a peevish remark by Bragg to Longstreet earlier in the afternoon that "there is not a man in the right wing who has any fight in him."[45] Not so by a long shot, to hear General Polk tell it. "The news from every part of the field [is] of the most cheering character," Polk was heard to say that afternoon before resorting to colorful farmhand language to urge on Frank Cheatham's 12th Tennessee Infantry: grind the enemy "as between the nether and upper millstone," he shouted. Polk all day, in fact, had been as ardent as if leading cheers. That morning Cheatham himself, while riding past his waking troops, had stirred them with an earthier exhortation: "Give them hell, boys, give them hell!" Just then, said a member of the 19th Tennessee Infantry, "General Polk came in full tilt on his heels and said, 'Give them what General Cheatham says; we will pay off old chores today.'" Hearing that, said the soldier, "there went up a 'Rebel Yell!'"[46]

As was true of Daniel Hill, General Longstreet's military experience and savvy naturally surpassed that of Polk, but as night closed in at Chickamauga the combined efforts of Longstreet's and Polk's two wings had crushed the Federals' lines. Leaving behind a treasure of booty for the victors to harvest, most of the defeated troops were soon streaming toward Chattanooga beneath a rising moon.[47] Only the stubborn men under George Thomas were able to stem in part the Confederate pursuit with their valiant stand atop Horseshoe Ridge and Snodgrass Hill. Casualties amounting to 16,000 for the Federals and 18,000 for the Confederates had paid the cost of two days of fighting. For the 20,000-odd men in General Polk's right wing, the loss was 32 percent of its total. It was the highest toll of the four major battles in which Polk had been engaged.[48]

Taking possession that night of entrenchments abandoned by Thomas's corps, General Polk, William Gale, and a few other members of Polk's staff, "cold, tired, hungry and wearied, sought any reasonably clear place to collapse." First, though, Polk sent Col. Philip B. Spence to Bragg's headquarters; Spence was to illustrate for Bragg the right wing's situation at day's end with sketches drawn in the sand. Then Gale made a fire and spread a blanket for Polk "within 10 yards of a dead Yankee, and one poor devil who lay within a few feet of us sobbing out his life all night long." Gale's further descriptions of the surroundings were just as grim. Sent by Polk after a while to look for his nephew Lucius Polk, Gale and his mare picked their way for a hour or so over the battlefield. "Such a ride as I had, does not often fall to the lot of man," he wrote to his wife, Kate.

> The moon was shining as clear as possible, and gave a most unearthly
> appearance to this horrid scene. Wounded, dying and dead men and
> horses were strewn around me and under me everywhere. . . . The
> field was yet hot and smoking from the last charge, and thousands
> were lying insensible, or in agony, where [for a] few short minutes they
> [had] stood in battle array. I can never forget the horrid indecency of
> death that was pictured on their agonized faces, upturned in the pale
> moonlight.[49]

Not discovered until the next day (but lying fewer than sixty yards from Polk's camp) was the body of Lt. William Richmond, Polk's aide-de-camp and his "dear and faithful and attached young friend. . . . One of the purest young men I ever knew." Long overdue from a courier mission to Hill's headquarters, he had apparently been ambushed while searching for Polk's bivouac; shot through the head and thigh, it was concluded he fell dead from his saddle. His body was then "stripped of everything he had on, save his boots, pants and shirt." Polk told Fanny he had "grieved for him as for a child." The fatherly general, in fact, "wept like a child," another aide, Henry Watterson observed. (Polk had shown bipartisan compassion that day. Amid the killing he was directing, he allowed a Yankee officer identifying himself as a friend of Crafts Wright—the West Pointer who had attended Leonidas's consecration in Cincinnati—to enter the Rebel lines to retrieve the body of a brother.)[50]

But there was work to be done before Monday's dawn. Not finding Polk's brigadier nephew, Gale returned to his own camp, and around midnight with Colonel Spence and General Polk he rode "among the dead and dying" in Thomas's entrenched line, looking for General Bragg's headquarters. Polk grumbled along the way, Spence remembered, at the great distance Bragg had separated himself from his front-line commanders.[51]

Relatively refreshed by supper and a brief rest (Polk was showing re-markably vigor for one who had slept little the night before and had fought a battle all day), Polk roused Bragg, who had gone to bed. Gale listened in the tent as Polk "urged upon Bragg the fact that the enemy was *routed* and flying precipitately from the field." Polk's plea was that Bragg order pursuit of the Federals before they reached their defensive works in Chattanooga, and he may have told Bragg to take note, as he later informed Jefferson Davis, that the moon was "never brighter—as bright to guide us in the pursuit as the enemy in their flight." Gale complained in his postwar recollection that "Bragg could not be induced to look at [the situation] in that light, and it was not done." Disgusted nineteen years later by the "vacillating imbecil-ity" of Bragg, he declared that Bragg at Chickamauga had "a better army than Hannibal and Scipio had to conquer Rome and Carthage."[52]

Early Monday morning, Brig. Gen. Nathan Bedford Forrest, atop the wooded heights of Missionary Ridge east of Chattanooga (having climbed a tree as well), confidently assured Polk that the Federals were clearly vis-ible in the valleys below, snaking toward the town. "I think they are evacu-ating as hard as they can go," Forrest said, and prisoners had likewise told him that "two pontoons had been thrown across [the Tennessee] for the purpose of retreating." From far in the distance axes could again be heard, persuading him the Yankees were felling trees to "obstruct our passing." Forrest concluded "we ought to press forward as rapidly as possible," and he urged Polk to pass the information to Bragg. Forrest was partly wrong, in that the Federals were fortifying Chattanooga, not fleeing through it, but either way Bragg left them alone to do as they pleased.[53]

Isham Harris, Tennessee's now out-of-office governor in the Federal-held state, was then serving as an aide at Bragg's headquarters. He would later tell Gale that "the commanding general [Sunday night] would not believe the Federals had been beaten, but insisted that we were to have a harder fight the next day . . . to hold our position."[54] With renewed fight-ing in mind, Bragg rode out after an early breakfast Monday to find James Longstreet at his bivouac. Persuaded like Forrest that the enemy was rac-ing toward Chattanooga in feckless disarray, Longstreet proposed that, rather than assaulting the Federals from the south below Chattanooga, he and Polk should cross the Tennessee River north of the town, get in their rear, and force them to abandon the city's fortifications.[55] With that accomplished—and should an opportunity present itself—Longstreet rec-ommended that a detachment follow the railroad leading to Knoxville and there destroy the Yankee army under Lt. Gen. Ambrose Burnside. The in-terview between the two men was possibly not as cordial as Longstreet's postwar accounts would have it. A private was standing near the generals and later provided fragments he overheard as the conversation escalated with rancor. Longstreet was astride his horse, according to the private, and was heard to say, "Yes, sir, but all *great* captains follow up a victory." Bragg was standing beside Longstreet's horse and his reply was inaudible to the attentive private, but he did hear Longstreet respond, "Yes, sir, you *rank* me, but you can't cashier me!"[56]

Civil or not, the discussion (according to Longstreet) concluded with Bragg's agreement "that such was probably our best move, and that he was about to give the necessary orders for its execution."[57] Accordingly, Longstreet and Polk made ready to move. Polk first hastily managed to inform Fanny of Sunday's outcome and to notify her of his intention to pursue the fleeing Yankees.[58] Later that day, however, making no mention of any pending sweep behind Rosecrans by his two wing commanders, Bragg issued a different order (one of many) directing Polk's wing to occupy the heights overlooking Chattanooga, a decision Polk's son described with veiled censure: "On the afternoon of the 21st the order to advance was given; it was not, however, to Chattanooga, but to occupy the high ground of Missionary Ridge." By that time Rosecrans was occupying, and at work strengthening, the Confederates' old Chattanooga fortifications.[59] Bragg's countermand of the proposed roundabout march was received with disgust by Longstreet and Polk, and while Bragg may have had his own defensible military reasons, it may also be that by then he was reacting to the curdled feelings he increasingly felt for his two wing commanders. In any case, he later took pleasure in saying that Longstreet's suggestion to cross the Tennessee River to get behind Rosecrans was a "visionary scheme" that was "utterly impossible for want of . . . military propriety."[60]

After Polk's headquarters were established on Missionary Ridge (so named for a theological seminary upon it), William Gale was awed by the sight below. "Our army van's headquarters are on top," he would soon tell his wife, "from which we have a perfect view of the enemy's line of entrenchments. It is very exciting to see the rascals just in front of us."[61] That the dug-in rascals were left unmolested by their nearby enemies would lead many under Bragg's authority to regard his leadership scornfully. Said Daniel Hill (though generously indicting himself as well): "Whatever blunders each of us in authority committed before the battles of the 19th and 20th [*sic*], and during their progress, the great blunder of all was that of not pursuing the enemy on the 21st." To the meticulous Chickamauga historian Archibald Gracie, that was putting it mildly. It was the "most stupendous blunder of the war," he wrote in 1911. More picturesque were the words of the editor of the *Memphis Daily Appeal*: not long after the battle he wrote that Bragg's failure to press the victory of September 20 had rendered Chickamauga in biblical terms "Dead Sea fruit in our hands." Capt. Robert W. Woolley of Breckinridge's command was more precise: the battle, he wrote, was "weak in conception, grand in execution and barren of results." As far as General Polk was concerned, it was yet another instance of the Confederacy's record of dilatory tactics, now exemplified by Bragg. As William Gale remembered, his father-in-law was wont to say: "If we fail, and our cause should be lost, on its tomb should be one epitaph only: '*Trop Tard.* Always too late.'"[62] Yet more demoralized than philosophical after Chickamauga, Polk must have thought at the time that Bragg was hell-bent toward failure. The bishop in him had "prayed long and earnestly that [God] might bless our arms," he confided to Chaplain Quintard shortly after the battle subsided, and he was at that point convinced that "God answered my prayers in giving us this great victory." Longstreet would shortly have other work for God to do: "Only the hand of God can save us or help us as long as we have our present commander," he advised the secretary of war.[63]

With his army virtually at rest, Bragg's headquarters on Monday issued various postbattle orders: the necessary details regarding the corralling of stragglers and prisoners, the burial of the dead, and the recovery of abandoned arms and ammunition on the battlefield. With that attended to, Bragg now had the leisure to attend to what seemingly was often on his mind: the settling of scores. The targets that Tuesday were two. One was Maj. Gen. Thomas Hindman, the man Bragg blamed for failing to spring the trap at McLemore's Cove earlier that September. The other was General Polk.[64] So before the day closed, Polk was ordered "to make as early as practicable a report explanatory of your failure to attack the enemy at daylight on Sunday last in obedience to orders."

Hearing nothing from Polk, Bragg on Friday, September 25, had the order repeated, this time ordering Polk to reply "without delay."[65] But Bragg was neither expecting, nor in a mood for, an acceptable explanation. Instead, he was already about to notify Jefferson Davis that he was finally fed up with Polk. (He had previously alerted Elise Bragg of his intentions on September 22, not forgetting to mention the ludicrous rocking chair incident.)[66] Bragg was to have his letter hand-delivered to the president by his aide, Lt. Col. William K. Beard, who could be counted on to amplify orally any censorious details in the text.

After a few preliminary sentences, Bragg got to his point: "Our greatest evil is *inefficient commanders.*" First citing D. H. Hill and Thomas Hindman, Bragg then lit into Polk: "Genl Polk, though gallant and patriotic, is luxurious in his habits, rises late, moves slowly, and always conceives his plans the best. He has proved an injury to us on every field where I have been associated with him." Hill was next for a going-over. Bragg thought him "despondent, dull, slow, and tho' gallant personally, is always in a state of apprehension. . . . His open and constant croaking would demoralize any command in the world." Discerning some value among other subordinates, Bragg wound up saying that, with Simon Buckner, John Hood, or Patrick Cleburne replacing Polk and Hill, "our strength would be far greater."[67]

Polk may be excused for failing to answer Bragg's two demands promptly. First, on Monday on Bragg's directive he had been preparing to press the tail end of an enemy rapidly securing itself behind the Chattanooga fortifications. And second, he had more pressing letters to write. Because even as Bragg was designing against him, Polk was scheming against Bragg. On the Saturday following the battle, he, Simon Buckner, Longstreet, and Hill—their fellowship stoked by mutual dislike of their leader—met, plotted, and apportioned writing assignments.[68] Buckner was to draft a petition to pass among the general officers expressing their displeasure with Braxton Bragg, as well as their wish for the president to remove him forthwith from the Army of Tennessee. Longstreet, though a newcomer, brought military stature and fresh enthusiasm to the anti-Bragg faction and would write both James Seddon, the secretary of war, and Robert E. Lee, Longstreet's friend and colleague from the war in Virginia, praying Lee would agree to, and the secretary approve, his transfer to the Army of Tennessee.[69] Polk would write *his* friend, the president, and also Lee, another, if more casual, friend from cadet days. The president was assured by Polk that Bragg's latest actions had "but deepened and confirmed my former conviction. He is not the man for the Station he fills. . . . He has had, as I believe, Genl Rosecranz' [sic] army twice at his mercy, and he has allowed it to escape both times. . . . Broken and scattered [and] routed, [the enemy] has been permitted to occupy Chattanooga without disturbance and fortify himself strongly." And to Lee on the same day, a similar but imploring message: Polk's "very familiar acquaintance with the mind and character of the officer commanding this army" convinced him "we must have a change before any permanent success can be had in this region." Uniting with Longstreet's appeal, Polk begged Lee to ask himself "whether, as a question of duty to our suffering command, it be not proper for you to come over and help us?"[70]

While members of Polk's cabal rubbed their hands expectantly, the denunciations of Bragg's handling of the aftermath of Chickamauga (a contest even Rosecrans had bemoaned as "a serious disaster" for his "overwhelmed Federals") made the rounds of the Richmond War Department.[71]

Longstreet's letter made a stir too, its "startling contents" noted soon after in the diary of John B. Jones, the ever-vigilant office clerk who twenty-seven months earlier had spotted Bishop Polk moseying about the War Department hallways as he was about to be commissioned a major general. Citing Longstreet's assertion how on the morning of September 21 he proposed to Bragg a pursuit of Rosecrans, only to be ignored, Jones opined that "if it be Longstreet [who is right], Bragg ought certainly to be relieved without delay; and the President cannot arrive in the field a moment too soon." Normally optimistic about the South's fortunes, Jones added: "I am filled with alarm for . . . the cause!"[72]

Buckner's petition, meanwhile, was passing from general to general. (It was the work of "imbeciles, traitors, rogues and intriguing politicians," as Bragg would lump the lot.)[73] Professing disingenuously that Bragg's poor health was the signers' main concern, the petition was a polished composition with an arresting flourish inspired by Europe's recent Crimean War. The peril in which Bragg's Confederates now found themselves—face to face with Yankees allowed to secure themselves in earthworks on the outskirts of Chattanooga—resembled the dark days of 1854 when British and French cavalry had hopelessly dashed against the massed Cossack and Russian cannons at Sebastopol, a tragic event familiar to soldiers and soon to be immortalized by the poet Alfred Lord Tennyson's *The Charge of the Light Brigade*.[74] Yet despite the letter's compelling prose, neither Buckner nor any of the other eleven signatories would admit to authorship, an admission deemed better left unsaid. Further, on prudent reflection, they would decide not to send it to the president after all; only its rumored existence would reach him.[75] Petitioned or not, Davis was soon having to weigh Polk's contentions in a follow-up letter asserting that Bragg's post-Chickamauga vacillation had not only wasted the victory he won on Sunday but also squandered the "heavy expenditure of the life-blood of the Confederacy [that had] bought and paid for the whole state of Tennessee, to the Mississippi River at the very least."[76]

A month would pass before General Lee, beset in Virginia both by the Yankee general George Meade and by a rheumatic back, answered General Polk. He tactfully declined the Tennessee invitation. Polk by then had got around to providing Bragg with an explanation of his movements on the night and morning of September 19–20. He shaded the report his way: it was General Hill's unknown whereabouts during the predawn darkness that had caused the delay on the morning of September 20. (Given to sardonic wit, Hill would later describe Polk's self-excusing report as "ingenious.")[77]

But blame whom he might, Polk's version mattered little to Bragg: if

Hill was responsible, then Polk, his superior, was responsible. Thereupon, reading what Polk had to say and declaring it "entirely unsatisfactory," Bragg later the same day stripped him of his command for "disobedience" and "neglect of duty" and ordered him off the premises to await his fate in Atlanta. General Bragg did, to his credit, entertain a moment's indecision before acting. David Urquhart was a confiding lieutenant colonel on Bragg's staff who before the war had been a wealthy sugar planter in Louisiana's Plaquemines Parish. In addition, he was a New Orleans socialite, just the kind of person to have been well acquainted with the bishop of the Episcopal diocese. Perhaps for the sake of that connection, Urquhart suggested that Bragg relent on suspending Polk; it might redound to Bragg and blight his popularity with the public. Bragg's hesitation was fleeting. "Urgent exactions of discipline" obliged him to proceed, he told Urquhart (and he told Davis later he was only sorry he hadn't dismissed Polk, the irritant, sooner).[78] Then continuing in a punishing mood, Bragg ordered Maj. Gen. Thomas Hindman to Atlanta as well, charging him with lack of aggression in McLemore's Cove. He was not deterred by knowing that Hindman would take to Atlanta the neck wound he had sustained fighting at Chickamauga.

24

"Fight Ever with True Hearts.
Your Friend, L. Polk" (1863)

Braxton Bragg—who before the war was a communicant of St. John's Episcopal Church in Thibodaux, Louisiana—would later think it "too bad that I had to arrest my own Bishop. Still, it had to be done."[1] Jefferson Davis would say otherwise. Even though it was to be a loose arrest without close confinement, the president quickly advised Bragg he had overstepped his authority and he would do well to back off promptly.[2] Whether Bragg was out of order or not, his arrested bishop, exuding aplomb, was scarcely fazed—and certainly not intimidated. Soon he was assembling double-barreled materials that in a court of inquiry would "vindicate my own conduct" while "establishing the truth . . . of [Bragg's] lack of capacity as a commanding general."[3]

Vindication, he would argue, rested on his contention that the man most responsible for the delay of the morning attack on Chickamauga's second day was his reluctant subordinate, Lt. Gen. Daniel Harvey Hill. Apparently not yet under suspicion by Bragg for his role in the anti-Bragg cabal and petition, Hill now had only to fend off Polk who, before his departure for Atlanta, desired "to propound" to Hill seven questions: Hill's answers, potentially incriminating, would explain Hill's baffling whereabouts throughout the Saturday night and Sunday morning of September 19–20. Hill responded warily, prefacing his remarks by saying: "Your inquiries embrace points upon which we have conversed, but I will answer them in order." His resentment at being questioned surfaced in his reply to Question 4: "What were the reasons for your unreadiness to attack the enemy at daylight [of September 20]?" Answer: "I had no orders to make such attack, which is a sufficient answer."[4]

Depositions, meanwhile, were being taken from others who had been up and about Polk's camp that murky night. Presiding over these sworn testimonies was Andrew Ewing, a former Tennessee congressman now the judge of the military court in Polk's corps.[5] Polk himself, meanwhile, put questions to his two other corps commanders, William Walker and Frank Cheatham—questions that might induce answers supporting Polk's version of his dutiful actions taken during the early morning of September 20.[6]

With these matters being attended to, Polk next prepared a calm farewell to the men of his corps for delivery the following day, September 30. An "unfortunate disagreement between myself and the commander-in-chief" was the cause of his being relieved, he began, but he would pass over the particulars except to "express the unqualified conviction of the rectitude of my conduct . . . on the field of Chickamauga." More to the point of his message to them, he wished his soldiers to know that, as he departed for Atlanta he bore heartfelt gratitude, precious memories, and deepest feelings of regret. "Our final victory is certain and assured," he said. "Fight on, and fight ever with true hearts . . . until your independence is achieved. . . . I leave you in the care of [Gen. Frank Cheatham] the bravest of the brave. . . . Your kindness, devotion and respect for me . . . is graven on my heart, and will be treasured there until it ceases to beat." He signed himself: "Your friend, L. Polk, Lieutenant General." For many left behind, the affectionate feelings were mutual.[7] What might be called a fan club, in fact, was soon formed by members of the Orleans Light Horse, Polk's escort troop. A committee of these cavalrymen would draft a resolution expressing "our confidence, respect and admiration for our friend and veteran leader, Lt. Gen. L. Polk, etc., etc." The encomium was addressed to any court of inquiry that might convene to examine Bragg's charges against their esteemed leader.[8] Polk would also hear from the chaplains association of his former corps. At a field meeting in December, the chaplains resolved to inform the general that his past kindnesses to them had been such as "to make us ever cherish the memory of our late commander."[9]

Polk headed down to the Georgia capital by train, arriving on the evening of October 1 almost alone in this rowdy, war-boom town of some 15,000 white and slave inhabitants. (William Gale and Harry Yeatman, the two in-law kinsmen serving as his aides, were the only staff members allowed to accompany him, a restraint on Bragg's part to avoid shorting his army further of valuable personnel.) Once arrived, though, Polk quickly acquired welcoming companionship: he was invited to take lodging in the home of John Sidney Thrasher and his wife. Thrasher was the influential general manager of the Confederate Press Association, a network of reporters and Southern newspapers, and Thrasher's sentiments were presumably more partial to Polk than to Bragg. For good measure, having the distinguished, if arrested, bishop-general under his roof doubtlessly gave him an enviable cachet among journalists.[10] That prestige would be augmented in November, when the famed John Bell Hood, who had lost a leg at Chickamauga, also came to the Thrasher home to recuperate. Graciously, Polk gave up his comfortable quarters to the wounded Texan. "The twin heroes of Chickamauga," an enthusiastic reporter was moved to say of the two houseguests.[11] Some other prisoners arriving in Atlanta that same week—Yankee captives taken at Chickamauga—did not fare as well as Polk. When they stepped out of boxcars at the crowded depot the men were met with "opprobrious epithets" and spit from the "rosy lips of Southern women," and they were targeted for stones by small boys as they were marched to an overnight holding pen. "After making allowance for [the spitters'] patriotic devotion," an Ohio sergeant drolly admitted to "having felt affronted."[12]

A tent was raised in the Thrashers' front yard for Polk's two staffers while the general's indoor room was soon "crowded with sympathizers and indignant friends."[13] Taking mulish pleasure in his predicament, Polk entertained his visitors with tales unflattering to Bragg and commending to himself. He continued to put as much in writing too. To President Jefferson Davis he wrote on October 6 that Bragg had shown "criminal negligence . . . rather incapacity at Chickamauga" and "should be replaced by General Lee or some other." (The "some other" Polk had in mind, as Davis would have reasoned, was Joseph E. Johnston, the soldier Polk respected but Davis could barely abide.)[14] Polk fumed even more in letters to his family. "You may be surprised to hear from me at this place," he began a letter to Fanny, his first since the suspension. His banishment, he said, was the fulfillment of General Bragg's "long cherished purpose to avenge himself on me for the relief and support I have given him in the past; attempts made twice before." (Here he was referring partly to the sudden order from Richmond in the summer of 1862 that he drop his command duties in Tupelo, Mississippi, to preside over a military court of inquiry in Jackson. Polk was sure that order, suddenly rescinded by someone in Richmond just as suddenly as it had come, had been Bragg's doing.) This time too, Polk told Fanny, Bragg's conniving would be foiled: "I defy his motive, and scorn the pitiful effort by which he has so long attempted to vent it. I beg you to be assured that I am entirely quiet and undisturbed."[15]

Undisturbed—but not cooled off. It was four days later when he wrote his daughter Fanny, "I certainly feel a lofty contempt for [Bragg's] puny efforts to inflict injury upon a man who has dry-nursed him for the whole period of his connexion [*sic*] with him, and has kept him from ruining the cause of the country by the sacrifice of its armies." Young Fanny should have no fear but that her father was "perfectly satisfied with my ability to take care of myself."[16] Writing on October 17 to Kenneth Rayner, his brother-in-law in Raleigh, he again referred to Bragg's two earlier efforts "to get rid of my presence." Jefferson Davis had by this time made Bragg agree to reinstate Polk, but Polk refused to cooperate. Thus, Polk could boast that Bragg's machinations would have failed yet again "if I would allow myself to serve under a man who has so entirely forfeited my respect by the arbitrary and reckless manner in which he has so publicly assailed me." Here in his draft to Rayner he added the words "I mean both himself and wife" but, with a gentlemanly second thought, lined them out. What assailing things Elise Bragg may have said that got back to Polk is not known, but they likely balanced nicely Polk's assessments of her husband. To Rayner he was now saying that Bragg was one whose "integrity of character and military capacity . . . were of the lowest order." As his rants continued into November, he would again write daughter Fanny to say Bragg was "a poor, feeble-minded, irresolute man of violent passions, unreasonable, and without resources, withal without elevation of character."[17]

Sowing scorn, Polk reaped serenity; by his own account he soon was "never in better health and . . . in marvelously fine spirits."[18] These spirits had been buoyed as well by assurances from Jefferson Davis (who had had to come to Georgia to deal with his wrangling generals) that his army future was secure. In his first month in exile, Polk would have at least three man-to-man talks with the president. One was during an overnight journey in Davis's private railcar as the president wound up a speechifying swing through the western Confederacy to boost public and military morale.[19]

In what was to become a Civil War version of shuttle diplomacy, Davis persuaded Polk to give up his initial demand for a court of inquiry just as he had pressured Bragg into dropping his charges against Polk. It was not the same thing as concord, but there was a surface appearance. Still, after first appeasing Polk in Atlanta, Davis upset him once he had moved on to Marietta to meet with Bragg. Addressing some of Bragg's soldiers then besieging Chattanooga, the president was quoted by a war correspondent that "notwithstanding the shafts of malice that had been hurled at him, [Bragg] had bravely borne it all, and the bloody field of Chickamauga plainly stamps him as a military commander of the first order." Upon returning to Atlanta on October 15, Davis was confronted by Polk, now highly indignant. Polk brandished a newspaper and insisted on knowing just whom Davis regarded as the hurlers of those "shafts of malice?" Polk himself? His fellow officers who shared displeasure with Bragg's generalship? Employing a tactic as useful then as nowadays among public figures when cornered, Davis told Polk he had been misquoted.[20]

While Davis had clumsily been doing what he could to placate Polk and Bragg, the existence of the other malcontents' petition against Bragg had leaked out. Bragg offered to resign, but that gesture was dismissed by Davis. Now well assured of the president's favor, Bragg began ridding himself of the worst of his critics. Polk having slipped the crook, Daniel Harvey Hill, he of the "open and constant croaking," became his backup scapegoat. Not only did Hill resist "prompt conformity to orders," but, Bragg told the president, he "weakens the *morale* and military tone of his command." (Bragg was sure that Hill, not Buckner, had drafted the critical petition.) Besides, Hill's caustic personality had rankled Bragg's nerves and apparently grated upon them for years after. Sourly he would declare to a friend ten years later that Hill had "greatly demoralized the troops he commanded, and sacrificed thousands at Chickamauga."[21] And so, with no formal charges ever made, and with Jefferson Davis obliging, Bragg drove Daniel Hill out of the Army of Tennessee, consigning him to Azazel in the military wilderness. In this affair, the Davis biographer William C. Davis deftly defines the president, who "ceased to be presidential for the most part, and reverted to being Jefferson Davis."[22]

It would develop, fortunately, that General Hill, after presidential punishment, soon had a change of heart regarding General Polk. He had at first suspected Polk of being in league with Bragg and Davis, conspiring to hang all the Chickamauga blame on him. To find out the truth of that, while passing through Atlanta en route to his home in North Carolina (where he was to await the "reassignment" that would never come), Hill paid Polk a visit. Polk "expressed [so] much friendship and kindness" to Hill that, before moving on, Hill heartily repented of the hostile feelings he had brought with him. Hill had discussed his "coalition" suspicions with fellow generals before leaving the Tennessee army, and, after seeing Polk, he wrote back to his friend John Breckinridge, "regret[ting] that I spoke unkindly of him in regard to the coalition" Bragg had propounded. Hill added: "I am satisfied that Polk is too much of a man to make a compromise. Please mention the matter to General Cleburne and tell him that I am now convinced that Gen'l Polk never became a part of [the plot]."[23]

While the intrigues of Bragg and his critics were playing out, General Polk's wife, bringing a domestic calm to the scene, had arrived in Atlanta from Asheville. The one room she shared with her husband in the Thrashers' home took some getting used to. Where she had come from, off on the fringes of the war in western North Carolina, she and her family were situated in a nineteen-room house, sustaining themselves "comfortably" by hiring out to others the labor of the slaves they owned. The Asheville house even compared favorably with the antebellum plantation mansion the Polks had owned on La Fourche Bayou, she told a former neighbor.[24] Now making the best of wartime circumstances, Fanny and Leonidas soon rented a vacant Atlanta house. A mattress and bedstead were provided by a friend, but "everything else was the camp equipage, of the plainest and scantiest description." Happy, of course, to be with her husband, she still "saw but little of him, [as] so many persons of every grade called to testify their respect for him." Still, she was welcome to sit in on visitors' meetings with Polk, even regarded, Gale quipped, as "a member of the staff." Thus, she was present when Jefferson Davis came around. Davis had kept insisting, she remembered, that her husband take back his old corps command under Bragg. "This Gen. Polk steadily declined," Fanny reported. "On one occasion [the president] said, '*Why* will you not return?'" "'Because,'" was the reply, "'I am tired of being dry nurse to Gen. Bragg.'" Fanny remembered that "the President laughed, and said that was unanswerable." Polk was getting good usage out of his jokey metaphor.[25]

The two men's conversation on October 15 was especially revealing of Davis's determination to keep Polk with the Tennessee army—and of Polk's quandary on staying in the military at all. Fanny's recollection (a decade later) of the conversation, though the words seem stilted and the exchanges somewhat out of logical sequence, appears essentially trustworthy. Davis, Fanny recalled,

> again urged his return [to Bragg's army], and finding him firm in his refusal, offered him the choice of three positions, one in Richmond [in her handwritten memoir she lined through the words "held afterwards by Gen. Bragg"], the Trans-Mississippi [Department], and the situation in Mississippi then held by Gen. Hardee. Gen. Polk declined to choose, and expressed the wish that his services should be dispensed with. "That I cannot do," said the President. "I have twice refused to receive your resignation. I need your services. I have known you from a boy and by the remembrances of those early years and our friendship I must beg you to resume your old command."

When her husband still balked at Davis's perseverance, Fanny pictured the next moment climactically: "'Mr. President,' said Gen. Polk, rising from his seat, 'because you have known me from a boy is the very reason you should not make this request. Knowing me as you do, I ask you frankly, do you think I can accept?' 'Well,' said the President, 'I do not think you can, but I must have you elsewhere.'"[26] Thereupon, it was tentatively agreed that Polk might serve best in Gen. Joseph Johnston's Army of Mississippi. William Hardee, whom he would replace, would take Polk's place with Bragg at Chattanooga. Only months before, Hardee had been glad to get out from under Bragg's thumb, but it was Bragg, in fact, who had on October 1 proposed a Polk-for-Hardee switch to Davis. The president now proceeded with his visitation to various Confederate centers: Mobile, Alabama, and Jackson, Mississippi, for example. Then, after consulting with Johnston in Meridian, Mississippi (and having an acquiescent Hardee waiting in Demopolis, Alabama), Davis sent word to Polk on October 23 that the swap was arranged. If convenient to Polk, they could discuss details when the president reached Montgomery on October 27. The president was accompanied by John C. Pemberton, the general who after a forty-six-day siege had lately surrendered Vicksburg to Grant. Davis had considered assigning Pemberton to Polk's old corps in the Army of Tennessee. That idea, however, met with such wide disapprobation among the military that it was quietly dropped.

For the Montgomery meeting with Davis, Polk took with him Lt. William Gale, now holding a commission and serving as the successor to the slain aide-de-camp William Richmond. Gale was greatly heartened by the Montgomery interview and a subsequent train ride with the president; so, too, was Polk, even accepting that Bragg was "to be retained '*conti qui conti.*'"[27] Writing Willie Huger, Gale's soon-to-be kinsman, about the meetings, Gale said "nothing gratified me more than the appearance of . . . perfect friendship, confidence and harmony existing between [Davis and Polk]. So far from losing in the collision with Genl. Bragg, I am sure Genl. Polk has gained immensely, the future looking good."[28] To his wife, Gale wrote: "The Genl and all of us think well of this [Mississippi assignment] and prefer it to Richmond. There is no doubt a field here where reputation can be made." Gale passed along the gossip he overheard, as well. The president assured Polk there would be no clash of personalities between Polk and Gen. Joe Johnston, the man Davis blamed for his inability to extricate General Pemberton from the siege of Vicksburg. General Johnston "will be only too glad to have someone of life and energy enough to relieve him of all responsibility," Gale heard Davis say, an utterance evidently bearing a double meaning. Moreover, the president "intimated that if things did not work well he would create a new department for your father."[29]

While awaiting his transfer, Polk and Fanny were dismayed by alarming news from the home front purporting that arsonists had struck again, this time at the home in Asheville shared by the Polks and Gales. It was suspected that a household slave named Josh was involved. All in the family were safe, but Kate Gale urged her husband not to tell her mother of the fire until her father had heard of it. Once word was out in the Atlanta household, William Gale informed Kate that his mother-in-law (who had escaped the arsonists' attack at Sewanee in 1861) reacted with far more self-control than the general. "I do not think any of you properly understand your mother," Gale enlightened his wife.

> I find she has a great deal the most fortitude and composure under difficulties, and I should always go to her first. This was eminently shown in this matter. Your mother was cool, composed and quiet, while your father and I were anything but so. Your father . . . could not and did not control his feelings, the tears almost bursting out, and his voice becoming husky as I read your letter [aloud]. . . . He fairly roared out to me, "Yes, sir, put your trust in God. . . . God is stronger than devils."[30]

The menfolk's first reactions turned out to be a lot more than was required. Details arriving from the Polks' daughters in Asheville suggested that perhaps it had not been arson after all and that they too had overreacted to whatever kind of fire it was. Susan Polk informed her mother that "their mountains, they now think, were 'molehills.'" Immediate thoughts of fleeing Asheville were given up. Fanny was relieved, and since no man of the family had been at the house (the ailing Hamilton had gone to Raleigh), she was philosophical about her daughters' understandable fright. "The only possible way in which I think I could have been of use," she said, "would have been in making you to see things more as they really are."[31]

Whatever the true circumstances of the nighttime fire (little that clarifies the issue can be found in the family correspondence), General Polk's initial agitation soon matured into determined action: except for the fact that he had no proof, he was of a mind to have the slave Josh hanged. He settled on having him sent to a slave market in Augusta and sold. Gale was dispatched to arrest him and see to the sale by advertising Josh "as a No. 1 cook who has served some time in a New Orleans restaurant." Of course, the fire might have been set by white North Carolina "Tories," Polk conceded, but he could not shake a conviction of treachery by Josh. He recalled to a daughter how this slave had once "seemed so devoted [to the family] that he fell on his knees in New Orleans and begged your mother to allow him to follow her. But the race to which he belongs is, in its peculiarities, really unfathomable, and I can believe most anything of them."[32] Something he could not have foreseen was that Josh would have the impudence to escape from Gale's custody while the two were on the way to Augusta. Kate Gale also could not fathom the black man's perfidy. "His ingratitude was deplored by all," she assured her children in her postwar memoir, "Recollections of Life in the Confederacy."[33]

Polk and Hardee changed places in early November, Fanny and the general leaving Atlanta by train for Mississippi on November 7. Before they left, Hardee had passed through and dined with them. Having discussed staffing matters, Hardee after dinner paid Polk a picturesque compliment, telling Fanny that "I told your husband he was a saint, and if he was a horse his fetlocks would touch the ground."[34] Hardee had reason to rethink Polk's saintliness within days. He had just arrived at Bragg's army when he received from Polk an angry letter written on November 5, the tone of which, Hardee complained, was not in keeping with what he had a right to expect from a "brother officer, and especially from you. It was unjust and, permit me to say, uncharitable."[35] The fact that Polk had allowed himself to offend his friend arose from Polk's seething suspicion that Braxton Bragg's latest meanness was spitefully depriving Polk of certain favorite staff officers whom he wanted transferred with him to Mississippi. Polk seems to have believed that Hardee supported Bragg's staffing decisions.[36] Insofar as Hardee was concerned, Polk's blaming him proved mostly wrong. Rather, because one of the retained officers whom Polk wished to take along was named "Lieut. Polk," Hardee had gone "in person [to Bragg] to learn the status of Lieut. Polk [and to] secure his transfer.[37] As far as was in my power," Hardee assured Polk, "[I] honestly and earnestly exerted myself to further your wishes. Conscious of having deserved well at your hands, imagine my surprise and my pain at receiving your very unkind letter."[38]

Polk's reaction to Hardee's rebuke could have been blushing chagrin, but his opportunity to make amends a few weeks later was missed. Hardee had by then wed the "almost beautiful" Mary Foreman Lewis, an Alabama belle of twenty-six whom the general had met the previous September. During their mid-January honeymoon train trip to Mobile, Hardee, Mary, and their wedding party (including best man Patrick Cleburne) were to pass through Polk's new headquarters town (Enterprise, Mississippi), with a layover of three-quarters of an hour. The telegram inviting Fanny and General Polk to toast the newlyweds at the train station was delayed in transit, however, and the rendezvous was missed. "So the Gen passed and nobody saw him," Fanny lamented to a daughter. "Most unfortunate." (More fortunate was General Cleburne. During the festive nuptial proceedings in Marengo County, Alabama, he fell in love with the maid of honor, Susan Tarleton. Now finding the Alabama belle he hoped someday to marry, Cleburne would die in battle at Franklin, Tennessee, before that day ever came.)[39]

On their way earlier to Enterprise in east-central Mississippi, the Polks had spent their second day out from Atlanta in Montgomery, Alabama, with Gen. Jones Mitchell Withers, a Polk comrade since Shiloh and a reliable anti-Bragg ally. They then moved on to Enterprise. Lying about 120 miles directly east of Union-held Vicksburg, Enterprise had lately become the temporary capital of Confederate Mississippi and was a kind of holding pen for 30,000 idle soldiers. Survivors of Vicksburg's siege and Port Hudson's subsequent fall to Grant, the troops had either been paroled or were awaiting exchange and constituted Polk's new army. Through the piney woods just to the south of Polk's headquarters was Meridian, a newly built rail junction and storage depot that was as important to the Confederates as anything they then held.

The Polks found lodging in a house "kindly offered us by [Brigadier General John W.] O'Ferrall," a resident of the town. Again tents went up in the front yard for Polk's office and his staff's living quarters. A friend in Mobile sent the Polks a jar of oysters; someone else sent a haunch of venison, a pair of wild ducks, lettuce and tomatoes, salad oil, and mustard and pepper. As Fanny remembered it, "Those were happy days passed in the log room sixteen feet square, lighted by one window, and I enjoyed it more than I can tell."[40] There had been some bad times, too, she admitted. Her husband was brought to bed not long after they had settled in by a severe "inflammation of the lungs," probably a flare-up of his chronic lung disability. Fanny took over as nurse, "and not having the fear of the medical doctors before my eyes," on her own she prescribed "aerials of begonia." As an herbal medicine (esteemed by some to this day), it either brought about, or did not greatly hinder, his recovery.[41] Lying ill while hoping the flower medicine worked, Polk would often say to his wife, "I am so glad you are here, so glad you are here." Much of their time together, said Fanny, "was passed in repeating [Prayer Book] collects, and in having me read the Bible to him, the lessons for the day and psalms and other parts which bore upon them. He seemed to commune constantly with God; and when I was not reading, I often heard him in prayer. He was daily fitting for heaven." The general spent other moments longing for homelife denied. With so much of his family far off in Asheville, "he feels cheated in losing so much of the childhood of his grandchildren." Some semblance of family life was supplied by Sally, their twenty-three-year-old daughter, who had come to Enterprise in

November. "She and her father had much to say," Fanny noted, but Sally's diversions were soon used up; by January her mother conceded: "She is having a very dull time and I am sorry your father sent for her."[42]

When Polk was able to arise wobbly from his sickbed, it was only to receive a setback of a different kind. Distressing word came from Chattanooga in late November. Braxton Bragg's army and many of Polk's old troops had been routed out of their rifle pits on the steep flanks of Lookout Mountain and Missionary Ridge. Gen. George Thomas, the Rock of Chickamauga, had chased them up and over the slopes. It was the final unraveling of Bragg's fleeting Chickamauga success two months before, and Bragg would soon be relieved consequently of his command and removed all the way to Richmond. Just before Christmas 1863, though, Polk received an uplifting letter about Chattanooga from John Henry Linebaugh, the journalist and former priest from Polk's diocese. "All say that we would not have been driven off so shamefully at the bottom of Lookout if 'Roderick' had been there," Linebaugh wrote.[43] Linebaugh's mention of "Roderick" was sure to have stirred General Polk's Scottish blood. Since his boyhood he had doted upon the writings of Sir Walter Scott, and fanciful Roderick Dhu had been among his heroes. In Scott's epic poem *The Lady of the Lake*, the exploits of Clan-Alpine's chieftain are recounted. Imprisoned after losing a duel with King James V of Scotland, Roderick Dhu's always-inspiring presence was lacking next day upon the battlefield when James's Lowlanders (think "Yankees," as Linebaugh did) charged up a mountainside, overwhelming the rebel Highlanders (Confederates). While Roderick languished in prison, Scott's minstrel sang the bad news: *"Clan-Alpine's best are backward borne—Where, where, was Roderick then!—One blast upon his bugle-horn / Were worth a thousand men."*[44]

For John Linebaugh and Leonidas Polk's other partisans, it was thus the Confederacy's misfortune at Chattanooga that on November 25 their favorite, inspiring general, shunted off to Mississippi, was fatefully absent on the rocky flanks of Lookout Mountain.

25

A "Monstrous Proposition . . . Revolting to Southern Sentiment" (1863–1864)

Whatever aches and pains Leonidas Polk had endured because of his inflamed lungs and the Confederates' disheartening defeat by the Yankees at Chattanooga (a reversal mitigated a little for Polk by Bragg's subsequent removal from his command), they were transitory. Headaches would shortly pile up, however, in his new posting "among the pines and in the sand of Mississippi," as William Gale described it. Not fully prepared for what he was getting into, Polk would later point out to an inspector general sent from Richmond that he had commenced his duties in Mississippi "with the unusual difficulties of a staff new to the locality, and as unacquainted as himself with the details of service in the territory."[1] And like the pines and sand, the Yankees themselves were plentiful in the region, swarming in Polk's way in February. Yet more immediate aggravations were plaguing the general's administration.

At the top on his list were the 10,000 military-age men (by Polk's estimate) who were idling in his department far from any combat where they could be put to good use. The more acceptable in this crowd were the paroled, but still loosely organized, troops milling around Enterprise and Meridian. They had been captured at Vicksburg or Port Hudson and had given their "paroles" (their words of honor) not to take up arms against the Union until the Confederate government had formally exchanged them for captured Yankees. The other idlers, whom Polk deemed completely unacceptable, were the deserters lying low in the region, as well as the many draft dodgers enjoying "the evils ensuing upon the inefficient administration of the conscript laws," as Polk had put it to Col. George Hodge, the inspector general dispatched from

Richmond.[2] (Electioneering for peace candidates was the pastime of some of these citizens.)[3]

Added to these manpower issues annoying Polk were the complaints of civilians opposed to slave-impressment demands put upon them by the army; the strictures against their trading with the enemy; and the galling reports that Yankee recruiters were successfully organizing mounted regiments in northern Alabama.[4] Finally, marauding Tory copperheads—sympathetic to the Union, hostile to the ruling secessionist state governments of Alabama and Mississippi, and in some cases opposed to slavery and champions of the black people in their midst—were gaining the upper hand in a few counties under Polk's administration. One feisty mother had even named her newborn Abe Lincoln. Mississippi's Jones County was the center of this virulent dissent, led by Newton Knight, a former Confederate soldier who earlier had been pressed into service by coercive recruiters. Deserting the army after the Confederates' drubbing at Corinth in the summer of 1862, Knight became the leader of some ninety-five disaffected rural poor Mississippians—"white trash" and "scalawags" their planter betters would have called them—who had become an insurgent devilment to Polk and his troops. It was even rumored that during Polk's military administration Jones County, Knight's home county, had declared itself seceded from the Confederacy altogether. If Jones County hadn't actually gone that far, the area was at least the battleground of the war within the war that Polk had stepped into.[5]

Given these mounting demands on his general, Lieutenant Gale had been premature in early December when he told his wife that "the truth is there is nothing for us to do. . . . We are laid on the shelf for the present, and no mistake."[6] He got it more accurately soon after when he described Polk's new theater as "a field . . . where [a] reputation can be made." Fanny Polk, a newly arrived visitor in Enterprise, saw as much right away. "There is an immense amount to be done," she discerned in the town that November. "But there seems no head." Her critical view (surely reflecting her husband's) referred obliquely to the general still in charge of the department: Joseph E. Johnston.[7]

To help end the turmoil in which he found himself, Polk in November instituted the first of his attempts to corral the absentee parolees and the "laggards and deserters" eligible for conscription. Getting his headquarters in Enterprise up and running, he first initiated Jefferson Davis's order to take "command of the prisoners captured and paroled at Port Hudson and Vicksburg." He sent out a directive addressed to all parolees throughout the region who might be expected to be in the reach of local newspapers.

It informed them that, while their exchanges were pending, they were not on leave and were to report for duty forthwith. The idea that many of the vacationing parolees entertained, "that you are free from all military control, so long as you are not exchanged, is fallacious," Polk's directive said. "Your duty . . . is . . . to return to your colors, where honor and patriotism alike call you." Two months later, honor and patriotism having failed to motivate as many as he had hoped, Polk reissued the circular, turning up the heat for noncompliance. Now officers and men had just fifteen days to report to Enterprise or be declared deserters subject to the harsh penalties that crime entailed.[8]

At that early stage, Polk had also concluded that, for him to succeed with the personnel problems in the department, it was essential to get out from under General Johnston's thumb. To that end, he was aided in early December 1863 by his behind-the-scenes efforts to have Johnston take over the still leaderless Army of Tennessee. Rarely inhibited by formalities of military protocol, Polk again offered unsolicited advice to his contact in Richmond, the Confederate president, signing his letter "very truly your friend." Fraternally granting that both he and Davis had "difficulties . . . in regard to the man," Polk nonetheless thought "Johnston is the person to whom you should offer the Army of Tennessee."[9] (William Hardee, when about to marry Mary Lewis, had already declined Davis's request that he replace Bragg.) There was one other issue to deal with. Inasmuch as Polk himself was logically the general to succeed Johnston at the head of the Army of Mississippi, he knew Davis might think him devious in promoting Johnston's appointment. So Polk reminded the president that, back when he had nothing to gain personally, "both in writing and verbally" he had several times before recommended Johnston. Polk hoped that he might now do so again "without the risk of [a] seeming indelicacy." Finally, allowing again for Davis's dislike of Johnston, Polk insisted that his own grasp of the sympathies of the Army of Tennessee—indeed, his understanding "of the [whole] country on the same subject"—required him to say that "your duty seems to your friend to be to yield to this general desire." Davis's "magnanimity" would doubtless allow him to make the appointment.[10]

Magnanimity played no role. Failing in persistent efforts to get others, including Robert E. Lee, to take the Army of Tennessee, and badgered by the Confederate Congress to come up with someone, Davis went along with Polk.[11] By the following week, December 16, he had put in motion the appointments of three high-ranking generals: The cashiered Bragg was to work as an adviser in Davis's office in Richmond; the disesteemed Johnston was to take over the Army of Tennessee in Georgia; and the bishop was to take charge of a newly configured and spread-out Department of the Southwest.

The responsibilities of Polk's new appointment were entrusted to the small-scale Army of Mississippi, a situation Polk was driven to complain about within weeks.[12] Scattered widely over the state, the little army comprised two infantry divisions (under Maj. Gens. William W. Loring and Samuel G. French) and two cavalry "departments": 7,500 troopers in southern Mississippi under Maj. Gen. Stephen Dill Lee, and 3,000 more in northern Mississippi and West Tennessee under the newly minted major general (rapidly up from private) Nathan Bedford Forrest, whose troopers were the scourge of hapless Yankees caught in the western Confederacy. In late January, Polk's jurisdiction over this assemblage was once again renamed: it was now the Department of Alabama, Mississippi, and East Louisiana.[13] At that time, imposing enemy concentrations were hunkering close to the Mississippi Confederates' Meridian headquarters. The Union's XVII Army Corps under Maj. Gen. James B. McPherson was stationed some 130 miles to the west in Vicksburg. The XVI Corps under Maj. Gen. Stephen A. Hurlburt was in Memphis, 200 miles to the northwest. Still more Federals were camped along the Tennessee River in northern Alabama.

Now undertaking to recharge the combative zeal of the soldiers in his Mississippi command, Polk on December 23 issued his General Orders No. 1. Forgoing Christmastide greetings, his religious sentiments were focused on the war and were all but identical to what they had been when he first took command of an army in the fall of 1861. Again, he inveighed against those who dishonored the Holy Bible: New England's barbarous horde of fanatics (the abolitionists) and the Middle-West's "infidels of German descent."[14] These hellish Yankees, he again reminded his soldiers, had come to the South to plunder her menfolk of their political rights, their property, their social life, their altars, and their womenfolk—*especially* their women, "who everywhere regard our invaders with loathing and abhorrence." Where God stood on the issue was clear, he added: "It was a maxim of the religion [even] of the heathen that the gods helped those that helped themselves. The teachings of purer and truer [Christian] faith have served to confirm and establish [this]."[15]

The commanding general's impassioned general orders notwithstanding, lingering dissatisfactions with camp life were still agitating some of his men. So a few days after his exhortation had been read to the army, Polk decided it might be useful to speak to his legions in person. In wintry weather, he "had them marched to one place and formed in hollow squares," William Gale reported. "He then mounted a table in the center [and] delivered a stump speech two hours long." Whatever rousing things their commander said to them, the chilled men were possibly glad to hear—and glad for sure once he finished: "The men gave him three cheers."[16]

Just before the end of the year, Polk had moved his headquarters from Enterprise to Meridian.[17] Meridian's hundred or so citizens had been drawn to the thirty-three-year-old village by the commercially promising junction of the state's recently built rail lines. Polk and Fanny and their daughter Sally occupied a one-story wing connected to a larger house owned by J. H. Gary, a prosperous resident. Polk's nearby headquarters house was a three-room cottage. Fanny recalled that, though her husband was worn down by the many burdens he had inherited, no day of his ended, no matter what the hour, that he did not awaken her "to have prayers." The prayers, she had noted with concern, included some for himself.[18]

Sometimes it must have seemed that results were in the hands of fickle fate. All of a sudden reappearing on Polk's horizon was Brig. Gen. Gideon Pillow, the irrepressibly egocentric subordinate who had once questioned Polk's sanity and fitness for command.[19] Now, three winters later, it was Pillow's own efficiency and fitness to command that were being critically reviewed by the War Department. Pillow had in recent months found a useful niche in his Volunteer and Conscript Bureau in the Army of Tennessee.[20] He was praised, in fact, in Alabama and Mississippi for his extralegal methods of corralling draft dodgers and deserters, which had placed about 25,000 fresh troops on the Confederate front lines. But his success had so aroused the jealousy of more conventional officers in the government's Bureau of Conscription in Richmond that they engineered his removal from the job.[21]

Pillow was ever one to rebound when knocked down. Brushing himself off, he offered the War Department an idea that would especially benefit his old adversary Polk. What the war in the West needed, he told authorities in Richmond, was a cavalry connection linking Joe Johnston's army in Georgia to Leonidas Polk's army in Mississippi. Pillow thought himself just the man to provide that link by commanding two brigades stationed in north-central Alabama below Huntsville and the Tennessee River. These troopers would shield the region's essential coal mines, ironworks and cotton mills from the hateful invader. Pillow sent similar messages to Polk and Johnston. Showing characteristic grace (and seeing how it might prove helpful) Polk telegraphed him: "I am disposed to think favorably of your proposition . . . and think you had better come to my headquarters that I may confer with you about it."[22] The reunion of the two in Meridian—the first since Pillow's Belmont accusations—was vintage Pillow and vintage Polk. Henry Yeatman, another of Polk's aides-de-camp, sat in on their ten-hour meeting and reported its highlights to Fanny Polk. She passed them along in a letter to a daughter. "Your father," she wrote,

> met [General Pillow] as if they had parted as ordinary acquaintances a few hours before. "Good morning, Gen.—take a seat—I received your dispatch," etc. When they had gotten through the business, Gen. Pillow laid his hand on your father's arm & said, "Now, Gen., you must permit me to explain the past, & tell you that I regret having acted [after Belmont] from misconception," etc. etc. . . . [He] finished by saying that his mind [at the time] was sore & "I think Gen. in my place you would have acted as I did."
>
> "'There we differ,' was your father's reply."

Fanny concluded: "Your father came out and told us he would dine with us, and we must be very civil."[23]

With Polk's endorsement, General Pillow soon set about establishing his pet project of a two-brigade guard of Alabama's iron and coal deposits. (Polk, indeed, thought he merited a division.)[24] But Pillow's initial optimism was soon dashed. Too many animosities in Richmond and military resentments in the Southeast were arranged against him, and as the months passed into summer his brigades never materialized. And by then Polk, his essential champion, had been killed.

Just as Gideon Pillow had been led to employ renegade recruitment methods by the Confederacy's growing manpower problems, so another of Polk's military associates (and a friend), Gen. Patrick Cleburne, had come up with an even more radical way to replenish the army's dwindling ranks. Cleburne proposed to thirteen fellow officers that the Confederate government remit the slave status of able-bodied black males and, giving them guns, send them into combat. Slaves were already being impressed for noncombat duties, thereby releasing white soldiers for fighting, while some other Southern blacks—either emancipated by Federal occupation forces or simply having escaped from their owners—were enlisting in the Union Army. To bolster his emancipation argument, Cleburne reasoned the black Yankee soldiers would lose heart and desert once Confederate blacks appeared in combat against them.[25] Cleburne knew he was handling highly combustible material, and he had first broached his idea in Dalton to a select assembly of Army of Tennessee generals, all of them Polk's former associates. But some of those gathered were aghast at what they were hearing and made sure that like-minded friends (such as President Davis himself) got word of the radical suggestion.

General Polk was among those alerted and was beseeched by one man to help undo somehow what he termed this "monstrous proposition . . . revolting to Southern sentiment." This ardent plea came from Polk's admiring friend, Brig. Gen. James Patton Anderson, a Tennessee physician-lawyer-politician-soldier who had served with Polk since Shiloh. "No one," Anderson now wrote, "knows better than yourself all the hidden powers and secret springs which move the great moral machinery of the South." (Polk may have nodded modest assent reading this plaudit.) So, Anderson agonized, what is to be done? "If this thing is once openly proposed to the Army, the total disintegration of that Army will follow in a fortnight," he said. "And yet to speak and work in opposition to it is an agitation of the question scarcely less to be dreaded." Anderson was sure that citizens and soldiers alike would heap so much wrath on Cleburne's head that it would crush "one of our bravest and most accomplished officers." Faced with that quandary, Anderson begged Polk in the letter, dated January 14, 1864, to "favor me by mail with some of the many thoughts which this subject will arouse in your mind."[26] However many thoughts Polk may have given the issue, they were evidently not communicated to Patton Anderson, at least in a timely manner.[27] Worried as much as anyone by the thinning Rebel ranks, he might well have been open to Cleburne's view; he had never revealed such loathing of blacks as had Anderson.

Inconceivable as the idea of arming slaves was to some, the antagonisms between Patrick Cleburne and Patton Anderson and between Cleburne and Bragg were not the only interpersonal conflicts disturbing the Confederacy; still high among Polk's priorities was the disarming of two of his battling friends, Jefferson Davis and Joseph Johnston. He was sure the lengthy, publicly known friction between the two was seriously subverting the South's prosecution of the war in the West, and he now resolved to attempt a reconciliation—a fitting role for a bishop. (Meridian's Episcopal parish, to which Polk must have repaired from time to time, was aptly named the Church of the Mediator.)

A few weeks earlier, to further his reconciling objective, Polk had talked with Edwin J. Harvie, a colonel on General Johnston's staff about to join his commander in Dalton. Polk outlined to Harvie the sly solution he wished to try: Harvie was to persuade Johnston to compose a letter to a friend known to be on equally good terms with Johnston and Davis—a letter to be shown subsequently to the president by the collaborating acquaintance. In the letter to this person (his identity is unknown) Johnston would concede ("without at all lowering the tone of a manly independence," in Polk's words) that the lack of "cordial feeling" between himself and Davis was "for himself . . . a subject of regret." For the public good, Johnston would be prompted to say he "was prepared to waive all that was past." Polk felt sure that, once these lofty sentiments were read by Davis, the "overture" would be received in the best spirit and the results would be "eminently conducive to the success of our military operations." As Polk was well aware of the prickly natures of both men, he did concede that Johnston's having to write such a self-subjugating letter might cost him "some sacrifices of feeling." It may have been just this cost that General Johnston was unwilling to pay; or it may be that he *did* write the letter and, after the mutual friend sent it along, Davis tossed it aside. What is sure, Polk's peacemaking was unavailing; the enmity between the two proud men would continue to flourish long after the war.[28]

General Polk was still trying to "familiarize himself with the novelties of his position" in Mississippi when in late January he was warned by General Johnston from Georgia "that there was every reason to believe the enemy were preparing a raid against the coal and iron fields of central Alabama." The Yankees would be coming down from northern Alabama.[29] While digesting that bad news, word came to Polk of other rumored Yankee movements, perils compassing Polk about from the Gulf Coast in the south, from Vicksburg in the west, and from Memphis in the north. Of all the reports, those concerning Vicksburg and Memphis were to prove the most accurate and immediately dire: a face-to-face confrontation with William T. Sherman was about to unfold. Denied reinforcements both by Johnston in Georgia and by Beauregard in South Carolina, themselves pressed hard by other Yankees, Polk was certain that Sherman was a formidable foe against whom he could not prevail. He set himself the task of making the best of a bad situation.

Sherman's pending campaign was to be a sampling of his concept of total war that he later exemplified in his 1864 sweep through Georgia and South Carolina. As practiced this time, it would be a demoralizing, thirty-day round-trip raid from Vicksburg with fewer than 750 casualties almost evenly divided between Federals and Confederates—but abundant personal loss and suffering by the "hostile people" who happened to live along Sherman's ravaging route. (Five thousand slaves, moreover, were caught up and carried along to freedom.)[30] Before setting out to prove the bishop's instincts right, Major General Sherman had defined what he hoped to achieve in the pending campaign in a dispatch to Ulysses S. Grant. Apart from his intention to demoralize thoroughly the citizens of Middle Mississippi ("Whenever a result can be achieved without a battle, I prefer it," he had written at about the same time), his destructive designs were aimed primarily at

Meridian. It was a railway hub bulging with engines and boxcars and was piled high with war matériel. Sherman and his army had just returned to Vicksburg flush with success in November's victory against Bragg at Chattanooga, and he now promised Grant he would lay to waste Mississippi's railroad system—"east and west, north and south"—in order to "isolate the State from the rest of the Confederacy."[31]

And just maybe, once in Meridian, he would make some more mischief, he told Grant and other interested generals. Having all but reached the Alabama state line, Sherman reckoned his infantry might then risk proceeding south and east. Awaiting him in Alabama were two prizes: Mobile on the Gulf Coast, a priceless supply-line seaport; and Selma in central Alabama, rich in coal and iron ore deposits, local foundries, military stores, and shipbuilding facilities. With the iron at hand to make the ships, and the Alabama River to float them to the sea, Selma shipwrights had just launched their best effort, the formidable ram CSS *Tennessee*, then the world's most powerful warship (and destined soon to play a starring role in the Battle of Mobile Bay).[32]

In a cautionary reaction, Grant would say that any expedition by Sherman beyond Meridian into Alabama should be undertaken very carefully, if at all. Thinking in the long term, Grant told General-in-Chief H. W. Halleck: "Sherman will be instructed, whilst left with large discretionary powers, to take no extra hazard of losing his army, or of getting it crippled too much for efficient service in the Spring against Joseph E. Johnston's Army of Tennessee."[33] Sherman's discretionary powers, in any case, would be subject to the effectiveness of a cooperating cavalry brigadier. William Sooy Smith, at the head of some 7,000 cavalry troops coming down from Memphis, was to coordinate his arrival in Meridian with Sherman's. Thereafter, the combined force—if they then chose to do so—could push Polk aside and roll unmolested into Alabama. True, General Smith's middle name led some Rebels to snigger, but he had graduated sixth in the 1853 class at West Point (Polk was eighth in his), and in the words of one Nathan Bedford Forrest biographer, Smith was a soldier "of capacity and courageous imagination." Forrest was now an essential component of Polk's new army, but Smith, nothing daunted, vowed to Sherman that he "would pitch into Forrest wherever I find him."[34] That was bravado with a catch. Sherman warned Smith that the reputation of the fearsome Confederate cavalry warrior was such that, in a fight, Forrest and his troopers could get the best of double their numbers. General Grant was of the same opinion, writing that "for the particular kind of warfare which Forrest had carried on, neither army could present a more effective officer than he was."[35] The best advice Sherman had for Smith was a three-step tactic: after Smith was attacked and, Sherman hoped, he had repelled Forrest, Smith "must in turn assume the most determined [counter] offensive, overwhelm him, and utterly destroy his whole force."[36]

As January 1864 drew to a close, spies in Vicksburg alerted Polk that Sherman's crushing expedition into the Mississippi interior was about to begin. At least four divisions of infantry, some 20,000 or more soldiers, would be headed toward Polk in Meridian.[37] (Rumors to that effect from General Forrest and others most likely had reached Polk earlier in the month.)[38] With the warnings accumulating on his desk, Polk had gone across Mississippi for a closer look—to the "front beyond Pearl River, in the neighborhood of Canton, northwest of Jackson." Becoming "satisfied that it is [the enemy's] intention to move . . . on this department at an early day, and in heavy force," he reminded his War Department that "the whole of my force is very small, inadequate to the emergency."[39] (On this point, Polk and Sherman were in full agreement. Sherman had already advised Grant that, barring early word of his invasion leaking to General Johnston in Georgia, who might then send reinforcements, "General Polk cannot have at Canton, Brandon and Meridian a force [adequate] to meet me.")[40] Polk thought it prudent to notify Jefferson Davis as well of his plight and did so directly a few days later, mentioning his worry that not just Sherman but other Yankee movements from northern Alabama were threatening the coal and iron center of that state. (And to do their manly part, almost 200 sixteen- and eighteen-year-old cadets at the University of Alabama had been called upon by Gideon Pillow to help man the ramparts in Selma.)[41]

With a timetable meant to be followed reliably by his subordinates, Sherman then launched the campaign on February 1, a troop of cavalry leading the way. A couple of days later, he rode out with the second of his two columns of infantry and artillery; they numbered in all about 26,000 infantry and 1,000 cavalry and departed in fair weather on good roads. Already behind schedule was William Sooy Smith's cavalry force of 7,000 riders and artillery assembling near Memphis. One of three brigades needed by Smith for the joint venture with Sherman was stationed in the far northwestern corner of Tennessee. Frozen mud along the banks of various Tennessee rivers along their path, ice in the water, and destroyed bridges so delayed the arrival of these men of the 4th Missouri that Smith's full aggregation of riders was a week late pulling itself together, and they did not mount up and head down into Mississippi until February 11. Getting wind of the Fourth Missouri's wintry travails, Sherman sputtered: "It is a disgrace to the cavalry arm of the service that they cannot cross a creek." Even crossing the state line into Mississippi gave some of the troopers pause as well. As the Forrest biographer Jack Hurst has written: "Smith seemed to take [Sherman's Forrest] warning much to heart. An eerie hint of dread pervades a Smith subordinate's description of crossing the Mississippi border into 'rough, hopeless, God-forsaken' Tippah County, the homeland of Forrest's youth. 'Its hills were steep, its mud was deep, its houses and farms were poor, its streams, torrents of muddy water, fast swelling from the thaw.'" By then, Sherman's fast-moving trans-Mississippi infantry was within striking distance of Meridian.[42]

When Sherman had organized the Meridian Campaign, he had ordered a train of 1,000 wagons; that was plenty for his ammunition but scarcely enough for his men's rations. The 23,500 soldiers crossing middle Mississippi were told to live off the land. "Celerity" was Sherman's defining word for the expedition, and he declared "not a tent, from the commander-in-chief down, was to be carried by the army."[43] At the same time, Federal Navy gunboats had commenced diversionary antics at Pascagoula, Mississippi, and in sight of Confederate fortifications on Mobile Bay, and two noisy land operations had begun elsewhere: the one from northern Alabama that had Polk worried, and another along the Yazoo River north of Vicksburg. These secondary operations, meant to obscure Sherman's intentions and to strain Confederate resources, gave considerable pleasure to the Federal admiral David Farragut. Assigned to play the deceptive role in Mobile Bay, he said, "I shall . . . amuse myself in that way for the next month."[44]

In a postwar recollection of the Meridian campaign from the Confederates' perspective, Polk's chief of cavalry, Maj. Gen. Stephen Dill Lee, sketched a laudatory portrait of his commander under Sherman's assault. He asserted, indeed, that Polk, assisted by Nathan Bedford Forrest, had "outgeneraled Sherman."[45] Polk from the outset (according to Lee) had "discredited what some of his spies told him was the enemy's target: Meridian." Instead, Polk deemed it improbable that Sherman intended to stop there. Such a shortsighted campaign with neither Mobile nor Selma as his actual targets, he reasoned, would neither benefit the Yankees nor much hurt the Confederacy. Confident he was right about Sherman's true designs (and certain he was outnumbered), Polk, "in the exercise of a wise discretion, determined from the first not to fight Sherman." Rather, he "plainly showed he did not want Sherman materially interfered with, but rather encouraged to move as far as he would." As General Lee nicely phrased it, his "entire cavalry force [was] to leave Sherman in his loneliness."[46]

Meanwhile, having had the defenses around Selma and Mobile strengthened by thousands of Alabama and Mississippi slaves impressed to carry out the labor, Polk would bide his time as the oblivious Yankees stretched their supply line from Vicksburg until it snapped. At that point, he would then spring his surprise, sending his Mississippi soldiers and a complement of others borrowed from the Army of Tennessee to fall upon the hapless foe. By such slyness, said Lee, Polk would "readily crush [Sherman's] ill-considered movement."[47]

Though later supporting Polk's plan, Lee did not at first agree with the wait-and-pounce strategy. Neither did Maj. Gen. William Loring, the nervy and widely experienced infantry leader of one of Polk's two divisions. Even before Sherman left Vicksburg, both Lee and Loring had urged Polk by dispatches to make a stand in the semicircle of breastworks and rifle pits facing west outside Jackson, Mississippi, some forty miles east of Vicksburg. (The deserted Confederate works were left over from the previous summer.) Polk's response is not recorded, but the two generals' advice was not taken.[48] Since Polk at the time was either in Meridian or Mobile, far removed from conditions lately unfolding on the front line, the generals' irritation with their commander can be imagined.

Stephen Lee's cavalry did confront and very slightly check the pace of Sherman's two massive columns of infantry once they departed Vicksburg. Other cavalry troopers harassed the marchers' flanks and rear, discouraging foraging parties from straying too far from the protection of the main column. The owners of plantations and farms closest to the roads, therefore, felt the full brunt of Sherman's total war: Smokehouses were emptied of hams and bacon, farmyards of chickens and turkeys; sawmills, warehouses, cotton gins, cotton bales, public buildings, and 2 millions bushels of corn were set afire; thousands of slaves were set free. Afterward, on their trudge back to Vicksburg with Sherman, the slaves' columns were said to stretch more than ten miles.[49] Polk nevertheless took some satisfaction in his cavalry's general success circumscribing the enemy. He boasted to the War Department that "a drove of hogs of mine was on the way east and pursued a route within six miles on an average of [Sherman's] line of march without molestation, and have arrived safely."[50]

If the Yankees' progress was impeded to some extent by Stephen Lee's cavalry harassment, it was assisted by an oversight on General Polk's part. The Southern Railroad of Mississippi, a line originating in Vicksburg and running east to Meridian, had been badly damaged by the summer battles of 1863, but the line retained potential benefit to the Confederates by connecting Clinton and Jackson to Meridian. On Christmas Eve 1863, more than a month before Sherman's expedition began, Polk had ordered Maj. Gen. Samuel French "to go to Jackson and put the railroad and the bridges in repair."[51] How far along French's infantrymen (assisted by impressed slaves) had gotten with their repairs isn't clear, but around February 1, 1864, Polk woke up to the value the repaired rail line would now have for the Yankees.[52] Immediately, he ordered Stephen Lee to commence "the thorough destruction of the railroad from Jackson to Vicksburg," wrecking the rails toward Sherman's front "as far west as possible."[53]

For his part, Sam French was to stop his repairing and join in Lee's wrecking, but the crucial moment had passed. By the time Polk's order reached French (on the afternoon of Friday, February 5), Sherman's infantry was in possession of the repaired western section of the trackage, marching along it straight toward Jackson. As John Howe, a chipper Yankee colonel would record, when his Illinois soldiers in the vanguard entered Clinton ten miles to the west, they were stepping along smartly behind their bands, the "music playing and the blue banner flung out to the breeze." With Sherman now bearing down on Jackson and only six miles out, French replied to Polk succinctly: "Your dispatch received. Impossible to comply."[54]

The Yankees were not only making good time; like Colonel Howe's men, they were also enjoying themselves. "We had some pretty skirmishes on our way out and handled the enemy's cavalry rather roughly," was how Sherman saw it.[55] A high point galling to the Southerners occurred on the morning of the second day, when the head of the column commanded by Maj. Gen. Stephen A. Hurlburt reached a plantation owned by Joseph Emory Davis, the Confederate president's older brother. Wanting to make a good defensive showing at such a symbolic site, but woefully outnumbered, Col. Peter Starke's Confederate cavalry brigade (native Mississippians, for the most part) was brushed aside by Hurlburt's men, who swept through the plantation like swarming locusts.[56] Sherman was cheered by such pushovers, but other times might lapse into exaggeration, as when he claimed his troops were "marching roughshod over all opposition."[57] Not all opposition. While Hurlburt was laying waste the Davis plantation, Brig. Gen. Lawrence Ross, commanding Texan cavalry at a distant point along the Yazoo River, "fought the [Yankees] on foot with pistols at 12 paces" and drove them off with "severe loss." Ross with his six-shooters was routinely ferocious.[58] He and his men a few weeks later fought a Federal cavalry force that this time was made up largely of regiments of United States Colored Troops mounted on mules. Putting these overmatched soldiers to flight (and worse) along the Benton–Yazoo City Road, Ross gloated in his official report that his horsemen had overtaken the enemy and had left "the road all the way to Yazoo City . . . literally strewed with their bodies." Col. James H. Coates, a better-equipped adversary who would fight Ross's men to a draw on March 5, protested to Ross during a battleground parley that he was convinced the slain soldiers on the Benton Road "had been brutally used . . . and murdered after having been taken prisoners." Ross did not deny it. He told his own commander that he did "not recognize Negroes as soldiers deserving the treatment accorded prisoners of war." Certainly General Polk also knew of these atrocities, for his aide William Gale wrote his wife on April 7 that "a company of Negroes with white officers (56 men) was attacked by Ross near Yazoo City, and as 6 got away, the others were all killed. [Ross's Texans] never take any prisoners. . . . His name is the terror of the Yazoo." The extent to which Polk objected to these measures is not known.[59]

Left undefended on Polk's orders, Jackson had been Sherman's first major stopping point. Confederate supplies had once been piled high in the town, but otherwise the state capital did not amount to much anymore, neither a prize to defend nor to capture. It had been fought over twice before and was so badly incinerated in the crossfire that it was now spoken of as Chimneyville. As Sherman drew near and the jeopardized stores were being hastily hauled to the eastern side of Jackson's Pearl River, the Confederate brigadier general Wirt Adams's 800 dismounted cavalrymen and Capt. Houston King's rifled artillery made a series of delaying demonstrations on the western side of town. Outmanned at least fifteen-to-one in the fights he picked, Adams was more calculating than crazy; he carefully measured the enemy's threat and withdrew his command gradually as Sherman came closer. (As Adams's commander, General Lee, put it: "Every man [knew] by actual observation the strength of the enemy.")[60] By the late afternoon of February 5, Adams's troopers were prudently scrambling over and through the empty breastworks, making haste to get out of the desolated town altogether.[61]

That same day, Polk from Mobile was urging General Loring to use his infantry to "detain the enemy as long as possible from getting into Jackson." If Polk "did not want Sherman materially interfered with," as Lee says, this order suggests that perhaps Polk was sometimes unsure of his resolve to lure Sherman into a trap. He further assured Loring that 6,000 reinforcements were hastening to the "front." (This front was more a moving line, redrawn eastward almost daily, and by then was about twelve miles east of Jackson.) Polk added that he was on his way to the front too.[62] The order came, of course, too late; by that evening, Samuel French and his feeble force of 2,200 soldiers had likewise evacuated Jackson, leaving it fully in Federal hands. Like old times and with what combustibles remained, it was soon on fire again.

As for the front, Polk did not get to it after all; an emergency necessitated his presence in Meridian. Behind his back, the Southern guerrillas in troublesome Jones County were maneuvering to assist Sherman's advance by burning down trestles on the Mobile & Ohio Railroad, a vital link with Mobile for the Confederates in Mississippi. Shorthanded though he already was, Polk drew 500 cavalry troops from Mobile's garrison and sent them on a retaliatory strike against the insurgent men and women inhabiting the piney woods of south-central Mississippi. The troopers under Col. Henry Maury (supplied with bloodhounds) were to dismount, the better to seek out and quash the region's "lawless banditti," as Polk colorfully termed them. Their particular target was to be Jones County, where anti-Confederate feelings ran highest and whose citizens made common cause with Confederate Army deserters and draft dodgers hiding out in swamps and woodlands. Polk provided Maury with six guides (Confederate soldiers whose houses had been burned and their families "insulted") and instructed him to deal with the region's outlaws "in the most summary manner"—code for the on-sight execution of any likely captives by shooting or hanging.[63]

Strewing their own destruction of towns and countryside by pillage and fire, meanwhile, the Federal soldiers out to quash Polk were now about halfway across the width of Mississippi. Just past Jackson, Sherman brought his original two columns together as one, now more like a sharp point, the better to ward off Lee's cavalry harassing his foraging parties. "They do not try to conceal that their destination is Meridian," a scout informed Polk on March 7, and Stephen Lee even expressed admiration for his foes: "It was impossible to damage the enemy much, as he marched in perfect order, his trains being divided between the brigades and kept in close order."[64]

Whatever Sherman's Alabama objectives might be beyond Polk's headquarters town, Polk had decided it was time for Fanny and Sally to return to Asheville. "Wife, have you ever thought what you would do if I should be killed, and this contest prove unsuccessful?" Polk asked shortly before they left. (It was "the only time he ever alluded to the possibility of our want of success," Fanny said later.) She replied, "If we were all ruined together, I think I shall go into the Santa Anna," her shorthand for New Orleans's St. Anna's Asylum for the Relief of Destitute Females and Their Helpless Children of all Religious Faiths. Fanny said she would remain there "until such time as my children can devise some means for my support." Tears in his eyes, Polk embraced his wife and commended her resolve, seeing in her a welcome strength in her "apprehension of evil." For her feminine toughness, the husband took some of the credit. "I have not lived in vain if you can say and feel this," he told her. It would be the last time the two would ever be together.[65]

With his wife and daughter on their way home, Polk set up temporary headquarters at Lake, Mississippi, a station on the Southern Railroad. That put him about twenty miles east of Morton, where midway across Mississippi the Confederate withdrawal and the Yankee advance had come to a standstill. Despite Lee's assertion that Polk "steadily adhered to his plan of non-interference," he again, as he had at Jackson, ordered that his army contest the way, once more handing the task to the pugnacious William Loring. This general immediately ordered rifle pits and breastworks dug along a mile-long crescent east of Morton. Thus sheltered, the 21,000 Confederates held on for two days, hoping reinforcements from Mobile might arrive in time.[66] The swarming Yankees, however, were slowed but not stopped by Loring's defensive line. (Stephen Lee was occupied elsewhere harrying Sherman's flanks and rear, and Lawrence Ross, riding hard from Yazoo County, was five days off.)[67] About to be overrun, surrounded, or passed by, Loring concluded with General French and the other commanders that their situation at Morton was untenable. They began their withdrawal at dusk on February 8, soldiers lighting numerous decoy campfires as though settling down for leisurely suppers. By morning, everyone was gone. The reinforcements from Mobile, still on the way, were about-faced and rushed back.

At the end of that day, February 9, the enemy locusts (35,000 by Polk's estimate) were passing by Morton, leaving it with empty smokehouses and smoking ruins. Now following the railroad tracks, their next destination was Lake Station. Polk and his escort troop pulled out of there not long before the Yankee "Signal Corps went through the town like a dose of salts," as a jocular Union officer said graphically. "Just as we were leaving I noticed a man hunting around to get some one to make an affidavit that there had been a town there."[68] One soldier with the withdrawing Confederates (he had barely arrived in Mississippi when he was sent back to Mobile) spoke for many when he said, "As Mississippians we were greatly hurt. . . . The whole state was to be abandoned without a single blow. . . . No wonder the hearts of her sons burned within them; no wonder if they learned to distrust the policy that gave their homes to the torch and their families to the tender mercies of the foe." Scores of his fellows, he was sure, would soon be deserting. He did not blame them.[69]

Doubtless aware of the mutterings of such soldiers, but feeling for his commander, General Loring would telegraph Polk a day or so later: "I see the papers are finding fault [with you]. If necessary I will come out with a statement showing that you did all you could with the force you had." Polk replied he had not seen the editorial reproaches but gracefully conceded that "it is natural that persons whose wishes are not realized should in their disappointment indulge in censure. The risk of incurring it is one of the penalties of position." Polk requested all the same that Loring send "such a statement as you propose. I will not publish it unless events should make it necessary."[70]

While General Polk presumably continued to plot a desperation ambush either at Selma or Mobile, Sherman was closing in on Meridian; Polk's immediate concern, therefore, was the evacuation of his headquarters town. Adding to his uncertainties of what to expect next, the Yankees, according to General French, had falsely "spread the report that they were en route for Mobile." Polk unfortunately amplified this misinformation by almost willfully refusing to comprehend dispatches from Lee disproving the rumor—dispatches Lee tried twice (with a little asperity) to clarify for Polk. Believing he had stated the situation clearly, but to make sure, Lee said, "[I] have examined my letters."[71] Lee, in fact, had told Polk specifically from the field that he suspected the intention of the enemy was to go to Meridian only. "He may then turn toward Mobile (but I doubt it)," Lee wrote.[72] But since the rumor supported what Polk had long expected, as Marie Riddle Bearss says in her study of the campaign, "Polk seemed to be the only Confederate leader who still believed that Sherman was headed for Mobile."[73] In General French's smug diary entry on the night of February 9, he wrote: "Gen. Polk . . . had been at Mobile, caught the contagion . . . and ordered me at once [to] proceed [there]."[74] The contagion might better be likened to a raging epidemic: Polk notified Gen. Dabney Maury, commander at Mobile, that the enemy, which he estimated at 35,000 infantry with sixty pieces of artillery, was rapidly approaching his coastline post. Polk was sending heavy reinforcements: Samuel French's infantry units and Francis Shoup's "imperfectly organized exchange brigade."[75] Col. Henry Maury and his bloodhounds were recalled from their pursuit of guerrillas in Jones County, and Mobile's noncombatants were urged by Polk "to leave at once."[76] Catching the contagion, too, was Jefferson Davis, who like a parent advised Polk that it was "needless to call attention to the importance of striking [the enemy] on the march, impeding his progress, and preventing him from using surplus supplies on his route. He should be met . . . before he reaches the Gulf and establishes a base."[77] Sound advice, surely. Still awaiting the return to Alabama of all the men loaned to Polk in Mississippi, Gen. Dabney Maury's "effective force for defense of Mobile was only about 2,500 men." Theoretically a dire situation, but as he was threatened merely by a false alarm, no harm done.[78] Sherman continued to hold the upper hand by default.

Within days, their Minié balls having had little effect, Loring's infantrymen had turned to fighting Sherman primarily with axes and matches, thereby felling trees and burning bridges to slow his progress into Meridian.[79] Other soldiers were meanwhile carting off to Alabama by wagon road and railway whatever the town contained that was of value: the sick and wounded, the military stores, the rolling stock of steam engines and cars. The whole lot, not counting the human cargo, was worth $12 million, Polk reckoned, and was being sent either south to Mobile (a half-million pounds of bacon headed there) or east to Demopolis in Alabama. Among other valuables merged into the military columns winding into Alabama, as General French was careful to note with an underline in his diary, were "Gen. Polk's headquarter wagons and cows." Artfully evident in his diary and his postwar memoir is the disdain that French, as a longtime professional soldier, felt for his bishop commander in Mississippi. That cool regard continued as he served under Polk in northern Georgia in the coming spring. Years later, with Polk dead and French free to indulge in lese majesty, he would pen these lyrical words in his 1901 autobiography:

> Gen. Polk had been an Episcopal bishop, and enjoyed the best the land afforded. The matins songs of the birds disturbed not his morning repose. The glorious sun rose too early for him to see it from the mountain top. It showed its face there at an unseemly hour. But when the "drowsy morn" was passed, and the milkmaid had drawn tribute from the cows, and the coffee pot was steaming on the hearth, and the light rolls were hot by the fire, and the plump, fine capon, with sides well lined with fat, was broiling on the coals, sending a savory odor through the apartments, the Bishop would arise, his face radiant with joy. He was a valiant trencherman, but when the repast was over he threw aside the surplice. The priest became a warrior when he girded on the saber, and sallied forth a paladin in the strife.[80]

Too bad that Braxton Bragg, who once limned Polk as "gallant and patriotic, [but] luxurious in his habits, rises late, [and] moves slowly," was no longer alive to enjoy French's more felicitous ridicule.

While withdrawing with their stores into Alabama in mid-February, Polk and his staff "did not get one night's sleep for eight days and nights," William Gale reported. Continued resistance in Mississippi would have been "madness," Gale said, but scurrying away to Demopolis was "humiliating."[81] Fully expanding into the vacuum the Rebels had left, Sherman loosed his army into Meridian on February 14. And in short order his men went to work burning down and ripping up their conquest. "For five days 10,000 men worked hard and with a will in that work of destruction, with axes, crowbars, sledges, clawbars, and with fire," Sherman reported. With no one to stop them, the soldiers over several days destroyed all train tracks of the four lines passing through the town: the Mobile & Ohio, the Meridian & Jackson, the Alabama & Mississippi River, and the Southern. The damage extended for miles in four directions and constituted, said Sherman, "the most complete destruction of railroads ever beheld."[82] Cross ties were stacked in open piles; the rails, balanced atop them, were weighted on each end, and the whole thing was set ablaze until the steel softened and drooped "30 to 40 degrees to the ground." Apparently no one thought to set fire to the deserted cottage that had served as Polk's headquarters.[83] Soon after the destruction had subsided, Sherman voiced his scorched-earth conviction that the key to the war's early end was visiting the rebellion directly upon the civilian population, declaring: "Meridian no longer exists." (For good measure, before abandoning what was left of Meridian, one of Sherman's arsonists specifically set fire to the house of a woman he said had spit in his face some months earlier when he was led through the town as a prisoner. Without being aware of it, he helped pay back the Atlanta women who in 1863 had spat upon other Union prisoners.)[84]

While the Yankees were cheerfully passing five days of pillaging, a spy reported that General Polk, along with 10,000 infantry and some 3,000 unarmed, still unexchanged parolees, were hunkered down in Demopolis. Polk, at least, was "living high" in "fine quarters," said Gale.[85] But he could hardly relax. On the one hand, he was anxious as to how his small army might fare if Sherman did indeed advance into Alabama toward Selma. On the other, he was fantasizing a bold expedition: if ever reinforcements arrived from Joe Johnston's Army of Tennessee, he would send Loring and French to chase Sherman back to Vicksburg and headlong into the Mississippi River. Polk's quandary was shortly solved by others. Gen. George Thomas, the Rock of Chickamauga, had 10,000 troops in Chattanooga poised to descend on Johnston in northern Georgia. Reinforcements for Polk in Alabama were therefore out of the question. And as for Sherman's advancing into Alabama? Still without Smith's essential cavalry, he gave up that game and was soon heading back to Vicksburg.

Polk had already apprehended Sherman's plight. "If we can destroy [Smith's cavalry], then the whole of Sherman's army must come to a bad end," Polk wired Nathan Bedford Forrest on February 20. "[He] seems to be lying quietly at Meridian awaiting for the coming of that column. If it be possible, let him never see it." Polk further urged Forrest to enlist civilian Mississippians willing to fight the Yankees on horses. "Urge all the people of the country through which you must pass to mount and take the field. . . . Let them ambuscade the enemy and assail him in bodies or singly."[86]

If failing badly to keep to Sherman's exacting schedule, Smith's cavalry brigades had not been dawdling along the way. They had been burning, plundering, and sowing destruction upon town and country as they rode south, and in the process they had picked up an encumbering train of hundreds of slaves, their wagons and mules added in. Craftily observed by Forrest, but not yet engaged by him (Forrest was falling back to concentrate his scattered riders and set up an ambush), Smith proceeded southward warily, contemplating Sherman's warning that Forrest "always attacked with a vehemence." On February 21, still some eighty miles short of Meridian, Smith decided to return to Memphis without even knowing what Sherman's latest plans might be. His about-face was not a moment too soon. Forrest's cavalry over the next several days fell upon the Yankee troopers relentlessly in running fights, first at Prairie Station, then at West Point, and lastly at Okolona. Stephen Lee's cavalry, after nipping at Sherman's retreating heels, hurried to Forrest's side on "jaded horses" but arrived too late—a disappointment to all but Smith and his riders, by then well on their way to the safety of Memphis. Having had about a third as many men as Smith's 7,000, Forrest so outthought and outfought the Yankees that Smith was sure he was the one put upon unfairly.[87] Sherman was disgusted with Smith, saying his absence in Meridian had cost him his supposed chance to "have utterly destroyed Polk's army." His anger at Smith would simmer for years.

The present time, though, had come for all involved to boast, not brood, about what-if's. And it was a refreshment that was shamelessly enjoyed by both commanders as they indulged wonderfully contradicting summations of the previous few weeks. Back in Vicksburg and claiming he had all but crippled the Confederacy's western rail system, Sherman wrote his wife Ellen that "I scared the Bishop out of his senses, he made a clean run." It was, all in all, "a pleasant excursion."[88] Polk, in turn, after repairing the mangled trackage within a few weeks, would write *his* wife a delusional letter: "Never was there a more gloomy prospect than that which surrounded me . . . and never did a brighter day shine than that which followed in the clear and manifest defeat and rout of that advancing army."

Viewing himself as David against Goliath, Polk likened the cavalry successes by Generals Forrest and Lee to David's pouch of slingshot stones: "I do not know when I have felt more dependent on God, or when I felt I had received so merciful a deliverance."[89] Polk thanked his soldiers as well for his and their deliverance: "Never did a grand campaign, inaugurated with such pretensions, terminate more ingloriously. . . . The lieutenant-general commanding offers his thanks to the whole army." A few days later, in another impassioned declaration, he proclaimed that "the brilliant and successful campaign just closed by Major General Lee and Major General Forrest was calculated to teach a useful lesson to our enemies. They came by the thousands with glistening bayonets and confident of their strength, . . . to overrun and desolate our country, if not to strike a death blow to our cause. They have been forced to return, beaten and distracted."[90] The bishop's bragging was a curious counterpoint to an episode the Yankee general had written off as an outing. The perils of pride being what they are, a few months later near Marietta, Georgia, William T. Sherman was to have the last word with Leonidas Polk.

26

Presidential Adviser—Army Strategies and Naval Plots (1864)

In correspondence back to Jefferson Davis in Richmond, Inspector General Col. George Hodge would say that, from his observations, ever since William T. Sherman had left Meridian and returned to Vicksburg, there was more chaos than order in Leonidas Polk's Western Department. General Polk, with his irrepressible optimism for future military successes that spring and summer, was not bothered by that assessment—an understandable attitude for one who, without blushing, had depicted General Sherman's relatively unmolested forces as "beaten and distracted." Further, with Sherman and Sooy Smith back where they came from, Polk had enthusiastically turned his attention to the rapid repair of the Mississippi railroads left tied in knots by the Yankees. That was no mean challenge. Sent on an inspection tour by his father, Lt. William Polk reported back that, along one thirty-mile stretch of track, rails had been bent, cross ties and bridges burned, telegraph poles chopped up, insulation glasses broken, wires snipped and melted, and the masonry reinforcements of tunnel entrances caved in. Meck begged leave to say in addition that the Federals' recent presence in the region had apparently invigorated the villainy of "the Tories and deserters who infest Jones County," 200 of whom had gone on a rampage against secessionist neighbors when their Yankee friends were gone.[1]

General Polk, accordingly, was obliged yet again, much to his irritation, to send cavalry troopers assisted by hunting dogs into the dissident regions of Mississippi. In addition to Jones County, other counties in the south and west of the state where swamp hideouts were plentiful were still overrun with the troublesome Tories, deserters, noncompliant conscripts, and guerrillas (some of whom already were interfering with repair of the torn-up railroads). With such anti-Confederate residents sometimes hoisting a United States flag in a public place (as Unionists did in both Jones and Smith Counties that March), a thoroughly fed-up loyalist (a district judge named Robert Hudson in Leake County) wrote Jefferson Davis to say that, while he was "no alarmist," he saw the whole state, following the example of "vastly rotten counties" like his, "drifting to the Yankees." Even former Confederate soldiers were among the brigands running loose, he declared, and Mississippi had become "almost a Sodom and Gomorrah." He recommended Davis remedy the "magnitude of these evils" with an "iron rule enforced with iron hand and hearts of stone."[2] Davis sent the letter on to Polk for action, and a few weeks later Polk obligingly set the dogs on the "Tories, conscripts and deserters" of northern Alabama, and he again ordered the severe punishment he had applied in Mississippi, ordering Gen. Philip Roddey to meet resistance "with death upon the spot."[3]

As the western army's scourge of the anti-Confederates continued, General Polk at length could see that progress was being made. Albeit self-anointed, he held more control over law and order than anyone else in the troubled region, and, just days before being transferred to Georgia to help Joe Johnston fend off Sherman, he was pleased to take credit for "re-establishing the ascendency of the civil power in [Mississippi and Alabama] courts."[4] To retain that ascendency, he had already set up nine military police subdivisions throughout Alabama, Mississippi, and eastern Louisiana, recycling available manpower to staff the units primarily with disabled soldiers. Over them all, as provost-marshal-general, he placed Maj. Jules Charles Denis.[5] Meanwhile, continuing to cope with the chronic shortage of troops in his department, Polk hounded all varieties of shirkers. Toward repentant deserters—those "misguided men" who had come "bitterly to regret their want of fidelity"—he held out this carrot: an offer of amnesty, scolding but all-forgiving, was extended to any soldier absent without leave (other than commissioned officers). While dubious of "the expediency of the measure," he said in his proclamation that he was giving it a chance in deference to the wishes of a joint petition from the "influential citizens of the Mississippi Legislature." Other times, as with draft dodgers, he brandished an egalitarian stick. Cavalry commanders were directed "to arrest every man capable of bearing arms from 17 to 50" in southwestern Mississippi and southeastern Louisiana, not excepting the sons of patrician planters in the region. "Young men as have good social positions and have hitherto evaded service were not to be spared," he declared. Again, resistance was to be answered with "death upon the spot."[6]

Otherwise, expunging deposits of Unionists (those "proclaiming them-selves 'Southern Yankees,'" as Polk sneered to Jefferson Davis) was natu-rally another of the commanding general's priorities, and most obliging in this assignment were Colonel Robert Lowry and his Mississippians (the fearsome colonel was later governor of their state). On one of their sor-ties they learned of a United States flag, homemade with hand-drawn stars, displayed on a Smith County dwelling. The cost of that patriotism to two Unionist leaders in the neighborhood was execution by hanging. On another raid in April the boast was made that Lowry's men had caught and hanged two teenage brothers. "The lieutenant-general commanding," Lowry would shortly be pleased to learn from Polk's adjutant, "directs me to say that he has received your several reports of your operations with great satisfaction, and conveys to you and your command his thanks."[7]

In assessing the department's manifold problems, Inspector General Hodge told the Richmond authorities that "the assumption of authority by the lieutenant general commanding" might strike an observer as "to some extent irregular," but overall Hodge judged Polk's actions to be "ex-pedient."[8] Rather pleased himself with the headway he was making, Polk asked Hodge to urge President Davis to be sure he read the inspector's affirmation of Polk's methods and successes. Two months later, on a Geor-gia battlefield, he was still feeling good about his Mississippi work, writing a daughter at the family's home in Asheville that his efforts in Mississippi had been, and were, "in the highest degree gratifying" to himself: "At least 5,000 men who were lost to the Confederacy now found themselves fight-ing on the front." Plus, his unrelenting pursuit of the region's "discon-tents" had lifted an "incubus" that had "rested upon the heart of the home population." It all went to show, said the ever-sanguine Southerner, that "the power of the Confederacy was not dead, but was not only living, but sharply elevating."[9]

Still, complete success sometimes eluded him, as day-to-day worries, big and small, had been continuous ever since he took over the Mississippi army. Had the piles of hides of slaughtered animals collected in Demopo-lis been efficiently converted to meet the Confederacy's critical shortage of leather? No, sir, concluded an investigator sent from Braxton Bragg's office in Richmond; he made a determination reflecting poorly on Polk's administration. "The number of hides lost, stolen or permitted to rot in this department would have supplied the army with shoes," he reported. He uncovered another scandal. In Mississippi and Alabama, certain army quartermaster officers—even some privates—were demanding foodstuff "tithes from farmers supplying produce to the military; the extorted proceeds were for their personal consumption."[10] Meanwhile, with the war not going all that well, and inflation climbing, profiteering by Mississippi planters flourished; they were surreptitiously selling their cotton (the one thing they had of negotiable value) to the Yankees, sending it by wagon into enemy-held Memphis. "Capture and confiscate all wagons and teams . . . engaged in this business," an irate Polk commanded Gen. James Chalmers. "Be vigilant."[11] And even loyal patriots were losing patience with soldiers camped in their fields, forever tramping to and fro across—and driving herds of livestock through—their gardens. Here was both an irritant to the citizenry and a nuisance for the army commander.

Helping the general bear up was his excellent aide-de-camp and son-in-law William Gale. He was more than content with his military duties, but to brighten his bedroom-office, he needed help from a modish invention. "If any photographist ever comes to Asheville," he wrote Kate Polk Gale in April, "I want you to have each one of the children taken and sent to me." While waiting for the family pictures, Gale began pondering the unrelenting issues his general had to deal with, and he thought it worthwhile to characterize for Kate a typical day in his father-in-law's headquarters house. The account, covering several pages of crisscrossed handwriting (the better to conserve his precious stationery), ran this way:

"We get up about 7 and have breakfast at 8. While we are taking our meals, the servants do up our rooms (for you must be informed that we use our rooms for offices)." After breakfast, Gale would arrange the general's papers so that he knew where each was, and at 10:00 A.M. Polk's staff members were ushered in to make whatever reports the general needed. "This usually occupies him until 12 when . . . visitors are to be admitted." By this time, Gale's bedroom office would be crammed with persons "anxious to see [General Polk], all of whom have first to state their business to me. . . . If, in my opinion, their business can only be transacted by the general in person, I admit them." Such meetings would carry on until 6:00 P.M., excepting when he and Gale would break for dinner, their main meal, at about 2:00 P.M. Barring any urgencies, Polk at 6:00 P.M. would stop work for a diverting horseback or buggy ride of four or five miles. He would return for tea: "A few moments of recreation at the table, and then to work again," wrote Gale. "The rule is not to see anyone after 6 in the evening, but he frequently yields." Normally, the nights were given over to correspondence. "His habit of late," Gale continued, "has been to make me write from his dictation, and from 8 until 1 or 2 will sit and write—or rather, he sits and dictates to me, and I write." Gale went on: "He often nods over his work, and waking up enquires, 'Where are you?,' and goes on again. I do not know how we all stand up under the constant labor and confinement, yet . . . I never was in better health."

Gale was never in better rapport with his general, either. "He has no secrets from me and freely discloses to me all his views, and in all questions of military or state policy asks my opinion. . . . In most of his important movements I am his only counselor. . . . We have our moments of relaxation, too, in which we joke and laugh and try to get rid of the heavy thoughts that [weigh] upon us." Moved to take a modest bow, Gale took a swipe at Harry Yeatman, the husband of Lucius Polk's daughter Mary and the second member of the general's staff having married into his family: "Harry occupies the same relative position [to the general] I do," Gale wrote, "but I do nearly all the work. . . . I came here to be useful. . . . I have succeeded, I think, very well."[12]

After Gen. Joe Johnston had seen how Polk's infantry had been shoved around by Sherman's Meridian raiders, he wrote to Braxton Bragg, now the president's military adviser, to suggest that Polk's army was "useless in Mississippi [but] would make a valuable addition to the Army of Tennessee," then marking time in Georgia.[13] The advice was eventually taken, but for his own part, Polk was completely unchastened by Sherman's visit. The roughing-up seemed instead to have galvanized Polk and triggered some strategic ideas of his own, which he now hoped to lay before the president. Johnston's army in northern Georgia was threatened that winter by the swelling mass of soldiers in Chattanooga, lately under U. S. Grant but soon to be bolstered by General Sherman and his "old and tried army on reassignment from Vicksburg." (Sherman took over in March when Grant was promoted to general in chief of all Federal armies and left for Virginia to contend with Robert E. Lee.) Most of the rest of Tennessee was in the Yankees' grip as well, the remarkable General Forrest being the only Confederate with the dash and cunning and ruthlessness to gallop into the state's western counties to do as he pleased. In league with the cavalry's Maj. Gen. Stephen Lee, Polk for some weeks had been analyzing this menacing situation, and in a letter on February 28 Jefferson Davis's "obedient servant" begged leave to detail his ideas on how to turn things around.

William Gale later summarized the message to the president for the benefit of his wife. In Polk's strategic thinking, Kate's father "took the ground viz. 'that no effectual opposition could be made [against] Gen. Sherman . . . directly in his front, but that his army might be destroyed or scattered'" by Polk's forces suddenly sweeping up from northern Mississippi. They would then pounce on the vulnerable backside of Sherman's divisions camped in East Tennessee and northern Alabama. Polk would need assistance for this coup; he wanted the president to assign him specifically Frank Cheatham's division, at the time attached to Johnston's Army of Tennessee. Formerly Polk's to command, these seasoned soldiers would not only enlarge Polk's firepower; inasmuch as they had been "raised by [Polk] chiefly in the western district of Tennessee," the general reckoned their battlefield renown would draw other Tennesseans into the Confederate ranks by the thousands, those "who had left . . . or never been in the service." Further augmented by James Longstreet coming out of Knoxville and approaching the enemy from the opposite direction, Polk envisioned his incursion squeezing toward Middle Tennessee until the combined armies would capture the vital Nashville & Chattanooga Railroad. Sherman would then be totally cut off from all the Northern states and the essential supplies they furnished, and General Johnston's army in Georgia would in short order be delivered from its predicament. Polk even suggested that a jaunty follow-up invasion of the North might then be in order.[14] All this conjecturing was a wasted effort on Polk's part: Davis either never saw his letter or read it and forgot about it. In any case, it went unanswered by anyone.[15]

Ignored strategy proposals aside, the president did not fail to make use of Polk during the weeks building up to his emergency assignment to Georgia in May. Skulduggery projects appealing to both men, Davis in several instances turned to his friend for help; Polk was eager to oblige. A scheme to recapture the Port of New Orleans, the loss of which two years earlier continued to gall the South, had come across Davis's desk in January. He referred the matter to Polk. The plot contemplated a military attack on the occupied city's garrison, abetted by a citizens' fifth-column insurgency. This ardent idea came from Thomas J. Reid Jr., a Rebel colonel from Arkansas who had been a prisoner of war in New Orleans after his surrender at Port Hudson in the summer of 1863. Reid was an observant captive, and once exchanged he lost no time writing directly to the president to share the military intelligence he had soaked up. New Orleans was not only lightly defended, he reported, but many of the Yankee troops charged with this important duty were black men, to Reid all but worthless for anything but field-hand donkeywork on a plantation. In addition, Reid had counted all the soldiers, artillery pieces, and warships stashed around the city and deemed the aggregate so insignificant that the Crescent City plum was hanging ripe for the picking. After a surprise coup by Confederate invaders, Reid avowed the city could be held securely by citizens enrolled in six secret, armed regiments that would be poised to materialize out of the shadows. Recapture by Yankee forces would be foiled by the simple expedient of setting fire to bridges spanning the Mississippi.

Davis was enough intrigued by this scenario that Reid was directed to report to Polk's headquarters for a hush-hush consultation; the general was authorized to act upon the plan with "the utmost secrecy" if he thought it feasible. He was even instructed to ask, if he needed it, for assistance from Franklin Buchanan, the admiral in charge of Confederate naval operations at Mobile. (Buchanan, famously, was the Southern hero whose ironclad CSS *Virginia* had run amok in 1862 through the Union's wooden warship fleet in the Chesapeake Bay. Subsequently, the ironclad USS *Monitor* fought Buchanan to a draw in one of naval history's best-known battles, and the sunken hulk lying on her side in the James River mud was aptly noticed by a *New York Times* reporter the day after Lee's surrender to Grant in April 1865.)[16]

As his earlier enthusiasm for the plotted kidnapping of Gen. William Rosecrans had shown, Polk was not one to shy from fanciful acts in warfare. So he now heartily subscribed to the intent of Reid's recovery of New Orleans. Considering that it had been the Polks' last Louisiana home (and that the bishop's clergy friends in the city were waging ongoing civil disobedience against the hated Federals), the retaking of the city was a topic that had lately "occupied much of my thoughts," Polk wrote back to Davis.[17] These thoughts might have been further nourished by a letter from his close bishop friend, Stephen Elliott. A man of certitude on many subjects, Elliott declared that the United States was about to call off the war, and he likened the recent days of its failing war effort to a satiric line by the Roman poet Horace: *Parturient montes; nascetur ridiculus mus* (roughly translated as "Mountains will labor, and an absurd little mouse will be born"). So sure was Elliott of his prediction that he could fancy any day now seeing "Lieutenant General [Polk] in Command, re-opening the Mississippi and re-uniting us with Louisiana, Texas and Arkansas."[18]

Polk had to like the sound of Elliot's words. But as for Thomas Reid, Polk thought the colonel was making too many easy assumptions. Polk deemed that New Orleans, even if recaptured, could not be held onto as easily as Reid supposed; it was essential that the Mississippi River coiling around the city first be returned to Rebel control. The Federal policing of the Mississippi between Memphis and New Orleans at the time was so strict that "it was difficult for even an individual to cross," General Stephen Lee had lately said, but Polk believed he had a solution. With Reid having provided an opening, Polk laid before the president in March his step-by-step specifics, which he had "been maturing" for some time, on just how such an integrated capture of river and city could succeed.[19]

Building on suggestions supplied him by Capt. John C. Kay, a Mississippi native with a flair for river warfare, Polk had devised a byzantine strategy.

First off, he told the president, consider that the Mississippi River in its south-ward flow crossed seven degrees of Confederate States latitude. Although all this stretch of waterway was controlled by the Yankees, Polk proposed that from Cairo, Illinois, to Manchac, Louisiana (just above New Orleans), the Confederates secretly assemble a dozen or more guerrilla squadrons along the riverbanks. These several hundred insurgents, "mounted infantry . . . of persons of all ages," were to be equipped with long-range rifles and artillery fieldpieces trained "on the principal bends of the river."[20] Assigned to either half-degree or quarter-degree segments of the sixty-degree latitu-dinal lines (an assigned sector would thus span either thirty or fifteen miles of riverbank), the shadowy paramilitary troops would attempt to sink every enemy transport that steamed past. The ideal ammunition to use, John Kay advised Polk, would be "liquid fire shells loaded with phosphorous, and splashed upon the passing wooden vessels." In short order, said Kay, navi-gation on the Mississippi would be so risky the Yankees would give it up.[21]

Polk's project had other features. When not sinking steamboats, his river guerrillas would neutralize the Federals' newly devised marine cavalry. This was a unit of mounted marines associated with a fleet of steamboat rams on the river, all commanded by Brig. Gen. Andrew Ellet Jr. The Mississippi Squadron, as it was called, was "a hybrid unit like nothing else in the U.S. armed forces," says the naval historian Gary Joiner.[22] The horse marines in Ellet's brigade, Polk told Davis, were a nuisance, providing protection along the Deep South river bottoms to treasonable Southern planters who had crept back to abandoned plantations in order to cultivate cotton they hoped to sell to the enemy. While some of Polk's guerrillas would keep the marines at bay, others would be sent to harass the pernicious disloyal plant-ers, obliging them to reconsider their marketing plans.[23]

All this was within reach, Polk estimated, if 3,000 to 6,000 men and boys were recruited for the mission; trial and error would fix the number needed. Then, once the Mississippi River's southern banks were largely back in Confederate hands, the only remaining trouble spots would be the Federal gunboats anchored at strategic points along the river's length. *Bear with me, Mr. President*, Polk may have thought as he laid out his ideas. To deal with the gunboat hitch, Polk had consulted Lt. Col. Frederic B. Brand, a prewar Polk family friend with naval experience. As a Louisiana-born graduate of Annapolis and a former officer in the United States Navy, Brand had won Southern acclaim the previous year in a river battle that resulted in his ram-ming and disabling a feared Yankee gunboat, the USS *Indianola*. (As booty, Brand dragged the stricken hulk to Palmyra Island near Jefferson Davis's plantation, but it sank anyway into the Mississippi mud.)[24] Now Brand and

Polk presented to the president a subtler, but no less effective, way of de-fanging the Yankee guard boats. As Polk explained it to Davis, he would arrange in St. Louis for the purchase of an ordinary, nonmilitary steamboat, the kind seen everywhere plying the Missouri and Mississippi Rivers. On its maiden voyage under new ownership, Polk's boat would round-to at a prearranged wood yard, whereupon 500 armed river men would clamber aboard and politely set ashore the dumfounded crew and civilian passen-gers. The civilian boat now in the hands of the pirates would then steam serenely downriver, a Trojan Horse with paddle wheels.

"It is the custom of such transports on the Mississippi," Polk went on, "to hail and round-to alongside [the Federal] gun-boats to get and put off mails." Thus, "it would not be difficult to board and capture the first [gun-boat] that should be encountered. . . . That being done . . . the 500 men . . . would be transferred to the prize, and it made to steam down to the next [gunboat] below." Polk's mail-delivery ruse would be then repeated serially down the Mississippi. As Polk put it: "The course by which [the first prize] was made ours would be pursued toward its consort, and so on for the rest."

Hindering the Yankees further, with no telegraph lines along the river, the alarm could not be flashed downstream. Polk reckoned that the several gunboats could be snuffed out like a row of candles. And then? As Colonel Reid had promised, "the capture of New Orleans would be an easy matter, and Port Hudson, Vicksburg, Helena and Memphis would follow . . . the future of the war dramatically turned around, the end practically in sight." QED. Brimming with exuberance, Polk signed off: "Hoping to hear from you at your early leisure."

In this hope he was again to be disappointed. Despite having asked for Polk's recommendations, Davis apparently made no response.[25] A month later, though, the president's new military adviser, Braxton Bragg—one al-ways happy to squelch his former subordinate—dismissed Polk's dream in an office notation to the president: "This whole proposal, both its practica-bility and policy, seem [sic] to me doubtful," he wrote. The capture of the gunboats "might be attended with temporary success," but the plan for raising the land forces along the river "would demoralize our troops." Why the riverbank squadrons would have depressed regular army soldiers is not explained by Bragg.[26]

The cold water dashed on General Polk by General Bragg did not dampen the president's continued reliance on Polk. No sooner had the pi-ratical hopes of reclaiming the Mississippi and New Orleans been scuttled than Davis asked Polk to evaluate another subversive undertaking.[27] Polk's provost marshal in Mississippi, Maj. Jules C. Denis, was quietly circulating a proposal to set fire to Nashville, Tennessee, for two years an occupied city that was full to bursting with military essentials for Sherman's 98,000 soldiers and 35,000 animals set to invade Georgia.[28]

If some called Nashville the peaceable Athens of the South, others said that, as a storehouse and arsenal, it was to General Sherman in Tennessee what Washington was to General Grant in Virginia. Sherman himself said his Nashville stores had provided his army with a "wonderful abundance."[29] In the city straddling the Cumberland River, the quantities of war-making facilities and piled-up supplies in the spring of 1864 were indeed wonderful: a ten-acre whitewashed corral capable of holding 7,000 horses and mules; a powder magazine under eight feet of earth that was fully half the size of a modern-day football field; a coal yard holding four million bushels; and warehouses packed with 24 million soldier rations, millions of bushels of corn and oats, and tens of thousands of tons of hay. Put it all together, as one general did on paper, and the train of wagons, ambulances, mules, and horses would stretch 283 miles. Best of all for Major Denis's incendiary designs, the storehouses held 2,000 bottles of Powell's American Liniment, a medicine for sore horses and whose flammable ingredients would greatly assist in spreading the major's conflagration. Complementing Nashville's stores were its radiating railroad lines and repair shops; trains ran, and provisions flowed, southward to the fields of war around the clock.[30]

Little wonder Davis considered setting fire to the city well worth the hazards. Did Polk in Mississippi think the time was ripe? Was Jules Denis the man to carry off this shenanigan? Polk's thoughts cannot be found. Diverting him was the presidential order to drop everything and rush to Joe Johnston's side; the advent of May and the blossoming of Georgia's peach trees found William T. Sherman letting loose his promised campaign against the Army of Tennessee.

27

"Old Friends Pleased to See Me Here"
(1864)

Throughout the late winter and early spring of 1864, the armies under Joe Johnston and Leonidas Polk—both squeezed into small clumps in Georgia, Mississippi, and Alabama—had been bracing for William T. Sherman's pending invasion from Tennessee, the Yankee commander's gaze presumed to be fixed on the prize of Atlanta. Suddenly jittery in Demopolis, General Polk on April 18 had sent an urgent note to Jefferson Davis: he suspected Sherman was about to throw no fewer than 20,000 troops into Alabama against Polk's comparatively little army of 8,000. Recollections of Sherman's recent Meridian raid informed Polk's thoughts when he told the president that "I hope I shall not again be subjected to the trial-of-feeling caused by having to deal with such a disparity of force." Still, hoping rather that he might yet be reinforced by Frank Cheatham and his veteran Tennesseans, Polk did venture to declare audaciously that he stood ready to "strike the enemy in flank and turn."[1] Polk's Southern blood was definitely up.

Soon learning that surrendering black soldiers had been victims of a purported massacre by Nathan Bedford Forrest's cavalry at Fort Pillow up in Tennessee, Polk sounded not the least bit perturbed. A stronghold on the Mississippi River built earlier by the Confederates and named after Polk's brigadier, the fort had lately surrendered to Federal gunboats. The occupying garrison included some 300 black soldiers (primarily runaway slaves) and a roughly equal number of white soldiers (primarily Tennessee Unionists). Several black women and children—soldiers' families—were there too. On April 12 the compound was stormed by 1,500 cavalrymen led by Forrest and Gen. James F. Chalmers. Overpowered in the fighting inside the walls, most of the surrendering black soldiers were given no quarter until two-thirds of them had been killed (against one-third of the Unionist whites). The river, Forrest was pleased to report to Polk, "was dyed with the blood of the slaughtered for 200 yards," and he trusted the assault "will demonstrate to the Northern people that negro soldiers cannot cope with Southerners." Chalmers later congratulated his troopers for teaching "the mongrel garrison of blacks and renegades a lesson long to be remembered." Polk heartily telegraphed Forrest that his "brilliant campaign . . . has given me great satisfaction," a sentiment resembling the equanimity with which he had accepted Lawrence Ross's deprecations against black Yankees the previous month in Yazoo City, Mississippi.[2] Jefferson Davis had a say as well, enforcing, as it were, the North's Fugitive Slave Law. He instructed Polk that any captured black soldiers who were runaways were to be returned to their former white owners.[3]

Meanwhile, Polk's daring offer to single-handedly take on Sherman's rumored Alabama invaders languished on the president's desk for more than a week before he passed it along to Bragg; naturally, Bragg dismissed it out of hand. Having under his thumb two of the generals he most detested, Bragg noted that "I cannot concur in [Polk's] apprehensions. [And] the transfer of [Frank Cheatham's] division to that locality would soon see another large portion of [his troops] on stolen horses marauding over the country."[4] Bragg was at least right in dismissing Polk's "apprehensions": the 20,000 Federals thought to be massing in northern Alabama proved a phantom force. The Confederates' misinformation was not altogether unusual in a region where confusion on both sides was pretty much the rule: at about the same time, a Federal general in Memphis advised a counterpart in Alabama that "I am credibly informed that Polk's force, 17,000 strong, [is headed for] Huntsville." There was no such force as that either, and it was not on the move.[5] What *was* true was that General Johnston's 55,000 Confederates in northwestern Georgia (under corps commanders William Hardee, John Bell Hood, and Joseph Wheeler) were facing the imminent advance of 100,000 Federals from their staging area in Chattanooga. Essentially picking up where the 1863 Battles of Chickamauga and Chattanooga had broken off, Sherman and his Yankees now had as their objectives four things: the capture of Atlanta, the destruction of the Army of Tennessee, the prevention of western Confederate troops' going to the aid of Robert E. Lee in Virginia, and the political support of President Lincoln.

The better to survey the landscape of his pending operations toward Atlanta, General Sherman on the last day of April had come down from his Nashville headquarters and ascended Chattanooga's Lookout Mountain with his chief of engineers. The two Union soldiers stood atop the same Tennessee eminence where, seven years before, Bishop Leonidas Polk, friends, and supporters had celebrated the Fourth of July as they envisioned a University of the South on the nearby Sewanee plateau. But the school's cornerstone having by now been obliterated by vandal Yankee soldiers, the Northern general and his engineer were deciding how best to get on with obliterating the Southern way of life.[6]

Coincidentally, *Harper's Weekly* had lately published a drawing by one of its field artists traveling with General Sherman's army. For his useful perspective, Theodore Davis had climbed to the top of northern Georgia's Ringgold Mountain and titled his drawing "Smoke of Enemy's Camps at Dalton." In the foreground, Lt. Henry W. Howgate's signalmen were shown training a mounted telescope on Buzzard's Roost Gap. The gap was one of the few passes through Rocky Face Ridge, a sheer-walled height of some 800 feet running north and south for twenty-five miles. It was then crawling with Confederate defenders. As the artist had been advised, it would likely be through Buzzard's Roost—a channel for both a road and a rail line—that Sherman would aim his first strike at Joe Johnston's Rebel army. Lieutenant Howgate's signalmen, in the meantime, were keeping abreast of the Rebels' private thoughts concerning their defensive measures; they had learned to decipher the Confederates' wigwag flag messages.[7]

Harper's Weekly having accurately set the scene, Gen. George Thomas's Army of the Cumberland set off from Ringgold on May 7; their destination was Buzzard's Roost Gap and the smoky Confederate entrenchments beyond. Supplied with 98,497 infantry and cavalry and 254 guns, Thomas was Sherman's spear point aimed at Joe Johnston's vitals. Firing from behind obstructions and breastworks, Gen. John Wharton's dismounted Confederates at the village of Tunnel Hill bravely delayed but scarcely impeded Thomas's initial thrust. The swarm of Yankees continued on down the rail line through the mountain toward the more heavily defended gap. Gen. Joe Wheeler, Wharton's commander, estimated "the relative numbers engaged were about ten to one, 5000 against 900." Against odds like that, the Rebel cavalry's only recourse was to fall back while inflicting as much damage as they could to the Federal onslaught.[8]

Faced with these realities, General Johnston in Dalton about seven miles below Tunnel Hill had by now "notified the ladies" present that it was time for them to be leaving the army for the safety of Atlanta.[9] For the time being, though, if outnumbered overall almost two-to-one, the Army of Tennessee assumed it had little to fear from the Federal forces rolling southward. Protected by Rocky Face Ridge, Johnston's men were effectively invulnerable from direct assault by anyone. Moreover, to Johnston's great pleasure, word came that additional fighters were hurrying to his side by rail and by foot. This was the Army of Mississippi under the personal command of Leonidas Polk. The Yankees, for their part, had heard the same news—if in an erroneous version—ten days earlier. While false rumors are routine in military affairs, the bearer was someone hardly to be expected or suspected: an unnamed "rebel chaplain." He had come into the Federal headquarters at Ringgold on April 22 to say that "part of Polk's corps" was at Dalton and that he estimated "Johnston's army at 60,000." Whether the chaplain intended to misinform the enemy or to betray the warrior bishop is not known.[10]

After having notified the Richmond War Department on May 6 that 10,000 of his infantrymen and 4,000 of his cavalry were on their way to Georgia, Polk and his staff set out on a virtually sleepless two-day journey, leaving Gen. Stephen Lee's cavalry troop to watch over his deserted department. (Seldom too busy in Richmond to find fault with Polk, Braxton Bragg two weeks later directly questioned Polk's authority and wisdom to have removed so many men from the Mississippi / Alabama region. The exchange of testy letters between the two petered out when, as his son puts it, Polk focused instead on fighting the enemy in Georgia and essentially "ignored [Bragg's] interference." It helped that President Davis, apparently failing to inform Bragg, had earlier left the question of numbers up to Polk.)[11]

As a general with gifts for waging war, Sherman well knew that the Rocky Face Ridge rearing up in front of George Thomas was a formidable impediment; accordingly, he had long since determined that the way to Atlanta was not to go through General Johnston's army but around it. To that end, while the Confederates on the ridge glared down balefully at Thomas, Sherman had already sent James McPherson's Army of the Tennessee along the western side of the ridges. This expedition brought the Yankees on Johnston's left flank and gave them access to the backside of Dalton, to Confederate stores heaped up there, and, most important, to the Western & Atlantic Railroad passing through Resaca. Stretching from Chattanooga to Atlanta, the Western & Atlantic was the essential supply line, whether southward or northward, of both Sherman's and Johnston's armies. As Philip Secrist, the author of a book-length study of the Resaca fighting, has said: "The Atlanta Campaign in a daily practical sense became a contest for control" of that railroad. Giving added point to the contest, the line was particularly vulnerable at Resaca, where it crossed the Oostanaula River on a covered, 600-foot-long wooden trestle.[12]

While worming his way toward Atlanta in five oblique moves on the flanks and rear of the Army of Tennessee, General Sherman first sent James McPherson through Resaca's Snake Creek Gap. Finding it amazingly undefended, McPherson's forces on May 8 arrived at what was virtually an open side door to the Confederate's right. That was "one of the great strategic marches of the war," and General Johnston's failure to guard the passage was "one of the great mistakes of the war," the historian Richard McMurry has said.[13] But wary of falling into a possible trap himself (some 4,000 of Polk's advance were already milling about Resaca and had mounted their artillery on heights west of the rail town), James McPherson's XV and XVI Corps, led by Maj. Gens. Grenville Dodge and John A. Logan (Polk's old foe from Belmont), made only a cautious, exploratory advance in the vicinity of Resaca and the railway on May 9. It was far from "the most vigorous attack possible" desired by Sherman. With too few men to break trackage once they reached the rail line, a troop of mounted infantry merely snipped telegraph lines to Dalton before they, and the rest of McPherson's force, drew back into the safety of Snake Creek to await support. And to await learning of Sherman's "much vexed" reaction to McPherson's failing to seize or break the railroad: "Well, Mac, you have missed the opportunity of a lifetime," Sherman said with self-control when next the two were face-to-face.[14] (For the Yankee quartermasters, every missed disruption of the road to Atlanta had consequences favorable to their Confederate counterparts: as Sherman's supply lines from Chattanooga stretched, Johnston's from Atlanta contracted.)

By that time, almost the full measure of Polk's Army of Mississippi was filling in the earthworks already built outside Resaca. Missing—and for days still to come—were two miserable brigades of Samuel French's division, standing in rain while awaiting rail transportation out of central Alabama. French peevishly laid the blame for the bad weather train troubles on Polk, and his cavalry troopers and infantrymen were to miss entirely the weekend's fighting around Resaca.[15]

As for Polk and his mounted escort, they had left Demopolis at four o'clock Monday morning (when Polk's 2:30 A.M. last-minute meeting with Stephen Lee and Nathan Bedford Forrest had at last wound up). Traveling continually from western Alabama, Polk's entourage reached Rome in west-central Georgia by noontime Tuesday, wearying hours either in the saddle or, briefly (for the general and four ranking aides, anyway), in a stagecoach. They made better time than most of their troops, but as the infantry and cavalry units began to arrive, Polk, the lifelong railway enthusiast, took pleasure in personally managing the further entraining of the men and horses to the Resaca front.[16] From Rome, Polk flashed a sanguine telegraphic all's-well to Jefferson Davis in Richmond, and on Wednesday morning, May 11, he and his staff moved on toward Resaca.[17]

The scramble to Johnston's aid had been uneventful save that in the rush someone had misplaced Polk's cipher box, leaving him at first unable to read coded messages brought to him.[18] With Polk now in command of Resaca, his irritation was offset by the gratifying welcome he soon encountered from "all my old friends much pleased to see me here again [with the Army of Tennessee]." Just as nice, he would tell Fanny a few days later, "the troops have received [me] with cordial demonstrations of pleasure." Cordial, indeed. A trooper in his escort, Charles Gallway of Louisiana, would write a friend that "I never witnessed such joy as that of General Polk's old corps as he passed at Resaca."[19]

That afternoon, May 11, another observant Louisiana soldier, while noting that under lowering rain clouds "everything is stripped for the fight," watched Polk and five other generals "together upon their horses, upon a rising ground, evidently very calmly surveying the scene of the expected conflict. . . . There is evidently a heavy thing on hand, for the troops are pouring in from Dalton. . . . The enemy's force is estimated at 150,000 with a large amount of artillery." The building tension eventually got the best of the soldier; he admitted to his diary that later that evening "I broke through my resolutions . . . and got drunk." Elsewhere on the field, an aide to General Johnston tersely complained, "enemy's sharpshooters in trees very annoying."[20]

Among the reconnoitering horsemen with Polk that afternoon was Gen. John Bell Hood, until that day in charge of keeping an eye on McPherson and, with three divisions, maintaining the defenses around Resaca; Hood had now handed that job to Polk, but for other reasons he was exceedingly glad to see the bishop general.[21] Relatively new to the Tennessee army when Polk had been banished by Bragg the previous fall, Hood had been twice wounded that year (he lost the use of his left hand at Gettysburg in July, his right leg altogether at Chickamauga in September) and was now facing yet another dangerous battle. The Confederacy's celebrated Civil War diarist Mary Chesnut seems to have had it right when she reckoned that by this time the doughty soldier was "scared into joining the Church"; a weeks-long religious revival among Confederate soldiers lining up for baptism in a Dalton creek about then may have also influenced Hood's decision. For whatever reason, he suddenly wanted to be baptized. And with Charles Quintard, chaplain-at-large of the Army of Tennessee, busy down in Atlanta ministering to hospitalized soldiers, who better to officiate than the fortuitously available general-bishop? Hood had become well acquainted with Polk during his post-Chickamauga convalescence in Atlanta when Polk gave up his room in John Thrasher's home to the wounded man. Here was the clergyman whom Hood soon "had grown to love . . . with my whole heart."[22]

As Thomas's front-line pressure at Dalton and McPherson's flanking movement at Snake Creek Gap had forced the Confederates to look both ways, Polk had been told to occupy Hood's defensive works east of Snake Creek Gap while Hood and one his divisions were to return to Dalton. The changeover accomplished, the two lieutenant generals took a train up to Dalton to confer further with Johnston about the Resaca situation. Shortly after midnight, Polk proceeded with the baptism Hood had asked for.[23]

In peacetime days, the bishop had seldom been a stickler for the fine points of liturgy, and on this night he showed similar latitude by dispensing with several rules set forth in the Book of Common Prayer regarding the baptism of "such as are of riper years." Among the allowances he made, "timely notice" had hardly been given the minister (himself), and the candidate (Hood), for all his sincerity, would scarcely have been able to fulfill the rubric that he prepare himself "by Prayers and Fasting, for the receiving of this Holy Sacrament." Nor were any required godparents "ready to present [him] at the Font" (in this instance a tin basin that somebody helpfully supplied).[24] Nevertheless it sufficed that the war-torn general leaning on crutches, as one "born in sin and seeking salvation," was firmly presented to the bishop by a few caring friends. One of these was Col. Henry Percy Brewster, once Gen. Sam Houston's personal secretary and now an aide and confidant of Hood's. He recorded the ceremony this way: "There stood the battered old hero (barely thirty years old). There the Warrior Bishop Polk. And there stood your humble servant, with a flaring yellow candle in one hand and a horse bucket of water in the other."[25] To Polk's question ("Dost thou renounce the devil and all his works, the vain pomp and glory of the world, with all covetous desires of the same, and the carnal desires of the flesh, so that thou wilt not follow, nor be led by them?") Hood replied, "I renounce them all." Said William Gale of the ceremony: "Most imposing."[26]

Figuratively exchanging miter for kepi as the night of May 11–12 wore on, a sleepless Polk made ready to rejoin his troops at Resaca, having to wait until 4 A.M. for a southbound train. Even then it took him two hours to cover the fifteen miles between the towns. Polk was none too soon getting back. Having been left to themselves on unfamiliar terrain, his troops, said Gale, had fallen into "confusion, well confounded, and if the enemy had made a bold attack . . . they would have taken the place in one hour."[27] Polk quickly set things aright, and though Sherman was in the area, the Yankees made no significant moves that day.

With a threat hanging over Resaca's road and rail bridges spanning the Oostanaula, the Confederates' essential link to Atlanta, Johnston had by now abandoned his fortifications on Rocky Face Ridge. Six months old, they were no longer relevant as Sherman's divisions had all but deserted Johnston's front and, by skirting the ridge, were headed south to bolster McPherson's corps in Snake Creek Gap. On the morning of May 12, Polk had been warned of this development, and the bulk of the Army of Tennessee in that night's darkness hurried southward too.[28]

By early afternoon on Friday, May 13, skirmishing, increasingly heavy, broke out along the Confederate line; it went on until nightfall. While no significant gains were made by the Federals, Polk himself was so exposed during Friday's shooting—his officer's uniform caught the eyes of alert Yankee marksmen—that two officers' horses on either side of him were shot and killed. The general credited his escaping a similar fate to "the Lord's hand defend[ing] me." He had yet another close call either that same day or the next. Polk had invited his friend Henry Watterson, the war correspondent now also serving Johnston as a scout and Polk as an aide, to share his lunch of guava jelly and bread. Watterson wrote this account of this battlefield meal to his fiancée Rebecca Ewing:

> While we were about to eat it, quite a brisk fire was opened on the place where we were standing. "General," said I, "this is rather uncomfortable. Suppose I look us up a cover." "Do so at once," said he, and I found a pretty shade spot behind a clump of trees, where we sat down to dinner. In a little while a shell came along and took the top off the very tree under which we were sitting, and scattering balls and branches in every direction. "Ugh!" says the General. "You are a fine fellow for selecting safe places. I expect we'd better go back to first principles."[29]

Three corps of Sherman's men—all his forces except those left behind to nip at Johnston's withdrawing rear—had flared through Snake Creek Gap by Saturday dawn, and they arrayed themselves in a concave line some four miles long. Soon they were face to face with the quickly reassembling Army of Tennessee, simultaneously arranging itself in a defensive semicircle on high ground north and west of Resaca. The Confederate line stretched between two rivers, Polk's corps nearest Resaca on the Confederate left (its own left protected from flank attack by the Oostanaula River); Hood's corps was on the right (his right on the Conasauga River); Hardee's corps connected the two. With their backs to the two rivers and overlooked by heights that the Yankees would shortly capture, the Confederates' position was less than perfect, but it would have to do. The two days of fighting that would then follow were to constitute the only part of the whole 125-day Atlanta Campaign in which all the opponents were engaged (excepting the still absent French command). But around Polk's headquarters, William Gale observed that the worry had been that "the enemy will not attack us here." What Gale more precisely complained of was the frustration Sherman aroused in Polk and his fellow officers by continuing to apply his hit-and-run flanking strategy, a tactic one historian likened not to a series of major battles but to a four-months-long skirmish over seventy miles of Georgia countryside. Rather than assault the defensive positions Johnston would establish at various points as he backed away toward Atlanta, Sherman was able repeatedly to shift his army farther south, maneuvering the Confederates out of their chosen works. Sherman's behavior did not sit well with the flummoxed Southerners. Doubtless speaking for Polk, Gale said: "We have been greatly perplexed by the enemy in his movement. We have offered battle often and invariably [he] demurred and compelled us to fall back."[30]

Protracted artillery and sharpshooting had caused considerable casualties to W. W. Loring's and James Cantey's divisions in Polk's lines by the close of Friday's fighting. After Polk and his staff had choked down their Saturday breakfast of hard bread, butter, and tea, they set out from their hillside headquarters to inspect the lines that protected the town proper.[31] Polk's dug-in infantry were already being peppered with skirmishers' fire from John Logan's XV Corps; during the night Yankee skirmishers had crept closer to the Rebel earthworks. But with little else to show for repeated attacks on the Rebel right and center (some so foolishly made across swampy ground against Hardee's elevated center that a Yankee brigadier who had ordered a foolhardy charge with heavy casualties was later dismissed for incompetency), Sherman was at least pleased to find John Logan's corps still on the move against Polk late in the day.[32] After wading through waist- to neck-deep Camp Creek, the Yankees around six o'clock on Saturday evening charged uphill about one-third of a mile against the heights held by Loring and Cantey—driving themselves with such vigor that as the night deepened they prevailed and, Logan would report, "at the point of the bayonet . . . planted their colors on the summits of the conquered hills."

Two desperate counterattacks by Polk's infantry filled the darkness with the red flames of hundreds of muskets, but Logan's men held their ground, much—for a certainty—to Polk's dismay. By 10 o'clock that night, in stark contrast to Gale's worry that the enemy would not fight, Logan could say "it was evident to the meanest comprehension among the rebels that night that the men who double-quicked across to their hills that afternoon had come to stay."[33] Further, with Sunday morning's light, Federal guns would now be able to lob shells over the heads of the Rebels on the critical rail and wagon bridges across the Oostanaula. Gale evidently had trouble accepting this. He wrote afterward in his diary that an afternoon charge by the enemy "was easily repulsed" and on Saturday night "[Brigadier General James] Cantey was ordered to . . . retake the hills . . . and the line was reestablished after a very severe conflict of an hour. Night closed the scene in this way." Gale's booster account of Polk's succeeding against Logan is unique among other witnesses and seems to contradict words attributed even to Polk, who lamented that the Federals have it "in their power at any moment . . . to burn our bridges and completely cut us off."[34] The Federals had even "effected a lodgement on the hill" opposite the headquarters house where Johnston and his ranking generals were to stay that night. Polk took up a position closer to the town and railroad. Johnston got busy that night having a pontoon bridge laid over the Oostanaula beyond the notice of Federal artillery.[35]

But something out of sight—and no less disadvantaging than shot and shell—had happened as well to the Confederates that Saturday afternoon. Five miles downstream from Resaca's battle chaos, Brig. Gen. Thomas W. Sweeney's troops in portable boats had rowed 100 yards over the Oostanaula River at Tanners Ferry. Designing to lay a pontoon bridge of their own, Sweeney in the face of light opposition had deposited two divisions into the Rebels' backyard. Overly edgy perhaps, the extended Federals became worried by a false report that they might be overrun by Rebels sent against them, withdrew back over the river, but then decided to cross once more. All to their good, it turned out.[36]

Sherman on Sunday, renewing the attack on the Rebel front, tried but failed again to break through Hood's and Hardee's lines. (For the fate of one Confederate cannoneer, his enemies came close enough: captured along with his guns, a tattoo on his arm was spotted by soldiers of the 105th Illinois Infantry. It read "FORT PILLOW," the Tennessee site of the Confederate massacre perpetrated the month previous. While begging for quarter, he was killed immediately by bayonets and bullets fired point-blank.)[37] But with Sherman to their front and Sweeney to their rear (even if Sweeney's hold at Tanners Ferry was insubstantial), it was all too much for the Rebels to contend with: Johnston and his generals consequently concluded Sunday that the Confederates' hold on Resaca had been pried loose, and they immediately set about gathering up their things and their wounded fellows and departing. Casualties were high, with about 7,000 for the Federals and about 5,000 for the Confederates. This was Johnston's second withdrawal in less than a week. Jefferson Davis, aided by hindsight at least, would later declare to William Gale that if Polk had been in command at Resaca instead of Johnston "I am sure he would have fought Sherman there." That is an interesting, if unprovable, claim. Perhaps the accord between Davis and Polk, so distinctly different from that between Davis and Johnston, might have led Polk to submit to Davis's urgings for an aggressive assault on the shifting strategy Sherman was using. That scarcely proves, however, that Polk would have prevailed at Resaca. To the contrary, the historian Philip Secrist surmises that, after the Yankees' gains on Polk's front Saturday evening, Sherman could have overrun Polk on Sunday, May 15; instead, Sherman spent that day in front of Polk's army entrenching his artillery and "thus lost a great opportunity to bag the entire Confederate army at Resaca."[38]

As it was, after a day of relative calm, Polk and the rest of the Army of Tennessee ever-so quietly pulled out of town on the night of May 15–16, with Polk and his staff being among the last to leave the trenches, the covered railroad trestle soon in ashes. "I held Resaca until General Johnston's forces passed the Oostanaula at that place" was General Polk's version of the nightlong withdrawal in a letter to his wife.[39] All of the Confederates then proceeded to Calhoun twenty miles south. But having given up the more easily defended hills and heights of northern Georgia, the rank-and-file Rebels now found themselves in open country, greatly exposed to the trailing enemy. Wheeler's cavalry did what it could to retard the Yankees (not unlike the assignments given the cavalry when Sherman's February raid was pressing across the middle of Mississippi). But if the enemy were cheered by the Rebels' withdrawal (and it made sense they would have felt that way), Gale, at least, supposed the last laugh was pending. Once a new defensive line had been formed on Monday afternoon at Calhoun, he boasted, "if the enemy will only come on us now, we will repay for all their jubilations." Lacking Gale's relish for conflict under any conditions, Johnston was dissatisfied with the scant defensive advantages Calhoun offered, and at half-past three in the morning (May 17) the order came to pack up and move on. "Under a continual strain since . . . we got to Resaca, . . . we have fought during the day and marched during the night," Gale summarized the campaign for his wife, and in the following weeks, he added: "We have never been out of the sound of a gun, or cannon, or both." His father-in-law too would soon be admitting the campaign "was by far the severest he has ever had since the war began."[40] As the two armies inched ever southward with only a few miles of no-man's land between them, the farming families still inhabiting the region (those less foresighted than their neighbors) began to scatter for whatever safety might be found. "We camped last night at Curtis near the farm of [Richard] Peters," Gale reported on May 17. An experienced Mississippi farmer before becoming an amateur soldier, Gale reverted to type when noting approvingly that Peters was "remarkable for his Cashmere goats."[41]

The destination for the Army of Tennessee was now Adairsville, seven miles farther south. Sticky as tar, the Yankees—infantry, cavalry, and artillery—were annoyed but not stopped by the small-arms fire of Joe Wheeler's backtracking cavalry "posted at every favorable position." The rearguard tactic, said Wheeler, merely "forced the enemy to advance in line all day."[42] Both armies arrived at Adairsville near sundown, whereupon heavy skirmishing broke out and continued until after dark. (That same day, to the west, an offshoot of Thomas's Army of the Cumberland had rather adventitiously come upon Rome and found there members of Samuel French's division still drying out and trying to catch up with Polk's army. Though checked by the arrival of Lawrence Ross's cavalry, the Yankees' attack was so vigorous that French, after 100 casualties, gave up the town and its prize of stores and communications. He then resumed his journey to Polk's side.)[43]

Presently at Adairsville, once the shooting had subsided, General Johnston sent for General Polk, in haste, to attend a conference of his lieutenant generals. They were to weigh the army's options: stand and fight or withdraw yet again for strategic reasons. A little later that night, incongruous battlefield surroundings still the norm, Johnston stood as the next in line to receive Bishop Polk's administration of Holy Baptism. Lydia Johnston, the general's wife, had taken note of John Bell Hood's previous sacramental alteration and, "full of all the sympathy of a loving, earnest wife" (as Lieutenant Gale expressed it), had now besought the bishop to perform the same rite for her husband. The soldier-husband had acquiesced. A little better organized than the rushed tin-basin baptism given John Hood, the ceremony had suitable light and ambience provided by a crucifix candlestick from Polk's field Communion set. Among the witnesses now were Hood and Hardee and Johnston's chief of staff, Brig. Gen. William W. Mackall. A sometime Bible reader, Mackall was apparently chary of organized religion and confessed that "I felt as if I was parting from an old friend."[44] Next day, William Gale telegraphed Mrs. Johnston in Atlanta, assuring her that her husband was now officially a redeemed lamb of Christ's flock. But if battle-field baptisms had united Joseph Eggleston Johnston and John Bell Hood as brothers in the Lord, friends in the here-and-now they failed to be. Quarrelsome postwar accusations engaged the two for years as they faulted one another for not having halted Sherman's inexorable advance into Georgia.[45]

With the latest nighttime baptism concluded in the headquarters tent, the Confederates, in General Mackall's words, "went to bed, as we call it, laying down on the floor and jumping up every few moments to read one dispatch and write another."[46] The burden of the outgoing dispatches to Richmond was that General Johnston and his generals had once more decided (though with Hardee dissenting) that the position of his outnumbered army was still untenable: the order was given to abandon Adairsville to the Yankees.

Like ten-mile legs of a triangle, two main roads led southward out of Adairsville, one southwest to Kingston, the other slightly southeast to Cassville. Having an ambush now in mind, Johnston sent only Hardee's corps, plus all the army's wagons, to Kingston. As that route paralleled Johnston's railroad supply line, and as Hardee had handled rear-guard duties since Resaca, Johnston guessed Sherman might be misled and obligingly decoyed toward Kingston. Which he was. Meanwhile, Hood and Polk took the road to Cassville, where the separated corps were to reunite.[47] Sherman, after briefly resting his troops at Adairsville on Wednesday, ordered Thomas's Army of the Cumberland, his largest, to pursue Hardee, the decoy. The rest of the Federals followed the road to Cassville that veered them away from Thomas. In due course, Sherman's columns, with rough country in between, were effectively isolated from one another. So far, Johnston's script was proceeding exactly as hoped. Hardee, meanwhile, with a half-day's lead, swung left after reaching Kingston and hurried east to rejoin Polk and Hood at Cassville. Gen. Samuel French had by then caught up with Polk, so at this point Joe Johnston had some 75,000 men at his command and a battleground to his liking. With the unsuspecting Yankee columns conveniently drifting apart, Johnston could savor the notion that on the morrow he would pounce on their flanks and destroy them. Drinking their Thursday morning coffee, indeed, the Rebels were treated to the reading of a spirited pep talk from their commander: "You will now turn and march to meet [the enemy's] advancing columns," he guaranteed them. "I lead you to battle!" Cheers were heard throughout the camp, though there may have been a question nagging some of the men: Why had their leader ordered them to throw up defensive breastworks?

Whatever happened in Cassville after breakfast—some of the accusations and recollections remain in unresolvable dispute, and General Polk left no record of the day—it did not advance the Confederate cause. The accepted facts explain enough. General Thomas discovered he had been duped into heading for Kingston, and he marched straightaway to Cassville; he arrived on Johnston's left flank early that day. Polk's skirmishers at midmorning advanced against the enemy in front of them, while to their right Hood (whether on his own or on Johnston's order can be debated) ventured northward from his earthworks at Cassville to make the proposed ambush on the left flanks of two undersized Yankee columns. Hood's role was crucial to Johnston's snare, but before he could pull it off he stopped in his tracks when told that other, unforeseen (and largely still unseen) Yankees were reportedly somewhere on his right flank and rear.[48] Rather than proceed into the perceived jaws of a bench vise, he wisely abandoned his mission and fell back out of imminent harm's way. However successful an ambush might have been, Johnston's was no longer possible.

With that development, Johnston had to adjust—albeit glumly—to Hood's turnaround. (Johnston would write years later, when thoroughly down on Hood, that had Polk been assigned to the flanking order he surely would have attacked, irrespective of the daunting Yankees in his rear.)[49] But now with no other recourse after his surprise had fizzled, Johnston rearranged his army so that by afternoon it had fortified a new and apparently strong position atop a ridge behind the town. He placed his corps, left to right, with Hardee, Polk, and Hood; French's lately arrived division occupied the heights in the middle. That done, Johnston told a visitor, Governor Isham Harris of Tennessee, that he would "be ready for, and happy to receive, [the] enemy next day."[50] If Johnston was well satisfied with the arrangement, so was Sherman, who had settled onto a roughly parallel and slightly higher ridge to the north. They showered artillery shells on one another all afternoon.[51]

Capt. Walter Morris, as Polk's chief of engineers, had been directed by Polk to make a surveillance of the Federal installations around Cassville. Morris concluded the enemy had done themselves proud, rendering the Confederates vulnerable to plunging artillery fire. Further, during supper at Polk's headquarters in the home of a Mr. Haisc, Johnston was given the disturbing news that in two places the Federal gunners had enfiladed the Confederate entrenchments, able to fire into the Rebel ranks from end to end. In a letter written five years after that night to William Gale, Johnston recalled that he was assured that the enfilading was "so severe . . . as to have produced demoralization of the exposed troops, especially . . . the enfiladed portion of General Polk's position."[52] Thus, he was told by his lieutenant generals and others present, that with the coming of daylight the trenches could not be held for long.

The talk of the conferring generals, if certain disputed testimony may be trusted, then took an interesting turn: while Johnston argued to lie low and remain in the entrenched lines, never mind the enfilading, Polk and Hood resisted.[53] The lieutenant generals asserted their trenches were little good for defense (especially those on the ridgetop occupied by French's artillery and infantry), but as Hood remembered the conference, he and Polk thought them fine *for launching an attack*. The two thus argued against retreat, plumping instead for a surprise headlong movement, either that night or in the morning, against the dug-in Yankees holding the opposite ridge.[54] If that was in fact what Hood and Polk urged (as Hood, on the "departed soul of the Christian and noble Polk," would later avow), Johnston must have regarded the idea as suicidal. He later wrote that no such recommendation had occurred, noting that it would have been "inexpressibly absurd" and "stupid."[55] Instead, he had slowly arrived at a third option—one of his favorites: retreat, this time over the Etowah River flowing south of Cassville. He explained that "after a discussion of about two hours, I yielded [on our remaining in the trenches], on the ground it would be hazardous to attempt to defend a position regarded as untenable by two of [my] three lieutenant-generals." Hardee, coming to the Haise house about eleven o'clock that night, was not in accord with Polk and Hood. His sector had been spared enfilading fire, and he was for staying put. His vote did not change the commanding general's decision, but it probably added to his increasingly favorable opinion of Hardee. Right after leaving Resaca, Johnston would write his wife that "[Hardee's] conduct in our recent difficult operations has been admirable, his bearing in danger high & in council fair & candid, between our Selves [I] would not give him [up] for both his compeers." (Hood and Polk, in other words.)[56]

Committed now to another dispiriting withdrawal ("I could not restrain my tears," Johnston's chief of staff, General William Mackall, said in a letter home), the Confederates at Cassville began a stealthy nighttime departure from their fortified ridges, leaving behind as well valuable war industries near the town: the Quimby Iron Works and the Etowah Manufacturing and Mining Company. Some troops were set to chopping trees as noisily as possible to suggest the army was strengthening its position—and to cover the rattling and squealing of artillery wheels on the move. Gale "was sent back to see that the men all kept quiet, and left their trenches with their arms at trail instead of [on] a shoulder, to keep them from being seen [glinting] in the moonlight." He reckoned "the enemy was not more than 300 yards distant in some places. I saw the last regiment down the mountain and then turned my horse's head toward our front." Over his journal that night, Gale closed the day's entry with a literary ornament, quoting (approximately) lines from a Longfellow poem: *"And they folded their tents / like the Arabs, / And silently stole away."*[57]

Hopeful as Johnston had been to lead his frustrated troops into battle Friday morning, staying on in those enfiladed trenches was not really a good idea. For if on that night some of Sherman's troops were indeed only 300 yards distant from the Confederates, others had crossed over the Etowah River while no one was looking, intent on creeping up behind the Confederates—a tactic Sherman would try more than once during the Atlanta Campaign. Still, as with any decision made by others, there was afterward dissension and blame-fixing noised abroad, and a tale-bearer informed Polk that people were saying he and Hood were responsible for the army's failure to stand and fight. "Is that so?" said Polk. "Well, you may say that I take all the blame upon myself." Privately, an aide protested. "Ah, well, let it go," said Polk. "My shoulders are no doubt broad enough to bear it."[58] No more cowed than Polk, General Johnston right after Cassville was not wholly convinced that he had been forced to withdraw. Once the war was over, though, and he and Sherman had become mutually respectful of one another, Johnston admitted to Sherman that soon after the fighting he had had to accept that rueful truth. Writing to another friend about Johnston's concession, Sherman noted that the Confederate general had come to see that "I had the Army and ability to do pretty much what I wanted."[59]

28

"Were It Not to Defend Our Soil and Families, I Should Fear the Curse of God" (1864)

Getting his Army of Mississippi to the relative safety of the southern side of Georgia's Etowah River, and burning his bridges behind him, General Polk on May 22 availed himself of a momentary pause in the Western Confederacy's continuing slide downhill: the loss of Chattanooga; the destruction of Meridian; Gen. Nathaniel Banks's gunboat invasion into the heart of Polk's Louisiana diocese. Accordingly, he took that Sunday off, during which he and a few staff members at the railroad town of Allatoona rode out amid his troops. His aide and son-in-law, William Gale, had begun keeping a diary two weeks previous and noted the fatigued soldiers on that Sunday morning were "bathing and recruiting." Members of Polk's staff were soon refreshed themselves while participating in a session of Morning Prayer in a regimental campground occupied by Brigadier General William Jackson's cavalry. The Reverend Alexander Gordon Bakewell, a Louisiana soldier-clergyman, was directed to officiate by Lieutenant General Leonidas Polk. Uniquely, the mandate was issued as well by Bakewell's bishop, the Right Reverend Leonidas Polk. The neophyte Minister Bakewell had been ordained in the Episcopal Church just nine days earlier, and as soldiers spread out on the slope of a forested hill, Sergeant Bakewell read the appointed Psalms and scripture lessons for Trinity Sunday; he then led prayers for his comrades' comfort and courage.

Sunday-morning church services were then in progress everywhere throughout the divided country, both Confederate and Union. One service not far from Allatoona had drawn in a goodly number of William T. Sherman's worshipful Yankees still encamped around the ruins of Cassville. "Had there been any church service in the village, many of the boys would have gone," Sgt. Rice C. Bull of the 123rd New York Infantry reported. "We had, however, service in the open near our camp. . . . When in camp, we were often called in a body to attend church, but in the field it was voluntary. It was surprising so many were at the service that morning."[1]

The spiritual repose bestowed on General Polk's staff and troops by the reverend sergeant sufficed for only a few hours. At half-past three that afternoon word was sent from Joe Johnston's headquarters to his three lieutenant generals to be ready to move with three days' rations in haversacks. Immediately after Monday's breakfast, local guides leading the way, Polk's command crossed Pumpkin Vine Creek using two bridges built on the spot. The destination now for the consolidated Army of Tennessee was the hilly and rocky area just above and northwest of Atlanta. The "many disloyal people" known to live thereabouts glowered at the secessionist passers-by from their porches.[2]

Settling "near New Hope Church outside Marietta," and with the Yankees not yet again threatening, General Polk used the break in fighting to tend to correspondence. Much of it concerned the batch of officious letters Braxton Bragg had lately sent second-guessing Polk's command decisions. More welcome was the loving letter from his ailing son Hamilton, who had been left behind on quartermaster duties in Alabama. "Please take good care of yourself and not unnecessarily expose yourself," the elder son counseled, such advice as the incautious father was not prone to heed. As for himself, Polk wrote to his wife, whose recent letter from Asheville had touched off "delightful reflections" of his and Fanny's May 6 wedding day thirty-four years before. As befitted a bishop-soldier and husband confronted by the distresses of Sherman's Atlanta Campaign, Polk was moved to theological musings upon the divine blessings of their life together (not forgetting that "we have had our trials, dear wife") and upon his current circumstances. Although he could say only for himself that "my whole soul hangs upon [God] like as a weaned child upon its mother's breast," it was a comfort to him that his fellow Episcopalian generals (Johnston, Hardee, and Hood) were now aligned with him religiously in their military labors. "Our whole hope and confidence is in God, upon whom we lean, and in whom we trust," he declared. "We consign ourselves, our army, and our cause to him . . . with the humble prayer that he will make it appear that he is our Saviour and Mighty Deliverer."[3]

Sunday's Morning Prayer service having raised the morale of some, it was insufficient to sustain the usually confident William Gale. On the previous Saturday night he had confided to his diary that under General

Johnston's leadership "things look bad for us in a military way. We all have gloomy anticipations. Genl J. is not the man we thought him. He lacks enterprise in the last degree. He hesitates and delays and retreats and waits for circumstances to force a fight upon him, instead of watching his chance and forcing the enemy to fight him at his own time and place." Gale's withering conclusion: "He has failed in this campaign beyond doubt, and I fear beyond repair. We must have a battle here soon or we are whipped without a fight." Pointedly, Gale had generous words for General Sherman in the same May 21 entry: the Union general marauding northern Georgia "has certainly managed his army well," he would write. "He understands the 'flanking' business thoroughly."[4]

Since rocky Allatoona and its narrow railroad pass had afforded the Confederates an impregnable defensive site for the time being, Sherman, after burning the Etowah Iron Works and pillaging Cassville, had also crossed the Etowah and now thrust his spear point to the west, hoping to get his regiments around and behind the artfully dodging Army of Tennessee. Sherman's prewar army duty in central Georgia had given him a helpful familiarity with the lay of the land, yet—not knowing for certain the present whereabouts of his foe—he was having to wrestle his cumbersome three-army command through the thickets and ravines of Paulding County before arriving himself near Dallas.[5] (Sherman had earlier conceded to his wife how much easier it had been the previous winter to snake a mere 20,000 men across the width of Mississippi during his "pleasant excursion" against Polk at Meridian.)[6]

After their Sunday leisure, General Jackson's rested Confederate troopers were mounting their saddles by Monday, May 24, and had soon discovered Sherman's westward-bearing whereabouts and relayed the word to Johnston. Hardee and Polk and Hood, in the words of Lt. Thomas Mackall, were thereupon directed to "join hands to be ready to fight in the neighborhood of Pickett's Mill and New Hope Church." In short order the Confederates were arrayed side by side in a line nine miles long, ready and set. As for Yankees, none was in sight.[7] One rumor had it that Sherman and his soldiers had all slipped away to Knoxville, Tennessee. Soon enough, that fanciful tale put to rest, the two armies stood face to face. The battle that William Gale had been longing for was at hand.

Sensing that what lay ahead might prove momentous, Pvt. Philip Stephenson, a teenage artillery loader from Arkansas who had been fighting in General Polk's ranks since the battle at Belmont, readied himself midweek by tidily washing his "only shirt in a little run that trickled by in the rear [of New Hope Church]." He put "it on again wet" as he hurried to his battery's position. According to his memoirs Private Stephenson's hunch that he was needed at the front proved true, and he was later to muse that while the little Methodist meetinghouse nearby might be well known "in heaven for the scenes of salvation, joy and peace enacted there in former times, [it was soon to be] known on earth as the storm center of one of the worst of human struggles."[8] William Gale, though—at Polk's side and often imperturbable—was not far from being a tourist, war or no war. With the worst fighting still a few days off, he chatted nonchalantly with his diary:

> MONDAY, MAY 23: *Marched 9 miles today and camped on a fine creek. Such delicious water as we get all along here.*

> TUESDAY, MAY 24: *Up at 3 A.M. Gen'l Hardee is on our right and Gen'l Hood bringing up the rear. I write this from Lost Mountain, which affords one of the finest views I ever saw. On the head branches of Powder Spring Creek, HdQtrs at Mr. Bagget's. Fine rain and a good night's rest. Nothing satisfactory about the movements of the enemy.*

> WEDNESDAY, MAY 25: *Up at daylight and in the saddle. The day passed off quietly until about 5 P.M. when a fierce assault was made on Major Gen'l Alexander Stewart, who repulsed the attack.* [Federal casualties amounted to 1,600; Stewart reported his loss at between 300 and 400, and as Sam Davis Elliott writes: "Stewart and his division had given the Army of Tennessee its first victory in the campaign in the space of three hours."[9]] *From prisoners taken, we learn that two corps were in front of us. Gen'ls Johnston, Hood, Polk, Hindman and Mackall all spent the night at the Widow Wigley's, one mile from New Hope Church. The attack is to be made on our side early tomorrow.* [Sherman disappointed Gale, using the next two days to shift to his left and redeploy.]

> THURSDAY, MAY 26: *Our center [is] at New Hope Church. Hardee occupies the left, Gen'l Polk the center, and Gen'l Hood the right. Our line is on a ridge dividing the water of Powder Spring Creek and Pumpkin Vine Creek 16 miles northwest of Marietta. All go to bed with the feeling that the long wished-for fight will come off today [Friday].*

Now Gale would be right. Sherman still had designs to get behind the Army of Tennessee by swinging around its far right flank at a point about two miles northeast of Polk's sector at New Hope Church; one landmark was the Widow Pickett's grist mill, its grindstones turned by the bucolic

Little Pumpkin Vine Creek. Sherman had supposed Joe Johnston's flank stopped short of Pickett's Mill. It did end there at one time, but General Johnston had extended his right just far enough to obstruct the Yankees, as Gale relates:

> FRIDAY, MAY 27: *At 3 P.M. a vigorous assault on our extreme right, held by Gen'l Hiram Granbury's Brigade and Gen'l Daniel Govan's. The enemy approached suddenly, and in three or more lines of battle, and were repulsed with such havoc as I have never seen on any field. They were under our fire for 3 and ½ hours. When he made the assault on Granbury, he got within 20 yards of our line.*

Dyed-in-the-wool Southerner that he was, usually thirsting for havoc against his Northern brethren, Gale was suddenly having trouble getting his feelings to behave. Stricken by what his fellow Confederates had wrought at New Hope Church, he wrote in his diary:

> *Some of the [enemy] were horribly mutilated, and nearly all were shot in the head or neck. I saw one man who had 11 balls in his head. Oh the horrid sight. Were it not to defend our soil and families I should fear the Curse of God would come upon us for such horrible butchery. Every principle of my nature revolts at the practice and institutions of war. God grant that we may soon have an end of this dreadful carnage.*

Two lines later Gale's mood has lightened: *Sam Smith participated in the fight. Sam is a good soldier and a good fellow.*[10]

Before the fighting had closed (carried on beneath a drumming downpour with thunderclaps vying with cannon roar, an awful noise heard in Atlanta miles away to the south), the area around the Methodists' meeting-house and grain mill had become the "Hell Hole." At New Hope Church and Pickett's Mill the Yankees sustained 1,600 losses killed, wounded, captured, or missing; the Confederates, protected by breastworks, lost 400 killed or wounded. Sherman's encircling scheme had derailed. The Confederate general William Mackall called the scene a "Golgatha . . . with the corpses of our inveterate foes piled together so thick that you would at first suppose that they had been collected from different parts of the field preparatory to interment."[11]

Gale's horror and moral shame were shared by Ambrose Bierce, a Federal Indiana officer on the scene (and a famed postwar author) whose *The Crime at Pickett's Mill* was an indictment of his own superiors for their foolish waste of US soldiers' lives that day. "The civilian reader," Bierce would write, "must not suppose when he reads accounts of military operations in which relative positions of the forces are defined . . . that these were matters of general knowledge to those engaged. It is seldom, indeed, that a subordinate officer knows anything about the disposition of the enemy's forces—except that it is unamiable—or precisely whom he is fighting." Blind to Sherman's overall strategies, the soldiers thrashing through thickets and underbrush would have scarcely known that they were attacking dug-in Arkansan and Texan troops all under General Patrick Cleburne's oversight—and all decidedly unamiable. It was not enough that these same determined infantrymen were largely the ones who had famously carried the day on Missionary Ridge during November's Battle of Chattanooga.

Whereupon, ordered by Brigadier Generals Thomas Wood and Richard Johnson, three brigades of Ohioans, Indianans, and Pennsylvanians recklessly charged into an array of Rebel muskets and artillery, one doomed brigade at a time. As the caustic Bierce would write: "With masses of idle troops behind in the character of audience," as each successive "swarm of men [came] struggling through the undergrowth of the forest, pushing and crowding, they were shot to pieces."[12] And when after nightfall that day's bloody blundering has been done, the Confederate flank had not been turned.[13] William T. Sherman chose not to breathe a word of that day's humiliation in his postwar *Memoirs*.

By the time the fighting at New Hope Church and Pickett's Mill had ended, William Gale was recovering his composure. He calmly recorded in his diary that he and his fellows were "up nearly all night engaged in making ready for a movement [by Hood] upon the enemy's left at dawn."[14] Their preparations proved a sleepless waste of time; the objective to circle Sherman's bloodied left flank was abandoned when it was learned that the enemy, having "the preponderance of force," had shifted left just enough to forestall any success the Confederates might have. By noontime, "in consequence of the insuperable obstacles with which the enemy has protected his left," General Polk urged his men to remain quiet and rest as much as possible. Rest was a fond hope. "The day wore off in the usual amount of skirmishing & cannonading," Gale complained, "annoying the troops and wearing out the men, adding to the daily list of killed and wounded."[15]

Short on supplies and frustrated in his attempt to get behind the Rebels, Sherman, to the relief of his hard-put quartermasters, would shortly sidle back toward the northeast to restore access to his supply-line railroad. He massed his troops at Big Shanty, and once the burned bridges had been rebuilt and the rail communication with Chattanooga was again intact, he would be able to send them grinding straight down the Western & Atlantic to Marietta and just beyond, he hoped, to Atlanta. (The first locomotive shrilling its whistle while soldiers shouted a welcome would chuff into Big Shanty on May 11.)

For the Confederates, the early days of June had been a succession of quiet times alternating with aimless shooting and dying, the whole over-seen by the endless rain. "The enemy is doubtless at some mischief," Gale had nervously recorded on Tuesday, May 31, but he slept well, and after awaking on June 1 he "sent for a nice breakfast." A letter from Kate brought news of the "darling little fellows"; these were the general's grandchildren living in Asheville, North Carolina. Heavy thundershowers on Thursday; the "day closed quiet." Rain all night on Saturday, June 4. "Rode with the General to the lines, found all quiet. Enemy very shy and are evidently wait-ing for reinforcements." (As indeed they were; 9,000 veterans in the XVII Corps were about to arrive in four days.) "Shy" was also Gale's way of guessing the Yankees milling about at Big Shanty were "recruiting" after the severe and fatiguing marching they had had.

Another Confederate "move to the rear," this time from the vicinity of New Hope Church, began late Saturday, June 4; it was a procedure in which Johnston's troops were by now proficient. Lest Sherman assault their migrating columns while they were vulnerable, the army was extricated from its latest emplacement in what William Polk would describe as "a movement of delicacy, requiring tact and celerity. General Polk gave close personal attention to the preparations necessary for withdrawing his com-mand," he wrote. "Roads were cut, bridges were built, guides were pro-vided, and a staff-officer was assigned to each division to conduct it over a road which [General Polk] himself had previously examined." With every-one poised and everything ready, Polk's officers and men set out at eleven o'clock that night, plunging into a mix of fog and persistent summer rain that was to continue intermittently for ten more days. As Meck Polk saw it, his father was as much a shepherd as a general that first night, personally leading his flock of 14,000 souls through the dark, the mud, and the confu-sion. "At dawn he left the men kindling their fires, went to an abandoned dwelling nearby, and throwing himself on his sheepskin, fell asleep." The most Gale could muster was a summary: "We had an awful night."[16]

In their newest position, shielding the rail-junction town of Marietta two miles farther south, the Confederates by Monday had established a ten-mile-long defensive line stretching from Lost Mountain in the west to Brush Mountain in the east. Polk's corps again held the center, now sitting athwart the Western & Atlantic Railroad. Gale's day had him "in the saddle

13 hours after being up all night." By Tuesday, Polk was lodged in better quarters—the home of John Kirk on Mud Creek near Kennesaw Mountain. Gale learned that Kirk "has given 8 sons & 1 son-in-law to the Cause, 5 of whom have been killed, variously at First and Second Manassas, and Chickamauga." Surmounting the Kirks' house now was Polk's Corps's new flag: a silver cross on a crimson background. Those colors, Polk informed the aides who had fashioned this flag to his latest exacting design, were the "emblems of Love and Mercy upon a field of blood." Kirk and his wife must have regarded the sanguinary symbolism over their roof with discomfort.[17]

The rain slacked off (a little), and with the front lines quiet, General Polk on Wednesday, June 8, gave a small dinner party, inviting aides and companionable colleagues. Hardee came but Hood, feeling unwell, declined. He missed a meal of ham, veal, chicken, potatoes, and peas prepared by Aaron, the multiuseful slave brought along to war by Gale. The good food and company (perhaps accompanied by some wine or whiskey) seem to have put Polk in far better spirits than he had been ten months previous when, evaluating the presidential leadership of Jefferson Davis, he had tartly told Stephen Elliott that Davis "was not quick to perceive coming events" and that "such a mind should [not] be allowed the untrammeled and final action of leading the Confederacy." This night with surpassing dewy-eyed bonhomie he expressed restored approval of the president, confiding to Hardee "that the longer the war lasted, the more he had cause to admire [Davis's] foresight, and particularly [his] just judgment of men." Hardee kindly passed along these compliments to Davis.[18]

Polk's mellow mood may have inclined his pastoral heart to provide a subsequent feast three days later to all the corps's rank and file. As cavalry officer Charles Gallway described the event to Willie Huger, Polk's son-in-law at home on leave at the time, "the troops had a barbecue along the lines, and to give you an idea of the family circle, there were one hundred and fifty beeves issued to Polk's infantry only. This was regardless of their [usual] rations, being the treat of the Candy General." As a result, straggling and grumbling on the march had been reduced to a minimum, Gallway was glad to report. It was yet another instance in which Gallway remarked on Polk's evident popularity with his soldiers.[19]

Polk had moved his headquarters on Friday four miles from Marietta, taking over the home of the Hardage family. Saturday was foggy, rainy, and quiet. "Enemy creeping up all about our front and pickets engaged," Gale wrote. "Heavy rain Saturday night. On Sunday, June 12, rain." (One Alabama soldier mentioned rain falling Wednesday, Thursday, Friday, Saturday, Sunday, and Monday.)[20] "For twelve days [the men] have been wet to the skin and all the time covered with mud," Gale noted. "The only consolation being that our enemy is suffering in the same degree, and that it is all for the cause which we have left home and friends and all." Waking as gloomy as the weather on that drizzly Sunday morning, Gale had brightened along with others when Bishop Polk (as he might properly be regarded under the circumstances) announced he would preside over Divine Worship for his headquarters staff and their hosts. Polk's reading of the Gospel assigned for the Third Sunday after Trinity—Jesus's proclamation of "joy in the presence of the angels of God over one sinner that repenteth"—would have been especially satisfying to the evangelical celebrant, and he probably preached a quick homily. It was the first time since the war began, according to Gale, that Polk had celebrated Communion from the Book of Common Prayer, even leading his martial flock a capella in a hymn. "His military life has not impaired his Church manner at all," Gale marveled. "He possesses as much of the truth and beauty of a true devotional manner as he ever did." Gale was left hoping that the exemplary display of holiness "by our beloved General and Bishop may not be lost on any of us."[21] The rain continued all night. Monday came, "rain all last night and still raining this morning—a wretched, miserable day."

But, blessedly, came Tuesday, June 14: "Rain over and gone." In the process earlier of repositioning themselves, one army cautiously advancing, one carefully backing up, the enemies had mutually wormed their ways southward toward Atlanta. ("Creeping" had been one of Gale's favorite words for the Yankees' maneuverings.) And no sooner had the Confederates dug in their new hillside defenses outside Marietta than the Union soldiers, like shadows cast by the new warming sun in the southern sky, presented dark-blue stretches along their hillsides about a mile and a half to the north. Roughly midway now between the two armies stood a woodsy conical mound some 300 feet high. Private Philip Stephenson likened it to "the apex of a triangle"; it rose from the plain about a mile forward of Polk's earthworks.[22] The local Georgians called the modest eminence Pine Mountain; Sherman would sometimes call it Pine Hill; Gen. Oliver O. Howard, Pine Top; Capt. David P. Conyngham, Pine Knob *and* Pine Top Mountain; Lt. Col. Joseph Fullerton, Pine Top Knob.

Having spotted the hill sooner than Sherman, and deeming it useful for scrutinizing his opponents not too many hundreds of yards away, General Johnston posted William Bate's infantry division atop the salient to detect any hostile goings-on. New Orleans's well-regarded Washington Artillery, and René T. Beauregard's South Carolina rifled battery, furnished artillery support. But since the Confederates were themselves in full view (and range) of Yankee artillery, and since, moreover, protection was lacking on the hill's flanks, life on the salient was nothing if not chancy. Still, while enjoying a lull in the fighting, General Bate's troops determined to make life in the trenches passably comfortable: the artillerymen in the two bunkers on the slope facing the Yankees had dug them deep enough to keep their heads out of sight and wide enough to stretch their legs.[23]

Of a mind to keep an eye on the Yankees himself (as well as on Bate's dangerously exposed division), General Polk on Saturday, June 11, had sent word to a daughter in Asheville asking that the "spy glass" he had left behind while on home leave be sent to him by a soldier messenger. As it had been "presented me by the ladies of New Orleans," Polk told young Fanny Polk, "I prize the glass very much." "Charge [the courier] to take good care of it."[24] By then, audacious Union soldiers ("creeping," probably) had been engaged in circling expeditions around Pine Mountain to view the Rebels' more formidable fortifications in its rear. (On their way to the hill's safer backside, the scouts exercised particular care not to alert the sharpshooters Bate had lodged on its front side.)

Apart from the usual skirmishing and the spying sorties, few outright threats had concerned the Confederates in recent days, so Johnston and his generals found time to think in long-range terms; Polk, for one, seized the moment by resuming his penchant for posting military advisories to the commander in chief. This time he would "respectfully" suggest that President Davis order Nathan Bedford Forrest to lead a cavalry raid behind Sherman's army to "operate on the enemy's communications between Chattanooga and Marietta." Such a force, he said, could be easily got up from idle troopers in northern Alabama. (Among these underemployed horsemen was a troop commanded by Gideon Pillow, with whom Polk was lately back in harmony.) General Hardee endorsed Polk's message to Richmond with the words: "I concur in the above."

Though going over his boss's head to the president was not a scruple that would necessarily have stopped him (Hood, too, had done that off and on since joining Johnston), Polk was not acting solely on his own initiative. Taking into account Hardee's concurrence, Polk was participating in a scheme to offset the president's mounting displeasure with Johnston's repetitive withdrawals down the center of Georgia. Polk and Hardee, indeed, may have been in cahoots with their commander, which could explain why Johnston that same day sent an almost identical suggestion regarding Forrest, not to Davis but to Braxton Bragg, the president's military adviser. Nonetheless, if a coordinated gambit by the three generals, it failed. Davis asked Bragg for his opinion of Polk's proposal, and Bragg, as usual with

Polk, replied phlegmatically with assorted reservations and quibbles. Consequently, the subject was dropped right there.[25] The fact that Sherman's supply line from Chattanooga was an obvious and worthwhile target for Confederate cavalry was well understood by the War Department, but by focusing on competing priorities in Mississippi and Alabama (where Joe Johnston had no say over Forrest), the authorities in Richmond never got around to cutting Forrest loose in Sherman's rear.[26]

Skirmishing on Polk's front began early Monday and continued late, with artillery picking up the beat at night. The general was occupied all day with his correspondence and troop movements, ordering his army to stretch itself to a single rank to accommodate a proposed assault by Hood on Sherman's left. He sent one letter to his daughter Lillie, recently married to Willie Huger; his affectionate advice included: "Do always what is right, not calculating what is expedient, . . . and with a pure heart and true devotion go straight forward and do it." At dusk he then rode out with Johnston and Hardee to inspect their several lines.[27] Near midnight, Polk retired to his bedroom in which Brig. Gen. Randall Lee Gibson, at Polk's invitation, had come to spend the evening. A sugar planter before the war, the younger general had been Polk's friend since Louisiana days, and late as it was (Gibson was already in bed), Polk was in a talkative mood, his typical cheerfulness shining through. As Gibson recalled their chat, Polk, now lying on his own bed, assured Gibson that, despite the Federals' recent successes against the Army of Tennessee, it was only a matter of time before he and Gibson and all their fellow Confederates "would surely achieve our independence, and what a day it would be when we could all return to the dear city of New Orleans, bringing peace and liberty to our people. [He] even described how Jackson Square would appear decorated by our banners, and filled with rejoicing people." Abruptly, though, Polk the general seemed to think better of his earthly aspirations; Polk the bishop took a different tack. "Rising up in bed," Gibson related, "[he] said, 'No, my dear boy, even this may never be. For experience in life and true philosophy have taught me to set my heart upon nothing, nothing in this world. Our triumphs, our joys can be celebrated only in the world and life to come.'"[28]

Earlier that Monday, while Polk had been occupied well behind the lines, Gen. Patrick Cleburne, just back on duty after an illness, took a convalescent gallop out to the summit of the Pine Mountain salient. There, Cleburne shrugged off warnings by posted artillerymen that Yankee gunners on a facing hill barely half a mile away had the Rebel parapets in range; instead, Cleburne and a staff officer peered over the logs of one of the gun emplacements to see what they could see. They may have then seen the telltale puff of gunpowder smoke from afar; they heard, for sure, the cannonball whistling over their heads and the second one close behind. "Let's get out of this," said Cleburne to his fully compliant companion. "I have seldom known one to go where he had no business, but that he got hurt."[29]

Encouraged by a promise of dry weather, four generals whose business was more than idle curiosity had likewise arranged to ascend Pine Mountain on Tuesday, June 14, General Polk among them. General Johnston had asked that they help him assess the wisdom of holding onto the isolated height, for the Federals were by then beginning to encroach alarmingly around its flanks.

Sometimes seen with a full beard, Polk that Tuesday was "clean-shaven, except little tufts of grey side whiskers," and after reading aloud morning prayers, followed by breakfast, he got ready to leave the Hardage house, first tucking into one coat pocket his prayer book, then in another four mint copies of *Balm for the Weary and the Wounded.* The just-published devotional pamphlet, edited by Chaplain Charles Quintard and given to Polk by him, contained eighty-five pages of sermon excerpts, hymns, poems, pithy sayings, and selections from the Book of Common Prayer. The soothing whole was Quintard's endeavor to lift up the flagging spirits, and to ease the pain and impatience, of diseased or injured Confederate soldiers "compelled to exchange active service in the field for the harder and more wearying service in the hospital." Polk had written his own name in one of the booklets, then inscribed the others to his officer colleagues Johnston, Hardee, and Hood, signing "with the compliments of Lieutenant-General Leonidas Polk." Chaplain Quintard was on Polk's mind another way that morning. He had telegraphed from Atlanta a promise to bring the general that day "the Blessed Sacrament," that is, Holy Communion.[30]

With those considerations attended to, Polk left his headquarters near Allatoona Creek, mounted his strawberry roan Jerry, and set out for the so-called Pine Mountain one mile north. Behind him rode his chief of staff, Thomas Jack; then came William Gale and Lt. Aristide Hopkins riding abreast; then two troopers who, like Hopkins, belonged to the Orleans Light Horse, Polk's security escort. Along the way, the riders mingled with the staffs accompanying Johnston, Hardee, and William Jackson, the cavalry brigadier. Though Johnston had specifically requested that the generals' companions not be numerous, as "to attract as little attention as possible," Pvt. Philip Stephenson, noting their arrival, said they in fact resembled "a considerable cavalcade."[31]

At the backside base of the hill, the group dismounted and walked to the summit, some carrying either their telescopes or field glasses. (Polk presumably was still awaiting delivery from Asheville of the prized "spy glass" he had sent for.) When earlier mounting their guns on parapets, the artillerymen had felled trees to form a defensive abatis and had left openings, or embrasures, in the parapets for firing their fieldpieces; the effect, as Gale considered, had "render[ed] the place very much exposed." Thus, like hosts welcoming guests to a party, the resident cannoneers of Lieutenant Beauregard's South Carolina Battery and the 5th Company of New Orleans's Washington Artillery courteously advised the visitors (as they had the day previous for Patrick Cleburne) to mind where they showed themselves, lest the enemy espy them. J. M. Crawford, a Georgia sharpshooter posted high on the hill, and well accustomed to finding himself in harm's way, was taken aback when the paternal Polk noticed and cautioned *him*. "Young man, you are exposing yourself unnecessarily, and had better get to cover." The enlisted man reminded Polk of his more crucial military worth, saying, "General . . . you are exposing yourself."[32] About then, Col. William S. Dilworth, acting commander of the 3rd Florida Infantry Brigade, "occupying the most prominent position on Pine Ridge" (yet another name for the hill), requested that the supernumeraries trailing their commanders not follow them to the highest point on the salient, reminding them that "a large crowd would be sure to attract the fire of the enemy."[33] By then the generals, according to a journalist, "being gathered in a knot, glided into a general and animated conversation, using their hands and glasses with a marked freedom, bespeaking rank and interest. The enemy could not fail to see them plainly, and whilst *they* were being observed, deliberately returned the observance, with full time for calculations and adjustments of their field pieces."[34]

This mutual scrutiny had begun as a frolic. Hours earlier, rank-and-file soldiers on both sides found their precarious closeness to each other entertaining. Sgt. Rice C. Bull of the 123rd New York Infantry reported it this way:

Whenever a Johnnie [Reb] showed himself to make observations or give signals with their flags, [our] shells began to drop on the crest of the hill. The boys located in the vicinity gathered around the battery to watch the sport. The Johnnies could see when the guns were fired from the smoke; we could see them dodge out of sight before the shells reached them. Often when a shell exploded or passed them, they would come out and wave their hats; they seemed as well pleased as we were.

By and by, Sergeant Bull glimpsed "a party of [Johnnie Reb] officers [coming] out in the open space."[35]

In the center of that open space, General Johnston planted himself above René Beauregard's log-and-dirt emplacement and trained his field glasses across the valley.[36] Watching Johnston, Gale too could see the enemy's "working parties and his flag." One look convinced Johnston "that the risk of holding the [exposed Pine Mountain] was much greater than any advantage it could give us."[37] The risk was increasing rapidly. Using an apt metaphor, a Yankee general, probably Oliver Otis Howard, was just then heard to say of the Confederates peering at his fortifications: "There are some big guns among that party."[38] General Sherman, nearby, took a look through his telescope; too far off to recognize faces, but not uniforms, Sherman said: "How saucy they are." Capt. David P. Conyngham, a correspondent for the *New York Herald*, recorded further dialog between Sherman and an Indiana artillery captain, Peter Simonson. "Captain Simonson," Sherman wanted to know, "can you send a shell right on top of that knob? I notice a battery there and several general officers near it."

"I'll try," Simonson replied. His gunners of the Fifth Battery, Light Artillery, Indiana Volunteers, previously told to conserve their limited ammunition, jumped to obey Sherman's overriding instructions.[39] Cpl. Benjamin Frank McCollum got busy adjusting the brass sights on his ten-pounder, an artillery rifle able with fair accuracy to fire a shell that was three inches across and seven inches long. He awaited Simonson's "fire" command. Sherman "looked on with his glass."

"'Ah, Captain, a little too high. Try again with a shorter fuse.'"

Corporal McCollum complied.

"Up went the glass to his eye."[40]

Implausibly, this drama was being observed by William Harrison Polk, a private in the 21st Illinois Infantry. He was a distant kinsman to the Confederate general being framed in the Yankee gun sight and was standing almost as close to the fieldpiece as the gunners themselves. He described what occurred: "I witnessed from a point only a few yards from the gun," he wrote in letter to Polk's son.

> [It was] a 10 pounder Parrott of the 5th Indiana Battery, Capt. Simonson [commanding]. A young deserter [had come] into our lines, and the man was handed a powerful field glass and asked to name who the [Confederate] officers were. He named them, and I remember he called your father's name last, saying: "General Johnston, General Hardee and

General Polk." Then Sherman said to the officer in command, "Turn a gun [to] the front and give the Bishop a morning salute!"[41]

Private Polk's letter continues: "The first shot went high, skipping over the top, when two of the [Confederate] officers walked away, the third lingering behind and retiring a little later, as I remember it. Simonson jumped off his horse and said: 'Let me sight that gun,' which he did very carefully."[42]

In contrast to the deadly intent of the Yankee artillerists on their crest, a pastoral calm had seemingly heartened some of the Confederates, a midday hush enveloping Pine Mountain and the valley below. A "grand panorama of war," came lyrically to Trooper Aristide Hopkins's mind. To William Gale, though, the noontime buzz of insects rather than the sizzle of shell fire led him to think the tranquility treacherous. It had "emboldened the sight-seers," he thought, lulling them into a lack of caution. As General Johnston and the others dawdled, or were folding their field glasses preparatory to moving on, Colonel Dilworth heard "a shower of Minié balls" from far-off sharpshooters fly past. A moment later "a solid shot from the enemy's battery came over our heads." Gale heard the "report of the rifled cannon borne upon the air, and at the same instant, almost, the whistling shell buried itself in the parapet near us." With that, the staff people, no longer bantering and carefree, began to duck and scatter. Dilworth was insistent that the generals follow them to cover. Johnston and the others obliged, heading to their tethered horses. They strolled, to be sure, with studied nonchalance so as not to betray any lack of manly composure that their own soldiers and subordinates might discern.[43]

Gale and Hardee angled off downhill together; Thomas Jack was elsewhere with Johnston. Alone, General Polk veered toward the crest of the hill, where he paused, a silhouette gazing at the enemy emplacements. Did Polk tarry to consider further the range of the Yankee guns, as Gale later speculated? Or was it "more probable," in keeping with the melodramatic funeral oration composed by Bishop Elliott, that Polk lingered "to spend a short interval in silent communion with God?"[44] Polk may well have been trusting that his charmed battlefield life would be spared yet again, mindful of his church's Litany that he had so often recited: "From . . . battle and murder, and from sudden death, good Lord deliver us."

Whatever had been General Polk's motive in lingering on the brow of ·the hill, Lieutenant Hopkins was keeping a dutiful eye on his general from a more-protected spot. Polk was known for his disregard of perils, but to Hopkins he was now displaying mere foolhardiness. That prompted the lieutenant to "try and draw him from [his] place of danger," and "in an instant I was at his side. But alas, too late."[45] Moments before, as the accounts by the *Herald*'s David Conyngham and by William Harrison Polk mutually attest, Corporal McCollum discharged the Parrott gun once more while General Sherman looked on. Away went the "morning salute," the iron shot in seconds careering through the bishop's upper torso. "That will do," said Sherman, shutting down his glass. "At once [your side] wigwagged the news to the rear," Private Polk recalled. "Captain Thayer, [our] Division Signal Officer, who had deciphered your code a few days before, spoke up and said: 'That shot killed General Polk.' Simonson, who was again sighting [McCollum's] gun, looked up and said: 'What is that?' Thayer repeated the remark. Simonson then turned from the gun, remarking: 'Thank God! They killed my brother yesterday, and I have killed a Lieutenant General.'"[46]

Gale at the time heard someone shout, "'One of the generals was killed.' I asked what general? 'General Polk!'" Gale broke toward the spot where he had last seen his father-in-law and met Aristide Hopkins, "pale and excited, calling to me that the General was killed." Gale saw Polk sprawled supine on the grass "nervously working his under jaw." The Right Reverend Warrior General Polk (as the mocking Ben Butler had once termed him) then lay still. Gale hurried off to get a litter.[47]

General Hardee was about to rush up to Polk when Colonel Dilworth "caught him by the arm and told him he must not expose himself." He then also urged Johnston not to go near Polk's body, reminding him "that our loss was sufficiently great already, that he could do no good. With much reluctance and hearts almost overcome with grief, [the two generals] complied with my request." By that time the Yankees had recommenced firing salvos against the hill.[48]

Braving the new barrage, members of Polk's Orleans Light Horse escort found a litter and scrambled to remove the body from the crest. They first carried it to Dilworth's brigade headquarters tent on the back side of the hill, then continued to Polk's headquarters cabin a mile to the south. Some who beheld the corpse, it was said, "gasped with horror." The missile passed through Polk's chest, "carrying away his heart," as Bishop Elliott reported, and while "not lacerating his chest at all, lacerating dreadfully his back." Captain Polk, arriving from an errand and less graphically than Elliott, telegraphed the news to his cousin Marshall Polk: "Father killed today instantly, being struck by a three inch rifle shot while reconnoitering enemy." Meck reckoned the experienced artillery officer could imagine the injury resulting from the solid missile.[49] The four Quintard booklets Polk had placed earlier in a right coat pocket were found and removed, and before day's end Polk's assistant adjutant general, Maj. Douglas West, sent them to their intended recipients. He remarked in his note to Hood that all four were "stained with hallowed blood, which he shed in the holiest of causes."[50] Not content with reality's harshness, Bishop Elliott soon would adorn his funeral oration by assuring those grieving that even in death Leonidas Polk's face "retain[ed] its last expression of prayerful faith, and the arms, though broken, [were] still crossed upon the breast." Elliott was evidently indulging a little poetic license or wishful thinking here: some soldiers had remembered Polk peering at the Yankees across the valley with his hands behind his back.[51] Imaginative in a different way would be a published sketch of Polk at the moment of the shell's impact. Showing his uniform and body still intact, the image the artist produced was meant to be as unoffending as possible; after all, it was published in *The Mountain Campaigns in Georgia*, an 1886 advertising booklet by the Western & Atlantic Railroad to popularize tourism along its historic right-of-way. Polk's arms are flung wide, but only his hat is sent flying.[52]

Leonidas Polk's death for some was all in a day's work. "We killed Bishop Polk yesterday, and have made good progress today," General Sherman informed Washington. But Confederates high and low were singularly affected by this latest news, even if already numbed by the relentless dying that was their lot. John Bell Hood, hardened soldier that he was, wrote General Johnston a few hours afterward that "I am too sad to come over this evening." To another officer Hood would confide: "I had grown to love Genl. Polk with my whole heart. He was so noble, so generous. And such an able soldier."[53] A private in the 13th Louisiana Infantry was more than just sorry. "I would lay down my life in a moment if it would bring Genl Polk back to life," he said. The urge for homicidal vengeance welled up in the breast of Lt. Charles Huger, the brother of Polk's son-in-law Willie Huger. "It almost makes me swear never to take another prisoner [alive]," Charles raged to his brother. "How those growling murderous hounds would rejoice if they only knew how much mischief they had done." Huger's grief spread throughout the 1st Louisiana, an infantry regiment largely made up of men from New Orleans: "Our brigade all seem to feel as if they had lost a protector, the only general in the army who took any interest in us." Huger's only comfort was his conviction that the general "could not have died more gloriously."[54] At his brother-in-law's fateful end, Kenneth Rayner, off in North Carolina, was "unnerved, riven with lightning." He was further troubled on theological grounds. As he recalled to a friend: "On several occasions, Gen. P. has made such narrow escapes, that it would seem as if Almighty Power had specially interposed in his favor. Inscrutable are the ways of Providence!" He was consoled to some extent that Polk's widow had "a very valuable plantation in Mississippi and some 150 slaves."[55]

When Gale found a moment to return to his diary that night—the entry is dated June 14 but covers June 15 and 16 as well—his spirit was as shattered as Polk's body. "Oh day of gloom! Oh black eclipse," he began. "Oh day of agony and deep distress! For today has fallen one of Earth's noblest and best, the bravest and truest of all our brave and true." He recalled his sprint past Hopkins to where Polk had lain and seeing "Oh God, the dreadful hole in his side, his broken arms, his grey head and streaming beard."[56]

Inasmuch as Federal signal corpsmen had been deciphering the Confederates' wigwags since early April, they read the flag messages asking that an ambulance be sent for Polk's body, an interception that supports the claim that word of Polk's death may have reached Washington at least as soon as Richmond.[57] The summoned ambulance wagon eventually took the body to Marietta, where it was placed in a make-do "plain box coffin," and that put in a larger box "filled around with [powdered] charcoal as a guard against odor and leakage." (It was "the best we could obtain," Gale apologized to his diary.)[58] Polk's son Meck, evidently in consultation with Gale, decided not to send Polk's body to Asheville, where Fanny and the family were. Gale was set against this as well: "I do not want him to go to Asheville, having always before me the outrage visited on the body of Genl A. S. Johnston." (What awful thing Gale remembered befalling the corpse of Sidney Johnston presumably had to do with its emergency embalming at Shiloh, reportedly with whiskey.) Meck and Gale then set about getting the double-box coffin loaded aboard the midnight train for Atlanta.[59]

After dark, the Confederates posted on Pine Mountain again stole away to a more defensible main line outside Marietta. Left behind to be found the next day by Yankees in the blood-matted grass where Polk had died were fragments of his ribs and arm bones; the *Herald*'s David Conyngham and a doctor friend saved them as souvenirs. Some Federal soldiers dipped handkerchiefs in Polk's gore: "Whether as a sacred relic, or to remind them of a traitor," Conyngham could not say. Nearby was the sorrowing scrawl by a Rebel soldier posted on a stake: "You damn Yankee sons of bitches has killed our old Gen. Polk."[60]

Chaplain Charles Quintard met the 3:00 A.M. train that bore the body to Atlanta. (He had canceled his intended visit to bring Polk Communion.) Accompanied by the chaplain and a citizen's committee appointed by Atlanta's mayor, the body was taken to St. Luke's Parish on Walton Street and placed on the chancel step to lie in state. As Polk would have appreciated, this unassuming little Episcopal Church, resembling a schoolhouse and only a few weeks old, fit the situation altogether. Meant to serve primarily war refugees flowing into Atlanta, St. Luke's was a monument to Quintard's persistent efforts to obtain cost-free lumber and nails to build it: this he achieved by preaching to, and by baptizing the children of, the merchants who sold the building materials. Soldier carpenters and handymen in the Atlanta garrison were "detailed," says Quintard, to raise the church, an interesting waiver of the Episcopalians' usually fussy adherence to separation of church and state.[61]

With the coming of daylight on June 15, despite Gale's demurring but at Quintard's "entreaty," the coffin on the chancel step was opened to public gaze. (When the body was embalmed is not mentioned by Gale.) Below the head, the torn remains were sensibly concealed beneath a Confederate flag covered in an array of magnolia blossoms and a cross of white roses. The general's sword lay alongside the casket. Throughout that morning and early afternoon, the sorrowful as well as the curious were permitted to thread up the church's northern aisle, past the body, and out down the southern aisle. Sallie Clayton, a teenage girl from a prominent Atlanta family, gazed forlornly upon the general's "bloodless face" and reported that she was but one among "many, many thousands who did so."[62] By afternoon, a funeral service, preliminary to another planned for Augusta, was conducted by Quintard and Army Chaplain (and later bishop of Georgia) John W. Beckwith of Demopolis. Though Quintard's eulogy was "hastily prepared" because of the many other things he was having to attend to (a news account reported), the printed version of what he said appeared in several Southern papers measuring thirty column inches of tightly spaced eight-point type. With his voluble extempore remarks at length concluded, coffin and hearse and pallbearers, four of them army generals, proceeded to the depot. A private car coupled to the 2:30 A.M. train to Augusta awaited.[63]

The daylong Atlanta obsequies were modest measured against what was to come in Augusta. Again, the funeral train was met by religious and secular dignitaries, the remains borne first to City Hall and thence, on Reynold's Street, to St. Paul's Church, a parish even older than the American nation. There, under the stained-glass gaze of many a saint and angel, the body remained two days lying in state, and then, encased in a leaden coffin, it was returned to a guarded "apartment" in City Hall—normally the grand-jury room. Elsewhere, Bishop Elliott was giving himself over wholeheartedly to planning the production of the second funeral.[64] By chance, just ahead on the calendar was the day in late June on which churches far and wide observe the Martyrdoms of Saints Peter and Paul; Elliott saw that as an ideal time to lay to rest the sainted Christian martyred by Northern heretics. Plus, the date provided extra time for people to come from distant points. Among those he first invited was the president of the Confederacy. That message was delayed, and once it arrived in Richmond, too little travel time remained for Davis's presence.[65] Fortunately, Lt. Gen. James Longstreet—Polk's fellow wing commander at Chickamauga and coantagonist against Braxton Bragg—had just arrived in Augusta to recuperate among family relations after being shot in the throat the previous month by confused fellow Confederates in Virginia's Wilderness. Agreeing to join the funeral procession, Longstreet (the military choice next best to a preoccupied Robert E. Lee) gave Elliott a certified celebrity. Lee, though "much grieved," was obliged to stick to his guns holding onto Richmond and a besieged Petersburg.[66]

All being ready and announced by cannon salutes, the cortege on June 29 moved out from the City Hall. A contemporary account goes this way: "At half-past nine o'clock A.M., the case enclosing the remains was brought and placed upon the hearse by soldiers. The hearse was draped in the flag of the Confederate States with its broad folds of white and its starry cross of Trust and Truth upon a field of blood, and surmounted with wreaths of bay and laurel, and a cross of evergreen and snow-white flowers." To the strains of Chopin's "Marche Funèbre," the military escort, led by the Palmetto Band, began its solemn procession. Behind, some on horseback, some walking, came an assemblage of ranking civic and state dignitaries, clergymen, doctors and lawyers, "other citizens," General Polk's military family, and pallbearers. "While the procession was passing along the streets of the city," newspaper readers were told,

> houses and balconies and walks were thronged with multitudes who had come out to pay the respects of loving homage to the departed Christian soldier. All places of business were closed. The band played appropriate dirges, and the bell of St. Paul's Church was tolled at intervals. As it came down Reynolds street, approaching the church, the Bishops of Georgia, Mississippi, and Arkansas, in their robes, attended by a company of surpliced Priests, moved from the vestry-room, and took their station in front on the church near the entrance-gate, while the company of Silver Greys [doddering Georgia militiamen over the age of forty-five] was drawn up on either side of the avenue as a special guard of honor. The bishops and clergy having met the corpse went before it into the church, the Senior Bishop [Stephen Elliott] repeating the words, "I am the Resurrection and the Life, saith the Lord," etc. The choir in plainsong then chanted the anthem, "Lord, let me know mine end."[67]

Midway through the service, when it came time for him to preach, the Right Reverend Mr. Elliott abandoned liturgical decorum and gave free vent to personal fury. Having eulogized his priestly brother (favorable comparisons to both Saint Stephen and Saint Paul were made), he stepped from behind his preaching desk and, turning to his left, bequeathed hellfire and damnation to all Christians living above the Mason-Dixon Line. He thundered to the gathered mourners:

> And now, ye Christians of the North, and especially ye priests and bishops of the Church who have lent yourselves to the fanning of the fury of this unjust and cruel war, do I this day, in the presence of the body of my murdered brother, summon you to meet us at the judgment-seat of Christ—that awful bar where your brute force shall avail you nothing; where the multitudes you have followed to do evil shall not shield you from an angry God; where the vain excuses with which you have varnished your sin shall be scattered before the bright beams of eternal truth and righteousness. I summon you to that bar in the name of that sacred liberty which you have trampled underfoot; in the name of the glorious Constitution which you have destroyed; in the name of our holy religion which you have profaned; in the name of the temples of God which you have desecrated; in the name of a thousand martyred saints whose blood you have wantonly spilled; in the name of our Christian virgins whom you have violated; in the name of our slaves whom you have seduced and then consigned to misery; and there I leave justice and vengeance to God.

As the sulphurous coda wafted Heavenward, tears rolled down the cheeks of a grieving Ella Thomas. Had she and the other properly brought-up Episcopalians not believed that applause in a church was irreverent, they would have given the bishop of Georgia a standing ovation. And had the bishop of Ohio been present, he *would* have stood up—and walked out. Charles McIlvaine was so offended after reading Elliott's harangue that he declined to sign a postwar invitation to the Southern bishops to attend a reconciling General Convention.[68]

Once more temperate speech had resumed in St. Paul's and appropriate prayers had been offered, the coffin was carried into the churchyard and lowered into a prepared grave just outside the chancel wall.[69] A final artillery salute was fired from nearby Washington Street, and before they left, family members laid Cape Jasmine bouquets on the covered grave.[70]

Reactions thereafter to Polk's death were to range from the anguished to the drily analytical. The Soldier Poet of the Confederacy, as Henry Flash liked to think of himself, penned a hopeful stanza in "Polk": "*Up in the courts of another world / That angels alone have trod, / He lives, away from the din and strife / Of this blood be-sprinkled sod— / Crowned with the amaranthine wreath / That is worn by the blest of God.*"[71] Moses Greenwood, a New Orleans businessman exiled to Mobile, had maintained contact with several members of New Orleans's Washington Artillery (his cannoneer son had died among them after his wounding at Chickamauga). The elder Greenwood received two letters regarding Polk's death with contrasting points of view. "It is a sad catastrophe, and has cast a gloom over the whole army [of Tennessee] as he was beloved by every man, both high and low," a combat-proven sergeant, Joseph Duggan, told Greenwood. "He was always kind and attentive to all. None were afraid to approach him." William Palfrey, a lieutenant who by his duties was privy to discussions among various generals, provided Greenwood with a frank but "fair evaluation" of the consequences of Polk's end. "While mourning our loss," Palfrey told Greenwood, "we cannot but return thanks to God for His great mercy in taking [of the four generals present on Pine Mountain] the one most easily spared." Doubtless reflecting opinions discretely whispered around his headquarters, Palfrey explained:

> In view of the position lately occupied by Genl. Polk, it may be said (with all respect for his many shining qualities) that his death was not inopportune. He was second in command, and in the event of any accident to Genl. Johnston—which, Heaven forbid—the charge of the army would have been in the hands of one not equal to the emergency. Genl. Polk lacked the qualities most essential for a great commander— quickness of perception, tact, enterprise and energy. He would have been at the mercy of a vigorous adversary. This is the general estimate of his military ability.[72]

Probably greater than anyone outside Polk's family was Henry Watterson's dismay. Having lately shared guava-jelly sandwiches with his commander under a shower of blasted tree limbs and artillery grape, the journalist had "always fancied somehow that there was safety within the magic circle of his presence." The notion now dashed, he summed up in the *Mobile Daily Advertiser and Register* all that Leonidas Polk might have desired in an epitaph: "HE WAS MY BISHOP, MY GENERAL AND MY FRIEND."[73]

Epilogue

A month after Polk had lost his life, and while Joe Johnston and John Bell Hood were in the process of losing Georgia and the whole war in the West to William Tecumseh Sherman, Dudley Gale held an extraordinary forty-five-minute conversation with Jefferson Davis. Dabbing at his eyes as he thought of the death of a friend since their teenage days at West Point, the president lamented the loss both to the Confederacy and to him personally. Davis was further distraught thinking about all that had happened that spring in the Confederate West before and after Polk's death. Gale watched as the president, who had continually tinkered with Joe Johnston's military decisions, "seemed to writhe in his chair in torture, as with a countenance of agony, while reflecting on Johnston's gradual backing away from Sherman's pressure." Davis then told Gale that if "I had known [General Johnston] would have retreated through Georgia to Atlanta before I ordered General Polk to join him, I could have permitted it, and at the same time sent General Polk around in Sherman's rear, either into Tennessee or to Chattanooga, which would have made Sherman's destruction sure." Gale told his wife Kate that Davis's concluding sentence "in this remarkable conversation" was "of great force because it is a complete vindication of your father. . . . Now that he is above the reach of all earthly honor, this tribute to his sagacity is given." Gale then reminded Kate of her father's bitter epitaph for the Confederacy: "*Trop tard*. Always too late." "Well may it be said, if [Davis] had only taken his advice. Now it was again 'too late, *trop tard*.'"[1]

Notes

Preface

1. Thomas B. Macaulay, *The History of England from the Accession of James II* (New York: Lovell, 1890), 2:466.

Prologue

1. Ella Gertrude Clanton Thomas, "The Journal of Ella Gertrude Clanton Thomas," 162, unpublished typescript, Manuscript Department, Duke University Library, Durham, NC; Catherine B. R. Smith, "Death and Funerals of Bishop-General Leonidas Polk," *Journal of the Augusta Richmond County Historical Society* 15 (January 1983): 31–41.

2. "Death of Lieut. Gen. Leonidas Polk," anonymous pamphlet bound with Stephen Elliott, *Funeral Services at the Burial of The Right Rev. Leonidas Polk, D.D. Together with the Sermon Delivered in St. Paul's Church, Augusta, Ga. on June 29, 1864: Being the Feast of St. Peter the Apostle* (Columbia, SC: Evans & Cogswell, 1864). The pamphlet is an undated reprint from the *Atlanta Appeal*. Judging from its reverential tone and the writer's apparent familiarity with Polk's ecclesiastical background, the author was probably John Henry Linebaugh, a wartime journalist and earlier an Episcopal priest in Polk's Louisiana diocese.

3. Allan Nevins and Milton Halsey Thomas, eds., *The Diary of George Templeton Strong* (New York: MacMillan Company, 1952), 4:28; *Harper's Weekly* 5 (27 July 1861): 467. Dispatch, Benjamin Butler to E. M. Stanton, 25 October 1862, in Benjamin F. Butler, *Private and Official Correspondence of Gen. Benjamin F. Butler: During the Period of the Civil War* (Norwood, MA: Plimpton Press, 1917), 2:407–408.

4. Letter, John Henry Linebaugh to LP, 20 December 1863. Unless otherwise noted, Leonidas Polk's correspondence is found in the Leonidas Polk Papers, 1767–1935, Southern Historical Collection, University of North Carolina. Catherine Ann Devereux Edmondston, "Dedication," in *The Morte d'Arthur; Its Influence on the Spirit and Manners of the Nineteenth Century* (Baltimore: Trumbull Brothers, 1872), 3. The book is dedicated to Frances Devereux Polk, the author's aunt and LP's widow. Letter, Patton Anderson to LP, 14 January 1864, OR 52/2:598–599.

5. For a discussion of the precise wording of the soldier's plaintive note see Richard M. McMurry, "Kennesaw Mountain," *CWTI* 8 (January 1970): 22, and Albert Castel, "Death Comes to the Bishop: When Luck Ran out for Leonidas Polk," in *Articles of War: Winners, Losers, and Some Who Were Both in the Civil War* (Mechanicsburg, PA: Stackpole, 2001), 150–160; Letter, William D. Gale to William M. Polk, 28 March 1882. In his biography of his father, William Polk modified Gale's wording to "a cannon-shot . . . opening a wide door, let free that indomitable spirit." William M. Polk, *Leonidas Polk, Bishop and General* (New York: Longmans, Green, and Company, 1915), 2:374; Frances Anne Devereux Polk (hereafter FAP), "Memoir," 48. Frances Polk's undated fifty-page handwritten memoir is among the Leonidas Polk Papers.

6. Elliott, *Funeral Services*, 26.

7. Examples of Polk's melancholy letters: already depressed by the loss of seventy slaves during an 1849 cholera epidemic in Louisiana, he wrote that the death of his wife's mother (from old age) left her "far better off than in this miserable world." Letter, LP to sister Susan Polk Rayner, 9 July 1849. Years before, after the death of two younger brothers, he wrote to another brother: "We do, indeed, seem but to be born to die. . . . It is indeed a dying world, . . . and every stroke bids us to prepare to meet our God." But to faithful Christians like himself, "the bed of death [is] a field of victory." Letter, LP to Lucius Polk, 9 November 1830. After the death of a niece: he urged

the father of the child, a US congressman, to consider that his political success was no substitute for dependence upon God, without whom ambition was "but to bestride a bubble which floats and bursts." Letter, LP to Susan Polk Rayner, 1 June 1855.

8. Letter, Peter L. Hornbeck to Isaac Bush, 17 July 1864, Bement Manuscripts, 1843–1891, Lilly Library, Indiana University, Bloomington.

1. Leonidas—A Name to Daunt the Northern Barbarians (1776–1825)

1. "Autobiography of Colonel William Polk," in William Henry Hoyt, ed., *The Papers of Archibald D. Murphey* (Raleigh: E. M. Uzzell, 1914), 2:402–404; Marshall D. Haywood, "William Polk," in Samuel A. Ashe, ed., *Biographical History of North Carolina* (Greensboro, NC: Charles L. Van Noppen, 1905), 2:361–362; *LPBG*, 2:40.

2. In 1789 William Polk married Griselda Gilchrist, with whom he had two sons, Thomas Gilchrist and William Julius; Griselda Polk died in 1799.

3. Leonidas's family and his friends probably pronounced the name as Lee-AHN-uh-dus as would approximate its Greek origin. In two letters to family members he signed himself "Leon."

4. Letter, LP to Sarah Polk, 10 March 1822.

5. The English educator Joseph Lancaster had devised the wall book system. David L. Swain, "An Address Delivered at the Opening of Tucker Hall," in *Early Times in Raleigh* (Raleigh: Walter, Hughes & Company, 1867), 36. Joseph Lancaster, *Scripture Reading Lessons* (British and Foreign School Society, 1814–1829), 65. This wall book lesson is in the Lancaster collection at the Huntington Library, San Marino, CA.

6. Letter, LP to William Polk, 31 March 1827.

7. Letter, Charles C. Jones to Ida Polk, 21 June 1886. As a student at Lehigh University, Jones discovered Thomas Polk's role in conveying Philadelphia's steeple bells to Bethlehem, Pennsylvania, for safekeeping, the Liberty Bell included.

8. Among the paintings adorning the rotunda walls beneath the dome, Leonidas closely scrutinized John Trumbull's *General George Washington Resigning His Commission to Congress, at Annapolis, Maryland, 3 December 1783*, finding amid the forty ladies and gentlemen assembled the artist's depiction of Continental Congressman Benjamin Hawkins, Leonidas's maternal uncle.

9. *Rendezvous for Taste: Peale's Baltimore Museum, 1814–1830* (Baltimore: Peale Museum, 1956), 8–9.

10. Letter, LP to William Polk, 10 March 1823, in *LPBG*, 1:66–67.

11. Letter, LP to Sarah Polk, 17 July 1823.

12. Letter, LP to Lucius Polk, 25 June 1823. Leonidas estimated that he was among seventy newcomers; the official count for his class was ninety-seven, with only thirty-two graduating.

13. Letter, Abner Hetzel to his father, 17 June 1823, excerpted in Sidney Forman, *Cadet Life at West Point Before the Mexican War* (West Point: United States Military Academy Printing Office, 1945), 6–7.

14. Letter, Abner Hetzel to his father, 17 June 1823, 6–7.

15. Letter, LP to William Polk, 14 January 1824.

16. Letters, LP to Sarah Polk, 17 July 1823, and LP to Lucius Polk, 25 June 1823.

17. For a description of Summer Camp conditions, see George S. Pappas, *To the Point: The United States Military Academy, 1802–1902* (Westport, CT: Praeger, 1993), 63, 119–122, 142–145.

18. Letters, LP to Lucius Polk, 25 June 1823, and LP to Sarah Polk, 16 April and 17 July 1823.

19. Letter, LP to Lucius Polk, 13 September 1823. George W. Cullum, *Biographical Register of the Officers and Graduates of the U.S. Military Academy at West Point, N.Y.*, 3rd ed. (Boston: Houghton, Mifflin, 1891), 1:329, 367–368. William Preston Johnston, *The Life of Gen. Albert Sidney Johnston* (New York: Appleton, 1878), 322.

20. Letters, LP to Lucius Polk, 13 September 1823, and LP to Sarah Polk, 20 September 1823.

21. Letter, LP to William Polk, 16 November 1823. William Polk had been involved in the creation of the University of North Carolina and was a member of the board of trustees when Leonidas was writing.

22. Special Order No. 50, 14 November 1824. Dim vestiges of the society continue at West Point in the guise of Hundredth Night Shows. Pappas, *To the Point*, 367.

23. Letter, LP to William Polk, 14 January 1824. The biblical quotation is from 1 Peter 4:12.

24. Letter, Lucius Polk to William Polk, 20 December 1823, quoting a letter from Rufus Haywood, PBEP.

25. Typical West Point menus for 1825, for which Leonidas and other cadets paid $10 a month, are found in "Report of the Board of Visitors, United States Military Academy, West Point, June 22, 1825," *ASP* 18:153–154.

26. *The Centennial of the United States Military Academy at West Point, New York, 1802–1902* (Washington, DC: Government Printing Office, 1904), 2:85.

27. Letters, LP to Sarah Polk, 16 April and 25 May 1824.

28. Letters, LP to Sarah Polk, 16 April 1824 and undated (internal evidence would place it on or about June 15). Leonidas commented favorably on the selection of Burges, a North Carolinian.

29. The fact that Sarah and William Polk had named their first son to honor Lucius Junius Brutus apparently did not sit well with Lucius Junius Polk. Years later, when his parents named a ninth son Charles James, Lucius offered to exchange names with his infant brother. Letter, Lucius Junius Polk to William Polk, 26 November 1828. Before Leonidas, a girl was born to the Polks. They gave her her own Roman name: Lucinda. She died in infancy.

30. Letter, LP to William Polk, 23 July 1824.

31. Daniel Smith Donelson, born in 1802, would graduate in 1825; he was later a Confederate brigadier general.

32. Letter, LP to William Polk, 23 July 1824. Leonidas evidently appreciated Worth's notice. At the beginning of the War with Mexico in 1846, Polk gave Worth his own saddle horse, an unusually fine animal.

33. Letter, LP to William Polk, 10 September 1824.

34. Charles H. Browning, "Lafayette's Visit to the United States in 1824–25," *The American Historical Register* 3 (1895): 167–173.

35. Letter, LP to William Polk, 10 September 1824.

36. Letter, LP to William Polk, 4 March 1825.

37. A second section was set up for those cadets who found Gregory's text daunting. Bewick Bridge's *A Treatise on Mechanics* was deemed the more accessible text. *Centennial of United States Military Academy*, 1:262–264.

38. Letter, LP to William Polk, 14 January 1825.

39. Jefferson Davis, "Autobiographical Sketch," in Haskell M. Monroe Jr. and James T. McIntosh, eds., *The Papers of Jefferson Davis* (Baton Rouge: Louisiana State University Press, 1971), 1:lxxx; Letter, Jefferson Davis to Stephen Elliott, 8 July 1864, in Dunbar Rowland, ed., *Jefferson Davis, Constitutionalist: His Letters, Papers and Speeches* (Jackson: Mississippi Department of Archives and History, 1923), 6:284.

40. Record of Delinquencies, 1822–1828. United States Military Academy Library.

41. Letter, LP to Sarah Polk, 18 April 1825.

42. Letter, LP to Sarah Polk, 18 April 1825; Letter, LP to William Polk, 4 December 1825.

43. Letter, LP to Sarah Polk, 18 April 1825.

44. Letter, LP to Lucius Polk, 15 July 1825.

45. Post Orders, 25 August 1825, United States Military Academy Archives; Letter, Sylvanus Thayer to William Polk, 26 September 1825; Letter, LP to William Polk, 4 December 1825, irritably quoting his father's vow to Thayer.

2. *"Opinions . . . Most Awfully Dangerous" (1826)*

1. Letter, LP to James Barbour, 23 January 1826, in *LPBG*, 1:82–85.

2. Post Orders No. 4, 13 December 1825, United States Military Academy Archives.

3. Letter, LP to William Polk, 12 May 1825.

4. Letter, LP to James Barbour, 23 January 1826, in *LPBG*, 1:82–89; Letter, LP to William Polk, 8 February 1826.

5. Letter, LP to William Polk, 2 April 1826.

6. William M. Polk, *The University of the South and The Race Problem* (Sewanee, TN: University of the South Press, 1893), 9.

7. Letter, LP to William Polk, 8 February 1826; Diary of Cadet S.P. Heintzelman, 5 February 1826, quoted in Douglas Southall Freeman, *R. E. Lee* (New York: Scribner's, 1934–1935), 1:57, n. 31.

8. FAP, "Memoir," 6.

9. Olinthus Gilbert Gregory, *A Treatise of Mechanics, Theoretical, Practical and Descriptive* (London: George Kearsley, 1815); *Centennial of the United States Military Academy*, 1:263–264.

10. *Register of Merit, 1817–1835*, United States Military Academy Archives.

11. John Watkins and Frederic A. Shoberl, eds., *A Biographical Dictionary of the Living Authors of Great Britain and Ireland* (London: Henry Colburn, 1816), 137; John Mason Good, Olinthus Gregory, and Newton Bosworth, *Pantologia: A New Cabinet Cyclopaedia* (London: J. Walker, 1819).

12. Olinthus Gilbert Gregory, *Letters on the Evidences, Doctrines and Duties of the Christian Religion*, 9th ed. (London: Henry G. Bohn, 1857).

13. Gregory, *Letters on the Evidences*, 431–443.

14. William Carus, ed., *Memorials of the Right Reverend Charles Pettit McIlvaine, D.D., D.C.L., LL.D.*, 2nd ed. (London: Elliot Stock, 1882), 36. See also E. Clowes Chorley, *Men and Movements in the American Episcopal Church* (New York: Scribner's, 1946).

15. *Collections of the Protestant Episcopal Historical Society for the Year 1851* (New York: Stanford & Swords, 1851), 1:69; Carus, *Memorials*, 9–11, 15–17.

16. Charles Francis Adams, ed., *Memoirs of John Quincy Adams* (Philadelphia: Lippincott, 1875), 5:230–231.

17. Carus, *Memorials*, 19; *Centennial of United States Military Academy*, 1:367–368.

18. Carus, *Memorials*, 27. The "infidel" lieutenant later came around to apologize, pressured to do so by his colleagues. McIlvaine's early trials at West Point are further related by him in a 12 December 1868 letter to the Rt. Rev. Charles T. Quintard, then Episcopal bishop of Tennessee. The letter was published twenty-two years later as "Leonidas Polk: The Bishop-General Who Died for the South," *SHSP* 18 (1890): 371–379. The letter is the source of the account of Leonidas Polk's religious odyssey at West Point.

19. Letter, James Milnor to Charles P. McIlvaine, 9 April 1821, in John Seely Stone, *A Memoir of the Life of James Milnor, D.D.* (New York: American Tract Society, 1848), 238.

20. Letter, McIlvaine to Quintard, 31 December 1868.

21. Letter, LP to William Polk, 11 May 1826.

22. Letter, LP to Lucius Polk, 25 August 1826. In comments about Leonidas's fervent evangelicalism at this point in his life, a passage in William Polk's biography reads this way: "He was beset by no doubts of the Christian religion; he took it for granted that the evangelicalism of his beloved pastor, McIlvaine, was the only true message of the gospel. . . . In after-years he outgrew not a little of the narrowness of evangelicalism." *LPBG*, 1:108. These observations relating to Polk's theological thinking betray the probable hand of the Reverend John Fulton, Polk's clerical protégé and friend in the 1850s. Fulton, as well as another writer named E. J. Biddle, collaborated with William M. Polk in the preparation of the biography solely under William Polk's name. Details of the joint authorship are found under the heading "Critical Essay on Authorities" by Joseph H. Parks in his own Polk biography, *General Leonidas Polk, C.S.A.: The Fighting Bishop* (Baton Rouge: Louisiana State University Press, 1992), 387–395.

23. Charles P. McIlvaine, *The Apostolic Commission: The Sermon at the Consecration of the Right Reverend Leonidas Polk, D.D., Missionary Bishop for Arkansas, in Christ Church, Cincinnati, Ohio, December 9, 1838* (Gambier: G. W. Myers, 1838).

24. Cadet Polk had a total of seventy-nine demerits for the 1825–1826 term. Martin Parks had eighty-four.

25. Carus, *Memorials*, 22.

26. Letter, McIlvaine to Quintard, 31 December 1868.

27. Letter, LP to William Polk, 11 May 1826. Most of the letter is in *LPBG*, 1:95–96.

28. Among the cadets now praying with Leonidas, who had become a kind of assistant to McIlvaine, was a roommate, a first-year plebe from Kentucky named Albert Taylor Bledsoe.

29. Perhaps McIlvaine was using the biblical "40" to denote a longish period of sacred days or years.

30. It is not known which other cadets were baptized that morning. McIlvaine said

thirteen years later in a sermon when Polk was ordained a bishop that "others" were baptized with him at West Point. McIlvaine, *Apostolic Commission*.

31. Letter, McIlvaine to Quintard, 31 December 1868.

32. Letter, McIlvaine to Quintard, 31 December 1868. Evidently Sylvanus Thayer was sympathetic to McIlvaine's evangelizing efforts; McIlvaine's friendly correspondence with Thayer later on strongly suggests he had the superintendent's support that year. See Letter, McIlvaine to Sylvanus Thayer, 15 October 1860, in Carus, *Memorials*, 210. Similarly, the Board of Visitors soon became supportive of ministry at the academy. About eighteen months after McIlvaine had left the academy for St. Ann's Brooklyn (November 1827), the visitors were irritated that a suitable chapel had not yet been built. "Report of the Board of Visitors, United States Military Academy, West Point, June 1829," *ASP*, 19:178.

33. After his demerit-marred tenure at West Point, Cadet Martin Parks headed for a career in the ordained ministry of the Episcopal Church. He died in 1853. Cullom, *Biographical Register*, 1:375–376.

34. Letter, McIlvaine to Quintard, 31 December 1868.

35. Letters, James Milnor to McIlvaine, 8 June, 14 June, and 17 June 1826, in Stone, *Memoir of James Milnor*, 263–264, 266–268.

36. Letters, LP to Lucius Polk, 25 August 1826, and LP to William Polk, 9 May 1827.

37. Letter, LP to William Polk, 5 June 1826.

38. Letters, Milnor to McIlvaine, 14 and 17 June 1826, in Stone, *Memoir of James Milnor*, 266–267.

39. Letter, Sarah Polk to Lucius Polk, 24 October 1826, PBMP.

40. Letter, Sarah Polk to Lucius Polk, 24 October 1826, PBMP.

41. Apparently, all saved correspondence between Leonidas and Frances Ann Devereux prior to their engagement in May 1828, and their marriage in 1830, was lost in an arson house fire in Sewanee, Tennessee, just before the outbreak of the Civil War.

42. Stephen F. Miller, *Recollections of Newbern 50 Years Ago* (Greenville, NC: J. Y. Joiner Library, 2006), 463.

43. FAP, "Memoir," 7.

44. Subsequently, Fanny left the Roman Catholics and aligned herself with Catherine, Leonidas, and other Episcopalians.

45. Letter, LP to William Polk, 5 September 1826.

46. Letter, LP to Lucius Polk, 25 August 1826; Letter, Alfred Balch to William Polk, 11 October 1826; Letter, Lucius Polk to William Polk, 16 November 1826, PBEP; Letter, Mary Polk to Lucius Polk, 13 December 1826, PBMP.

3. "Board, Room, Servant, and All Other Like Necessities" (1826–1830)

1. Polk family children who died in infancy: Lucind Davis, c. 1804; John Hawkins, c. 1814; Philemon Hawkins, c. 1820; Sarah, c. September 1826; Charles James (sometimes incorrectly identified as Charles Junius), c. November 1828. See *The New England Historical and Genealogical Register* 77 (1923) and internal evidence of letters.

2. Letter, Sarah Polk to Lucius Polk, 24 October 1826, PBMP; Letter, LP to Luicus, 25 August 1826.

3. Letter, LP to William Polk, 4 September 1826. His passing mention of the McIlvaine family deaths is his only allusion to the chaplain.

4. Stephen Ambrose describes the course as intended to be "the capstone of a man's education." *Duty, Honor, Country: A History of West Point* (Baltimore: Johns Hopkins University Press, 1999), 96.

5. As far as the 1826 Board of Visitors was concerned, the study of "English grammar, rhetoric, the constitutional law of the United States, and political economy" did not directly serve the objective of a military academy. "Report of the Board of Visitors, United States Military Academy, West Point, June 24, 1826," in *ASP*, 18:385.

6. Letter, LP to William Polk, 26 December 1826. Perversely, by Leonidas's lights, the 1826 Visitors had recommended that only cadets excelling in engineering, the academic elite of the school, be held over a fifth year—and only for additional, intensive studies in *that* field.

7. Letter, LP to William Polk, 26 December 1826.

8. Letter, LP to William Polk, 26 March 1827.

9. Letter, LP to William Polk, 31 March 1827.

10. Letters, LP to William Polk, 12 December 1826, 26 March 1827, and 31 March 1827.

11. *Catalogue of the Mount Pleasant Classical Institution* (Amherst, MA: n.p., 1828), quoted by Clifford E. Clark Jr., *Henry Ward Beecher: Spokesman for a Middle-Class America* (Urbana: University of Illinois Press, 1978), 13.

12. Sylvanus Thayer was born in Braintree, Massachusetts.

13. Amherst College, *Catalogue of the Corporation, Faculty and Students* (October 1827). Colton's Episcopalian, evangelical leanings helped arrange that he and Leonidas would cross paths frequently in the future.

14. Letter, LP to William Polk, 31 March 1827.

15. William Polk's letter to which Leonidas makes reply is lost; the son's answer on 9 May 1827 contains his rebuttals and supplies the supposed thrust of the missing letter.

16. Francis Fellowes was born in November 1803.

17. Letter, LP to William Polk, 9 May 1827.

18. The Lenten season in Raleigh was having an impact on Leonidas's sister Mary as well. She was greatly disturbed that a convicted Raleigh felon, a slave named Ned, was to be hanged publicly on sacred Good Friday.

19. These letters from Leonidas's parents are lost; their contents are inferred from his responses.

20. Letter, LP to William Polk, 22 June 1827. In his letter to William Polk, 23 October 1827, Leonidas alludes to his mother's request "that I should see you before I resigned my commission."

21. Writing Lucius later in the summer, Colonel Polk sounded more or less resigned to Leonidas's "determination . . . to pursue the study of Theology and practice in the Ministry of the Episcopal Church. Hence, I may fairly presume, he has abandoned all thoughts of Tennessee and, for the present at least, all attention to worldly matters." Letter, William Polk to Lucius Polk, 20 July 1827, PBEP.

22. Letter, LP to William Polk, 22 June 1827. Henry Atkinson Hawkins, born 20 September 1811, was the son of Benjamin F. Hawkins, the brother of Sarah Hawkins Polk.

23. Elizabeth Reid Murray, *Wake: Capital County of North Carolina* (Raleigh, NC: Capital County Publishing, 1983), 221.

24. Letters, LP to William Polk, 14 July 1827, and William Polk to Lucius Polk, 1 September 1827.

25. On the Fairmount Waterworks, see John Cotter, *The Buried Past* (Philadelphia: University of Pennsylvania Press, 1992).

26. Letter, LP to William Polk, 30–31 July 1827. Also see "Cotton Seed Gas," *Register of the Arts and Sciences* 4 (19 August 1827): 151.

27. William Arba Ellis, ed., *Norwich University: 1819–1911: Her History, Her Graduates, Her Roll of Honor* (Montpelier, VT: Capital City Press, 1911), 1:42–43.

28. Letters, LP to William Polk, 30–31 July 1827, and 3 August 1827. Leonidas overstated the inadequacy of the Partridge academy library.

29. Letter, LP to William Polk, 17 August 1827. See Freeman, *R. E. Lee*, 1:68. Freeman does not say where Lee spent his furlough, only that he returned to West Point on 28 August 1827.

30. Charles B. Stuart, *Lives and Works of Civil and Military Engineers of America* (New York: D. Van Nostrand, 1871), 190. John Childe later became known as an inventive railroad civil engineer.

31. The claim in D. M. Wilson, *Three Hundred Years of Quincy: 1625–1925* (Boston: Wright and Potter, 1926) that this was America's first railroad is open to question; in Pennsylvania, the Mauch Chunk Gravity Railroad was constructed in May 1827 to carry coal from Carbondale mines to the Lehigh River nine miles away. Arthur Schlesinger Jr., ed., *The Almanac of American History* (New York: Putnam, 1983), 21. See also John W. Starr Jr., *One Hundred Years of American Railroading* (New York: Dodd, Mead and Company, 1929), 27ff.

32. Letter and rail diagram, LP to William Polk, 22 August 1827. Cadet Lee's recollection of Lieutenant Polk's remarks was given after the Civil War to William M. Polk by E. J. Biddle, a journalist who was an early participant in William Polk's plans to write a biography of his father. Biddle wrote on 12 May 1886: "Among those I have seen much of here [in Roxbury, Mass.] is General Lee, who was for two years at West Point with your father. . . . While Genl Lee was at home [*sic*] for his leave at the end of the second year [1827], they met by agreement in Boston and Genl Lee (whose father, like your grandfather, had been an officer under Washington and a member of the Order of the Cincinnati) took Lt. Polk to see the granite quarries at Quincy where there was a railroad. Genl Lee says he distinctly remembers your father speaking of the interest he felt in the matter, and that turning to him, he said: 'Lee, [et cetera].'" Omitting Lee's name, William Polk paraphrased the conversation, also misdating it "1832 or 1833." *LPBG*, 1:150.

33. Letters, LP to William Polk, n.d. [c. 3 August 1827], in *LPBG*, 1:103; and LP to William Polk, 17 August 1827. See also Henry Adams, *The Birthplaces of Presidents John and John Quincy Adams* (Quincy, MA: Adams Memorial Society, 1936).

34. The school *did* flourish for a brief while and continued up and down for almost 100 years.

35. Letter, LP to William Polk, 30 August 1827; Robert Remini, *The Election of Andrew Jackson* (Philadelphia: Lippincott, 1963), 15 and 56–57.

36. Letter, LP to William Polk, 30 August 1827.

37. Richard L. Blanco, ed., *The American Revolution, 1775–1783: An Encyclopedia* (New York: Garland, 1993).

38. James Fenimore Cooper, *The Last of the Mohicans* (Garden City, NY: International Collectors Library, 1985), Preface, 4.

39. Letters, LP to William Polk, 30 August 1827 and 14 September 1827. I have supposed Leonidas went by boat as he says he employed "five miles land carriage" between Lake George and Lake Champlain. James Fenimore Cooper and his friends took a steamboat up Lake George in 1824. Cooper, *The Last of the Mohicans,* "Historical Introduction," xxxiii.

40. Letter, LP to William Polk, 14 September 1827.

41. The ups and downs of the Ohio River prior to dams and locks are noted by Walter Havighurst, *River to the West: Three Centuries of the Ohio* (New York: Putnam, 1970), 277.

42. John Loudon McAdam, who developed the process, specified that all stones used in surfacing a road be no more than one inch on any dimension. See W. J. Reader, *Macadam: The McAdam Family and the Turnpike Roads: 1798–1861* (London: Heinemann, 1980). Letter, LP to William Polk, 23 October 1827.

43. Letter, LP to William Polk, 23 October 1827.

44. Letter, LP to William Polk, 23 October 1827.

4. *"'Minding High Things' Too Much" (1828–1830)*

1. Letter, Marshall T. Polk to Lucius Polk, 11 December 1828; Letter, LP to Lucius Polk, 3 July 1828.

2. Letters, LP to William Polk, 17 May 1828 and 17 August 1828.

3. "Record of Confirmations by Bishop Ravenscroft, P.B. Wiley Deacon, March 24, 1828: George E. Badger, citizen of Raleigh N.C.; Mary Badger, wife of G. E. Badger; Leonidas Polk, cit. of Raleigh," St. John's Episcopal Church, Fayetteville, NC, Parish Register (photocopy).

4. *Journal of the Proceedings of the Annual Convention of the Episcopal Church in the State of North Carolina* (Fayetteville, NC: Carney and Dismukes, 1828).

5. *Journal of the Proceedings of the Annual Convention of the Episcopal Church in the State of North Carolina*, 188; Guion Griffis Johnson, *Ante-Bellum North Carolina: A Social History* (Chapel Hill: University of North Carolina Press, 1937), 183.

6. Marshall De Lancey Haywood, *Lives of the Bishops of North Carolina* (Raleigh, NC: Alfred Williams & Company, 1910).

7. FAP, "Memoir," 7.

8. FAP, "Memoir," 7; Letter, LP to Lucius Polk, 18 February 1828, New-York Historical Society Collections.

9. Letter, Mary Polk Badger to Lucius Polk, 17 June 1828, PBMP.

10. Letter, LP to Lucius Polk, 3 July 1828, GWPP. The bridegroom's few sentences about his marriage plans are buried within a rambling disquisition concerning the raising of oats, alfalfa, lucern, and millett.

11. FAP, "Memoir," 7.

12. Letter, William Polk to Lucius Polk, 6 March 1829. Leonidas's two returns from his seminary in Virginia would take place in March and September.

13. Letters, LP to Lucius Polk, 17 November 1828, and LP to William Polk, 7 October 1828.

14. Adams, *Memoirs of John Quincy Adams*, 5:230–231

15. Letter, William Polk to Sarah Polk, 23 February 1822.

16. Letter, LP to William Polk, 5 November 1828. The fact that Leonidas mentions, but does not name, the "two other gentlemen" with whom he saw President Adams suggests they were McIlvaine and Milnor.

17. Letter, LP to William Polk, 5 November 1828.

18. Letters, LP to Lucius Polk, 17 November 1828, and LP to William Polk, 10 February 1829.

19. Letter, LP to Sarah Polk, 10 January 1829.

20. Letter, Sarah Polk to Lucius Polk, 22 November 1828.

21. Letter, LP to McIlvaine, 1 December 1828, Leonidas Polk Papers, 1828–1871, Perkins Library, Duke University. Leonidas's biblical quotations (some of them paraphrases) are taken from Epistles to the Hebrews 12:2; Romans 12:16; and Philippians 2:7. His source was the 1611 Authorized Version of the Bible.

22. Entries in McIlvaine's diary include such confessions as "I feel that I am too anxious to please" (13 November 1827) and "I go to the throne of grace trusting too much to my own heart" (26 January 1829). Carus, *Memorials*, 32 and 42.

23. McIlvaine was a vice president of the national ACS in 1845–1860. William Polk was vice president of the North Carolina chapter in 1818; see Murray, *Wake*, 165. Polk was president in 1829.

24. For more on the motives of ACS members, see Lawrence J. Friedman, *Inventors of the Promised Land* (New York: Alfred A. Knopf, 1975), 185–219; Douglas R. Egerton, "Its Origin Is Not a Little Curious: A New Look at the American Colonization Society," *Journal of the Early Republic* 5(4) (1985): 463–480; and Barry Gewen, "Absolute Values," *The New York Times Book Review*, 24 March 2002, 11.

25. Among the ACS's clergy members were Bishops William Meade of Virginia and James Otey of Tennessee. Even Raleigh's Parson McPheeters belonged. See William A. R. Goodwin, *History of Theological Seminary in Virginia and Its Historical Background* (New York: Gorham, 1923–1924), 1:383; and Eric Burin, *Slavery and the Peculiar Solution* (Gainesville: University Press of Florida, 2005), 17.

26. Letter, LP to William Polk, 21 January 1829, in *LPBG*, 1:111.

27. John Macpherson and not George Badger got the cabinet post. At about the same time, a very distant Polk relative, Josiah L. F. Polk, asked Colonel Polk to use his influence to land him a patronage job as well. Letters, Josiah Polk to William Polk, 6 March and 1 May 1829. Josiah could sit at a desk and write for up to fourteen hours a day, he claimed, and was familiar with Indian affairs. Colonel Polk dutifully wrote a recommendation of his cousin, but when Josiah took it to the White House, President Jackson was too occupied with affairs of state to read it.

28. *LPBG*, 1:107. Edward Butler and Leonidas were later Louisiana planters, and Butler's son Eddy was killed at the Battle of Belmont in 1861 while under General Polk's

command. Some fifty years after Colonel Polk's stationed-at-the-seminary remark, Edward Butler recounted the story in a letter to William M. Polk.

29. Letters, LP to William Polk, 10 June and 25 July 1829. Hawkins later washed out of West Point for keeps. "List of Cadets at West Point in 1828, and the Rule in Making Appointments and Filling Vacancies," *ASP*, 18:800. He and his brother Ben subsequently settled in the Republic of Texas where Leonidas, by then a missionary bishop, would visit them.

30. Letter, William Polk to Lucius Polk, 6 March 1829, GWPP.

31. Letter, LP to Charles McIlvaine, 2 February 1830.

32. The seminary itself conceded the damaging effect of Reuel Keith's absence. "Systematical Divinity has been passed over in a manner somewhat more general than usual . . . but the most important subjects . . . have been thoroughly studied," a professor reported to the next diocesan convention. *Journal of the Proceedings of the Convention of the Protestant Episcopal Church of the Diocese of Virginia* (Richmond, VA: Warrock, 1830), 10.

33. *Journal of the Proceedings of the Convention of the Protestant Episcopal Church of the Diocese of Virginia*.

34. Letter, LP to Charles McIlvaine, 2 February 1830. As was often the case, Leonidas's quotations from Scripture were paraphrases. His "fields white with the harvest" is an approximation of Jesus's words "the fields . . . are white already to harvest." (John 4:35.)

35. Letter, LP to William Polk, 10 June 1829 and 3 February 1830. Leonidas had promised the previous June to help with surveying his land when he should be next at home.

36. Letter, LP to William Polk, 3 February 1830.

37. T. Frederick Davis, "Pioneer Florida," *Florida Historical Quarterly* 24 (1946): 292–294. Federal Writers Project, *Florida: A Guide to the Southernmost State* (New York: Oxford University Press, 1939), 276. Prince Murat was also a nephew of Napoleon Bonaparte. Gay Wilson Allen, *Waldo Emerson* (New York: Viking Press, 1981), 96–100. William H. Gilman and Alfred R. Ferguson, eds., *The Journals and Miscellaneous Notebooks of Ralph Waldo Emerson* (Cambridge, MA: Belknap Press, 1963), 5:3, 115. Elliott J. Mackle, "The Eden of the South, Florida's Image in American Travel Literature and Painting, 1865–1900" (PhD diss., Emory University, 1977), 32, n. 3. Frederick Ives Carpenter, *Emerson Handbook* (New York: Handpicks House, 1953), 144.

38. In whatever way the Polks' "family malady" might be diagnosed by modern medicine, it was a pulmonary affliction that caused Leonidas considerable illness.

39. Letter, LP to Sarah Polk, 3 March 1830. He concluded his admonitions with an anguished hope that the preachments to his parents were always "productive of peace and ease to your declining years. . . . In the survey of my past life, nothing so much pains me as the recollections of occasions when from misjudgments or the criminal impetuosity of my naturally ardent dispositions, I have said or done things . . . which must have pained you. I entreat you to erase this recollection from your memory."

40. Letter, LP to William Polk, 3 February 1830.

41. George D. Fisher, *History and Reminiscences of the Monumental Church from 1814 to 1878* (Richmond: Whittet & Shepperson, 1880), 1.

42. Letter, LP to McIlvaine, 21 July 1830. For his first three sermons Polk apparently took liberties with the official lectionary of the Book of Common Prayer that

appointed biblical texts related to Easter rather than the ones he chose. On Easter Day, for example, his sermon was based on John 3:16, then as now a favorite with evangelical Christians. Perhaps he had written the sermon while still at the seminary. FAP, "Memoir," 8.

5. "At Any Moment Our Brightest Hopes May Be Nipt in the Bud" (1830–1832)

1. FAP, "Memoir," 8.

2. Letter, LP to McIlvaine, 21 July 1830. In England, meanwhile, McIlvaine was deploring the high-church services he had attended in Winchester and Exeter Cathedrals where chanting men's and boys' choirs, "approximating much too nearly the pageantry and formality of the Romish church," were a scandalous substitute for "preaching the Gospel to perishing souls." Stone, *Memoir of James Milnor,* 399.

3. 1 Timothy 4:12.

4. FAP, "Memoir," 8–9. Leonidas gave Fanny an account of his Raleigh visit, which she recorded.

5. Letter, "Lucius J. Polk from his affectionate brother, A. H. P." 8 September 1830, PBMP.

6. Letter, LP to William Polk, 4 November 1830.

7. Letter, LP to Lucius Polk, 9 November 1830.

8. His symptoms are mentioned in FAP, "Memoir," 10, and in Letter, LP to McIlvaine, 9 October 1831.

9. Hamilton was born 27 January 1831 in Richmond.

10. Letter, LP to Lucius Polk, 10 February 1831.

11. Igniting the revival's fire in New York City was the Reverend William Patton, pastor of Central Presbyterian Church on Broome Street in Greenwich Village.

12. Letter, LP to McIlvaine, 24 March 1831. There is no letter of reply from McIlvaine.

13. FAP, "Memoir," 9.

14. William S. Perry, *The Bishops of the American Church* (New York: Christian Literature Company, 1897), 75.

15. FAP, "Memoir," 9. "Several uncles" had also died, she added, but she did not name them.

16. Sheila M. Rothman, *Living in the Shadow of Death: Tuberculosis and the Social Experience of Illness in American History* (Baltimore: Johns Hopkins University Press, 1994), 20.

17. Irwin Richman, *The Brightest Ornament: A Biography of Nathaniel Chapman, M.D.* (Bellefonte, PA: Pennsylvania Heritage, 1967), 72.

18. Such was Chapman's medical knowledge that a fellow physician had said it resembled "an electron [which] shines with no borrowed light but with an innate lustre." Richman, *The Brightest Ornament,* 72 and 84.

19. FAP, "Memoir," 11. Tartar emetic plasters, composed of antimony and potassium tartrate, were used not only to induce vomiting but also, in smaller doses, for sweating and expectoration. W. A. Newman Dorland, *American Illustrated Medical Dictionary* (Philadelphia: Saunders, 1941). In New York, Leonidas would consult a third physician, but his identity is not known.

20. FAP, "Memoir," 10.

21. Letter, LP to Lucius Polk, 7 October 1831. The notes were in consideration of the slaves Leonidas had previously sold to Lucius, and Leonidas apparently carried with him a letter written by his politically well-connected brother-in-law, George Badger, that would give him access to bankers.

22. Letters, LP to McIlvaine, 9 October 1831, and LP to William Polk, 16 October 1831, in *LPBG*, 1:130.

23. Letter, LP to McIlvaine, 9 October 1831.

24. FAP, "Memoir," 11.

25. William Sweetser, *A Treatise on Consumption, With Directions for the Consumptive Visiting the South of Europe* (Boston: T. H. Carter, 1836), 174.

26. Letters, LP to Lucius Polk, 7 October 1831, and LP to William Polk, 18 September 1831, GWPP. Fanny in her memoir says he was "totally overcome by sea sickness, spending 19 days" in his berth. In another letter of his own he said only that "at the close of the voyage and for the first few days I was on ship, I was quite unwell." LP to McIlvaine, 9 October 1831.

27. Letter, LP to Lucius Polk, 7 October 1831.

28. A years-long deferral of preaching was mentioned by Leonidas to McIlvaine, but to Lucius he said the doctor in Paris had merely advised he suspend "preaching, etc., a while at least."

29. Letter, LP to Rufus Polk, 7 November 1831. America's Dr. Sweetser would have concurred with Broussais, but with two caveats: consumptive travelers in Italy should stay off the ashy slopes of Mt. Vesuvius when visiting Pompeii and should cut short sightseeing visits to churches. Chilly marble floors could be death-dealing.

30. Journal entry, 2 October 1831, in *LPBG*, 1:129–130.

31. Journal entry, 10 October 1831, in *LPBG*, 130.

32. Journal entry, 11 October 1831, in *LPBG*, 130.

33. Journal entry, 18 October 1831, in *LPBG*, 132. Fellenberg was a radical Swiss educator whose school had been in operation for about thirty years when Leonidas visited. Fellenberg was a follower, too, of Switzerland's Johann Heinrich Pestalozzi, another educational reformer whose teaching theories Leonidas would apply in his Columbia (Tennessee) Female Institute five years later. For mention of the *Pestalozzian* method in use at the Columbia Female Institute, see Eva Pearl Quillen, "A Study of the Life of Franklin Gillette Smith" (master's thesis, Tennessee Polytechnic Institute, 1960), 24.

34. Journal entry, n.d. [c. 15 December 1831], in *LPBG*, 1:132–133. St. Paul does not write that while living in Rome he preached in the Forum, though Leonidas asserts "who may doubt that he did so?"

35. Letter, LP to William Polk, 24 December 1831.

36. Journal entry, n.d. [c. 31 December 1831], in *LPBG*, 1:133. "Much, very much do I see in it to deplore," he wrote on New Year's Eve, "with the keenest, bitterest regret. . . . I can only be relieved from the unhappiness of such a retrospect by humbly casting myself at the foot of the Mercy-seat."

37. Journal entry, n.d. [c. 22 January 1832], in *LPBG*, 135.

38. Letter, LP to McIlvaine, 27 March 1832.

39. Letter, Andrew Jackson to William Polk, 11 April 1832, GPP. Mary Eastin was a

daughter of William Eastin and Rachel Donelson, Rachel Jackson's niece. In the bridegroom's care, Jackson sent to Tennessee a silver medallion of his own likeness, a gift to Lucius's brother and the president's namesake, seven-year-old Andrew Jackson Polk.

40. Letter, FAP to Mary Eastin Polk, 19 August 1832, DPP.

41. Letter, LP to William Polk, 21 April 1832, GWPP. See also Murray, *Wake*, 287–288, and Cornelius Oliver Cathey, *Agricultural Developments in North Carolina 1783–1860* (Chapel Hill: University of North Carolina Press, 1956), 168. Cathey writes: "There is no evidence anyone made any money out of silk culture in the state."

42. Letter, LP to Sarah Polk, 5 May 1832. In a letter to McIlvaine (31 May 1832) Leonidas mentions specifically the Church Missionary Society, the London Missionary Society, and the British and Foreign Bible Society as participants in the composite meetings.

43. Letter, McIlvaine to Quintard, 31 December 1868; FAP, "Memoir," 12.

44. Stone, *Memoir of James Milnor*, 344–345. Letter, LP to McIlvaine, 31 May 1832.

45. FAP, "Memoir"; Letter, LP to FAP, 30 May 1832, in *LPBG* 1:139–140. Because in William Polk's biography his father's letters are often shortened, it cannot be known whether the few sentences published about slavery were all there were in the original. (In the biography, the text was taken from one of the few antebellum letters from Leonidas to Fanny available to their son. Most of his letters to her were lost in a household fire at Sewanee at the outbreak of the Civil War.)

46. Letter, LP to FAP, 1 June 1832, in *LPBG*, 1:140.

47. Letter, LP to FAP, 3 June 1832, in *LPBG*, 141–142.

48. John Julian, *A Dictionary of Hymnology* (London: John Murray, 1925), 764. James Montgomery had once worked as a newsman in Sheffield with Joseph Gales, a journalist hounded out of town by political enemies, then landing on his feet to found the *Raleigh Register* and become close to the Polk family. So close, in fact, that Joseph and his wife Winifred had just that spring presented Leonidas and Fanny with a pair of Spode pitchers as a wedding present. The pitchers, to bring things full circle, were first given to the Galeses by Montgomery. Letter, FAP to Gale Ring, 1 September 1889. Ring was a granddaughter of Leonidas and Fanny.

49. Rufus W. Griswold, ed., *Sacred Poets of England and America* (New York: Appleton, 1850), 370.

50. More properly known as Graitney, a history of Greta Green as a marriage mill is found in H. V. Morton, *In Scotland Again* (New York: Dodd, Mead, 1934), 7–12. Letter, LP to Sarah Polk, 12 August 1832.

51. G. W. H. Davidson, "The Library of Robert Leighton (1611–1684), Bishop of Dunblane," *HMPEC* 28 (1959): 216–266. Leonidas does not name Dunblane as one of his stopping points, though the cathedral town lies squarely along the road he was following.

52. Letter, LP to Sarah Polk, 12 August 1832. He finished the letter in Philadelphia.

53. Unlike the servant Paul whom Leonidas employed in Italy, "the boy" is not named.

6. "A Disposition to Be Pulling Down and Fixing Things Better" (1832–1836)

1. The *Sheffield* was one of two vessels with that name making the Atlantic run in 1832. *Lloyd's Register of Shipping, 1832* (London: W. Marchant, 1832).

2. After coming north in July, Fanny had visited a Mrs. Rutgers in New Jersey and a Mrs. (Frances?) Whitney in New Haven.

3. Fanny's health is also mentioned in a letter from Mary Brown Polk Badger to Mary Eastin Polk, 20 June 1832.

4. Letter, Mary Brown Polk Badger to Mary Eastin Polk, 20 June 1832; Letter, LP to Sarah Polk, 12 August 1832.

5. Letter, FAP to Mary Eastin Polk, 6 December 1832, YPP.

6. Due to turmoil in the Diocese of Ohio, McIlvaine had not yet been ordained to the episcopacy when the Polks visited.

7. Letter, LP to Sarah Polk, 14 October 1832.

8. Letter, LP to Rufus Polk, 28 February 1832; Letter, William Polk to Sarah Polk, 27 July 1828.

9. Letter, William Polk to Lucius Polk, 15 November 1832, YPP; Letter, William Polk to Sarah Polk, 27 July 1828.

10. Letter, John Devereux to William Polk, 21 November 1832. The enforced migration of the coastal slaves of the Carolinas by Leonidas Polk was a small example of the pending flood of millions of African Americans being resettled from the East Coast to the cotton and sugar plantations of the inland United States. Ira Berlin, *The Making of African America: The Four Great Migrations* (New York: Viking, 2010).

11. Letter, William Polk to Sarah Polk, 10 July 1828, "Letters and Diaries of the George W. Polk Family," *Historic Maury* 28 (1986): 22. Polk had received acreage from North Carolina, either before or after an earthquake. At the time, he had some 5,000 acres just around Reel Foot Lake. Also see Hillsman Taylor, "The Night Riders of West Tennessee," *West Tennessee Historical Society Papers* 6 (1952): 79.

12. Letter, LP to Rufus Polk, 28 February 1833. Leonidas had hoped to be on the road by March 20 and expected to be at Lucius's by April 20. They seem to have left later, and certainly the trip took longer. Lucius in March advised Mary Polk to take care of Leonidas's furniture when it arrived; "it is very fine and must be protected," he wrote on 21 March 1833, YPP.

13. FAP, "Memoir," 12. In Fanny's stoic words: "Our journey was long owing to my extreme illness on the road and the death of a little boy born near Knoxville." Earlier along the way, however, while still within North Carolina, she had reported feeling better. "We have heard again from . . . Fanny," Mary Polk Badger wrote her husband on April 25. "Her indisposition arose from some derangement of the liver. There was no fear of an accident [miscarriage?]." Letter, LP to Sarah Polk, 28 May 1833.

14. In the summer of 1829 (Letter, William Polk to Lucius Polk, 20 June 1829), Colonel Polk had sent his slave carpenters and masons to Tennessee to build Lucius's home, Hamilton Place, finished late in 1832, and "he wished to do the same for us," Fanny later recorded. FAP, "Memoir," 13. Chelsey Mosman, journal entry, 29 August 1862, in Arnold Gates, ed., *The Rough Side of War: The Civil War Journal of Chelsey A. Mosman, 1st Lieutenant, Company D, 59th Illinois Infantry Regiment* (Garden City, NY: Basin,1987), 24. Mosman added: "Splendid pike, fine residences on each side. Through this forest would appear the splendid homes. Saw [Leonidas] Polk's and General [Gideon] Pillow's residences."

15. St. Peter's cornerstone was laid in 1831 by the Right Reverend William Meade, Leonidas's bishop friend from Virginia. *Journal of the Proceedings of the Fifth Annual Con-*

vention of the Clergy and Laity of the Protestant Episcopal Church in the State of Tennessee (Nashville: Nye & Company, 1833).

16. James Walker had come to Columbia around 1810 as a newspaperman from Rockbridge, Virginia, and married Jane Maria Polk, a sister of James K. Polk. In 1835 the Walkers would name their eleventh child, who lived less than a year, Leonidas Polk Walker. Elbert L. Watson, "James Walker of Columbia," *THQ* 23 (1964): 24–37.

17. At the time, Colonel Polk owned some 5,000 acres just around Reel Foot Lake, later a prime resort area in Tennessee. Letter, William Polk to Sarah Polk, 10 July 1828, "Letters and Diaries," 22.

18. FAP, "Memoir," 12.

19. Parks, *General Leonidas Polk*, 66. William Polk's naming his plantation Rattle and Snap suggests a dice game had been involved in its acquisition.

20. Letter, William Polk to Sarah Polk, 4 July 1833, GPP. For the definitive word on steam doctors, see John S. Haller Jr., *The People's Doctors: Samuel Thomson and the American Botanical Movement, 1790–1860* (Carbondale: Southern Illinois University Press, 2000).

21. Letter, LP to Sarah Polk, 17 August 1833.

22. Limestone for the foundation was quarried on the place. Letter, LP to William Polk, 7 October 1833.

23. Letter, LP to Sarah Polk, 15 September 1833. Taking after Sarah Polk's interest in railroads, Leonidas within a year would be promoting a railroad connecting Columbia to the Tennessee River—just what cotton shippers could use.

24. Stephens was the third Episcopal priest to settle in Tennessee, arriving there in 1829. For deserting his father's Baptist Church in Virginia, he had been disinherited. William B. Sprague, *Annals of the American Episcopal Pulpit* (New York: R. Carter & Bros., 1859), 521; *Journal of Fifth Convention in Tennessee* (1833), 7.

25. Bishop Otey diary, 16 November 1833, quoted by William M. Green, *Memoir of Rt. Rev. James Hervey Otey: The First Bishop of Tennessee* (New York: J. Pott & Co, 1885), 152. In Bolivar, Stephens's fortunes were little changed; St. James Church, organized by him and thirty-seven founding members in 1834, had only fourteen communicants sixteen years later. Arthur Howard Noll, *History of the Church in the Diocese of Tennessee* (New York: J. Pott & Co, 1900), 102.

26. A letter dimissory from the Diocese of Virginia transferring Leonidas to Tennessee arrived in December 1833.

27. *Journal of the Proceedings of the Sixth Annual Convention of the Clergy and Laity of the Protestant Episcopal Church in the State of Tennessee* (Nashville: Harell, Hunt & Company, 1834), 24. Letter, LP to Susan Polk, 22 September 1834. Leonidas had also organized his people to put on a parish "fare" that raised $1,100 for the building fund.

28. Letter, LP to Sarah Polk, 2 February 1834. Colonel Polk had declined in health since his return to Raleigh from the Tennessee west; growing worse in early January, he died on January 14 at seventy-five.

29. Letter, LP to Sarah Polk, 18 May 1834. Leonidas suggested his mother help pay off Lucius's debts with money borrowed from the estate of their father. Lucius had moved to Mississippi that winter of 1833–1834 and then as suddenly moved back to Mount Pleasant by early spring 1834.

30. Larry J. Daniel and Lynn N. Bock, *Island No. 10: Struggle for the Mississippi Valley* (Tuscaloosa: University of Alabama Press, 1996), 4ff.

31. FAP, "Memoir," 13. Letter, Mary Polk Badger letter to George Badger, 26 April 1834, PBMP. Letter, LP to Sarah Polk, 18 April 1834.

32. Letter, LP to Sarah Polk, 28 July 1834. Date of completion figured from letter from FAP to Laura Johnson, 18 May 1836, in which she says the house is about ready; she is ordering furnishings. But not until 18 July 1837 do they move in. Letter, LP to Sarah Polk, 28 July 1837.

33. James Patrick, *Architecture in Tennessee, 1768–1897* (Knoxville: University of Tennessee Press, 1981), 72. What Ashwood Hall originally looked like is now hard to say. The only known photograph (Patrick, 172) was taken after Leonidas's brother Andrew Jackson Polk had bought the house and, with considerable money at hand, had remodeled it extensively. It burned to the ground in 1874.

34. Alfred Leland Crabb, "Twilight of the Nashville Gods," *THQ* 15 (1956): 291. Fogg was a Unionist when the Civil War broke out and was to lose a son fighting for the Confederacy. Fletch Coke, "Christ Church, Episcopal, Nashville," *THQ* 38 (1979): 141ff. Donald Smith Armentrout, *James Hervey Otey: First Episcopal Bishop of Tennessee* (Knoxville: Episcopal Dioceses in Tennessee, 1984), 27.

35. Mary Fogg's Patriot ancestors were Edward Rutledge and Arthur Middleton. Crabb, "Twilight of Nashville Gods," 292.

36. Letter, LP to Sarah Polk, 28 July 1834.

37. Armentrout, *James Hervey Otey*; Green, *Memoir of James Hervey Otey*, 86.

38. See Polk's "Committee Report on the Rev. Rector of Trinity Church, Clarksville," *Journal of the Proceedings of the Seventh Annual Convention of the Clergy and Laity for the Protestant Episcopal Church in the State of Tennessee* (Nashville: S. Nye & Company, 1835), 31–36.

39. *Journal of Sixth Convention in Tennessee* (1834), 28.

40. Committee appointments are found throughout *Journal of Sixth Convention in Tennessee*, 22–31. The Standing Committee had the authority in most things to act in the name of the convention throughout the year. Copy of proceedings, LP to Sarah Polk, 28 July 1834.

41. Lewis Cecil Gray, *History of Agriculture in the Southern United States to 1860* (Washington, DC: Carnegie Institution of Washington, 1933) 2:820–821. See also James F. Hopkins, *A History of the Hemp Industry in Kentucky* (Lexington: University of Kentucky Press, 1951).

42. For a history of the Columbia Railroad, see Philip M. Hamer, *Tennessee: A History 1673–1932* (New York: American Historical Society, 1933), 421ff.

43. "Bishop's Address," *Journal of Seventh Convention in Tennessee* (1835), 5.

44. Letter, FAP to Mary Eastin Polk, 7 December 1834. The physician Fanny criticized was Dr. John Beckwith, one of Raleigh's leading (and most versatile) physicians. He had perfected an operation for removing cataracts and restoring sight and marketed nationally his "Beckwith's Anti Dyspeptic Pills." Murray, *Wake*, 442.

45. Marilou Alston Rudulph, "George Cooke and His Paintings," *Georgia Historical Quarterly* 44 (1960): 119. George's brother John had been ordained in 1824.

46. Letter, Lucius Polk to Mary Ann Eastin Polk, 22 December 1834. If any of these

paintings survive, their whereabouts are unknown by me. But Leonidas liked Cooke's work so well that he had him make another portrait a few years later when he had been ordained a bishop of the Episcopal Church. That portrait, dated 1841, is reproduced in Rudulph, "George Cooke and His Paintings," 122–123.

47. Letter, Sarah Polk to Mary Eastin Polk, 29 December 1834.

48. Lucius, anxious to get home to Mary Ann, remained in Washington after the others left, staying at Gadsby's Hotel on Pennsylvania Avenue. But at President Andrew Jackson's insistence, he moved to 1600 Pennsylvania Avenue for a few days of Executive Mansion parties and companionship before he would head west for home. Letter, Lucius Polk to Mary Ann Eastin Polk, 14 January 1835.

49. Letter, Mary J. Lucas to Susan Polk, 2 March 1835. The same friend, a Raleigh music teacher, was delegated by Sarah Polk to write immediately to young Susan in Philadelphia to discard her woolen mourning clothes as soon as warm weather came. "For the last four years [in memory of Hamilton] you have worn little else," she reminded Susan "and [your mother] very much fears your health may suffer for it."

50. FAP, "Memoir," 13.

51. Letter, LP to Susan Polk, 23 October 1835, mentioning "Mary's and Grizzie's eyes"; Letter, Sarah Polk to Mary Eastin Polk, 19 February 1836.

52. Polk had first been elected to represent his diocese on the GTS board at the diocesan convention in Jackson, Tennessee, in June 1835. Another board member was a longtime Raleigh family friend, Duncan Cameron, who in a few years' time would have loaned LP several thousand dollars. Letter, LP to Sarah Polk, 28 September 1842. *Journal of the Proceedings of the Bishops, Clergy and Laity of the Protestant Episcopal Church in the United States of America in a General Convention* (New York: Protestant Episcopal Press, 1835), 612–613.

53. Until 1835 all US Episcopal dioceses were coextensive with state boundaries. The unmanageable size of some of them resulted in legislation that year creating separated, regional dioceses within the same state. Meanwhile, the wanton neglect of would-be Episcopalians settling on the fringes of the United States, one missionary said, would never have occurred had these unchurched legions lived instead in Siberia or India. The Reverend Joseph Doddridge, quoted by Walter H. Stowe, "A Turning Point: The General Convention of 1835," *HMPEC* 4 (1935): 152, 163, 168, 177.

54. Julia Hawks and Frances Devereux, among other charitable acts, had joined other Newbern women in presenting a quadrant to the University of North Carolina for use by the students. Kemp P. Battle, *History of the University of North Carolina* (Raleigh, NC: Edwards and Broughton, 1907–1912), 1:131–132.

55. Letter, FAP to Sarah Polk, 5 February 1836.

56. FAP, "Memoir," 14.

57. Patrick, *Architecture in Tennessee*, cites the "First Annual Catalogue" to identify Drummond and Lutterloh as the builders of the institute building. Letter, FAP to Sarah Polk, 5 February 1836.

58. Letter, LP to Sarah Polk, 11 February 1836.

7. "How Happily the Days of Thalaba Went By" (1836–1838)

1. FAP, "Memoir," 14. Fanny Polk remembered, apparently incorrectly, that the Wednesday Evensong had been in May.

2. Letter, Lucius Polk to Sarah Polk, 25 April 1836, PYP. Dating this attack, the first of three in close succession, is problematical. On Friday, April 8, Leonidas had written his mother that "all of us are well," perhaps believing the illness had passed and was not worth mentioning. Letter, LP to Sarah Polk, 8 April 1836, GWPP. In any case, Lucius Polk, himself writing Sarah Polk on April 21, says that Leonidas's first attack occurred "about four weeks ago." But inexplicably he then says a second attack had occurred a week previous [that would be on April 13], "two weeks after the first attack." The third, which he witnessed, occurred "yesterday, April 20." Letters, Lucius Polk to Sarah Polk, 21 April and 25 April 1836, YPP.

3. For reasons Lucius's correspondence does not make clear, O'Reily was not a physician in whom he had complete confidence; still, the doctor had previously won Leonidas's trust and gratitude for bringing Fanny safely through her latest pregnancy—and for refusing payment.

4. FAP, "Memoir," 15. See also Letters, Lucius Polk to Sarah Polk, 21 April and 25 April 1836; Parks, *General Leonidas Polk*, 74; Leon S. Bryan Jr., "Blood-letting in American Medicine, 1830–1892," *Bulletin of the Institute of the History of Medicine* 38 (1964): 516–529. Letter, FAP to Sarah Polk, 2 April 1836.

5. Letter, Lucius Polk to Sarah Polk, 25 April 1836, YPP. The visitor was probably James Chamberlain Jones, an area farmer, politician, and early railroad enthusiast. He may have been involved with Leonidas in the nascent Columbia Railroad Company.

6. A probable diagnosis of Leonidas's illness was made in 1997 by a California physician who had read Lucius Polk's letters: "My best guess . . . is that he suffered from . . . complex partial seizures or temporal lobe epilepsy. . . . The cause is unknown, and treatment with medications even today is unpredictable. It does seem to be self-limiting, but is exacerbated by fatigue, hyperventilation, and stress. [The condition] is almost impossible to diagnose [even] with hard data." Letter, Dorothy Young Riess, MD, Pasadena, CA, to the author, 24 March 1997. FAP "Memoir," 15.

7. Letter, Adlai O. Harris to James K. Polk, 13 April 1836, in Herbert Weaver and Kermit Hall, eds., *Correspondence of James K. Polk* (Nashville: Vanderbilt University Press, 1975), 3:698. Fanny, in her "Memoir," gives $30,000(!) as the amount of Leonidas's loan to Harris (15). And see Letter, LP to Charles McIlvaine, 10 August 1840, in which Leonidas estimates his loss. "I would do again what I did then," he told McIlvaine four years later, "for I thought I was doing a good work."

8. Letter, FAP to Sarah Polk, 2 April 1836, GWPP; *Journal of the Proceedings of the Eighth Annual Convention of the Clergy and Laity of the Protestant Episcopal Church in the State of Tennessee* (Nashville: Bynum and Cameron 1836), 6. In his report, LP mentioned that the children's instruction was oral, suggesting he abided by the Southern custom of discouraging literacy among slaves. Tennessee's slave code, by contrast, did not forbid teaching slaves to read and write. Randall M. Miller and John David Smith, eds., *Dictionary of Afro-American Slavery* (New York: Greenwood Press, 1998), 211 and 718ff.

9. Letter, LP to Sarah Polk, 8 April 1836, GWPP. Ropewalks were so well known

that the poet Henry W. Longfellow was moved to use their operations as a melancholy metaphor for a tedious life. See Longfellow, *The Early Poems of Henry Wadsworth Longfellow* (London: Pickering and Company, 1878). "The Rope Walk," written in 1854, begins: "In that building long and low, / With its windows all a-row, / Like the port-holes of a hulk, / Human spiders spin and spin."

10. Letter, LP to Sarah Polk, 8 April 1836, GWPP.

11. Letters, FAP to Sarah Polk, 5 February 1838, and 2 April 1836, GWPP.

12. St. Peter's was probably without any clergy until Otey had returned to Columbia from a Southern visitation and promotion of his Literary and Theological Seminary plan; Otey then preached Sundays May 12 through July 10. "Bishop's Address," *Journal of Eighth Convention in Tennessee* (1836), 18–24.

13. "Bishop's Address," *Journal of Eighth Convention in Tennessee* (1836); "Affairs of the Church: Tennessee," *The New-York Review* 2 (April 1838): 509.

14. Letter, LP to Sarah Polk, 24 November 1836, GWPP.

15. FAP, "Memoir," 16. Fanny modified the line from Southey's poem *Thalaba the Destroyer* (1801), which reads: "How happily the *years* of Thalaba went by." Robert Southey, *Thalaba the Destroyer* (London: T. N. Longman and O. Rees, 1801), Third Book, stanza 15, line 228.

16. Letter, LP to James Otey, 29 September 1837.

17. Letters, LP to Sarah Polk, 12 December 1837; Sarah Polk to Mary Eastin Polk, 14 February 1838, YPP.

18. Letter, Joseph Hubbard Saunders to "My dearest and beloved wife Laura," 15 September 1838, William Laurence Saunders Papers, 1767–1905, Perkins Library, Duke University. Alas for Saunders's demurral, he paid a high price. While caring for his flock during a calamitous yellow fever epidemic in 1839, he caught the disease himself and died in a delirium a week later, his toxic body hastily buried by parishioners beneath the church floorboards. Discovered in 1988, his bones were barely three inches deep. See *Downtown Crowd*, June 1988 (Pensacola [Florida] Downtown Improvement Board).

19. James Otey, "Bishop's Annual Address," *Journal of the Proceedings of the Eleventh Annual Convention of the Clergy and Laity of the Protestant Episcopal Church in the Diocese of Tennessee* (Nashville: S. Nye & Company, 1839), 15.

20. FAP, "Memoir," 17.

21. Polk's parochial report to the Tennessee diocesan convention in Clarksville. The Polk family correspondence in the fall of 1838 is thin inasmuch as Sarah Polk, Susan Polk, and most of Leonidas's brothers were all living near one another in Maury County.

22. Polk bid farewell to his twenty-four parish families, obliging Bishop Otey and the Reverend William T. Leacock, a schoolmaster recently arrived from Kentucky, to share parish duties.

23. Walter H. Stowe, "Polk's Missionary Episcopate," *HMPEC* 7 (1938): 343. Joseph Parks and Glenn Robins believe that the missionary and evangelical zeal shared by Bishops Otey and McIlvaine was instrumental in the choice of Polk. Glenn M. Robins, "Leonidas Polk and Episcopal Identity: An Evangelical Experiment in the Mid-Nineteenth Century South" (PhD diss., University of Southern Mississippi, 1999), 62.

John Thomas Wheat, rector of Christ Church in Nashville, and Thomas Maney, a Tennessee lawyer, informed Polk of his election.

24. FAP, "Memoir," 17.

25. "Consecration of Bishop Polk," *SOM* 4 (1839): 28. The Reverend Edward W. Peet, a colleague of McIlvaine's, read the biblical passages. Vera Lea Dugas says the Polks arrived in Cincinnati in late October. "The Ante-Bellum Career of Leonidas Polk," *Louisiana Historical Quarterly* 32 (1949): 286.

26. George Smythe, *History of the Diocese of Ohio Until the Year 1918* (Cleveland: Diocese of Ohio, 1931), 221. In 2018 the plaque honoring Bishop Polk's consecration in Christ Church, now a cathedral, was removed because of its racial overtones. The cathedral also plans to remove a Robert E. Lee stained-glass window.

27. Pope Leo XIII in 1896 declared Anglican orders defective. McIlvaine's hope that someday "all others become Episcopal" was expressed in a cornerstone address at Bexley Hall at Gambier, Ohio, 23 October 1839. Smythe, *History of Diocese of Ohio*, 230. For lavish praise of the sermon, see Letter, William Whittingham to McIlvaine, 3 April 1839, Episcopal Diocese of Maryland Archives, Baltimore. For those critical of McIlvaine's remarks, see Smythe, *History of Diocese of Ohio*, 230.

28. "Miscellaneous: Bishop Polk," *SOM* 4 (1839): 89–92.

29. I. J. Austin, "Obituary: Crafts James Wright, Class of 1828," *15th Annual Reunion of The Association of Graduates of the United States Military Academy* (East Saginaw, MI: Courier, 1884), 59. Wright later married McIlvaine's sister-in-law, Harriet Coxe.

30. *OR*, 10/1:159–160. The 13th Missouri was redesignated the 22nd Ohio Infantry in July 1862. Colonel Wright would be commended with his regiment for gallantry by Brig. Gen. William T. Sherman.

31. Harry E. Pratt, "Albert Taylor Bledsoe: Critic of Lincoln," *Transactions of Illinois State Historical Society* 41 (1934): 153. See also the entry on Bledsoe in Dumas Malone, ed., *Dictionary of American Biography* (New York: Scribner's, 1934), 2:364.

32. "Arkansas" was shorthand usage for the sprawling Southwest territory Polk would oversee as bishop.

33. The history of the centuries-old ordination hymn, and its many translations from Latin, is found in Julian, *Dictionary of Hymnology*, 1207ff. On vestments see Massey Shepherd Jr., *The Oxford American Prayer Book Commentary* (New York: Oxford University Press, 1950), 555.

34. John Johns, *A Memoir of the Rt. Rev. William Meade* (Baltimore: Innes, 1867). The descent of bishops of the American Episcopal Church is found in Perry, *Bishops of the American Church*, and in Hermon G. Batterson, *A Sketch Book of the American Episcopate* (Philadelphia: Lippincott, 1891).

35. Letter, LP to Sarah Polk, 31 December 1838; Letter, LP to McIlvaine, 10 August 1840. The for-sale plantation was in Mississippi.

8. *"Not a Common Preacher; He Was Good for Something" (1839–1841)*

1. Catherine Clinton, *The Plantation Mistress: Woman's World in the Old South* (New York: Pantheon Press, 1982). Letters, FAP to Sarah Polk, 5 March 1839 and 25 March 1839. "Mrs. Dutton" was probably the widowed mother of Thomas Dutton, a Raleigh

teacher known to Leonidas and Sarah Polk. Letter, LP to R. B. Buchanan, 8 September 1839, Autograph Collection, Pierpont Morgan Library, New York.

2. Most pressing was his letter to the Diocese of Louisiana agreeing to assume its episcopal oversight. Letter, LP to the Reverend N. S. Wheaton, President of the Louisiana Diocese Standing Committee, 14 February 1839. William Samuel Slack, "Bishop Polk and the Diocese of Louisiana," *HMPEC* 7 (1938): 362.

3. Letter, LP to Sarah Polk, 31 December 1838. Leonidas, Lucius, their half-brother William J. Polk, their mother, and James Walker, their cousin by marriage, were among the turnpike's private investors.

4. The acquisition of the Madison County plantation is first mentioned by Rufus Polk to Sarah Polk, 1 February 1839. He calls it a "purchase." Letter, LP to Sarah Polk, 4 November 1840. The acreage is also referred to by Lucius, Letter to Mary Polk, 27 March 1841, GWPP. As the brothers soon realized, the remoteness of the plantation (a railroad was still twenty years in the future) rendered the shipping of cotton to New Orleans economically unfeasible.

5. Letters, FAP to Sarah Polk, 28 January, 5 and 25 March 1839. Polk paid Brewster $600 and supported his family, an expense reckoned by Fanny at about $200; Brewster also was entitled to one-tenth of the profits the mills made.

6. Letter, LP to Foreign Committee of Board of Missions, 10 January 1839, *SOM* 4 (1839): 88. The committee had asked Polk in early January to go to Texas, and Louisiana had invited him to visit just prior to his departure in February. Letter, LP to Foreign Committee of Board of Missions, 10 January 1839, *SOM* 4 (1839), 87. In addition, Mississippi's Standing Committee had asked him to visit *them*. "Report of Bishop Polk," *Journal of the Proceedings of the Bishops, Clergy and Laity of the Protestant Episcopal Church in the United States of America* (New York: Swords, Stanford, 1841), 157–172.

7. Letter, LP to Board of Missions, 16 March 1839, *SOM* 4 (1839): 141. Armentrout, *James Hervey Otey*, 181. Also see James H. Stone, "The Economic Development of Holly Springs During the 1840s," *Journal of Mississippi History* 32 (1970): 341.

8. Randolph, Tennessee, eventually disappeared. Armentrout, *James Hervey Otey*, 173.

9. Foster took over the church in Holly Springs on March 1, 1839. Armentrout, *James Hervey Otey*, 173. But his leap was without enough of a look. Ten months later the wages provided his planter congregants were so meager that only the goodwill of a local merchant prevented him and his family from going hungry.

10. Polk did not relate his tavern adventure to his mother; Fanny Polk provided the details in her memoir. FAP, "Memoir," 18–19.

11. E. Clowes Chorley, "The Church in Arkansas and Its Bishops," *HMPEC* 15 (1946): 320. Letter, LP to Sarah Polk, 18 March 1839.

12. Letter, LP to Board of Missions, 12 July 1839, *SOM* 4 (1839): 306. He reported from his home in Tennessee.

13. Letter, LP to N. S. Wheaton, 14 February 1839; Slack, "Bishop Polk," 362; "Report of Bishop Polk," 157–162.

14. An analysis of the land dispute is given by Louis Wiltz Kemp, *The Signers of the Texas Declaration of Independence* (Houston: Anson Jones Press, 1944), 98. Polk set foot in Texas almost exactly three years since the spring of 1836 when the Texas Revolution

had convulsed in three massacres: Texans at the Alamo, Texans at Goliad, and Mexican soldiers at San Jacinto.

15. "Map Illustrating Indian Territory and Plan of the Defenses of the Western Frontier," *SOM* 8 (1843): 165.

16. Letter, LP to Board of Missions, 12 July 1839, *SOM* 4 (1839): 308, and "Intelligence: Bishop Polk," *SOM* 6 (1841): 152. See also "Report of Bishop Polk."

17. FAP, "Memoir," 23–24.

18. Letter, LP to Board of Missions, 12 July 1839, *SOM* 4 (1839): 310, and Letter, LP to Sarah Polk, 5 April [1839], in *LPBG*, 1:169.

19. Letter, LP to Board of Missions, 12 July 1839, *SOM* 4 (1839): 309–310.

20. Letter, James H. Otey to Board of Missions, 3 June 1842, *SOM* 7 (1842): 202–203. Letter, LP to Sarah Polk, 28 July 1839, GWPP. Armentrout, *James Hervey Otey*, 100. See also Green, *Memoir of James Hervey Otey*, 159.

21. Slack, "Bishop Polk," 361. See W. Darrell Overdyke, *Louisiana Plantation Homes: Colonial and Ante-Bellum* (New York: Architectural Book Publishing Company, 1965), and Betty Carter and Hodding Carter, *So Great a Good: A History of the Episcopal Church in Louisiana and of Christ Church Cathedral, 1905–1955* (Sewanee, TN: University Press, 1955), 47.

22. Andrew Forest Muir, "William Fairfax Gray, Founder of Christ Church Cathedral, Houston," *HMPEC* 28 (1959): 379.

23. Letter, LP to Foreign Committee of Board of Missions, 17 May 1839, *SOM* 4 (1839): 198; James P. Baughman, *Charles Morgan and the Development of Southern Transportation* (Nashville: Vanderbilt University Press, 1968), 24–27.

24. C. Bradford Mitchell, ed., *Merchant Steam Vessels of the United States, 1790–1868* (Staten Island, NY: Steamship Historical Society of America, 1975), 253.

25. Letter, LP to Foreign Committee of Board of Missions, 17 May 1839, *SOM* 4 (1839): 199.

26. Writers' Program of the WPA, *Houston: A History and Guide* (Houston: A. Jones Press, 1942), 239.

27. Muir, "William Fairfax Gray," 358. Letter, LP to Foreign Committee of Board of Missions, 17 May 1839, *SOM* 4 (1839): 199.

28. Muir, "William Fairfax Gray," 361. Polk would later fret about the amount of time his reports required and that he could never seem to satisfy all his readers: some wanted much more detail, others far less. Letter, LP to Board of Missions, 18 May 1840, *SOM* 5 (1840): 268.

29. WPA, *Houston: A History and Guide*, 256.

30. FAP, "Memoir," 26–27. Fanny misremembered the date of this encounter, thinking it had occurred during Polk's brief 1839 visitation, not during his return to Texas in February 1841.

31. Polk called it a "stroke of the sun," though clinically speaking a sunstroke or heatstroke is normally more severe—involving coma and convulsions, for example—than the effects he reported.

32. Had they been able to, they would have gone up the Colorado River to Bastrop, then to Austin, the new seat of Texas's government, thence east to Washington on the Brazos ["Brassos," he wrote], thence farther east to Nacodoches, San Augustine, and Sabine Town. From there they would have reentered Louisiana.

33. Letter, LP to Foreign Committee of Board of Missions, *SOM* 4 (1839): 313. Letters, LP to McIlvaine, 21 July 1830, and 10 August 1840, in *LPBG*, 1:164. Leonidas was reminded, he wrote, of a taunt made by the "Romanist bishop of Ohio, to Campbell, the Baptist [when] discussing . . . celibacy of the clergy. He asked Campbell if he did not think St. Paul would have cut a fine figure, while visiting the churches of Asia, with a wife and seven screaming children following in his train!"

34. Letter, LP to Sarah Polk, 28 July 1839.

35. Luke 16:8b.

36. Letter, LP to Foreign Committee of Board of Missions, 24 July 1839, *SOM* 4 (1839): 333–335.

37. Jill K. Garrett, "St. John's Church, Ashwood," *THQ* 29 (1970): 8.

38. Hopkins's architectural skills and ceremonial taste are examined in James F. White, "Theology and Architecture in America: A Study of Three Leaders," in Stuart C. Henry, ed., *A Miscellany of American Christianity: Essays in Honor of H. Shelton Smith* (Durham: Duke University Press, 1963), 362–390. See also John Henry Hopkins, *Essay on Gothic Architecture* (Burlington: Smith & Harrington, 1836). In his text, Hopkins counseled against too many windows, as well as windows extending too low to the floor; all allowed the distractions of the out-of-doors to intrude, hence "unfriendly to devotion." As to creature comforts in the wintertime, he preferred "the practice of our ancestors who used no artificial heat whatsoever in the house of God. But if this be too much to expect from the effeminacy of our day," he grudgingly allowed that warm-air ducts be installed beneath the floor of the nave. Hopkins's manly hardiness would desert him in old age. During Vermont's exceedingly cold winter of 1868–1869, he caught pneumonia and died.

39. On his way through Virginia, it is likely that he stopped to recruit at his own seminary in Alexandria.

40. The pregnancy ended in the birth of a girl her parents named Sarah, after her paternal grandmother.

41. Letter, LP to Board of Missions, 18 May 1840, *SOM* 5 (1840): 274–275. Also see Peter J. Hamilton, *Mobile of the Five Flags: Mobile from the Earliest Times to the Present* (Mobile, AL: Gill Printing Company, 1913), 233–236.

42. Letter, LP to Board of Missions, 21 July 1840, *SOM* 5 (1840): 287. The quotation is from Psalm 119:71. Also see D. Clayton James, *Antebellum Natchez* (Baton Rouge: Louisiana State University Press, 1968), 267–271.

43. Letter, LP to Lucius Polk, 2 April 1840.

44. Fanny mentions Polk's visit to the debtor's jail without naming the prisoner. FAP, "Memoir," 27. See Stuart O. Landry, *Imprisonment for Debt in Louisiana* (New Orleans: Pelican, 1964), 13–16.

45. Letter, LP to Board of Missions, 21 July 1840, *SOM* 5 (1840): 284. Polk had written his report at his home in Tennessee.

46. Letter, LP to Charles McIlvaine, 10 August 1840.

47. Letters, LP to Sarah Polk, 1 January 1841, 10 February 1841, in *LPBG*, 1:167–168. The carriage horses had formerly belonged to Sarah Polk.

48. Letter, LP to Sarah Polk, 18 January 1841 [*sic*], in *LPBG*, 166–167. The printed date may be incorrect as Polk says in his report to the General Convention that he was in the Indian Territory visiting the Cherokee chief John Ross on that date. The tone of the

letter suggests he wrote it on New Year's Day. Moreover, the Reverend W. H. C. Yeager, in a letter to the missionary society dated Little Rock, 1 January 1841, says "Our Bishop ... is here at present." Letter, W. H. C. Yeager to Board of Missions, 1 January 1841, *SOM* 6 (1841): 105. In the same letter, Yeager reveals the bishop's gift of $800. Fanny mentions it in her "Memoir" as well; his salary, she adds, was $2,500 per annum.

49. Letter, William Scull to Board of Missions, 9 September 1840, *SOM* 5 (1840): 345.

50. Biographical notes on Sophia Sawyer are found in Teri L. Castelow, "'Behold Me and This Great Babylon I Have Built': The Life and Work of Sophia Sawyer, 19th Century Missionary and Teacher Among the Cherokees" (PhD diss., Florida State, 2005). Earlier, Sawyer had gotten into trouble in Georgia for teaching slave children to read, against Georgia law.

51. "Supplemental Report," LP to Board of Missions, *SOM* 8 (1843): 313. Inspired by Sawyer's zeal and success, and perhaps by Polk's prodding, William Scull opened a complementary academy for Indian boys in Fayetteville later that year.

52. "Church Missions Among the Indians," *SOM* 8 (1843): 76. The unnamed author lamented that even by 1843 "we have not a single Missionary west of the Mississippi to baptize [the Indians] into Christ."

53. "Report of Bishop Polk," 170.

54. For some of the worst antagonisms among the Cherokees regarding the relocation treaty, see Gary Moulton, *John Ross, Cherokee Chief* (Athens: University of Georgia Press, 1978), 136.

55. "Report of Bishop Polk," 170.

56. "Intelligence: Bishop Polk," *SOM* 6 (1841): 152. Polk's quotations are from Isaiah 30:21 and the "Ordering of Priests" in the Book of Common Prayer.

57. He visited the families of Benjamin and Henry Hawkins in Arkansas and William B. Hawkins in Bowie County in Texas. Visits at his relatives are alluded to both in a letter to Sarah Polk and in his report to the 1841 General Convention. Letter, LP to Sarah Polk, 10 February 1841, in *LPBG*, 1:168; "Report of Bishop Polk," appendix, 170.

58. "Report of Bishop Polk," appendix, 171. Letter, LP to Sarah Polk, 10 February 1841, in *LPBG*, 1:168.

59. Letter, LP to Sarah Polk, 10 February 1841, in *LPBG*, 1:167–168.

60. Letter, LP to Susan Polk, 7 April 1841.

9. *"As It Is My Duty to Live Here, I Will Try My Best to Like It"* (1841–1849)

1. The Diocese of Louisiana at the time had too few ordained clergymen to elect its own bishop.

2. The village was named for Henry Schuyler Thibodaux and was incorporated as Thibodauxville. As did others, Polk sometimes spelled it Thibeaudauxville, even Thibodeaux. In 1918 the town name was officially changed to Thibodaux. In the text, I have used the spellings variously employed by the people mentioned.

3. The nearness of New Orleans so appealed to Lucius that, in his enthusiasm, he wrote Mary that "Thibodeaux was only 14 miles from the city." Letter, Lucius Polk to Mary Eastin Polk, 27 March 1841, GWPP.

4. Letter, Lucius Polk to Mary Eastin Polk, 27 March 1841, ᴳWPP.

5. Letter, Mary Eastin Polk to Lucius Polk, 13 April 1840, GWPP.

6. Letter, LP to Susan Polk, 7 April 1841.

7. Letter, LP to Susan Polk, 7 April 1841. The bayou's water level, held by a levee, would have been only slightly lower than Porter's front yard. A dam later built at the Mississippi River source of La Fourche Bayou has altered many of the stream's bucolic characteristics that Bishop Polk found appealing in the 1840s.

8. James Porter, his older brother Alexander, and a sister had been in the bayou region for about two decades. Letter, FAP to Mary Polk, 20 January 1843, mentions Porter's being a widower.

9. When Pollock died intestate in 1839, his sizable North Carolina estate was divided among various Pollock and Devereux kinfolk, and Fanny and Leonidas took their share in cash and slaves: $50,000 and 161 slaves reckoned at the same amount. As was largely true of Leonidas Polk's slave holdings, one-fifth of all slave-owning clergymen in the South shortly before the Civil War had "obtained them from either the dowries or inheritances of their wives." Larry Tise, *Proslavery: A History of the Defense of Slavery in America, 1701–1840* (Athens: University of Georgia Press, 1987), 151.

10. The purchase details are in David Plater, *"The Remarkably Neat Church in the Village of Thibodaux": An Antebellum History of St. John's Episcopal Church* (Lafayette: University of Southwestern Louisiana Press, 1994), 40 and 82, n. 77. See also Parks, *General Leonidas Polk*, 93–94 and 112–113. How the financial details were worked out without Fanny's being there is interesting (if there was relevant correspondence between the bishop and her, it is missing), but mortgage and sale papers dated April 17, 1841, are in the Lafourche Parish Records.

11. Letter, LP to Sarah Polk, 15 July 1841. Polk's description of the family caravan was a loose paraphrase from Exodus in the Hebrew Bible. Leonidas underlines an intriguing sentence in the letter which remains unfathomable: "We come with all the children, little Sally, wet nurse and all. I don't mean the little foster baby and her nurse, too, for they, we think, can be very well taken care of at home, and must be left." In surviving correspondence, this is the only reference I have seen to a foster child being raised by Fanny and Leonidas. Perhaps he means a slave child.

12. Samuel Farmar Jarvis, *A Chronological Introduction to the History of the Church: Being a New Inquiry into the True Dates of the Birth and Death of our Lord and Saviour Jesus Christ* (New York: Harper, 1845).

13. "Canon," *Journal of Proceedings of Bishops, Clergy and Laity* (1841), 113.

14. The slaves inherited by the Polks were not later sold when the family's failing finances became dire in the late 1840s. Parks, *General Leonidas Polk*, 111–112.

15. Letter, Lucius Polk to Mary Polk, 5 March 1842, YPP; FAP, "Memoir," 31.

16. According to a priest officiating, Bishop Polk arrived at St. Paul's on January 20 "in the midst of our services, having encountered extreme difficulty and fatigue in the prosecution of his journey." Letter, John Burke to the Board of Missions, 20 January 1842, *SOM* 7 (1842): 69.

17. "Bishop's Address," *Journal of the Fourth Convention of the Diocese of Louisiana* (New Orleans: Diocese of Louisiana, 1842), 30–32. The reference to "sincere milk . . ." is from 1 Peter 2:2. Reacting, perhaps, to critics, Polk evidently wanted no one to mistake

where he stood theologically, pointedly reminding a later convention: "My own views were well known to you before I was invited to take charge of this diocese, and have been explicitly recorded in [my] address in 1842." "Bishop's Address," *Journal of the Sixth Annual Convention of the Protestant Episcopal Church of the Diocese of Louisiana* (New Orleans: T. Rea, Printer, 1844), 15.

18. "Bishop's Address," *Journal of the Fifth Annual Convention of the Diocese of Louisiana* (New Orleans: George Young, 1843), 5.

19. Fanny names the places in Scotland Leonidas said he intended to visit. Letter, FAP to Mary Eastin Polk, 19 August 1832, DPP. Dunblane is not on her list, but several nearby lochs and towns are. The owners' naming of plantations in one Louisiana parish for practical and romantic reasons is discussed in Jeffrey Alan Owens, "Naming the Plantation: An Analytical Survey from Tensas Parish, Louisiana," *Agricultural History* 68, 4 (1994): 46–69.

20. The bishop's hope for the Donaldsonville parish was in "trusting God would bless it as a magnet for the planters living within reach along both Bayou La Fourche and the Mississippi River."

21. Parks, *General Leonidas Polk*, 99, citing an account of the worship service in the *Columbia Guardian*, 15 October 1842.

22. FAP, "Memoir," 32. Letter, LP to Lucius Polk, 29 June 1843, GWPP. Polk's surviving correspondence does not record whether Andrew Jackson Polk, another of his full brothers but never "nearest and dearest" to him, was ever baptized. The consecration of St. John's is related in Garrett, "St. John's, Ashwood."

23. Letter, LP to Sarah Polk, 28 September 1842.

24. The bishop's week-by-week calendar for 1842 is included in his "Bishop's Address," *Journal of Fifth Convention of Diocese of Louisiana* (1843), 4–11.

25. Letters, FAP to Mary Eastin Polk, 8 January and 20 January, 1843. Nephew William Polk, son of Thomas Gilchrist Polk and then twenty-one, would spend the next three years helping manage Uncle Leonidas's sugaring operations before striking out on his own. As for Fanny's disappointment, one historian of Louisiana architecture, who had never seen Leighton Place in its dilapidated stage, rhapsodized about it after visiting one late afternoon some seventy-five years after the Polks had lived there. "The long shadows with streaks of emerald green stretched themselves the length of the broad lawn. The light in the moss and the thick foliage of the live oaks possessed an almost dramal quality. . . . The house has an air of snuggling close to the ground under the far-reaching branches and the deep shadows of its encompassing trees. It is a house with a personality, not gay, but serene in the sweet, deep, impenetrable calm." William P. Spratling and Natalie Scott, *Old Plantation Houses in Louisiana* (New York: William Helburn, 1927), 89–90.

26. Edward L. Bond, *St. James Episcopal Church, Baton Rouge* (Baton Rouge: The Church, 1994), 18. "Bishop's Address," *Journal of Fifth Convention of Diocese of Louisiana* (1843), 4–11.

27. Slaves on neighboring plantations, hearing that Sunday was a day off for those at Leighton Place, were soon wanting the same. Letter, Charles Goodrich to FAP, 3 December 1867. FAP, "Memoir," 45.

28. Neither Chaplain Wall nor Bishop Polk was ever known to call slavery sacred,

but that set them apart from George Freeman, the rector of Christ Church in Raleigh. He assured his congregation that "in the Episcopal Church [the slaveholder] would find asylum from the taunts and reproaches of the civilized world; [and] from her altars he could gather balm for his wounded conscience." Slavery was sanctioned by God, Freeman assured the faithful, and approved by Jesus Christ. The North Carolina bishop Levi Silliman Ives was so comforted by Freeman's sermon that he called for its publication so that masters throughout the South could find repose in the Church's balm. See William Jay, "A Letter to the Rt. Rev. L. Silliman Ives," in *Miscellaneous Writings on Slavery* (Boston: J. P. Jewett & Company 1853), 453–489. Freeman succeeded Polk as bishop of the Southwest.

29. "Bishop's Address," *Journal of Fifth Convention of Diocese of Louisiana* (1843), 8; to further appease nervous slave owners, Polk urged his clergy to remind them that the original Apostles had, when preaching salvation, avoided social issues. They "did not condescend . . . to dogmatize on the civil relations or rights of individuals."

30. Felicity Allen, *Jefferson Davis, Unconquerable Heart* (Columbia: University of Missouri Press, 1999), 621, n. 23.

31. Letter, LP to Sarah Polk, 9 June 1843; Letter, LP to Lucius Polk, 29 June 1843, GWPP.

32. Letter, LP to Otey, 7 August 1843.

33. Letter, LP to Sarah Polk, 23 September 1843.

34. Letter, LP to Lucius Polk, 24 November 1856, GWPP. Leonidas paraphrases Paul's letter from prison in Philippians 4:12.

35. Letters, LP to Sarah Polk, 9 June 1843 and 23 September 1843.

36. "Bishop's Address," *Journal of Sixth Convention of Diocese of Louisiana* (1844), 9–11. A lasting friendship developed between Polk and George Guion; it included Guion's significant financial and moral support in the 1850s of Polk's budding University of the South.

37. David Plater, in *Remarkably Neat Church*, suggests that Polk was influenced by the Greek Revival style of New Orleans's Christ Church, the newly built cathedral of the diocese on Bourbon and Canal. In any case, a renovation of St. John's in 1855—to enlarge its seating capacity for the growing parish—resulted in its present-day "Classical Revival" style.

38. Charles Menard, *Annales de l'Eglise de St. Joseph* (1843), 24. I am indebted to Michael Foret, archivist at Nicholls State University in Thibodaux, for the translated quotation.

39. Letters, LP to Lucius Polk, 13 December 1843, and FAP to Mary E. Polk, 22 February 1844. The well-to-do socializing friends Leonidas mentioned included Elise Ellis and husband Braxton Bragg, at the time a planter in La Fourche Parish.

40. Letters, LP to Susan Polk Rayner, 10 January 1844, and LP to Lucius Polk, 11 April 1844.

41. Solving a problem for a region short on timber, the church for Matagorda was "designed, cut and framed in New York, and then shipped in sections" to Texas in 1839–1840. Bishop Polk consecrated the erected building on 25 February 1844. See DuBose Murphy, "Caleb S. Ives, Pioneer Missionary in Texas," *HMPEC* 6 (1937): 244.

42. Letter, LP to Lucius Polk, 6 June 1844; Letter, Lucius Polk to Mary Eastin Polk, 23 July 1844. Fanny, eight months pregnant, was summering in Tennessee when her father died and was reluctant to travel after Leonidas joined her; her father's funeral went on

without them. Fanny gave birth at Ashwood Hall to William Mecklenburg Polk on August 15.

43. Samuel Wilberforce, *A History of the Protestant Episcopal Church in America* (London: James Burns, 1844), 422–425. William Jay, "Introductory Remarks to the Reproof of the American Church Contained in the Recent 'History of the Protestant Episcopal Church in America' by the Bishop of Oxford [Samuel Wilberforce]," *Miscellaneous Writings on Slavery*, 412–414. A sermon appendix to an American edition of Wilberforce's book (New York: Stanford & Swords, 1849) chides Polk by name for owning slaves (345).

44. Letter, Richard King to William Whittingham, 16 November 1846, Leonidas Polk Papers, 1838–1865, Archives of the Episcopal Diocese of Maryland, Episcopal Diocesan Center.

45. Clarence A. Walworth, *The Oxford Movement in America, or, Glimpses of Life in an Anglican Seminary* (New York: Catholic Book Exchange, 1895), 27. Exalting "the Church above Christ . . . making her, not Him, the dispenser of renewing and sanctifying grace" was the way Polk's friend James Milnor put the Christmas Eve bell-ringing issue. Quoted in Stone, *Memoir of James Milnor*, 571–572.

46. For various accounts of the whole messy period, see Powel Mills Dawley, "Little Oxford," ch. 6, *The Story of the General Theological Seminary* (New York: Oxford University Press, 1969); Richard G. Salomon "The Episcopate on the Carey Case," *HMPEC* 18 (1949): 240–279; E. Clowes Chorley, "The Oxford Movement in the Seminary," *HMPEC* 5 (1940): 177–201; and George E. DeMille, *The Catholic Movement in the American Episcopal Church* (Philadelphia: Church Historical Society, 1941).

47. "Bishop's Address," *Journal of Sixth Convention of Diocese of Louisiana* (1844), 14–16. Polk's fine sentiment was not evident months later, however, when Polk allied himself with McIlvaine and other virulent low churchmen in an "unchaste conduct" trial against the high-church bishop of New York, Benjamin Onderdonk. The ecclesiastical trial on probable trumped-up charges in New York dragged on for four titillating weeks (the proceedings covering 333 closely printed pages), and Leonidas was not able to return to Fanny and their baby boy Willy until early January 1845.

48. Solon Robinson, "Agricultural Tour South and West—No. 7," *American Agriculturist* 8 (1849): 219.

49. Letter, LP to Susan Rayner, 8 December 1847. "The Old North State" is a North Carolina anthem.

50. Letter, LP to Charles McIlvaine, 18 May 1848.

51. Robinson does not say when he first learned of the bishop-planter. He had passed through the "Polk neighborhood" in Middle Tennessee in 1845, and, when beginning another Southern tour in November 1848, he encountered on his steamboat from St. Louis William Julius Polk, Leonidas's half-brother then farming in Arkansas. "Agricultural Tour South and West—No. 2," *American Agriculturist* 8 (1849): 51; "Agricultural Tour South and West—No. 3," *American Agriculturist* 8 (1849): 92.

52. Solon Robinson, "Mr. Robinson's Tour, No. 11" *American Agriculturist* 8 (1849): 337–338.

53. E. D. Fenner, "Report on Epidemic Cholera in the City of New Orleans, 1848–'49," *Southern Medical Reports* (New Orleans: B. M. Norman, 1850), 1:125–159. See also

Charles E. Rosenberg, *The Cholera Years: The United States in 1832, 1849, and 1866* (Chicago: University of Chicago Press, 1962), 105.

54. "Bishop's Address," *Journal of the Proceedings of the Eleventh Annual Convention of the Protestant Episcopal Church in Louisiana* (New Orleans: Spencer & Middleton, 1849), 9. The biblical quotation is from Micah 6:9.

55. William A. Booth, "On the Cholera of La Fourche Interior," in *Southern Medical Reports*, 1:196–235.

56. Williams was to die in a steamboat explosion later in 1849, but his estate subsequently sued Polk for $1,116 in unpaid medical bills. A court reduced the judgment to $425, finding that Williams had occasionally been inebriated while ministering to the sick on Leighton Plantation. Plater, *Remarkably Neat Church*, 61–62.

57. Booth, "On the Cholera," 235. The epidemic struck Leighton Place on May 17 and lasted until June 7. FAP, "Memoir," 35–36. That was the day neighbor Braxton Bragg married Elise Ellis at Evergreen.

58. Booth, "On the Cholera," 235. To the convention the following year, incorporating scripture, the bishop said: "I desire to record here my unfeigned gratitude and thanksgiving to Almighty God our Heavenly Father, for his pity and compassion toward me . . . 'in sparing me when I deserved to be punished, and in the midst of his judgments for having remembered mercy.'" "Bishop's Address," *Journal of the Proceedings of the Twelfth Annual Convention of the Protestant Episcopal Church in Louisiana* (New Orleans: H. Spencer & Company, 1850), 15.

59. Polk gave slightly different statistics. Letter, LP to Susan Rayner, 9 July 1847. "Of all the population on my place white and black amounting to between 360 or 370, I suppose not more than, say, 50 who did not have the disease. Of this number, we lost 70 of all ages, 25 children, 29 men and 16 women. Among them we had some of the best people, but generally they were among the old and feeble and the young, and of all that died . . . there were about 28 only who could be called hands." Fanny wrote that seventy-six died of cholera and thirty more of "secondary" causes. FAP, "Memoir," 35.

60. "We deem it our duty to state that we suggested this prescription to Bishop Polk and his physicians," wrote Dr. Erasmus Darwin Fenner, a North Carolinian likely to have been known to Polk from their schoolboy days in Raleigh. "Happening to be [at Leighton Place] when the epidemic was raging, and finding the cases so very unmanageable after the attack was declared, we advised the trial of premedication. We offered the above mixture as a mere suggestion, stating frankly at the time, that we had no experience to refer to, and that we had serious doubts as to the value of any sort of preventive medication. We were not surprised at the result; but we still think that, under the circumstances, it was worth the trial." Booth, "On the Cholera," 213, editor's note.

61. Richard Follett, *The Sugar Masters: Planters and Slaves in Louisiana's Cane World, 1820–1860* (Baton Rouge: Louisiana State University Press, 2005), 191–192. Polk's experimental cholera cure is mentioned by fellow planter Elu Landry in his estate dairy and ledger, 11 July 1849.

62. Parks, *General Leonidas Polk*, 111–112. Letter, LP to Susan Rayner, 9 July 1849.

63. Fanny mentions the $5,000 doctor's bill, plus a "very large" apothecary bill. FAP,

"Memoir," 36. "Last Will and Testament," 14 November 1849, and "Codicil: To Whom It May Concern," 1 September 1858.

10. *"From This Time Forward We Were Beggars" (1850–1857)*

1. Valcour Aime, *Plantation Diary of the Late Mr. Valcour Aime* (New Orleans: Clark & Hopeline, 1878), 137, entry for May 8. The ruined sugarhouse Aime mentioned probably belonged to a C. Nicholas, or Nicholls.

2. *New Orleans Daily Delta*, 9 May 1850, morning edition, 1.

3. Letter, Charles Goodrich to FAP, 3 December 1867. Soon thereafter, Goodrich provided Mrs. Polk with twenty pages of anecdotal recollections regarding her late husband.

4. *LPBG*, 1:206–207. The neighbor is not identified. But George Guion, whose plantation Ridgefield was nearby, is a likely candidate.

5. Letter, Charles Goodrich to FAP, 3 December 1867. Goodrich, born in Connecticut, like Polk had attended the theological seminary in Virginia.

6. In her memoir, Fanny Polk uses the word "cyclone." That term is anachronistic as far as 1849 is concerned; it came into general use in the 1870s when she was writing. See foreword in David M. Ludlum, *Early American Tornadoes, 1586–1870* (Boston: American Meteorological Society, 1970). William M. Polk, who was probably at home during the storm, uses the older word "tornado." *LPBG*, 1:206. Bishop Polk called it a "hurricane" in a letter to James Robb, 4 October 1851.

7. FAP, "Memoir," 38.

8. FAP, "Memoir," 38–39. The alleged defrauder's name could not be established; Fanny seems to implicate John Williams, a New Orleans businessman who would later buy Leighton Place. In a letter to James Robb, 4 October 1851, The Historic New Orleans Collection (hereafter THNOC), Leonidas calculated his latest losses at Leighton Place because of disease, storms, and cold weather as "upwards of 100 Negroes, together with two crops worth 60M dollars," plus unspecified machinery and buildings wrecked by the 1850 tornado.

9. "Report of the Committee on Education," *Journal of the Proceedings of the Fourteenth Annual Convention of the Protestant Episcopal Church in Louisiana* (New Orleans: B. M. Norman, 1852), 31–32. Scoffing at the social prestige attached in Louisiana to substantial slave- and landholdings, a contemporary journalist opined: "These very large sugar plantations are all humbug, and show a silly vanity." *West Baton Rouge Sugar Planter*, 13 February 1858, quoted by Joseph R. Razek, *Accounting on the Old Plantation: A Study of the Records of William J. Minor and Other Sugar and Cotton Planters* (New Orleans: University of New Orleans, 1981).

10. See the Bishop's Addresses in *Journal of the Seventh Annual Convention of the Protestant Episcopal Church in the Diocese of Louisiana* (New Orleans: T. Rea, 1845), 12–13; *Journal of the Eighth Annual Convention of the Protestant Episcopal Church in Louisiana* (New Orleans: B. M. Norman, 1846), 8–9; *Journal of Twelfth Convention in Louisiana* (1850), 21–22; and *Journal of the Fourteenth Convention in Louisiana* (1852), 28–30. See also Robert Campbell Witcher, "The Episcopal Church in Louisiana, 1805–1861" (PhD diss., Louisiana State University, 1969), 244–272. The sentiments of Polk's Education Committee

members sometimes resembled those published in the March issue of *De Bow's Review*, the New Orleans–based journal of resolute Southernness. In that issue, J. D. B. De Bow decried the shipping off of Southern boys to schools in the North. "There they go," De Bow wrote, mocking the upward-striving sons of Louisiana planters, "crowding Dartmouth and Harvard, and Brown and Yale, and Amherst and Middlebury." Southern schools might be lacking in excellence, but "better it would be for us that our sons remained in honest ignorance and at the plow handle, than that their plastic minds be imbued with doctrines subversive of their county's peace and honor." "Home Education at the South," *De Bow's Review* 10 (1851): 362.

11. "Report of the Committee on Education," *Journal of Seventh Convention in Diocese of Louisiana* (1845), 16–17. Also see William H. Nelson, *A Burning Torch and a Flaming Fire: The Story of Centenary College of Louisiana* (Nashville: Methodist Publishing House, 1931), 101. Fanny wrote that, in the winter of 1850–1851, "[I] for the first time heard my husband speak of his wish to establish a University which should enlist the sympathies of all the [Southern] states." At one point, she remembered, the bishop considered purchasing Jefferson College "for the diocese . . . [and] then thought of purchasing it himself, and removing there. But the heavy losses induced by the cholera [in 1849] prevented more than the thought of this." FAP, "Memoir," 34. No other record was found of Polk's ever having designs on Jefferson College. Fanny may have confused his frustrated attempt to buy Franklin College in 1853.

12. *Journal of the Proceedings of the Thirteenth Annual Convention of the Protestant Episcopal Church in Louisiana* (New Orleans: H. Spencer, 1851), 26.

13. "Report of the Committee on Education," *Journal of Fourteenth Convention in Louisiana* (1852), 31–43. William Lacey's report, running twelve pages, deemed that girls were already adequately educated in Louisiana.

14. "Bishop's Address," *Journal of the Proceedings of the Fifteenth Annual Convention of the Protestant Episcopal Church in Louisiana* (New Orleans: Crescent, 1853), 17–22. Letter, LP to James Robb, 31 October 1852, THNOC. James Robb was just the man for the bishop to confide in regarding his financial difficulties. In the spring of 1854, Robb was listed as a vestryman of Trinity Episcopal Church in New Orleans, the parish where Polk, moving to the city in the winter of that year, would become rector about January 1, 1855. See "Bishop's Address," *Journal of the Proceedings of the Seventeenth Convention of the Protestant Episcopal Church in the Diocese of Louisiana* (New Orleans: B. M. Norman, 1855), 21. The diocesan Treasurer's Report in 1855 shows Robb donated $500—more than most parishes gave—to the bishop's meager annual salary of about $1,900.

15. Elijah Guion, "Report of the Committee on Education," *Journal of Fifteenth Convention in Louisiana* (1853), 23–25.

16. When Franklin College in Opelousas came up for sale by the state, Polk appointed wealthy friends to negotiate for its purchase. The work of the Franklin College special committee appointed in 1853 "had yet to be acted upon" by the following year. *Journal of the Proceedings of the Sixteenth Annual Convention of the Protestant Episcopal Church in Louisiana* (New Orleans: Sherman and Wharton, 1854), 39. Also see Edwin W. Fay, *The History of Education in Louisiana* (Washington, DC: Government Printing Office, 1898), 53–54, 143.

17. FAP, "Memoir," 39, and Letter, FAP to Winchester Hall, 7 January 1872. In 1872,

Fanny was providing information to Hall for his proposed biography of Leonidas Polk. Hall was so fond of Fanny that she was the godmother of one of Hall's sons. Hall and William M. Polk, however, had a postwar falling-out over Hall's copyrighted but unpublished manuscript. See Letters, Winchester Hall to FAP, 20 July 1869, and William M. Polk to Winchester Hall (undated, c. 12 December 1880).

18. Letters, LP to Lucius Polk, 19 May 1853, GPP, and 25 July 1853, BEFP. Crowding his time unremittingly were Polk's other efforts to expand his diocese. Under him for eleven years, it had grown from "two churches in buildings to 17, with another 23 unhoused congregations, and from none to 19 congregations of plantation slaves." The two parochial clergy he inherited now numbered twenty-six, plus himself.

19. W. W. Pugh, "Reminiscences of an Old Fogy," ch. 10, Assumption (Parish) Louisiana *Pioneer*, 1 October 1881. Before the Civil War, the various Pugh families in the bayou regions were among Louisiana's wealthiest. Flaunting its wealth and independence defined Christ Church Napoleonville in its early days. Indifferent to diocesan doings, parish delegates rarely attended conventions or sent parochial reports.

20. Clarissa Elizabeth Leavitt Town, "Diary" (typescript), 24–27 March 1853, THNOC. Town was the mother-in-law of Archibald Lamon, the rector of St. John's Church in the village, who had been Leonidas's classmate at the Virginia Theological Seminary. "Bishop's Address," *Journal of Fifteenth Convention in Louisiana* (1853), 20.

21. "Bishop's Address," *Journal of Sixteenth Convention in Louisiana* (1854), 17.

22. Jo Ann Carrigan, "Yellow Fever, 1853: A Fatherly Correction?" *Louisiana History* 10 (1969): 352; idem, *The Saffron Scourge* (Lafayette: University of Southwestern Louisiana, 1994), 67; Letter, LP to Stephen Elliott, 2 October 1855.

23. Letter, LP to My Dear bishop, 12 December 1853. Alexander Dobb's wife died, too, of yellow fever shortly after her husband. Memorial plaque, Trinity Church, New Orleans.

24. The 1855 report of the Committee on Assessments refers to the $4,000 salary approved by the previous convention. *Journal of Seventeenth Convention in Louisiana* (1855), 16. The Bishop received $1,308 in 1853 and $1,999 in 1854. *Journal of Sixteenth Convention in Louisiana* (1854), 32.

25. Apart from loans from James Robb and John Williams, Polk had borrowed $18,500 from Bernard A. Soulie, a commission merchant and real-estate broker. Soulie was a "free Creole of color"; Polk had helped organize a congregation for free blacks in 1855. Soulie, at any rate, was among the city's wealthiest men of any race. Polk's loan note to Soulie is in THNOC.

26. P. A. Champomier, *Statement of the Sugar Crop Made in Louisiana* (New Orleans: Magne & Weisse, 1851–1857). Williams's production of sugar in 1861 and molasses was almost double that of his next highest neighbor.

27. Letter, LP to James Robb, 6 October 1854, THNOC.

28. "Bishop's Address," *Journal of Seventeenth Convention in Louisiana* (1855), 21. Fanny's memoir says her husband before becoming ill had been ministering to a member of the household of Judge George S. Guion, the Polks' next-door neighbors on Ridgefield Plantation.

29. Parks, *General Leonidas Polk*, 112–113.

30. Hamilton married Emily Beach in Connecticut in June.

31. The Church of the Holy Trinity had been founded in 1847 by Roderick H. Ranney, a pioneer Episcopal priest in the Southwest. Having certain high-church inclinations, he and Polk were usually cool toward one another. Letter, Roderick Ranney to Bishop William Whittingham, 28 December 1844, Leonidas Polk Papers, Episcopal Diocese of Maryland. A year after hiring Polk, the Trinity parish was almost out of money and cut his salary in half. On the Trinity choir, see Dugas, "Ante-Bellum Career," 325–327.

32. Letter, LP to James Robb, 6 October 1854. In the summer of 1861, while in Memphis with her husband, Fanny mentions in a letter to daughter Kate Polk Gale that a Mr. Sully was terminating the Polks' lease on their New Orleans home. This may be George Washington Sully, a Garden District cotton broker. Letter, FAP to Kate Gale, 19 August 1861.

33. Letter, FAP to Meck Polk, 4 March 1866; Letter, LP to Stephen Elliott, 2 October 1855.

34. Letter, LP to Stephen Elliott, 2 October 1855. Perhaps Polk and Colton simply were not destined to work together (see chapter 16); a year later, the bishop's assistant had left New Orleans for the Diocese of Virginia. Bishop's Address, *Journal of the Proceedings of the Eighteenth Convention of the Protestant Episcopal Church in the Diocese of Louisiana* (New Orleans: B. M. Norman, 1856), 24.

35. Parks, *General Leonidas Polk*, 115.

36. "Bishop's Report," *Journal of Seventeenth Convention in Louisiana* (1855), 22.

37. "Parochial Report: St. Thomas' Church," *Journal of Eighteenth Convention in Diocese of Louisiana* (1856), 55–56. Brought up among French Canadians, Williamson was also pastor of the L'Eglise Protestante Française in New Orleans.

38. "Parochial Report: St. Thomas' Church," *Journal of Seventeenth Convention in Diocese of Louisiana* (1855), 54.

39. Jennings's first arrest is cited by Timothy Reilly, "Genteel Reform Versus Southern Allegiance: Episcopalian Dilemma in Old New Orleans," *HMPEC* 44 (1975): 448, n. 44. Jennings's second arrest is recounted in Roger A. Fischer, "Racial Segregation in Ante Bellum New Orleans," *American Historical Review* 74 (1969): 936.

40. Timothy Reilly, "The Louisiana Colonization Society and the Protestant Missionary," *Louisiana History* 43 (2002): 433ff. *LPBG*, 1:226. While Polk's denunciations of slavery first appear in the biography authored by his son William, the actual writer of these particular pages was John Fulton, the bishop's protégé and confidant in the late 1850s. Fulton was born in Scotland and was ordained priest by Bishop Polk in 1857. He became Polk's assistant at Trinity Church in New Orleans about the same time. Fulton was to collaborate extensively on William M. Polk's biography after the war, supplying two full chapters recounting the bishop's Louisiana ministry. For Bishop McIlvaine's antislavery position, see Diana Hochstedt Butler, *Standing Against the Whirlwind: Evangelical Episcopalians in Nineteenth-Century America* (New York: Oxford University Press, 1995), 136–177.

41. Letter, LP to Stephen Elliott, 20 August 1856. In his study of the religious and racial tensions in antebellum New Orleans, Timothy Reilly writes: "Unfortunately, the genteel reform begun by Polk was almost completely nullified by his Southern patriotism, an emotional force which eventually pivoted the Bishop into an attack against his original [pro-black] objectives." "Genteel Reform," 443. At Polk's funeral, Bishop Elliott

preached that he and Polk believed the Civil War was essential for defending the "sacred trust of slavery, yes!—a thousand times yes." Polk's outburst regarding the slave owner as victim is comparable to Robert E. Lee's views in Elizabeth Brown Pryor, *Reading the Man: A Portrait of Robert E. Lee Through His Private Letters* (New York: Viking, 2007), 146.

42. "Bishop's Address," *Journal of Seventeenth Convention in Diocese of Louisiana* (1855), 32.

43. Letters, LP to Kenneth Rayner and James Robb, 30 July 1857, and Stephen Elliott, 23 July 1856. In the early 1830s, the Evangelical Oberlin College in Ohio became the first college in America to admit women; only other colleges with denominational bases first followed Oberlin's then-radical lead. Polk's university, however, did not admit women as full-time students until 112 years after Polk had broached the idea.

44. "Bishop's Address," *Journal of the Proceedings of the Nineteenth Convention of the Protestant Episcopal Church in the Diocese of Louisiana* (New Orleans: B. M. Norman, 1857), 28–29.

45. Letter, LP to Stephen Elliott, 20 August 1856. Probably reasoning that Polk's discussion of "the negro question" might detract from his father's postwar memory, William M. Polk excluded it from the text of this letter that he included in his 1895 biography. *LPBG*, 1:237ff. Polk's belief that a "wall as high as the heavens stood between Northern and Southern Episcopalians" was disputed by a Boston Unitarian editor who later observed "the least offensive of Protestant denominations at the South is the high and dry Episcopal Church, so conservative [and] ecclesiastically established that it can take little notice of what is politically or socially unjust." See Chester Forrester Dunham, *The Attitude of the Northern Clergy toward the South, 1860–1865* (Toledo, OH: Gray, 1942), 100.

46. When Bishop Elliott's school was flourishing in the 1840s, *Spirit of Missions* lauded his "testing the sufficiency of slave labour to support it." *SOM* 8 (1843): 75. The Montpelier Institute succumbed to financial reversals in the early 1850s.

47. Letter, LP to Stephen Elliott, 31 January 1857.

48. FAP, "Memoir," 42.

49. Though there were numerous springs in the region to choose among, it is probable that the Polks went to White Sulphur Springs in the Greenbrier Mountains. Besides being in vogue just then for its mineral waters and its large and sociable hotel dining and ballrooms, its amenities included a "Louisiana Row" of guest cottages. See J. J. Moorman, *The Virginia Springs and Springs of the South and West* (Philadelphia: Lippincott, 1859).

50. "Bishop's Address," *Journal of Nineteenth Convention in Diocese of Louisiana* (1857), 19.

51. FAP, "Memoir," 43. Potter's increasing opposition to slavery later put him and Bishop Polk at odds, as it did with the Vermont bishop John Henry Hopkins, who defended slavery on biblical grounds. In a public spat, Hopkins reminded Potter that he had entertained Christian slaveholders in his Philadelphia home (he meant Polk, for one) and should have taken the occasion to criticize them to their face. The text of Hopkins's quarrel with Potter was published in the *Boston Liberator*, 11 November 1863, 33.

52. FAP, "Memoir," 42. Perhaps it was Fanny's own ambivalence toward the university that colored her recall of the Philadelphia convention.

53. "Bishop's Address," *Journal of Nineteenth Convention in Diocese of Louisiana* (1857),

19–20. Among Louisiana convention delegates listening to Polk's report was the bishop's future nemesis, Col. Braxton Bragg, a member of the congregation of St. John's Church in Thibodaux. Bragg had lately married a local heiress and had become a La Fourche planter; their plantation was not far from where the Polks had previously lived.

54. To give the text of Polk's original circular letter more persuasive punch, it was reworked by Bishops Otey and Polk. George R. Fairbanks, *History of the University of the South* (Jacksonville, FL: H. & W. B. Drew, 1905), 21. Polk uses the title "Address to the Southern States" in his May 30, 1857, letter to President James Buchanan. Each of the nine bishops was billed $14.89 for the printing cost.

55. Letter, LP to Stephen Elliott, 31 January 1857.

56. Letter, LP to Kenneth Rayner, 30 July 1857.

57. Letter, LP to Kenneth Rayner, 3 December 1857. Certain sentences from this letter and a previous one to Rayner on July 30 were conflated in *LPBG*, 248–249.

58. The nature of Fanny's eye disease could not be determined. Isaac Hays, whom she identifies in her memoir as "Dr. Hayes, the occulist" (43), was a protégé of Nathaniel Chapman, the Philadelphia physician who three decades earlier had advised Leonidas on his lung disease.

59. Letter, James Otey to John Armfield, 13 February 1857, JHOP. In July of the same year, when the name "University of the South" had been proposed to the Board of Trustees, Otey in a dedicatory sermon even more forcefully rejected the assertion making the rounds that "Southern men [who] have contemplated evil to this Union" were behind the school's founding and naming. "The name is one of convenient description; it is no party war-cry," he said. Green, *Memoir of James Otey*, 64–65. Green, the bishop of Mississippi, had first proposed the name that was later officially adopted; he also denied that it was intended to suggest any anti-Northern feeling.

60. Letter, LP to Stephen Elliott, 31 January 1857.

61. "Bishop's Address," *Journal of the Proceedings of the Twentieth Convention of the Protestant Episcopal Church in the Diocese of Louisiana* (New Orleans: K. Fuhri, 1858), 21.

62. In her study of John Armfield, Isabel Howell concludes that Armfield and Polk almost certainly first met in Alexandria around 1830. Howell, "John Armfield, Slave Trader," *THQ* 2 (1943): 18. For a recent examination of Armfield's dominating role in slave-trading, see Edward Ball, "Retracing Slavery's Trail of Tears," *Smithsonian Magazine* 46(7) (2015): 58–82.

63. George W. Featherstonhaugh, *Excursion Through the Slave States* (New York: Harper, 1844), 46. The author, a famed geologist, gives a droll account of his several days on the stage road in 1833 with Armfield and a few other rough-hewn traveling companions who, from his bearing and English accent, supposed him to be effete. He was provoked in a Tennessee tavern by one of them. The man carried a dirk and a pistol and declared "I allow you are a damned old rascal!" Featherstonhaugh, then fifty-three, promptly popped the younger man with "two 'straightforwarders,' right and left, and down he went on the floor into an ocean of tobacco spit, quite puzzled to imagine how he got there." In his twenties the scientist had studied boxing in England under "Gentleman" John Jackson, the eighteenth-century British champion whose pugilism students had also included Lord Byron.

64. Isabel Howell speculates that the Armfield family, when in New Orleans, some-

times attended Trinity Church while Polk was rector. Howell, "John Armfield of Beersheba Springs," *Tennessee Historical Quarterly* 2 (1944): 26–27.

65. The word "Sewanee" is attributed to an Indian tribe once inhabiting the southeastern United States.

66. Letter, James Otey to John Armfield, 13 February 1857, JHOP.

67. Margaret Brown Coppinger et al., *Beersheba Springs: 150 Years, 1833–1893* (Beersheba Springs, TN: Beersheba Springs Historical Society, 1983), 19. In addition to the lumber and coal, Tracy promised free shipping up the mountain for building materials. On his horseback outing, Polk was accompanied by Vernon K. Stevenson, the president of the Nashville & Chattanooga Railroad Company whose rail spur ran up the mountain. Polk's confident utterance was reported by another member of the scouting party, the geologist J. M. Safford. See Fairbanks, *History of University of the South*, 30. Letter, James Otey to John Armfield, 11 May 1857, JHOP. For Armfield's pledge of $25,000, see Daniel Wilson Randle, "A Question of Style: The Architectural Competition for the Central Building of the University of the South (1860)" (master's thesis, University of Texas, 1978), 51. His written pledge is in the Sewanee archives.

68. Letters, LP to James Buchanan, 30 May 1857, and Secretary John Appelton to Envoy John Mason, John Young Mason Letterbooks, Virginia Historical Society Photocopies, MSS5:2/M3815, 4–5.

69. Herbert Wender, *Southern Commercial Conventions, 1837–1859* (Baltimore: Johns Hopkins University Press, 1930), 153.

70. For a study of the Southern Commercial Convention before and after the Civil War, see Vicki Vaughn Johnson, *The Men and Vision of the Southern Commercial Conventions, 1845–1871* (Columbia: University of Missouri Press, 1992).

71. Letter, LP to Stephen Elliott, 14 August 1857, Elliott Family Papers. Leonidas Polk's and John Perkins Jr.'s committee memberships are listed in "Proceedings of the Southern Convention," *De Bow's Review* 23 (1857): 315–316, 440. Robert Dabney Calhoun, "The John Perkins Family of Northeast Louisiana," *Louisiana Historical Quarterly*, 19 (1936): 70–88; Sarah A. Dorsey, *Recollections of Henry Watkins Allen* (New York: M. Doolady, 1866), 397, 410.

72. Letter, LP to Elliott, 14 August 1857, Elliott Family Papers.

73. Hugh Davey Evans, "The Southern University," *The Monitor* 36 (4 September 1857): 426. Evans was not alone in his questioning that a creditable university could be improvised on the spot rather than evolve slowly over a span of years. Three years later this criticism, still being heard, was addressed and refuted at some length in the cornerstone-laying ceremonies in October 1860, by F. A. P. Barnard. See Fairbanks, *History of University of the South*, 54–57.

74. Letter, LP to Stephen Elliott, 27 September 1857. Polk's KJV quotation from Isaiah 45:9 goes like this: "Woe unto him that striveth with his Maker! Let the potsherds strive with the potsherds of the earth. Shall clay say to him that fashioneth it, What makest thou?"

11. A University Takes Root in Terra Incognita (1857–1860)

1. Letter, LP to Kenneth Rayner, 3 December 1857. Writing Rayner from Selma, Alabama, Polk mentions visiting "my son William in a school nearby." Howard College, a Baptist school in nearby Marion, became a military institute soon after the start of the Civil War and probably was young Polk's school.

2. Isabell Howell, "John Armfield of Beersheba Springs," *THQ* 3 (1944): 57; Fairbanks, *History of University of the South*, 30. In his study of Sewanee's architectural beginnings, Daniel Randle wrote that Armfield, before developing Beersheba Springs, had managed estates in Louisiana, and the connections he made there apparently "helped make Beersheba popular among a small element of aristocratic Southern planters, most of whom, if not all, were Episcopalians." Randle, "A Question of Style," 46.

3. Letter, LP to Stephen Elliott, 15 May 1858; *New York Journal of Commerce*, 20 August 1859. Before the coal line was built, only the Chattanooga–McMinnville Stage Road connected the woodland plateau to civilization.

4. Letter, LP to F. A. P. Barnard, 4 March 1858, Columbiana Manuscripts, 1572–1986, Columbia University. Barnard was an Episcopal priest, a mathematician, and a future president of Columbia College in New York City. Though a Yankee, he was held in high regard by the founding trustees of the University of the South. Bishop William Mercer Green of Mississippi told him in 1859 that he "was the only man of science of which [the South] can at present boast." Letter, Green to Barnard, 29 May 1859. Green also dangled the presidency of the new university before his friend. David G. Sansing, *The University of Mississippi: A Sesquicentennial History* (Jackson: University Press of Mississippi, 1999), 95.

5. The boarding-house arrangement was important enough to the founders that it would become prescribed by the university's 1860 statutes.

6. Stephen Elliott, "The Choice of a Site for The University: An Address, 1858," in Lily Baker et al., eds., *Purple Sewanee* (Sewanee, TN: Association for the Preservation of Tennessee Antiquities, 1961), 10–11. The address was made during a Board of Trustees meeting on July 3, 1858, in Beersheba Springs. When published, it bore the names of several of the trustees, but the rhetoric is pure Elliott.

7. Letter, LP to Stephen Elliott, 15 May 1858; "Bishop's Address," *Journal of the Proceedings of the Twenty-First Convention of the Protestant Episcopal Church in the Diocese of Louisiana* (New Orleans: B. Albertson, 1859), 18–19; Letter, LP to Charles R. Barney, 27 November 1858. See also the undated letter quoted by Howell, "John Armfield of Beersheba Springs," 57.

8. "Bishop's Address," *Journal of Twentieth Convention in Diocese of Louisiana*, 24. In a fragmented letter dated June 18, 1859, probably to James Otey, Polk reported having $320,000 in hand. I am indebted to Glenn Robins for the quotations from the 1860 fund-raising brochure, "Address of the Commissioners for Raising the Endowment of the University of the South." See Robins, "Leonidas Polk and Episcopal Identity," 168.

9. "Bishop's Address," *Journal of Twentieth Convention in Diocese of Louisiana*, 23.

10. Caleb Dowe, "Report of the Committee on the State of the Church," *Journal of the Proceedings of the Twenty-Second Convention of the Protestant Episcopal Church in the Diocese of Louisiana* (New Orleans: Isaac T. Hinton, 1860), 32.

11. The nascent State Seminary of Learning & Military Academy eventually became Louisiana State University in Baton Rouge.

12. Letter, LP to Charles R. Barney, 23 July 1858. There is no record of how Gorgas assisted Barney. An expert in munitions, he may have consulted on the use of blasting powder for road construction on the domain. After the war, he returned to Sewanee as a member of the faculty.

13. Letters, LP to Charles R. Barney, 8 July 1860 and 4 July 1859.

14. Letter, Charles R. Barney to LP, 23 April 1860. How Barney was a colonel could not be learned; perhaps it was in a militia in Maryland, his home state. During the Civil War a Charles R. Barney, presumably the same man, was a major in the Nitre and Mining Department of the Confederacy.

15. Letter, LP to Stephen Elliott, 20 September 1858. The publishing of the maps in Baltimore almost came to a halt when Elliott became convinced the printers were overcharging and lying. Conceding as much, Polk insisted to Elliott that the maps were invaluable in fund-raising, and the printers must be paid to finish the job. "While it is as a part of our purposes to get up an establishment to abate lying and to foster a becoming sense of self-respect, I do not think this is the point at which to begin the work. Let them lie and play the sharp. We can better afford this than to do without [their] work." Letter, LP to Stephen Elliott, 27 November 1858.

16. Letter, LP to Stephen Elliott, 24 July 1858, typescript.

17. Letter, R. B. Roberts for John Armfield to Charles Barney, 7 August 1858. For a glimpse of the goings-on, see Herschel Gower and Jack Allen, eds. *Pen and Sword: The Life and Journals of Randal W. McGavock* (Nashville: Tennessee Historical Commission, 1959), 483.

18. By June 18, Polk had "secured $320,000 of the $500,000" endowment capitalization required "as the lowest limit at which we will begin to build. I think I shall be able to obtain in one . . ." [letter fragment breaks off]. LP to unidentified recipient, 18 June 1859. These "subscriptions . . . were principally obtained from the wealthy planters of Louisiana, on the coast and upon the Mississippi and Red Rivers. Comparatively few . . . were obtained in the cities." *Proceedings, Board of Trustees of the University of the South*, July 1870, 28, University of the South Archives.

19. Codicil, 1 September 1858, attached to Last Will and Testament, 14 November 1849. Polk's expense account was approved in *Proceedings, Board of Trustees of the University of the South*, 10–12 August 1850, 9.

20. Letter, LP to Kate Polk Gale, 22 September 1859, GPP; Letter, LP to Alexander Bache, 4 November 1859, Huntington Library, San Marino, CA; FAP, "Memoir," 43.

21. Letter, Meck Polk to LP, 11 September 1859; Letter, LP to James Robb, 30 October 1859, THNOC. Mercer Otey and Meck were in the class of 1863; Rufus was in the class of 1864. Though none graduated, all wound up in the Confederate Army and were granted honorary degrees by the school. Virginia Military Institute Archives.

22. Letter, David Swain to Thomas Ruffin, 10 October 1859, in J. G. de Roulhac Hamilton, ed., *The Papers of Thomas Ruffin* (Raleigh, NC: Edwards and Broughton, 1918–1920), 3:48; "Bishops Address," *Journal of Twenty-Second Convention in Diocese of Louisiana*, 19; *Journal of the Proceedings of the Bishops, Clergy, and Laity of the Protestant Episcopal Church* (Philadelphia: King & Baird, Printers, 1860).

23. Letters, LP to Alexander Dallas Bache, 4 November 1859 and 6 December 1859, Huntington Library. Letter, LP to Stephen Elliott, 4 November 1859.

24. "Constitution Committee Report," *Proceedings, Board of Trustees of University of the South*, 8 February 1860, 6; Fairbanks, *History of University of the South*, 36; Letter, LP to Kate Polk Gale, 8 January 1860. James Lawrence Cabell, a professor at the University of Virginia, faulted three of Sewanee's statutes: (1) the numerical ranking of students based on the West Point system: "Repressive. . . . We tried the system . . . then abandoned it by universal consent"; (2) the vice chancellor being charged with disciplining the university's professors: "More mischievous than the disease"; and (3) tenure for professors lasting only five years: "Very objectionable. You won't find good teachers consenting to such terms." Letter, Cabell to LP, 18 April 1860. Later Polk got essentially the same criticisms from Albert Taylor Bledsoe, Polk's roommate at West Point and also then teaching at the University of Virginia. Letter, Bledsoe to LP, 11 September 1860.

25. Letter, William Mercer Green to F. A. P. Barnard, 1 March 1860, Columbiana Manuscripts. Green's dismissive reference to Lee may have been related to his own urging that the presidency go to Barnard, then chancellor of the University of Mississippi.

26. Letter, LP to Kate Polk Gale, 8 January 1860; FAP, "Memoir," 43.

27. Polk says of Hopkins: "In my rambles in the North, I had induced [him] to go out to the mountain to lay out the grounds for our future purposes." Letter, LP to Kate Polk Gale, 8 January 1860.

28. Letters, LP to James Robb, 30 October 1859, THNOC, and LP to Charles Barney, 30 October 1859.

29. John Henry Hopkins Jr., *The Life of the Late Right Reverend John Henry Hopkins, First Bishop of Vermont* (New York: F. J. Huntington, 1873), 314.

30. Letter, John Hopkins Sr. to FAP, 14 February 1867.

31. Letter, LP to Kate Gale, 1 January 1860. Among other amenities Polk mentioned to Kate: future residents building homes on the university grounds would have the assistance of "landscape gardeners for their tasteful arrangement and improvement."

32. Letter, LP to Katherine Polk Gale, 8 January 1860; Letters, John Hopkins to LP, 26 March 1860 and 25 July 1860; *Proceedings, Board of Trustees of the University of the South*, 9–12 October 1860, 12.

33. Letter, LP to Lucius Polk, 26 February 1860.

34. Letter, Francis Smith to LP, 26 March 1860, Virginia Military Institute Archives.

35. Thomas Wharton was among the professional architects competing for a design prize offered by the university trustees; he evidently was known personally to Bishop Polk. See Randle, "A Question of Style," 96, 119. Another architect competing for the University of the South prize and not yet known to Polk was William S. Rosecrans, a West Point graduate and a military engineer. Randle, "A Question of Style," 273. During the Civil War Lieutenant General Polk and Major General Rosecrans, United States Army, fought one another on various battlefields.

36. Bills of Lading, 23 May 1860 et seq.

37. Letter, LP to Susan Polk Rayner, 9 July 1860.

38. The safe apparently failed to protect early university documents. Minutes of board meetings in 1860 were evidently destroyed by fire. See *Proceedings, Board of Trustees of the University of the South*, 27 January 1862, 15.

39. I. T. Miller, quoted in Lily Baker et al., *Purple Sewanee,* 16; Arthur Ben Chitty, *Reconstruction at Sewanee* (Sewanee, TN: University Press, 1954), 63. Bishop Polk's hope to transplant some of Oxford University's architecture onto the Cumberland Plateau was fulfilled posthumously to some extent after the Civil War. The chapel and its tower, Sewanee historian Chitty has written, "are a modified derivative of St. Mary the Virgin there," and even the Phi Delta Theta fraternity house "borrowed from Founder's Tower at Oxford, its bay window and buttresses." Arthur Ben Chitty, "Sewanee: Then and Now," *THQ* 38 (1979): 383.

40. Letters, LP to Benjamin Smith, 22 September 1860, and LP to James Robb, 5 September 1860. Another man invited was Christopher Memminger of South Carolina, later the Confederacy's secretary of the treasury. Memminger's reply to James Otey regretting his inability to attend the dedication was found four war years later in the trampled mud of the uncompleted Sewanee campus. Edgar Legare Pennington, "The Battle at Sewanee," *THQ* 9 (1950): 238.

41. Letter, LP to Charles Barney, 2 September 1860.

42. "Bishop's Address," *Journal of the Proceedings of the Twenty-Third Convention of the Protestant Episcopal Church in the Diocese of Louisiana* (New Orleans: Bulletin Book & Job Office, 1861), 18. The weatherboarding used to construct the dining shelter was recycled by Bishop Polk after the crowd had dispersed; he applied it to his own cabins. Letter, Charles Barney to George Fairbanks, 2 January 1861.

43. Chitty, *Reconstruction at Sewanee,* 62–66; Fairbanks, *History of the University of the South,* 5; Hester Elliott Shoup, "The Laying of the Cornerstone," in Lily Baker et al., eds., *Purple Sewanee,* 14–16; Randle, "A Question of Style," 96.

44. Pennington, "The Battle at Sewanee," 239. The "consecrated lore" on Sewanee Mountain that coins were among the stone's contents is carefully refuted (along with other fanciful "facts") in Merritt R. Blakeslee, *The Pillaging and Destruction of the Cornerstone of the University of the South, July 1863* (Sewanee, TN: Sewanee History Project, 2010).

45. *Journal of Twenty-Third Convention in Diocese of Louisiana,* 19. More quotations from Smith's oration are found in Randle, "A Question of Style," 175. A list of the men known to be present for the laying of the cornerstone is in Randle's appendix 3, 288–290.

12. *"My Dear General, Consider Me at Your Service" (1860–1861)*

1. *Proceedings of the Board of Trustees of the University of the South* (Nashville: Bang, Walker and Company, 1860), Executive Committee, 13 October 1860. Anderson's design was destroyed by Union troops during the war. Randle, "A Question of Style," 142.

2. Letter, FAP to James Robb, 2 November 1860, THNOC.

3. Letter, James Otey to LP, 8 December 1860, in Green, *Memoir of Bishop Otey,* 91. Also see Armentrout, *James Hervey Otey,* ch. 5.

4. Letter, Charles Barney to George Fairbank, 2 January 1862.

5. Letter, John Rowland to LP, 20 October 1860, in *LPBG,* 1:215–216. To his punctilious credit, Rowland had led his parish in Williamsport to be the only one in the diocese not in arrears in financial support of the bishop. *Journal of Twenty-First Convention in Diocese of Louisiana,* 31.

6. Letter, LP to James Buchanan, 26 December 1860; an amended draft is in Leonidas Polk Papers, 1856–1868, Library of Congress. The letter's text is essentially the same in *LPBG*, 1:299–301. The prayer is found in *LPBG*, 303. An example of the divided thinking early in the Southern Episcopal Church is Bishop Otey's asserting one month earlier that "I want to see Buchanan impeached and tried for neglecting to enforce the laws [against secessionist South Carolina]. Had he done his duty as [Millard] Fillmore and [Andrew] Jackson, and throttled nullification, all this fuss had been ended long ago." Letter, James Otey to Edward C. Burks, 23 November 1860, in Armentrout, *James Hervey Otey*, 85.

7. Thomas A. Adams was a wealthy insurance company president; his home in New Orleans was close to where the Polks had lived. "Diary" entries, 1 January to 20 January 1861. A prayer for "the President of the United States, and all others in authority" was obligatory for all ministers conducting certain services from the Book of Common Prayer. Polk subsequently directed his clergy to pray for the "President of the Confederate States."

8. A calendar of the steps taken toward secession in Louisiana in January and February 1861 is found in "The Secession of Louisiana," *OR* 1:489–501.

9. The diocesan administration of Christianity's geographical realms, borrowed from secular governments, was adopted by bishops in the third century C.E. Polk's protégé at Trinity Church, the Reverend John Fulton, first defended his bishop's action but later, having studied ecclesiastical law, termed Polk's theory of diocesan independency an "infelicitous" idea.

10. The unnamed delegate was quoted by the Reverend George M. Randall, "A Mitred Major-General," *The Church Monthly* (August 1861): 57. The typescript of Randall's scornful column is at the Virginia Historical Society.

11. The fairest pro-and-con analysis of Polk's position (and that of more passive bishops) is probably Bishop Joseph Blount Cheshire, *The Church in the Confederate States* (New York: Longmans, Green & Company, 1912). A more flattering picture of Polk is provided by John Fulton, himself a player in the secession goings-on. Fulton, "The Church in the Confederate States," in William Steven Perry, ed., *The History of the American Episcopal Church, 1783–1883* (Boston: James R. Osgood & Company, 1885), 561–592.

12. Letter, James Otey to "My dear Bishop," 18 March 1861, typescript, JHOP. Polk's assertion—that the Southern dioceses now consider themselves "separated, not divided" from their Northern brethren—drew Otey's biblical condemnation. "Allow me to say," he wrote, "that [separation] is an unfortunate selection of a word—see Jude 19." The New Testament verse he cites refers to godless, arrogant heretics who "separate themselves" from the true Church.

13. LP, "Diary," 23 March 1861. The quotation is found in Cheshire, *Church in Confederate States*, 18–19. They were, by their own fiat, the senior bishops in the new configuration of Southern dioceses.

14. Letter, LP to James Otey, 24 April 1861, JHOP. Only the beginning of the letter has been preserved. Polk's research attempts to bolster his action on historical grounds was frustrated by the penetrating dampness of New Orleans. Most of the books from his library, which he had left in storage when he had moved to Sewanee, were ruined by damp, mold, and book worms. "Some of them are not books any more," Fulton

wrote, "unless a squaw lump of manure deserves that name." Letter, John Fulton to LP, 7 April 1861.

15. Armentrout, *James Hervey Otey*, 91, 97 n. 24, citing *Memphis Daily Appeal*, 26 May 1861.

16. Letter, FAP to LP, 15 April 1861, GPP; Letter, FAP to Susan Polk Badger, 16 April 1861.

17. Merritt R. Blakeslee, "'The Spirit of Hell Itself Was Never More Exhibited': The Firing of the Polk and Elliott Homes at University Place, Night of Fort Sumter, 1861," in *Upon the Debatable Ground: Sewanee and the Lower Cumberland Plateau During the Civil War*, manuscript in preparation. Blakeslee, a meticulous researcher, examines the arson, possible motives, and consequent reactions of the involved victims and neighbors in his manuscript. Attempts by the arsonists on subsequent nights to set other fires on the campus, he writes, were thwarted by barking dogs and fire-resistant building materials. Letter, LP to FAP, 18 July 1861.

18. Letters, LP to FAP, 26 and 27 April 1861; *LPBG*, 1:323–324, 326–327.

19. Letters, LP to Francis H. Smith, 14 and 17 April 1861, Virginia Military Institute Archives. Because of the slow mails, Polk did not know that even before his withdrawal letter arrived at VMI Meck for a second time had been dismissed by the school. Still, because he had reduced his demerits somehow, he had been reinstated. See also Letters, LP to FAP, 22 and 26 April 1861; *LPBG*, 1:323–324.

20. Letter, LP (aboard the steamer *Hodge*) to James Robb, Chicago, 25 April 1861, THNOC; Letter, Thomas A. Adams to LP, 13 August 1861.

21. Letter, Meck Polk to LP, 18 April 1861 [fragment]. Meck's role in the melee is reported in William Couper, *One Hundred Years at V.M.I.* (Richmond: Garrett and Massie, 1939), 2:85, n. 31. Letter, George Cary Eggleston to William M. Polk, 19 July 1907; Letter, Meck Polk to FAP, 28 May 1861.

22. LP, "Diary," 2 May 1861. Hearing of the arson at Sewanee on 26 April, he had told his diary on the next day: "So troubled could not write my address." "Diary," 27 April 1861.

23. "Bishop's Address," *Journal of Twenty-Third Convention in Diocese of Louisiana*, 19.

24. Polk's dismissal of Paul Hebert notwithstanding, other Louisianans were persuaded by his heart and will; the colonel was promoted to brigadier general and put in charge of the state's military forces in August 1861.

25. At some point around this time Polk wrote also to Albert Sidney Johnston, urging him to leave California and come home to the Confederacy and assume a military role. E. W. Munford in a letter to Polk dated 4 September 1861 says he has learned from "Judge [Alexander M.] Clayton . . . that you had in advance of us all [written] General Johnston and the President urging [his appointment] for the common good." OR 52/2:140.

26. Letter, LP to Jefferson Davis, 14 May 1861, printed in *The Collector* 47 (November 1932), 2. As to Johnston's asserted preeminence to lead the Confederate military, Albert Bledsoe that same week was urging Davis himself to become general in chief. Letters, Bledsoe to Davis, 10 May 1861, and Davis to LP, 22 May 1861, in *PJD*, 7:159, 174.

27. Letter, LP letter to Stephen Elliott, 22 June 1861.

28. Letter, LP to FAP, 19 June 1861.

29. Letter, LP to FAP, 19 June 1861.

30. Letter, Meck Polk to FAP, 28 May 1861. Zollicoffer, a Tennessee congressman and editor before the war, was a Polk family friend; Meck told his mother he had "found a good bed" at Camp Trousdale in Middle Tennessee.

31. The draft of the letter dated 27 May 1861 breaks off in the second paragraph and may never have been finished and mailed. It is not found in Secretary Walker's correspondence in the OR.

32. Thomas Lawrence Connelly, *Army of the Heartland: The Army of Tennessee, 1861–1862* (Baton Rouge: Louisiana State University Press, 1967), 25, 41. First rejecting secession in February, Middle and West Tennesseans after Fort Sumter voted on June 8 to leave the Union by a vote of 104,000 to 47,000. But East Tennesseans in thirty-four counties voted 33,000–14,000 to *stay* in the United States; some East Tennessee counties then even tried to secede from their Rebel state. Among the powerful antisecessionists in East Tennessee was Leonidas Polk's second cousin William Hawkins Polk, youngest brother of President James K. Polk. Later in that summer of 1861 he was defeated in his gubernatorial race against Isham Harris, who was reelected. Typical of the conflicts dividing families in the Civil War, W. H. Polk's nephew, Marshall Tate Polk, would become an artillery officer under Leonidas Polk's command.

33. Stanley F. Horn, ed., *Tennessee's War 1861–1865, Described by Participants* (Nashville: Tennessee Civil War Centennial Commission, 1965), 19.

34. Grady McWhiney, *Braxton Bragg and Confederate Defeat* (New York: Columbia University Press, 1969), 232.

35. Letter, LP to Isham Harris, 19 June 1861, Tennessee State Library and Archives. The telegram sent earlier on June 19 is mentioned in this follow-up letter.

36. Letters, LP to Stephen Elliott, 22 June 1861, and LP to FAP, 22 June 1861.

37. Beth Crabtree and James Patton, eds., *Journal of a Secesh Lady* (Raleigh: North Carolina Department of Archives and History, 1979), 733. On Sidney Johnston "as royal Arthur," see Benjamin Franklin Cooling, *Forts Henry and Donelson—Key to the Confederate Heartland* (Knoxville: University of Tennessee Press, 1987), 41.

38. In a letter to Albert Sidney Johnston almost six months later, Polk recounts in some detail his June talks with Jefferson Davis. *LPBG*, 1:372–373.

39. Letter, LP to FAP, 19 June 1861. No source was found for McIlvaine's musket remark, but McIlvaine just about then had reminded Ohio's Episcopalians at their diocesan convention that "our duty in this emergency is bravely, earnestly, to sustain our government in its administration in the use of all lawful means to preserve the integrity of the Union." Whitelaw Reid, *Ohio in the War* (New York: Moore, Wilstach & Baldwin, 1868), 1:270. See also Kara M. McClurken, "For Love of God and Country: McIlvaine's Mission," *Anglican and Episcopal History* 49 (2000): 315–347.

40. Letter, LP to Stephen Elliott, 22 June 1861. Meade's disparaging references to McIlvaine, as well as to Bishops Alfred Lee of Delaware and William Whittingham of Maryland, are omitted from the printed text of this letter in *LPBG*, 1:359. (About the time Meade was belittling McIlvaine, McIlvaine was appositely lamenting that "Meade, my most intimate brother bishop, the near friend of so many years, is now the Bishop of a seceded state . . . and his beloved Theological Seminary in Alexandria may be taken for barracks of Virginia troops. . . . Oh, may God give us a just and righteous peace.")

Letter, Charles McIlvaine to William Carus, 3 May 1861, in Carus, *Memorials of Charles McIlvaine*, 215.

41. Letter, Jefferson Davis to William M. Polk, 15 December 1879. William Meade, *Address on the Day of Fasting and Prayer Appointed by the President of the Confederate States, June 13, 1861, Delivered at Christ Church, Millwood, Va. by Bishop Meade* (Richmond: Enquirer Book and Job Press, 1861), 6–9.

42. Letter, William Meade to LP, August 1861, in *LPBG*, 1:366. In some accounts of the meeting, Meade reputedly advised Polk *against* accepting the commission. See, e.g., Randall, "A Mitred Major-General," 57.

43. In a letter to Davis the following fall, Polk reminds the president of the adage he had used in the June meeting in Richmond. LP to Davis, 6 November 1861, *OR* 4:522. The saying is attributed to Judge John Bradshaw in the seventeeth-century trial of England's Charles I, although usually given as "rebellion to tyrants is obedience to God." Polk, when attempting to resign from the army by letter four months later, recalled to Davis his "strong conviction to the sentiment," repeating the quotation. A historian who enjoys needling Leonidas Polk's Civil War duty has written that Polk thought incorrectly he was quoting the Bible when he mentioned "resistance to tyrants." Given Polk's familiarity with scripture, this assumption by Steven Woodworth is probably what's incorrect. Steven E. Woodworth, *While God Is Marching On: The Religious World of Civil War Soldiers* (Lawrence: University Press of Kansas, 2001), 120–121.

44. Letter extract, Jefferson Davis to William M. Polk, n.d., in *LPBG*, 2:362. Either Davis misremembered Polk's Latin, or Polk himself got it a little wrong. Cicero is credited with the martial sanction *Pro aris et focis pugnare*—to fight in defense of one's altars and hearths. Letter, Davis to William Polk, 15 December 1879.

13. "I Am Afraid of the Polkism of Your Nature" (1861)

1. Walter Goodman, president of the Mississippi Central Railroad Company, got back in touch with Polk in July to recapitulate a conversation they had had in June in Richmond regarding the manufacture in Holly Springs, Mississippi, of rifles, bayonets, and "large shot and shell of any size and description." Letter, W. Goodman to LP, 12 July 1861, *OR* ser. 4, 1:467.

2. John B. Jones, *A Rebel War Clerk's Diary at the Confederate States Capital* (Philadelphia: Lippincott, 1866), 1:53, entry for 21 June 1861. Failing twice to induce Polk to accept the rank of brigadier general, Jefferson Davis instructed the War Department to issue Polk's major-general commission. Letter, Samuel Cooper to LP, 25 June 1861. *OR* 52/2:115.

3. Randall, "A Mitred Major-General."

4. *Southern Illustrated News*, 15 November 1862. Engravers would sometimes carelessly reverse Stuart's portrait, parting Polk's hair on the left.

5. *LPBG*, 2:54–59; Margaret Sumner McLean, "A Northern Woman in the Confederacy," *Harper's Magazine*, February 1914, 440–451. McLean was the wife of the Confederate colonel Eugene E. McLean.

6. Frank Moore, ed., *The Rebellion Record: A Record of American Events* (New York: Putnam, 1861–1868), 2:14, "Diary of Events," 30 June 1861.

7. Gary W. Gallagher, ed., *Fighting for the Confederacy: The Personal Recollections of Edward Porter Alexander* (Chapel Hill: University of North Carolina Press, 1989), 288–289. Polk was promoted from major general to lieutenant general in 1862.

8. William C. Davis, *Jefferson Davis: The Man and His Hour* (New York: HarperCollins, 1991), 376. Letter, Stephen Elliott to LP, 6 August 1861.

9. Letter, LP to Albert Sidney Johnston, 9 November 1961, *LPBG*, 1:372–373; Letter, Stephen Elliott to LP, 6 August 1861.

10. Letter, William S. Leacock to LP, 1 July 1861.

11. Letter, McIlvaine to Charles Wesley Andrews, 6 August 1861, Charles Wesley Andrews Papers, 1808–1901, Perkins Library, Duke University. When Andrews's incendiary anti-Union sermon was published in pamphlet form his name was omitted from the title page. Before long, General Polk was being credited as the author.

12. *Harper's Weekly*, 27 July 1861, 467. *London Herald*, unsigned clipping, August 1861, quoting Col. Charles Frederick Henningsen, Amos G. Browning Papers, 1860–1913, Perkins Library, Duke University.

13. Jones, *A Rebel War Clerk's Diary*, 1:53, entry for 21 June 1861.

14. Letter, LP to John Fulton, 4 February 1862, in *LPBG*, 1:369.

15. Polk's Mississippi Valley command was first defined on 4 July 1861, *OR* 4:362, and expanded on 2 September 1861, *OR* 3:687.

16. Kate Polk Gale, "My Recollections of Life in the Southern Confederacy, 1861–1865," typescript, GPP; Connelly, *Army of the Heartland*, 47; Stanley F. Horn, *The Army of Tennessee: A Military History* (New York: Bobbs-Merrill, 1941), 25, quoting Brig. Gen. Nathaniel Lyon.

17. Horn, *Tennessee's War*, 191, quoting Maj. Joseph Vaulx; Letter, R. E. Lee to Mary Custis Lee, 8 July 1861, Virginia Historical Society, photocopy.

18. Horn, *Tennessee's War*, 191–192. Two years later, caught in a Federal officer's uniform in Tennessee, Williams was convicted and hanged as a Confederate spy. Lee would later say of his cousin Orton's curtailed career: "My blood boils at the thought of this atrocious outrage." Michael Korda, *Clouds of Glory: The Life and Legend of Robert E. Lee* (New York: Harper, 2014), 608.

19. A fragment of Polk's first, tentative draft text is found in the Leonidas Polk Papers. As published, the text is found in General Orders No. 1, Headquarters Dept. No. 2, Memphis, Tenn., July 13, 1861, *OR* 4:368–369. See also Eugene D. Genovese, "Religion in the Collapse of the American Union," in Randal Miller, Harry Stout, and Charles Wilson, eds., *Religion and the American Civil War* (New York: Oxford University Press, 1998), 74–88.

20. See Dunham, *Attitude of Northern Clergy*, 101–102.

21. Letter, William Seawell to LP, 24 July 1861; Parks, *Leonidas Polk*, 171.

22. Telegram, LP to Jefferson Davis, 9 July 1861, *OR* 4:365. See also *LPBG*, 2:5, and Noel C. Fisher, *War at Every Door: Partisan Politics and Guerilla Violence in East Tennessee, 1860–1869* (Chapel Hill: University of North Carolina Press, 1997), 46 and 197, n. 14.

23. Letter, LP to Jefferson Davis, 7 August 1861, *OR* ser. 4, 1:535. Among the Leonidas Polk Papers is a risqué poem concerning a certain bureaucrat named Jon Harelson (or John Harrolson) whose wartime assignments in Selma, Alabama, included encouraging citizens to save their urine, another source of saltpeter. The concluding stanzas:

We thought the ladies did enough
At sewing shirts and kissing,
But you have put the lovely dears
To patriotic pissing.

Jon Harelson, Jon Harelson,
Can't you suggest a neater
And faster method for our folks
To make up your salt-petre?

Indeed the thing's so very odd,
Gunpowder-like and cranky,
That, when a lady lifts her shift,
She shoots a horrid Yankee!

24. Dillard Jacobs, "Outfitting the Provisional Army of Tennessee: A Report on New Source Materials" *THQ* 40 (1981): 259.

25. Testimony, John T. Shirley, Navy Department Investigation, 26 February 1863, *ORN* ser. 2, 1:780.

26. *Journal of the Congress of the Confederate States of America, 1861–1865* (Washington, DC: Government Printing Office, 1904–1905), 1:371, 396. Also see William N. Still Jr., *Iron Afloat: The Story of Confederate Armorclads.* (Nashville: Vanderbilt University Press, 1971), 16, 62; William N. Still Jr., ed., *The Confederate Navy: The Ships, Men and Organization, 1861–65* (Annapolis: Naval Institute Press, 1997); *ORN* ser. 2, 1:253.

27. John Houston Bills, "Diary," 9 October 1861, quoted by John Cimprich, *Slavery's End in Tennessee, 1861–1865* (University: University of Alabama Press, 1985), 14.

28. For a good account of torpedoes and mines in the Civil War, see Milton F. Perry, *Infernal Machines: The Story of Confederate Submarine and Mine Warfare* (Baton Rouge: Louisiana State University Press, 1965).

29. Maury's son Richard tells the story of the June 1861 James River demonstration in Maury in "The First Marine Torpedoes Were Made in Richmond, Va. and Used in James River," *SHSP* 31 (1903): 326–328. Also see Letters, LP to Judah P. Benjamin, 10 October 1861, *ORN* 22:793; Isaac N. Brown to LP, 2 August 1861, *ORN* 22:791; M. F. Maury to LP, 4 December 1861, *ORN* 22:806 and *OR* 52/2:227. Unable to come to Columbus, Maury dispatched his trusted associate Isaac Brown.

30. Connelly, *Army of the Heartland*, 39. Caught in the middle, border-state Kentuckians on the whole were more pro-Kentucky than either pro-South or pro-North. The fact that their neutrality was not being taken seriously by the North that summer is indicated by Abraham Lincoln's itchy memorandum dated July 27, six days after First Manassas. Roy P. Bassler, ed., *The Collected Works of Abraham Lincoln* (New Brunswick, NJ: Rutgers University Press, 1953–1955), 4:457.

31. Letter, Charles Wickliffe to LP, 6 August 1861, *OR* 4:381. Wickliffe became military governor of Columbus in the fall of 1861 and was killed at Shiloh in April 1862.

32. Letter, Samuel Tate to LP, 12 July 1861. Hardee was a graduate of West Point, later a commandant of the academy, and the author of *Rifle and Light Infantry Tactics*,

the authoritative training manual followed throughout the war by both Federal and Confederate soldiers.

33. Reviewing the faltering Missouri invasion, on August 8 Polk reminded Gideon Pillow that "the difficulty with me after I took command . . . was to see my way clear, with the force at my command . . . that there was in hand strength enough to make that move [into Missouri] and [also] hold the positions we had on the river, and in the interior of this state." Dispatch, LP to Pillow, 9 August 1861, Leonidas Polk Papers, Library of Congress.

34. Letter, G. Gantt to Leroy P. Walker, 23 July 1861, *OR* 4:372.

35. Letter, LP to G.W. Randolph, 22 July 1862, in which he spells out his distemper with Pillow after serving with him, *OR* 3:317–324. Letter, Henry Clay Yeatman to Mary Polk Yeatman, April 1861, YPP. Nathaniel C. Hughes and Roy P. Stonesifer Jr., *The Life and Wars of Gideon J. Pillow* (Chapel Hill: University of North Carolina Press, 1993), 118.

36. Dispatch, Gideon Pillow to Jefferson Davis, 16 May 1861, *OR* 52/2:100–101.

37. Letter, Jefferson Davis to LP, 2 September 1861, in *LPBG*, 2:14–15. For an overview of Pillow's and Polk's relationship, and for an understanding of the curious campaign in Missouri that was to follow, I am indebted to Hughes and Stonesifer, *Life and Wars of Gideon Pillow*, and to Nathaniel C. Hughes, *The Battle of Belmont: Grant Strikes South* (Chapel Hill: University of North Carolina Press, 1991).

38. Dispatch, LP to Secretary of War Leroy P. Walker, 23 July 1861, *OR* 3:612–614.

39. Dispatch, William Hardee to LP, 29 July 1861, *OR* 3:619. At the time in his headquarters town, John Frémont had jailed the editor of the secessionist newspaper, the *St. Louis Republican*. Andrew Rolle, *John Charles Frémont* (Norman: University of Oklahoma Press, 1991), 192.

40. Dispatch, LP to Secretary Walker, 23 July 1861, *OR* 3:612–613; Dispatch, Pillow to LP, 16 August 1861, *OR* 3:654–655. At this time, the Federal general Ulysses S. Grant set about establishing his headquarters at Cairo on September 4. John Frémont, meanwhile, had lately been mulling exploits on a scale even grander than the Confederates'. He would split the Confederacy asunder by sweeping down the Mississippi, capturing New Orleans, and from there encircling Dixie in a counterclockwise squeeze before marching on Richmond, ending the war. Rolle, *John Charles Frémont*, 193–194.

41. Telegram, Pillow to LP, 28 July 1861, *OR* 3:619.

42. Dispatch, LP to Secretary Walker, 28 July 1861, *OR* 3:617. Connelly estimates Jackson's exaggeration at about 50 percent. *Army of the Heartland*, 49.

43. Dispatch, LP to Secretary Walker, 28 July 1861, *OR* 3:617. While Polk weighed his next move, Ohio's Bishop McIlvaine was in northern Virginia ministering to the US casualties from the Manassas battlefield. "There you have my approximations of Bishop Polk's war work," he afterward told a friend. Letter, McIlvaine to Charles Wesley Andrews, 13 August 1861, Charles Wesley Andrews Papers.

44. Dispatches, Pillow to LP, 2 and 5 August 1861, *OR* 3:626, 630.

45. Dispatch, LP to Pillow, 3 August 1861, Perkins Library, Duke University. Sixty feet of the chain and its eastern anchor were uncovered by a landslide in Columbus in 1926. Shortly after its installation, the chain was swept from its moorings by the river's current. "Obstructing Federal Gunboats," *Confederate Veteran* 34 (1926): 221; Alfred T. Mahan, *The Navy in the Civil War: The Gulf and Inland Waters* (New York: Scribner's,

1883), 64–65; Report, U. S. Grant to Chauncey McKeever, 18 October 1861, *OR* 3:248. A "secret agent" had informed Grant of a "chain brought up to Columbus" to obstruct navigation. Dispatch, LP to S. R. Mallory, 25 September 1861, *OR* 3:707. Also see Katherine Brash Jeter, *A Man and His Boat: The Civil War Career of Lieutenant Jonathan H. Carter, CSN* (Lafayette: Center for Louisiana Studies, 1996).

46. Letter, Lundsford Yandell Jr. to Sally Yandell, 10 August 1861, Yandell Family Papers, 1823–1877, Filson Historical Society.

47. Letter, Thomas Yeatman to LP, 1 August 1861, YPP.

48. Dispatch, LP to Gideon Pillow, 3 August 1861, Leonidas Polk Papers, Duke University; Special Order No. 3, 7 August 1861, Leonidas Polk Papers, Library of Congress; Dispatch, William Hardee to T. C. Hindman, 13 August 1861; Letter, Jefferson Davis to LP, 2 September 1861, in *LPBG*, 2:14–15. The complete manuscript is in LP Papers.

49. Dispatches, Gideon Pillow to LP, 11 August and 12 August 1861, *OR* 3:642, 645.

50. Dispatch, LP to Pillow, 26 August 1861, *OR* 3:683–684.

51. Dispatch, LP to Pillow, 15 August 1861, *OR* 3:650.

52. Dispatch, Pillow to LP, 16 August, 1861, *OR* 3:654. Pillow even confided his insubordinate intentions to Brig Gen. M. Jeff Thompson. Thompson dispatch to Maj. J. H. Miller, 17 August 1861, *OR* 3:659.

53. Dispatch, LP to Pillow, 16 August 1861, *OR* 3:653.

54. Dispatch, R. P. Neely to LP, 19 August 1861, *OR* 3:662. For several days previous, Pillow had had his eye on Neely's 4th Tennessee because it was "entirely composed of Americans," which made it distinct from the Irish immigrant soldiers composing J. Knox Walker's 2nd Tennessee. Dispatch, Pillow to LP, 11 August 1861, *OR* 3:643.

55. Dispatch, Unsigned to Pillow, 19 August 1861, *OR* 3:662.

56. Dispatch, Pillow to LP, 20 August 1861, *OR* 3:664–665.

14. *"I Beg Leave to Tender My Resignation"* (1861)

1. Dispatch, Lewis G. DeRussy to Gideon Pillow, 21 August 1861, *OR* 3:668. DeRussy was a Louisianan known to Polk before the war, probably in Natchitoches.

2. Dispatch, Gideon Pillow to L. P. Walker, 21 August 1861, *OR* 3:666–667.

3. Rolle, *John Charles Frémont*, 193–195.

4. Dispatch, LP to Pillow, 29 August 1861, Huntington Library.

5. Letter, Samuel Tate to D. M. Currin, 23 August 1861, *OR* 4:396.

6. Letter, LP to Davis, 29 August 1861, *OR* 3:687–688. A manuscript copy is not included in the Leonidas Polk Papers. Details of Johnston's cross-country journey are given in Johnston, *The Life of Albert Sidney Johnston*, 275ff.

7. Dispatch, LP to Davis, 4 September 1861, *OR* 4:181. The existence of a lost dispatch is supported by Polk's mention of it. He wrote: "Referring you to my dispatch of the 2d, I have the honor to be, respectfully, your obedient servant, L. Polk." According to a footnote in *OR* 4:181, the September 2 dispatch was "not found" when the records were compiled two decades after the war.

8. Letter, Davis to LP, 2 September 1861, in *PJD*, 7:318; *LPBG*, 2:14.

9. Letter, Davis to LP, 2 September 1861, in *LPBG*, 2:14, 14–15.

10. Letter, Mrs. E. W. Phelps to LP, 5 August 1861. Miss Brockenbrough was doubtless a member of the prominent family of Richmond.

11. Letter, Mrs. M. M. B. Stafford to LP, 7 September 1861. Fred Stafford had been a cadet with Meck Polk at VMI.

12. Letter, Mrs. M. MacGregor to LP, 19 August 1861.

13. Letter, S. B. Hawkins to LP, 29 July 1861. Letter, Bishop William Meade to LP, August 1861, in *LPBG*, 1:366.

14. Letter, George W. Stickney to LP, 19 August 1861. Stickney earlier was rector of St. Matthew's in Houma, Louisiana.

15. Purdy resumed his ministry among fellow Unionists in Mount Sterling, Kentucky. See also postwar letter, E. James Purdy to Andrew Johnson, 24 May 1865, in LeRoy P. Graf and Ralph W. Haskins, eds., *Papers of Andrew Johnson* (Knoxville: University of Tennessee Press, 2000), 8:108.

16. For Pillow's role in the Civil War, see especially Hughes and Stonesifer, *Life and Wars of Gideon Pillow*. Also see Benny F. Craig, "Northern Conquerors and Southern Deliverers: The Civil War Comes to the Jackson Purchase," *Register of the Kentucky Historical Society* 73 (1975): 17; Moore, *The Rebellion Record*, 2:164; Dispatches, Buckner to B. Magoffin and Lloyd Tilghman, both 15 June 1861, *Supplement to the OR* 1:200–202.

17. William W. Freehling, *The Reintegration of American History* (New York: Oxford University Press, 1994), 233. For a fact, Lincoln is known to have written, "I think to lose Kentucky is nearly the same as to lose the whole game." Letter, Lincoln to Orville H. Browning, 22 September 1861, in Basler, *Collected Works of Lincoln*, 4:532.

18. Hughes, *Battle of Belmont*, 4.

19. Letter, James H. Polk letter to "My dear Sallie," 27 January 1862, "Letters and Diaries of George Polk Family," 22. James was the son of George and Rebecca Polk.

20. Dispatch, Frémont to U. S. Grant, 28 August 1861, *OR* 3:141–142. Like Pillow, Frémont had been itching to invade western Kentucky for weeks. On 9 August he said that "I want to occupy the Mississippi River part of Kentucky, and would prefer to do it with Kentucky men, that is, Federal troops recruited in Kentucky." Dispatch, Frémont to Montgomery Blair, *OR* 3:432.

21. Dispatch, G. Waagner to Frémont, 2 September 1861, *OR* 3:152.

22. Letter, Davis to LP, 2 September 1861; Letter, LP to FAP, 18 September 1861; Letter, Davis to William M. Polk, 15 December 1879.

23. Dispatch, Isham Harris to LP, 4 September 1861, *OR* 4:180; Dispatch, Isham Harris to Davis, 4 September 1861, *OR* 4:188–189. Dispatch, LP to Isham Harris, 4 September 1861, *OR* 4:180.

24. Jefferson Davis's handwritten endorsement (5 September 1861) on telegram from Harris to Davis, 4 September 1861, is quoted in *PJD*, 7:325. Also see Steven E. Woodworth, "'The Indeterminate Quantities': Jefferson Davis, Leonidas Polk, and the End of Kentucky Neutrality," September 1861, *Civil War History* 38 (1992): 292; idem, *No Band of Brothers: Problems in the Rebel High Command* (Columbia: University of Missouri Press, 1999), 14ff.

25. Dispatch, Leroy P. Walker to LP, 4 September 1861 [*sic*], *OR* 4:180. (The date shown in the *OR* is logically incorrect; it should read 5 September 1861.) See Wood-

worth, "Indeterminate Quantities," 293. Walker to Isham Harris, 5 September 1861, *OR* 4:189.

26. Telegram, LP to Davis, 4 September 1861, *OR* 4:181.

27. Telegram, Davis to LP, 5 September 1861, in *PJD*, 7:327.

28. Telegram, LP to Davis, 6 September 1861, in *PJD*, 7:328. In this telegram Polk claims Federal intentions to occupy Paducah were "in course of execution prior to my movement on Columbus." The assertion seems questionable.

29. Telegram, LP to Beriah Magoffin, 8 September 1861, *OR* 52/2:141. Pillow's and Polk's Kentucky invasion and the attendant telegraphic wordplay is detailed in Woodworth, "Indeterminate Quantities." See also dispatch, Buckner to S. Cooper, 13 September 1861, *OR* 4:189. Polk was dubious of Buckner's argument that a Confederate withdrawal from Kentucky would be politically shrewd and productive.

30. John Y. Simon, ed., *The Papers of Ulysses S. Grant* (Carbondale: Southern Illinois University Press, 1969), 2:193. Grant credited his taking possession of Paducah ahead of approaching Confederates solely on information given him by the spy Charles de Arnaud. Letter, Grant to de Arnaud, 30 November 1861, in Simon, ed., *The Papers of Ulysses S. Grant*, 3:243. De Arnaud's account of the role he played is in *The Union, and its Ally, Russia* (Washington, DC: Gibson Bros., 1890).

31. Grant took the best troops he had to Paducah, leaving behind "the raw, unarmed and ragged." Dispatch, Grant to Chauncey McKeever, 9 October 1861, in Simon, *Papers of U. S. Grant*, 3:30.

32. A good account of Grant's occupation of Paducah is E. B. Long, "The Paducah Affair: Bloodless Action that Altered the Civil War in the Mississippi Valley," *The Register of the Kentucky Historical Society* 70, 4 (1972): 253–276. Long believes the reported number of Confederates marching on Paducah was exaggerated.

33. Leland R. Johnson, *Engineers on the Twin Rivers: A History of the U.S. Army Engineers Nashville District, 1769–1978* (Nashville: US Army Engineer District, 1978), 82; Dispatch, Grant to Chauncey McKeever, 9 October 1861, in Simon, *Papers of U. S. Grant*, 3:30; Dispatch, W. J. Waldron to LP, 26 September 1861, *OR* 52/2:155.

34. Dispatch, Grant to Charles F. Smith, 10 September 1861, in Simon, *Papers of U. S. Grant*, 2: 227–228; William B. Feis, *Grant's Secret Service* (Lincoln: University of Nebraska Press, 2002), 32.

35. Polk probably reached Columbus on Saturday, September 6. *OR* 3:699. The candy order was signed by September 9, 1861.

36. Davis, *Jefferson Davis*, 377. Dispatch, Jefferson Davis to LP, 13 September 1861, *OR* 4:89.

37. Leroy Walker's resignation had come about from his falling out of favor with the president. What weight Polk's name was given as his replacement is not known. He was mentioned in one contemporary newspaper, as shown by an undated clipping in the Polk file in the General Theological Seminary Library in New York City.

38. William G. Stevenson, *Thirteen Months in the Rebel Army by An Impressed New Yorker* (New York: A. S. Barnes & Burr, 1862), 77–78. Stevenson's book contains a few minor factual errors, and his saying Polk was considered for secretary of state may be only his misunderstanding of the secretary of war rumor.

39. Letter, LP to FAP, 25 September 1861. No mention is made to her of his desire to resign.

40. Polk's springtime correspondence with Johnston in California urging him to come home to the Confederacy and assume a military role was not found. Such correspondence is mentioned only obliquely by E. W. Munford writing to Polk on September 4, 1861. He says he has learned from "Judge [Alexander M.] Clayton . . . that you had in advance of us all [written] General Johnston and the President urging [his appointment] for the common good," OR 52/2:140. Munford was among the men urging Bishop Polk to join the Confederate Army.

41. Letter, LP to John M. Johnston, Chairman of Committee, Senate of Kentucky, 9 September 1861, OR 4:186–187. Dispatch, Davis to Albert Sidney Johnston, 17 December 1861, OR 52/2:240.

42. Connelly, Army of the Heartland, 53.

43. Letter, LP to FAP Memphis, 18 September 1861. Letter, Marshall T. Polk to "My Dearest Wife," 9 October 1861, courtesy of the private collection of Ted Yeatman. Marshall was a graduate of West Point and his father had been Polk's roommate at the University of North Carolina. Dispatch, Grant to Frémont, 10 September 1861, in Simon, Papers of U. S. Grant, 3:225.

44. Letters, LP to FAP, 18 and 25 September 1861. Daniel and Bock, Island No. 10, 12.

45. E. G. W. Butler Jr. to "My Dear Mother," 27 September 1861, THNOC, MS 662. His father was a West Point graduate, and various grandfathers and uncles had been active in the Revolutionary War.

46. Johnston, Life of Gen. Albert Sidney Johnston, 322ff.

47. Letter, LP to Albert Sidney Johnston, 1 April 1862, OR 7:923; LPBG, 2:58.

48. Dispatch, Adolphus Heiman to LP, 14 October 1861, OR 4:446.

49. Letter, LP to FAP, 25 September 1861. He wrote: "My Dear Wife, You have seen that I am here [Columbus] and why I came here. I shall use [Columbus] as a starting point for going farther, as my opinion is that a forward movement is the one for our cause."

50. Daniel and Bock, Island No. 10, 9.

51. Dispatch, Asa Gray to E. D. Blake, 18 September 1861, OR 3:703.

52. Dispatch, W. W. Mackall to LP, 17 October 1861, OR 4:456. Shortly, Polk was taking heat from civilians, too. The Woods-Yeatman foundry in Nashville wrote Polk that its iron-rolling mill near Fort Donelson was in imminent danger of capture. "There is not a solitary man [at the fort] that knows how to load, handle, or direct [the fort's guns]. . . . Logs of wood blackened would do just as well [to] frighten the Lincolnites." Letter, Woods-Yeatman Company to LP, 14 November 1861, NA RG109, Confederate Papers Relating to Citizens or Business Firms, M. 346, Roll 1, 140.

53. Fanny at least was better off in Nashville than if she had heeded the advice of a well-meaning diocesan friend in New Orleans. Richard Nugent, a banker and the treasurer of the Louisiana diocese, had suggested that Fanny and the girls settle in Mississippi. Learning of this, Polk was "vexed" and "indignant," for he knew the recommended area to be swampy and lying "in the direct line of the contemplated [Yankee] invasion, surrounded by vast plantations of Negroes." Letters, FAP to LP, 14 and 13 October 1861; LP to FAP, 19 October 1861.

54. Dispatch, LP to Secretary of the Navy S. R. Mallory, 15 October 1861, *OR* 4:448. Tony Gibbons, *Warships and Naval Battles of the Civil War* (New York: Gallery Books, 1989), 14–15.

55. Letter, LP to Jefferson Davis, 2 November 1861, *OR* 4:499. William B. Richmond had been treasurer of the Episcopal Diocese of Tennessee before the war, doubtless where Polk had first known him. See Arthur Howard Noll, ed., *Doctor Quintard: Chaplain C. S. A. and Second Bishop of Tennessee: Being His Story of the War (1861–1865)* (Sewanee, TN: University Press, 1905), 89.

56. Dispatch, W. W. Mackall to LP, 31 October 1861, *OR* 4:491; Dispatch, LP to Mackall, 31 October 1861, *OR* 4:491–492.

57. Dispatches, Mackall to LP, 4 November 1861, *OR* 4:513; LP to Albert Sidney Johnston, 4 November 1861, *OR* 4:513; Mackall to LP, 5 November 1861, *OR* 4:517. Pillow and his troops left Columbus the morning of November 7; Polk recalled them within an hour or so.

58. Draft letter, LP to Davis, 6 November 1861; see also *OR* 4:522.

59. F. D. Jodon, "Recollections of the War," *Confederate Veteran*, 9 (1901): 14. Another Rebel soldier in Columbus created an exotic, erroneous provenance for the "Lady Polk," saying it had been made in England by Whitworth Foundry and was one of four similar heavy guns sneaked into the Confederacy by the *Bermuda*, a blockade runner calling at Charleston, South Carolina. Stevenson, *Thirteen Months in the Rebel Army*, 65–66. In fact, the gun and its twin, the "Lady Polk Jr.," had been made in Richmond by the Tredegar Iron Works.

60. U. S. Grant's sequence of orders in early November is found in Simon, *Papers of U. S. Grant*, 3:143ff.

15. The Battle of Belmont—Strutting and Bonhomie (1861)

1. Dispatch, Chauncey McKeever to Grant, 1 November 1861, in Simon, *Papers of U. S. Grant*, 3:143–144, 146.

2. Grant's first report on the Battle of Belmont was sent to Washington on November 10, 1861; his revised report, in which the two o'clock message is first mentioned, is dated November 17, 1861, but was in fact composed by Grant's staff in April 1864. No corroboration of the wake-up message has ever surfaced, and Grant's recent biographers and historians are largely agreed that Grant made it up. In the revised report, Grant also alludes to an equally mysterious telegram he says he received from Frémont's St. Louis headquarters on November 5. Again, there is no documentary evidence of any such telegram being sent from St. Louis or received in Cairo, Grant's headquarters. Full particulars of these questionable messages are provided in William B. Feis, "Grant and the Belmont Campaign: A Study in Intelligence and Command," in Steven E. Woodworth, ed., *The Art of Command in the Civil War* (Lincoln: University of Nebraska Press, 1998), 17–49. See also Simon, *Papers of U. S. Grant*, 3:141–156; Hughes, *The Battle of Belmont*; Ronald C. White, *American Ulysses* (New York: Random House, 2016); and Brooks D. Simpson, *Ulysses S. Grant: Triumph Over Adversity, 1822–1865* (New York: Houghton Mifflin, 2000). Simpson maintains that either an oral or a written message was indeed delivered to Grant in the early morning of November 7 (477, n. 7).

3. Dispatch, LP to W. W. Mackall, 10 November, *OR* 3:305. Polk's report on the Battle of Belmont is in *OR* 3:306–310. The Yankee columns alarming Jeff Thompson were under Col. Richard Oglesby. With changing wartime fortunes, Polk's headquarters house in Columbus became the headquarters of the Union brigadier general Clinton B. Fisk, who described it as "the best Secesh house in town." Dispatch, Fisk to Sam Curtis, 27 December 1862, *OR* 17/2:495.

4. Report, Maj. Henry Winslow to LP, 1 December 1861, *OR* 3:360.

5. Col. Charles Wickliffe twice communicated with Polk on or about November 7 regarding an enemy column moving west toward Columbus from Paducah. Dispatch, Wickliffe to LP, 7 November 1861, *OR* 3:733.

6. Though there is no other evidence that the Federals actually planned to assault the rear of Polk's fort that day, Polk would later report that one of his officers captured during the battle overheard his captors denouncing fellow "officers charged with attacking Columbus from the Kentucky side for failing in that attempt." Dispatch, LP to Secretary of War G. W. Randolph, 22 July 1862, *OR* 3:323.

7. Hughes, *Battle of Belmont*, 82–83.

8. William M. Polk, observing that Pillow had plenty of time to array his troops in more defensible positions (Pillow would dispute this), charitably suggests that Pillow's own personal courage may have led him to expect "the same capacity for resistance to be found among the untested soldiers under his command, even in the exposed positions he selected." *LPBG*, 2:43.

9. Letter, U. S. Grant to Jesse Root Grant [his father], 9 November 1861. Simon, *Papers of U. S. Grant*, 3:137.

10. Dispatch, Col. Thomas J. Freeman to LP, 23 February 1862, *OR* 3:341.

11. Hughes, *Battle of Belmont*, 119. The battery had not been used effectively against Grant's columns—parked, in effect, in Camp Johnston, as Hughes puts it, possibly because the Confederates had run out of powder.

12. Report of Engagement at Belmont, Col. Henry Dougherty, 22nd Illinois Infantry, *OR* 3:291ff; Hughes, *Battle of Belmont*, 119.

13. Hughes, *Battle of Belmont*, 121, quoting Cpl. Bill Onstot. This soldier's dispassion was reminiscent of the Confederates' "high glee" at Bethel Church in June when they had "seemed to enjoy [killing Yankee soldiers] as much as boys do rabbit-shooting."

14. Dispatch, Pillow to LP, 11 August 1861, *OR* 3:642–643.

15. Hughes, *Battle of Belmont*, 142

16. Hughes, *Battle of Belmont*, 147.

17. Alexander P. Stewart, "The Bursting of the 'Lady Polk,'" in Bromfield L. Ridley, *Battles and Sketches of the Army of Tennessee* (Mexico: Missouri Printing and Publishing Company, 1906), 26.

18. Dispatch, Col. Jacob G. Lauman, 7th Iowa, to U. S. Grant, 10 November 1861, *OR* 3:296.

19. Hughes, *Battle of Belmont*, 157, quoting Capt. Charles Wesley Frazer in a letter written 9 November 1861.

20. Marcus J. Wright, "The Battle of Belmont," *SHSP* 16 (1888): 82. In Frank Cheatham's subsequent conversations with Hatch and Grant, the Federal officers identified themselves as the running men.

21. Belmont report, LP to War Department, 10 November 1861, *OR* 3:308. LP sent Davis a less-detailed account of the battle on November 8, 1861. *PJD*, 7:402. Dispatch, Col. Jacob G. Lauman, 7th Iowa, to U. S. Grant, 10 November 1861, *OR* 3:296.

22. Charles W. Wills, *Army Life of an Illinois Soldier* (Washington, DC: Globe Printing Company, 1906), 43. Grant reported that "there was no hasty retreat or running away."

23. During the nine hours of the fight, according to casualty figures as assembled by Nathaniel Hughes, 90 Federal soldiers had been killed and about 400 were wounded. Of the approximately 5,000 Confederates engaged, 105 were killed, 419 wounded, and 117 were missing. *Battle of Belmont*, 184–185; Report of Lieut. Col. Robert H Barrow, *OR* 10/1:420.

24. The Federal physician was Maj. John Brinton, who wrote Polk the next day quoting Major Butler's farewell "best love" to his parents: "Tell my father I died . . . at the head of my men." Letter, John Brinton to LP, 8 November 1861; John H. Brinton, *Personal Memoirs* (New York: Neal Publishing Company, 1914), 80–81. The dying officer was a son of Polk's planter friend in Louisiana, Edward George Washington Butler.

25. McLean, "A Northern Woman," 440–451; *LPBG*, 2:54–59. McLean's diary excerpts, published in 1914, differ in some respects from the version published in William Polk's biography.

26. Letter, LP to Albert Sidney Johnston, 9 November 1861, in *LPBG*, 1:372–373.

27. General Orders No. 20, 12 November 1861, *OR* 3:310. The full quotation ("We must, we can, and we will be free") is attributed to the town council of Leominster, Massachusetts, in 1766.

28. *Boston Evening Transcript*, 6 December 1861, reprinting an item from the *Cincinnati Gazette*, and in Moore, *The Rebellion Record*, 3:71. Dispatch, LP to Grant, 10 November 1861, *OR* ser. 2, 1:517.

29. Johnston, *Life of Albert Sidney Johnston*, 377.

30. Dispatch, Brig. Gen. J. Trudeau to LP, 10 November 1861, *OR* 52/2:204.

31. Letter, LP to "My Dear Kate," 28 November 1861, Illinois State Historical Library; Letter, LP to "My Dear Daughter" [Sally Polk?], 29 November 1861.

32. A cartel governing the parole and exchange of prisoners of war would be drawn up between the United States and the Confederate States in July 1862. This codifying of an informal process already in practice had been delayed by the United States' resistance to dealing with what it regarded as a group of insurgents, not a legal government. See Lonnie R. Speer, *Portals to Hell: Military Prisons of the Civil War* (Mechanicsburg, PA: Stackpole Books, 1997), 97–98.

33. Christopher Losson, *Tennessee's Forgotten Warriors: Frank Cheatham and His Confederate Division* (Knoxville: University of Tennessee Press, 1989), 38.

34. *Nashville Union and American*, 19 September [*sic*] 1861, quoted by Horn, *The Army of Tennessee*, 66.

35. Col. Napoleon Buford proposed the toast. William M. Polk, "General Polk and the Battle of Belmont," in *BLCW*, 1:357.

36. T. Michael Parrish and Robert M. Willingham Jr., eds., *Confederate Imprints: A Bibliography of Southern Publications from Secession to Surrender* (Austin, TX: Jenkins Publishing Company, 1987), no. 6827.

37. Dispatch, LP to Grant, 19 December 1861, *OR* ser. 2, 1:530.

38. Letter, LP to FAP, 15 November 1861, and *LPBG*, 2:48. Some twenty years later, in an account of Belmont that included portions of this letter, Polk's son would judiciously modify his father's airy evaluation of Grant. In the sanitized version, Grant's "sad" look was rendered "grave," and Polk's "I think him rather second-rate" became "I was favorably impressed with him; he is undoubtedly a man of much force." The modified text appears also in William Polk, "General Polk and the Battle of Belmont," 356–357. Grant's near-miss of a bullet in his back was recounted by him in his memoirs. A Confederate friend from Grant's West Point days told him of Polk's flippant remark while he and Grant were conferring during the truce negotiations. See Ulysses S. Grant, *Personal Memoirs* (New York: Charles L. Webster & Company, 1885–1886), 1:281.

39. *LPBG*, 2:45–46. William Polk later added the name of Lynch Dixon to the fatalities. Another version has Rucker saying to Polk, "General, isn't this hell?" to which Polk, perhaps a little too drolly for the occasion, is said to have replied, "Rucker, it smells like it." Philip B. Spence, "Service for the Confederacy," *Confederate Veteran* 8 (1900): 373. Colonel Spence had been a member of Polk's staff. Letter, William Polk to Winchester Hall, 11 August 1879.

40. Letter, A. B. Gray to Col. DeRussy, 20 August 1861, *OR* 4:390; A. G. G., "The Bursting of the 'Lady Polk,'" *Confederate Veteran* 12 (1904): 118–119. Three months after A. G. G.'s recollection was published, William Pickett provided his own details for the *Confederate Veteran*, challenging several of A. G. G.'s "material facts." Pickett makes no mention of John McCown and heard "nothing said to ruffle the General's temper." Further, he says no warning was made to Polk of anything's being wrong with the gun, nor of any danger in firing it. "General Polk . . . would not have risked the lives of those around him merely to gratify a whim," he wrote. William Pickett, "The Bursting of the 'Lady Polk,'" *Confederate Veteran* 12 (1904): 277–278. M. A. Miller, another survivor (one not mentioned by Rucker), concurs with Pickett: "I was on the spot at the time . . . and never heard of any such conversation [between Polk and McCown] having taken place." Lastly, he said that Polk would not have ignored the advice of a man with General McCown's knowledge of artillery. To say otherwise "seems an unwarranted reflection on General Polk's intelligence." At the very least, Miller reasoned, had Polk been concerned he would have directed that a slow-burning fuse be used so that everyone could take cover; instead, a lanyard attached to a firing device was yanked for instantaneous ignition. Marsh A. Miller, "Another Account," *Confederate Veteran* 12 (1904): 279. See also Jodon, "Recollections of the War."

41. Letter, LP to FAP, 12 November 1861, in *LPBG*, 2:44. Kate Polk Gale, "My Recollections of Life in the Southern Confederacy, 1861–1862," typescript, GPP.

42. Charles B. Dew, *Ironmaker to the Confederacy: Joseph R. Anderson and the Tredegar Iron Works* (New Haven: Yale University Press, 1966), 135. The "Lady Polk's" twin 128-pounder, the "Lady Polk Jr.," would itself explode on March 19, 1862, while defending Island No. 10 against a Yankee siege. Daniel and Bock, *Island No. 10*, 97.

43. Connelly, *Army of the Heartland*, 104.

44. Dispatch, LP to Sidney Johnston, 28 November 1861, *OR* 3:305; Dispatch, LP to W. W. Mackall, 26 November 1861, *OR* 7:705.

45. Dispatches, Pillow to Major Mackall, 13 November 1861, *OR* 4:550; Pillow to Colonel Lynch Dixon, Pillow to Isham Harris, and Pillow to Mississippi's Governor John J.

Pettus, all 17 November 1861, *OR* 4:560–561; LP to Secretary of War S. Cooper, 14 November 1861, *OR* 4:553.

46. Letter, Samuel Tate to E. E. Munford, 30 November 1861, *OR* 52:222.

47. Dispatch, Davis to LP, 12 November 1861, *OR* 4:539.

48. Dispatch, Christopher Memminger to LP, 12 November 1861, in *LPBG*, 1:374–375. Memminger had been invited to the cornerstone laying at Sewanee, but he declined.

49. Letter, LP to FAP, 9 December 1861.

50. Dispatches, LP to Sidney Johnston, 28 November 1861, *OR* 3:305; LP to Davis, 8 December 1861, *OR* 7:746.

51. Dispatches, LP to Davis, 30 November 1861, in *PJD*, 7:433; LP to Davis, 8 December 1861, *OR* 7:746. This is second mention of Davis's November 12 letter. Letter, LP to Jefferson Davis, 30 January 1862, Jefferson Davis Papers, 1841–1938, Perkins Library, Duke University.

16. *"I Have Saved the Army from Divers Disasters" (1862)*

1. General Orders No. 21, 4 December 1862, *OR* 7:736; Letter, LP to FAP, 25 November 1861, in *LPBG*, 2:53.

2. Dispatch, Brig. Gen. James D. Trudeau to LP, 2 December 1861, *OR* 52/2:224.

3. Letter, LP to FAP, 1 January 1862, in which he wrote that Pillow had broached making an expedition to Cairo "during my illness."

4. Polk's various battle flags (the material, colors, and number of stars were to change) are illustrated at www.confederate-flags.org. The first shipment to Polk left Memphis on January 30, 1862. The familiar Confederate flag bearing a diagonal St. Andrew's cross, and officially adopted, was chosen by Gen. P. G. T. Beauregard some weeks before Polk came up with his own design. Also see Devereaux D. Cannon Jr., *Flags of the Confederacy: An Illustrated History* (Gretna, LA: Pelican Publications, 1988).

5. The silk sash was sent to him by a New Orleans Episcopalian "not well-acquainted" with the bishop, but an admirer all the same. Letter, Mrs. J. T. Belknap to LP, 19 December 1861.

6. Letter, LP to FAP, 25 December 1861.

7. Letter, Lundsford P. Yandell Jr. to "My Dear Father," 15 December 1861, Yandell Family Papers.

8. Dispatch, Edward Fontaine to LP, 28 November 1861, *OR* 7:708; Dispatch, Capt. Montgomery Lynch to LP, 1 December 1861, *OR* 7:728–729. Three weeks after writing Polk, Fontaine, in a letter to Thomas Moore, the governor of Louisiana, eerily predicted the succession of forthcoming Confederate defeats—Forts Henry and Donelson, Bowling Green, and Nashville—that would contribute to, and coincide with, the fall of Memphis and that of New Orleans. Letter, Edward Fontaine to Thomas O. Moore, 18 December 1861, *OR* 6:783.

9. Letter, LP to FAP, 6 January 1862. Polk had also ordered roads approaching Columbus to be mined. Two runaway slaves reaching Cairo reported the submerged torpedoes to the authorities there, but "in such exaggerated terms" that "great consternation prevailed." Dispatch, M. Jeff Thompson to LP, 26 December 1861, *OR* 7:722.

10. J. H. Townsend and James. E. Montgomery, both steamboat captains, apparently

explained their idea to Polk in Columbus a day or so after Christmas; Polk's letter to Davis endorsing the scheme is dated December 27, 1861, *OR* 7:798. Called both the Montgomery Fleet and the River Defense Fleet, the boats were involved in river battles at, for example, Fort Pillow and Memphis. See Michael Gillespie, "The Novel Experiment: Cotton-Clads and Steamboatmen," *CWTI* 22 (December 1983): 34; Chester G. Hearn, *Ellet's Brigade: The Strangest Outfit of All* (Baton Rouge: Louisiana State University Press, 2000), 30–37.

11. Letter, LP to Secretary of War G. W. Randolph, 22 July 1862, *OR* 3:318.

12. Dispatches, Gideon Pillow to Judah Benjamin, 16 January 1862; Sidney Johnston to Secretary of War J. P. Benjamin, 25 December 1861, *OR* 7:792–794; Johnston to Pillow, 26 December 1861, *OR* 7:797; LP to Johnston, 30 December 1861, *OR* 7:808.

13. According to Polk, Pillow's original reasons for resigning had only to do with President Davis; it was a fortnight later that Pillow decided to blame Polk for his unhappiness in the army. Dispatch, LP to Secretary of War G. W. Randolph, 22 July 1862, *OR* 3:317–318.

14. Dispatch, Pillow to Secretary of War J. P. Benjamin, 16 January 1862, *OR* 3:313–316. Polk's Belmont report, 10 November 1861, *OR* 3:306–310.

15. Dispatch, Jefferson Davis to LP, 7 February 1862, in *PJD*, 8:39. In quoting Davis's letter in his Polk biography, William Polk omitted Davis's sarcasm referring to Pillow. *LPBG*, 1:384.

16. Letter, LP to FAP, 6 January 1862. Pillow's initial resignation letter was not found by the *OR* compilers after the war, but his subsequent explanation of his action is in his January 16, 1862, letter to Secretary Benjamin.

17. Letter, LP to FAP, 15 February 1862.

18. Letter, LP to Jefferson Davis, 30 January 1862, Jefferson Davis Papers.

19. Letter, LP to FAP, 31 January 1862.

20. Letter, LP to John Fulton, 4 February 1862, in *LPBG*, 1:369.

21. Letter, John Perkins Jr. to LP, 1 February 1862, in *LPBG*, 1:381–382.

22. Letter, A. T. Bledsoe to LP, 3 February 1862, in *LPBG*, 1:383.

23. Letter, Jefferson Davis to LP, 7 February 1862, in *PJD*, 8:39. Also, Jefferson Davis to LP, 7 February 1862, in *LPBG*, 1:384. As the victor of First Manassas, Beauregard was greatly admired just then in Northern Virginia; Davis's motive for sending him away to the West is a matter historians debate.

24. Don C. Seitz, *Braxton Bragg, General of the Confederacy* (Columbia, SC: State Company, 1924), 86.

25. The issue of Crittenden's alleged intoxication at Mill Springs is carefully examined in Kenneth A. Hafendorfer, *Mill Springs: Campaign and Battle of Mill Springs, Kentucky* (Louisville, KY: KH Press, 2001), 537–538.

26. Dispatch, Gideon Pillow to W. D. Pickett, 6 February 1862, *OR* 7:859. Hughes and Stonesifer reckon that Zollicoffer's death gave Pillow the face-saving excuse he desired to report back for duty under Johnston. *Life and Wars of Gideon Pillow*, 209–210.

27. "Defence [sic] of the Cumberland," *Nashville Republican Banner*, 2 November 1861. An eight-foot rise in the Cumberland was said to be necessary to clear Polk's barge obstructions. William D. Pickett, *Sketch of the Military Career of William J. Hardee* (Lexington, KY: James D. Hughes, 1910), 6. Polk in April 1862 would remind Sidney Johnston

that he, Polk, had no responsibility over Henry and Donelson prior to Johnston's taking command of the region the previous fall. Letter, LP to Sidney Johnston, 1 April 1862, *OR* 7:923. He makes no mention of Fort Heiman.

28. John W. Emerson, "Grant's Life in the West and his Mississippi Valley Campaigns," *The Midland Monthly* 10 (1898): 417.

29. Gower and Allen, *Pen and Sword*, 593. McGavock's journal entries chronicling the capture of Fort Donelson present, in the accurate words of his editors, "some of the most graphic eyewitness reporting available in the literature on the Civil War" (582). Also see John Procter, "A Blue and Grey Friendship: Grant and Buckner," *The Century Illustrated Monthly Magazine* 53 (1897): 944; Howard Criswell Jr., "A Conversation with the Past," *CWTI* 29 (1990): 56–63.

30. Cooling, *Forts Henry and Donelson*, xiii. Cooling's book is a definitive study of the two forts and their fall.

31. John K. Bettersworth, *Confederate Mississippi* (Baton Rouge: Louisiana State University Press, 1943), 214.

32. Letter, Symmes E. Brown to "My Own Dear One," 24 February 1864, in John D. Milligan, ed., *From the Fresh-Water Navy, 1861–64: The Letters of Acting Master's Mate Henry R. Browne and Acting Ensign Symmes E. Brown* (Annapolis: United States Naval Institute, 1970), 32. Letters, Andrew Foote to "My Dear Wife," 23 February 1862; Andrew Foote to Gideon Welles, 23 February 1862, *ORN* 22:626–627. Dispatches, LP to The Commanding Officer, US Forces, Cairo, 22 February 1862; Flag-Officer Andrew H. Foote and Brig. Gen. George W. Cullum to LP, 23 February 1862; LP to Foote and Cullum, 23 February 1862; Foote and Cullum to LP, 24 February 1862; Maj. Gen. H. W. Halleck to Cullum, 24 February 1862, all *OR* ser. 2, 3:312–315.

33. Letter, FAP to Susan Rayner, 20 March 1862. The identity of the post commander could not be established. Col. Andrew Jackson Lindsay was one of Polk's cavalry commanders at Shiloh the following April. If General Polk had any twinges of guilt regarding the fall of Forts Henry and Donelson and the consequent panic in Nashville, they do not appear in his letters.

34. LP to "a member of his family," 16 February 1862, in *LPBG*, 2:77.

35. Alfred Roman, *The Military Operations of General Beauregard* (New York: Harper & Brothers, 1884), 1:233. Beauregard's concerns about Columbus—as well as his corollary ambitions to gain full control of military affairs in the West—are examined in detail by Connelly, *Army of the Heartland*, ch. 7.

36. Dispatches, LP to Davis, 11 March 1862, *OR* 10/2:311; Beauregard to Sam Cooper, Richmond War Department, in Roman, *Military Operation of Beauregard*, 2:77.

37. *LPBG*, 2:80–81. William Polk adds in a note on page 81: "The work was not only rapid, but thorough. This is shown . . . by the fact that the critics in our own lines—who, just then, were very active—could pick no flaw." Letter, LP to "My dear daughter," 9 March 1862.

38. Dispatches, Andrew Foote to Gideon Welles, 4 March 1862; George Cullum to Henry Halleck, 4 March 1862, both *OR* 7:435–437. Dispatches, LP to J. P. Benjamin, 17 March 1862, *OR* 52/2:288, and LP to Benjamin, 18 March 1862, *OR* 7:437.

39. Letter, Sarah Anne Ellis Dorsey to LP, 20 February 1862. Dorsey assured Polk that "no ignoble hands" had been employed in the banner's manufacture and concluded her

note saying: "After you lay down your arms, let [the banner] be deposited as a memorial in one of the churches in New Orleans."

40. Among the engineers stiffening the fortifications that spring around New Madrid was Bishop Polk's former right-hand man at the University of the South, Charles Barney. He was now a captain in the Confederate Army and had briefly served with Polk in Columbus before being sent to New Madrid. Letter, Charles Barney to George R. Fairbanks, 19 December 1861.

41. Dispatch, E. W. Gantt to LP, 28 February 1862, *OR* 8:763.

42. Dispatch, LP to John P. McCown, 9 March 1862, *OR* 8:772.

43. Letter, LP to "My beloved daughter," 9 March 1861. Two days later LP told Jefferson Davis: "At Island No. 10 I have erected a series of batteries, which make the passage down the river by boats as difficult as at Columbus, and which can be held by a much smaller force." Dispatch, LP to Davis, 11 March 1862, *OR* 10/2:311.

44. Dispatch, E. W. Gantt to LP, 28 February 1862, *OR* 8:763.

45. Letter, William M. Polk to "My Dear Sister," 29 March 1862. After the war, Beauregard declared McCown's efforts at New Madrid "the poorest defense made by any fortified post during the whole course of the war." Horn, *Army of Tennessee*, 144. As for the rat-tail spikes, the Yankees reported they were able to extract most of them from the disabled cannons.

46. By the Mississippi River's whimsical whirls, what was in 1862 the Mississippi's tenth island downstream from the Ohio River has since been detached from Tennessee and attached to the shore of Missouri. See Daniel and Bock, *Island No. 10*; Charles M. Evans, *The War of the Aeronauts* (Mechanicsburg, PA: Stackpole Books, 2002). Rufus Polk was an artillery officer and may have felt the brunt of Colonel Buford's target-spotting from on high.

17. Shiloh (1862)

1. Letter, Davis to Johnston, 12 March 1862, *PJD*, 8:92. Dispatch, Johnston to Davis, 18 March 1862, in Bromfield Ridley, ed., *Battles and Sketches of the Army of Tennessee* (Mexico: Missouri Printing and Publishing Company, 1906), 81.

2. The north-south Mobile & Ohio and the east-west Memphis & Charleston (the *truly* essential rail link to Richmond) crossed one another at Corinth. Polk began his move toward Corinth on March 12. LP to Beauregard, 12 March 1862, *OR* 18:776. His first use of Corinth as his address is March 26: Special Order No. 445, *OR* 8:804.

3. Letter, Braxton Bragg to Brig. Gen. Sam Jones, 27 February 1862, quoted in Seitz, *Braxton Bragg: General of the Confederacy*, 87.

4. *Agree* to name? Maybe. Beauregard, a Napoleonic figure, is usually credited by historians with applying the name "Army of the Mississippi" on 5 March 1862. The *OR* Index, however, credits Bragg. In any case, the second "the" in the army's name was subsequently dropped by the Confederacy. The name, thus, was no longer confused with the Federal "Army of the Mississippi." As regards the organizational structure in Corinth, Thomas Connelly, in an essay critical of Johnston, contends that *because* of their problematic organization the Confederates began losing the Battle of Shiloh even before it took place. See Connelly, "The Johnston Mystique," *Civil War Times* 5 (February 1967): 15–23.

5. Hardee to Bragg, 1 April 1862, *OR* 10/2:379. Crittenden was the older brother of Thomas Leonidas Crittenden, a major general in the Union Army. The brothers were the sons of John Jordan Crittenden, a pro-Union Kentucky senator and congressman.

6. *OR* 10/1:396, 398.

7. Apart from the Tennessee regiments, three others, Polk noted in his report, were from Arkansas, Louisiana, and Mississippi. He forgot to mention that the 7th Kentucky Infantry was a part of his 2nd Brigade, Second Division, *OR* 10/1:405.

8. For a detailed biographical note on Robert Russell see Hughes, *Battle of Belmont*, 237, n. 11.

9. The identity of William Stephens is found in William Anderson, ed., "The Civil War Reminiscences of John Johnston," *THQ* 13 (1954): 78

10. Dispatch, Grant to H. W. Halleck, 21 March 1862, *OR* 10/2:55. Also see Lloyd Lewis, *Sherman: Fighting Prophet* (New York: Harcourt, Brace, 1932), 217.

11. "General Polk passed [Bethel] by train to Corinth this evening." Journal of Major-General Bushrod Rust Johnson, 21 March 1862, *Supplement to the OR* 1:657–658.

12. Letter, William D. Gale to "Dear Wife," 14 May 1867. Bayard was an esteemed French knight of the sixteenth century. In compliance with an order from General Johnston, one of Gale's first assignments was to record Polk's dictation regarding the fall of Forts Henry and Donelson.

13. McWhiney, *Braxton Bragg and Confederate Defeat*, 213.

14. Letters, Braxton Bragg to Elise Bragg, 10 March and 25 March 1862, quoted in McWhiney, *Braxton Bragg and Confederate Defeat*, 216.

15. Grady McWhiney, "Braxton Bragg at Shiloh," *THQ* 21 (1962): 22, n. 11.

16. Letter, Bragg to Elise Bragg, 20 March 1862, quoted in T. Harry Williams, *P.G.T. Beauregard: Napoleon in Gray* (Baton Rouge: Louisiana State University Press 1954), 123. Bragg would once say (and Beauregard was pleased later to quote him) that he had never felt any jealousy toward Beauregard. Letter, Bragg to John Forsyth, 17 July 1862, in Roman, *Military Operations of General Beauregard*, 1:592.

17. Dispatch, LP to Johnston, 1 April 1862, *OR* 8:923. Letter, LP to Davis, 11 March 1862, *OR* 10/2:311–312.

18. Albert Sidney Johnston, Special Orders 5, 1 April 1862, *OR* 10/2:381.

19. G.T. Beauregard, "The Campaign of Shiloh," *Battles and Leaders*, 1:579. Lew Wallace's movement was in fact a reconnaissance, but it set in motion all the mayhem that followed.

20. When Capt. Adolph Metzner, an artist in the 32nd Indiana Infantry, came upon the Polks' St. John's Church in Ashwood, Tennessee, he unpacked sketch paper and pencils to portray the graveyard and its tranquil sanctity. Other soldiers in Buell's army gaily sacked the church, wrenching loose the organ pipes for souvenirs. Michael A. Peake, *Blood Shed in This War: Civil War Illustrations by Captain Adolph Metzner, 32nd Indiana* (Indianapolis: Indiana Historical Society Press, 2010), 217. Also see George W. Polk, "St. John's Church, Maury County, Tennessee," *Tennessee Historical Magazine* 7 (1921): 152.

21. Thomas Jordan, "Notes of a Confederate Staff-Officer at Shiloh," *BLCW*, 1:594.

22. Jordan's oral transmission of the orders was later put into writing. Circular Dispatch, Thomas Jordan to Polk, Bragg, and Hardee, 2 April 1862, *OR* 10/2:383. Some

versions of these predawn events portray Johnston as reluctant to mount an attack and was persuaded to do so only by Thomas Jordan's arguments. But Johnston had already shown himself ready to attack Grant (see his order of April 1); had he any hesitation at all, it must have been because Van Dorn's 20,000 soldiers from Arkansas had not arrived in Corinth. Breckinridge was notified after midnight, April 3. See William C. Davis, *Breckinridge: Statesman, Soldier, Symbol* (Baton Rouge: Louisiana State University Press, 1974), 302–303.

23. Special Orders No. 8, Corinth, 3 April 1862, by command of General A. S. Johnston, signed Thomas Jordan, *OR* 10/1:392–395. Also see Johnston, *Life of Sidney Johnston*, 555–557. Johnston's son in this 1878 biography gives his father all the credit for the composition of all orders during that predawn dark, orders that directed the march to Shiloh as well as the battle plan. Colonel Jordan, saying that the orders were the cooperative efforts of Beauregard and himself, testily disputed Preston Johnston's claims in an 1885 magazine article. Thomas Jordan, "The Campaign and Battle of Shiloh," *The United Service* 12 (1885): 273. See also Jordan, "Notes of a Confederate Staff-Officer at Shiloh," *BLCW*, 1:594.

24. As clear an explication of the proposed line of march as can be found is in T. Harry Williams, "Beauregard at Shiloh," *Civil War History* 1 (1955): 17–34. In some Civil War reports and histories the spelling of Michie's is given as Mickey's. The present-day village in Tennessee is spelled Mitchie.

25. Some early accounts of Shiloh say the attack was always scheduled to begin on Saturday morning, not sometime Friday. These assertions are refuted by most present-day historians. See, e.g., Charles P. Roland, "Albert Sidney Johnston and the Shiloh Campaign," *Civil War History* 4 (1958): 368, n. 40. Also, McWhiney, *Braxton Bragg and Confederate Defeat*, 222–223.

26. Dispatch, Bragg to division commanders, 3 April 1862, in Seitz, *Braxton Bragg*, 102.

27. McWhiney, *Braxton Bragg and Confederate Defeat*, 222.

28. O. Edward Cunningham, *Shiloh and the Western Campaign of 1862* (Baton Rouge: Louisiana State University Press, 1966), 182.

29. Jordan, "Campaign and Battle of Shiloh," 273.

30. Jordan, "Campaign and Battle of Shiloh," 273; Cunningham, *Shiloh and Western Campaign*, 180.

31. Beauregard, "Campaign of Shiloh," 582–583.

32. Being blamed for tardiness is recurrent in Polk's military history; it was said not only about the march out of Corinth but also about his movements on the second day of Shiloh and on the second day of Chickamauga. See, e.g., Gallagher, *Fighting for the Confederacy*, 288–289.

33. Polk's official Shiloh Report, *OR* 10/1:407. Also see Roman, *Military Operations of General Beauregard*, 1:278.

34. Horn, *Army of Tennessee*, 125–126; Johnston, *Life of Gen. Johnston*, quoting Gen. William Preston, 569. William Preston, in a letter after the war to Polk's son, remembered General Johnston's saying, "Polk is a true soldier and friend." *LPBG*, 2:103. Beauregard later disputed Johnston's boastful "million" remark. Wrote Beauregard: "Johnston was too wise a man . . . to make the foolhardy remark attributed to him." "The Shiloh Campaign, Part II" *The North American Review* 142 (1886): 162.

35. Stevenson, *Thirteen Months in the Rebel Army*, 145–147. Lt. George Baylor, Johnston's senior aide-de-camp, described the generals' roadside meeting differently: it took place in "Gen. Johnston's tent," he "vividly recalled" thirty-five years later. George Withe Baylor, "With Gen. A.S. Johnston at Shiloh," *Confederate Veteran* 5 (1897): 609–610.

36. Scattered firefights between small parties of scouting Federals and Confederates had been popping up for several days, but none resulted in the Federals' taking alarm. Cunningham, *Shiloh and the Western Campaign*, 183ff.

37. Simpson, *Ulysses S. Grant*, 129; Ulysses S. Grant, *Memoirs and Selected Letters* (New York: Viking Press, 1990), 1:225. Grant and Sherman both repeatedly fulminated in after years that they were perfectly prepared for the Confederate onslaught. Horn, *Army of Tennessee*, 126.

38. James Lee McDonough, *Shiloh: In Hell Before Night* (Knoxville: University of Tennessee Press, 1977) 86–87; *OR* 10/1:282, 284. Everett Peabody's men delayed Hardee's advance enough to be given credit for helping their fellows prepare to meet the advancing Confederates. *OR* 10/1:278.

39. Peabody's exploits that morning are related fondly in Carlton L. Smith, *Peabody at Shiloh: A Short Study of Courage and Injustice* (Harvard, MA: Tahanto Trail, 1983). The injustice the author mentions relates to Prentiss's failure in his official report to give Peabody credit for first spotting Hardee's advancing troops. See B. M. Prentiss's Shiloh Report, 17 November 1862, *OR* 10/1:277–278.

40. Address, Albert Sidney Johnston to "Soldiers of the Army of the Mississippi," 3 April 1862, *OR* 10/1:396. Johnston's phrase "agrarian mercenaries" traces back to *lex agraria*, a Roman law for dividing conquered lands.

41. Though Johnston had planned for the three corps under Hardee, Polk, and Bragg to be massed abreast with Breckinridge in reserve, Beauregard subsequently imposed the linear model, with or without Johnston's concurrence. See Charles P. Roland, *Jefferson Davis's Greatest General: Albert Sidney Johnston* (Abilene, TX: McWhiney Foundation Press, 2000), 66–68, and Timothy Smith, *Shiloh: Conquer or Perish* (Lawrence: University Press of Kansas, 2014), 62. Beauregard was at pains to explain his thinking. See Alexander Chisolm, "The Shiloh Battle-Order and the Withdrawal Sunday Evening," *BLCW*, 1:606. General Bragg had an opinion, too, regarding Beauregard's rearrangement: "[Johnston's] original plan was admirable—*the elaboration simply execrable*." Smith, *Shiloh: Conquer or Perish*, 62.

42. An engaging description of Hardee's *Tactics* is in chapter 4 of Nathaniel Hughes, *General William J. Hardee: Old Reliable* (Baton Rouge: Louisiana State University Press, 1992).

43. *LPBG*, 2:105.

44. Dispatch, R. H. Brewer to Maj. George Williamson, 19 April 1862, *OR* 10/1:461. Brewer was an 1858 graduate of West Point and was later attached to LP's staff.

45. John G. Biel, "The Battle of Shiloh: From the Letters and Diary of Joseph Dimmit Thompson," *THQ* 17 (1958): 256. Polk's distinctive flag with its starry vertical cross was noticed, too, about then by a New Orleans reporter and aesthete who pronounced it "a tasteful banner" in his battlefield account. Alexander Walker of the *New Orleans Delta* described Polk's flag in his "Narrative of the Battle of Shiloh," in H. C. Clarke, *Diary of the War for Separation* (Vicksburg, MS: Clarke's Southern Publishing House, 1862), 119.

46. Gen. John McClernand, Shiloh Report, *OR* 10/1:115.

47. Sam Davis Elliott, *Soldier of Tennessee: General Alexander P. Stewart and the Civil War in the West* (Baton Rouge: Louisiana State University Press, 1999), 29.

48. LP's Shiloh report, *OR* 10/1:407, 445. Capt. Marshall T. Polk was the son of Leonidas's college roommate of the same name and was the nephew of President James K. Polk. Marshall's father and Leonidas attended the University of North Carolina in the 1820s. Young Marshall's leg was amputated after his wounding, and upon his subsequent release from prison, he returned to Polk's army, becoming a member of Polk's staff. *LPBG*, 2:114, n. 2.

49. Williams, "Beauregard at Shiloh."

50. Mildred Throne, "Iowa and the Battle of Shiloh," *Iowa Journal of History* 55 (1957): 209.

51. "Report of Col. John Logan, Thirty-second Illinois Infantry," *OR* 10/2:215; "Report of Maj. Gen. Leonidas Polk, C.S. Army, commanding First Corps," *OR* 10/2:405–412.

52. Alexander Walker, "Narrative of Battle of Shiloh," 135. The batteries Walker mentioned were commanded by Smith Bankhead, Melancthon Smith, and Marshall Polk. Smith Bankhead's battery included 2nd Lt. William Polk.

53. Beauregard's Shiloh report, *OR* 10/1:389

54. *LPBG*, 2:105.

55. LP, Shiloh report, *OR* 10/1:408. Lt. Col. Andrew Blythe had organized Blythe's Mississippi Infantry Regiment in 1861. After his death, it eventually became the 44th Mississippi.

56. Robert M. Russell, Shiloh report, *OR* 10/1:419.

57. Beauregard's report, *OR* 10/1:389. Hardee's horse, "my beautiful black, was shot in the shoulder," but Hardee minimized his own arm wound, saying it was "very slight." Hughes, *General William J. Hardee*, 112–113. The mortality of horses was huge; in his corps alone, Capt. Smith Bankhead, the chief of Polk's artillery, reported that 139 of his 347 caisson horses were killed. *OR* 10/1:413.

58. Polk's official casualties were 385 killed, 1,953 wounded, and 19 missing. Letter, LP to daughter Fanny Polk, 15 April 1862.

59. Letter, LP to FAP, 10 April 1862, in *LPBG*, 2:114.

60. Diary of John Euclid Magee, entry for 6 April, *Supplement to the OR* 1:652–653.

61. Benjamin Prentiss, as noted, was the commanding officer of Everett Peabody, who had encountered advancing Confederates in the dark before Sunday's dawn.

62. The Federals first occupied the Sunken Road about 9:30 A.M. Cunningham, *Shiloh and the Western Campaign*, 334. Benjamin Prentiss's Shiloh report, *OR* 10/2:279.

63. Col. W. B. Bell, Eighth Iowa Infantry, in Mildred Throne, "Comments on the 'Hornet's Nest'—1862 and 1887," *Iowa Journal of History* 55 (1957): 272–273.

64. Report of Col. John D. Martin, Second Confederate Infantry, *OR* 10/1:621. Also see report of Col. Isaac L. Dunlop, *OR* 10/1:624. Some have suggested Johnston's risk-taking was a reaction to the criticisms he had lately endured.

65. Roland, *Jefferson Davis's Greatest General*, 79. Like Polk, Albert Sidney Johnston had rashly put himself in dangerous positions better left to officers not bearing the supreme commander's responsibilities. He was felled by the wound just below the knee in his booted leg. The bullet tore the right popliteal artery, and the location of the wound

went undetected by his aides until it was too late. Jack D. Welsh presents the possibility that "the altered sensation in his leg from the nerves damaged by his 1837 dueling wound [inflicted by Gen. Felix Houston] prevented him from realizing in the excitement of the battle how badly he had been wounded." *Medical Histories of Confederate Generals* (Kent, OH: Kent State University Press, 1995), 119. Besides the fatal wound, Welsh reports, Johnston had been struck three times by less lethal bullets and a shell fragment.

66. In his description of the fight around the Sunken Road, Col. W. B. Bell of the Eighth Iowa Infantry seems to attribute the "Hornet's Nest" nickname to the perilous life *inside* his curved-back defensive line, the Federal defenders finding themselves as the fight began to go against them "under fire from three directions." Throne, "Comments on the 'Hornet's Nest,'" 273.

67. Report of Col. J. L. Geddes, submitted 13 November 1862 after his exchange as a prisoner of war. *OR* 10/1:165–167. So proud were Iowans of their defense of the Hornet's Nest that survivors formed "Iowa's Hornet's Nest Brigade" in the 1880s. Throne, "Comments on the 'Hornet's Nest.'"

68. Samuel R. Edgington, *First Reunion of Iowa's Hornet's Nest Brigade, Held at Des Moines, Iowa, 1887* (Oskaloosa, IA: 1888), 20; Mildred Throne, "Erastus B. Soper's History of Company D, 12 Iowa Infantry, 1861–1866," *Iowa Journal of History* 56 (1958): 181.

69. LP's Shiloh report, *OR* 10/1:410; Report of Col. A. J. Lindsay and Report of Lt. Col. John H. Miller, First Mississippi Cavalry, *OR* 10/1:459–461.

70. Report of Col. R. M. Russell, Twelfth Tennessee, commanding First Brigade, 18 April 1862, *OR* 10/1:416–419.

71. Elliott, *Soldier of Tennessee*, 49.

72. James G. Smart, ed., *A Radical View: The "Agate" Dispatches of Whitelaw Reid, 1861–1865* (Memphis: Memphis State University Press, 1976), 1:132.

73. Letter, LP to "My Dear Fanny," 15 April 1862.

74. Smart, *A Radical View*, 1:152.

75. Because the Confederate battle plan did not develop as Johnston had hoped—to fold back the Federal left and thrust the army away from its supplies and reinforcements at Pittsburg Landing—the Yankees had in fact been able to retreat to the relative safety of just that place.

76. Many accounts of Shiloh, particularly the final hours of the first day, are nothing if not matters of dispute—no less by those who were there than by later historians. That the Yankee gunboats' shelling was noisy and annoying, but because of high aim of insignificant effect, is widely held, for example. And if contemporary military historians are divided on whether Grant was on the verge of defeat when Beauregard backed off his exhausted troops, General Polk's opinion is illuminative: "We had one hour or more of daylight still left . . . and nothing seemed wanting to complete the most brilliant victory of the war but to press forward and make a vigorous assault on the demoralized remnant of [the enemy's] forces." Polk's Shiloh report, September 1862, *OR* 10/1:410. (Inexplicably, or perhaps because of postbattle weariness, he wrote just the opposite to Fanny days after the battle, claiming Grant's whole force would have been captured "if we had had an hour more of daylight." Letter, LP to FAP, 10 April 1862, in *LPBG*, 2:115.) His son Meck, who was there, too, says that "the corps commanders . . . who [later]

wrote upon the subject [and with whom he sides] concur in saying there was abundant daylight [left] for fighting." In *LPBG*, 2:116.

77. Jordan, "Notes of a Confederate Staff-Officer," 602.

78. LP's Shiloh report, *OR* 10/1:410. Frank Cheatham's biographer terms Cheatham's return to his morning campground inexplicable." Losson, *Tennessee's Forgotten Warriors*, 50.

79. LP's Shiloh report, *OR* 10/1:411.

80. Smart, *A Radical View*, 1:158.

81. Jordan, "Notes of a Confederate Officer," 603

82. Beauregard's approved version of Polk's disappearance and return is in Roman, *Military Operations of General Beauregard*, 1:313. Roman was Beauregard's postwar amanuensis who recounted Beauregard's wartime exploits rather immodestly, as approved and perhaps dictated by the general. In his official report in the *OR*, Beauregard makes no mention of Polk's absence or tardy return to the battlefield. Polk's version of his goings and comings is in *OR* 10/1:410–411 and seems corroborated by Cheatham, *OR* 10/1:440–441. Alexander Walker says Polk and Cheatham had gone to the rear Sunday night in anticipation of a forceful attack Monday morning on the Confederates' left flank, but this version appears to be his own understanding. Walker, "Narrative of the Battle of Shiloh," 147–148.

83. Letter, LP to FAP, 10 April 1862, in *LPBG*, 2:114.

84. Polk's Shiloh report, *OR* 10/1:411. Also see McWhiney, *Braxton Bragg and Confederate Defeat*, 328, n. 66.

85. Jordan, "Notes of a Confederate Officer at Shiloh," 603.

86. Horn, *Tennessee's War*, 97, quoting the Federal captain Ephraim A. Otis regarding a statement allegedly made by Sherman; Horn, *Army of Tennessee*, xii.

87. Ben L. Bassham, ed., *Conrad Wise Chapman's Civil War Memoir: Ten Months in the "Orphan Brigade"* (Kent, OH: Kent State University Press, 1999), 72. Chapman's drawings and paintings of Civil War scenes established him, in the words of his biographer, as "the most important artist of the Confederacy." He had hoped after the war to memorialize Albert Sidney Johnston at the Battle of Shiloh in a painting depicting the general leading a charge, but he never did so.

88. Of the very many accounts of the Battle of Shiloh penned since 1862, few are more recent (and none more singular) than geoscientist Philip Kemmerly's learned disquisition on the swamps, sodden, gluey soils, and porous sediments underlying the battlefield that variously affected for ill the necessary maneuverings of the opposing fighters and their draft animals. Kemmerly, "Into the Muck and Mire: Mud, Soils, and Sediments of Shiloh," *THQ* 73 (2014): 2–31.

18. "I Am as Happy as I Generally Am" (1862)

1. Roman, *Military Operations of General Beauregard*, 1:358; Letters, LP to "My Beloved Daughter," 9 March 1862, and LP to daughter Frances Polk, 15 April 1862.

2. Horn, *Army of Tennessee*, 149; Richard Barksdale Harwell, ed., *Kate: The Journal of a Confederate Nurse* (Baton Rouge: Louisiana State University Press, 1959), 23.

3. Letter, LP to Susan Polk Rayner, 10 July 1862.

4. Letter, FAP to LP (with "PS" from Sallie), 24 April 1862, GPP. Also see Gale, "My Recollections." Kate Gale remembered, too, that her mother was able to smuggle letters out of New Orleans after it was occupied.

5. George W. Cable, "New Orleans Before the Capture," in *BLCW*, 2:20.

6. The April burning of cotton in New Orleans was the "finishing blow to General Polk's fortune." See *LPBG*, 2:119. In early June, Meck Polk was dispatched to New Orleans on furlough to console his family on their financial reversals. One report valued the burned cotton at $2 million. Elliott Ashkenazi, ed., *The Civil War Diary of Clara Solomon: Growing up in New Orleans* (Baton Rouge: Louisiana State University Press, 1995), entry for May 4, 1862. See also Charles East, ed., *The Civil War Diary of Sarah Morgan* (Athens: University of Georgia Press, 1991), entry for April 26, 1862.

7. By Command of Major-General Polk, Special Orders No. 75, Camp Near Tupelo, Mississippi, 23 June 1862, *OR* 17/2:622.

8. Dispatch, LP to Davis, 15 April 1862, *OR* 10/2:420. Richmond had been treasurer of Bishop Otey's Diocese of Tennessee. Sam Davis Elliott, ed., *Doctor Quintard, Chaplain C.S.A. and Second Bishop of Tennessee: The Memoir and Civil War Diary* (Baton Rouge: Louisiana State University Press, 2003), 78.

9. There is no record of Davis's replying.

10. The background of muddled boat-building preceding the fall of New Orleans is told by Chester G. Hearn, *The Capture of New Orleans, 1862* (Baton Rouge: Louisiana State University Press, 1995).

11. General Polk's involvement with the ironclads CSS *Tennessee* and CSS *Arkansas*, as well as with the CSS *Eastport*, is related in earlier chapters.

12. Letter, LP to "My Dear Daughter," 3 June 1862, in *LPBG*, 2:118.

13. Letter, Elise Bragg to Braxton Bragg, 15 April 1862, in McWhiney, *Braxton Bragg and Confederate Defeat*, 255.

14. Horn, *Army of Tennessee*, 147.

15. Butler's General Orders No. 28, 15 May 1862, *OR* 10/2:531; John Gordon Law, "Diary of Rev. J. G. Law," *SHSP*, 12 (1884): 23. Polk's motto is similar to Beauregard's General Orders No. 44, 19 May 1862: "Men of the South: Shall our mothers, our wives, our daughters, and our sisters be thus outraged by the ruffianly soldiers of the North, to whom is given the right to treat at their pleasure the ladies of the South as common harlots? Arouse, friends!" *OR* 10/2:531.

16. Roman, *Military Operations of General Beauregard*, 1:376–399. Dispatch, John Pope to Henry Halleck, 1:30 A.M., 30 May 1862, *OR* 10/2:225. A quarrel between two regiments as to which deserved the honor of being first to reach the Rebels' abandoned works was resolved by Pope.

17. Dispatch, Davis to Bragg, 20 June 1862, *OR* 17/2:614.

18. General Orders No. 89, 2 July 1862, *OR* 17/2:636. Dispatches, Bragg to S. Cooper, 29 June 1862 and 9 August 1862, *OR* 17/2:627–628, 673. Connelly, *Army of the Heartland*, 197.

19. Letters, LP to "My Dear Daughter," 3 June 1862, in *LPBG*, 2:118; William P. Johnston to Jefferson Davis, 15 July 1862, *OR* 10/1:780–786. Johnston had been sent to Mississippi on a fact-finding tour after the evacuation of Corinth, and in his generally positive report on the new location he pointed out that the bake ovens were turning out corn bread, which the soldiers preferred to wheat-flour bread. William M. Polk, with his

father in Tupelo, thought his father's cheerfulness "was scarcely justified by the conditions then being forced upon the people in that quarter of the Confederacy." Instead, he said, it illustrated "Gen. Polk's unvarying attitude toward even his own family [that] if matters were not all right, they soon would be."

20. Roy O. Hatton, ed., "Camille Polignac's Diary, Part I," *CWTI* 19 (August 1980): 17.

21. Letter, James H. Polk to "My father," Saltillo, Mississippi, 21 July 1862, "Letters and Diaries." Persimmon beer was made from baked cakes of mashed fruit and wheat bran that were then broken up and allowed to ferment in water.

22. Letter, LP to Susan Rayner, 10 July 1862.

23. Because he was Lt. Mercer Otey's father (and the father-in-law of Col. Daniel C. Govan of Arkansas), Otey may have been forced to leave occupied Memphis by an edict from Grant, while briefly in command there, "expelling the families of Confederate soldiers from the city." Law, "Diary of Rev. J. G. Law," 215.

24. For Mrs. Johnstone's residence, see Elliott, *Doctor Quintard, Chaplain*, 47. Quintard had visited Otey at Mrs. Johnstone's before Polk arrived. Polk's July 6 letter to Otey is lost and is known only by Otey's July 15 reference to it and by his paraphrasing.

25. Letter, Otey to LP, 15 July 1862.

26. The biblical quotation is from the 120th Psalm, which concludes: "I am for peace; but when I speak, they are for war."

27. Letter, LP to Secretary of War G. W. Randolph, 22 July 1862, *OR* 3:317–324.

28. This intriguing event is known only by reading postwar correspondence of Polk's son and biographer, William Polk. Writing an inquiring letter on 19 December 1875 to "My Dear Col." (almost certainly General Polk's wartime chief of staff, Col. William Williamson), William Polk asks for details of his father's reaction when the court summons was received at his headquarters in Tupelo. It was, the son says, "one of Bragg's indirect attacks" on his father. If Williamson sent an answer, it is not in the Leonidas Polk Papers. This was not the only time General Polk was hypocritically recommended for a judicial post. After the Battle of Perryville in October, David W. Yandell, a prominent surgeon in William Hardee's corps who was highly critical of Polk's generalship, urged a friend on Jefferson Davis's staff to have Polk appointed to a *permanent* court of inquiry where he could "do more service . . . than in command of troops." Letter, David W. Yandell to William Preston Johnston, 8 November 1862, A. S. Johnston and W. P. Johnston Papers, Mrs. Mason Barrett Collection, Howard-Tilton Library, Tulane University.

29. Documentary mention of the August 12 court of inquiry in Jackson is not in *OR*. Further supporting the two Polks' contention that Bragg had hoped to "shelve" General Polk is the absence of Polk's name in Special Orders No. 4, 21 July 1862. This order from Bragg's headquarters specified how various commanders, each mentioned by name, were to make a pending move to Chattanooga, Tennessee. Even Maj. Gens. Samuel Jones and Frank Cheatham, two of Bragg's "incumbrances," are given assignments. No mention, though, of the so-called second in command general. *OR* 17/2:656–657. Of related interest is that, on July 24, by General Orders No. 103, Bragg orders Maj. Gens. Earl Van Dorn and John Breckinridge and Brig. Gen. Daniel Ruggles to sit on a court of inquiry of George Crittenden, the time and place to be determined by Van Dorn. *OR* 17/2:658. Breckinridge was promoted to major general after Shiloh.

30. Richard Taylor, *Destruction and Reconstruction: Personal Experiences of the Late War* (New York: D. Appleton, 1879), 100. In his account of this staff dinner that took place in late July or early August in Chattanooga, Taylor discreetly inserted a blank in place of the disdained general's name. A friend of Bragg, Taylor attributed Bragg's "sour and petulant temper" to "many years of dyspepsia." Letter, LP to daughter Fanny, 10 October 1863. Possibly relevant, too, were the carbuncles "in so sensitive a place" afflicting Bragg earlier that year. Elise Bragg to Braxton Bragg, quoted by Earl J. Hess, *Braxton Bragg: The Most Hated Man of the Confederacy* (Chapel Hill: University of North Carolina Press, 2016), 31–32.

31. Military Commission Investigating Maj Gen. D. C. Buell, *OR* 16/1:9. Gen. John Pope, at President Lincoln's direction, had been sent to Virginia to take on Robert E. Lee; U. S. Grant was to stay put in northern Mississippi.

32. Dispatch, Lincoln to Halleck, 8 June 1862. *OR* 10/2:277.

33. *Guide to the Civil War in Tennessee* (Nashville: Civil War Centennial Commission, 1962), 11.

34. Buell to Henry Halleck, 14 July 1862, *OR* 16/3:143. The source of the fright, probably, was the arrival on July 3 of 3,000 troops in John P. McCown's division. Dispatch, Kirby Smith to Davis, 14 July 1862, *OR* 16/2:726.

35. Diary of Lizzie Hardin, 1862, quoted by Hambleton Tapp, "The Battle of Perryville, October 8, 1862," *Filson Club History Quarterly* 9 (1935): 159.

36. Dispatches, Kirby Smith to Bragg, 20 and 24 July 1862, *OR* 16/2:730, 734.

37. Special Orders No. 4, *OR* 17/2:656.

38. Bragg left behind Sterling Price with 16,000 men in Tupelo and Earl Van Dorn with 20,000 in Vicksburg to keep an eye on U. S. Grant. Dispatch, Bragg to Beauregard, 22 July 1862, *OR* 52/2:331. At 775 miles, it was to be the longest single troop movement in the whole war; Bragg had tested the feasibility of the route by sending McCown's division to Chattanooga on June 26. Dispatch, Kirby Smith to Davis, 14 July 1862, *OR* 16/2:726.

39. Connelly, *Army of the Heartland*, 193.

40. See Kirby Smith to Davis, 11 August 1862, especially note 16, in *PJD*, 8:331–335.

41. Dispatch, Bragg to Kirby Smith, 10 August 1862, *OR* 16/2:748.

42. James Lee McDonough, *War in Kentucky: From Shiloh to Perryville* (Knoxville: University of Tennessee Press, 1994), 116, 146. General Polk's luckless nephew Lucius Eugene Polk received the second of his four war wounds at Richmond.

43. While Polk was on furlough in Raleigh in the fall of 1862, his criticisms of the Kentucky campaign were expressed in person to Kenneth Rayner. Rayner, in turn on November 23, 1862, relayed them by letter to a friend, Judge Thomas Ruffin. See Hamilton, *Papers of Thomas Ruffin*, 3:270. When the University of the South was being organized, Ruffin had been a member of Bishop Polk's board of trustees.

44. Letter, LP to Susan Polk Rayner, 22 August 1862.

45. General Orders No. 1, 29 August 1862, *OR* 16/2:788. Any armed man out of ranks without permission would be suspected of being a bushwhacker and was to be "arrested as a marauder."

46. Dispatch, Bragg to Kirby Smith, 10 August 1862, *OR* 16/2:749.

47. Dispatches, Lincoln to Buell, 8 September 1862; Buell to Lincoln, 10 September 1862, *OR* 16/2:496, 500.

48. Dispatches, Brig. Gen. J. T. Boyle to Col. S. D. Bruce, 10 September 1862, and Bragg to Polk, 7 September 1862, *OR* 16/2:502, 799.

49. The succession over several weeks of Bragg's and Buell's moves and counter-moves, and the thinking behind them, is told engagingly in McDonough, *War in Kentucky*.

50. Dispatch, Bragg to LP, 11 September 1862, *OR* 16/2:811.

51. Dispatch, Bragg to LP, 7 September 1862, *OR* 16/2:799. Colonel Michael Shoemaker testimony, Buell Commission inquiry, *OR* 17/1:128.

52. Headquarters Dept. No. 2, Glasgow, KY, 14 September 1862, *OR* 16/2:822–823.

53. Dispatch, Bragg to LP, 11 September 1862, *OR* 16/2:811.

54. R. Lockwood Tower, ed., *A Carolinian Goes to War: The Civil War Narrative of Arthur Middleton Manigault* (Columbia: University of South Carolina Press, 1983), 37.

55. As noted above (note 43), Polk's criticisms of the Kentucky campaign were relayed by Rayner to Thomas Ruffin. Rayner reminded Ruffin that as Polk was "second in command, [he] of course feels himself greatly restrained by professional etiquette and propriety in speaking out openly, but he would have spoken freely and unreservedly to you, as he did to me." Hamilton, *Papers of Thomas Ruffin*, 3:270.

56. The letter by Cooney, dated October 2, 1862, is reprinted as an appendix to Jon L. Wakelyn, "The Civil War and Catholics," in Michael Glazier and Thomas Shelley, eds., *The Encyclopedia of American Catholic History* (Collegeville, MN: Liturgical Press, 1999), 348–349.

57. Before surrendering, Col. Wilder charmingly asked for—and was given—permission to inspect the magnitude of the besieging Confederate forces. Seeing for himself that he hadn't a chance, he agreed to Bragg's unconditional terms. The episode was later related with sensitivity by Gen. Simon Bolivar Buckner (Wilder's escort around the Confederate works) in "Last Surviving Lieutenant General: Visit to the Home of Gen. S. B. Buckner," *Confederate Veteran* 17 (1909): 85. See also Bragg's Kentucky Campaign, *OR* 16/1:1090.

58. E. T. Sykes, "A Cursory Sketch of General Bragg's Campaigns," *SHSP* 11 (1883): 466.

59. Lt. Gen. Joseph Wheeler, "Bragg's Invasion of Kentucky," in *BLCW*, 3:10. Buell, coming up from Bowling Green, had been on his way to attack Bragg at Glasgow when Bragg veered to Munfordville. See Don Carlos Buell, "East Tennessee and the Campaign of Perryville," in *BLCW*, 3:41.

60. Sworn testimony, 10 January 1863, F. A. Smith to Buell Commission, *OR* 16/1:292. Bragg was making himself at home in Smith's private house. Citizen Smith, less than pleased, was passing on to the Federals everything of interest being said by Bragg in his hearing. Arndt M. Stickles gives the owner of the house as *Mrs.* F. A. Smith. See Stickles, *Simon Bolivar Buckner: Borderland Knight* (Chapel Hill: University of North Carolina Press, 1940), 204.

61. Dispatch, Bragg to Adjutant-General, Richmond, 25 September 1862, *OR* 16/2:876.

62. Nathaniel C. Hughes, ed., *Liddell's Record* (Baton Rouge: Louisiana State University Press, 1985), 83.

63. Proclamation, 4 September 1862, *PJD*, 8:377.

64. McWhiney, *Braxton Bragg and Confederate Defeat*, 292; McDonough, *War in Ken-*

tucky, 181–185; Horn, *Army of Tennessee*, 170–172. Earl J. Hess neither faults nor acquits Bragg's departure from Munfordville. *Braxton Bragg*, 61–62.

65. J. Montgomery Wright, "Notes of a Staff-Officer at Perryville," in *BLCW*, 3:60.

66. McWhiney, *Braxton Bragg and Confederate Defeat*, 297.

67. Dispatch, Bragg to Adjutant General, C.S. Army, 25 September 1862, *OR* 16/2:876. Dispatch, Kirby Smith to Bragg, 18 September 1862, quoted in Horn, *Army of Tennessee*, 174–175. Bragg's elegant phrasing is a variant of bucolic words addressed to him the previous week by Kirby Smith, who wrote: "The Kentuckians' . . . hearts are evidently with us but their blue grass and fat cattle are against us."

68. Dispatch, LP to Bragg, 30 September 1862, *OR* 16/2:892. Polk and other Confederates hoped that, with Lincoln's proclamation, first reported on September 22, 1862, but not to take effect until January 1, 1863, the Union's president had shot himself in the foot. Rank-and-file Federal soldiers, they reasoned, might be willing to die to preserve the Union but not to abolish slavery. At a meeting of Lincoln's cabinet on September 22, indeed, Postmaster General Montgomery Blair said that "he was afraid of the [damaging political] influence of the Proclamation on the Border States and on the Army, and stated at some length the grounds of his apprehensions." David Donald, ed., *Inside Lincoln's Cabinet: The Civil War Diaries of Salmon P. Chase* (New York: Longmans, Green, 1954), 152. James M. McPherson discusses the Federal armies' generally positive reaction to the proclamation in *Battle Cry of Freedom: The Civil War Era* (New York: Oxford University Press, 1988), 557ff.

69. Dispatch, Bragg to LP, 1 October 1862, *OR* 16/2:895.

70. Seitz, *Braxton Bragg*, 184.

71. Polk was in command of the Army of the Mississippi from September 28 until November 7; when Polk left Knoxville for Richmond and a meeting with Jefferson Davis, Bragg resumed full command. Dispatch, Thomas Jack to LP, 12 February 1863.

72. Dispatch, Bragg to LP, 30 September 1862, *OR* 16/2:891.

73. The transmittal of dispatches between Bragg and Polk was almost glacial that week. Polk's September 30 dispatch regarding Lincoln's Emancipation Proclamation had taken two days and nights to reach Bragg in Lexington, scarcely sixty miles away. Dispatch, Bragg to LP, 2 October 1862, Leonidas Polk Papers, Library of Congress. Polk did not reply to Bragg's September 30 dispatch until Thursday, October 2, presumably because it had been delayed arriving.

74. Dispatch, LP to Bragg, 2 October 1862, *OR* 16/2:898.

75. Dispatch, LP to Bragg, 2 October 1862, *OR* 16/2:898, and Dispatch, Bragg to LP, 4 October 1862. "Yours of the 2d A.M. . . . just received here." *OR* 16/2:905.

76. Dispatches, Bragg to LP, 2 October 1862, *OR* 16/2:896–897; Hughes, *General William J. Hardee*, 124 and n. 21; Dispatch, LP to Bragg, 3 October 1862, *OR* 16/2:901. One member of the council, Brig Gen. Patton Anderson, admitted to Bragg later that he was at first reluctant to consider disobeying Bragg's order to attack Buell's flank, fearing that to do so would expose Kirby Smith's army to "embarrassment," if not defeat, in Frankfort. Later in the discussion, he concurred with Polk. Dispatch, Anderson to Bragg, 15 April 1863, *OR* 16/1:1099.

77. Dispatch, LP to Bragg, 3 October 1862, *OR* 16/2:901.

78. Horn, *Army of Tennessee*, 181.

79. Sykes, "Cursory Sketch," 470.

80. Dispatch, Bragg to LP, 7 A.M., 4 October 1862, *OR* 16/2:904.

19. Perryville—"The Most Exciting Few Moments of My Life" (1862)

1. First elected as lieutenant governor, Richard Hawes had been preceded as governor by the secessionist George W. Johnson, who died of wounds sustained at Shiloh. With the collapse of Kentucky's neutrality in early 1862, Hawes fled the state to avoid arrest by Federal occupation troops. W. Buck Yearns, ed., *The Confederate Governors* (Athens: University of Georgia Press, 1985), 81ff.

2. *Daily National Intelligencer*, 15 October 1862, 2. The *Intelligencer* was quoting a Kentucky paper. Being governor-in-exile, Hawes, also a major in Bragg's army, attempted, not very successfully, to maintain a shadow government for Kentucky secessionists.

3. Hughes, *Liddell's Record*, 85.

4. Taking with them everything of use to an army, the Confederates left behind in Bardstown only broadsheet proclamations urging citizens to "rise in their might, rally to [Bragg's] standard, and aid him to expel the invader from their sacred soil." Wilbur F. Hinman, *The Story of the Sherman Brigade* (Alliance, OH: Hinman, 1897), 291.

5. Hughes, *Liddell's Record*, 85. Liddell dates this incident as not long after he left Bardstown, and Maj. Gen. George Thomas's rather unspecific report of a skirmish near Bardstown, Kentucky (4 October 1862, *OR* 16/1:1019) *may* refer to this incident. Polk's keeping the officers' horses was not the usual practice during the Civil War. On October 3 in a skirmish at Cedar Church, Kentucky, Col. Minor Milliken of the 1st Ohio Cavalry captured twenty-two Confederate cavalry officers and men. The three officers' horses (without saddles and bridles) were returned to them immediately. Milliken to Capt. William Kesley, 3 October 1862, *OR* 16/1:1018–1019. The "McClellan trees" mentioned by Liddell referred to the famous cavalry saddle designed before the Civil War by George B. McClellan, then a captain in the United States Army. With some design variations, it was still use by cavalrymen well into the twentieth century.

6. Dispatch, LP to Bragg, 6 October 1862, James W. Eldridge Manuscripts, 1797–1902, Henry E. Huntington Library, box 47.

7. More successful in coming up from behind, a paymaster from Louisville caught up with the ambling 64th Ohio Infantry and disbursed four months' back pay. Almost to a man, the soldiers consigned their pay to an agent to send to their families at home. Hinman, *Story of the Sherman Brigade*, 291.

8. Dispatch, Buell to Halleck, 13 October 1862, *OR* 16/2:612.

9. Hinman, *Story of the Sherman Brigade*, 292.

10. Kenneth Hafendorfer, *Perryville: Battle for Kentucky* (Louisville: KH Press, 1991), 95; *LPBG*, 2:114, n. 2.

11. Letter, LP to FAP, 7 October 1862.

12. Bragg's Perryville report No. 2, 20 May 1863, *OR* 16/1:1092.

13. Hughes, *Liddell's Record*, 86.

14. LP's Perryville report, *OR* 16/1:1109; Dispatch, Polk to Hardee, 17 April 1863, *OR*

16/1:1102. When writing their official reports, Civil War generals—Leonidas Polk and Braxton Bragg included—reliably remembered past events in a way that burnished their leadership.

15. Dispatch, LP to Bragg, 11 P.M., 6 October 1862, OR 16/1:1095.

16. Braxton Bragg, Perryville report No. 1, 12 October 1862, OR 16/1:1087–1088, and report No. 2, 20 May 1863, OR 16/1:1092; Confidential circular, 7 October 1862, OR 16/1:1095. It seems clear that Hardee and Polk were as poorly informed about the enemy's location as Bragg. See McWhiney, *Braxton Bragg and Confederate Defeat*, 310.

17. Hughes, *General William J. Hardee*, 125

18. Perryville calendar, OR 16/1:1022; Dispatch, Bragg to LP, 7 October 1862, 5:40 P.M., OR 16/1:1096.

19. Bishop Otey was perhaps a closer friend of the family of the bride, Elise Ellis. Bragg was later to be baptized during the war (by Chaplain Charles Quintard) and confirmed by the Georgia bishop Stephen Elliott on June 2, 1863. See Elliott, *Doctor Quintard*, 69–71 and n. 21.

20. Dispatches, Bragg to LP, 7 October 1862, 5:40 P.M., OR 16/1:1096; LP to Hardee, 17 April 1863, OR 16/1:1102.

21. Bragg, Perryville report No. 1, 12 October 1862, OR 16/1:1088; Dispatch, Bragg to Davis, 22 May 1863, OR 52/2:817–819; McWhiney, *Braxton Bragg*, 307. Bragg, like Polk, resisted contrary opinions. Bragg's chief of staff, William W. Mackall, explained: "Between ourselves," he told his wife in September 1863, "if [Bragg] don't want news to be true, he will listen to nothing—'It can't be so' is his reasoning, and if it prove true he is not prepared to meet it." Quoted by June I. Gow, "Chiefs of Staff in the Army of Tennessee Under Braxton Bragg," *THQ* 27 (1968): 358. Dispatch, Hardee to William P. Johnston, Jefferson Davis's aide, quoted by Hughes, *General William J. Hardee*, 134–135.

22. LP's Perryville report, OR 16/1:1109–1110.

23. Liddell's Perryville report, OR 16/1:1158; McDonough, *War in Kentucky*, 216–219.

24. Dispatch, Hardee to Bragg, 7 October 1862, 7:30 pm, OR 16/1:1099; Hughes, *General William J. Hardee*, 127.

25. Dispatch, LP to Hardee, 17 April 1863, OR 16/1:1102. Bragg uses the word "disobedience" in his dispatch to Hardee, 13 April 1863, OR 16/1:1098. In an unfortunate memory lapse, Polk subsequently forgot just what Bragg had ordered on Friday night, October 7, namely, "you had better . . . give the enemy battle immediately." Writing his official report on Perryville in November from memory, Polk says he was directed to attack the enemy next morning; OR 16/1:1109. Bragg quotes Polk's report but changes Polk's word "directed" to "ordered"; OR 16/1:1098. Polk later realized his error.

26. Elliott, *Doctor Quintard*, 52; Perryville inquiry testimony, Col. Daniel McCook, 52 Ohio Infantry, OR 16/1:238; Col. Aytch [Samuel R. Watkins], "An Adventure of General Leonidas Polk at the Battle of Perryville," *Southern Bivouac* 2 (1884): 403.

27. McDonough, *War in Kentucky*, 223.

28. Dispatch, LP to Bragg, 8 October 1862, 6 A.M. OR 16/1:1096.

29. LP's Perryville report, November 1862, OR 16/1:1109–1112.

30. Thomas Claibourne was a member of General Buckner's staff. His account of the roadway meeting is in "Battle of Perryville, Ky.," *Confederate Veteran* 16 (May 1908): 225–227. It was several weeks after the battle that Polk disclosed in his official report that

he and his subordinate commanders had decided on the morning of October 8 not to follow their commanding officer's October 7 instructions to give the enemy battle immediately. This public revelation by Polk displeased Bragg greatly. In May 1863, seeking evidence against Polk, he would inveigh against all those present at the breakfast council for their conspiratorial disobedience. The secrecy of councils among military men was usually regarded as sacred, he wrote to Hardee (and to the others in a circular letter), and Polk had both violated the code and humiliated his superior. Dispatch, Bragg to Hardee, 13 April 1863, *OR* 16/1:1097–1098. Others to whom Bragg's circular was addressed were Patton Anderson, Daniel Donelson, B. R. Johnson, A. P. Stewart, and Simon Buckner.

31. Kenneth Noe, *Perryville: This Grand Havoc of Battle* (Lexington: University Press of Kentucky, 2001), 423, n. 40. Grady McWhiney supposes "Bragg must have been furious" at Polk's lack of activity when he arrived in Perryville on the morning of October 8. McWhiney, *Braxton Bragg*, 312. But in Bragg's first official report the matter is not mentioned, and in his second, written in May 1863 (*OR* 16/1:1092), Bragg does not record any stronger feeling than of being "surprised" and "impatient" at Polk's delays in attacking the enemy. As for Claibourne, he was famously known to fellow Confederates as the man who ordered the premature burning of an essential bridge during General Beauregard's secret nighttime withdrawal from Corinth the previous May. Trouble was, six loaded supply trains had not yet crossed. There was nothing left for Claibourne to do but incinerate the valuable trains.

32. Hughes, *Liddell's Record*, 89. In his official report of the battle, Liddell says it was General Buckner who told him to withdraw. *OR* 16/1, 1158. Perhaps Buckner had failed to say he was relaying an order from Polk.

33. Joseph Wheeler, Perryville report, 30 October 1862, *OR* 16/1:897–898. Confronting partly dismounted cavalry of the 1st Kentucky and 7th Pennsylvania (Thomas Leonidas Crittenden's II Corps), Wheeler's cavalry, greatly outnumbered, deceived and chased the Yankees for two miles.

34. Bragg, Perryville reports No. 1 and No. 2, *OR* 16/1:1087, 1092.

35. Bragg, Perryville report No. 2, *OR* 16/1:1092–1093.

36. LP, Perryville report, *OR* 16/1:1110.

37. Bragg, Perryville report No. 1, 12 October 1862, *OR* 16/1:1087–1088.

38. Bragg, Perryville report No. 2, 20 May 1863, *OR* 16/1:1093.

39. Bragg, Perryville report No. 1, 12 October 1862, *OR* 16/1:1087–1088. McWhiney supposes Bragg must have been furious—not merely "impatient"—at Polk's lack of activity when he arrived in Perryville on the morning of the 8th. See *Braxton Bragg and Confederate Defeat*, 312.

40. Buell was later removed from his command following a lengthy investigation of his mismanagement of Bragg's Kentucky invasion.

41. LP's Perryville report, *OR* 16/1:1110.

42. B. F. Cheatham, "The Battle of Perryville," *Southern Bivouac* 1(11) (April 1886): 704–705.

43. Hughes, *Liddell's Record*, 91.

44. Capt. Percival Oldershaw, Perryville report, *OR* 16/1:1060.

45. Dispatch, A. S. Marks to Brig. Gen. B. R. Johnson, 12 October 1862, *OR* 16/1:1128–1129.

46. My account draws on Hughes, *Liddell's Record*, 92–93; Liddell's Perryville report, *OR* 16/1:1158; Arthur Fremantle, *Three Months in the Southern States, April–June 1863* (Omaha: University of Nebraska Press, 1991), 165–167; Aytch, "Adventure of General Polk"; and William Mercer Otey, "Organizing a Signal Corps," *Confederate Veteran* 7 (1899): 549–550. Fremantle and Otey claim their information came directly from Polk.

47. Liddell compresses the story in his official report, *OR* 16/1:159. Whether confused or intending a ruse, the Federal soldier heard by Liddell to cry out "You are firing on your friends!" was arguably either Lt. Col. Squire Keith of the 22nd Indiana Infantry or Col. Michael Gooding, who commanded the 13th brigade opposing Liddell. See Noe, *Perryville*, 312.

48. The *Knoxville Daily Register* reported Polk's close call in its October 29, 1862, edition. Noe, *Perryville*, 435, n. 91.

49. Hughes, *Liddell's Record*, 94–95; Noe, *Perryville*, 437, n. 29. In a curious, uncorroborated anecdote of that late afternoon of utter confusion, William M. Polk says that before his own misadventure General Polk himself had taken Michael Gooding prisoner when the Yankee colonel strayed into the Confederate lines. *LPBG*, 2:161–162.

50. Otey, "Organizing a Signal Corps." Otey errs in saying Tanner was a lieutenant colonel that day; he attained that rank later in the war. Not citing Otey's account, the Perryville historian Kenneth Noe has written that Lt. Col. Squire Keith, the regiment's regular commander killed that afternoon, was still alive when Polk appeared. *Perryville*, 435, n. 91. Randolph Marshall affirms that Tanner succeeded Squire Keith as commander of the regiment that afternoon but does not give the time. *An Historical Sketch of the Twenty-Second Regiment, Indiana Volunteers* (Madison, IN: Courier Company, 1884), 24. Marshall had been a lieutenant in the regiment and gave his sketch as an address at an 1877 reunion. See also Col. Michael Gooding's report, *OR* 16/1:1079–1081. With the evidence now available, *proving* which officer Polk encountered appears irresolvable.

51. Hughes, *Liddell's Record*, 100.

52. Letter, LP to FAP, 14 June 1863, in *LPBG*, 2:214–215.

53. Elliott, *Doctor Quintard*, 55–56. Col. Lucius E. Polk, Leonidas's nephew, was wounded at Perryville and was possibly treated by Dr. Quintard. The text of Polk's prayer, its source unknown, is given on a historical marker in front of the Harrodsburg parish church.

54. Dispatch, Benjamin Butler to E. M. Stanton, 25 October 1862, in Jessie Ames Marshall, ed., *Private and Official Correspondence of Gen. Benjamin F. Butler: During the Period of the Civil War* (Norwood, MA: Plimpton Press, 1917), 2:407–408. See also *OR* ser. 2, 4:650. The six miscreant priests were the Reverend Messrs. Chaplin Southwood Hedges, Charles Whitehorn Hilton, William Thomas Leacock, Amos Dunham McCoy, Charles Goodrich, and John Fulton. For more on the episode, see Suzanne Hiller Herrick, *Leacocks, Including the Manuscript Entitled The Three Clergymen of New Orleans and Gen. Benjamin F. Butler by Helen Gray* (San Rafael, CA: SJB, 1994), 151. William Leacock had named a son Leonidas Polk Leacock.

55. *Southern Churchman* (Richmond, Virginia) 28(42): 2, 17, and 24 October 1862.

56. Fellow convention delegate George Templeton Strong had an opinion about Vinton: "He has no common sense whatever." Diary entries for November 10, 1862, and August 18, 1865, Nevins and Thomas, *Diary of George Templeton Strong*, 3:273, 4:28. Strong

had had little stomach for Polk as well since 1844, when Benjamin Onderdonk, Strong's New York bishop, was brought to ecclesiastical trial and sentenced by Polk and other Evangelical bishops for immoral conduct. Diary entry for November 10, 1844, in Nevins and Thomas, *Diary of George Templeton Strong*, 1:249–250.

57. Kentucky's Garret Davis and others had lately expelled Senator Jesse Bright of Indiana from the US Senate because of his pro-Confederacy sentiments. See *The Congressional Globe: Containing the Debates and Proceedings of the Second Session of the Thirty-Seventh Congress* (City of Washington: Congressional Globe Office, 1862). Senator Bright's feelings were indeed pro-Southern: just before the war began, he had introduced a firearms inventor to Jefferson Davis.

58. Vinton's remarks and the text of the letter were published in "Letter from Bishop General Polk," *The Liberator* 32(45) (7 November 1862): 177. The manuscript letter itself is now in the John C. Breckenridge Collection of the Chicago Historical Society. Filed with the letter is an unsigned note by an archivist who surmised the letter "was probably written by some soldier under [Polk's] command who assumed his name without authority. Though not authentic, it is worthy of preservation as reflecting the excitement of the time when it was written." For his part, General Polk denounced both the letter as a "fabrication throughout" and its presentation by Francis Vinton on the convention floor.

59. *Pastoral Letter of the Bishops of the Protestant Episcopal Church in the United States of America to the Clergy and Laity of the Same, Friday, October 17, 1862* (New York: Baker & Godwin, 1862). Softening somewhat his condemnation of Polk, McIlvaine concluded: "To hate rebellion . . . is duty; but to hate those engaged therein, is the opposite of Christian duty. Nothing can release us from the charge . . . to love even our greatest enemies." His complete text is available online at www.anglicanhistory.org

60. Letter, William H. Seward to McIlvaine, 29 November 1862. Newspaper clipping in Archives of the Episcopal Church, Austin, TX.

20. *"I Believe I Have Been of Some Use to the Republic"* (1862–1863)

1. McWhiney, *Braxton Bragg and Confederate Defeat*, 1:319; Hafendorfer, *Perryville: Battle for Kentucky*, 401. Buell's losses were 845 killed, 2,851 wounded, and 515 captured or missing. Bragg's losses were 510 killed, 2,635 wounded, and 251 captured or missing.

2. Dispatch, Brig. Gen. A. T. Boyle to Lincoln, 12 October 1862, *OR* 16/2:609; *LPBG*, 2:158–159.

3. McWhiney, *Braxton Bragg and Confederate Defeat*, 322. Joseph H. Parks, *General Edmund Kirby Smith, C.S.A.* (Baton Rouge: Louisiana State University Press, 1954), 237–239.

4. The date of Polk's promotion was October 10, 1862. The retreat began on October 13.

5. Noll, *Doctor Quintard*, 64.

6. Letter, LP to "My dear daughter," 25 May 1863. Bishop Polk had a rented cow while at Sewanee. Bill (invoice), Jonathan Dykes to LP, $7 for two months and ten days, 1 January 1860.

7. Dispatch, Kirby Smith to LP, 17 October 1862, *OR* 16/2:959. Philip Spence, "Campaigning in Kentucky," *Confederate Veteran* 9 (1901): 22–23.

8. *PJD*, 8:408–410.

9. Letters, LP to FAP, 24 October 1862; William Gale to Kate Polk Gale, 23 October 1862. He identifies "Thom Polk as his wife's cousin." Probably this is Sgt. Thomas M. Polk, a member of Company K, 48th Tennessee Infantry, which had fought at Perryville. Kate Polk Gale, "My Recollections," 9.

10. The four slaves—three women (one with a child) and a man—had been given a choice of staying behind, according to Gale in her memoir, but had decided not to. Had they stayed in New Orleans, within weeks they would have been set free on January 1, 1863, the day Lincoln issued his Emancipation Proclamation. The vessel on which the family left the city was probably owned by a certain Bodenald, a Lake Pontchartrain fisherman who was said to have often smuggled letters in and out of the city for the Polks. Kate Polk Gale, "My Recollections," 9. A witness to the Polks' departure described the boat as "a miserable flat."

11. Kate Polk Gale, "My Recollections," 9; Letter, William Gale to Kate Polk Gale, 23 October 1862, GPP. Poverty Hall was owned by Josiah Gale. Crabtree and Patton, *Journal of a Secesh Lady*, 497.

12. Emily Beach Polk and her sons, Frank Devereux and George Beach Polk, had been living in Maury County, Tennessee, probably in the home of Lucius Polk.

13. Letter, LP to Daughter Fanny, 21 December 1862.

14. Letter, David W. Yandell to William Preston Johnston, 8 November 1862, Johnston Papers. Yandell had been medical director of the Confederacy's so-called Army of the West before Albert Sydney Johnston's death at Shiloh.

15. Bragg's first Perryville report, 12 October 1862, *OR* 16/1:1088.

16. Horn, *Army of Tennessee*, 172–176.

17. Letter, Elise Bragg to Braxton Bragg, 16 October 1862, in McWhiney, *Braxton Bragg and Confederate Defeat*, 324–325.

18. Letter, Bragg to Gen. S. Cooper, 22 October 1862, *OR* 16/2:974.

19. Special orders No. 29, 4 November 1862, *OR* 20/2:388.

20. *LPBG*, 2:158.

21. Dispatch, LP to Davis, 4 February 1863, *OR* 20/1:698.

22. McWhiney, *Braxton Bragg and Confederate Defeat*, 329. Historian Steven Woodworth has expressed his dismay that, after Polk's "disobedience" in the Perryville campaign, Davis "failed even to rebuke Polk, let alone remove him from his responsible position." Woodworth, *Jefferson Davis and His Generals: The Failure of Command in the West* (Lawrence: University Press of Kansas, 1990), 160.

23. Bragg assumed command of the new Department of Tennessee on August 6. *OR* 23/2:954. Circular letter, Bragg to William Hardee, *OR* 16/1:1097–1098. For his failures in Kentucky, General Buell would fare worse than either Bragg or Polk: Lincoln fired Buell and replaced him with Gen. William S. Rosecrans.

24. Crabtree and Patton, *Journal of a Secesh Lady*, 306.

25. Bragg complained of Polk's missing Kentucky campaign report to Jefferson Davis on 17 January 1863. *PJD*, 9:29 and 31, n. 8.

26. Letter, Kenneth Rayner to Thomas Ruffin, 23 November 1862, in Hamilton, *Papers of Thomas Ruffin*, 3:270. Dispatch, Maj. Gen. George H. Thomas to Col. J. P. Garesche, Chief of Staff, 11 December 1862, *OR* 20/2:156. "Polk's division," as Thomas misunder-

stood it, was more exactly a division under Benjamin Cheatham and was the principal component of Polk's right wing. (Polk's official opinion of the Kentucky invasion will never be known; he apparently never got around to the writing chore of producing it.)

27. Letter, FAP to LP, 17 December 1862; Gale, "My Recollections," 18.

28. Letter, LP to FAP, 23 [and 24–25] December 1862; Gale, "My Recollections," 17; Letter, LP to "My dear daughter," 21 December 1862. The "remarkable tonic effect of General Electrization" is explained by A. D. Rockwell, *Electricity as a Means of Diagnosis* (New York: Trow & Smith, 1869).

29. Dispatch, Braxton Bragg to Sam Cooper, 22 November 1862, *OR* 20/2:416.

30. Letter, James Hall to "Father," 14 December 1862, in Charles T. Jones Jr., ed., "Five Confederates: The Sons of Bolling Hall in the Civil War," *Alabama Historical Quarterly* 24 (1962): 166.

31. Letter, LP to FAP, 17 December 1862, in *LPBG*, 2:169.

32. Walter Durham, *Nashville: The Occupied City* (Nashville: Tennessee Historical Society, 1985), 139, quoting the *Daily Ohio State Journal*, 17 December 1862.

33. Peter Cozzens, *No Better Place to Die: The Battle of Stones River* (Urbana: University of Illinois Press, 1990), 38; Horn, *Army of Tennessee*, 192.

34. As Craig Symonds points out, in Bragg's "bold, if not reckless, move to Murfreesboro, Bragg's smaller army was much closer to the Federal supply base at Nashville than to its own in Chattanooga." Symonds, *Joseph E. Johnston: A Civil War Biography* (New York: W. W. Norton, 1992), 189.

35. James Lee McDonough gives Mattie's age as seventeen. See *Stones River: Bloody Winter in Tennessee* (Knoxville: University of Tennessee Press, 1980), 46. Other sources give her birth date as June 21, 1840.

36. Letter, C. B. Hilliard to Mattie Morgan, 18 December 1862, quoted by James A. Ramage, *Rebel Raider: The Life of General John Hunt Morgan* (Lexington: University Press of Kentucky, 1986), 134 and 278, n. 2; Letter, Basil W. Duke to "My Dear Steele," 26 April 1893. The illustration of the dancers trampling the US flag appeared in 1878 in William Cullen Bryant and Sidney Howard Gay, *A Popular History of the United States* (New York: Charles Scribner's Sons, 1880), 4:535. "Needless to say," scoffed Capt. William M. Polk, the engraving was "fictitious." *LPBG*, 2:177.

37. Letter, LP to "My Dear Daughter," 21 December 1862. William Richmond's rank was first lieutenant. In official documents, he is variously referred to as a captain or a lieutenant; even General Polk calls him "Col. Richmond" in a letter.

38. Letter, LP to Frances D. Polk, 21 December 1862. Andrew Johnson, ruling with a heavy Federal hand, was as irksome to most Nashville citizens as Benjamin Butler was to the secessionists in New Orleans. Like Butler, Johnson had weeded disloyal clergymen from the city's pulpits. Durham, *Nashville: Occupied City*, 143–160.

39. *OR* 15:906–908.

40. Dispatch, John Austin Wharton to LP, 24 December 1862, *OR* 20/2:461. Polk's reply to Wharton, if any, could not be found. By Bragg's order, a deserter from another unit was in fact shot on December 26. The execution triggered an implacable anger in the soldier's commander, Maj. Gen. John Breckinridge, against Bragg. Cozzens, *No Better Place to Die*, 42.

41. Letter, LP to FAP, written over 23, 24, and 25 December 1862.

42. Bragg's cavalry was at about half its usual strength. At the time of Rosecrans's approach to Murfreesboro, some 5,000 cavalry troopers under Nathan Bedford Forrest and John Hunt Morgan were far off on separate raids of their own. For a good account of these and other cavalry operations at the time in Bragg's army, see Edwin Bearss, "Cavalry Operations in the Battle at Stones River," *THQ* 19 (1960): 23–53, 159–184.

43. E. Bearss, "Cavalry Operations in the Battle at Stones River," *THQ* 19 (1960): 23–53, 159–184. Earl J. Hess suspects Rosecrans's forces considerably outnumbered the Confederates. See "Braxton Bragg and the Stones River Campaign," in Kent T. Dollar, Larry H. Whiteaker, and W. Calvin Dickinson, eds., *Border Wars: The Civil War in Tennessee and Kentucky* (Kent, OH: Kent State University Press, 2015), 199. Hess's study is a persuasive, balancing defense of the many critical assessments by historians of Bragg's generalship at Stones River.

44. Letter and clipping, McIlvaine to LP, 19 May 1863, in LP Papers. McIlvaine's letter to Polk was passed through the lines of the opposing armies, but an answer from Polk might have been interdicted. Occasionally in his biography, William Polk protected his father's image by deleting passages from letters that would reflect badly upon him. The fact that, in this instance, he neither mentioned nor destroyed McIlvaine's letter and the damning clipping suggests he found the captain's story too far-fetched to be given credence—or even to be denied.

45. Bragg's biographer, Grady McWhiney, thinks Bragg, missing "the most obvious lesson of Shiloh and Perryville," failed to entrench his infantry around Murfreesboro and thereby lost the battle. McWhinney, *Braxton Bragg and Confederate Defeat*, 348. As regards the particular front-line placement of the division under Maj Gen Jones M. Withers, Polk said this was his decision, but Bragg in a footnote to his own report corrects Polk, saying the decision was *his*. LP, Murfreesboro report, *OR* 20/1:686.

46. Joe Wheeler's Murfreesboro report, 29 Janaury 1863, *OR* 20/1:960–961. Wheeler says that by the morning of December 31, when Hardee was attacking McCook, his cavalry had returned to the Murfreesboro area and was fighting the enemy "north of Overall's Creek." James McDonough, though, citing "missed opportunities" by the Rebels, faults Wheeler: "Wheeler, making his spectacular attention-grabbing ride . . . did not arrive on the field of battle until early afternoon." McDonough, *Stones River*, 146. However, Edwin Bearss says that "two crack infantry brigades sent to deal with Wheeler were consequently absent from Rosecrans' front line when the battle began on the 31st." E. Bearss, "Cavalry Operations at Stones River," 116.

47. Rosecrans's discrete silence is noted by Kenneth P. Williams, *Lincoln Finds a General* (New York: Macmillan, 1956), 4:260.

48. David J. Eicher, *The Longest Night: A Military History of the Civil War* (New York: Simon & Schuster, 2001), 420.

49. W. J. Worsham, *Old Nineteenth Tennessee Regiment, C.S.A. June 1861–April 1865* (Knoxville: Paragon, 1902), 22. Worsham is quoting a little inexactly John R. Thompson's Civil War poem "Museum in Camp."

50. W. D. B. [William Dennison Bickham], *Rosecrans' Campaign with the Fourteenth Army Corps, or the Army of the Cumberland* (Cincinnati: Moore, Wilstach, Keys, 1863), 207; Bickham, "The Battle of Stone [*sic*] River, by Our Correspondent," the *Cincinnati Daily Commercial*, 8 January 1863, 1; Garesche, who also received Communion from Fr.

Cooney that morning, was decapitated hours later by cannon fire while riding close beside Rosecrans.

51. At a meeting of generals on the night of December 30, Polk countered Bragg's original idea to attack Rosecrans' left flank, and Bragg agreed. McWhiney, *Braxton Bragg*, 349. In his own Murfreesboro report, Polk took no credit for what proved to be a significant suggestion.

52. Dispatch, Bragg to Maj. Gen. Jones Withers, 30 December 1862, *OR* 20/2:469.

53. Bragg, Murfreesboro report, 23 February 1863, *OR* 20/1:664; Bickham, "The Battle of Stone River," 1.

54. McDonough, *Stones River*, 85, quoting Col. William H. Gibson. The Federal general Richard Johnson estimated the 10,000 rampaging, screaming Confederates at 35,000.

55. McDonough, *Stones River*, 97–98; LP, Murfreesboro report, 28 February 1863, *OR* 20/1:687; Earl J. Hess, *Banners to the Breeze: The Kentucky Campaign, Corinth, and Stones River* (Lincoln: University of Nebraska Press, 2000), 206; Samuel Watkins, *"Company Aytch," Maury Grays, First Tennessee Regiment, or, a Sideshow of the Big Show* (Jackson, TN: McCowat-Mercer Press, 1952), 54.

56. LP, Murfreesboro report, *OR* 20/1:687.

57. LP, Murfreesboro report, *OR* 20/1:687.

58. Leonidas Polk, in his report, mentions *two* men waving flags to determine whose battery was firing on them: Sergeant Oakley of the 4th Tennessee Confederate Infantry and Sgt. M. C. Hooks of the Ninth Tennessee Infantry. *OR* 20/1:688. The unidentified private is quoted in *Confederate Veteran* 2 (1894): 68.

59. LP, Murfreesboro report, *OR* 20/1:687, 693.

60. Horn, *Army of Tennessee*, 143.

61. McDonough, *Stones River*, 131.

62. Cozzens, *No Better Place to Die*, 153.

63. John Houston Savage, Murfreesboro report, *OR* 20/1:717. See Thomas A. Head, *Campaigns and Battles of the Sixteenth Regiment, Tennessee Volunteers* (Nashville: Cumberland Presbyterian Publishing, 1885), 105.

64. LP, Murfreesboro report, *OR* 20/1:690.

65. John J. Hight, *History of the Fifty-Eighth Regiment of the Indiana Volunteer Infantry* (Princeton, NJ: Clarion, 1895), 117–118.

66. LP, Murfreesboro report, *OR* 20/1:690; G. C. Kniffin, "The Battle of Stone's River," in *BLCW*, 3:626.

67. Faulting Polk, Cozzens has written that "the ease with which the Federals repulsed [a] fourth attack was ridiculous." *No Better Place to Die*, 164. Hess more recently has said bluntly: "The dreadful waste of life [at the Round Forest was] attributable to Polk's decision to attack piecemeal." *Banners to the Breeze*, 214. Though partially agreeing, McWhiney mentions a mitigating issue raised by Kenneth Williams, "a careful student of the battle who examined the fought-over ground." Williams's analysis supports to some extent the piecemeal tactic adopted by Polk, for he concluded that "there seems to have been room for no more than a two-brigade front, and how close one assault can follow another must always be a matter of dispute. A long interval favors the defender, but a short one can cause the second assault to become disorganized by

men from the one that has failed." McWhiney, *Braxton Bragg and Confederate Defeat*, 365, quoting Williams, *Lincoln Finds a General*, 4:273. Polk makes no mention of a confined battlefield; he blames in his report the *delayed arrival* of Breckinridge's brigades as the real problem. Evening the argument out, McDonough faults both Bragg and Polk. *Stones River*, 146. See also Hess, "Braxton Bragg and the Stones River Campaign," 197.

68. Col. William B. Hazen, Murfreesboro report, *OR* 20/1:544.

69. Col. William B. Hazen, Murfreesboro report, *OR* 20/1:545–547.

70. *LPBG*, 2:193.

71. "For four hours this little wood [Round Forest] obsessed Bragg, and his obsession cost him the battle," Peter Cozzens has concluded. *No Better Place to Die*, 150. Similarly, McDonough has argued that had Bragg employed the strength of Breckinridge's reserves in "rejuvenating [Hardee's] original Confederate thrust against the Yankee right and occupying the Nashville pike . . . it is doubtful that the Federal army could have withstood it." *Stones River*, 146.

72. Jill K. Garrett, ed., *Confederate Diary of Robert D. Smith* (Columbia, TN: Capt. James Madison Sparkman Chapter, United Daughters of the Confederacy, 1975). Entry for January 1, 1863. Smith was the son of the Reverend Franklin Smith, principal of Polk's Female Institute in Columbia, Tennessee; James Lee McDonough surmises that had Bragg been in Rosecrans's place, it is likely he would have withdrawn. "Cold Days in Hell: The Battle of Stones River," *Civil War Times Illustrated* 25 (1986): 36.

73. Elliott, *Doctor Quintard*, 60. Willie (as he was called) was soon back in the thick of battles, shot in the remaining leg before the war was over. (Three of his brothers were killed during the war.) His marriage to Lilly Polk took place on April 27, 1864, a few weeks before General Polk's death. The Huger couple would name a daughter Leonide.

74. McDonough, "Cold Days in Hell," 40. The casual acquisition of this high ground by the Federals, one of Bragg's staff members later said, was decisive in the Confederates' ultimate loss of the battle. Cozzens, *No Better Place to Die*, 175.

75. William C. Davis, *The Orphan Brigade: The Kentucky Confederates Who Couldn't Go Home* (Garden City, NY: Doubleday, 1980), 155–161.

76. LP, Murfreesboro report, *OR* 20/1:691.

77. Pillow had arrived at Murfreesboro just that morning and talked Bragg into giving him a command. Hughes and Stonesifer, *Life and Wars of Gideon J. Pillow*, 263.

78. McWhiney disputes Breckinridge's own estimate of his strength, saying it was considerably in excess of Breckinridge's "4,500 effectives." *Braxton Bragg and Confederate Defeat*, 367, n. 58.

79. McDonough, "Cold Days in Hell," 42.

80. McDonough, "Cold Days in Hell," 41. Cozzens, *No Better Place to Die*, 191, provides the figure of forty-five cannons.

81. Davis, *The Orphan Brigade*, 157–160.

82. Williams, *Lincoln Finds a General*, 4:281.

83. Bickham, "The Battle of Stone River."

84. See the exchange of dispatches, Cheatham to Bragg via Polk, and Polk to Hardee throughout the early of hours of January 3, 1863, *OR* 20/1:700–701.

85. Bragg, Murfreesboro report, 23 February 1863, *OR* 20/1:669; Dispatch, LP to

Cheatham, 3 January 1863, *OR* 20/2:479; McWhiney, *Braxton Bragg and Confederate Defeat*, 371.

86. McWhiney's estimate of the remarkably similar losses in killed and wounded at Stones River: Confederates: 1,274 killed, 7,969 wounded, 1,071 captured or missing; Federal: 1,730 killed, 7,802 wounded, 3,717 captured or missing. McWhiney, *Braxton Bragg and Confederate Defeat*, 371. On those left behind, see Bragg, Murfreesboro report, *OR* 20/1:669.

87. *LPBG*, 2:181–182.

88. Letter, Lincoln to Rosecrans, 31 August 1863, quoted by T. Harry Williams, *Lincoln and his Generals* (New York: Alfred Knopf, 1952), 208–209.

21. General Rabbitt Escapes a Guerrilla Snare (1863)

1. Dispatch, Davis to Bragg, 15 January 1863, *OR* 52/2:409.

2. John M. Huger obituary, *The New York Times*, 25 February 1874, 2.

3. Letter, John Middleton Huger to LP, 15 February 1863.

4. The $50 bill was authorized by the state of Louisiana and issued in Confederate-controlled Shreveport, dated March 10, 1863. Grover Criswell Jr., *Confederate and Southern States Currency* (St. Petersburg, FL: Krause, 1964), 152.

5. McWhiney, *Braxton Bragg and Confederate Defeat*, 375, quoting George Brent diary, 10 January 1863. Bragg later that year banned the *Rebel* on army campgrounds until Watterson resigned. See Joseph Frazier Wall, *Henry Watterson, Reconstructed Rebel* (New York: Oxford University Press, 1956), 41–44.

6. Circular letter, Braxton Bragg to LP et al., 11 January 1863, *OR* 20/1:699.

7. Horn, *Army of Tennessee*, 223.

8. Dispatches, Breckinridge and Hardee to Bragg, 12 January 1863, *OR* 20/1:682–683; Cheatham and Cleburne to Bragg, 13 January 1863, *OR* 20/1:684.

9. Letter, Davis to Johnston, 22 January 1863, *PJD*, 9:36.

10. Writing Polk after Easter of that year, Fanny Polk told her husband that grandson "Frank was made happy by dyed eggs with 'Jenny Rabbit's' name and picture on one, and has put one away to send by the first opportunity to 'Gen. Rabbitt [*sic*].'" Letter, FAP to LP, 10 April 1863, GPP.

11. Letter, William Gale to Kate Polk Gale, 24 January 1863, GPP. Gale does not say how he learned of the guerrilla threat. Polk was apparently unfazed by the bushwhackers; he sent his son Meck to Asheville on a twenty-day furlough shortly after his own return. Letter, LP to FAP, 16 February 1863.

12. Letter, W. B. Richmond to Susan Polk Rayner, 9 March 1863.

13. Letter, LP to FAP, 27 August 1863; Letter, LP to "My Dear Daughter," 25 May 1863. Polk's field bed may have been the one left behind at the Battle of Belmont by the Federal general John McClernand. Fanny and Sallie Polk had come to Shelbyville by May 7, returning to Asheville about May 24.

14. Letter, LP to daughter Frances. 10 October 1863; FAP, "Memoir," 46.

15. Circular Letter, Bragg to LP et al., 30 January 1863, *OR* 20/1:701; Letter, LP to Bragg, 31 January 1863, *OR* 20/1:702.

16. *LPBG*, 2:205.

17. Letter, LP to Davis, 4 February 1863, *OR* 20/1:698. Polk sent this letter by mail and had William Richmond, an aide-de-camp, hand-carry a copy to Davis.

18. Letter, Johnston to Louis T. Wigfall, in Craig Symonds, *Joseph E. Johnston*, 195, 199.

19. Letter, Johnston to Davis, 12 February 1863, in *PJD*, 9:59.

20. Dispatch, Johnston to Davis, 3 February 1863, in *PJD*, 9:48–50.

21. Dispatch, Davis to Johnston, 19 February 1863, in *PJD*, 9:66–68.

22. Symonds, *Joseph E. Johnston*, 196.

23. Letter, LP to Davis, 30 March 1863, *OR* 23/2:729–730. As in February, Polk both mailed this letter and had a copy hand-carried to Davis by Lt. William Richmond.

24. Letter, William Gale to LP, 27 March 1863. Though others had come in for censure, Polk and Hardee were "specially commended" in Bragg's report for "valor, skill and ability displayed . . . throughout the engagement." Letter, Johnston to Davis, 10 April 1863, in *PJD*, 9:137–138.

25. Letter, LP to Bragg, 2 April 1863, Tennessee State Library and Archives.

26. Letter, Johnston to Davis, 10 April 1863, in *PJD*, 9:137–138. Johnston's wounds are described in Symonds, *Joseph E. Johnston*, 172.

27. Letter, William P. Johnston to Rosa D. Johnston, 3 April 1863, in *PJD*, 9:119–120 and n. 1. Letter, LP to FAP, 30 March 1863, in *LPBG*, 2:211–212.

28. Johnston's report to Davis concerning strictly military facts is found at *OR* 23/2:757–761.

29. Letter, LP to Davis, 30 March 1863, *PJD*, 9:118–119. So keen was Polk for enforcing conscription and the rounding up of deserters that he recommended to the War Department that Gideon Pillow be made a major general to run the Confederacy's Conscript Bureau. Letter, LP to Adjutant & Inspector General Samuel Cooper, 21 July 1863, *OR* 23/2:921.

30. Horn, *Army of Tennessee*, 226.

31. William M. Lamers, *The Edge of Glory: A Biography of William S. Rosecrans, U.S.A.* (New York: Harcourt, Brace, 1961), 244.

32. Lieutenant Colonel Malone was on duty under Brig. Gen. John Wharton, then at Unionville, on March 13. Dispatch, Wharton to LP, 13 March 1863, *OR* 23/1:146, and *OR* 23/2:694. Adding to the unfolding drama, a soldier claiming to be Rosecrans's orderly had been captured and was being held in Shelbyville. Wharton had hoped to meet with Polk and Malone in Shelbyville on March 15, presumably to discuss the kidnap plot, but there is no further mention of that meeting. Dispatch, John Wharton to LP, 14 March 1863, *OR* 23/2:694–695.

33. Draft letter, LP to Lt. Col. James C. Malone, 16 March 1863.

34. Letters, William Gale to Kate Polk Gale, 1 March 1863 and 1 August 1863, GPP; Kate Cumming, *Gleanings from Southland* (Birmingham, AL: Roberts & Son, 1895), 135.

35. For the exchange of kidnap letters between Polk and Malone, 16–17 March 1863, see *OR* 23/2:701–702.

36. Letters, Lt. Col. T. F. Sevier to Assistant Adjutant General Maj. Thomas Jack, 10 March 1863, and LP to Thomas Jack, 10 March 1863, *OR* ser. 2, 5:846–847; Letter, LP to Thomas Jack, 10 March 1863.

37. Letter, LP to "My Beloved Wife," 16 February 1863, Tennessee State Library and Archives; Letter, FAP to Kate Polk Gale, 14 May 1863.

38. Letters, LP to FAP, 16 February 1863, Tennessee State Library and Archives; LP to FAP, 26 March 1863, GPP; LP to "My Dear Daughter," 25 May 1863; LP to FAP, 26 March 1863.

39. Letters, LP to FAP, 26 March 1863, GPP; LP to "My Dear Daughter [Susan?]," 6 April 1863.

40. Letters, LP to FAP, 26 March 1863; LP to Patton Anderson, 17 June 1863, OR 20/1:695–696. The Confederate War Department was not especially pleased with Polk after all. His Murfreesboro report had appeared in newspapers without the department's sanction. See William Richmond's explanation to Secretary of War James Seddon, 15 June 1863, OR 20/1:703–704. Seddon drily termed the explanation "little satisfactory."

41. Letters, LP to FAP, 11 and 16 April 1863, in LPBG, 2:212–213. Altimore was the servant who carried Fanny from the burning house at Sewanee.

42. Bragg, Murfreesboro report, 12 October 1862, OR 16/1:1088. When Bragg showed Polk his first Perryville report before forwarding it to Richmond, Polk reportedly said, "emphatically, I had [credited] him more, and myself much less, than justice." Letter, Bragg to Davis, 22 May 1863, OR 52/2:817–819.

43. Circular Letter, Bragg to Hardee et al., 13 April 1863, OR 16/1:1097. Polk was excluded.

44. Dispatches, Hardee to LP, 14 April 1863, OR 16/1:1098; LP to Hardee, 17 April 1863, OR 16/1:1101.

45. Horn, Army of Tennessee, 227; Dispatch, Bragg to Davis, 22 May 1863, OR 52/2:817–819.

46. Elliott, Doctor Quintard, 69–70.

47. Polk had invited Elliott and his daughter Hettie to come to Shelbyville while Fanny and her girls were there. He apparently came alone just as the female Polks were leaving for Asheville. Letter, LP to Stephen Elliott, 7 May 1863. Elliott also preached that Sunday, and Polk, Bragg, and Hardee were in the congregation. See Hess, Braxton Bragg, 143.

48. Fremantle, Three Months in the Southern States, 147–148, 162.

49. Letter, Bragg to Quintard, n.d., quoted by Edgar Legare Pennington, "The Confederate Episcopal Church and the Southern Soldiers," HMPEC 17 (1948): 374.

50. Fremantle, Three Months in the Southern States, 148.

51. Worsham, Old Nineteenth Tennessee Regiment, 79.

52. William Mercer Otey, "Operations of the Signal Corps," Confederate Veteran 8 (1900): 129. Why Yankee cavalry troopers did not attempt to destroy the railroad tunnel at Cowan, Tennessee, when they were in the neighborhood on June 29 is not recorded.

53. Elliott, Doctor Quintard, 76–77. Harvey Washington Walter was Bragg's judge-advocate. See List of Staff Officers of the Confederate States Army (Washington, DC: Government Printing Office, 1891), 172.

54. Report of Col. John T. Wilder, 17th Indiana Mounted Infantry, OR 23/1:461. Wilder was on the campus grounds on June 29.

55. Pennington, "Battle at Sewanee," 238–239.

56. Otey, "Operations of the Signal Corps," 129. "Inspiration Point" may be "Polk's Lookout" named on a postwar map of the campus. Otey's version of the layover is at

variance with Lt. William Richmond's notes in *OR* 23/1:625; Richmond says he and Polk arrived at University Place at 2:00 A.M. A typographical error, probably. See also Fairbanks, *History of University of the South*. A prewar university executive and later a Confederate major, Fairbanks does not mention fetching buttermilk for General Polk on July 3.

57. The number of Rebel deserters turning themselves over to the enemy was remarked upon by several soldiers. See Merrit R. Blakeslee, *"A Rite Sharp Little Fight": Skirmish on Sewanee Mountain, July 4, 1863* (Sewanee, TN: Sewanee History Project, n.d.), 14 and n. 52; Dispatch, Wheeler to Polk, 4 July 1863, *OR* 23/1:616.

58. Pennington, "Battle at Sewanee," 217–243.

59. Dispatch, Thomas Jack to Wheeler, 4 July 1863, *OR* 23/1:625.

60. Edward P. Williams, *Extracts from Letters to A. B. T. from Edward P. Williams during His Service in the Civil War, 1862–1864* (New York: For Private Distribution, 1903), 83–84.

61. Pennington, "Battle at Sewanee," 239; William S. Slack, "A Fragment: of the Cornerstone," in Baker et al., *Purple Sewanee*, 29. A definitive account of the cornerstone's fate is in Blakeslee, *Pillaging and Destruction of the Cornerstone*, 14.

22. *"I Am Somewhat Afraid of Davis" (1863)*

1. Letter, LP to Kenneth Rayner, 14 August 1863; Letter, LP to Kate Polk Gale, 12 July 1863, GPP. A lighthearted tone was being taken by Braxton Bragg as well. In the words of Bragg biographer Judith Lee Hallock, "He cavalierly informed his superior officer in Richmond, Virginia, Adjutant General Samuel Cooper that in the retreat from Tullahoma his army lost 'nothing of importance.'" Hallock, *Braxton Bragg and Confederate Defeat*, vol. 2 (Tuscaloosa: University of Alabama Press, 1991), 7.

2. *LPBG*, 2:119.

3. Letter, LP to Kenneth Rayner, 14 August 1863.

4. Letter, LP to Stephen Elliott, 15 August 1863. The copy of the Rayner letter sent to Elliott is missing, but a brief excerpt of its text, in William Polk's biography of his father, is identical to lines in the Rayner letter. *Leonidas Polk*, 2:118–119. Polk grants Elliott permission to show his letter to Rayner to the Confederate senator Robert Barnwell "and men of that ilk." Ezra Warner and W. Buck Yearns, eds., *Biographical Register of the Confederate Congress* (Baton Rouge: Louisiana State University Press, 1975).

5. To resume fighting, these paroled men had to be exchanged for Federal prisoners held by the Confederates—a problematic process Polk would be charged with resolving in the winter of 1863–1864. Polk condemned a West Pointer, Gen. John Pemberton, for his handling of the Vicksburg defense and the surrender of 29,500 officers and men to Grant. See Letter, LP to Kenneth Rayner, 14 August 1863. A balanced portrayal of Pemberton's career is in Michael B. Ballard, *Pemberton: A Biography* (Jackson: University Press of Mississippi, 1991).

6. Letter, LP to Davis, 26 July 1863, *OR* 23/2:932–933.

7. Letter, LP to Hardee, 30 July 1863.

8. Letter, Hardee to LP, 27 July 1863.

9. Letter, LP to Davis, 9 August 1863, Leonidas Polk Papers, Duke University. Bragg had made a similar proposal to Joe Johnston in July. Horn, *Army of Tennessee*, 239.

10. Richmond's authorities, preoccupied with Vicksburg and Gettysburg, were not answering Bragg's mail either, as Bragg complained to Beauregard about that time. Horn, *Army of Tennessee*, 239.

11. Letter, LP to Stephen Elliott, 15 August 1863.

12. Pillow's success in furnishing Bragg's army with many hundreds of fresh troops is examined by Hughes and Stonesifer, *Life and Wars of Gideon Pillow*.

13. Harwell, *Kate: Journal of a Confederate Nurse*, 117; Cumming, *Gleanings from Southland*, 114.

14. Letter, H. D. Clayton et al. to General S. Cooper, 25 July 1863, *OR* ser. 4, 2:670. Henry De Lamar Clayton was a brigadier general; after the war, he became president of the University of Alabama.

15. Dispatch, Cooper to Bragg et al., 6 August 1863, *OR* ser. 4, 2:695.

16. Howell Purdue and Elizabeth Purdue, *Pat Cleburne: Confederate General* (Hillsboro, TX: Hill Junior College Press, 1972), 229–230, n. 9. The authors' "fair inference" is that Cleburne wrote prayers and hymns for the CSC. Also see Elliott, *Doctor Quintard*, 81–82.

17. Distracted by his visiting family, Polk was less than fully focused during August. Until he noticed the mistake, he had signed off a chatty letter to his daughter in Raleigh, Susan Rayner, by writing "L. Polk, Lt. Gen." LP to Susan Polk Rayner, 15 August 1863, in LP Papers.

18. Hughes, *Liddell's Record*, 135.

19. McWhiney, *Braxton Bragg and Confederate Defeat*, 389; Cumming, *Gleanings from Southland*, 122. As well as Wilder's 17th Indiana, the Federal force seen by Otey's lookouts included Capt. Eli Lilly's 18th Indiana Battery. *OR* 30/1:445. The Yankees' appearance in front of Chattanooga was meant primarily to unnerve and mislead the Confederates as to where Rosecrans might cross the Tennessee River.

20. Roy Morris, "That Improbable, Praiseworthy Paper: *The Chattanooga Daily Rebel*," *CWTI* 23 (1984): 16–24; Otey, "Operations of the Signal Corps," 129–130. Signalman Otey, exonerated by the artillery raining on Chattanooga, was a little miffed that the headquarters staff had ignored his warning. Years later he playfully got even, treating the readers of the *Confederate Veteran* to his recollection of the town's bombardment by quoting poetry from Lord Byron's *Childe Harold Pilgrimage* (canto 3, stanza 24). In the poet's portrayal of a Flemish ballroom in Brussels, one fateful midnight in 1815, Napoleon Bonaparte's salvos opening the Battle of Waterloo jolted the heedless dancers to a sudden halt: "Ah! Then and there was hurrying to and fro, / And gathering tears, and tremblings of distress. . . ."

21. The last Confederates left the town on 9 September. "Extracts from Notes of Lt. W. B. Richmond, Aide-de-Camp to General Leonidas Polk," *OR* 30/2:71.

22. Letter, LP to FAP, 25 August 1863.

23. Letter, LP to FAP, 27 August 1863.

24. Letter, LP to FAP, 27 August 1863. Polk seems to forget he had told Fanny two days before that "we hear of a few Federals crossing the river below [downstream] in the neighborhood of Bridgeport and Shell Mound."

25. *LPBG*, 2:255.

26. E. T. Wells, "The Campaign and Battle of Chickamauga," *The United Service* 16 (1896): 208.

27. Daniel Harvey Hill, "Chickamauga—The Great Battle of the West," *BLCW*, 3:641.

28. Peter Cozzens, *This Terrible Sound: The Battle of Chickamauga* (Urbana: University of Illinois Press, 1992), 29.

29. "Extracts from Notes of Lt. W. B. Richmond," *OR* 30/2:71.

30. "Extracts from Notes of Lt. W. B. Richmond," *OR* 30/2:71.

31. "Extracts from Notes of Lt. W. B. Richmond," *OR* 30/2:72.

32. Steven E. Woodworth, *Six Armies in Tennessee* (Lincoln: University of Nebraska Press, 1998), 67. Actual desertions had been so numerous earlier in the summer that Polk had assigned cavalrymen to patrol the banks of the Tennessee River. Hallock, *Braxton Bragg and Confederate Defeat*, 31. An amnesty for deserters and AWOL soldiers was announced by Bragg in August. *OR* 23/2:954.

33. Letter, LP to FAP, 10 September 1863.

34. Letter, Tom Hall to "Father," 6 September 1863, in Jones, "Five Confederates," 179.

35. Letter, LP to FAP, 10 September 1863.

36. An account of the unfolding in McLemore Cove is in Howard Popowski, "Opportunity: The Clash at Dug Gap," *CWTI* 22 (Summer 1983): 16–19. See also Thomas L. Connelly, *Autumn of Glory: The Army of Tennessee, 1862–1865* (Baton Rouge: Louisiana State University Press, 1971), 178–186.

37. Letter, William Gale to Kate Polk Gale, 15 September 1863, GPP.

38. "Extracts from Notes of Lt. W. B. Richmond," *OR* 30/2:74.

39. W. M. Polk, "General Bragg and the Chickamauga Campaign: A Reply to General Martin," *SHSP* 12 (1884): 382.

40. Letter, Gale to Kate Polk Gale, 15 September 1863, GPP; Letter, Bragg to E. T. Sykes, 8 February 1873, *SHSP* 12 (1884): 222.

41. Dispatch, Brent to Hindman, 10 September 1863, *OR* 30/2:301. In the dispatch announcing Crittenden's move south, Bragg urges Hindman to wrap up quickly the entrapment he had supposedly accomplished in McLemore's Cove.

42. Report of Maj. Gen. Thomas L. Crittenden, 1 October 1863, *OR* 30/1:603–604.

43. Donald E. Reynolds and Max H. Kele, eds., "With the Army of the Cumberland in the Chickamauga Campaign: The Diary of James W. Chapin, Thirty-Ninth Indiana Volunteers," *Georgia Historical Quarterly* 59 (1975): 234.

44. "Extracts from Notes of Lt. W. B. Richmond," *OR* 30/2:76.

45. William Miller Owen, *In Camp and Battle with the Washington Artillery of New Orleans* (Boston: Ticknor & Company, 1885), 272. See Shakespeare's *As You Like It*, Act II, scene vii, line 150: A "man in his time plays many parts, / His acts being seven ages." The fourth age is as "a soldier, / Full of strange oaths, and bearded like the pard." In other words, a panther.

46. St. John Liddell says Polk's headquarters were at the church itself; other records give the home of Mrs. Susan Parks [*sic*]. The 1850 census for Walker County, Georgia, Peavine Division, lists the household of Moses and Susan Park with eight children. Owning a house large enough for Polk's headquarters, Susan Park was possibly widowed by 1863.

47. William M. Polk, "General Polk at Chickamauga," *BLCW*, 3:663.

48. Hughes, *Liddell's Record*, 140, 173.

49. Dispatch, LP to Bragg, 12 September 1863, *OR* 30/2:44. The dispatch is dated 8 P.M., but Lt. William Richmond, who delivered it, says he left Polk's headquarters at 10:35. See "Extracts from Notes of Lt. W. B. Richmond," *OR* 30/2:76.

50. "Extracts from Notes of Lt. W. B. Richmond," *OR* 30/2:76; Dispatch, Bragg to LP, 12 September 1863, "12 o'clock at night," *OR* 30/2:49.

51. Circular, Thomas M. Jack, AAG, by command of Lieutenant-General Polk, 12 September 1863, 11:30 P.M., *OR* 30/2:49.

52. William Polk, "General Bragg and Chickamauga Campaign," 385.

53. Hill, "Chickamauga—The Great Battle of the West," 643.

54. Polk, "General Bragg and Chickamauga Campaign," 387.

55. Polk, "General Bragg and Chickamauga Campaign," 386; Report of General Bragg, 28 December 1863, *OR* 30/2:30–31. William Polk adds that Bragg's blaming his father "was never communicated to General Polk officially," and General Polk "never saw Bragg's report on the Chickamauga campaign." Captain Polk concludes, in his "Reply to General Martin" (who in an earlier issue of *SHSP* had cited "General Polk's failure to attack Crittenden's corps in its isolated position"), by saying: "This, Mr. Editor, is my version of this portion of the Chickamauga campaign. If I am in error, I wish to be put right, for I have no desire to do General Bragg injustice." "General Bragg and Chickamauga Campaign," 389. William Polk makes similar points in Hill, "Chickamauga—The Great Battle of the West," 663.

56. See especially Peter Cozzens's scornful assessment of Polk's operations at Rock Spring Church in *This Terrible Sound*, 82–85, indicting him for being both disobedient and fainthearted. Hallock finds William Polk's reasoning less than convincing. *Braxton Bragg and Confederate Defeat*, 62.

57. Hill, "Chickamauga—The Great Battle of the West," 663.

58. *LPBG*, 2:242.

59. Hughes, *Liddell's Record*, 114.

60. Linebaugh renounced his priest's vows before Stephen Elliott, Polk's partner bishop in the Sewanee school. Linebaugh's visits "every day with Polk and Fanny in Shelbyville" are mentioned in a letter from FAP to Kate Polk Gale, 14 May 1863, GPP.

61. George Sisler, "The Arrest of a *Memphis Daily Appeal* War Correspondent on Charges of Treason," *West Tennessee Historical Society Papers* 11 (1957): 76–92. An unlikely traitor, Linebaugh's Confederate army son had been killed in battle.

62. Dispatches, Col. Alex. McKinstry to Francis [*sic*] M. Paul, 3, 23, and 24 June 1863, *OR* 23/2:860, 885. McKinstry thought better of this planted news story after he discerned that "the knowing ones" in the Northern press had seen through its falsity. Accordingly, he asked Paul to print "somethings to the effect" that Breckinridge had been "recalled" to Johnston in Mississippi.

63. Wall, *Henry Watterson*, 37, 44.

64. *LPBG*, 2:245; Cozzens, *This Terrible Sound*, 89.

65. Circular, Headquarters Army of Tennessee, 18 September 1863 [night of 17 September], *OR* 30/2:31.

66. Wells, "Campaign and Battle of Chickamauga," 208.

67. *LPBG*, 2:247.

68. Cozzens, *This Terrible Sound*, 128.

69. *LPBG*, 2:248–249; Dispatch, George Thomas to John Palmer, 19 September 1863, *OR* 30/1:124.

70. *LPBG*, 2:250.

71. Dispatch, Hindman to Lt. Col. G. Moxley Sorrel, 25 October 1863, *OR* 30/2:302.

72. Purdue and Purdue, *Pat Cleburne: Confederate General*, 218.

73. Letter, W. D. Gale to Kate Polk Gale, 21 September 1863.

74. Letter, J. Frank Wheless to W. D. Gale, 8 October 1867.

75. Letter, W. D. Gale to Kate Polk Gale, 21 September 1863.

76. *LPBG*, 2:250.

77. Letter, Wheless to Gale, 8 October 1867.

23. Bragg's Designs for a Satisfying Sabbath Disintegrate (1863)

1. Purdue and Purdue, *Pat Cleburne, Confederate General*, 220.

2. Hill, "Chickamauga—Great Battle of the West," 650–651.

3. Hill, "Chickamauga—Great Battle of the West," 652.

4. James Longstreet, *From Manassas to Appomattox* (Bloomington: Indiana University Press, 1960), 438; G. Moxley Sorrel, *Recollections of a Confederate Staff Officer* (Jackson, TN: McCowat-Mercer Press, 1968), 183–184.

5. Archer Anderson, "Campaign and Battle of Chickamauga," *SHSP* 9 (1881): 409.

6. The contradictions found in various Chickamauga reports are comprehensively discussed by Thomas Connelly, *Autumn of Glory*, ch. 9, "The Chaos of Chickamauga."

7. *LPBG*, 2:241, 255, 265–266. Hill's biographer Hal Bridges questions the accuracy of William Polk's surmises of Bragg's enmity toward Hill during the time of Chickamauga. See Hal Bridges, *Lee's Maverick General: Daniel Harvey Hill* (Lincoln: University of Nebraska Press, 1991), 207. But also see Bragg's acerbic letter to Maj. E. T. Sykes, 8 February 1873, in *LPBG*, 2:309.

8. How close Polk's camp was to Alexander's Bridge is a subject of conflicting reports, ranging from a mere 150 feet up to a half-mile. Contending even in 1893 that "so many falsehoods have been published concerning the relation of those headquarters to the line," Polk's son William "deemed it proper" to insert in his biography the authoritative statement of Polk's engineer, Capt. W. J. Morris, who spots the bivouac along a road "within fifty yards of the [Alexander's] bridge. A part of the staff slept on either side of the road." *LPBG*, 2:253–254. Whatever the case, some people looking for Polk in the early morning could not find him. Connelly, *Autumn of Glory*, 214.

9. Dispatch, LP to Lt. Col. George William Brent [i.e., Bragg], 28 September 1863, *OR* 30/2:47.

10. Dispatch, LP to Hill, 30 September 1863, *OR* 30/2:63. Polk recalled in this note that Hill had previously said to him conversationally, "If you communicated [orders] to [Anderson], they were not communicated by him to me."

11. Connelly, *Autumn of Glory*, 212–213.

12. Dispatch, LP to Hill, 30 September 1863, *OR* 30/2:63; Dispatch, Hill to LP, 30 September 1863, *OR* 30/2:64; Hill, "Chickamauga—Great Battle of the West," 653; Dispatch, LP to Brent, 28 September 1863, *OR* 30/2:47.

13. Bridges, *Lee's Maverick General*, 300–301, n. 30; Anderson, "Campaign and Battle of Chickamauga," 410.

14. Deposition, L. Charvet, 30 September 1863, *OR* 30/2:59.

15. Circular dispatch, Thomas Jack [Polk] to Hill, Cheatham, and Walker, 19 September 1863, *OR* 30/2:52.

16. Dispatch, LP to Brent, 7 October 1863, *OR* 30/2:48.

17. Deposition by Courier J. A. Perkins, 30 September 1863, *OR* 30/2:60.

18. Unsigned letter fragment to "My Dear Willie," 11 October 1863. The writer was Charles Gallway corresponding with his friend Willie Huger, Polk's future son-in-law. Other letters "To my dear Willie" signed by Gallway are also in the Leonidas Polk Papers. These letters were gathered by William Polk, the brother-in-law of Huger. It is evident that the unsigned writer of the October 11 letter, as well as Willie Huger, was at General Polk's headquarters on the night of September 19–20. On the first page of the manuscript, William Polk has written: "All in this letter covered by statements sworn to."

19. Dispatch, Cheatham to LP, 30 September 1863, *OR* 30/2:63.

20. Deposition of John H. Fisher, 29 September 1863, *OR* 30/2:57–58; Statement of Lt. Col. Thomas M. Jack, 29 September 1863, *OR* 30/2:58.

21. Deposition of L. Charvet, Orleans Light Horse, 30 September 1863, *OR 30/2: 58*; Letter, Charles Gallway to "My Dear Willie," 11 October 1863.

22. High on Polk's list of favorite officers, Wheless had previously been a banker in Nashville and had been severely injured at Perryville; he was now serving Polk in the less-demanding role of staff officer and had been at the general's side at sundown. Polk would shortly recommend Wheless to Jefferson Davis as a paymaster in the Confederate Navy. Letter, LP to Davis, 5 November 1863, Rowland, *Jefferson Davis, Constitutionalist*, 6:78.

23. Letter, Gallway to "My Dear Willie," 11 October 1863; Statement of J. Frank Wheless, 30 September 1863, *OR* 30/2:61

24. Dispatches, Thomas Jack to Cleburne and Breckinridge, 20 September 1863, 5:30 A.M., *OR* 30/2:52. Polk's archived order reads "attack . . . as soon as you are in position." But in referring to this order in an explanatory letter demanded by Bragg, Polk on September 28 says his order to Cleburne and Breckinridge was to "make attack at once." In Polk's defense, this wording may reflect what Polk was *thinking* at the dawn dictation to Thomas Jack and later wished he had said explicitly. Polk to George Brent, 28 September 1863, *OR* 30/2:47.

25. Statement of J. Minick Williams, 30 September 1863, *OR* 30/2:60. Williams says the orders he carried were in writing; Polk's assistant adjutant general, Thomas Jack, says they were "verbal," meaning, presumably, oral. Just another of the night's inconsistencies. Statement of Thomas Jack, 29 September 1863, *OR* 30/2:58.

26. Statement of J. Frank Wheless, 30 September 1863, *OR* 30/2:61.

27. Lt. Gen. Daniel H. Hill, Chickamauga report, n.d., *OR* 30/2:141. Hill's undated report was found among the papers of General Polk after his death in 1864. Hill says "I saw the order [for a daylight attack] for the first time nineteen years afterward reading Captain William M. Polk's letter to the Southern Historical Society." "Chicka-

mauga—Great Battle of the West," 653. Hill's reference is to William Polk, "The Battle of Chickamauga," *SHSP* 10 (1882): 1–25. The order is mentioned on page 19.

28. Hill, "Chickamauga—Great Battle of the West," 653; Hill's Chickamauga report, *OR* 30/2:141.

29. Y. R. LeMonniere, "Gen. Leonidas Polk at Chickamauga," *Confederate Veteran* 24 (1916): 17. The French example of talking one's way out of a jam refers to the sixteenth-century author François Rabelais. Once when traveling toward Paris, the oft-told story goes, he ate a full meal at an inn and could not pay. To extricate himself he led the innkeeper to believe he was on his way to poison the French king. Whereupon the innkeeper had him arrested and transported (at no cost to Rabelais) to the capital. There the amused king set Rabelais free.

30. LeMonniere, "Gen. Leonidas Polk at Chickamauga," 17.

31. Letter, Gallway to "My Dear Willie," 11 October 1863. William M. Polk would say an arrest would *not* have been his father's way of handling such a situation. *LPBG*, 2:296–297.

32. Hill, Chickamauga report, *OR* 30/2:141.

33. Hill, "Chickamauga—Great Battle of the West," 653; Letters, Bragg to Elise Bragg, 22 and 27 September 1863, in Hallock, *Braxton Bragg and Confederate Defeat*, 72; Letter, Bragg to Davis, 25 September 1863, *PJD*, 9:405.

34. Sykes, "Cursory Sketch of General Bragg's Campaigns," 493, quoting an excerpt from Bragg's letter to him dated February 8, 1873. (William Polk includes the complete letter in *LPBG*, 2:308–313.) Letter, George C. Binford to R. A. Lancaster, 11 October 1863, Virginia Historical Society. Binford wrote detailed accounts of Confederate battles (and passed along rumors) to his cousin Bob and opined that, but for Polk's Sunday morning "tardiness and negligence" at Chickamauga, the Confederates would already be occupying Louisville.

35. William Polk, "General Polk at Chickamauga," 663, and *LPBG*, 2:265–266.

36. William Polk, "General Polk at Chickamauga," 663, and *LPBG*, 2:265–266. In a lengthy footnote, Captain Polk categorically disputes all the farmhouse allegations.

37. For details of an imbroglio involving Lee and two Polk cousins, see Letter, James Hilliard Polk to William M. Polk, 23 August 1913, "Letters and Diaries of the George W. Polk Family," 23 (1987): 23.

38. Hill, "Chickamauga—Great Battle of the West," 654.

39. Horn, *Tennessee's War*, 212, quoting Dana, an assistant secretary of war for the Federal government at Chickamauga.

40. Newspaper clipping (undated) and letter, Maj. W. W. Carnes to William M. Polk, 20 June 1884. Letter, William Gale to William M. Polk, 15 December 1884. In this letter Gale offers to assist William Polk in the article on Chickamauga he was then preparing for publication in *Battles and Leaders*.

41. Hill, "Chickamauga—Great Battle of the West," 656.

42. *LPBG*, 2:277.

43. Hill, "Chickamauga—Great Battle of the West," 656–659. Bridges notes Hill's "charity" in his numerous postwar writings regarding "those who had been killed in battle or had died before he wrote about them." Bridges, *Lee's Maverick General*, 275.

44. In the assault on the Federal left under a "terrible volley of grape, canister and

small arms," Lucius Polk ordered artillery rolled into position by men instead of horses, the men presenting smaller targets. In the face of the Rebels' double charges of canister from less than 200 yards, "the enemy's line wavered," the brigadier reported, and he was among those who charged into their breastworks. Report of Brig. Gen. Lucius E. Polk, 10 October 1863, OR 30/2:176–178. At the conclusion of the fight, the thirty-year-old Polk called Major Carnes to his side and addressed an exultant message to his uncle commander: "Go back and tell the old general that we have passed two lines of [Thomas's] breastworks, [and] that we have got them on the jump." W. W. Carnes, "Chickamauga," SHSP 14 (1886): 405.

45. Longstreet, *From Manassas to Appomattox*, 452. Longstreet says Bragg was some two miles in the rear of the fighting when he made the disparaging remark about the men of Polk's wing and was in no position to evaluate their mettle. Hallock disputes Bragg's absence from the front, calling it a myth originated by Longstreet, either deliberately or "in his dotage [he] truly misremembered." *Braxton Bragg and Confederate Defeat*, 2:80–81.

46. Losson, *Tennessee's Forgotten Warriors*, 111; W. J. Worsham, *Old Nineteenth Tennessee Regiment*, 88–99. Fremantle wrote that Frank Cheatham "does all the [corps's] necessary swearing . . . which General Polk's clerical character incapacitates him from performing." *Three Months in the Southern States*, 116. Others allege Polk had said "Give them what General Cheatham says" at Perryville and Murfreesboro.

47. Donald Bridgman Sanger, a professional soldier and historian and one of Longstreet's biographers, asserts that Polk made several tactical mistakes during the day that Longstreet, had he been in Polk's place, would have avoided. Sanger, *James Longstreet: Soldier* (Baton Rouge: Louisiana State University Press, 1952), 209 and n. 12.

48. Cozzens, *This Terrible Sound*, 534; LPBG, 2:286.

49. Letter, William Gale to Kate Polk Gale, 28 September 1863, GPP.

50. Letters, LP to FAP, 27 September 1863; William Gale to Kate Polk Gale, 25 September 1863; William W. Carnes to William M. Polk, 26 August 1884; Henry Watterson to Rebecca Ewing, 3 October 1863, typescript, Filson Historical Society. Also see I. J. Austin, "Obituary of Crafts James Wright, Class of 1828," 52–64 in *15th Annual Reunion of the Association of Graduates of the United States Military Academy* (East Saginaw, MI: Courier, 1884), 59.

51. Letters, William Gale to William Polk, 28 March 1882; Philip Spence to William Polk, 5 August 1874.

52. Letters, LP to Davis, 6 October 1863, OR 30/2:67–68; William Gale to William M. Polk, 28 March 1882. Gale may have forgotten in making his colorful comparison that Hannibal, with or without his famous elephants, failed to conquer Rome.

53. John A. Wyeth, *That Devil Forrest: Life of General Nathan Bedford Forrest* (Baton Rouge: Louisiana State University Press, 1989), 259. Dispatches, Nathan Bedford Forrest to LP, 21 September 1863, OR 30/4:675, 681.

54. Letter, William Gale to William Polk, 28 March 1882.

55. Report of Lt. Gen. James Longstreet, October 1863, OR 30/2:287–290; LPBG, 2:283. What other objectives Longstreet had in mind is unclear; he gave contradictory statements in later years.

56. The eavesdropping soldier, John McPherson Pinckney of Hood's Texas brigade,

is quoted in James Goggin, "Chickamauga—Reply to Major Sykes," *SHSP* 12 (1884): 222. General Breckinridge was also present, according to Pinckney.

57. Report of Lt. Gen. James Longstreet, *OR* 30/2:289–290; Letter, Longstreet to J. A. Seddon, 26 September 1863, *OR* 30/4:705–706; Circulars, George William Brent to various commanders, both 22 September 1863, *OR* 30/4:689.

58. Letter, LP to FAP, 21 September 1863.

59. *LPBG*, 2:283. Earlier Monday, Bragg had directed Polk, as of daylight Tuesday, to "drive the enemy as far as possible." Even as Polk was preparing to execute this new order with Frank Cheatham's division, another order from Bragg stated that Polk's right wing "resting [its] right at [Chickamauga Station] will form his line extending up the west side of the river." By this arrangement, Polk's force was brought to a standstill while his ordnance officers were told to see to the burial of the dead and to the collection of abandoned enemy "guns and accouterments lying on the battlefield." 21 September 1863, *OR* 30/2:53. And then came the Missionary Ridge order.

60. Bragg, Chickamauga report, 28 December 1863, *OR* 30/2:37.

61. Letter, William Gale to Kate Polk Gale, 28 September 1863, GPP.

62. Hill, "Chickamauga—Great Battle of the West," 662; Archibald Gracie, *The Truth About Chickamauga* (Boston: Houghton Mifflin, 1911), iii; Editorial, *Memphis Daily Appeal* [published in Atlanta], 2 October 1863. See also Letter, William Gale to William M. Polk, 15 December 1884. Gale recalled seeing the words "barren of results" applied to Chickamauga "in some Richmond papers." Letter, William Gale to William M. Polk, 27 November 1884.

63. Quintard's eulogy at St. Luke's Church, Atlanta, 15 June 1864, *The Church Intelligencer*, 14 September 1864; Report of Lt. Gen. James Longstreet, October 1863, *OR* 30/2:287–290; Letter, Longstreet to J. A. Seddon, 26 September 1863, *OR* 30/4:705–706.

64. Hallock, *Braxton Bragg and Confederate Defeat*, 89. Circular, Brent to LP et al., 21 September 1863, *OR* 30/4:679; Kinloch Falconer to LP, 21 September 1863, *OR* 30/4:680.

65. Dispatches, George Brent [Bragg] to LP, 22 and 25 September 1863, *OR* 30/2:54.

66. Connelly, *Autumn of Glory*, 235; Hallock, *Braxton Bragg and Confederate Defeat*, 72, n. 16; Cozzens, *This Terrible Sound*, 529.

67. Letter, Bragg to Davis, 25 September 1863, *PJD*, 9:404–406. Hallock ascribes the same letter from Bragg to Secretary Seddon. *Braxton Bragg and Confederate Defeat*, 95.

68. Dispatch, Brent to LP, 21 September 1863, *OR* 30/2:53. Simon Buckner is listed among the conspirators on Saturday in Jeffry D. Wert, *General James Longstreet: The Confederacy's Most Controversial Soldier* (New York: Simon & Schuster, 1993), 325. Buckner's presence was not mentioned, however, by Polk when he wrote Jefferson Davis on October 6, 1863, *OR* 30/2:67–68.

69. Letter, Longstreet to J. S. Seddon, 26 September 1863, *OR* 30/4:705–706. An all-but-illegible microfilm of the pencil draft of the letter, with many changes in Polk's handwriting, is in the Houghton Library, Harvard University. Jeffry Wert cites Longstreet's writing Lee.

70. Letters, LP to Davis, 27 September 1863, *PJD*, 9:410; LP to Lee, 27 September 1863, in *LPBG*, 2:289–290.

71. Dispatch, Rosecrans to Henry W. Halleck, 20 September 1863, *OR* 30/1:142.

72. Jones, *Rebel War Clerk's Diary*, 2:65–66, 8 October 1863. Instead of naming the

letter's author, Jones discretely left a blank in his published diary; a 1935 edition of this book, annotated by Howard Swiggett, identifies Polk as having written the letter.

73. Letter, Bragg to E. T. Sykes, 8 February 1873, in Goggin, "Chickamauga—Reply to Major Sykes," 222.

74. Tennyson would write his poem about the siege of Sebastopol in the Crimean War in 1864.

75. Petition to Jefferson Davis, 4 October 1863, *OR* 30/2:65. The authorship of the petition is still unsettled by historians. An unsigned draft in Buckner's handwriting, first dated October 3, then changed to October 4, with numerous other changes, is in the Simon Bolivar Buckner Collection, Henry E. Huntington Library, SB214. Maj. A. C. Avery, one of Hill's aides and later a North Carolina Supreme Court justice, said in 1893, "Buckner drew the petition." See "On the Life and Character of Lieut.-General D. H. Hill," *SHSP* 21 (1893): 143–144. A signed copy of the petition, in different handwriting, is in Daniel Harvey Hill Papers, Virginia State Library and Archives. Buckner's signature, leading a list of eleven others, appears where a writer would ordinarily sign a letter. The last page of this version with signatures is photocopied in Bridges, *Lee's Maverick General*, 237. The eleven other signers: Pat Cleburne, Randall Gibson, William Preston, James Longstreet, Bushrod Johnson, Archibald Gracie Jr., D. H. Hill, Marcellus Stovall, J. A. Smith, John C. Brown, and Lucius E. Polk, nephew of General Polk. Lucius has sometimes been confused by historians with his uncle, already under arrest in Atlanta, who did not sign.

76. Letter, LP to Davis, 6 October 1863, *OR* 30/2:67–68. This letter, written from Atlanta after his arrest, "recapitulates" much of his September 27 letter to Davis.

77. Dispatch, LP to George Brent, 28 September 1863, *OR* 30/2:47; Bridges, *Lee's Maverick General*, 230, 304, n. 14.

78. Letter, Bragg to E. T. Sykes, 8 February 1873, in Goggin, "Chickamauga—Reply to Major Sykes," 222. Suspensions of Polk and Hindman, 30 September 1863, charges and specifications against Polk, and orders to proceed with his personal staff to Atlanta are in *OR* 30/2:55–56. Also see David Urquhart, "Bragg's Advance and Retreat," in *BLCW*, 3:608.

24. "Fight Ever with True Hearts. Your Friend, L. Polk" (1863)

1. Bragg's "too bad" is quoted only in a draft version of William M. Polk's biography, its source unknown, but it is not used in the published version. Technically, Bragg "suspended" Polk, a procedure Polk protested was against army regulations. He "*should be placed under arrest and charges preferred*," Polk insisted at the time, hoping to bring the matter before a military court. Jefferson Davis saw to it that this would not happen.

2. Dispatches, Davis to Bragg, 1 October 1863, *OR* 30/2:55; Davis to Bragg, 3 October 1863, *OR* 52/2:535.

3. Letter, LP to Davis, 6 October 1863, *OR* 30/2:67–68. This letter, on the heels of his letter to the President on September 27, amplifies Polk's account of Bragg's hesitant behavior after the Battle of Chickamauga.

4. Letters, LP to Hill, 29 September 1863, *OR* 30/2:56; Hill to LP, 30 September 1863, *OR* 30/2:64.

5. Though now on Polk's staff, Andrew Ewing had opposed Polk's invasion of neutral Kentucky in 1861 and at the time was sent by the Tennessee governor Isham Harris to urge Polk's withdrawal. Letter, Harris to Jefferson Davis, 13 September 1861, *OR* 4:190.

6. Dispatches, LP to Walker and Cheatham, *OR* 30/2:57; Cheatham to LP, *OR* 30/2:63 (Walker's reply to LP was not found); Ewing depositions, *OR* 30/2:57–62.

7. Polk's farewell, *OR* 30/2:64–65.

8. Letter, Lt. P. M. Kenner et al. to Court of Enquiry, 9 October 1863.

9. Letter, Chaplains Association to LP, 1 December 1863.

10. More on Thrasher and the Confederate Press Association is found in Ford Risley, "The Confederate Press Association," *Civil War History* 47 (2001): 222–239.

11. Richard M. McMurry, *John Bell Hood and the War for Southern Independence* (Lexington: University Press of Kentucky, 1982), 80. The journalist was probably John H. Linebaugh.

12. Asa B. Isham, Henry M. Davidson, and Henry B. Furness, *Prisoners of War and Military Prisons* (Cincinnati: Lyman & Cushing, 1890), 168–169. Extenuating, perhaps, the boorish behavior of the depot women was the report that they had gone to meet the train thinking it was bringing wounded Confederates from Chickamauga, not Federal prisoners.

13. Letter, LP to Kenneth Rayner, 17 October 1863, GPP.

14. Letter, LP to Davis, 6 October 1864, *PJD*, 10:11–12, and explanatory notes regarding versions of this letter. The letter reflects most of the criticisms of Bragg Polk made in his letter to Davis on September 27. A draft in pencil, heavily modified, is in Leonidas Polk Papers, Library of Congress. Symonds makes the interesting assertion in his biography of Joseph E. Johnston that "those who got along best with Davis were men who were willing to subordinate their own views and personalities to the president." Leonidas Polk could not be accused of any such deference. Symonds, *Joseph E. Johnston: A Civil War Biography*, 226.

15. Letter, LP to FAP, 3 October 1863. Polk's vague allusion to a second instance of Bragg's attempting to get rid of him cannot be substantiated. William Polk connected it to Polk's and Bragg's getting in one another's way on the roads leading to Shiloh. *LPBG*, 2:298, n. 1. If Bragg at the time had appealed to P. G. T. Beauregard to dismiss Polk, it is not known. Alternatively, General Polk may have been referring to an effort by Bragg to have Polk dismissed when the Army of Tennessee retreated from Kentucky after Perryville.

16. Letter, LP to Frances D. Polk, 10 October 1863.

17. Letter, LP to Rayner, 17 October 1863, GPP; Letter, LP to "My Dear Daughter," 15 November 1863.

18. Letter, LP to FAP, 10 October 1863.

19. The first two meetings took place in Atlanta on 8 and 15 October; the train ride, from Montgomery, Alabama, to Atlanta, was on October 27–28. William Gale (and possibly Polk's wife) had accompanied him to Montgomery. Letter, William Gale to Kate Polk Gale, 29 October 1863, GPP. See also *PJD*, 10:35–36.

20. The *Atlanta Rebel* clipping, dated October 14, 1864, is in Leonidas Polk Papers. It is accompanied by a handwritten copy of the denial item published in the *Savannah Republican* on October 16 and by a note in William M. Polk's handwriting that reads:

"Gen. Polk considered the dispatch of which the above is a denial as a reflection upon himself and the general officers who had expressed dissatisfaction with Genl Bragg's management [of the Battle of Chickamauga] and asked [the president] if he had used such language. Whereupon the President authorized the above denial."

21. Dispatch, Bragg to Davis, 11 October 1863, *OR* 30/2:148; Letter, Bragg to Sykes, 8 February 1873, quoted in *LPBG*, 2:310.

22. William C. Davis, *Jefferson Davis: The Man and His Hour* (New York: HarperCollins, 1991), 532. Davis speculates that Hill's subsequent punishment—being ousted from the army and not being confirmed as a lieutenant general by the Confederate senate—provided the vacancy President Davis needed to push the promotion of a friend, the "lionized John B. Hood" (547–548). The Hill biographer Hal Bridges has written in a similar vein. By Bragg and Davis, Hill was "accused, tried, convicted and sentenced to professional disrepute in the official records of the Confederacy and in any history that might be written from them. . . . [The] case was closed, with no loose ends, except possibly a few in the realm of conscience." Bragg's antagonists were by now pretty much dispersed; Hindman, chastened, was allowed to return. Bridges, *Lee's Maverick General*, 247–248. The whole unsavory episode is carefully examined in Bridges's book.

23. Letter, Hill to Breckinridge, 26 October 1863, *The Historical Magazine*, 3rd ser., 1/2 (1872): 119. The letter is also quoted by *LPBG*, 2:297. Of course, Polk *did* blame Hill for the delay, though he did not conspire with Bragg to cause Hill's ostracism.

24. Letter, FAP to "My Dear Harriette" [Young], 27 November 1863, GPP. Harriette Young was a friend from the Polks' sugar-plantation days in Thibodaux, Louisiana.

25. FAP, "Memoir," 46; Letter, William Gale to Kate Polk Gale, 29 October 1863, GPP.

26. FAP, "Memoir," 47.

27. "*Conti qui conti*"—cost what it may. Letter, William Gale to Kate Polk Gale, 29 October 1863, GPP.

28. Letter, William Gale to William Huger, 31 October 1863.

29. Letter, William Gale to Kate Polk Gale, 29 October 1863, GPP.

30. Letter, William Gale to Kate Polk Gale, 29 October 1863, GPP.

31. Letter, FAP to Lillie Polk, 21 November 1863. In her long, chatty letter, Lillie's mother recounted an anecdote she found amusing regarding a Federal soldier, an escaped slave formerly owned by William Gale. The soldier had returned to the occupied Mississippi Delta "in full uniform talking very big to recover from an illness," she continued coolly, and while convalescing, "he was taken off and hung [hanged] by some parties."

32. Letter, LP to "My dear daughter," 15 November 1863. Bishop Polk had suspected a slave named Jackson to have been involved in the Sewanee fire; Fanny adamantly contradicted him on this suspicion, and at her insistence he dropped the charges after arresting the man. Letter, LP to FAP, 18 July 1861.

33. Gale, "Recollections of Life," 23.

34. Letter, FAP to Lillie Polk, 21 November 1863.

35. Letter, Hardee to LP, 23 November 1863.

36. Among others on Polk's list was Charles Quintard. An aide wrote the chaplain on November 5 from Atlanta that "the general wants you with him but does not know how to arrange it." C. T. Quintard Papers, 1857–1899, Perkins Library, Duke University.

37. "Lieut. Polk" is not otherwise identified by Hardee. That he was twenty-year-old Rufus King Polk, 10th Tennessee Infantry, General Polk's nephew (son of George W. Polk), seems likely.

38. Letter, Hardee to LP, 23 November 1863.

39. Nathaniel Hughes, *General William J. Hardee*, 186–189; Letter, FAP to "My Dear Child," 21 January 1864; Purdue and Purdue, *Pat Cleburne, Confederate General*, 285–287, 433.

40. Letter, FAP to Lillie D. Polk, 21 November 1863; FAP, "Memoir," 47–48.

41. FAP, "Memoir," 47–48. The "aerial portions [of begonia—*B. Fimbristipulata*] are used as an alternative, to clear heat, eliminate toxins, promote blood circulation, treat coughing of blood." See Michael Tierra, *Flowers as Medicine*, www.planetherbs.com.

42. Letter, Marshall Polk to Eva, 2 December 1863, typescript from Ted Yeatman; FAP, "Memoir," 48; Letter, FAP to "My Dear Child," 21 January 1864.

43. Letter, John H. Linebaugh to LP, 20 December 1863.

44. Walter Scott, *The Lady of the Lake*, in *The Poetical Works* (Edinburgh: Adams and Charles Black, 1851), canto 6, stanza 18.

25. A "Monstrous Proposition . . . Revolting to Southern Sentiment" (1863–1864)

1. Letter, William Gale to Kate Polk Gale, 8 December 1863, GPP; Dispatch, Col. George B. Hodge to Gen. Samuel Cooper, 2 May 1864, *OR* 39/2:568.

2. Dispatch, Col. George B. Hodge to Gen. Samuel Cooper, 2 May 1864, *OR* 39/2:570.

3. Writing the Richmond War Department, 6 August 1863, Maj. W. T. Walthall, Commandant of Alabama, warned that noncombatants voting for "Peace Candidates, were skewing state elections for loyal Confederate candidates." *OR* ser. 4, 2:726.

4. Dispatch, Hodge to Cooper, *OR* 39/2:570.

5. Bettersworth, *Confederate Mississippi*, 222. For Jones County's wartime convulsions, see Victoria E. Bynum, *The Free State of Jones: Mississippi's Longest Civil War* (Chapel Hill: University of North Carolina Press, 2001.)

6. Letter, William Polk to Kate Polk Gale, 8 December 1863, GPP.

7. Letter, FAP to Lillie D. Polk, 21 November 1863.

8. LP, Circulars to Paroled and Exchanged Prisoners, 20 November 1863, *OR* ser. 2, 6:542–543; 11 January 1864, *OR* ser. 2, 6:833- 834.

9. Letter, LP to Davis, 8 December 1863, *OR* 31/3:796.

10. Letter, LP to Davis, 8 December 1863, *OR* 31/3:796.

11. Davis, *Jefferson Davis: Man and His Hour*, 529–530.

12. Dispatch, LP to Davis, 14 January 1864, in *LPBG*, 2:324; *PJD*, 10:172.

13. 28 January 1864, *OR* 31/3:857. Polk and Forrest had fought together at Chickamauga. For Forrest's promotion, see *OR* 31/3:816.

14. Polk's theological disdain of the immigrant Germans in the Union Army was in part associated with his rejection of "higher criticism" of the Bible, a nonliteralist form of scriptural scholarship then gaining adherents among German theologians.

15. General Orders No. 1, 23 December 1863, *OR* 31/3:857; Dispatch, Davis to LP, 18

January 1864, *PJD*, 10:184. A warm note expressing the president's "gratification" at the spirit of Polk's motivating message soon arrived from Davis.

16. Letter, William Gale to Kate Polk Gale, 3 January 1864, GPP.

17. FAP, "Memoir," 48.

18. FAP, "Memoir," 48. Fanny recorded the evenings' routine in her memoir: "The outpouring of his heart to his maker as a very present help, who knew all, and yet to whom as to a friend it was his delight to unburthen his heart, his dependence upon God, his cheerful submission to his will, feeling it was his duty to do everything he could, and then leave the result in God's hands, insured contentment in all that occurred."

19. Dispatch, Gideon Pillow to Judah P. Benjamin, 16 January 1861, OR 3:313–316. His 1861 assertions to the War Department had accused Polk at the Battle of Belmont of negligent failure to reinforce Pillow's beleaguered troops.

20. Dispatch, Gideon Pillow to Gen. Samuel Cooper, 23 October 1863, OR ser. 4, 2:884.

21. Hughes and Stonesifer, *Life and Wars of Gideon Pillow*, 259–275.

22. Letter, Pillow to Gen. Samuel Cooper, 15 January 1864; Dispatch, LP to Pillow, 15 January 1864, OR 32/2:562–563. General Johnston, while approving Pillow's plan, was reluctant to supply a cavalry brigade.

23. Letter, FAP to "My Dear Child," 21 January 1864. Pillow also expressed to Polk at their meeting his appreciation that Polk in July had recommended to the War Department that Pillow be put in charge of a reorganized conscription program for the whole Confederacy and promoted to major general. See, Dispatch, LP to Samuel Cooper, 21 July 1863, OR 23/2:921–922.

24. Dispatch, LP to Stephen D. Lee, 26 April 1864, OR 32/3:825.

25. Dispatch, Johnston to Davis, 2 January 1864, OR 30/2:510. Johnston suggested to the president that the noncombat use of slaves be greatly expanded by "judicious legislation," freeing at once 10,000 to 12,000 (white) men for fighting. Johnston further recommended that, should the slave soldiers desert the army, their owners should be punished if they failed to send them back.

26. Dispatch, Anderson to LP, 14 January 1864, OR 52/2:598–599.

27. If, in fact, Polk ever answered at all, no account is known of his position. But see *LPBG*, 2:341. Polk's son seems to suggest that Anderson's confidence in Polk's opinions would indicate he sided with Anderson. If so, no matter; the revolutionary idea, before it got very far, was quashed that winter by presidential fiat. But it became a law of the declining Confederacy fourteen months later (13 March 1865). See, e.g., *PJD*, 10:178–179. Polk's nephew Brig. Gen. Lucius Polk stood among the Tennessee army generals who did support Cleburne. Polk's military friend William Hardee was another.

28. Dispatch, LP to Colonel Harvie, 21 January 1864, OR 32/2:593–594. Even before this intrigue, Harvie asked the president's brother Joseph to try to reconcile Davis and Johnston. Gilbert E. Govan and James W. Livingood, *A Different Valor: The Story of General Joseph E. Johnston, C.S.A.* (New York: Bobbs-Merrill, 1956), 229.

29. Dispatch, George B. Hodge to Gen. Samuel Cooper, 2 May 1864, OR 39/2:568–569. Colonel Hodge, as an assistant inspector general, recapitulates in this dispatch his visit to Polk's headquarters in January.

30. Margie Riddle Bearss, *Sherman's Forgotten Campaign* (Baltimore: Gateway Press, 1987), 9. Bearss says "the region through which [Sherman's] soldiers marched in February 1864 . . . was left more scourged and desolated than the area he covered in the March to the Sea or in the Carolinas." (A less than sympathetic critique of Sherman's concept of total war is John Bennett Walters, "General William T. Sherman and Total War," *Journal of Southern History* 14:447–480.) The estimate of slaves freed by Sherman's infantry runs from 5,000 to 8,000. Gen. Sooy Smith's cooperating cavalry reportedly liberated about another 1,000. See John F. Marszalek, *Sherman: A Soldier's Passion for Order* (New York: Free Press, 1993), 255; Report of Maj. Gen. William T. Sherman, 27 February 1864, *OR* 32/1:173; Sally Jenkins and John Stauffer, *The State of Jones: The Small Southern County That Seceded from the Confederacy* (New York: Doubleday, 2009), 168.

31. Dispatches, Sherman to Grant, 19 January 1864, *OR* 32/2:146; Sherman to D. D. Porter, 19 January 1864, *OR* 32/2:147; Sherman to Nathaniel Banks, 16 January 1864, *OR* 32/2:113.

32. Jack Friend, *West Wind, Flood Tide: The Battle of Mobile Bay* (Annapolis: Naval Institute Press, 2004), 42–43.

33. Dispatch, Grant to Halleck, 15 January 1864, *OR* 32/2:99–101.

34. Robert S. Henry, *"First with the Most" Forrest* (Indianapolis: Bobbs-Merrill, 1944), 220; Dispatch, William Sooy Smith to Sherman, *OR* 32/2:251.

35. Grant, *Personal Memoirs*, 2:108–109. Forrest's warrior effectiveness may have depended in part on cosmetics. A soldier in the ranks with an eye for the telling detail noticed one day that the nearly white-haired cavalryman blackened his beard; the soldier supposed the fortyish Forrest "gets dye enough from Memphis to keep it so." Letter, Walter to Cousin Susan, 28 January 1864, private collection of Nathaniel Hughes, Chattanooga, Tennessee.

36. William T. Sherman, *Memoirs of General William T. Sherman by Himself* (Bloomington: Indiana University Press, 1957), 1:389–390.

37. Dispatch, LP to Samuel Cooper, 26 January 1864, *OR* 32/2:616–617..

38. Wirt Adams notified Polk of similar "reliable information" on January 23. Dispatch, Adams to Thomas Jack, 23 January 1864, *OR* 32/2:607. Crist writes that Nathan Bedford Forrest's chief of scouts reported rumors "as early as 8 January of Union plans to advance from Memphis and Vicksburg." *PJD*, 10:224, n. 8.

39. Dispatch, LP to Samuel Cooper, 26 January 1864, *OR* 32/2:616.

40. Dispatch, Sherman to Grant, 24 January 1864, in Brooks D. Simpson and Jean V. Berlin, eds., *Sherman's Civil War: Selected Correspondence of William T. Sherman, 1860–1865* (Chapel Hill: University of North Carolina Press, 1999), 589. The version of the dispatch in *OR* 32/2:201 renders "meet me" as "beat me." The Simpson and Berlin version is found, too, in Simon, *Papers of Ulysses S. Grant*, 10:22.

41. Dispatches, LP to Davis, 31 January 1864, *OR* 32/2:637; Thomas Rosser to Thomas Jack, 27 January 1864, *OR* 32/2:626. Also see Hughes and Stonesifer, *Life and Wars of Gideon Pillow*, 279.

42. Dispatch, Sherman to Commanding Officer at Columbus, Kentucky, 2 February 1864, *OR* 32/2:315–316; Stephen Lee, Meridian report, *OR* 32/1:365–367; Jack Hurst, *Nathan Bedford Forrest: A Biography* (New York: Knopf, 1993), 148. Several other accounts of Smith's expedition into Mississippi are in Moore, *Rebellion Record*, 8:469–495.

43. M. Bearss, *Sherman's Forgotten Campaign*, 243; Special Field Orders No. 11, Sherman, *Memoirs of General Sherman*, 1:450.

44. Arthur W. Bergeron Jr., *Confederate Mobile* (Jackson: University Press of Mississippi, 1991), 130.

45. Stephen D. Lee, "Sherman's Meridian Expedition," *SHSP* 8 (1880): 49–61. Written in 1879, Lee's magazine article was meant to controvert an address delivered to the society by Brig. Gen. James R. Chalmers. In it, Chalmers extolled his commander Nathan Bedford Forrest for his significant role against Sherman's Meridian Campaign while, in the same context slighting Polk, mentioning him but once. James R. Chalmers, "Forrest and His Campaigns," *SHSP* 7 (1879): 451–486. Still, Lee's claim that Polk "from the first cunningly meant to entrap Sherman in Alabama" is evident neither in Polk's own accounts of the campaign nor in Stephen Lee's own official *OR* report, which he wrote for Polk in April 1864. Bearss scoffs at Lee's assertion that Polk "outgeneraled Sherman." M. Bearss, *Sherman's Forgotten Campaign*, 240.

46. Lee, "Sherman's Meridian Expedition," 58.

47. Dispatches, LP to Thomas Jack, 28 January 1864, and Col. Thomas Rosser to Jack, 7 January 1864, *OR* 32/2:626, 629.

48. Dispatches, Loring to Stephen D. Lee, 31 January 1864; Lee to Thomas Jack, 1 February 1864; *OR* 32/2:637, 648.

49. Dispatch, Sherman to Maj. Gen. Halleck, 29 February 1864, *OR* 32/2:498.

50. Dispatch, LP to War Department, 22 February 1864, *OR* 32/2:338.

51. Samuel G. French, *Two Wars: An Autobiography* (Nashville: Confederate Veteran Press, 1901), 185, Diary entry, "December 24 [1863]."

52. Dispatch, W. D. Gale to Samuel French, 22 January 1864, *OR* 32/2:601.

53. Dispatches, LP to Gen. Samuel Cooper, and LP to Stephen Lee, 1 February 1864, *OR* 32/2:648.

54. Dispatches, French to William Loring, 5 February 1864; French to LP, 5 February 1864; *OR* 32/2:677, 676. Report of Lt. Col. John H. Howe, 124th Illinois Infantry, *OR* 32/1:235.

55. Letter, Sherman to Ellen Ewing Sherman, 7 February 1864, in Simpson and Berlin, *Sherman's Civil War*, 602. From Jackson, Sherman wrote this during his return toward Vicksburg.

56. Sherman's Meridian campaign report, *OR* 32/2:175; M. Bearss, *Sherman's Forgotten Campaign*, 59.

57. Dispatch, Sherman to Brig Gen. J. M. Tuttle, 6 February 1864, *OR* 32/2:340.

58. Lee, "Sherman's Meridian Expedition," 52. In Lee's official report, he says Ross's Texans with their six-shooters fought the enemy at "20 paces." *OR* 32/1:365.

59. Dispatches, Stephen Lee to LP, 4 February 1864, *OR* 32/1:357; James Coates to Lawrence Ross, 4 March 1864, *OR* 32/1:327; Lawrence Ross to Brig Gen. W. H. Jackson, 5 March 1864, *OR* 32/1:385–386. Letter, William Gale to Kate Polk Gale, 7 April 1864, GPP.

60. Stephen Lee, Meridian campaign report, 18 April 1864, *OR* 32/1:365.

61. Wirt Adams report, 12 March 1864, *OR* 32/1:371–374.

62. Dispatch, LP to Loring, 5 February 1864, *OR* 32/2:676. Polk's various orders cannot always be reconciled with Stephen Lee's recollections of the events.

63. Dispatch, LP to Gen. Dabney Maury [Col. Henry Maury's brother], 7 February 1864, *OR* 32/2:688.

64. Stephen Lee, Meridian campaign report, *OR* 32/1:366.

65. FAP, "Memoir," 49–50. St. Anna's was situated not far from where the Polks had lived in the 1850s.

66. Dispatch, Thomas Jack to Maj. Gen. John Forney, 8 February 1864, *OR* 32/2:695.

67. Stephen Lee, Meridian campaign report, 18 April 1864, *OR* 32/1:365–366; Dispatch, Lee to LP, 10 February 1864, *OR* 32/1:358; Dispatch, Thomas Jack to John Forney, 8 February 1864, *OR* 32/2:695.

68. Dispatch, Capt. Lucius M. Rose to Capt. O. H. Howard, 8 March 1864, *OR* 32/2:222.

69. M. Bearss, *Sherman's Forgotten Campaign*, 109, quoting William Pitts Chambers, 46th Mississippi Infantry.

70. Dispatches, William Loring to LP, 12 February 1864, and LP to William Loring, 12 February 1864, *OR* 32/2:722, 724, and 725.

71. French, *Two Wars*, 189; Dispatch, Lee to LP, 11 February 1864, *OR* 32/2:718–719; Dispatches, Lee to LP, 10 and 11 February 1864, *OR* 32/1:358–359.

72. Dispatch, Lee to LP, 10 February 1864, *OR* 32/1:358.

73. M. Bearss, *Sherman's Forgotten Campaign*, 116.

74. Samuel French, *Two Wars*, 189–190. Excerpts from his diary were published by French years later. Often critical of Polk, French may have doctored his diary entry after the fact.

75. Dispatches, Thomas Jack to John H. Forney, 8 February 1864; LP to T. F. Sevier, 8 February 1864, "12 at night"; *OR* 32/2:695.

76. Dispatch, LP to D. H. Maury, 9 February 1864, *OR* 32/2:701.

77. Dispatch, Davis to LP, 13 February 1864 [received 15 February], *OR* 32/2:729. Not content with that, Davis on February 16 advised Polk once again how to prevent Sherman's "reaching Mobile." He urged him, too, to "beware lest his movement in that direction be a feint and his real purpose be to move eastward" (751).

78. Dispatches, LP to D. H. Maury and Maury to Samuel Cooper, both 9 February 1864, *OR* 32/2:701.

79. Dispatch, LP to William Loring, 12 February 1864, *OR* 32/2:723–724.

80. French, *Two Wars*, 189–190. On the day of Polk's death on Pine Mountain in Georgia, French would write more charitably in his diary: "Thus died a gentleman and a high Church dignitary. As a soldier he was more theoretical than practical" (202).

81. Letter, William Gale to Kate Polk Gale, 18 February 1864, GPP. For three Army of Tennessee generals on night duty away in Dalton, Georgia, the bad news telegraphed from Alabama was hard to assimilate. Joseph Johnston's chief of staff, Brig. Gen. William W. Mackall, would give this account of the "amusing scene" involving him, Johnston, and Brig. Gen. Benjamin Ewell, Johnston's adjutant general: "I [had] left my glasses at home; Joe had mislaid his, and there was only one pair to the three [of us], when some important dispatches came in. Joe read a little, then I took the glasses and read a little, and finally he went to bed, and left Ewell and myself to put [the dispatches] in cipher. I would take [the glasses] to write, then Ewell to decipher, and so we worked along till twelve at night. We are anxious about General Polk's movements." William

W. Mackall, *A Son's Recollections of His Father* (New York: Dutton, 1930), 204. An illustration of the Confederate cipher "dictionaries" Mackall might have used can be found in Beauregard, "Campaign of Shiloh," 581.

82. Sherman report, 27 February 1864, *OR* 32/1:173.

83. Meridian report of Capt. Andrew Hickenlooper, 25 March 1864, *OR* 32/1:217. Local tradition in Meridian holds that Polk's headquarters cottage survived the war and was subsequently incorporated into a twenty-room mansion known as Merrehope.

84. Sherman report on Meridian expedition, 7 March 1864, *OR* 32/1:176; Richard L. Howard, *History of the 124th Regiment Illinois Infantry* (Springfield, IL: H. W. Rokker, 1880), 195–196.

85. Dispatch, G. M. Dodge to Maj. Gen. J. B. McPherson, 8 April 1864, *OR* 32/3:294; Letter, William Gale to Kate Polk Gale, 18 February 1864, GPP.

86. *LPBG*, 2:327; Dispatches, LP to Forrest and LP to Stephen Lee, both 20 February 1864, *OR* 32/2:779, 781.

87. Robert S. Henry, *As They Saw Forrest* (Jackson, TN: McCowat-Mercer Press, 1956), 151; Hurst, *Nathan Bedford Forrest*, 155–156; Lee, Meridian report, *OR* 32/1:367–368.

88. Letter, William T. Sherman to Ellen E. Sherman, 10 March 1864; Simpson and Berlin, eds., *Sherman's Civil War*, 605.

89. Letter, LP to FAP, March 9 1864, GPP. For Polk as the ablest Civil War general at utilizing railroads, see Jeffrey N. Lash, *Destroyer of the Iron Horse: General Joseph E. Johnston and Confederate Rail Transport, 1861–1865* (Kent: Kent State University Press, 1991), foreword and 138.

90. LP, General Orders No. 22, 26 February 1864, and Special Orders No. 63, 3 March 1864, *OR* 32/1:345, 356. Letter, Sherman to Ellen Ewing Sherman, 10 March 1864, in M. A. DeWolfe Howe, ed., *Home Letters of General Sherman* (New York: Scribner's, 1909), 284.

26. Presidential Adviser—Army Strategies and Naval Plots (1864)

1. Dispatch, First Lt. A. H. Polk [*sic*] to Lt. Col. Theodore F. Sevier, 3 March 1864, *OR* 32/3:579. Sevier was an inspector general on Polk's staff. The *OR* incorrectly attributes the damage assessment to A. H. Polk, Meck's brother. See *LPBG*, 2:346. See also dispatch, LP to Gen. S. Cooper, 3 March 1864, *OR* 32/3:580.

2. Letter, Judge R. S. Hudson to Jefferson Davis and forwarded to LP, 14 March 1864, *OR* 32/3:625.

3. Dispatch, LP to French, 24 April 1864, *OR* 32/3:825.

4. Dispatch, LP to Hodge, 28 April 1864, *OR* 32/3:836–837.

5. General Orders No. 43, 10 March 1864, *OR* 32/3:611.

6. *A Proclamation of Amnesty Made at the Behest of the Mississippi Legislature*, Demopolis (AL), 16 April 1864. See, similarly, Col. Robert Lowry's proclamation "To the Citizens of Smith County," 10 April 1864, *OR* 52/2:658. Dispatch, Thomas M. Jack to Col. J. S. Scott, 25 April 1864, *OR* 32/3:819–820.

7. Dispatch, LP to Davis, 21 March 1864, *OR* 32/3:663; Jenkins and Stauffer, *State of Jones*, 193; Bynum, *Free State of Jones*, 118–119; Dispatch, Thomas M. Jack to Col. Robert Lowry, 25 April 1864, *OR* 32/3:820.

8. Dispatch, Col. George B. Hodge to Gen. S. Cooper, 2 May 1864, *OR* 39/2:571.

9. Dispatch, LP to Hodge, 28 April 1864, *OR* 32/3:836–837. Letter, LP to "My dear daughter," 11 June 1864. In his biography, William Polk changed his father's words to "the power of the Confederacy is not dead, but is not only living, but moving." *LPBG*, 2:339.

10. Dispatch, George William Brent to Bragg, 1 May 1864, *OR* 39/2:565–566.

11. Dispatch, LP to James Chalmers, 2 May 1864, *OR* 39/2:575.

12. Letters, William Gale to Kate Polk Gale, 7 and 29 April 1864, GPP.

13. Dispatch, Johnston to Bragg, 27 February 1864, *OR* 32/2:809.

14. Letter, LP to Davis, 28 February 1864, *OR* 32/2:813; Letter, William Gale to "My Darling Kate," 30 July 1864. Suggesting the influential role he must have played shaping Polk's counsels, Stephen Lee urged Polk on April 25 to reconsider (and act on) *"my recommendation* for mounting such an invasion of Tennessee behind Sherman's army." Dispatch, Lee to Thomas Jack, 25 April 1864, *OR* 32/3:822.

15. Cast aside, perhaps, but not lost. The letter appears in *OR* 32/2:813. Jefferson Davis's next letter *to* General Polk was written in April, finding fault with his ineffective suppression of guerrilla activity in western Mississippi's Adams, Williams, and Felicia Counties. See *PJD*, 10:382–383.

16. Letters, Col. Thomas J. Reid Jr. to Jefferson Davis, 8 January 1864, *OR* 34/2:846–848; G. W. C. Lee to LP, 9 January 1864, *OR* 34/2:846. Still pushing his idea, Reid would write Davis again, on 29 August 1864, *PJD*, 10:629. The CSS *Virginia* was formerly the USS *Merrimac*. Rechristened by the Confederates after her capture, the vessel is best remembered by her previous name. *New York Times*, 10 April 1865, page 1.

17. Unsigned letter, New Orleans clergyman to LP, 16 May 1864. See also Letter, Charles Goodrich et al. to Brig. Gen. Shepley, 2 October 1862 and Letter, LP to Davis, 21 March 1864, *OR* 34/2:1064–1067.

18. Letter, Stephen Elliott to LP, 8 January 1864.

19. Letter, LP to Davis, 21 March 1864, *OR* 34/2:1064; Lee, "Sherman's Meridian Expedition," 50.

20. Dispatch, Col. George B. Hodge to Gen. S. Cooper, 2 May 1864, *OR* 39/2:568–571. Inspector general Hodge summarized Polk's scheme in his report to the War Department in Richmond.

21. Dispatch, Capt. John C. Kay, Commanding River Rangers, to LP, 14 January 1864, *OR* 52/2:599–601.

22. Gary Joiner, *Mr. Lincoln's Brown Water Navy: The Mississippi Squadron* (Lanham, MD: Rowman & Littlefield, 2007), 67–68.

23. Letter, LP to Davis, 21 March 1864, *OR* 34/2:1064–1067. Alfred Ellet was a formidable family name in the Civil War. Alfred and his brother Charles, who had developed the Ram Fleet, manned these vessels that won the Battle of Memphis against conventional Confederate gunboats. Now Alfred commanded a fleet of riverboats charged with sweeping the Mississippi's banks clear of Confederate guerrillas and other troublesome sorts. For up-to-date histories of the Ellets, see Hearn, *Ellet's Brigade*, and Joiner, *Mr. Lincoln's Brown Water Navy*.

24. Dispatch, Lt. Col. Fred. B. Brand to Jefferson Davis, 9 April 1865, *OR* ser. 4, 3:1180. See also Napier Bartlett, "Capture of the Federal Ironclad Gunboat *Indianola*," *Military Record of Louisiana* (New Orleans: L. Graham & Company, 1875).

25. Capt. John C. Kay, who had proposed with Polk to enlist guerrillas along the Mississippi, was at least granted permission to form a small group of irregulars by the War Department in March. His compensation was to be 50 percent of the value of enemy property destroyed. J. A. Seddon, 12 March 1864, *OR* ser. 4, 3:210.

26. Endorsement, Bragg to Davis, 26 April 1864, written on LP's letter to Davis, 21 March 1864. *PJD*, 10:288.

27. Dispatch, Davis to LP, 3 May 1864, *OR* 52/2:665. Scarcely slackening the arduous pace he kept up as president, Davis was writing Polk shortly after his five-year-old son Joseph Evan Davis had fallen from a porch at the Executive Mansion onto pavement; he died a few hours later, the night of April 30. There is no record that Polk sent the Davises condolences, though it seems most unlikely that he would have failed to do so.

28. Jesse C. Burt, "Sherman's Logistics and Andrew Johnson," *THQ* 15 (1956): 205.

29. James R. Rusling, *Men and Things I Saw in Civil War Days* (New York: Eaton & Mains, 1899), 184; William Sherman, Atlanta campaign report, *OR* 38/1:62.

30. Walter T. Durham, *Reluctant Partners: Nashville and the Union* (Nashville: Tennessee Historical Society, 1987), ch. 7; James A. Hoobler, *Cities Under the Gun: Images of Occupied Nashville and Chattanooga* (Nashville: Rutledge Hill Press, 1986); Rusling, *Men and Things I Saw*, 188.

27. "Old Friends Pleased to See Me Here" (1864)

1. Dispatch, LP to Davis, 18 April 1864, *OR* 32/3:790.

2. Dispatch, Forrest to LP, 15 April 1864, *OR* 32/1:609; Proclamation, James Chalmers to Soldiers, 20 April 1864, *OR* 32/1:623; Dispatch, LP to Forrest, 24 April 1864, *OR* 32/1:619. Documented accounts of the Fort Pillow massacre are found in Richard L. Fuchs, *An Unerring Fire: The Massacre at Fort Pillow* (Rutherford, NJ: Fairleigh Dickinson University Press, 1994); John Cimprich and Robert C. Mainfort Jr., "Fort Pillow Massacre: A Statistical Note," *Journal of American History* 76 (1989): 830–837; and Albert Castel, *Winning and Losing in the Civil War* (Columbia: University of South Carolina Press, 1996), 35ff.

3. Dispatch, Davis to LP, 23 April 1864, *PJD*, 10:359.

4. Dispatch, Bragg to Davis, 26 April 1864, *OR* 32/3:791. Another general high on Bragg's distaste list was John C. Breckinridge. After the war Bragg wrote a friend: "In France or Germany, either [Cheatham or Breckinridge] would have been shot in six hours. With us they pass for heroes." Losson, *Tennessee's Forgotten Warriors*, 131.

5. Dispatch, Samuel Hurlburt to James B. McPherson, 19 April 1864, *OR* 32/3:419.

6. Albert Castel, *Decision in the West: The Atlanta Campaign of 1864* (Lawrence: University Press of Kansas, 1992), 120. "Bishop's Address," *Journal of Eighteenth Convention in Diocese of Louisiana* (1858), 21.

7. Situated in a high-ground terrain ideal for signal observations, Lieutenant Howgate, with another signal officer, had a few weeks earlier broken the wigwag code the Confederates were using at Dalton. As the US general Albert Myer wrote in a postwar account of Signal Department operations: "Every [Confederate] item of information conveying valuable hints to our commanders was promptly deciphered and delivered almost as quickly in our Headquarters as in those of the enemy." Myer report, *Supple-*

ment to the OR, 10:622. Also see John E. Hoover, "Introduction" to Myer Report, *Supplement to the OR*, 10:279–292. Dispatch, Thomas to Sherman, 13 April 1864, *OR* 32/3:341.

8. Sherman, Atlanta campaign report, 15 September 1864, *OR* 38/1:63; Nathaniel C. Hughes, *Jefferson Davis in Blue: The Life of Sherman's Relentless Warrior* (Baton Rouge: Louisiana State University Press, 2002); 238; Wheeler, Reports, 1 June 1864, *OR* 38/3:944.

9. Letter extract, 2 May 1864, in Mackall, *A Son's Recollections*, 208.

10. Dispatch, Maj. Gen. George H. Thomas to Maj. Gen. Sherman, 22 April 1864, *OR* 32/3:444.

11. The number of Polk's cavalry was 6,000 according to Craig Symonds in *Stonewall of the West: Patrick Cleburne and the Civil War* (Lawrence: University Press of Kansas, 1997), 206; *LPBG*, 2:348. The running correspondence is found in *OR* 38/4:684, 733–737. Bragg on May 23, 1864, disputed Polk's claim that Davis had authorized Polk's decision, but whether from misunderstandings, or willfulness, or hindsight the generals and the president remembered the details of Polk's move to Georgia in different, seemingly self-serving, ways (737). Also see Castel, *Decision in the West*, 127, and Connelly, *Autumn of Glory*, 332.

12. Philip L. Secrist, *The Battle of Resaca: Atlanta Campaign, 1864* (Macon, GA: Mercer University Press, 1998), 5. A photograph of the covered bridge is on page 45.

13. Richard McMurry, *Atlanta 1864: Last Chance for the Confederacy* (Lincoln: University of Nebraska Press, 2000), 63–66. An interesting analysis of Sherman's indirect methods and their impact upon later warfare is in James M. McPherson's "Blitzkrieg in Georgia," *The New York Review of Books* 47 (30 November 2000): 36–38.

14. McMurry, *Atlanta 1864*, 67; Castel, *Decision in the West*, 150.

15. French, *Two Wars*, 193.

16. William Gale, "Diary," 9, 10, and 11 May. An eighteen-page typescript of Gale's dairy, covering the period of May 7–June 14, 1864, is in the University of the South Archives. The entries were written sometimes in the present tense, other times in the past tense; it is not clear whether they were written on a daily basis, were recollections written later, or are a combination of both. Also see Lash, *Destroyer of the Iron Horse*, 138. Lash calls Polk the "most enterprising and successful [Civil War] railroad general."

17. Letter, LP to FAP, 27 May 1864. Polk and Lieutenant Gale were unaware until the mail caught up with them that, in Asheville, Kate Polk Gale had given birth to a girl on May 10. Mother and father contrived the name "Leonide" for the infant. "I think the name very pretty," the child's namesake would say when he next wrote Fanny on May 27. Letter, LP to Fanny, 27 May 1864. See also Letter, Lilly Polk Huger to William M. Polk, 29 October 1866.

18. Dispatches, LP to Davis and LP to Johnston, 10 May 1864, *OR* 38/4:688.

19. Letters, LP to FAP, 21 May 1864; Charles Gallway to "My dear Willie," 14 June 1864.

20. F. Jay Taylor, ed., *Reluctant Rebel: The Secret Diary of Robert Patrick* (Baton Rouge: Louisiana State University Press, 1959), 164–165, entries for May 11 and 12; Lt. T. B. Mackall, "Journal of Operations of the Army of Tennessee, May 14–June 4, 1864," *OR* 38/3:984, entry for May 31. See also R. S. Bevier, *History of the First and Second Missouri Confederate Brigades* (St. Louis: Bryan, Brand & Company, 1879), 235.

21. The brigadier generals with Polk (in addition to Hood) were James Cantey, J. Warren Grigsby, and Alfred J. Vaughan Jr., plus Maj. Gen. William H. Martin.

22. C. Vann Woodward, ed., *Mary Chesnut's Civil War* (New Haven: Yale University Press, 1981), 731; Letter, Lt. Thomas J. Stokes to "My Dear Sister," 28 April 1864, in Editors of Time-Life Books, *Voices of the Civil War: Atlanta* (Alexandria, VA: Time-Life, 1996), 21; Dispatch, John Bell Hood to Douglas West, 16 June 1864, GPP. A facsimile of Hood's note to West is reproduced in Jerry Frey, *In the Woods Before Dawn: The Samuel Richey Collection of the Southern Confederacy* (Gettysburg, PA: Thomas Publications, 1994), 153.

23. McMurry, *John Bell Hood*, 102. In August, Hood would be confirmed in the Episcopal Church by Bishop Henry C. Lay, among Polk's friends (142).

24. *The Book of Common Prayer and Administration of the Sacraments and Other Rites and Ceremonies of the Church, According to the Use of the Protestant Episcopal Church in the United States of America* (Philadelphia: Hall & Sellers, 1790). It seems likely Bishop Polk was using one of the recently published Confederate prayer books imported from England by blockade runners. The text of these books was identical to the authorized 1790 edition except for word changes on the title page, as well as three prayers for the "President of the Confederate States of America." See G. MacLaren Brydon, "The Confederate Prayer Book," *HMPEC* 17:339ff; *LPBG*, 2:354.

25. C. Vann Woodward, ed., *Mary Chesnut's Civil War*, 616. Hood's dependence upon Polk the bishop was not equated to Polk the general. McMurry points out that "once he joined the army in Georgia, Polk, like [William] Hardee, often found himself ignored by Johnston, who continued to consult and rely heavily on Hood." McMurry, *Atlanta 1864*, 68.

26. William Gale "Diary," 11 May 1864.

27. William Gale "Diary," 12 May 1864.

28. Dispatch, W. W. Mackall to LP, 12 May 1864, *OR* 38/4:698.

29. Letter, William Gale to Kate Polk Gale, 27 May 1864, GPP. Gale credited enemy sharpshooters with the near misses. Letter, LP to FAP, 21 May 1864; Letter, Henry Watterson to Rebecca Ewing, 12 June 1864, Filson Historical Society. In another version of the anecdote, General Polk is quoted as saying: "Come! we may as well take ourselves back to the front." *LPBG*, 2:353. A slightly different *third* version is in J. Cutler Andrews, *The South Reports the Civil War* (Princeton, NJ: Princeton University Press, 1970), 447, quoting the *Augusta Daily Constitutionalist*, 21 June 1864.

30. Letter, William Gale to Kate Polk Gale, 27 May 1864, GPP.

31. Sydney Kerksis, *The Atlanta Papers* (Dayton, OH: Morningside, 1980), 6; Letter, William Gale to Kate Polk Gale, 14 May 1864, GPP; W. W. Loring, Resaca report, *OR* 34/3:875.

32. Donald B. Connelly, *John M. Schofield and the Politics of Generalship* (Chapel Hill: University of North Carolina Press, 2006), 96; Castel, *Decision in the West*, 150–160, 197. The brigadier was Henry Moses Judah, a West Point graduate in 1843.

33. Maj. Gen. John A. Logan, Atlanta campaign report, 13 September 1864, *OR* 38/3:93–94. Lt. T. B. Mackall's account of this assault on Polk's line is found in *OR* 38/3:979–980.

34. Castel, *Decision in the West*, 167–168.

35. Maj. Gen John A. Logan, Resaca report, 13 September 1864, *OR* 38/3:93–94; William Gale "Diary," entry for "14th, Saturday [14 May 1864]"; McMurry, *Atlanta 1864*, 70; Mackall, "Journal of Operations," *OR* 38/3:979.

36. Reports of William T. Sherman, 8 June 1864, *OR* 38/1:59, 64.

37. Private Robert H. Strong, 105th Illinois Infantry, Editors of Time-Life Books, *Voices of the Civil War*, 47.

38. Richard M. McMurry, "Resaca: 'A Heap of Hard Fiten,'" *CWTI* 9 (November 1970): 4–14; Philip Lee Secrist, "Battle of Resaca," in David S. Heidler and Jeanne T. Heidler, eds., *Encyclopedia of the American Civil War* (Santa Barbara, CA: ABC-CLIO, 2000), 4:1630; Secrist, *The Battle of Resaca*, 57; Letter, Jefferson Davis to William Gale, 30 July 1864.

39. Letter, LP to FAP, 21 May 1864, in *LPBG*, 2:363.

40. Gale, "Diary," "Monday 16"; Letter, William Gale to Kate Polk Gale, 27 May 1864, GPP.

41. Gale, "Diary," "Tuesday 17."

42. Wheeler, Resaca report, *OR* 38/3:945.

43. Gale, "Diary," 18 May; French, *Two Wars*, 195.

44. Gale "Diary," 18 May; Letter extract, 18 May 1864, in Mackall, *A Son's Recollections*, 210. Polk's wartime communion set was sold at auction in New York in 2005. Hood's and Johnston's baptisms apparently inclined William Hardee toward religion, too. Already baptized, he would shortly have Bishop Polk confirm him as a communicant of the Church. Hughes, *General William J. Hardee*, 209.

45. See, e.g., Richard M. McMurry, "The Mackall Journal and Its Antecedents," *CWH* 20 (1974): 315–316. As Mackall was on Johnston's staff, McMurry posits Johnston influenced the journal's bias against Hood.

46. Letter extract, 18 May 1864, Mackall, *A Son's Recollections*, 210.

47. Lee Kennett, *Sherman: A Soldier's Life* (New York: HarperCollins, 2001), 13. To the mortification of some Cassvillians in the 1860s, the town was named for Lewis Cass, a noted Yankee politician. Just after the start of the Civil War an attempt was made to change the town's name to Manassas, site of the Confederates' early big victory in Virginia.

48. Johnston maintained for years that Hood had overreacted to a "false report." Later evidence proved that a Yankee brigade, lost on back roads, was indeed behind Hood. See Symonds, *Joseph E. Johnston*, 293.

49. Letter, Joseph E. Johnston to William Gale, 24 May 1869, in *LPBG*, 2:357. Johnston's hindsight confidence in Polk and Johnston's antipathy toward Hood resembles Jefferson Davis's saying that, had Polk been in command at Resaca, he would have prevailed where Johnston had failed.

50. Mackall, "Journal of Operations," *OR* 38/3:984.

51. Letter, Walter J. Morris to William M. Polk, 25 June 1878. William Polk quotes Morris in *LPBG*, 2:378. Richard McMurry, in what he terms "one of the strangest [days] of the war," provides a chronology of the day, along with a description of the lay of the land, in his "Cassville," *CWTI* 10 (1971): 4.

52. Letter, J. E. Johnston to William Gale, 24 May 1869, quoted by *LPBG*, 2:356. The letter, answering one from Gale, seems intended to corroborate Gale's own recollections of the day and night of May 19, 1864. Contra Gale, Richard McMurry says Polk's headquarters was the "little cabin of William McKelvey. The McKelveys had fled south." "Cassville," 4–5.

53. Thomas Connelly indicts just about everyone involved in the conference—if not for misremembering, then for fabricating facts. *Autumn of Glory*, 348–352.

54. Horn, *Army of Tennessee*, 329; McMurry, *John Bell Hood*, 109. Johnston's letter to Gale does not mention either Hood or Polk that night urging an attack rather than a withdrawal. Johnston does write to Gale (albeit ambiguously), "You say truly that General Polk advocated offensive fighting," but whether he was generalizing or was referring to Polk's advice that night is not clear. In any case, such a detail of the events on the night of 19–20 May is missing from Joseph E. Johnston, *Narrative of Military Operations* (New York: Appleton, 1874).

55. John Bell Hood, *Advance and Retreat: Personal Experiences in the United States and Confederate States Armies* (New Orleans: Hood Orphan Memorial Fund, 1880), 108. Letter, J. E. Johnston to Charles G. Johnson, 19 June 1874, *SHSP* 21 (1893): 319–320.

56. Letter, Johnston to Lydia Johnston, his wife, 16 May 1864, quoted by McMurry, *Atlanta 1864*, 94–95.

57. Letter extract, 21 May 1864, Mackall, *A Son's Recollections*, 211. Gale, "Diary," 20 May. Gale's quotation was roughly correct: in *The Day is Done*, Longfellow had written: "And the night shall be filled with music, / And the cares, that infest the day, / Shall fold their tents, like the Arabs, / And as silently steal away."

58. *LPBG*, 2:362–363.

59. Stanley P. Hirshon, *The White Tecumseh* (New York: John Wiley & Sons, 1997), 226.

28. *"Were It Not to Defend Our Soil and Families, I Should Fear the Curse of God" (1864)*

1. William Gale, "Diary," Sunday, 22 May 1864; *LPBG*, 2:357–358. The typescript of Gale's diary among the Leonidas Polk Papers is considerably condensed compared to William Polk's quotation. K. Jack Bauer, ed., *Soldiering: The Civil War Diary of Rice C. Bull, 123rd New York Volunteers Infantry* (San Rafael, CA: Presidio Press, 1970), 113.

2. Mackall, "Journal of Operations," Sunday, 22 May 1864, *OR* 38/3:985; Circular, Douglas West, 23 May 1864, *OR* 38/4:738.

3. Letters, Hamilton Polk to LP, 25 May 1864; LP to FAP, 27 May 1864, both in LP Papers.

4. Gale, "Diary," "Saturday [May] 21st" and "Tuesday 24." In condensing quotations from Gale's diary, I have omitted showing ellipses.

5. John E. McKay, "Atlanta Campaign," in Heidler and Heidler, *Encyclopedia of the American Civil War*, 1:134.

6. Letters, Sherman to Ellen Ewing Sherman, 22 May 1864 and 10 March 1964, in Howe, *Home Letters of General Sherman*, 293 and 284.

7. Mackall, "Journal of Operations," Monday, 23 May 1864, *OR* 38/3:986.

8. Nathaniel Hughes, ed., *The Civil War Memoir of Philip Daingerfield Stephenson* (Baton Rouge: Louisiana State University Press, 1995), 186–187.

9. Elliott, *Soldier of Tennessee*, 189.

10. Gale, "Diary," "Wednesday 25."

11. Mackall, *A Son's Recollections*, 211.

12. Ambrose Bierce, "The Crime at Pickett's Mill," *The Collected Works of Ambrose Bierce* (New York: Neale Publishing Company, 1909), 1:287. The essay was written in 1888.

13. Symonds, *Stonewall of the West*, 214.

14. Gale, "Diary," "Friday the 27th" and "Saturday the 28th."

15. *LPBG*, 2:359; Circular, LP to divisions, 28 May 1864, *OR* 38/4:746.

16. Castel, *Decision in the West*, 272; *LPBG*, 2:359–360; Gale, "Diary," "Sunday 5th."

17. Gale, "Diary," "Monday 6," and "Tuesday, 7th;"; *LPBG*, 2:369. The description of the flag was provided by Stephen Elliott in a letter to his wife on June 16, the day after Polk's death. Elliott says he was told of the flag by William Gale, who in his diary quoted Polk's description of the flag as "Purity upon a field of blood." Elliott's letter photocopy is in the University of the South Archives.

18. Letter, LP to Stephen Elliott, 15 August 1863. Writing to Jefferson Davis on June 22, Hardee recalled Polk's words from "only a day or two before his decease." *PJD*, 10:478.

19. Letter, Gallway to "My Dear Willie," 14–15 June 1864.

20. Lewis Wynne and Robert Taylor, eds., *This War So Horrible: The Civil War Diary of Hiram Smith Williams* (Tuscaloosa: University of Alabama Press, 1993), 89.

21. Gale, "Diary," "Sunday 12." The account of the worship service is a compilation of excerpts from Gale's "Diary" and *LPBG*, 2:370. Though neither mentions the Holy Communion service specifically, an exceptional worship service seems clearly meant by Lieutenant Gale. Furthermore, Aristide Hopkins, another lieutenant on Polk's staff, says that on the following Tuesday (the day of Polk's death) Polk had "said morning prayers as usual that morning." Aristide Hopkins, "Address to United Sons of Confederate Veterans," Beauregard Chapter, New Orleans, 10 April 1907, typescript, Aristide Hopkins Collection, Tulane University.

22. Hughes, *Civil War Memoir*, 189.

23. Nathaniel C. Hughes, *The Pride of the Confederate Artillery: The Washington Artillery in the Army of Tennessee* (Baton Rouge: Louisiana State University Press, 1997), 188.

24. Letter, LP to Miss F. D. Polk, 11 June 1864. Polk was presumably referring to a collapsible telescope.

25. Dispatches, LP to Jefferson Davis, Joseph Johnston to Davis, 13 June 1864, *OR* 38/4:774, 772; Bragg to Davis, 14 June 1864, in *PJD*, 10:464.

26. See McMurry, *Atlanta 1864*, 98–99.

27. Letters, Charles Gallway to "My Dear Willie," 14–15 June 1864; LP to Lillie Huger, 13 June 1864, in *LPBG*, 2:367.

28. Letter, R. L. Gibson to FAP, 26 December 1873. In his letter to Polk's widow, Gibson added: "I do not give his words perhaps exactly, but as much as my memory, filled with many sad scenes, may retain of that after-midnight conversation in bed." Gibson was later a member of the US Congress.

29. Irving A. Buck, *Cleburne and His Command* (Jackson, TN: McCowat-Mercer Press, 1959), 222–223. As assistant adjutant general to Cleburne, Buck was most likely Cleburne's unnamed companion on Pine Mountain.

30. Noll, *Doctor Quintard*, 98–99.

31. Hopkins, "Address to United Sons of Confederate Veterans"; Hughes, *Civil War Memoir*, 189.

32. *Confederate Veteran* 8 (1900): 532. Polk's warning eerily resembles Hamilton Polk's admonishing letter to his father a few weeks earlier. Lieutenant Beauregard was a son of Gen. P. G. T. Beauregard; Private Stephenson, a teenager, thought him "young looking and 'frenchified.'"

33. For Dilworth's words and actions, I have relied on his own account in "Statement of Colonel William S. Dilworth, Third Florida Infantry, on the death of General Leonidas Polk, June 14, 1864," *Supplement to the OR* 7:89, and on Albert Castel's detailed "Who Killed the Bishop?" The same essay later appeared as "Death Comes to the Bishop: When Luck Ran Out for Leonidas Polk," in *Articles of War: Winners, Losers, and Some Who Were Both in the Civil War* (Mechanicsburg, PA: Stackpole Books, 2001), 150–160. Dilworth's own statement is interesting in that he prefaces a June 26, 1864, letter to *The Southern Recorder* by saying that none of the previously published reports he had seen "were exactly correct."

34. The journalist, writing for the *Augusta Constitutionalist* and signing himself "Grape," was almost certainly Henry Waterson, reporting from Atlanta and writing "A Full and Circumstantial Account of the Fall of Lt. General Leonidas Polk, Atlanta, June 15, 1864." A handwritten copy of "Grape's" newspaper dispatch is in the Leonidas Polk Papers. The writer says his information had "just been related to me by one of the party who was nearest [Polk] at the moment." Assuming the writer was Henry Watterson (for a family emergency Watterson had shortly before left his staff post with General Johnston and gone to Atlanta), his eyewitness source would have been William Gale.

35. Bauer, *Soldiering: The Civil War Diary of Rice C. Bull*, 126.

36. Hughes, *Civil War Memoir*, 189; Letter, Joseph E. Johnston to Winfield Peters, 25 September 1890, clarifying and correcting a newspaper article Peters had written for the *Baltimore Sun*. Peters sent the letter to William Polk on May 10, 1893.

37. Gale, "Diary," "Tuesday 14th"; Letter, Johnston to Peters, 25 September 1890, in LP Papers.

38. Aristide Hopkins says he learned of these remarks from members of Peter Simonson's Fifth Battery, Light Artillery, Indiana Volunteers. He errs, apparently, attributing the quotation to George Thomas, not thought to be present. Gen. Oliver Otis Howard was the more likely speaker. See Oliver Otis Howard, *Autobiography* (New York: Baker & Taylor, 1907), 1:563.

39. David P. Conyngham, *Sherman's March Through the South* (New York: Sheldon & Company, 1865), 111. Though portions of Captain Conyngham's memoir may resemble storybook prose, this episode with Sherman and Simonson has the ring of verisimilitude. Further, as a professional journalist, as well as an aide-de-camp to Sherman, Conyngham claims in his preface to be an "eye-witness of . . . most of the incidents described" and that he had adhered to "strict fidelity to truth, believing this to be the duty of the historian" (6).

40. Conyngham, *Sherman's March*, 111. Gunners of Battery M, First Illinois Light Artillery, posted beside the Fifth Indiana, take credit, too, for Polk's death: "On the 14th we shelled the mountain, killing Lieutenant General Leonidas Polk." "History of First Light Artillery," *Report of the Adjutant General of the State of Illinois* (Springfield, IL: H. W. Rokker, 1886), 8:666.

41. Letter, William Harrison Polk to William M. Polk, 28 October 1908. Polk began this sentence "Then Stanley said. . . ." As no one with that name is known to have been present, Polk presumably had intended to write "Then Sherman said." Letter, William Harrison Polk to William M. Polk, 21 October 1908. See also William R. Polk, *Polk's Folly: An American Family History* (New York: Doubleday, 2000), 272.

42. Letter, William Harrison Polk to William M. Polk, 28 October 1908. None of William Harrison Polk's account was quoted in William M. Polk's biography. He jotted at the top of the first page of the letter "Not used." And in contrast to Private Polk's recollections of repartee between Simonson and Sherman, Sherman in his official report merely wrote that "during a sharp cannonading from General Howard's right, or General Hooker's left, General Polk was killed on the 14th." Report of Maj. Gen. W. T. Sherman, 15 September 1864, OR 38:1, 67.

43. "Statement of Colonel William S. Dilworth," *Supplement to the OR* 7:89.

44. Elliott, "Occasion of His Death," *Funeral Services at the Burial of Polk*, 5.

45. Hopkins, "Address to United Sons of Confederate Veterans."

46. It was Simonson's brother-*in-law* who had been killed, William H. Polk explained. A Confederate sharpshooter would kill Peter Simonson himself, an esteemed artillery chief, on May 16. See Maj. Gen. David S. Stanley, First Division, Fourth Army Corps, "Operations Report," 3 May–26 July, OR 38/1:223.

47. Gale, "Diary," "Tuesday 14th"; Dispatch, Benjamin Butler to E. M. Stanton, 25 October 1862. Butler, *Private and Official Correspondence*, 2:407–408.

48. "Statement of Colonel William S. Dilworth," *Supplement to the OR*, 7:89.

49. Letter, Stephen Elliott to Wife, 16 June 1864. Elliott's description of Polk's wounds was based on information he got from William Gale. Telegram, William M. Polk to Lt. Col. Marshall T. Polk, Aberdeen, Mississippi, 16 [*sic*] June 1864. William Gale wrote in his diary on the night of June 14 that it was the second shot that hit Polk. General Johnston in a letter to Winfield Peters thirty-six years later says a second shot had passed harmlessly overhead and that the third shot killed Polk. Letter, Joseph E. Johnston to Winfield Peters, 25 September 1890. The fieldpiece in question has been variously termed by witnesses and later historians as either a Parrott gun or a Rodman. Philip Stephenson, an artillery loader, said the shell was from a Parrot. Hughes, *Civil War Memoir*, 189. The regimental history of the Fifth Indiana says "at Pine Mountain, the shot that killed Lieutenant General Polk, of the rebel army, was fired from one of the Rodman guns of the Fifth Battery." W. H. H. Terrell, *Report of the Adjutant General of the State of Indiana* (Indianapolis: Samuel M. Douglass, 1866), 400.

50. Letters, Douglas West to Hood, Hardee, and Johnston, 15 June 1864. Quintard was widely known in Rebel ranks for his *The Confederate Soldier's Pocket Manual of Devotions*, a similar tract published in 1863.

51. Stephen Elliott, "Occasion of His Death," *Funeral Services at the Burial of Polk*, 5.

52. Joseph M. Brown, *The Mountain Campaigns in Georgia; or, War Scenes on the W&A*

(Buffalo: Matthews, Northrup & Company, 1886). The sketch is unsigned, but Mc-Murry in *Atlanta 1864* identifies the artist as Alfred R. Waud.

53. Dispatches, Hood to Johnston, 14 June 1864; Hood to Maj. Douglas West, 16 June 1864, GPP. A facsimile of Hood's note to West is in Frey, *In the Woods Before Dawn*, 173

54. Charles L. Huger to "Dear Willy [Huger]," 15 June 1864, in LP Papers. Charles's brother William was also a lieutenant in the First Louisiana Infantry; he lost a leg after being wounded at Murfreesboro.

55. Letter, Kenneth Rayner to Thomas Ruffin, 15 June 1864, in Hamilton, *Papers of Thomas Ruffin*, 3:391. As valuable as Fanny Polk's Mississippi lands may have been before the war, they were greatly diminished (and the slaves set free) once the war was over.

56. Gale, "Diary," "Tuesday, 14th." Years later Gale could write more temperately that "the manner of his death had something in it suitable to his greatness of soul, and it seems not improper that a shell should open wide the door that let his spirit out." Letter, William Gale to Meck Polk, 28 March 1882.

57. Dispatch, Capt. J. C. Van Duzer to Majors Eckert and Beckwith, 14 June 1864, OR 38/4:479: "Our signal officers read the enemy flags, and in this way we learn that the rebel general Polk was killed today and his remains sent to Marietta. The messages were from Hood." The Federal claim of the intercepted messages was heatedly disputed later by Johnston, who declared that the report of Confederate signalmen seen on Pine Mountain was a "fabrication." Van Duzer, however, makes no mention of where the Confederate signalmen were posted. Letter, Joseph E. Johnston to Winfield Peters, 25 September 1890. See also "Myer Report," *Supplement to the OR* 10:622.

58. Sgt. Joseph Duggan described the coffin as "handsome." Letter, Sgt. Joseph Henry Duggan to Moses Greenwood, 14 June 1864, Moses Greenwood Papers, THNOC, MSS 222, folder 70.

59. Meck's presence was mentioned by "Grape" in his news story for the *Augusta Constitutionalist*. Gale, "Diary," "Tuesday, 14th."

60. Conyngham, *Sherman's March Through the South*, 113; Richard M. McMurry, "Kennesaw Mountain," 22.

61. Harwell, *Kate: Journal of a Confederate Nurse*, 197; Elliott, *Doctor Quintard*, 83. See also Robert Scott Davis Jr., ed., *Requiem for a Lost City: A Memoir of Civil War Atlanta* (Atlanta: Mercer University Press, 1999), 96 and n. 52, 114. Alas for all concerned, the finished structure, having been consecrated by Polk's bishop friend Stephen Elliott, survived Sherman's Atlanta Campaign only slightly longer than did General Polk; it was damaged by shell fire in the next few weeks and was then consumed in the fallen city's mid-November conflagration.

62. Davis, *Requiem for a Lost City*, 96–97, 114–115. "It was the first and only time for some years to come that flowers were used in Atlanta on a funeral occasion," Clayton noted. Later, when in Augusta, Sallie Clayton frequently visited Polk's grave in the churchyard behind St. Paul's (139). Editor Davis suggests that in her life Sallie Clayton had many traits exhibited by Scarlet O'Hara in *Gone with the Wind*.

63. Quintard's sermonic address, as "substantially taken down" by a reporter, was published first in the *Atlanta Confederacy* (undated clipping), then reprinted in the *Church Intelligencer*, 14 September 1864. The four generals were Maj. Gen. Gustavus W. Smith of the Georgia State Militia, Brig. Gen. Marcus J. Wright, Brig. Gen. Daniel Ruggles,

and Brig. Gen. Daniel H. Reynolds. Col. Benjamin Ewell, Johnston's assistant adjutant general, also accompanied the hearse. Elliott, *Doctor Quintard*, 86.

64. Florence F. Corley, *Confederate City, Augusta, Georgia, 1860–1865* (Columbia: University of South Carolina Press, 1960), 80.

65. Letter, Jefferson Davis to Elliott, 8 July 8 1864, *PJD*. Davis added that the press of his duties would have prevented his coming to Georgia anyway.

66. Wert, *General James Longstreet*, 390–391. Lee had expressed his grief to both Braxton Bragg and Jefferson Davis on the day following Polk's death. Letters, Robert E. Lee to Bragg and Davis, June 15, 1864, in Clifford Dowdey, ed., *The Wartime Papers of R. E. Lee* (New York: Little Brown & Company, 1961), 781–783.

67. Details of the funeral procession through the streets of Augusta are found variously in Corley, *Confederate City*; "The Journal of Ella Gertrude Clanton Thomas," Ella Gertrude Clanton Thomas Papers, 1848–1906, Perkins Library, Duke University; and Smith, "Death and Funerals of Bishop-General Leonidas Polk." The flag described was the rectangular "Stainless Banner" adopted by the Confederate Congress on May 1, 1863. Stonewall Jackson was killed the next day (by friendly fire), and as his body was enshrouded in the first flag made in this design, it became known also as the "Jackson Flag." Richard N. Current, ed., *Encyclopedia of the Confederacy* (New York: Simon & Schuster, 1993), 2:585.

68. Elliott, *Funeral Services at the Burial of Polk*, 26; "The Journal of Ella Gertrude Clanton Thomas," 162. Thomas paraphrased Elliott's sermon in her diary, writing that Elliott had charged the Yankees with violating "Christian virgins" rather than "Christian women." A few days after the funeral, Thomas resumed rolling cartridges with other Augusta women for the army. Letter, McIlvaine to Presiding Bishop John Henry Hopkins, 1 July 1865, Archives of the Episcopal Diocese of Maryland, and note 71 below.

69. Smith, "Death and Funerals of Bishop-General Leonidas Polk," 42. Polk's outdoor grave and that of his wife, who was buried beside him after her death in 1873, ended up *indoors* after the chancel was extended eastward in 1916. The graves were consequently then *beneath* the new chancel floor. In 1945 the Polks' remains were reburied in Christ Church Cathedral in New Orleans. Charles Quintard, apparently mistakenly, says the original burial was *in* the chancel of St. Paul's. Elliott, *Doctor Quintard*, 87.

70. Letter, William Gale to Kate Polk Gale, n.d. [early August 1864], GPP. Having visited the grave at St. Paul's a month after the funeral, Gale told his wife that "the grave is just as you left it with a bunch of cape jasmines at each end."

71. Henry Lynden Flash, "Polk," *Poems* (New York: Neale Publishing Company 1906), 156.

72. Letters, Sgt. Joseph Henry Duggan to Moses Greenwood, 14 June 1864; William Palfrey to Moses Greenwood, 22 June 1864, Moses Greenwood Papers, THNOC, MSS 222, folder 70. Palfrey was adjutant general to Brig. Gen. Francis Shoup.

73. Andrews, *South Reports the Civil War*, 447, quoting *Mobile Daily Advertiser and Register*, 21 June 1864. Watterson signed this dispatch "Shadow," one of his noms de plume. "Shadow's" identity is more probable than provable. Andrews suggests that "Shadow" and "Grape" (another nom de plume familiar to Confederate readers) were *both* Henry Watterson (543–551). George Sisler, however, has proposed that John Linebaugh, another correspondent sympathetic to the South, was "Shadow." See Sisler, "Arrest of

a Memphis *Daily Appeal* War Correspondent." Yet Sisler's theory has been challenged by B. G. Ellis and S. J. Dick in "Who Was Shadow? The Computer Knows: Applying Grammar-Program Statistics in Content Analyses to Solve Mysteries About Authorship," *Journalism and Mass Communication Quarterly* 73 (1996): 947–963. The authors' conclusion: Henry Watterson, not John Linebaugh, was "Shadow."

Tributes paid Polk did not include the government of the Confederate States of America. Strapped for cash, the CSA owed the dead soldier $3,157.48 in back pay and allowances and dragged its bureaucratic feet for more than five months before settling up with his widow. At the time of his death, General Polk's monthly salary was $300. His allowances included a stipend for housing. Polk's service record is found in the National Archives, M331, roll no. 199, and includes imploring correspondence from Polk's son Hamilton to his North Carolina congressman asking his intervention with the paymaster authorities in Richmond. Hamilton wrote that in fact his father was owed $3,605.44. The Diocese of Louisiana, moreover, had not settled back pay due Bishop Polk's widow as late as early 1867. Letter, Emily Donelson Polk Williams to Susan Rebecca Polk Campbell, 25 February 1867, BEP.

Epilogue

1. Letter, William Gale to "My Darling Kate," 30 July 1864.

Bibliography

Adams, Charles Francis, ed. *Memoirs of John Quincy Adams.* Vol. 5. Philadelphia: Lippincott, 1875.

Adams, Henry. *The Birthplaces of Presidents John and John Quincy Adams.* Quincy, MA: Adams Memorial Society, 1936.

"Affairs of the Church: Tennessee." *The New-York Review* 2 (April 1838): 508–509.

A. G. G. "The Bursting of the 'Lady Polk.'" *Confederate Veteran* 12 (1904): 118–119.

Aime, Valcour. *Plantation Diary of the Late Mr. Valcour Aime.* New Orleans: Clark & Hopeline, 1878.

Allen, Felicity. *Jefferson Davis, Unconquerable Heart.* Columbia: University of Missouri Press, 1999.

Allen, Gay Wilson. *Waldo Emerson.* New York: Viking Press, 1981.

Ambrose, Stephen E. *Duty, Honor, Country: A History of West Point.* Baltimore: Johns Hopkins University Press, 1999.

American State Papers: Documents, Legislative and Executive of the Congress of the United States. 38 vols. Washington, DC: Gales & Seaton, 1832–1861.

Amherst College. *Catalogue of the Corporation, Faculty and Students.* 1827.

Anderson, Archer. "Campaign and Battle of Chickamauga." *SHSP* 9 (1881): 386–418.

Anderson, William, ed. "The Civil War Reminiscences of John Johnston." *THQ* 13 (1954): 65–82.

Andrews, J. Cutler. *The South Reports the Civil War.* Princeton: Princeton University Press, 1970.

Angellotti, Mrs. Frank M. "The Polks of North Carolina and Tennessee." *The New England Historical and Genealogical Register* 77 (1923): 133–145, 213–227.

Armentrout, Donald Smith. *James Hervey Otey: First Episcopal Bishop of Tennessee.* Knoxville: Episcopal Dioceses in Tennessee, 1984.

Ashe, Samuel A., ed. *Biographical History of North Carolina.* 8 vols. Greensboro: Charles L. Van Noppen, 1915.

Ashkenazi, Elliott, ed. *The Civil War Diary of Clara Solomon: Growing Up in New Orleans.* Baton Rouge: Louisiana State University Press, 1995.

Austin, I. J. "Obituary of Crafts James Wright, Class of 1828." In *15th Annual Reunion of* the *Association of Graduates of the United States Military Academy*, 52–64. East Saginaw, MI: Courier, 1884.

"Autobiography of Colonel William Polk." In *The Papers of Archibald D. Murphey*, ed. William Henry Hoyt. Vol. 2, 400–410. Raleigh: E. M. Uzzell, 1914.

Avery, A. C. "On the Life and Character of Lieut.-General D. H. Hill." *SHSP* 21 (1893): 110–150.

"Aytch" [Samuel R. Watkins]. "An Adventure of General Leonidas Polk at the Battle of Perryville." *Southern Bivouac* 2 (1884): 403–404.

Baker, Lily, et al., eds. *Purple Sewanee*. Sewanee, TN: Association for the Preservation of Tennessee Antiquities, 1961.

Ball, Edward. "Retracing Slavery's Trail of Tears." *Smithsonian Magazine* 46, 7 (2015): 58–82.

Ballard, Michael B. *Pemberton: A Biography*. Jackson: University Press of Mississippi, 1991.

Bartlett, Napier. "Capture of the Federal Ironclad Gunboat Indianola." In *Military Record of Louisiana*, 44–54. New Orleans: L. Graham & Company, 1875.

Basler, Roy P., ed. *The Collected Works of Abraham Lincoln*. 9 vols. New Brunswick, NJ: Rutgers University Press, 1953–1955.

Bassham, Ben L., ed. *Conrad Wise Chapman's Civil War Memoir: Ten Months in the "Orphan Brigade."* (Kent, OH: Kent State University Press, 1999.

Batterson, Hermon G. *A Sketch Book of the American Episcopate*. Philadelphia: Lippincott, 1891.

Battle, Kemp P. *History of the University of North Carolina*. Vol. 1, *From Its Beginnings to the Death of President Swain, 1789–1868*. Raleigh, NC: Edwards & Broughton Printing, 1907.

Bauer, K. Jack, ed. *Soldiering: The Civil War Diary of Rice C. Bull, 123rd New York Volunteer Infantry*. San Rafael, CA: Presidio Press, 1970.

Baughman, James P. *Charles Morgan and the Development of Southern Transportation*. Nashville: Vanderbilt University Press, 1968.

Baylor, George. "With Gen. A. S. Johnston at Shiloh." *Confederate Veteran* 5 (1897): 609–613.

Bearss, Edwin. "Cavalry Operations in the Battle at Stones River." *THQ* 19 (1960): 23–53, 110–144.

Bearss, Margie Riddle. *Sherman's Forgotten Campaign*. Baltimore: Gateway Press, 1987.

Beauregard, G. T. "The Campaign of Shiloh." In *BLCW*. Vol. 1, 569–593.

———. "The Shiloh Campaign. Part II." *The North American Review* 142 (1886): 159–184.

Beilein, Joseph, et al. "The Free State of Jones: A Roundtable." *Civil War History* 63 (2017): 400–420.

Bergeron, Arthur W. Jr. *Confederate Mobile*. Jackson: University Press of Mississippi, 1991.

Bergeron, Paul. "My Brother's Keeper: William H. Polk Goes to School." *North Carolina Historical Review* 44 (1967): 188–204.

Berlin, Ira. *The Making of African America: The Four Great Migrations*. New York: Viking, 2010.

Bettersworth, John K. *Confederate Mississippi*. Baton Rouge: Louisiana State University Press, 1943.

Bevier, R. S. *History of the First and Second Missouri Confederate Brigades*. St. Louis: Bryan, Brand & Company, 1879.

Bickham, William D. "The Battle of Stone River, by Our Correspondent." *The Cincinnati Daily Commercial*, 8 January 1863, 1.

———. *Rosecrans' Campaign with the Fourteenth Army Corps, or the Army of the Cumberland*. Cincinnati: Moore, Wilstach, Keys, 1863.

Biel, John G., ed. "The Battle of Shiloh: From the Letters and Diary of Joseph Dimmit Thompson." *THQ* 17 (1958): 250–274.

Bierce, Ambrose. *The Collected Works of Ambrose Bierce*. New York: Neale Publishing Company, 1909.

Blakeslee, Merritt R. *The Pillaging and Destruction of the Cornerstone of the University of the South, July 1863*. Sewanee, TN: Sewanee History Project, 2010.

———. *"A Rite Sharp Little Fight": Skirmish on Sewanee Mountain, July 4, 1863*. Sewanee, TN: Sewanee History Project.

———. "'The Spirit of Hell Itself Was Never More Exhibited': The Firing of the Polk and Elliott Homes at University Place, Night of Fort Sumter, 1861." In *Upon the Debatable Ground: Sewanee and the Lower Cumberland Plateau During the Civil War*. Forthcoming.

Blanco, Richard L., ed. *The American Revolution 1775–1783: An Encyclopedia*. New York: Garland Publishing Company, 1993.

Bond, Edward L. *St. James Episcopal Church, Baton Rouge: A History, 1844–1944*. Baton Rouge: St. James Episcopal Church, 1994.

The Book of Common Prayer and Administration of the Sacraments and Other Rites and Ceremonies of the Church, According to the Use of the Protestant Episcopal Church in the United States of America. Philadelphia: Hall & Sellers, 1790.

Booth, William A. "On the Cholera of La Fourche Interior." In *Southern Medical Reports*. Vol. 1, 196–235. New Orleans: B. M. Norman, 1849.

Bridges, Hal. *Lee's Maverick General: Daniel Harvey Hill*. Lincoln: University of Nebraska Press, 1991.

Brinton, John H. *Personal Memoirs*. New York: Neal Publishing Company, 1914.

Brown, Joseph M. *The Mountain Campaigns in Georgia; or, War Scenes on the W & A*. Buffalo: Matthews, Northrup & Company, 1886.

Browning, Charles H. "Lafayette's Visit to the United States in 1824–25." *The American Historical Register* 3 (1895): 151–194.

Bryan, Leon S. Jr. "Blood-letting in American Medicine, 1830–1892." *Bulletin of the Institute of the History of Medicine* 38 (1964): 516–529.

Bryant, William Cullen, and Sidney Howard Gay. *A Popular History of the United States*. Vol. 4. New York: Scribner's, 1880.

Brydon, G. MacLaren. "The 'Confederate Prayer Book.'" *HMPEC* 17 (1948): 339–344.

Buck, Irving A. *Cleburne and His Command*. Jackson, TN: McCowat-Mercer Press, 1959.

Buell, Don Carlos. "East Tennessee and the Campaign of Perryville." In *BLCW*. Vol. 3, 31–51.

Burin, Eric. *Slavery and the Peculiar Solution*. Gainesville: University Press of Florida, 2005.

Burt, Jesse C. "Sherman's Logistics and Andrew Johnson." *THQ* 15 (1956): 195–215.

Butler, Benjamin F. *Private and Official Correspondence of Gen. Benjamin F. Butler during the Period of the Civil War.* 5 vols. Norwood, MA: Plimpton Press, 1917.

Butler, Diana Hochstedt. *Standing Against the Whirlwind: Evangelical Episcopalians in Nineteenth-Century America.* New York: Oxford University Press, 1995.

Bynum, Victoria E. *The Free State of Jones: Mississippi's Longest Civil War.* Chapel Hill: University of North Carolina Press, 2001.

Cable, George W. "New Orleans Before the Capture." In *BLCW.* Vol. 1, 14–21.

Calhoun, Robert Dabney. "The John Perkins Family of Northeast Louisiana." *Louisiana Historical Quarterly* 19 (1936): 70–88.

Carnes, W. W. "Chickamauga." *SHSP* 14 (1886): 398–407.

Carpenter, Frederick Ives. *Emerson Handbook.* New York: Handpicks House, 1953.

Carrigan, Jo Ann. *The Saffron Scourge.* Lafayette: University of Southwestern Louisiana, 1994.

———. "Yellow Fever, 1853: A Fatherly Correction?" *Louisiana History* 10 (1969): 352.

Carter, Betty, and Hodding Carter. *So Great a Good: A History of the Episcopal Church in Louisiana and of Christ Church Cathedral, 1905–1955.* Sewanee, TN: University Press, 1955.

Carus, William, ed. *Memorials of the Right Reverend Charles Pettit McIlvaine, D.D., D.C.L.* 2nd ed. London: Elliot Stock, 1882.

Castel, Albert. *Articles of War: Winners, Losers, and Some Who Were Both in the Civil War.* Mechanicsburg, PA: Stackpole Books, 2001.

———. *Decision in the West: The Atlanta Campaign of 1864.* Lawrence: University Press of Kansas, 1992.

———. *Winning and Losing in the Civil War.* Columbia: University of South Carolina Press, 1996.

Castelow, Teri L. "'Behold Me and This Great Babylon I Have Built': The Life and Work of Sophia Sawyer, 19th Century Missionary and Teacher Among the Cherokees." PhD diss., Florida State University, 2005.

Cathey, Cornelius Oliver. *Agricultural Developments in North Carolina, 1783–1860.* Chapel Hill: University of North Carolina Press, 1956.

The Centennial of the United States Military Academy at West Point, New York, 1802–1902. Vol. 2. Washington, DC: Government Printing Office, 1904.

Chalmers, James R. "Forrest and His Campaigns." *SHSP* 7 (1879): 451–486.

Champomier, P. A. *Statement of the Sugar Crop Made in Louisiana.* New Orleans: Magne & Weisse, 1851–1857.

Cheatham, B. F. "The Battle of Perryville." *Southern Bivouac* 4 (1886): 704–705.

Chernow, Ron. *Grant.* New York: Penguin, 2017.

Cheshire, Joseph Blount. *The Church in the Confederate State.* New York: Longmans, Green & Company, 1912.

Chisolm, Alexander. "The Shiloh Battle-Order and the Withdrawal Sunday Evening." In *BLCW.* Vol. 1, 606.

Chitty, Arthur Benjamin Jr. *Reconstruction at Sewanee.* Sewanee, TN: University Press, 1954.

———. "Sewanee Then and Now." *THQ* 38 (1979): 383–400.

Chorley, E. Clowes. "The Church in Arkansas and Its Bishops, 1835–1946." *HMPEC* 15 (1946): 318–354.

———. *Men and Movements of the American Episcopal Church*. New York: Scribner's, 1946.

———. "The Oxford Movement in the Seminary." *HMPEC* 5 (1936): 177–201.

Cimprich, John. *Slavery's End in Tennessee, 1861–1865*. University: University of Alabama Press, 1985.

Cimprich, John, and Robert C. Mainfort Jr. "Fort Pillow Massacre: A Statistical Note." *Journal of American History* 76 (1989): 830–837.

Claibourne, Thomas. "Battle of Perryville, Ky." *Confederate Veteran* 16 (May 1908): 225–227.

Clark, Clifford E. Jr. *Henry Ward Beecher: Spokesman for a Middle-Class America*. Urbana: University of Illinois Press, 1978.

Clarke, H. C. *Diary of the War for Separation*. Vicksburg, MS: Clarke's Southern Publishing House, 1862.

Clinton, Catherine. *The Plantation Mistress: Woman's World in the Old South*. New York: Pantheon, 1982.

Coke, Fletch. "Christ Church, Episcopal, Nashville." *THQ* 38 (1979): 141–157.

Collections of the Protestant Episcopal Historical Society for the Year 1851. Vol. 1. New York: Stanford & Swords, 1851.

The Congressional Globe: Containing the Debates and Proceedings of the Second Session of the Thirty-Seventh Congress. City of Washington: Congressional Globe Office, 1862.

Connelly, Donald B. *John M. Schofield and the Politics of Generalship*. Chapel Hill: University of North Carolina Press, 2006.

Connelly, Thomas Lawrence. *Army of the Heartland: The Army of Tennessee, 1861–1862*. Baton Rouge: Louisiana State University Press, 1967.

———. *Autumn of Glory: The Army of Tennessee, 1862–1865*. Baton Rouge: Louisiana State University Press, 1971.

———. "The Johnston Mystique." *CWTI* 5 (February 1967): 15–23.

"Consecration of Bishop Polk." *SOM* 4 (1839): 28.

Conyngham, David P. *Sherman's March Through the South*. New York: Sheldon & Company, 1865.

Cooling, Benjamin Franklin. *Forts Henry and Donelson: The Key to the Confederate Heartland*. Knoxville: University of Tennessee Press, 1987.

Cooper, James Fenimore. *The Last of the Mohicans*. Garden City, NY: International Collectors Library, 1985.

Coppinger, Margaret Brown, et al. *Beersheba Springs: 150 Years, 1833–1983*. Beersheba Springs, TN: Beersheba Springs Historical Society, 1983.

Corley, Florence F. *Confederate City, Augusta, Georgia, 1860–1865*. Columbia: University of South Carolina Press, 1960.

Cotter, John. *The Buried Past*. Philadelphia: University of Pennsylvania Press, 1992.

"Cotton Seed Gas." *Register of the Arts and Sciences* 4 (19 August 1827): 151.

Couper, William. *One Hundred Years at V. M. I.* 4 vols. Richmond, VA: Garrett and Massie, 1939.

Cozzens, Peter. *No Better Place to Die: The Battle of Stones River*. Urbana: University of Illinois Press, 1990.

———. *This Terrible Sound: The Battle of Chickamauga*. Urbana: University of Illinois Press, 1992.

Crabb, Alfred Leland. "Twilight of the Nashville Gods." *THQ* 15 (1956): 291–305.

Crabtree, Beth, and James Patton, eds. *Journal of a Secesh Lady*. Raleigh, NC: Department of Archives and History, 1979.

Craig, Benny F. "Northern Conquerors and Southern Deliverers: The Civil War Comes to the Jackson Purchase." *Register of the Kentucky Historical Society* 73 (1975): 17–30.

Crist, Lynda Laswell, et al., eds. *The Papers of Jefferson Davis*. Vols. 7–10. Baton Rouge: Louisiana State University Press, 1992–1999.

Criswell, Grover Jr. *Confederate and Southern States Currency*. St. Petersburg, FL: Krause Publications, 1964.

Criswell, Howard Jr. "A Conversation with the Past." *CWTI* 29 (March–April 1990): 56–63.

Cullum, George W. *Biographical Register of the Officers and Graduates of the U.S. Military Academy, 1802–1890*. 3rd ed. Vol. 1. Cambridge, MA: Houghton, Mifflin, 1891.

Cumming, Kate. *Gleanings from Southland*. Birmingham, AL: Roberts & Son, 1895.

Cunningham, O. Edward. *Shiloh and the Western Campaign of 1862*. Baton Rouge: Louisiana State University Press, 1966.

Current, Richard N. *The Encyclopedia of the Confederacy*. Vol. 1. New York: Simon and Schuster, 1993.

Daniel, Larry J., and Lynn N. Bock. *Island No. 10: Struggle for the Mississippi Valley*. Tuscaloosa: University of Alabama Press, 1996.

Davidson, G. W. H. "The Library of Robert Leighton (1611–1684), Bishop of Dunblane." *HMPEC* 28 (1959): 216–266.

Davis, Jefferson. "Autobiographical Sketch." In *The Papers of Jefferson Davis*, ed. Haskell M. Monroe Jr. and James T. McIntosh, lxvii–lxxxiv. Baton Rouge: Louisiana State University Press, 1971.

Davis, Robert Scott Jr., ed. *Requiem for a Lost City: A Memoir of Civil War Atlanta*. Atlanta: Mercer University Press, 1999.

Davis, T. Frederick. "Pioneer Florida." *Florida Historical Quarterly* 24 (1946): 287–294.

Davis, William C. *Breckinridge: Statesman, Soldier, Symbol*. Baton Rouge: Louisiana State University Press, 1974.

———. *Jefferson Davis: The Man and His Hour*. New York: HarperCollins, 1991.

———. *The Orphan Brigade: The Kentucky Confederates Who Couldn't Go Home*. Garden City, NY: Doubleday, 1980.

———, ed. *Diary of a Confederate Soldier: John S. Jackman of the Orphan Brigade*. Columbus: University of South Carolina Press, 1990.

Dawley, Powel Mills. *The Story of the General Theological Seminary*. New York: Oxford University Press, 1969.

de Arnaud, Charles A. *The Union, and Its Ally, Russia*. Washington, DC: Gibson Bros., 1890.

De Bow, J. D. B. "Home Education at the South." *De Bow's Review* 10 (1851): 362–363.

DeMille, George E. *The Catholic Movement in the American Episcopal Church*. Philadelphia: Church Historical Society, 1941.

Dew, Charles B. *Ironmaker to the Confederacy: Joseph R. Anderson and the Tredegar Iron Works*. New Haven: Yale University Press, 1966.

Donald, David, ed. *Inside Lincoln's Cabinet: The Civil War Diaries of Salmon P. Chase*. New York: Longmans, Green, 1954.

Dorland, W. A. Newman. *American Illustrated Medical Dictionary*. Philadelphia: Saunders, 1941.

Dorsey, Sarah Anne Ellis. *Recollections of Henry Watkins Allen*. New York: M. Doolady, 1866.

Dowdey, Clifford, ed. *The Wartime Papers of R. E. Lee*. New York: Little Brown & Company, 1961.

Dugas, Vera Lea. "The Ante-Bellum Career of Leonidas Polk." *Louisiana Historical Quarterly* 32 (1949): 245–356.

Dunham, Chester Forrester. *The Attitude of the Northern Clergy Toward the South, 1860–1865*. Toledo, OH: Gray, 1942.

Durham, Walter. *Nashville: The Occupied City*. Nashville: Tennessee Historical Society, 1985.

———. *Reluctant Partners: Nashville and the Union*. Nashville: Tennessee Historical Society, 1987.

East, Charles, ed. *The Civil War Diary of Sarah Morgan*. Athens: University of Georgia Press, 1991.

Editors of Time-Life Books. *Voices of the Civil War: Atlanta*. Alexandria, VA: Time-Life Books, 1996.

Edmonston, Catherine Ann Devereux. "Dedication." In *The Morte d'Arthur; Its Influence on the Spirit and Manners of the Nineteenth Century*, 3. Baltimore: Trumbull Brothers, 1872.

Egerton, Douglas R. "Its Origin Is Not a Little Curious: A New Look at the American Colonization Society." *Journal of the Early Republic* 5 (1985): 463–480.

Eicher, David J. *The Longest Night: A Military History of the Civil War*. New York: Simon & Schuster, 2001.

Elliott, Sam Davis. *Doctor Quintard, Chaplain C. S. A. and Second Bishop of Tennessee: The Memoir and Civil War Diary*. Baton Rouge: Louisiana State University Press, 2003.

———. *Soldier of Tennessee: General Alexander P. Stewart and the Civil War in the West*. Baton Rouge: Louisiana State University Press, 1999.

Elliott, Stephen. *Funeral Services at the Burial of The Right Rev. Leonidas Polk, D.D. Together with the Sermon Delivered in St. Paul's Church, Augusta, Ga. on June 29, 1864: Being the Feast of St. Peter the Apostle*. Columbia, SC: Evans & Cogswell, 1864.

Ellis, B. G., and S. J. Dick. "Who Was Shadow? The Computer Knows: Applying Grammar-Program Statistics in Content Analyses to Solve Mysteries about Authorship." *Journalism and Mass Communication Quarterly* 73 (1996): 947–963.

Ellis, William Arba, ed. *Norwich University, 1819–1911: Her History, Her Graduates, Her Roll of Honor*. Vol. 1. Montpelier, VT: Capital City Press, 1911.

Emerson, John W. "Grant's Life in the West and his Mississippi Valley Campaigns." *The Midland Monthly* 10 (1898): 26–36, 121–131, 225–233, 315–327, 409–430, 507–521.

Evans, Charles M. *The War of the Aeronauts*. Mechanicsburg, PA: Stackpole Books, 2002.

Evans, Hugh Davey. "The Southern University." *The Monitor* 36 (4 September 1857): 426.

Fairbanks, George R. *History of the University of the South.* Jacksonville, FL: H. & W. B. Drew, 1905.

Fay, Edwin W. *The History of Education in Louisiana.* Washington, DC: Government Printing Office, 1898.

Featherstonhaugh, George W. *Excursion through the Slave States.* New York: Harper & Bros., 1844.

Federal Writers Project. *Florida: A Guide to the Southernmost State.* New York: Oxford University Press, 1939.

Feis, William B. "Grant and the Belmont Campaign: A Study in Intelligence and Command." In *The Art of Command in the Civil War,* ed. Steven E. Woodworth. Lincoln: University of Nebraska Press, 1998.

———. *Grant's Secret Service.* Lincoln: University of Nebraska Press, 2002.

Fenner, E. D. "Report on Epidemic Cholera in New Orleans in 1848–9." *Southern Medical Reports.* Vol. 1, 125–158. New Orleans: B. M. Norman, 1850.

Fischer, Roger A. "Racial Segregation in Ante Bellum New Orleans." *American Historical Review* 74 (1969): 926–937.

Fisher, George D. *History and Reminiscences of the Monumental Church, Richmond, Va., from 1814 to 1878.* Richmond, VA: Whittet & Shepperson, 1880.

Fisher, Noel C. *War at Every Door: Partisan Politics and Guerilla Violence in East Tennessee, 1860–1869.* Chapel Hill: University of North Carolina Press, 1997.

Flash, Henry Lynden. "Polk." In *Poems,* 156. New York: Neale Publishing Company, 1906.

Follett, Richard. *The Sugar Masters: Planters and Slaves in Louisiana's Cane World, 1820–1860.* Baton Rouge: Louisiana State University Press, 2005.

Forman, Sidney. *Cadet Life at West Point Before the Mexican War.* West Point: United States Military Academy Printing Office, 1945.

Freehling, William W. *The Reintegration of American History.* New York: Oxford University Press, 1994.

Freeman, Douglass Southall. *R. E. Lee: A Biography.* 4 vols. New York: Scribner's, 1934–1935.

Fremantle, Arthur J. L. *Three Months in the Southern States, April–June 1863.* Omaha: University of Nebraska Press, 1991.

French, Samuel G. *Two Wars: An Autobiography.* Nashville: Confederate Veteran Press, 1901.

Frey, Jerry. *In the Woods Before Dawn: The Samuel Richey Collection of the Southern Confederacy.* Gettysburg, PA: Thomas Publications, 1994.

Friedman, Lawrence J. *Inventors of the Promised Land.* New York: Knopf, 1975.

Friend, Jack. *West Wind, Flood Tide: The Battle of Mobile Bay.* Annapolis: Naval Institute Press, 2004.

Fuchs, Richard L. *An Unerring Fire: The Massacre at Fort Pillow.* Rutherford, NJ: Fairleigh Dickinson University Press, 1994.

Fulton, John. "The Church in the Confederate States." In *The History of the American Episcopal Church, 1783–1883,* ed. William S. Perry. Vol. 2, 561–592. Boston: James R. Osgood & Company, 1885.

Gallagher, Gary W., ed. *Fighting for the Confederacy: The Personal Recollections of Edward Porter Alexander*. Chapel Hill: University of North Carolina Press, 1989.

Garrett, Jill K. "St. John's Church, Ashwood." *THQ* 29 (1970): 3–23.

———, ed. *Confederate Diary of Robert D. Smith*. Columbia, TN: Capt. James Madison Sparkman Chapter, United Daughters of the Confederacy, 1975.

Gates, Arnold, ed. *The Rough Side of War: The Civil War Journal of Chelsey A. Mosman, 1st Lieutenant, Company D, 59th Illinois Infantry Regiment*. Garden City, NY: Basin Publishing Company, 1987.

Genovese, Eugene D. "Religion in the Collapse of the American Union." In *Religion and the American Civil War*, ed. Randal M. Miller, Harry Stout, and Charles Wilson, 74–88. New York: Oxford University Press, 1998.

Gewen, Barry. "Absolute Values." *The New York Times Book Review*, 24 March 2002, 11.

Gibbons, Tony. *Warships and Naval Battles of the Civil War*. New York: Gallery Books, 1989.

Gillespie, Michael. "The Novel Experiment: Cotton Clads and Steamboatmen." *CWTI* 22 (December 1983): 34–36.

Gilman, William H., and Alfred Ferguson, eds. *The Journals and Miscellaneous Notebooks of Ralph Waldo Emerson*. Cambridge, MA: Belknap Press, 1963.

Glazier, Michael, and Thomas J. Shelley, eds. *Encyclopedia of American Catholic History*. Collegeville, MN: Liturgical Press, 1997.

Goggin, James. "Chickamauga—A Reply to Major Sykes." *SHSP* 12 (1884): 219–224.

Good, John Mason, Olinthus Gregory, and Newton Bosworth. *Pantologia: A New Cyclopaedia*. 12 vols. London: J. Walker, 1819.

Goodwin, William A. R. *History of The Theological Seminary in Virginia and Its Historical Background*. 2 vols. Rochester, NY: Du Bois Press, 1923–1924.

Govan, Gilbert E., and James W. Livingood. *A Different Valor: The Story of General Joseph E. Johnston, C.S.A.* New York: Bobbs-Merrill, 1956.

Gow, June I. "Chiefs of Staff in the Army of Tennessee Under Braxton Bragg." *THQ* 27 (1968): 341–60.

Gower, Herschel and Jack Allen, eds. *Pen and Sword: The Life and Journals of Randal W. McGavock*. Nashville: Tennessee Historical Commission, 1959.

Gracie, Archibald. *The Truth About Chickamauga*. Boston: Houghton Mifflin, 1911.

Graf, LeRoy P., and Ralph W. Haskins, eds. *Papers of Andrew Johnson*. Knoxville: University of Tennessee Press, 2000.

Grant, Ulysses S. *Memoirs and Selected Letters*. New York: Viking Press. 1990.

———. *Personal Memoirs*. 2 vols. New York: C. L. Webster & Company, 1885–1886.

Gray, Lewis Cecil. *History of Agriculture in the Southern United States to 1860*. Washington, DC: Carnegie Institution of Washington, 1933.

Green, William Mercer. *Memoir of Rt. Rev. James Hervey Otey, D.D., LL.D.: The First Bishop of Tennessee*. New York: J. Pott & Company, 1885.

Gregory, Olinthus Gilbert. *Letters on the Evidences, Doctrines and Duties of the Christian Religion*. 9th ed. London: Henry G. Bohn, 1857.

———. *A Treatise of Mechanics, Theoretical, Practical and Descriptive*. London: George Kearsley, 1815.

Griswold, Rufus W., ed. *Sacred Poets of England and America*. New York: Appleton, 1850.

Guide to the Civil War in Tennessee. Nashville: Civil War Centennial Commission, 1962.

Hafendorfer, Kenneth A. *Mill Springs: Campaign and Battle of Mill Springs, Kentucky*. Louisville: KH Press, 2001.

———. *Perryville: Battle for Kentucky*. Louisville: KH Press, 1991.

Haller, John S. Jr. *The People's Doctors: Samuel Thomson and the American Botanical Movement, 1790–1860*. Carbondale: Southern Illinois University Press, 2000.

Hallock, Judith Lee. *Braxton Bragg and Confederate Defeat*. Vol. 2. Tuscaloosa: University of Alabama Press, 1991.

Hamer, Philip M. *Tennessee: A History 1673–1932*. New York: American Historical Society, 1933.

Hamilton, J. G. de Roulhac, ed. *The Papers of Thomas Ruffin*. 4 vols. Raleigh: Edwards & Broughton Printing Company, 1920.

Hamilton, Peter J. *Mobile of the Five Flags: Mobile from the Earliest Times to the Present*. Mobile, AL: Gill Printing Company, 1913.

Harwell, Richard Barksdale, ed. *Kate: The Journal of a Confederate Nurse*. Baton Rouge: Louisiana State University Press, 1959.

Hatton, Roy O., ed. "Camille Polignac's Diary, Part I." *CWTI* 19 (August 1980): 14–18.

Havighurst, Walter. *River to the West: Three Centuries of the Ohio*. New York: Putnam, 1970.

Haywood, Marshall De Lancey. *Lives of the Bishops of North Carolina*. Raleigh: Alfred Williams & Company, 1910.

Head, Thomas A. *Campaigns and Battles of the Sixteenth Regiment, Tennessee Volunteers*. Nashville: Cumberland Presbyterian Publishing House, 1885.

Hearn, Chester G. *The Capture of New Orleans 1862*. Baton Rouge: Louisiana State University Press, 1995.

———. *Ellet's Brigade: The Strangest Outfit of All*. Baton Rouge: Louisiana State University Press, 2000.

Henry, Robert S. *As They Saw Forrest*. Jackson, TN: McCowat-Mercer Press, 1956.

———. *"First with the Most" Forrest*. Indianapolis: Bobbs-Merrill, 1944.

Herrick, Suzanne Hiller. *Leacocks, Including the Manuscript Entitled The Three Clergymen of New Orleans and Gen. Benjamin F. Butler, Written by Helen Gray*. San Rafael, CA: SJB, 1994.

Hess, Earl J. *Banners to the Breeze: The Kentucky Campaign, Corinth, and Stones River*. Lincoln: University of Nebraska Press, 2000.

———. "Braxton Bragg and the Stones River Campaign." In *Border Wars: The Civil War in Tennessee and Kentucky*, ed. Kent T. Dollar, Larry H. Whiteaker, and W. Calvin Dickinson. Kent, OH: Kent State University Press, 2015.

———. *Braxton Bragg: The Most Hated Man of the Confederacy*. Chapel Hill: University of North Carolina Press, 2016.

Hight, John J. *History of the Fifty-Eighth Regiment of the Indiana Volunteer Infantry*. Princeton: Clarion, 1895.

Hill, Daniel H. "Chickamauga—The Great Battle of the West." In *BLCW*. Vol. 3, 638–662.

Hinman, Wilbur F. *The Story of the Sherman Brigade*. Alliance, OH: Hinman, 1897.

Hirshon, Stanley P. *The White Tecumseh*. New York: John Wiley & Sons, 1997.

"History of First Light Artillery." In *Report of the Adjutant General of the State of Illinois*. Vol. 8, 660–667. Springfield: H. W. Rokker, 1886.

Hoobler, James A. *Cities Under the Gun: Images of Occupied Nashville and Chattanooga*. Nashville: Rutledge Hill Press, 1986.

Hood, John Bell. *Advance and Retreat: Personal Experiences in the United States and Confederate States Armies*. New Orleans: Hood Orphan Memorial Fund, 1880.

Hopkins, James F. *A History of the Hemp Industry in Kentucky*. Lexington: University of Kentucky Press, 1951.

Hopkins, John Henry. *Essay on Gothic Architecture*. Burlington, VT: Smith & Harrington, 1836.

Hopkins, John Henry Jr. *The Life of the Late Right Reverend John Henry Hopkins, First Bishop of Vermont*. New York: F. J. Huntington, 1873.

Horn, Stanley F. *The Army of Tennessee: A Military History*. New York: Bobbs-Merrill, 1941.

———, ed. *Tennessee's War 1861–1865, Described by Participants*. Nashville: Tennessee Civil War Centennial Commission, 1965.

Howard, Oliver Otis. *Autobiography*. New York: Baker & Taylor, 1907.

Howard, Richard L. *History of the 124th Regiment Illinois Infantry*. Springfield, IL: H. W. Rokker, 1880.

Howe, M. A. DeWolfe, ed. *Home Letters of General Sherman*. New York: Scribner's, 1909.

Howell, Isabel. "John Armfield of Beersheba Springs." *THQ* 3 (1944): 46–64, 156–167.

———. "John Armfield, Slave Trader." *THQ* 2 (1943): 3–29.

Hughes, Nathaniel C. *The Battle of Belmont: Grant Strikes South*. Chapel Hill: University of North Carolina Press, 1991.

———. *General William J. Hardee: Old Reliable*. Baton Rouge: Louisiana State University Press, 1992.

———. *Jefferson Davis in Blue: The Life of Sherman's Relentless Warrior*. Baton Rouge: Louisiana State University Press, 2002.

———. *The Pride of the Confederate Artillery: The Washington Artillery in the Army of Tennessee*. Baton Rouge: Louisiana State University Press, 1997.

———, ed. *The Civil War Memoir of Philip Daingerfield Stephenson, D.D.* Baton Rouge: Louisiana State University Press, 1995.

———, ed. *Liddell's Record*. Baton Rouge: Louisiana State University Press, 1985.

Hughes, Nathaniel C. and Roy P. Stonesifer Jr., *The Life and Wars of Gideon J. Pillow*. Chapel Hill: University of North Carolina Press, 1993.

Hurst, Jack. *Nathan Bedford Forrest: A Biography*. New York: Knopf, 1993.

Isham, Asa B., Henry M. Davidson, and Henry B. Furness. *Prisoners of War and Military Prisons*. Cincinnati: Lyman & Cushing, 1890.

Jacobs, Dillard. "Outfitting the Provisional Army of Tennessee: A Report on New Source Materials." *THQ* 40 (1981): 257–271.

James, D. Clayton. *Antebellum Natchez*. Baton Rouge: Louisiana State University Press, 1968.

Jarvis, Samuel Farmar. *A Chronological Introduction to the History of the Church: Being a New Inquiry into the True Dates of the Birth and Death of our Lord and Saviour Jesus Christ*. New York: Harper, 1845.

Jay, William. *Miscellaneous Writings on Slavery*. Boston: J. P. Jewett & Company, 1853.

Jenkins, Sally, and John Stauffer. *The State of Jones: The Small Southern County That Seceded from the Confederacy*. New York: Doubleday, 2009.

Jeter, Katherine Brash. *A Man and His Boat: The Civil War Career of Lieutenant Jonathan H. Carter, CSN*. Lafayette: Center for Louisiana Studies, 1996.

Jodon, F. D. "Recollections of the War." *Confederate Veteran*, 9 (1901): 14.

Johns, John. *A Memoir of the Rt. Rev. William Meade*. Baltimore: Innes, 1867.

Johnson, Guion Griffis. *Ante-Bellum North Carolina: A Social History*. Chapel Hill: University of North Carolina Press, 1937.

Johnson, Leland R. *Engineers on the Twin Rivers: A History of the U.S. Army Engineers, Nashville District, 1769–1978*. Nashville: US Army Engineer District, 1978.

Johnson, Robert Underwood, and Clarence Clough Buel, eds. *Battles and Leaders of the Civil War: Being for the Most Part Contributions by Union and Confederate Officers*. 4 vols. New York: Century Company, 1884–1887.

Johnson, Vicki Vaughn. *The Men and Vision of the Southern Commercial Conventions, 1845–1871*. Columbia: University of Missouri Press, 1992.

Johnston, Joseph E. *Narrative of Military Operations*. New York: Appleton, 1874.

Johnston, William Preston. *The Life of Gen. Albert Sidney Johnston*. New York: Appleton, 1878.

Joiner, Gary. *Mr. Lincoln's Brown Water Navy: The Mississippi Squadron*. Lanham, MD: Rowman & Littlefield, 2007.

Jones, Charles T. Jr., ed. "Five Confederates: The Sons of Bolling Hall in the Civil War." *Alabama Historical Quarterly* 24 (1962): 133–231.

Jones, John B. *A Rebel War Clerk's Diary at the Confederate States Capital*. Philadelphia: Lippincott, 1866.

Jordan, Thomas. "The Campaign and Battle of Shiloh." *The United Service* 12 (1885): 262–280.

———. "Notes of a Confederate Staff-Officer at Shiloh." In *BLCW*. Vol. 1, 594–603.

Julian, John. *A Dictionary of Hymnology*. London: John Murray, 1925.

Kemmerly, Philip. "Into the Muck and Mire: Mud, Soils, and Sediments of Shiloh." *THQ* 73 (2014): 2–31.

Kemp, Louis Wiltz. *The Signers of the Texas Declaration of Independence*. Houston: Anson Jones Press, 1944.

Kennett, Lee. *Sherman: A Soldier's Life*. New York: Harper Collins, 2001.

Kerksis, Sydney C. *The Atlanta Papers*. Dayton, OH: Morningside Bookshop, 1980.

Kniffin, G. C. "The Battle of Stone's River." In *BLCW*. Vol. 3, 613–632.

Korda, Michael. *Clouds of Glory: The Life and Legend of Robert E. Lee*. New York: Harper, 2014.

Lamers, William M. *The Edge of Glory: A Biography of William S. Rosecrans, U.S.A.* New York: Harcourt, Brace, 1961.

Lancaster, Joseph. *Scripture Reading Lessons*. British and Foreign School Society, 1814–1829.

Landry, Stuart O. *Imprisonment for Debt in Louisiana*. New Orleans: Pelican Publishing Company, 1964.

Lash, Jeffrey N. *Destroyer of the Iron Horse: Gen. Joseph E. Johnston and Confederate Rail Transport, 1861–1865*. Kent, OH: Kent State University Press, 1991.

"Last Surviving Confederate General: Visit to the Home of Gen. S. B. Buckner." *Confederate Veteran* 17 (1909): 61–64, 83–85.

Law, John Gordon. "Diary of Rev. J. G. Law." *SHSP* 12 (1884): 22–28.

Lee, Stephen D. "Sherman's Meridian Expedition." *SHSP* 8 (1880): 49–61.

LeMonniere, Y. R. "Gen. Leonidas Polk at Chickamauga." *Confederate Veteran* 24 (1916): 17–19.

"Letter from Bishop General Polk." *The Liberator* 32, 45 (7 November 1862): 177

"Letters and Diaries of the George W. Polk Family." *Historic Maury* 22 (1986): 1–29; 23 (1987): 1–28.

Lewis, Lloyd. *Sherman: Fighting Prophet*. New York: Harcourt, Brace, 1932.

List of Staff Officers of the Confederate States Army. Washington, DC: Government Printing Office, 1891.

Lloyd's Register of Shipping, 1832. London: W. Marchant, 1832.

Long, E. B. "The Paducah Affair: Bloodless Action that Altered the Civil War in the Mississippi Valley." *The Register of the Kentucky Historical Society* 70 (1972): 253–276.

Longfellow, Henry W. *The Early Poems of Henry Wadsworth Longfellow*. London: Pickering and Company, 1878.

Longstreet, James. *From Manassas to Appomattox*. Bloomington: Indiana University Press, 1960.

Losson, Christopher. *Tennessee's Forgotten Warriors: Frank Cheatham and His Confederate Division*. Knoxville: University of Tennessee Press, 1989.

Ludlum, David M. *Early American Tornadoes, 1586–1870*. Boston: American Meteorological Society, 1970.

Macaulay, Thomas B. *The History of England from the Ascension of James II*. Vol. 2. New York: Lovell, 1890.

Mackall, William W. *A Son's Recollections of His Father*. New York: Dutton, 1930.

Mackle, Elliott J. "The Eden of the South, Florida's Image in American Travel Literature and Painting, 1986–1900." PhD diss., Emory University, 1977.

Mahan, Alfred T. *The Navy in the Civil War*. Vol. 3: *The Gulf and Inland Waters*. New York: Scribner's, 1883.

Malone, Dumas, ed. *Dictionary of American Biography*. New York: Scribner's, 1934.

Marshall, Jessie Ames, ed. *Private and Official Correspondence of Gen. Benjamin F. Butler: During the Period of the Civil War*. 5 vols. Norwood, MA: Plimpton Press, 1917.

Marshall, Randolph V. *An Historical Sketch of the Twenty-Second Regiment, Indiana Volunteers*. Madison, IN: Courier Company, 1884.

Marszalek, John F. *Sherman: A Soldier's Passion for Order*. New York: Free Press, 1993.

Maury, Richard. "The First Marine Torpedoes Were Made in Richmond, Va. and Used in James River." *SHSP* 31 (1903): 326–328.

McClurken, Kara M. "For Love of God and Country: McIlvaine's Mission." *Anglican and Episcopal History* 49 (2000): 315–347.

McDonough, James Lee. "Cold Days in Hell: The Battle of Stones River." *CWTI* 25 (1986): 12–51.

———. *Shiloh: In Hell Before Night*. Knoxville: University of Tennessee Press, 1977.

———. *Stones River: Bloody Winter in Tennessee*. Knoxville: University of Tennessee Press, 1980.

———. *War in Kentucky: From Shiloh to Perryville*. Knoxville: University of Tennessee Press, 1994.

McIlvaine, Charles P. *The Apostolic Commission: The Sermon at the Consecration of the Right Reverend Leonidas Polk, D.D., Missionary Bishop for Arkansas, in Christ Church, Cincinnati, Ohio, December 9, 1838*. Gambier, OH: G. W. Myers, 1838.

———. "Leonidas Polk: The Bishop-General Who Died for the South." *SHSP* 18 (1890): 371–379.

McKay, John E. "Atlanta Campaign." In *The Encyclopedia of the American Civil War*. Vol. 1, 128–146. Santa Barbara, CA: ABC-CLIO, 2000.

McLean, Margaret Sumner. "A Northern Woman in the Confederacy." *Harper's Magazine*, February 1914, 442–443, 451.

McMurry, Richard M. *Atlanta 1864: Last Chance for the Confederacy*. Lincoln: University of Nebraska Press, 2000.

———. "Cassville." *CWTI* 10 (December 1971): 4–9.

———. *John Bell Hood and the War for Southern Independence*. Lexington: University Press of Kentucky, 1982.

———. "Kennesaw Mountain." *CWTI* 8 (January 1970): 19–34.

———. "The Mackall Journal and Its Antecedents." *Civil War History* 20 (1974): 311–328.

———. "Resaca: 'A Heap of Hard Fiten.'" *CWTI* 9 (November 1970): 4–12.

McPherson, James M. *Battle Cry of Freedom: The Civil War Era*. New York: Oxford University Press, 1988.

———. "Blitzkrieg in Georgia." *The New York Review of Books* 47 (30 November 2000): 36–38.

McWhiney, Grady. *Braxton Bragg and Confederate Defeat*. Vol. 1. New York: Columbia University Press, 1969.

———. "Braxton Bragg at Shiloh." *THQ* 21 (1962): 19–30.

Meade, William. *Address on the Day of Fasting and Prayer Appointed by the President of the Confederate States, June 13, 1861, Delivered at Christ Church, Millwood, Va. by Bishop Meade*. Richmond: Enquirer Book and Job Press, 1861.

Miller, Marsh A. "Another Account." *Confederate Veteran* 12 (1904): 279.

Miller, Randall M., and John David Smith, eds. *Dictionary of Afro-American Slavery*. New York: Greenwood Press, 1998.

Miller, Stephen F. *Recollections of Newbern 50 Years Ago*. Greenville, NC: J. Y. Joiner, 2006.

Milligan, John D., ed. *From the Fresh-Water Navy, 1861–64: The Letters of Acting Master's Mate Henry R. Browne and Acting Ensign Symmes E. Browne*. Annapolis: United States Naval Institute, 1970.

"Miscellaneous: Bishop Polk." *SOM* 4 (1839): 89–92.

Mitchell, C. Bradford, ed. *Merchant Steam Vessels of the United States, 1790–1868*. Staten Island, NY: Steamship Historical Society of America, 1975.

Moore, Frank, ed. *The Rebellion Record: A Diary of American Events*. 11 vols. New York: Putnam, 1861–1868.

Moorman, J. J. *The Virginia Springs and Springs of the South and West*. Philadelphia: Lippincott, 1859.

Morris, Roy. "That Improbable Praiseworthy Paper: *The Chattanooga Daily Rebel*." *CWTI* 23 (November 1984): 16–24.

Morton, H. V. *In Scotland Again*. New York: Dodd, Mead, 1934.

Moulton, Gary. *John Ross, Cherokee Chief*. Athens: University of Georgia Press, 1978.

Muir, Andrew Forest. "William Fairfax Gray, Founder of Christ Church Cathedral, Houston" *HMPEC* 28 (1959): 341–380.

Murphy, DuBose. "Caleb S. Ives, Pioneer Missionary in Texas." *HMPEC* 6 (1937): 240–248.

Murray, Elizabeth Reid. *Wake: Capital County of North Carolina*. Raleigh: Capital County Publishing, 1983.

Nelson, William H. *A Burning Torch and a Flaming Fire: The Story of Centenary College of Louisiana*. Nashville: Methodist Publishing House, 1931.

Nevins, Allan, and Milton Halsey Thomas, eds. *The Diary of George Templeton Strong*. 4 vols. New York: MacMillan, 1952.

The New England Historical and Genealogical Register 77 (1923).

Noe, Kenneth. *Perryville: This Grand Havoc of Battle*. Lexington: University Press of Kentucky, 2001.

Noll, Arthur Howard. *History of the Church in the Diocese of Tennessee*. New York: J. Pott & Company, 1900.

———, ed. *Doctor Quintard, Chaplain C.S.A. and Second Bishop of Tennessee: Being His Story of the War (1861–1865)*. Sewanee, TN: University Press, 1905.

"Obstructing Federal Gunboats." *Confederate Veteran* 34 (1926): 221.

Official Records of the Union and Confederate Navies. Washington, DC: Government Printing Office, 1894–1922.

Otey, William Mercer, "Operations of the Signal Corps." *Confederate Veteran* 8 (1900): 129–130.

———. "Organizing a Signal Corps." *Confederate Veteran* 7 (1899): 549–551.

Overdyke, W. Darrell. *Louisiana Plantation Homes: Colonial and Ante-Bellum*. New York: Architectural Book Publishing Company, 1965.

Owen, William Miller. *In Camp and Battle with the Washington Artillery of New Orleans*. Boston: Ticknor & Company, 1885.

Owens, Jeffrey Alan. "Naming the Plantation: An Analytical Survey from Tensas Parish, Louisiana." *Agricultural History* 68 (1994): 46–69.

Pappas, George S. *To the Point: The United States Military Academy, 1802–1902*. Westport, CT: Praeger, 1993.

Parks, Joseph H. *General Edmund Kirby Smith, C.S.A.* Baton Rouge: Louisiana State University Press, 1954.

———. *General Leonidas Polk, C.S.A.: The Fighting Bishop*. Baton Rouge: Louisiana State University Press, 1992.

Parrish, T. Michael, and Robert M. Willingham Jr., eds. *Confederate Imprints: A Bibliography of Southern Publications from Secession to Surrender*. Austin, TX: Jenkins Publishing Company, 1987.

Pastoral Letter of the Bishops of the Protestant Episcopal Church in the United States of America to the Clergy and Laity of the Same, Friday, October 17, 1862. New York, Baker & Godwin, 1862.

Patrick, James. *Architecture in Tennessee, 1768–1897.* Knoxville: University of Tennessee Press, 1981.

Peake, Michael A. *Blood Shed in This War: Civil War Illustrations by Captain Adolph Metzner, 32nd Indiana.* Indianapolis: Indiana Historical Society Press, 2010.

Pennington, Edgar Legare. "The Battle at Sewanee." *THQ* 9 (1950): 217–243.

———. "The Confederate Episcopal Church and the Southern Soldiers." *HMPEC* 17 (1948): 356–383.

Perry, Milton F., *Infernal Machines: The Story of Confederate Submarine and Mine Warfare.* Baton Rouge: Louisiana State University Press, 1965.

Perry, William S. *The Bishops of the American Church, Past and Present.* New York: Christian Literature Company, 1897.

———, ed. *The History of the American Episcopal Church, 1783–1883.* 2 vols. Boston: James R. Osgood & Company, 1885.

Pickett, William D. "The Bursting of the 'Lady Polk.'" *Confederate Veteran* 12 (1904): 277–278.

———. *Sketch of the Military Career of William J. Hardee.* Lexington: James E. Hughes, 1910.

Plater, David D. *"The Remarkably Neat Church in the Village of Thibodaux": An Antebellum History of St. John's Episcopal Church.* Lafayette: University of Southwestern Louisiana, 1994.

Polk, George W. "St. John's Church, Maury County, Tennessee." *Tennessee Historical Magazine* 7 (1921): 147–153.

Polk, William M. "The Battle of Chickamauga." *SHSP* 10 (1882): 1–25

———. "General Bragg and the Chickamauga Campaign: A Reply to General Martin." *SHSP* 12 (1884): 378–390.

———. "General Polk and the Battle of Belmont." In *BLCW.* Vol. 1, 348–357.

———. "General Polk at Chickamauga." In *BLCW.* Vol. 3, 662–663.

———. *Leonidas Polk, Bishop and General.* 2 vols. New York: Longmans, Green, and Company, 1915.

———. *The University of the South and the Race Problem.* Sewanee, TN: University of the South Press, 1893.

Polk, William R. *Polk's Folly: An American Family History.* New York: Doubleday, 2000.

Popowski, Howard. "Opportunity: Clash at Dug Gap." *CWTI* 22 (Summer 1983): 16–19.

Pratt, Harry E. "Albert Taylor Bledsoe: Critic of Lincoln." *Illinois State Historical Society Transactions* 41 (1934): 153–183.

"Proceedings of the Southern Convention." *De Bow's Review* 23 (1857): 315–316, 440.

Procter, John R. "A Blue and Grey Friendship: Grant and Buckner." *Century Illustrated Monthly Magazine* 53 (April 1897): 942–949.

Pryor, Elizabeth Brown. *Reading the Man: A Portrait of Robert E. Lee through His Private Letters.* New York: Viking, 2007.

Pugh, W. W. "Reminiscences of an Old Fogy, Chapter 10." *Assumption Pioneer,* 1 October 1881.

Purdue, Howell, and Elizabeth Purdue. *Pat Cleburne: Confederate General*. Hillsboro, TX: Hill Junior College Press, 1972.

Quillen, Eva Pearl. "A Study of the Life of Franklin Gillette Smith." Master's thesis, Tennessee Polytechnic Institute, 1960.

Ramage, James A. *Rebel Raider: The Life of General John Hunt Morgan*. Lexington: University Press of Kentucky, 1986.

Randall, George M. "A Mitred Major-General." *The Church Monthly* (August 1861): 57–58.

Randle, Daniel Wilson. "A Question of Style: The Architecture Competition for the Central Building of the University of the South (1860)." Master's thesis, University of Texas, 1978.

Razek, Joseph R. *Accounting on the Old Plantation: A Study of the Records of William J. Minor and Other Sugar and Cotton Planters*. New Orleans: University of New Orleans, 1981.

Reader, W. J. *Macadam: The McAdam Family and the Turnpike Roads, 1798–1861*. London: Heinemann, 1980.

Reid, Whitelaw. *Ohio in the War*. New York: Moore, Wilstach & Baldwin, 1868.

Reilly, Timothy. "Genteel Reform Versus Southern Allegiance: Episcopalian Dilemma in Old New Orleans." *HMPEC* 44 (1975): 437–450.

———. "The Louisiana Colonization Society and the Protestant Missionary." *Louisiana History* 43 (2002): 433–477.

Remini, Robert. *The Election of Andrew Jackson*. Philadelphia: Lippincott, 1963.

Rendezvous for Taste: Peale's Baltimore Museum, 1814–1830. Baltimore: Peale Museum, 1956.

Reynolds, Donald E., and Max H. Kele, eds. "With the Army of the Cumberland in the Chickamauga Campaign: The Diary of James W. Chapin, Thirty-Ninth Indiana Volunteers." *Georgia Historical Quarterly* 59 (1975): 223–242.

Richman, Irwin. *The Brightest Ornament: A Biography of Nathaniel Chapman, M.D.* Bellefonte: Pennsylvania Heritage, 1967.

Ridley, Bromfield L. *Battles and Sketches of the Army of Tennessee*. Mexico: Missouri Printing and Publishing Company, 1906.

Risley, Ford, "The Confederate Press Association." *Civil War History* 47 (2001): 222–239.

Robins, Glenn M. "Leonidas Polk and Episcopal Identity: An Evangelical Experiment in the Mid-Nineteenth Century South." PhD diss., University of Southern Mississippi, 1999.

Robinson, Solon. "Agricultural Tour South and West—No. 2." *American Agriculturist* 8 (1849): 51–53.

———. "Agricultural Tour South and West—No. 3." *American Agriculturist* 8 (1849): 90–92.

———. "Agricultural Tour South and West—No. 7." *American Agriculturist* 8 (1849): 219–220.

———. "Mr. Robinson's Tour, No. 11." *American Agriculturist* 8 (1849): 337–338.

Rockwell, A. D. *Electricity as a Means of Diagnosis*. New York: Trow & Smith, 1869.

Roland, Charles P. "Albert Sidney Johnston and the Shiloh Campaign." *Civil War History* 4 (1958): 355–382.

———. *Jefferson Davis's Greatest General: Albert Sidney Johnston*. Abilene, TX: McWhiney Foundation Press, 2000.

Rolle, Andrew. *John Charles Fremont: Character as Destiny*. Norman: University of Oklahoma Press, 1991.

Roman, Alfred. *The Military Operations of General Beauregard in the War Between the States*. New York: Harper & Brothers, 1884.

Rosenberg, Charles E. *The Cholera Years: The United States in 1832, 1849, and 1866*. Chicago: University of Chicago Press, 1962.

Rothman, Sheila M., *Living in the Shadow of Death: Tuberculosis and the Social Experience of Illness in American History*. Baltimore: Johns Hopkins University Press, 1994.

Rowland, Dunbar, ed. *Jefferson Davis, Constitutionalist: His Letters, Papers, and Speeches*. 10 vols. Jackson: Mississippi Department of Archives and History, 1923.

Rudulph, Marilou Alston. "George Cooke and His Paintings." *Georgia Historical Quarterly* 44 (1960): 117–153.

Rusling, James R. *Men and Things I Saw in Civil War Days*. New York: Eaton & Mains, 1899.

Salomon, Richard G. "The Episcopate on the Carey Case." *HMPEC* 18 (1949): 240–279.

Sanger, Donald Bridgman. *James Longstreet: Soldier*. Baton Rouge: Louisiana State University Press, 1952.

Sansing, David G. *The University of Mississippi: A Sesquicentennial History*. Jackson: University Press of Mississippi, 1999.

Schlesinger, Arthur Jr., ed. *The Almanac of American History*. New York: Putnam, 1983.

Scott, Walter. *Poetical Works*. Edinburgh: Adams and Black, 1851.

Secrist, Philip L. "Battle of Resaca." In *Encyclopedia of the American Civil War*, ed. David S. Heidler and Jeanne T. Heidler. Vol. 4, 1630. Santa Barbara, CA: ABC-CLIO, 2000.

———. *The Battle of Resaca: Atlanta Campaign, 1864*. Macon: Mercer University Press, 1998.

Seitz, Don C. *Braxton Bragg, General of the Confederacy*. Columbia, SC: State Company, 1924.

Shepherd, Massey H. Jr. *The Oxford American Prayer Book Commentary*. New York: Oxford University Press, 1950.

Sherman, William T. *Memoirs of General William T. Sherman by Himself*. Bloomington: Indiana University Press, 1957.

Simon, John Y., ed. *The Papers of Ulysses S. Grant*. Carbondale: Southern Illinois University Press, 1969.

Simpson, Brooks D. *Ulysses S. Grant: Triumph Over Adversity, 1822–1865*. New York: Houghton Mifflin, 2000.

Simpson, Brooks D., and Jean V. Berlin, eds. *Sherman's Civil War: Selected Correspondence of William T. Sherman, 1860–1865*. Chapel Hill: University of North Carolina Press, 1999.

Sisler, George. "The Arrest of a Memphis *Daily Appeal* War Correspondent on Charges of Treason." *West Tennessee Historical Society Papers* 11 (1957): 76–92.

Slack, William Samuel. "Bishop Polk and the Diocese of Louisiana." *HMPEC* 7 (1938): 360–377.

———. "A Fragment: of the Cornerstone." In *Purple Sewanee*, ed. Lily Baker, et al., 29. Sewanee, TN: Association for the Preservation of Tennessee Antiquities, 1961.

Smart, James G., ed. *A Radical View: The "Agate" Dispatches of Whitelaw Reid, 1861–1865.* 2 vols. Memphis: Memphis State University Press, 1976.

Smith, Carlton L. *Peabody at Shiloh: A Short Study of Courage and Injustice.* Harvard, MA: Tahanto Trail, 1983.

Smith, Catherine B. R. "Death and Funerals of Bishop-General Leonidas Polk." *Journal of the Augusta Richmond County Historical Society* 15 (1983): 31–41.

Smith, Timothy B. *Shiloh: Conquer or Perish.* Lawrence: University of Kansas Press, 2014.

Smythe, George. *A History of the Diocese of Ohio Until the Year 1918.* Cleveland: Diocese of Ohio, 1931.

Sorrel, G. Moxley. *Recollections of a Confederate Staff Officer,* ed. Bell Irvin Wiley. Jackson, TN: McCowat-Mercer Press, 1968.

Southey, Robert, *Thalaba the Destroyer.* London: T. N. Longman and O. Rees, 1801.

Speer, Lonnie R. *Portals to Hell: Military Prisons of the Civil War.* Mechanicsburg, PA: Stackpole Books, 1997.

Spence, Philip. "Campaigning in Kentucky." *Confederate Veteran* 9 (1901): 22–23.

———. "Service for the Confederacy." *Confederate Veteran* 8 (1900): 373–374.

Sprague, William B. *Annals of the American Episcopal Pulpit.* New York: R. Carter and Bros., 1859.

Spratling, William P., and Natalie Scott. *Old Plantation Houses in Louisiana.* New York: William Helburn, 1927.

Starr, John W. Jr. *One Hundred Years of American Railroading.* New York: Dodd, Mead and Company, 1929.

Starr, S. Frederick. *Southern Comfort: The Garden District of New Orleans, 1800–1900.* Cambridge, MA: MIT Press, 1989.

Stevenson, William G. *Thirteen Months in the Rebel Army by an Impressed New Yorker.* New York: A. S. Barnes & Burr, 1862.

Stewart, Alexander P. "The Bursting of the 'Lady Polk.'" In *Battles and Sketches of the Army of Tennessee,* ed. Bromfield Ridley, 25–28. Mexico: Missouri Printing and Publishing Company, 1906.

Stickles, Arndt M. *Simon Bolivar Buckner: Borderland Knight.* Chapel Hill: University of North Carolina Press, 1940.

Still, William N. Jr. *Iron Afloat: The Story of Confederate Armorclads.* Nashville: Vanderbilt University Press, 1971.

———, ed. *The Confederate Navy: The Ships, Men and Organization, 1861–65.* Annapolis: Naval Institute Press, 1996.

Stone, James H. "The Economic Development of Holly Springs during the 1840s." *Journal of Mississippi History* 32 (1970): 341–361.

Stone, John Seely. *A Memoir of the Life of James Milnor, D.D.* New York: American Tract Society, 1848.

Stowe, Walter H. "Polk's Missionary Episcopate." *HMPEC* 7 (1938): 340–359.

———. "A Turning Point: The General Convention of 1835." *HMPEC* 4 (1935): 152–179.

Stuart, Charles B. *Lives and Works of Civil and Military Engineers of America.* New York: D. Van Norstrand, 1871.

Supplement to the Official Records of the Union and Confederate Armies. 100 vols. Wilmington, NC: Broadfoot Publishing Company, 1994–1998.

Swain, David L. "Address Delivered on the Occasion of the Erection of the Monument to Jacob Johnson in the Raleigh Cemetery." In *Early Times in Raleigh: Addresses Delivered by the Hon. David L. Swain*, comp. R.S. Tucker, 3–21. Raleigh: Walters, Hughes, 1867.

Sweetser, William. *A Treatise on Consumption, with Directions for the Consumptive Visiting the South of Europe*. Boston: T. H. Carter, 1836.

Sykes, E. T. "A Cursory Sketch of General Bragg's Campaigns." *SHSP* 11 (1883): 466–474.

Symonds, Craig L. *Joseph E. Johnston: A Civil War Biography*. New York: W. W. Norton, 1992.

———. *Stonewall of the West: Patrick Cleburne and the Civil War*. Lawrence: University Press of Kansas, 1997.

Tapp, Hambleton. "The Battle of Perryville, October 8, 1862." *Filson Club History Quarterly* 9 (1935): 158–181.

Taylor, F. Jay, ed. *Reluctant Rebel: The Secret Diary of Robert Patrick*. Baton Rouge: Louisiana State University Press, 1959.

Taylor, Hillsman. "The Night Riders of West Tennessee." *West Tennessee Historical Society Papers* 6 (1952): 77–86.

Taylor, Richard. *Destruction and Reconstruction: Personal Experiences of the Late War*. New York: Appleton, 1879.

Terrell, W. H. H. *Report of the Adjutant General of the State of Indiana*. Indianapolis: Samuel M. Douglass, 1866.

Throne, Mildred. "Comments on the 'Hornet's Nest'—1862 and 1887." *Iowa Journal of History* 55 (1957): 249–274.

———. "Erastus B. Soper's History of Company D, 12 Iowa Infantry, 1861–1866." *Iowa Journal of History* 56 (1958): 153–187.

———. "Iowa and the Battle of Shiloh." *Iowa Journal of History* 55 (1957): 209–274.

Tise, Larry E. *Proslavery: A History of the Defense of Slavery in America, 1701–1840*. Athens: University of Georgia Press, 1987.

Tower, Lockwood, ed. *A Carolinian Goes to War*. Columbia: University of South Carolina Press, 1983.

Urquhart, David. "Bragg's Advance and Retreat." In *BLCW*. Vol. 3, 600–609.

Wakelyn, Jon L. "The Civil War and Catholics," in Michael Glazier and Thomas Shelley, eds., *The Encyclopedia of American Catholic History* (Collegeville, MN: Liturgical Press, 1999), 348–349.

Walker, Alexander. "Narrative of the Battle of Shiloh." In *Diary of the War for Separation*, ed. H. C. Clarke, 114–160. Vicksburg, MS: Clarke's Southern Publishing House, 1862.

Wall, Joseph Frazier. *Henry Watterson, Reconstructed Rebel*. New York: Oxford University Press, 1956.

Walters, John Bennett. "General William T. Sherman and Total War." *Journal of Southern History* 14 (1948): 447–480.

Walworth, Clarence A. *The Oxford Movement in America, or, Glimpses of Life in an Anglican Seminary*. New York: Catholic Book Exchange, 1895.

Warner, Ezra, and W. Buck Yearns, eds. *Biographical Register of the Confederate Congress*. Baton Rouge: Louisiana State University Press, 1975.

The War of the Rebellion: A Compilation of the Official Records of the Union and Confederate Armies. 70 vols. Washington, DC: Government Printing Office, 1880–1901.

Watkins, John, and Frederic A. Shoberl, eds. *A Biographical Dictionary of the Living Authors of Great Britain and Ireland*. London: Henry Colburn, 1816.

Watkins, Samuel. *"Company Aytch," Maury Grays, First Tennessee Regiment, or, A Sideshow of the Big Show*. Jackson, TN: McCowat—Mercer Press, 1952.

Watson, Elbert L., "James Walker of Columbia." *THQ* 23 (1964): 24–37.

Weaver, Herbert, and Kermit L. Hall, eds. *Correspondence of James K. Polk*. Nashville: Vanderbilt University Press, 1975.

Wells, E. T. "The Campaign and Battle of Chickamauga." *The United Service* 16 (1896): 205–233.

Welsh, Jack D. *Medical Histories of Confederate Generals*. Kent, OH: Kent State University Press, 1995.

Wender, Herbert. *Southern Commercial Conventions, 1837–1859*. Baltimore: Johns Hopkins University Press, 1930.

Wert, Jeffry D. *General James Longstreet: The Confederacy's Most Controversial Soldier*. New York: Simon & Schuster, 1993.

Wheeler, Joseph. "Bragg's Invasion of Kentucky." In *BLCW*. Vol. 3, 1–25.

White, James F. "Theology and Architecture in America: A Study of Three Leaders." In *A Miscellany of American Christianity: Essays in Honor of H. Shelton Smith*, ed. Stuart C. Henry, 362–290. Durham: Duke University Press, 1963.

White, Ronald C. *American Ulysses*. New York: Random House, 2016.

Wilberforce, Samuel. *A History of the Protestant Episcopal Church in America*. London: James Burns, 1844.

———. *A History of the Protestant Episcopal Church in America*. New York: Stanford and Swords, 1849.

Williams, Edward P. *Extracts from Letters to A. B. T. from Edward P. Williams during His Service in the Civil War*. New York: For Private Distribution, 1903.

Williams, Kenneth P. *Lincoln Finds a General*. New York: Macmillan, 1956.

Williams, T. Harry. "Beauregard at Shiloh." *Civil War History* 1 (1955): 17–34.

———. *Lincoln and His Generals*. New York: Knopf, 1952.

———. *P.G.T. Beauregard: Napoleon in Gray*. Baton Rouge: Louisiana State University Press 1954.

Wills, Charles W. *Army Life of an Illinois Soldier*. Washington, DC: Globe Printing Company, 1906.

Wilson, D. M. *Three Hundred Years of Quincy: 1625–1925*. Boston: Wright and Potter, 1926.

Witcher, Robert Campbell. "The Episcopal Church in Louisiana, 1805–1861." PhD diss., Louisiana State University, 1969.

Woodward, C. Vann, ed. *Mary Chesnut's Civil War*. New Haven: Yale University Press, 1981.

Woodworth, Steven E. "The Indeterminate Quantities: Jefferson Davis, Leonidas Polk, and the End of Kentucky Neutrality, September 1861." *Civil War History* 38 (1992): 289–297.

———. *Jefferson Davis and His Generals: The Failure of Command in the West*. Lawrence: University Press of Kansas, 1990.

———. *No Band of Brothers: Problems in the Rebel High Command*. Columbia: University of Missouri Press, 1999.

———. *Six Armies in Tennessee*. Lincoln: University of Nebraska Press, 1998.

———. *While God is Marching On: The Religious World of Civil War Soldiers*. Lawrence: University Press of Kansas, 2001.

Worsham, W. J. *Old Nineteenth Tennessee Regiment, C.S.A. June 1861–April 1865*. Knoxville: Paragon 1902.

Wright, Marcus J., "The Battle of Belmont." *SHSP* 16 (1888): 69–82.

Wright, Montgomery. "Notes of a Staff-Officer at Perryville." In *BLCW*. Vol. 3, 60–61.

Writers' Program of the WPA. *Houston: A History and Guide*. Houston: A. Jones Press, 1942.

Wyeth, John A. *That Devil Forrest: Life of General Nathan Bedford Forrest*. Baton Rouge: Louisiana State University Press, 1989.

Wynne, Lewis, and Robert Taylor, eds. *This War So Horrible: The Civil War Diary of Hiram Smith Williams*. Tuscaloosa: University of Alabama Press, 1993.

Yearns, W. Buck, ed. *The Confederate Governor*. Athens: University of Georgia Press, 1985.

Index

Gale, William Dudley, *continued*
   family and, 303; sharpshooters and,
   535n29; Sherman and, 408
Gales, Joseph, Jr., 6, 443n48
Gales, Winifred, 443n48
Gallway, Charles, 333, 336, 394, 412, 519n18
Galveston, 87, 88, 107
Garrison, William Lloyd, 273
Gary, J. H., 362
Geddes, James, 235
General Convention, 69, 78, 119, 127, 425,
   453n48
General Theological Seminary, 42, 71, 91,
   108
George (slave), 203
George III (king), 37
Gettysburg, 312, 394, 515n10
Gibson, Randall Lee, 415, 523n75, 538n28
Gilbert, Charles C., 264, 265; McCook and,
   267–268; Perryville and, 262
Gilchrist, William Julius, 431n2
Gilham, William, 152
Glasgow, 251, 252, 253
Gone with the Wind (movie), 541n62
Gooding, Michael, 271, 504n47, 504n49
Goodman, Walter, 474n1
Goodrich, Charles, 115, 116, 460nn3–4
Goodwin, Daniel, 272
Gorgas, Josiah, 137, 468n12
Gosling, William, 297, 301, 304, 307
Govan, Daniel C., 269, 270, 409, 497n23
Grace Episcopal Church, 176
Gracie, Archibald, Jr., 342, 523n75
Graham & Son, 206
Granbury, Hiram, 409
Grant, Ulysses S., 178, 180, 181, 185, 188,
   198, 203, 206, 228, 234, 236, 238, 249,
   300, 365, 367, 368, 383, 477n40, 483n20,
   484n22, 491n22, 492n37, 497n23,
   498n31; Beauregard and, 494n76;
   Belmont and, 304, 482n2, 485n38;
   Buckner and, 215; Camp Johnston
   and, 483n11; Columbus and, 199, 200,
   214, 478n45; Corinth and, 223; Fort
   Donelson and, 215; Frémont and,
   482n2; Meridian and, 366; Middle
   Tennessee and, 225; Nashville and, 216;

orders from, 482n60; Paducah and, 183,
   480nn30–31; Polk and, 195, 197, 201,
   202, 204, 313; Sherman and, 232; Shiloh
   and, 223; surrender to, 385; Vicksburg
   and, 312, 313, 353, 498n38; Wallace and,
   229
"Grape," 539n34, 541n59, 542n73
"Grave, The" (Montgomery), 59
Graves, Rice, 330
Gray, Asa, 185, 205
Gray, Millie, 88
Gray, William Fairfax, 88
Great Mammoth Cave, 252
Great Religious Charities, 58
Green, William Mercer, 467n4, 469n25
Green River, 253
Greenwood, Moses, 426
Gregory, Olinthus Gilbert, 12, 17, 18, 21,
   29, 58, 433n37
Gretna Green, 60, 443n50
Grigsby, J. Warren, 535n21
guerrillas, 281, 297, 372, 374, 379, 386,
   511n11, 532n15, 533n25
Guion, George Seth, 106, 457n36, 460n4,
   462n28
Gulf Coast, 89, 91, 92, 115, 117, 365, 366
Gulf of Mexico, 98, 116, 242

Haise house, 402, 403
Hall, James, 280, 462n17
Halleck, Henry W., 214, 243, 366
Hallock, Judith Lee, 514n1, 517n56, 521n45,
   522n67
Hamilton, James Alexander, 11
Hamilton, Robert, 86
Hamilton Place, 64, 65, 68
Hanson, Roger, 292–293
Hardage house, 412, 416
Hardee, Mary Foreman Lewis, 355, 360
Hardee, William J., 169, 216, 221, 222,
   225, 229, 230, 236, 242, 248, 250, 253,
   261, 269, 274, 276, 286, 287, 296, 300,
   305, 352, 390, 397, 398, 401, 402, 403,
   406, 407, 408, 412, 415, 416, 418, 419,
   492n41, 497n28, 510n71, 512n24,
   513n47; advance by, 492n38; Army of
   the Mississippi and, 249; Bragg and,

Tullahoma, 295, 299, 300, 306, 308, 514n1
Tunnel Hill, 391
Tupelo, 244, 248, 249, 250, 349, 497n19,
497n28, 498n38

Union Army, 2, 148, 209, 220, 490n5; slaves
in, 363
Union City, 178, 179, 180
United States Colored Troops, 370
United States Military Academy (West
Point), 35, 38, 42, 45, 54, 86, 92;
education at, 29, 31, 48; influenza
epidemic at, 16–17; Polk at, 2, 4–6, 10,
13, 14, 17, 18, 22, 24, 26, 28, 32, 34
United States Navy, 167, 220, 386
University of Alabama, 367, 515n14
University of North Carolina, 5, 7, 34,
432n21, 447n54, 493n48
University of the South, 68, 90, 119, 133,
144, 150–151, 160, 241, 250, 311, 317,
391, 457n36, 465n59, 469n35, 489n40,
498n43; establishing, 461n11; evolution
of, 134, 135; naming, 136
University of Virginia, 124, 143, 160
University Place, 139, 146, 149, 514n56
Urquhart, David, 346
USS Indianola, 386
USS Merrimac, 532n16
USS Monitor, 385

Van Buren, Martin, 34, 36
Van Cleve, Horatio, 285–286
Van Dorn, Earl, 222, 242, 249, 277, 491n22,
497n29, 498n38
Van Duzer, J. C., 541n57
Vaughan, Alfred J., Jr., 288, 535n21
Vaught, Nathan, 68
Vermont Episcopal Institute for Boys, 141,
142
Vicksburg, 87, 97, 104, 153, 244, 277, 304,
314, 325, 356, 358, 359, 361, 366–370,
376, 377, 379, 383, 387, 498n38; raid
from, 365; surrender of, 353; victory at,
312, 313
Vinton, Francis, 272–273, 504n56, 505n58
Virginia Military Institute (VMI), 139, 140,
142, 151, 152, 472n19, 479n11

Virginia Theological Seminary, 42,
462n20
Volunteer and Conscript Bureau (Army of
Tennessee), 362

Walker, Alexander, 232, 322, 323, 333,
473n31, 492n45, 493n52, 495n82
Walker, James, 65, 66, 140, 445n16, 451n3
Walker, Jane Maria Polk, 67, 445n16
Walker, Knox, 181, 199
Walker, Leroy Pope, 155, 160, 175, 181,
480n37
Walker, William H. T., 322, 326, 328, 330,
333, 348
Wall, William Spencer, 104, 113, 456–
457n28
Wallace, Lew, 225, 229, 230, 237
Wallace, W. H. L., 235
Walter, Harvey, 309
War of 1812: 6, 7, 10
War of the Rebellion: A Compilation of
the Official Records of the Union and
Confederate Armies, The, 179–180, 232
Wartrace, 308
War with Mexico, 144, 224, 432n32
Washington, George, 7, 12, 203, 296
Washington Artillery, 413, 417, 426
Watkins, Samuel, 271
Watson Battery, 197, 198, 199
Watterson, Henry, 296, 318, 319, 324–325,
340, 396, 426, 511n5, 539n34, 543n73
Waud, Alfred R., 541n52; drawing by, 193
(fig.)
Welsh, Jack D., 494n65
Wert, Jeffry, 522n69
West, Douglas, 420–421, 535n21
Western & Atlantic Railroad, 392, 411, 412,
421
Western Department, 182, 209, 244, 379
"West Indies, The" (Montgomery), 59
Wharton, John A., 260, 267, 283, 287, 391,
512n32; deserters and, 282; Perryville
and, 268; Polk and, 285, 507n40
Wharton, Thomas, 469n35
Wheat, John Thomas, 449–450n23
Wheeler, Joseph, 253, 256, 257, 266, 283,
285, 390, 391, 399, 400, 503n33, 508n46